VISIBLE TRACES

RARE BOOKS AND SPECIAL COLLECTIONS FROM THE NATIONAL LIBRARY OF CHINA

中國國家圖書館善本特藏珍品菁美展覽圖錄

VISIBLE TRACES

RARE BOOKS AND SPECIAL COLLECTIONS FROM THE NATIONAL LIBRARY OF CHINA

中國國家圖書館善本特藏珍品菠美展覽圖錄

Compiled and edited by Philip K. Hu

胡廣俊 編著

Queens Borough Public Library, New York
National Library of China, Beijing
Morning Glory Publishers, Beijing

皇后區公共圖書館・紐約
中國國家圖書館・北京
朝華出版社・北京
聯合出版

This publication is issued in conjunction with the exhibition *Visible Traces: Rare Books and Special Collections from the National Library of China*

Queens Library Gallery
Queens Borough Public Library
Jamaica, New York
December 10, 1999-March 15, 2000

The exhibition has been organized by the Queens Borough Public Library, New York, and the National Library of China, Beijing, and will also be shown at the Getty Gallery, Central Library, Los Angeles Public Library, Los Angeles, California, April 15-June 25, 2000.

Exhibition catalogue:
All works in the exhibition are selected by Rare Book and Special Collections Department of the National Library of China

Introductory essay in Chinese by the National Library of China
Bilingual catalogue essays and all reference matter compiled and edited by Philip K. Hu
Copy edited by Susan Dewar and Bruce Doar

The exhibition and the exhibition catalogue, part of an ongoing collaboration between the Queens Borough Public Library and the National Library of China, have been supported in part by The Henry Luce Foundation, Inc., The E. Rhodes and Leona B. Carpenter Foundation, The Himalaya Foundation, and the Decentralization Program, a regrant program of the New York State Council on the Arts, administered by the Queens Council on the Arts. Additional support for the symposium organized by the Queens Borough Public Library on February 19, 2000 has been provided by grants from HSBC Bank U.S.A. and The Starr Foundation.

Illustrations on front and back covers: 6 woodblock-illustrated leaves from cat. no. 10: *Manual of Weiqi Strategies Carefully Edited by the Gentleman Zuoyin* (2 *juan*); Ming dynasty (1368-1644), Wanli period (1573-1619); compiled by Wang Tingna (ca. 1569-after 1628); proofread and edited by Zhan Guoli; illustrated by Wang Geng (1573-1620); engraved by Huang Yingzu (1563 or 1573-1644); Xin'an, Anhui province: Wang shi Huancui tang, 1609.

Cover design: Judy Hong, New York
The catalogue has been designed by Wang Chen and Xu Jun at Beijing Leefung-Asco Great Wall Graphics Co., Ltd., using Adobe Pagemaker 6.5C on Power Macintosh G3 computers.

The color photographs of all the works in the exhibition were taken by Feng Jinchuan of Jabel Photo Service, Beijing, with the assistance of Zhao Chunhou.

Published by the Queens Borough Public Library, New York, the National Library of China, Beijing, in association with Morning Glory Publishers, Beijing

Distributed by Art Media Resources, Ltd., Chicago

First edition, first printing, 2000

ISBN: 0-964-53371-5

Printed and bound in the People's Republic of China

Contents
目 錄

賀詞

經過貴我兩館的共同努力和緊密配合，中國國家圖書館藏珍品今天在這裡展出并與熱情奔放的美國觀眾見面了。我代表中國國家圖書館并以我個人名義表示熱烈的祝賀。祝賀展覽圓滿成功，祝賀由此建立起來的兩館關系不斷發展。

中國是有五千年歷史的文明古國。在中華民族的開化史上有素稱發達的農業和手工業，有許多偉大的思想家、科學家、發明家、政治家、軍事家、文學家和藝術家，有豐富的文化典籍。這些典籍，從古老的甲骨刻辭、青銅器銘文、早期石刻文字，中經竹簡、木牘、縑帛的發展，直至盛行的手寫紙書、雕印紙書和活字排印的紙書，歷經幾千年，前後賡續不斷，多如重山，浩如煙海。它不僅是中國文明的忠實紀錄，也是人類文明的重要組成部分。

今天，我們不遠萬里，遠涉重洋，將這些典籍中的珍品，在國際大都會紐約皇后區圖書館展出，是一九四九年以來的第一次。我們愿它能給美國人民帶來東方文明的陶冶和享受，播灑下中國人民的友情，建立起兩館和兩國之間友好往來的紐帶。讓文明之花永遠盛開。

中國國家圖書館副館長
周和平

Message

As a result of the hard work and close cooperation between the Queens Borough Public Library and the National Library of China, treasures from the collections from the National Library of China are now being presented to an enthusiastic American public. I wish to express heartfelt congratulations on behalf of the National Library of China and also from my personal standpoint. We hope that the exhibition will be a great success and that it will lead to the continued development of relations between our libraries.

China is an ancient and cultured country with some five thousand years of history. The civilization of the Chinese people, well known for its advanced agricultural practices and handicraft industries, has produced many great thinkers, scientists, inventors, politicians, military strategists, littérateurs, and artists. It also possesses a wealth of books and cultural records. These cultural records began with texts inscribed on ancient oracle bones, inscriptions on bronze vessels, and early stone inscriptions. Later, there appeared inscriptions on bamboo and wooden slips as well as on silk. Eventually, manuscripts on paper, woodblock-printed books on paper, and books printed with movable-type on paper all flourished. Through the course of several thousand years, all these writings formed unbroken chains as numerous as mountains and as vast as the seas. They are not only reliable records of Chinese civilization, but constitute an important component of human civilization at large.

Now, unhindered by the distance of a myriad miles across the oceans, these treasures of books and records are being presented, for the first time since 1949, at the Queens Borough Public Library in the international metropolis of New York City. It is our hope that the civilization of the East embodied by these exhibits will bring pleasure and enjoyment to the American people, convey the friendship of the Chinese people, and strengthen the bond between our libraries and our nations. May the flower of civilization bloom forever!

Zhou Heping
Deputy Director
The National Library of China

Foreword

The written word has always been highly revered in Chinese culture. There is early evidence of glyphs some 6,100 years ago. Beautifully printed books were published in China hundreds of years before Gutenberg. Up until the modern day, examples of exquisite calligraphy, writing, and printing are valued for their form as well as their content. It is appropriate, then, that although *Visible Traces: Rare Books and Special Collections from the National Library of China* showcases art objects in their truest sense, this exhibition has been arranged library-to-library, rather than through an art museum, since it is our libraries that are devoted to the written word.

The priceless treasures on display are from the collection of the National Library of China in Beijing. Most of them have not been shown outside of China in more than fifty years, and none of them have never been seen anywhere in North America. The exhibition has been made possible through a unique inter-library cooperation agreement between the Queens Borough Public Library (New York) and the National Library of China. That agreement has paved the way for the two library systems to exchange printed and electronic information, to assist each other in obtaining library materials, to exchange professional information, and more.

On behalf of the Queens Borough Public Library, we are especially pleased to make this opportunity available to our community. Many in our communities trace their roots to China and feel a special cultural bond. It is also an occasion for scholars and appreciators of fine art and the book arts to view ancient objects that are seldom seen, even in China. The pieces on display are culturally important and extremely rare, including examples of ethnic literature.

It is gratifying to be exhibiting these treasures in a public library, where Western culture traditionally expresses its reverence for the written word. We thank our colleagues at the National Library of China for their professionalism and trust which made this exhibition possible, particularly Mr. Zhou Heping and Ms. Sun Liping. We also thank The Henry Luce Foundation, The Himalaya Foundation, and the Decentralization Program, a regrant program of the New York State Council on the Arts, administered by the Queens Council on the Arts, for their generosity in underwriting the costs of *Visible Traces: Rare Books and Special Collections from the National Library of China*. We hope it is the first of many fruitful collaborations.

Gary E. Strong
Library Director
The Queens Borough Public Library

Acknowledgments

The exhibition *Visible Traces: Rare Books and Special Collections from the National Library of China* transcends time and space. Its scope spans centuries and crosses cultures, languages, and ethnic traditions in China.

First and foremost, recognition for extraordinary vision must be given to Madame Sun Beixin and Mr. Zhou Heping, both Deputy Directors of the National Library of China in Beijing. I met Madame Sun at the First China–U.S. Conference on Library Cooperation in October 1996 and began discussions on how our two library systems might exchange materials, information, and staff. A cooperative agreement was signed in December 1997. It paved the way for all that ultimately became the exhibition, catalogue, symposium, and a great deal more.

Customarily, this kind of exhibition is reserved for academic institutions and some of the larger museums. After all, the exhibition includes rare, priceless objects that are displayed, interpreted, and given cultural context. The Queens Library's Board of Trustees gave unwavering support to the exhibition and to the Interlibrary Cooperation Agreement because they understood that a public library is not just a place to borrow books, but also a place to gain information and insight. Sometimes that is more readily accessible in three dimensions. The breadth and value of the Trustees' understanding cannot be underestimated.

Most of the objects that make up *Visible Traces: Rare Books and Special Collections from the National Library of China* have never before been seen outside of Asia. Arranging for their transport and display took a quantum leap of trust on the parts of both the National Library of China and the Queens Borough Public Library. Special credit goes to Ms. Sun Liping, Director of the International Cooperation Division, National Library of China, and to Dr. Sherman Tang, Director–Central Library, the Queens Borough Public Library, for all their work in successfully negotiating the necessary contracts and permissions, as well as the regulations of their respective governments to make the exhibition a reality.

There are many, many people on the staffs of both libraries whose hard work have made *Visible Traces* possible. Special thanks go to Mr. Zhang Zhiqing, Associate Research Librarian, and Mr. Zhao Qian, Assistant Research Librarian, both of the Rare Book and Special Collections Department at the National Library of China. Much gratitude also goes to Carol Sheffer, Deputy Director–Planning and Development, the Queens Borough Public Library; Mindy Krazmien, Exhibitions Manager, Queens Library Gallery; and Sarah Paul, Assistant Exhibitions Manager, Queens Library Gallery.

This catalogue will permit the valuable work that went into *Visible Traces* to be studied long after the exhibition has closed. Countless hours went into its research and production. It would not have been possible without the very specialized expertise of Philip K. Hu, Ph.D. candidate at the Institute of Fine Arts, New York University, who served as the compiler and editor of this catalogue. He worked closely with Jeffrey Moy, President of Art Media Resources in Chicago and with Shane Suvikapakornkul, Marketing Manager of Art Media Resources, in arranging for the publication of the catalogue. Judy Hong, graphic designer, is responsible for the superb design of the catalogue's cover and the Gallery brochure. Thanks go to them all.

Several people worked with the Queens Borough Public Library to make the exhibition a success. The exhibition brochure was researched and written by Richard A. Pegg, independent scholar. Jody Hanson custom-designed mounts and frames for each piece, an exacting task which contributed to both the conservation and the exquisite presentation of each individual piece. She also led a team of expert arthandlers, including Mark McLoughlin and Donald Groscost, in the daunting task of installing scrolls and books that had no formal history of display. Their hard work made the exhibition come alive.

A symposium on February 19, 2000, at Queens' flagship Flushing Library, brings together a number of noted scholars in the field of Chinese books, maps, epigraphical and pictorial rubbings, as well as texts and illustrations from China's ethnic minorities. Among those presenting papers are: Chun Shum [Shen Jin], Curator, Rare Books Collection, Harvard-Yenching Library, Harvard University; J. Sören Edgren, Editorial Director, Chinese Rare Books Project, Princeton University; Robert E. Harrist, Jr., Associate Professor of Chinese Art, Columbia University; Robert E. Hegel, Professor of Chinese Language and Literature, Washington University, St. Louis; Evelyn S. Rawski, University Professor of History, University of Pittsburgh; and Qian Zhao, Assistant Research Librarian, National Library of China.

In addition to interpretive programming for adults, educational materials were prepared for elementary and secondary school students. Invaluable assistance was given by Namji Kim Steinemann, Heather Clydesdale, and the Education Division of the Asia Society, New York City. We thank them very much.

Thanks also go to the legions of people on the staffs of the Queens Borough Public Library, the National Library of China, and the Queens Library Foundation, who worked on the physical installation, wrote grant proposals, worked on marketing materials, generously contributed their ideas, and took on countless other tasks that made the exhibition such a success. I hope we have made your efforts worthwhile.

Of singular importance, of course, is funding to support such an ambitious endeavor. A major part of this exhibition is funded by grants from The Henry Luce Foundation and The E. Rhodes and Leona B. Carpenter Foundation. *Visible Traces* was also made possible with funds from the Himalaya Foundation and the Decentralization Program, a regrant program of the New York State Council on the Arts, administered by the Queens Council on the Arts. Additional support for the symposium was provided by grants from HSBC Bank U.S.A. and The Starr Foundation. Without their generosity, *Visible Traces* would never have materialized.

To all those who have come from near and far to view the exhibit, study the artifacts, and exchange ideas at the symposium, I wish to express my gratitude for your interest and support.

Gary E. Strong
Library Director
The Queens Borough Public Library
February 2000

Editor's introduction and acknowledgments

During the summer of 1998 I had the opportunity to collaborate with the Queens Borough Public Library in presenting the exhibition *Shanghai Library Treasures: Historical Rubbings and Letters*. That exhibition, held at the Queens Library Gallery for a short period in July 1998, featured a very fine selection of rubbings and manuscripts. Conducting research on the objects and closely studying them at Queens gave me fresh insights on Chinese epigraphy and calligraphy that could not have been gained solely through the study of books and reproductions. When I was contacted by Dr. Sherman Tang, Director-Central Library, the Queens Borough Public Library, about collaborating on a planned exhibition from the National Library of China, there was no doubt in my mind that this would prove to be even more of a learning experience and I immediately agreed to participate.

Visible Traces: Rare Books and Special Collections from the National Library of China is an exhibition that coincides with the ninetieth anniversary of the largest repository of books and documents in the People's Republic of China and one of the most important collections in the world. The National Library of China was originally established on September 9, 1909 by imperial decree as the Capital Library (Jingshi tushu guan). It was installed on the premises of Guanghua Temple beyond Di'an Gate and the renowned bibliophile and epigrapher Miao Quansun (1844-1919) was appointed as imperial librarian. Apart from inheriting a part of the Southern Song and the bulk of the Ming and Qing imperial collections formerly housed in the Wenyuan Pavilion within the palace complex, the library also absorbed the collections of the Grand Secretariat (Neige), the Hanlin Academy (Hanlin yuan), and the Imperial Academy (Guozi jian). To these were added portions of several important private collections as well as more than 8,000 priceless scrolls recovered from Dunhuang.

After the fall of the Qing dynasty in 1911, the Capital Library was opened to the general public on August 27, 1912. In 1916, it was designated a depository library, thus assuming the role of a national library for the first time. Soon thereafter, an entire set of the imperially commissioned "Complete Library of the Four Treasuries" (*Siku quanshu*) that had been deposited in the Wenjin Pavilion of the Imperial Summer Resort at Chengde (Bishu shanzhuang) was brought to the Capital Library. The library was later transferred to the site of the southern school (nan xue) of the Imperial Academy (Guozi jian) at Fangjia hutong, within the old city walls near the Anding Gate, where it reopened to the public on January 26, 1917.

After Nanjing became the capital of Nationalist China in 1927, a new National Central Library (Guoli zhongyang tushu guan) was established there, though formal library services would only commence in February 1936. Beijing was renamed Beiping ("Northern Peace") and from July 1928 the Capital Library became known as the National Library of Peiping (Guoli Beiping tushu guan). In January 1929 it moved to Juren Hall in Zhongnanhai. Later that year, the library absorbed the Beihai Library (Beihai tushu guan), which had been established in 1926 as the Beijing Library (Beijing tushu guan). A grand new library building on Wenjin Street was completed in 1931; it was designed in traditional Chinese architectural style and set within beautifully landscaped grounds on the western side of Beihai Park. The early years of this phase of the library's history are described in such works as *The National Library of Peiping and Its Activities* (Beiping: National Library of Peiping, 1931) and *A Short Sketch of the National Library of Peiping* (Beiping: National Library of Peiping, 1931), while many scholarly studies based on its extraordinarily rich collections appeared in *Guoli Beijing tushu guan yuekan* (*Bulletin of the Metropolitan Library*) (vol. 1, no. 1 through vol. 3, no. 1; monthly from May to August 1920, bimonthly from September-October 1920) and *Guoli Beiping tushu guan guan kan* (*Bulletin of the National Library of Peiping*) (vol. 3, no. 2 through vol. 11, no. 1; bimonthly through January-February 1937).

With the outbreak of the Sino-Japanese War in 1937, the National Library of Peiping implemented a decentralization and evacuation policy. Administrative offices were set up in Hong Kong and Shanghai, but in 1938 the greater part of the library's personnel and collections were relocated far to the south in Kunming, Yunnan province. Despite wartime difficulties, the library continued to put out publications; these are listed in *Guoli Beiping tushu guan chuban shuji mulu*, rev. ed. [N.p. (Kunming): N.p. (Guoli Beiping tushu guan Kunming banshi chu), 1939]. For safekeeping purposes, the rarest editions were sent first to Hong Kong in 1938, then to Shanghai in 1941, and eventually to the Library of Congress, Washington, D.C., in 1942, where they were microfilmed in their entirety. Following the Japanese surrender and the liberation of Beiping, the library repossessed its Wenjin Street premises in October 1945.

After the founding of the People's Republic of China on October 1, 1949, the library was appropriately renamed as the Beijing Library (Beijing tushu guan) on March 6, 1950, as the city of Beiping reverted to its former appellation and reassumed its status as the national capital. The documentary history of the library from the time of its establishment in 1909 through 1966 may be studied in *Beijing tushu guan guan shi ziliao huibian (1909-1949)*, compiled and edited by Beijing tushu guan yewu yanjiu weiyuan hui, 2 vols. (Beijing: Shumu wenxian chuban she, 1992) and *Beijing tushu guan guan shi ziliao huibian (er) (1949-1966)*, compiled and edited by Beijing tushu guan guan shi ziliao huibian (er) bianji weiyuan hui, 2 vols. (Beijing: Beijing tushu guan chuban she, 1997).

The large-scale expansion of the Beijing Library was first proposed by Premier Zhou Enlai (1898-1976). The current premises, occupying 7.42 hectares on Baishiqiao Road in northwestern Beijing and capable of accommodating 20 million volumes, opened to the public in 1987. The old library complex on Wenjin Street became a branch library. The Beijing Library's new facilities have been summarized in a report by Jin Zhishun, "New Building of National Library of China: A Survey," in *Proceedings of the Fourth International Conference of Directors of National Libraries in Asia and Oceania, December 5-9, 1989* (Beijing: National Library of China, 1989), documented in *Beijing tushu guan xin guan jianshe ziliao xuan bian*, compiled by Li Jiarong et al. (Beijing: Shumu wenxian chuban she, 1992).

On December 12, 1998, the library was once again renamed, becoming the National Library of China (Zhongguo guojia tushu guan), fully reflecting its preeminent role and the importance of its mission. With some 21.6 million volumes/items at the end of 1998 and a projected annual increase of 600,000 to 700,000 volumes/items, it now ranks as the fifth largest national library in the world. A succinct account of its history as well as an overview of its facilities and future goals may be found in a bilingual introductory

volume entitled *Zhongguo guojia tushu guan* (National Library of China), edited by Li Zhizhong (Beijing: Zhongguo guojia tushu guan, 1999). In addition, more than 350 of the library's finest rare books and items from its special collections have recently been published in a lavish, color-illustrated catalogue, *Zhongguo guojia tushu guan guji zhenpin tulu*, edited by Ren Jiyu (Beijing: Beijing tushu guan chuban she, 1999).

* * *

In the original scheme of things, I was asked to prepare a basic checklist of the exhibits and write brief entries on each item for a brochure and wall labels for the installation. It soon became very clear, however, that the historical importance and quality of the exhibits from the National Library of China merited in-depth research. The checklist grew into catalogue entries, and as more and more information became available on individual items, the catalogue entries rapidly developed into more substantial essays. In the beginning, there were plans to include only the most basic texts in Chinese, such as the main titles and the names of authors and illustrators. But full appreciation of a great deal of the selected objects hinges upon the reading and understanding of the texts embodied within them, whether in the form of manuscripts, printed books, rubbings, maps, or sutras. This being the case, the already much expanded catalogue instantly doubled in size by becoming a bilingual one with titles, physical descriptions, and narrative text also in Chinese.

Many visitors to library exhibitions will surely relate to the frustration felt by not being able to see, and therefore not being able to know, what is contained within pages not opened up for display. This drawback is further compounded in the case of rare books and manuscripts which in most cases cannot simply be looked up at one's neighborhood library, or even at large academic libraries. Hence it seemed necessary to produce fairly substantial accounts of the works. The tasks I set out to accomplish included the following: locating the objects within relevant cultural contexts; supplying accurate physical descriptions in terms of format, materials, and dimensions; providing as much information about the nature and content of each work as space and time allowed; producing transcriptions and translations of key textual passages so that the works might speak a little for themselves; and finally, furnishing the reader with a range of bibliographical references to aid in further research.

The National Library of China had convened a committee of specialists within the Rare Books and Special Collections Department (shanben tecang bu) to curate the exhibition. After five months of research, a checklist of exhibit items was proposed to the Queens Library in October 1998. The items were arranged within four groupings: rare books and manuscripts (shanben), cat. nos. 1-23; epigraphical and pictorial rubbings (jinshi), cat. nos. 24-46; maps and atlases (yutu), cat. nos. 47-58; and texts and illustrations from China's ethnic minorities (shaoshu minzu yuwen), cat. nos. 59-68. These groupings were carefully selected to reflect the objects' placement under the curatorship of individual sections (zu) within the Rare Books and Special Collections Department of the National Library of China. An introductory essay entitled "China's Ancient Books and Records: A Kaleidoscopic Picture," which appears in this catalogue in English translation as well as the original Chinese, discusses a selection of the exhibits under these four groupings.

Within each section, I rearranged the sequence of items in a chronological manner. The manuscripts and rare printed editions are presented by the order of their known or presumed date of execution or publication. The most ancient artifacts in the exhibition, inscribed oracle bones from the Shang dynasty (cat. no. 24A-B), are placed at the beginning of the section on rubbings as an introduction to epigraphy. Apart from one rubbing taken during the Yuan (1279-1368), all the other rubbings in this section were made during the Ming (1368-1644) and Qing (1644-1911) periods. I have used the explicitly known date, attributed date, or probable date of execution of the original artifact as a guide. Thus, the oracle bones are followed by rubbings taken from inscribed bronze vessels, rubbings of terminal roof tiles, stamped bricks, and bronze mirrors, and so on. The rubbing of Zhao Mengfu's inscription of the *Daode jing* (cat. no. 40) is placed according to the date of the engraving of the stones and not the probable date of the canonical text itself, which is of course much older.

In compiling the catalogue essays, my aim was to provide the following kinds of data ranging from the general to the specific: basic contextual information on the period, region, or original location of the work; brief biographical remarks on known authors, compilers, editors, illustrators, engravers, and printers; concise descriptions of the overall content of the work whenever feasible; and finally, identification of the specific folios, details of illustrations, and sections of scrolls that were chosen for reproduction. The cata-

logue essays, drawn from sources in a variety of languages, were developed independently in English and Chinese. They are not "parallel" essays like those found in many bilingual exhibition catalogues; the English is not a direct translation of the Chinese, or vice versa. Nevertheless, readers will find that most of the important information pertaining to the object at hand should be present in both versions. Readers will also notice that certain essays are longer in English than in Chinese, or the other way around. As a rule, I have neither rendered into English certain lengthy blocks of Chinese texts which are given in transcribed and punctuated form, except for obviously important passages, nor have I transliterated some long lists of names and terms which would be extremely tedious strings of romanized text if provided in full. Documentary information such as the legends of seals are not transcribed or translated into English. Likewise, many of my discursive passages in English have not been rendered into Chinese.

Following the catalogue essays is a section entitled "Sources, References, and Related Readings" in which the principal research materials consulted are arranged chronologically by date of publication. Readers should be aware that the references and illustrations listed may refer to the exemplar being catalogued, or to an identical edition in another collection, or to a similar edition or rubbing elsewhere, or to other editions, rubbings, and scrolls which are useful for making visual, textual, and documentary comparisons. Whenever a reference does not include specific page numbers, it may be assumed that the entire monograph or text is relevant to the object at hand. It is my hope that anyone wishing to pursue the study of any item in greater depth will find the indicated sources to be useful starting points.

The bibliography provided at the end of this volume, despite its length, is far from exhaustive. It lists the books, articles, and catalogues which I was able to consult during the course of research. In only a handful of cases have I included works not examined in person, when it was certain that they were of absolute relevance, and only when accurate and complete citations could be obtained. The bibliography contains all works cited in the previous section of references to the catalogue essays, but it also includes many useful reference works, encyclopaedias, and specialized dictionaries which are related to one or more specific items in the exhibition. Full citations, including series titles and numbers, are supplied throughout, and characters are provided for all works in Chinese and Japanese.

* * *

In an exhibition of this kind, where the timeline stretches across an enormous swath of Chinese civilization from the Shang through the Qing, each object is a window that opens onto a much wider world. The corresponding literature is so vast that many lifetimes would not be sufficient to uncover the tip of the iceberg of sinology. Fortunately, there exist many fine reference works which allow quick access not only to many branches of the vast body of knowledge about China, but also to the rich collections of the National Library of China. In compiling the essays for this catalogue, I have found Endymion Wilkinson's *Chinese History: A Manual* (Cambridge, Mass.: Harvard University Asia Center, 1998) to be a singularly indispensable tool in navigating the deep and less familiar waters of sinology; the forthcoming revised and enlarged edition of this remarkable reference work is eagerly anticipated.

The study of Dunhuang manuscripts (cat. no. 1) is now a well established and internationally represented branch of inquiry with an enormous corpus of secondary and tertiary materials; a small selection is listed in the corresponding reference notes. Likewise, the Jin *Tripitaka* of Zhaocheng (cat. no. 2), rediscovered some time after the great Dunhuang finds, now boasts a substantial bibliography that reflects its importance. The literature on rare Chinese printed editions is extremely copious, with voluminous catalogues available for many of the most important collections. The rare books (excluding manuscripts) held by the National Library of China, now amounting to some 275,000 volumes, have been catalogued according to the traditional four-fold classification scheme (*jing, shi, zi, ji*) several times since the early twentieth century, for example, in *Jingshi tushu guan shanben jianming shumu* (4 *juan*), compiled and edited by Xia Zengyou (Beijing: Jingshi tushu guan, 1916); *Guoli Beiping tushu guan shanben shumu* (4 *juan*), compiled and edited by Zhao Wanli [N.p. (Beiping): N.p. (Guoli Beiping tushu guan), 1933] and a supplement, *Guoli Beiping tushu guan shanben shumu yi bian xu mu* (4 *juan*) [N.p. (Beiping): N.p. (Guoli Beiping tushu guan), 1937]; and most recently in the five-volume *Beijing tushu guan guji shanben shumu*, compiled by Beijing tushu guan [Beijing: Shumu wenxian chuban she, n.d. (1987)], which lists more than 11,000 rare editions (excluding Dunhuang manuscripts, the Jin *Tripitaka*, other manuscript materials, and post-1912 books) collected between 1910

and 1986. The so-called "ordinary old books and records" (*putong guji*), numbering some 200,000 titles and including a great deal of Qing stitch-bound editions, are being separately catalogued according to modern subject divisions in an ongoing series of 15 volumes entitled *Beijing tushu guan putong guji zongmu*, compiled by Beijing tushu guan putong guji zu (Beijing: Shumu wenxian chuban she, 1990-).

Among the most noteworthy recent catalogues of Chinese rare books is the annotated record of the Harvard-Yenching Library's rare Song, Yuan, and Ming editions compiled by Shen Jin [Chun Shum], *Meiguo Hafo daxue Hafo Yanjing tushu guan Zhongwen shanben shu zhi* (Shanghai: Shanghai cishu chuban she, 1999); a catalogue of the rare Qing editions at Harvard is currently in preparation. A number of exhibition and collection catalogues merit special mention for their high standards of documentation or illustration: *Chinese Rare Books in American Collections*, an exemplary catalogue by J. Sören Edgren (and featuring several illuminating essays on related topics by other scholars and collectors) that accompanied a landmark exhibition at New York's China Institute in America in late 1984 and early 1985; *Chûgoku kodai hanga ten*, the catalogue of an exhibition of Chinese illustrated books from the National Library of China and various Japanese collections compiled by Machida shiritsu kokusai hanga bijutsukan and Takimoto Hiroyuki (Machida, Japan: Machida shiritsu kokusai hanga bijutsukan, 1988), which contains several well written essays; *Impressions de Chine*, the informative and exquisitely illustrated catalogue by Monique Cohen and Nathalie Monnet that was published in conjunction with an exhibition showcasing the Chinese treasures held by the Bibliothèque Nationale (now the Bibliothèque Nationale de France) in Paris during fall 1992; and Andrew C. West's *Catalogue of the Morrison Collection of Chinese Books* (London: School of Oriental and African Studies, University of London, 1998), which is notable for its bilingual listings.

The long tradition of Chinese epigraphical studies is reflected in a very substantial corpus of catalogues and studies devoted to the subject as well as an enormous number of facsimile reproductions of rubbings. The National Library of China has the world's largest collection of inscribed oracle bones (34,512 individual pieces), and most of the more than 70,000 rubbings taken from such bones are published in the *Jiagu wen he ji*, compiled by the Chinese Academy of Social Sciences under the direction of Guo Moruo and the editorship of Hu Houxuan [N.p. (Beijing): Zhonghua shuju, 1978-

1983]. Among the best introductory texts to the study of stelae (*bei*) and model calligraphies (*tie*) based on rubbings are Ma Ziyun, *Beitie jianding qianshuo* (Beijing: Zijin cheng chuban she, 1985) and Ma Ziyun and Shi Anchang, *Beitie jianding* (Guilin, Guangxi: Guangxi shifan daxue chuban she, 1993). One of the first systematically published collections of Chinese rubbings was the *Catalogue of Chinese Rubbings from Field Museum*, researched by Hoshien Tchen and M. Kenneth Starr, prepared by Alice K. Schneider, and edited by Hartmut Walravens (Chicago: Field Museum of Natural History, 1981). This selectively illustrated compilation lists the extraordinary collection assembled largely by Berthold Laufer (1874-1934) in the early twentieth century. Since the mid-1980s, the National Library of China (under its previous name, Beijing Library) has undertaken several large-scale publications of its unrivaled collection of some 269,000 rubbings, and in doing so has made the rubbings much more accessible to researchers. *Beijing tushu guan cang qingtong qi mingwen taben xuanbian*, compiled and edited by Beijing tushu guan jinshi zu (Beijing: Wenwu chuban she, 1985), features a selection of rubbings taken from inscribed bronze vessels and musical instruments; Beijing *tushu guan cang shike xu lu*, edited by Xu Ziqiang (Beijing: Shumu wenxian chuban she, 1988), documents the inscriptions on a wide range of important engraved stone stelae; the monumental 100-volume series *Beijing tushu guan cang Zhongguo lidai shike taben huibian*, compiled and edited by Beijing tushu guan jinshi zu (Zhengzhou, Henan: Zhongzhou guji chuban she, 1989-1991), catalogues in a chronological manner thousands of epigraphical and pictorial rubbings in the library's collection; *Beijing tushu guan cang muzhi tapian mulu*, edited by Xu Ziqiang, compiled by Ji Yaping and Wang Xunwen (Beijing: Zhonghua shuju, 1990), focuses on the library's extensive collection of rubbings taken from grave epitaphs; *Beijing tushu guan cang huaxiang taben huibian*, compiled by Beijing tushu guan shanben bu jinshi zu, chief compiler: Ji Yaping (Beijing: Shumu wenxian chuban she, 1993), reproduces rubbings with figural subjects in ten volumes; *Beijing tushu guan cang qingtong qi quanxing tapian ji*, compiled and edited by Beijing tushu guan, 4 vols. (Beijing: Beijing tushu guan chuban she, 1997), contains a fine selection of reproductions of so-called "full-figured rubbings" (*quanxing ta*) in the National Library of China.

The study of Chinese maps and cartographic history has also reached a high level, where fine scholarly essays are accompanied by excellent reproductions. The most useful sources are *Zhongguo gudai ditu ji: Zhan guo-Yuan* [(*An Atlas of Ancient Maps in China—From the Warring States to the Yuan Dynasty (476 B.C.-A.D. 1368)*]; *Zhongguo gudai ditu ji: Ming dai* [(*An Atlas of Ancient Maps in China—The Ming Dynasty (1368-1644)*]; and *Zhongguo gudai ditu ji: Qing dai* [(*An Atlas of Ancient Maps in China—The Qing Dynasty (1644-1911)*], all published under the editorship of Cao Wanru et al. [Beijing: Wenwu chuban she (Cultural Relics Publishing House), 1990, 1995, and 1997 respectively]. To date, the most authoritative and comprehensive treatment of Chinese cartography in a Western language are Cordell D.K. Yee's contributions to *The History of Cartography*, edited by J.B. Harley and David Woodward, volume 2, book 2, *Cartography in the Traditional East and Southeast Asian Societies*, edited by Joseph E. Schwartzberg and Cordell D.K. Yee (Chicago and London: The University of Chicago Press, 1994). More than 6,800 Chinese and foreign maps from the National Library of China, out of a total of more than 105,000, are listed in *Yutu yao lu: Beijing tushu guan cang 6827 zhong Zhong wai wen gujiu ditu mulu*, compiled by Beijing tushu guan shanben tecang bu yutu zu (Beijing: Beijing tushu guan chuban she, 1997). A selection of illustrations of maps from the National Library of China and other collections is presented in the bilingual catalogue *Heyue cang zhen: Zhongguo gu ditu zhan (History through Maps: An Exhibition of Old Maps of China)*, edited by Ding Xinbao (Joseph S.P. Ting) [Hong Kong: Linshi shizheng ju (Provisional Urban Council), 1997], as well as in the lavishly illustrated volume, *Zhonghua gu ditu zhenpin xuanji*, compiled and edited by Zhongguo cehui kexue yanjiu yuan (Harbin: Ha'erbin ditu chuban she, 1998) and its English edition, *China in Ancient and Modern Maps*, compiled by the Ancient Map Research Team of Chinese Academy of Surveying and Mapping, translated by Chen Gengtao and Wang Pingxiang (London: Published for Sotheby's Publications by Philip Wilson Publishers Limited, 1998).

The final section of the exhibition and catalogue, "Texts and Illustrations from China's Ethnic Minorities," is a very small selection from the library's holdings of more than 118,297 books in languages of ethnic minorities, not counting manuscripts and other non-book materials. The non-Chinese scripts featured include Sanskrit, Tibetan, Tangut, Mongolian, Manchu, Yi, Dai, as well as Naxi pictographic and Geba scripts. These objects presented the greatest challenge in conducting research for the individual essays, and I have relied heavily on the scholarly works of numerous specialists in China, Japan, and the West. There are too many authoritative works to mention here by title; I trust that my debts to all of them have been properly acknowledged in the reference notes corresponding to the catalogue essays as well as in the full bibliographical listings.

* * *

This catalogue would not have been possible without the involvement of many people. First of all I wish to express my sincere thanks to Gary E. Strong, Library Director, the Queens Borough Public Library, and Sherman Tang, Director–Central Library, the Queens Borough Public Library, for inviting me to participate in this exciting project and for their trust and encouragement. My academic base, the Institute of Fine Arts, New York University, has been most supportive. Prof. James R. McCredie, director of the IFA, and Prof. Jonathan Hay, associate professor of fine arts at the IFA, very kindly arranged for me to collaborate with the Queens Borough Public Library. I am also grateful to Mr. H. Christopher Luce, director of The Henry Luce Foundation, New York, for his friendship over the years and his enthusiastic support of this exhibition. A substantial grant from the Luce Foundation effectively transformed what would have been a simple checklist and brochure into this fully illustrated, bilingual catalogue.

Part of August 1999 was spent at the National Library of China in Beijing to document and study the exhibits as well as to select illustrations and supervise photography for the catalogue. During this time I enjoyed the warm hospitality extended by Mr. Huang Runhua, director of the Rare Books and Special Collections Department, and his deputy, Mr. Zhang Zhiqing. A basic checklist of the exhibits in Chinese was prepared under the editorship of Mr. Ren Jiyu, director of the National Library of China; the co-editors were Huang Runhua, Chen Hanyu, and Zhang Zhiqing. The editorial committee for the checklist consisted of Chen Hongyan, Zhao Qian, Ji Yaping, Su Pinhong, Zheng Xianlan, and Cheng Youqing, with the contributors being Huang Runhua, Chen Hanyu, Zhang Zhiqing, Zhao Qian, Ji Yaping, and Yang Huaizhen. Many other staff members of the library are to be thanked for their assistance in fetching items to and from the storage facilities and for their help during the photography sessions: Jin Jing, Zhang Musen, Li Xiaoming, Jia Shuangxi, Li Jinhua, Wang Yanping, Huang Jian, Wu Yuanzhen, Shi Baiyan, Yang Huaizhen, He Youguang, Liu Zhongmin, and Chen Jian. I am also grateful to Ms. Sun Liping, director of the library's International Cooperation Division, and her capable staff members Mr. Wang Du and Ms. Zheng Buyun, for lending logistical support as well as making arrangements for my accommodation and transportation. All the photographs that appear in this volume are the work of Mr. Feng Jingchuan, who labored professionally and tirelessly along with his assistant, Ms. Zhao Chunhou, during the very tightly scheduled photography sessions.

I am deeply indebted to Dr. J. Sören Edgren, editorial director of the International Chinese Rare Books Project, Princeton University, for freely sharing his profound knowledge of Chinese bibliography and connoisseurship skills in old and rare editions as well as supplying me with all manner of relevant literature. He kindly reviewed the preliminary checklist, descriptive information for the exhibits and wall labels, as well as my translation of the National Library of China's introductory essay, drawing my attention to a number of infelicities. He also graciously allowed me to join him in studying and examining many of the rare books and manuscripts prior to their installation at the Queens Library Gallery. The Research Libraries Group's RLIN computerized database of Chinese rare books administered by Dr. Edgren was an indispensable tool for checking basic bibliographic information. I also wish to thank Prof. Melanie Trede at the Institute of Fine Arts, New York University, for helping me with a text in German; Dr. Colin Mackenzie of the Asia Society Galleries for answering many questions pertaining to bronzes and archaeology; and Prof. Katherine N. Carlitz from the University of Pittsburgh for supplying an important bibliographical reference for a woodblock-printed edition. I am indebted to Mr. Qian Zhijian at the Institute of Fine Arts, New York University, for his help in checking several classical Chinese passages for accuracy in transcription and punctuation.

Access to the holdings of numerous libraries in the United States facilitated much of the research for this catalogue. The administrative and office staff of the IFA's Stephen Chan Library of Fine Arts have made my work there a pleasure. Sharon Chickanzeff, the library director, and Clare Hills-Nova, the reference librarian, lent their unwavering support and understanding as I constantly exceeded my allotted reserve shelf space with ever-growing stacks of books, notes, and papers. Cara Scouten was indefatigable in helping me to obtain many books through interlibrary loan, and John Maier kindly allowed me to peruse some newly arrived library acquisitions prior to cataloging and binding.

I am grateful for reading privileges at Columbia University, where many long but enjoyable hours were spent looking up books and periodicals in the C.V. Starr East Asian Library, the Nicholas Murray Butler Library, and the Avery Architectural and Fine Arts Library. At the Starr Library, home of a superb sinological collection, I wish to thank Ms. Zhang Rongxiang and Mr. Alexander Brown at the circulation desk for their help with obtaining materials held at an offsite location, Ms. Ria Koopman-de Bruijn for cheerfully retrieving rare Chinese editions from the Kress Room, and Mr. Kenneth B. Harlin for allowing me to stay until the very last minute before closing time on many occasions.

The New York Public Library was also one of my main research bases. I wish to thank Dr. John M. Lundquist of the Oriental Division for his encouragement, for lending me a useful rare book dealer's catalogue, and for allowing me to see the division's impressive holdings during a tour of the normally inaccessible stacks. His efficient staff, including Ms. Ankie Chung, Mr. Todd Thompson, and Dr. Sunita Vaze, processed hundreds of closed-stack and locked-cage paging requests all summer long with patience and fortitude. Several Ming and Qing editions from the Spencer Collection were made available for study by print specialist Elizabeth Wyckoff and librarian Margaret Glover in the Print Room of the Division of Art, Prints & Photographs, while a variety of old and newly published works on cartography were consulted at the Map Division. Elsewhere in New York City, I was able to draw on the resources of the Thomas J. Watson Library at The Metropolitan Museum of Art and the Art Reference Library of the Brooklyn Museum of Art. Thanks to Prof. François Louis at the Bard Graduate Center for the Decorative Arts, I was able to consult an illustrated catalogue published in the People's Republic of Mongolia at his institution's library.

At Princeton University, I benefited from visits to the Gest Oriental Library, Marquand Art Library and its Far Eastern Seminar Collection, as well as Firestone Library. Dr. Martin Heijdra, Chinese & East Asian Studies Bibliographer and Head of Public Services at Gest Oriental Library made available a newly acquired publication from Hong Kong and enlightened me on some of the more esoteric items in this catalogue. I would like to thank Dr. Mi Chu Wiens, China specialist at the Asian Division, Library of Congress, for taking out rare editions and supplying several bibliographic references. While at the Library of Congress, I was also most fortunate to encounter Mr. Zhu Baotian, one of the few authorities on Naxi civilization, who kindly reviewed the Chinese text of the last two catalogue essays and shared many insights on this unique minority culture from southwestern China. Lily Kecskes,

Head, Library & Archives at the Freer Gallery of Art and the Arthur M. Sackler Gallery, Smithsonian Institution, Washington, D.C., extended unexpected courtesies during my brief visit to the library. Many useful sources on Chinese cartography and bibliography were found at the Joseph E. Regenstein Library and the East Asian Library of The University of Chicago; I am also grateful to Prof. Emeritus Tsuen-hsuin Tsien for dispensing words of wisdom and allowing me to consult an important out-of-print exhibition catalogue from Japan. A number of rather rare publications were consulted at the Ryerson and Burnham Library at The Art Institute of Chicago. At the University of Minnesota, Twin Cities Campus, Minneapolis, I spent a productive week conducting research at the East Asian Library, the Ames Library of South Asia, and the Meredith O. Wilson Library.

I am grateful to Mr. Jiang Cheng'an of Morning Glory Publishers, Beijing, for his enthusiastic support in publishing this catalogue. His capable assistant, Ms. Zheng Wenlei, also played an important role in the production process. I was most fortunate to have Susan Dewar and Bruce Doar as copy editors; their very sharp eyes and superb command of the bilingual material at hand saved me from many glaring errors, though any that remain are solely my responsibility. I also wish to express my sincere appreciation to Jeffrey Moy and Shane Suvikapakornkul of Paragon Book Gallery and Art Media Resources, Ltd. in Chicago for helping me to obtain several recently published works urgently needed for research, for liaising with the publisher on behalf of the Queens Borough Public Library, and for acting as distributors of the catalogue.

Mindy Krazmien, exhibitions manager of the Queens Library Gallery, is to be commended for her unbridled enthusiasm and great professionalism throughout the planning, transportation, and installation phases of the exhibition. Sarah Paul, the gallery's assistant exhibitions manager, has also been of great help, particularly in making color transparencies and digitized images available to me during the course of writing the catalogue essays. Mindy and Sarah also worked closely with graphic designer Judy Hong to produce the attractive cover design of this catalogue as well as the complimentary brochure, exhibition poster, and related gallery paraphernalia. I would like to thank Richard A. Pegg for his work on the brochure and the text of the introductory wall panels in the gallery. Exhibition installers Jody Hanson, Donald Groscost, and Mark McLoughlin worked long and hard to produce a strikingly handsome installation at the Queens Library Gallery.

Two venerable cultural institutions in Manhattan collaborated with the Queens Library Gallery and the Queens Borough Public Library in enabling the exhibition to engage a wider audience in New York City. A K-12 education package was produced by the Education Division of the Asia Society, where Namji Kim Steinemann, Heather Clydesdale, Grace Norman, and their colleagues are to be thanked for their outstanding efforts. France Pepper, program coordinator at the China Institute in America, made special arrangements for me to deliver a slide presentation there as part of the Institute's Winter 1999/2000 series of art lectures.

I have benefited from the kindness of many other friends and colleagues during the six months of catalogue preparation. Daniel Dennehy offered cheerful encouragement on many a late night at the Institute of Fine Arts. Yonatan Radzin provided swift solutions to various computer hardware and software problems. Eileen Hsu and David Kamen were generous with their hospitality and their impressive collection of books. In addition, I would like to express my appreciation to Miriam Wattles and Koizumi Hideo, Melanie Trede and Lorenz Bichler, Ansgar Simon and Hong Tieu, Roberta Wue, Nixi Cura, Francesca Dal Lago, Yeewan Koon, Qian Zhijian, Yoohyang Do, Irene S. Leung, John C. Carpenter, Sofia Sanabrais, Michael A. Brown, Adriaan Waiboer, Lothar von Falkenhausen, James G. Doyle, Alfreda Murck, Alain Thote, Ho Teng Fai, Goh Tiow Hua, and Lim Mei Yin for their genuine friendship and moral support. Finally, I wish to thank my parents and close family members who have put up with me as I indulged my interests in architectural design, architectural history, art history, and now, as I plunge into the bottomless ocean that is sinology. This catalogue is dedicated to my family with much love and gratitude.

Philip K. Hu
Institute of Fine Arts
New York University

Chronology
中國歷史年代表

商	Shang		ca. 1600-ca. 1100 B.C.	北朝	Northern Dynasties	386-581
周	Zhou		ca. 1100-256 B.C.	北魏	Northern Wei	386-534
西周	Western Zhou		ca. 1100-771 B.C.	東魏	Eastern Wei	534-550
東周	Eastern Zhou		770-256 B.C.	西魏	Western Wei	535-556
春秋		Spring and Autumn	770-476	北齊	Northern Qi	550-577
戰國		Warring States	475-221 B.C.	北周	Northern Zhou	557-581
秦	Qin		221-206 B.C.	隋	Sui	581-618
漢	Han		206 B.C.-A.D. 220	唐	Tang	618-907
西漢	Western Han		206 B.C.-A.D. 8	五代	Five Dynasties	907-960
新	Xin		A.D. 9-24	後梁	Later Liang	907-923
東漢	Eastern Han		A.D. 25-220	後唐	Later Tang	923-936
三國	Three Kingdoms		220-280	後晉	Later Jin	936-946
魏	Wei		220-265	後漢	Later Han	947-950
蜀	Shu		221-263	後周	Later Zhou	951-960
吳	Wu		222-280	宋	Song	960-1279
西晉	Western Jin		265-316	北宋	Northern Song	960-1127
南朝	Southern Dynasties		420-589	南宋	Southern Song	1127-1279
東晉	Eastern Jin		317-420	遼	Liao	916-1125
劉宋	Liu Song		420-479	西夏	Xi Xia	1038-1227
南齊	Southern Qi		479-502	金	Jin	1115-1234
梁	Liang		502-557	元	Yuan	1279-1368
陳	Chen		557-589	明	Ming	1368-1644
				清	Qing	1644-1911

中國古代典籍：一幅色彩斑斕的圖畫

中國國家圖書館撰

一、中國古代書籍文化的特點

人類歷史，大都依靠文字得以流傳，書籍是文字的載體。在紙發明以前，古代中國人曾使用龜甲、獸骨、青銅、石料、竹木、磚瓦、縑帛等材料鐫刻、鑄造或書寫文字。刻寫在龜甲、獸骨上的「甲骨文」距今三千多年，已是有系統的成熟文字。它與古埃及的象形文字和古巴比倫的楔形文字一樣，在世界文明史上佔有重要地位。公元前十六世紀至公元前五世紀的中國商周時期，記載事件、紀念祖先、表彰功德的銘文還被鑄在青銅禮器和樂器上，稱為「金文」或「鐘鼎文」。由於材料和制作方法不同，金文比甲骨文圓潤，構字方法更為進步。公元前221年秦統一六國，推行「書同文」政策，用秦小篆替代六國文字，使漢字進一步規範化。秦始皇經常巡游各地，利用天然石壁刻文記事。這種摩崖石刻後來發展為在磨制的石碑上刻字，漢朝把儒家經典刻在石上，做為向全國推廣的正本。碑刻促進了文字、繪畫和書法藝術的發展。為了逼真、完整地保存鐘鼎、碑刻資料，傳拓技術被發明，可以復制金石上的紋飾和文字。但在公元三世紀前，最為人們廣泛採用的文字載體是竹木和縑帛。其中，把文字寫在經過「殺青」處理的竹簡上，用麻繩或絲綫依次將竹簡連編成策的方法，在世界範圍內僅為中國人採用；帛書在其他國家也很罕見。直到公元前後和公元七世紀，紙和印刷術在中國被發明，以後作為記錄載體和生產方式傳播到全世界，人類文明才最終邁出了關鍵性的一步。

紙可能是古代婦女在漂絮的勞動中發明的。漂絮時，絮絲粘在有網格的蓆席上，就形成了紙狀物。公元105年，蔡倫改進造紙法，使能夠書寫文字的紙批量生產。紙比起笨重的竹木簡和昂貴的縑帛來，具有輕便、價廉等優點，是書寫理想材料。到三世紀，紙的應用已十分廣泛，最終代替了竹簡和縑帛。中國古代的紙品很多，開始是麻紙，隨後又出現了皮紙和竹紙。優質的紙堅韌、潔白、平滑，千年不壞，有力促進了文化的發展。

雕版印刷術大約發明於公元七世紀的隋唐之際，鈐印、傳拓、鏤板都可能是雕版印刷術的源頭。到十世紀的宋代，雕版技術已發展到完美的地步，造紙、制墨、刻版、印刷等技術工藝都達到了很高水平。現存的宋刻本，字體端麗，刀法圓熟，紙堅刻軟，墨色光潔，受到歷代藏書家的推崇。公元1041至1048年間，畢升發明了泥活字印刷術，後來又出現了木活字、金屬活字，使印刷技術進入了一個新時代。伴隨印刷術的發展，人們開始注意色彩的運用。1605年出版的《程氏墨苑》，附有五十幅彩色插圖，多為四色、五色印成。印刷方法是在一塊印板上，刷上不同的顏色，然後一次印出。多色套印是雕版印刷術的革命，在中國起源很早。史料記載八世紀有一位婦女用雕鏤木板法，曾在絲織品上套印彩色花卉獻給皇后。十世紀的北宋使用的紙質錢幣已用黑紅、黑紅藍三色套印。到十四世紀的明代，出現了許多著名的書坊和套印作品。十七世紀上半葉，還出現了「餖版」和「拱花」。餖版是套色印刷前，將每種顏色各刻一塊木板，印刷時依次套印，一幅圖往往要刻三、四十塊板子，先後輕重印六、七十次。用這種方法印刷，一朵花或一片葉可以分出顏色深淺，陰陽向背，最能保持中國繪畫的本色和精神。拱花是把紙放在刻好的版上，在白紙上加壓，白紙上就可顯現凸出的花紋，是一種無色印刷，用這種方法襯托畫中的白雲、流水、花葉的脈紋，顯得更真實、素雅。明代的《十竹齋書畫譜》、《十竹齋箋譜》和清代的《芥子園畫傳》都是套印、餖版、拱花技術的代表作品。

中國的木刻版畫肇始於唐代(618-907年)，發現於敦煌的868年刻印的《金剛經》中就有十分成熟的木刻佛像。木刻版畫發展到明代(1368-1644年)，在技術上達到高峰，出現了許多著名的畫家和刻工。建安派、金陵派和徽派版畫體現了不同風格。其中徽派作品綫條細膩，刀法婉麗，背景繁復，人物生動，是中國版畫的杰出代表，在世界版畫發展史上也是很突出的。

古代中國人在造紙和印刷術上走在了世界的前面，紙的使用比歐洲人要早一千年，雕版印刷早六百年，活字印刷早四百年，雖然西方人在工藝上進行了改進，但基本概念源於中國，如今，一般學者都認為，紙和被稱為「文明之母」的印刷術是中國對世界作出的最重要和最基本的貢獻。它們與指南針、火藥一起引發了現代文明。

以上我們看到了中國古代書籍文化受科技、歷史等諸多因素的影響，所具有的獨創性和進步性。此外，中國古代書籍文化還具有連續性的特點:比如，雖然簡策早就被紙張所代替，卷軸裝也變成了册頁裝，但通行的方法仍是把豎的漢字約束在行格里，行與行都用墨綫分開，保持着過去簡策制度的遺跡，而且一直流傳到近、現代。又譬如漢字，雖然在發展過程中有形體、意義和數量的變化，但現代中國人仍然不難理解古代漢語的字義和語法。從甲骨文到今天規範的漢字，中國文字的傳統是一脈相承的，不象世界上其他古代文明那樣都先後消亡了。統一的語言文字促進了統一的中華民族文化體系的形成。從書籍的內容上看，中國歷史從公元前722年以來，幾乎沒有一年缺少編年的記錄。史學家司馬遷在公元前90年撰成的《史記》中，記載了公元前十六至公元前十一世紀的殷商世系，與現代考古發掘的成果大致吻合。說明了中國人對祖先及其創造的精神財富的尊崇和敬畏，也體現了一種嚴格的科學精神。中國古代文明的另一特點是豐富性。著名的錢存訓教授對中國古代書籍的數量進行統計後認為：「中國書籍的產量，直到十五世紀末年，比世界上各國書籍的總數還要多。而中國叢書、類書卷帙之浩繁，亦少有其他文字的著作可以比擬」。中國哲學、宗教著作內容深刻，極富東方色彩；古典文學是世界文學遺產中的瑰寶；史書和地方文獻類型完善，記載詳實；工藝百科描述細膩，富於實證。由此產生了許多世界一流的學者和作家，為人類進步作出了很大貢獻。

二、中國國家圖書館的善本特藏和赴美展覽

中國國家圖書館（原北京圖書館）始建於1909年，前身是清學部所轄「京師圖書館」，發展至今已擁有二千一百萬冊的館藏，數量上在亞洲名列第一。其中，被稱為「善本特藏」的善本古籍、金石拓片、古代輿圖和中國少數民族文獻是館藏精華，也是中國古代書籍的代表。

善本古籍

「善本」在古代漢語中最初的含義，是指「經過嚴格校勘，無文字訛脫的書本」（李致忠《古書版本學概要》）。現在則把古代典籍中具有歷史文物性、學術資料性和藝術代表性的部分稱為「善本」。中國國家圖書館藏古籍善本近三十萬冊，直接繼承了南宋以來歷代皇家珍藏，更廣泛繼承了明清以來中國許多私人藏書家的畢生所聚。敦煌遺書、《趙城金藏》、《永樂大典》、《四庫全書》並為四大專藏；古代戲曲小說、方志家譜完整而有特色；名刊名抄、名家校跋本頗為豐富。

這次赴美展出六十八件展品中古籍善本佔三分之一，能夠比較系統地反映中國書籍發展的歷史、版本價值和藝術特色。展品年代最早的一件古籍善本是唐武則天證聖元年（695年）的敦煌寫經《妙法蓮華經》卷第五，經文書寫恭正，富有古韻，雖歷經千年，紙張仍保存完好。另一件佛教文獻屬於著名的《趙城金藏》，刊刻於金皇統九年至大定十三年（1149-1173年），仍採用「卷軸裝」，反映了佛教在中國北方傳播的盛況和雕版技術的高超。宋慶元二年（1196年）刻印的《歐陽文忠公集》是宋刻本中的代表作之一，出版者周必大是江西版刻名家，全書在校、寫、刻、印、紙、墨等各方面都很考究。元大德三至四年（1299-1300年）江浙等處行中書省刻印的《大德重校聖濟總錄》，是元代官刻本中的精品。宋元刻本大多採用冊頁裝幀，行

格之間都用墨線分開，還保留簡策制度的遺跡。

套印本和木刻版畫在這次展覽中有充分展現，匯集了眾多精品。套印文字的明天啟元年（1621年）吳興著名的閔氏家族出版的《唐詩艷逸品》和清內府刻五色套印《古文淵鑒》，後者正文用墨色，注文用朱、黃、橙、綠分色套印，技術純熟。套印花卉、石竹、翎毛、器物的有明崇禎十七年（1644年）胡正言刻印的《十竹齋書畫譜》和清康熙三十五年（1701年）的《芥子園畫傳二集》，兩者都是多色套印，色彩絢麗，是中國印刷史上劃時代的作品，反映了明、清兩代套印技術的最高水平。《文美齋百華詩箋譜》還採用了餖版和拱花工藝，使作品具有立體感。

木刻版畫在明萬曆間（1573-1619年）發展到高峰，涌現出許多著名的版刻家和版畫作品。杭州著名書坊容與堂刻印了許多小說、戲曲，多配有精美插圖，《李卓吾先生批評忠義水滸傳》就是其中一種。王驥德香雪居刻本《新校注古本西廂記》講述大家閨秀崔鶯鶯與平民書生張生的愛情故事，版畫優美動人。著名的徽派版畫在展品中有十分全面的反映。安徽許多書坊如程氏滋蘭堂、汪氏環翠堂、汪氏玩虎軒等都是刻印版畫的名坊，《新編目連救母勸善戲文》豪放有力，是早期徽派的代表。程氏滋蘭堂的《程氏墨苑》由著名的刻版師雕刻，印刷色彩考究精良，達到了很高的藝術水平。休寧汪氏環翠堂的《坐隱先生精訂捷徑奕譜》和新安汪氏玩虎軒的《有象列仙全傳》富麗精工，是徽派版畫的上品。《元曲選圖》收元曲一百種，配有婉麗纖細的版畫插圖，反映出萬曆後期徽派版畫的風格。

金石拓片

中國國家圖書館藏金石拓片約二十六萬件，其中有甲骨三萬六百五十一片，以及許多海內外罕見的碑拓和青銅器全形拓本。名人金石專藏中精品眾多。此外，北京房山石經拓本、龍門山石窟全山造像題記拓本、歷代墓碑、墓誌、造像、畫像、銅陶磚瓦，以及名人字畫等都十分珍貴。

甲骨和金石拓片最能反映紙發明以前的各種文字載體。此次展出三千多年前刻有文字的龜甲和獸骨各一，經考訂為商代武丁和祖庚、祖甲時期。上面的「甲骨文」是研究商代社會歷史的重要資料。有關商周青銅器的全形拓本四幅來自羅振玉、王懿榮、端方等金石名家舊藏，附有眾多名人題跋，完整地反映出青銅器的全貌。珍貴的石刻文字內容豐富，書法典雅，具有重要的史料價值和很高的藝術價值。《樊敏碑》立於東漢建安十年（205年）三月，從中可以了解漢末社會動亂情況，如張角領導的黃巾農民起義和西北邊疆羌族的活動。《比丘慧成為亡父始平公造像記》刻於北魏太和二十二年（498年），陽文正書，是著名的「龍門四品」之一。在龍門二千餘品造像記中，僅此和《孫秋生等造像記》題有書者姓名。清代收藏家贊譽此造像記的書法「字形大小如星散天，體勢顧盼如魚得水」。《蘭亭修禊圖》刻於明永樂十五年（1417年），清乾隆嘉慶年間（1736-1820年）拓，描繪東晉著名書法家王羲之與詩人謝安、孫綽等四十一人在浙江紹興蘭亭飲酒賦詩，創作《蘭亭序》的盛況。此圖展現了蘭亭的幽雅環境，在崇山峻嶺、茂林修竹之間，人物沿淙淙曲水或坐或臥，或談或飲，形態多樣，栩栩如生。石刻傳拓技藝也在這次展覽中得到體現，如《印心石屋圖》用烏金精拓，《漢君車畫

像》用朱拓，《蘭亭修禊圖》以深淺兩色套拓，都很有特色。這次展覽還展出了磚文、瓦文和鏡銘三種集拓，均為收藏名家、傳拓高手陳介祺所輯拓，拓本着墨均勻，感覺凝重，也體現了磚瓦作為文字載體的特點。

古代輿圖

中國古代輿圖歷史悠久。文獻記載：公元前十一世紀的西周初年，周、召二公為營造東都洛邑繪制了「洛邑圖」，這是最早有文字記載的城市建設圖，極為珍貴。1977年在河北平山縣三汲村出土了戰國時期（公元前475年至公元前221年）的「兆域圖」，是中國現存最早的原始地圖。這是一幅用金銀片鑲嵌在青銅版上的陵墓建築平面圖，圖形和注記表明了此圖是按一定比例尺和方向制作的。在古代中國，輿圖作為國家疆土的象徵、土地主權的憑證，具有神聖地位，周朝（公元前十一世紀至公元前771年）天子分封諸侯時，同時將所分屬地圖賜給他們，如發生爭執，則「以圖正之」。輿圖在軍事上也早有運用，中國古代著名的軍事家孫武所著的《孫子兵法》中附有地圖九卷，另一位軍事家孫臏所著的《孫臏兵法》也附地圖四卷。公元前221年秦始皇建立統一的中央集權國家後，開始繪制全國地圖，需要各地的地圖資料作基礎，逐漸形成了地圖造送制度。自東漢（公元25至220年）開始各地一年一度向中央進獻地圖，唐、宋均有這種制度，到明代改為三年一送。明代羅洪先（1504-1564年）繪制了《廣輿圖》，共四十四幅，對以後地圖編制產生了較大影響。1582年後，西方利瑪竇等傳教士相繼來華，帶來了西方的地圖投影和經緯測量等制圖方法，清代在全國組織了大規模的經緯度測量和三角測量，分別於1708至1718年和1760至1762年繪制了康熙《皇輿全覽圖》和乾隆《內府輿圖》，使中國地圖學有了新發展。

中國國家圖書館藏中國古代輿圖約三萬多件。1136年用「計里畫方」法繪制的《禹跡圖》在地圖學史上具有經典意義。清代康熙年間七米見方的絹底繪畫《福建輿圖》氣勢恢宏，裝飾豪華，是圖中極品。特別該圖首次描繪清政府在收復後的台灣設置一府三縣的概貌，很有價值。本世紀三十年代訪求的近萬件清「樣式類」圖是皇家園林、陵寢等建築的系統圖樣，研究價值很高。

這次展覽的《平江圖》採用平面和主體形象結合的手法，詳細繪出了蘇州城的城郭、街道、府衙、廟宇、河流、橋梁等人文、自然景觀共計六百四十餘處。此圖是現在僅存的幾幅宋代地圖之一，也是中國傳世最大、最完整的古代石刻城市地圖，對研究中國古代城市布局、宋代經濟文化和地圖繪制水平，都有重要參考價值。另一展品《江西全省圖說》共三十七幅，採用中國古代地圖的傳統形象繪法，精細描繪了江西各府、縣境內的山嶺、河流、湖泊、城池、村寨等，色彩鮮艷、繪畫生動逼真，是研究古代地方行政歷史沿革、地理風貌以及社會經濟的重要參考文獻。《盛朝七省沿海圖》是由海防圖沿襲下來的沿海形勢圖的代表作。反映中國東北至海南沿海形勢，繪制精致，尤其對沙洲、暗沙、島嶼等繪制詳細。後列台灣圖、台灣後山圖、澎湖和瓊州府圖，對澳門也加繪城牆和建築物，十分醒目。

中國古代少數民族文獻

中國是統一的多民族國家。各民族共同創造了燦爛輝煌的文化。內容豐富、形式各異的民族古文字，據不完全統計，約有近三十種。如佉盧文在公元前已傳入中國；粟特文有二至三世紀的銘文；焉耆—龜茲文有五世紀的文獻；古藏文、突厥文、回鶻文、契丹文、西夏文、傣文等已有一千幾百年或近一千年的歷史。這些不同的文字留下豐富的文獻，從形式上可以分為：一、圖書類：包括各種論著、工具書和宗教典籍等；二、檔案類：包括文書、契約、函牘等；三、金石類：包括碑刻、墓志、印信、錢幣等；四、題記類：包括壁畫題記、石壁墨書等。在語言文字學、哲學宗教、文學藝術、歷史考古、天文歷法和醫學等方面都有重要的價值。

中國國家圖書館是中國最大的中國古代少數民族文獻收藏基地，所收文獻數量很大，版本珍貴。本次展覽中的「東巴圖」和「東巴經」是中國雲南麗江地區納西族的文獻。使用古老的圖畫文字寫成，是研究古代納西族的資料寶庫。彩繪的東巴文《創世紀》記載了納西族關於世界的形成、人類產生的傳說，很有研究價值。傣族貝葉經是用鐵筆在貝多羅樹葉上刻寫文字而成的，十多頁綫裝成冊，數冊成套或一、二十冊成套，上下用竹或木片夾好，裝幀優雅古樸，有的在側面塗上黑漆或金粉，精致美觀。貝葉經的主要內容是佛教經典，不僅保存了小乘佛教經典比較早期的面貌，而且包含了許多傣族地區歷史、地理、語言、文學的資料，有很高的史料價值。此次展出的《舍利偈頌》，是佛經論藏之一，經文以傣文拼寫巴利語，成書於十九世紀末。党項族是十一世紀中國西北的少數民族，使用一種自創的西夏文字。這種文字早已死亡，迄今發現的數千卷冊的西夏古文獻是研究古代西北地區少數民族社會面貌的珍貴史料，它的內容包括佛教經典、儒家經典、法律文書、經濟檔案、碑刻銘記等。此次展出的《梁皇寶懺》十卷中的一卷就是從漢文佛經翻譯的集錄佛經語句編成的懺法書。

建立了中國最後一個封建王朝清朝的滿族，1599年創制了自己的文字—滿文，此後的三百年間，滿漢文字并行，成為官方使用的重要語言。中國國家圖書館收藏有幾百萬種圖書和上千種滿、漢文拓片，是全國滿文圖書收藏最多的單位。此次展出的兩件滿漢文合璧的文獻，一件是乾隆年間的奏摺，另一件是皇帝向五品以上高級官員及其先代和妻室頒發的誥命，用五色錦緞制成，不但有文獻資料價值，本身也是一件精美的文物。

中國國家圖書館這次在美國舉辦中國古代書籍展覽，是中美兩國文化交流的盛事，中國是歷史悠久的文明古國，內涵豐富、形式多樣的文化典籍是中國古代文明的重要方面。相信通過這個展覽，可以使美國人民更直觀地了解中國古代文化的情況，從而為更好地觀察了解現代中國創造條件，這也是我們所誠摯希望的。

China's Ancient Books and Records: A Kaleidoscopic Picture

National Library of China

1.　Special characteristics of China's ancient books and records

The history of mankind has been largely transmitted through the act of writing, with books being the principal medium for the written word. Prior to the invention of paper, the ancient Chinese utilized the plastrons or carapaces of turtles, bones of animals, bronze, stone, bamboo, bricks and tiles, silk, and other materials for engraving, incising, or writing inscriptions. Although the so-called "oracle-bone inscriptions" were incised upon the shells of turtles and animal bones more than three thousand years ago, they were already a systematic and mature form of writing. Together with the hieroglyphic characters of ancient Egypt and the cuneiform characters of ancient Babylon, they occupy an important position in the history of world civilization. In China during the Shang and Zhou periods (16th century-5th century B.C.), records of historical events, commemorations of ancestors, and citations of merit and virtues were incised upon bronze ritual vessels and musical instruments; they are known as "inscriptions on metal" (*jinwen*) or "inscriptions on bells and tripods" (*zhongding wen*). Due to differences in material and methods of writing, bronze inscriptions are more rounded and fluid than those found on oracle bones while the method of composing characters became more advanced. In 221 B.C., the Qin unified six separate states and promulgated the policy of "writing using the same script" (*shu tong wen*). The small seal script (*xiao zhuan*) of the Qin replaced the scripts used in the six states, thus further regularizing the form of Chinese characters. The first emperor of the Qin often made inspection tours to various locales, during which he would have records engraved upon natu-rally formed rock faces. These "cliff inscriptions" (*moya shike*) later developed into characters engraved on smooth, finished stone stelae. During the Han dynasty, the Confucian classics were engraved on stone, becoming the master source used for the promotion of Confucianism across the country. Stelae inscriptions enhanced the development of the arts of writing, pictorial illustration, and calligraphy. The technique of making rubbings was invented for the purpose of faithfully and comprehensively preserving the documentation on inscribed bronzes and engraved stelae, and it can reproduce in facsimile the decorative elements and inscriptions on metal and stone surfaces alike. However, prior to the third century A.D., the most widely used type of writing surfaces were bamboo slips and fine silk. The Chinese were the only people in the world who employed the method of inscribing texts on bamboo strips that were first dehydrated using the *shaqing* method and then fastened together with hemp strings or silken threads, while silk manuscripts were very rarely used in other countries. Between the time of Christ and the seventh century, paper and the technology of printing were invented in China; only when this medium for writing and this method of reproduction were transmitted to other parts of the world did human civilization finally reach a crucial stage of development.

Paper may have been invented by women of ancient times in the course of their cotton wadding activities. While wadding cotton, cotton fibers would become glued to the meshed screens, forming a paper-like substance. In A.D. 105, Cai Lun refined the method of papermaking, enabling paper which could be used for writing to be produced in large quantities. Compared to bulky bamboo slips and costly fine silk, paper had the advantages of being both lightweight and inexpensive, and therefore an ideal material for writing. By the third century, the use of paper had become very widespread, eventually replacing bamboo slips and fine silk altogether. There were many types of paper in ancient China, beginning with hemp paper, followed later by mulberry paper and bamboo paper. The best papers were resilient, pristinely white, smooth and flat. Able to endure for a thousand years, the finest papers greatly enhanced the development of culture.

The technique of printing with engraved woodblocks was invented sometime in the seventh century during the transitional period between the Sui and Tang dynasties. Seals, rubbings, and engraved boards may all have been the sources of woodblock-printing technology. By the Song dynasty in the tenth century, the technique of engraved woodblock printing had become fully developed; the crafts of papermaking, ink making, woodblock engraving, printing, and other technologies all attained very high standards. Extant Song editions have regularized and beautiful characters, carving that exhibits great skill, sturdy papers and fine engraving, as well as clear and distinct ink impressions; they have been held in great esteem by book collectors of successive periods. Between 1041 and 1048, movable clay type was invented by Bi Sheng, and thereafter wooden movable type and metal movable type appeared, enabling printing technology to enter a new phase. Along with the development of printing techniques, emphasis began to be placed on the use of color. The *Cheng shi mo yuan* (Ink Garden of the Cheng Family) of 1605 has fifty illustrations that are either four-color or five-color. The method of printing involved the brushing of different pigments onto a single block so that all the colors were printed in a single impression. Polychrome woodblock printing (*caise taoyin*), which has early origins in China, revolutionized the technology of engraved woodblock printing. Historical records state that in the eighth century, a woman used engraved wooden blocks to print various colored floral and plant motifs on woven silks for presentation to the empress. By the tenth century, Northern Song paper currency was being printed with multiple blocks in black and red ink as well as in black, red, and blue inks. By the Ming period in the fourteenth century, many prominent commercial booksellers had emerged as well as color-printed works (*taoyin zuopin*). In the first half of the seventeenth century, the techniques of *douban*

("assembled blocks") and *gonghua* ("embossed patterns") also appeared. *Douban* involves multiple blocks each applied with a single color prior to printing. During the printing process the blocks are separately impressed; a single illustration could entail the carving of thirty or forty blocks and a total of sixty or seventy impressions that were variously light and heavy. Using this method of printing, a single blossom or an individual leaf could display a wide range of shades and contrasting tonalities, thus enabling the original colors and characteristics of Chinese painting to be preserved. *Gonghua* is the technique of applying blank papers to a finished woodblock and exerting pressure on the sheets so that embossed designs appear on the paper surfaces, a type of printing without color (blind printing). Using this method, the lines of clouds and bodies of water, and the veins of flowers and leaves in pictures could be set off and made to appear even more realistic and refined. The *Shizhu zhai shuhua pu* (The Ten Bamboo Studio Manual of Calligraphy and Painting) and the *Shizhu zhai jian pu* (The Ten Bamboo Studio Manual of Letter-Writing Papers) of the Ming dynasty, as well as the *Jiezi yuan hua zhuan er ji* (The Mustard Seed Garden Manual of Painting, Second Series) of the Qing dynasty are all representative works which utilized the printing techniques of multiple blocks, *douban*, and *gonghua*.

Woodblock illustration in China had its beginnings during the Tang period (618-907). The *Jin'gang jing* (Diamond Sutra) engraved and printed in the year 868 that was discovered at Dunhuang already contains very well developed Buddhist figural woodcuts. Woodblock illustrations continued to develop until the Ming dynasty (1368-1644), when techniques reached their apogée and there emerged many famous illustrators and engravers. The Jian'an, Jinling (Nanjing), and Huizhou schools of woodblock illustration displayed distinctive characteristics. Works of the Huizhou school exhibit very fine linework, superb engraving techniques, richly illustrated pictorial backgrounds, and lively figures; in addition to being outstanding representatives of Chinese woodblock illustration, they also occupy a special place in the historical development of woodblock illustration worldwide.

The ancient Chinese were pioneers of papermaking and printing technology. The use of paper in China preceded its use by Europeans by a millennium, engraved woodblock printing by six hundred years, and movable-type printing by four hundred years. Although Westerners greatly improved the technical aspects of printing, the basic concepts originated in China. Nowadays, most scholars concede that paper and printing (known as the "mother of civilization") are the most important and the most fundamental contributions made by China to the world. Together with the compass and gunpowder, paper and printing were the initiators of modern civilization.

From the above discussion it may be observed that many technological and historical factors influenced the book and documentary culture of ancient China, and that it was an innovative and progressive culture. In addition, ancient Chinese book and documentary culture also possesses the unique characteristic of continuity. For example, although writings on bambooslips were long ago replaced by those on paper, and although the handscroll format metamorphosed into albums mounted with individual leaves, the writing of Chinese characters in vertical columns with the columns delineated in black remained essentially unchanged. The traces of ancient bamboo slips have thus been preserved and indeed continuously transmitted right up to modern times. Another example is that Chinese characters, in spite of many changes in form, meaning, and sheer quantity over the course of their development, can still be read and understood with relative ease by contemporary Chinese people, whether in terms of meaning or grammar. From oracle-bone inscriptions to the standardized Chinese script in use today, the tradition of Chinese writing is one of singular continuity, unlike the writings of many other ancient civilizations of the world which have become extinct. A unified language and writing system has enabled the formation of a unified Chinese culture. In terms of the content of books and documents, there is virtually not a single year of Chinese history from 722 B.C. onwards that lacks written records. The *Shi ji* (Records of the Grand Historian) completed by Sima Qian in 90 B.C. already listed the genealogy of the Shang royal house (16th-11th century B.C.) which has largely been corroborated by modern archaeological finds. This not only makes clear how the Chinese revered and respected their ancestors, as well as the essence and material wealth of their creations, but also reflects a certain spirit of scientific rigor. Another special feature of China's ancient civilization is its sheer richness. According to the well respected Professor Tsien Tsuenhsuin, who has studied the production figures of China's ancient books and documents, the quantity of Chinese books and documents printed through the end of the fifteenth century exceeds the number produced by all other countries in the world combined, and the comprehensiveness and richness of Chinese collectanea

and encyclopaedias know few rivals in other languages. The content of China's philosophical and religious works is profound and its classical literature a great treasure in the body of world literature. its historical works and various types of regional documents are comprehensive, containing detailed and accurate records. and its technological crafts and encyclopaedic fields of learning are minutely described on a strong evidential foundation. From this tradition came many world-class scholars and authors who have made significant contributions to the improvement of mankind.

2.   Rare books and special collections of the National Library of China and their exhibition in the United States

The National Library of China (formerly known as the Beijing Library) was founded in 1909 by the Qing ministry of education as the Capital Library (Jingshi tushu guan). The library now has in its possession more than 21 million volumes, the largest collection in Asia. The highlights are the special collections, which include rare books and manuscripts, epigraphical and pictorial rubbings, ancient maps, and documents from China's ethnic minorities; together they are representative of ancient Chinese book and documentary culture.

Rare books and manuscripts

In classical Chinese, the earliest use of the term *shanben* ("rare books" or more literally, "fine editions") refers to the books that have been "closely scrutinized and collated so that no part of the text is missing" (see Li Zhizhong, *Gu shu banben xue gaiyao*). Nowadays the term *shanben* is extended to include all ancient materials that possess demonstrable value as historical and cultural relics, contain important resources for scholarly study, or are representative works with a high artistic quality. Using this definition, the National Library of China has close to 300,000 *shanben* volumes; this is partially the result of inheriting successive imperial collections beginning with the Southern Song, and partially the legacy of many great libraries assembled by private book collectors from the Ming and

Qing dynasties onwards. Four major special collections are the Dunhuang scrolls and documents, the *Zhaocheng Jin Zang* (Jin-dynasty *Tripitaka* of Zhaocheng), the *Yongle dadian* (Yongle Encyclopaedia), and the *Siku quanshu* (Complete Library of the Four Treasuries). In addition, there are comprehensive and notable collections of ancient dramatic and novelistic literature, local gazetteers, and genealogies. There is also a wealth of works that were printed by renowned publishers, copied in manuscript by eminent personalities, or annotated and inscribed by famous people.

Of the sixty-eight items showcased in this exhibition in the United States, a third belong to the category of rare books and manuscripts, making it possible to demonstrate in a systematic manner the historical development, the value of individual editions, and the artistic features of Chinese books. The earliest item in this category is a Tang-dynasty manuscript handscroll from Dunhuang dated 695, which contains *juan* 5 of the *Miaofa lianhua jing* (Sutra of the Lotus of the Wonderful Law) in a formal calligraphic style that resonates with a sense of antiquity. Although the scroll is well over a thousand years old, the paper is remarkably well preserved. Another of the exhibited items, also a Buddhist text, is *juan* 103 from the famous *Zhaocheng Jin Zang* (Jin-dynasty *Tripitaka* of Zhaocheng), which was printed between 1149 and 1173 and mounted as a handscroll; it not only reflects the transmission and flourishing of Buddhism in northern China, but also demonstrates the high level of woodblock engraving. The *Ouyang Wenzhong gong ji* (Collected Works of Ouyang Xiu) printed in 1196 is a representative work of the Song dynasty. Published by the renowned Jiangxi scholar and printer Zhou Bida, it shows the great discrimination exercised in the editing of the text, in the drafting of the master copy, in the engraving of the blocks, in the printing, as well as in the choice of paper and ink. The *Dade chongjiao Sheng ji zonglu* (Comprehensive Record of Imperially Sanctioned Remedies Revised during the Dade Reign Period), printed between 1299 and 1300 in Hangzhou, is a fine example of officially sponsored publishing during the Yuan dynasty. The majority of Song and Yuan editions were bound in the "butterfly" format (*hudie zhuang*), with the columns demarcated by inked lines, thus preserving traces of texts written on bamboo slips.

Multiple-block printing and engraved woodblock illustrations are comprehensively represented in the present exhibition by many fine examples. Among the works of a purely textual nature printed with multiple blocks are the *Tang shi yan yi pin* (Exemplars of the

Beautiful and the Refined in Tang Poetry) of 1621 by a member of the renowned Min family of Wuxing, and the *Yuzhi Guwen yuanjian* (Imperially Commissioned Profound Mirror of Ancient Essays). In the latter, the main texts are printed in black ink, but the marginal annotations appear in red, yellow, orange, and green, using a refined and well developed multiple-block technique. Multiple-block prints of flowers and plants, rocks and bamboo, birds and animals, as well as objects are featured in Hu Zhengyan's *Shizhu zhai shuhua pu* (The Ten Bamboo Studio Manual of Calligraphy and Painting) of 1644 and the *Jiezi yuan hua zhuan er ji* (The Mustard Seed Garden Manual of Painting, Second Series) of 1701, both of which employed polychrome multiple-blocks with exquisite colors. They are epoch-making works in the history of Chinese printing, reflecting the highest standards of multiple-block printing techniques achieved during the Ming and Qing periods. The *douban* and *gonghua* techniques were also used for the *Wenmei zhai Bai hua shi jian pu* (The Hundred Flowers Poetry-Writing Paper from the Wenmei Studio), giving the compositions a sense of three-dimensionality.

Illustrations made from engraved woodblocks reached a developmental peak during the Wanli period (1573-1619) of the Ming dynasty. Rongyu tang, the The famous Hangzhou bookseller, printed numerous novels and dramatic works which were accompanied by fine illustrations, such as the *Li Zhuowu xiansheng piping Zhongyi Shuihu zhuan* (Outlaws of the Marsh from the Hall of Loyalty and Righteousness, with Commentaries by the Gentleman Li Zhuowu). The *Xin jiaozhu guben Xixiang ji* (Newly Annotated Edition of the Story of the Western Wing, Based on Classic Editions), printed by Wang Jide's Xiangxue ju, not only tells the love story of Cui Yingying, the daughter of an important family, and the less privileged Student Zhang, but also illustrates it with beautiful and moving pictures. The renowned Huizhou school of woodblock illustration is comprehensively treated in this exhibition. The Zilan tang of the Cheng family, the Huancui tang of the Wang family, and the Wanhu xuan of the Wang family are among the well known booksellers of Anhui province that specialized in illustrated editions. The bold and energetic illustrations in the *Xin bian Mulian jiu mu quan shan xiwen* (New Compilation of the Text to the Play about Mulian Rescuing His Mother and Exhorting the World to Goodness) exemplify the style of the early Huizhou school. The woodblock illustrations in the Zilan tang's *Cheng shi mo yuan* (Ink Garden of the Cheng Family) were carved by the finest engravers, while the color printing therein was particularly well executed and attained a very high level of artistry. The *Zuoyin xiansheng jingding jiejing yi pu* (Manual of Weiqi Strategies Carefully Edited by the Gentleman Zuoyin) printed by the Huancui tang of the Wang family of Xiuning and the *You xiang Liexian quan zhuan* (Complete and Illustrated Biographies of Transcendents) published by the Wanhu xuan belonging to the Wang family of Xin'an are also splendid works and may be counted among the best of Huizhou-style woodblock-illustrated editions. The one hundred plays collected in the *Yuan qu xuan* (Selected Yuan Dramas) are beautifully evoked in a pictorial manner within the *Yuan qu xuan tu* (Illustrations from Selected Yuan Dramas), reflecting the style of Huizhou-style woodblock compositions during the late Wanli period.

Epigraphical and pictorial rubbings

The National Library of China possesses about 260,000 items of epigraphical and pictorial rubbings. Among these are 35,651 rubbings taken from oracle bones, as well as rubbings of stelae inscriptions and "full-figured rubbings" (*quanxing ta*) of bronze vessels and musical instruments rarely seen in collections either inside or outside China. There are also numerous fine pieces from the specialized collections of famous epigraphers. In addition, there are valuable rubbings of classic texts engraved on stone at Fangshan near Beijing, rubbings of inscriptions accompanying Buddhist images from the entire site of the Longmen Grottoes, rubbings of tombstones, memorial tablets, statues, stone pictorial reliefs, bronzes, pottery, bricks, and tiles, as well as inscriptions and illustrations made by famous scholars.

Rubbings of oracle bones and bronze inscriptions are best able to convey the characteristics of various writing styles and writing media prior to the invention of paper. The inscribed fragments from a turtle plastron and an ox scapula exhibited here date back more than 3,000 years; studies have shown them to be from the reign of Wu Ding and from the period between the reigns of Zu Geng and Zu Jia during the Shang dynasty. The so-called "oracle-bone inscriptions" (*jiagu wen*) found on such fragments constitute important materials for the study of Shang social history. The four examples of "full-figured rubbings" of Shang and Zhou bronzes come from the collections of Luo Zhenyu, Wang Yirong, Duanfang,

and other renowned epigraphers. They are accompanied by colophons and inscriptions made by many famous scholars and demonstrate the artistic value of bronzes in a comprehensive way. Chinese writings engraved on stone are not only rich in terms of content and elegant in terms of calligraphy, but are also of great importance as historical materials and have significant aesthetic value. From the *Han gu lingxiao Ba jun taishou Fan Min fujun bei* (Epitaph of Fan Min, Governor of Ba Commandery during the Han Dynasty), which was erected in the year 205 during the Eastern Han, it is possible to gain certain insights into social upheavals of late Han times such as the Yellow Turbans peasant rebellion led by Zhang Jiao and the activities of the Qiang people in the northwestern border region. The *Biqiu Huicheng wei wang fu Luozhou chishi Shiping gong zaoxiang tiji* (Inscription for a Buddhist Image Constructed by the Monk Huicheng to Commemorate His Late Father, the Duke of Shiping and Regional Inspector of Luozhou), with regular-script calligraphy carved in relief in 498 during the Northern Wei, is one of the "Four Exemplary Inscriptions of Longmen" (*Longmen si pin*). Among the more than two thousand inscriptions accompanying Buddhist statues at Longmen, only this and the *Sun Qiusheng deng zaoxiang ji* (Inscription for a Buddhist Image Constructed by Sun Qiusheng and Others) are supplied with the names of the calligraphers. The calligraphy of this Longmen inscription has been praised by a Qing-dynasty collector thus: "The characters vary in size like stars scattered in the heavens; their formal gestures glance around like fish splashing about in the water." The *Lanting xiuxi tu* (Illustration of the Spring Purification Gathering at the Orchid Pavilion) was engraved in 1417 during the Ming dynasty, while the rubbing was taken sometime during the Qianlong or Jiaqing reigns of the Qing dynasty (between 1736 and 1820). It depicts a gathering for composing poetry and drinking wine attended by the renowned Eastern Jin calligrapher Wang Xizhi and forty-one others, including the poets Xie An and Sun Chuo, which took place at the Orchid Pavilion at Shaoxing in Zhejiang and for which Wang drafted the famous *Lanting xu* ("Preface to the Orchid Pavilion Gathering"). The illustration portrays the secluded environment of the Orchid Pavilion where the figures are seen sitting, reclining, chatting, or drinking alongside a gurgling stream amidst the lofty mountains, towering hills, thick groves, and tall bamboo, with varied yet lifelike expressions. Special techniques for making rubbings from engraved stones are also represented in this exhibition, such as the *Yinxin shi wu tu shuo* (Illustrations and Records of the Yinxin

Stone Dwellings) with its very finely executed "black gold rubbings" (*wujin ta*) made with lustrous black ink on thick paper and burnished with a polishing shell, the *Han jun che huaxiang* (Illustration of a Han Dynasty Procession) in the form of a vermilion rubbing (*zhu ta*), and the duotone rubbing of the *Lanting xiuxi tu* (Illustration of the Spring Purification Gathering at the Orchid Pavilion) which distinguishes darker and lighter areas. This exhibition also showcases selected sets of rubbings of stamped bricks, terminal roof tiles, and inscribed bronze mirrors assembled by Chen Jieqi, a great collector and a skilled master at making rubbings. His rubbings are not only very evenly inked and dignified in appearance, but also show the special characteristics of bricks and tile-ends as a medium for inscriptions.

Maps and atlases

Ancient Chinese cartography has a long history. According to documentary records, in the eleventh century B.C. during the early years of the Western Zhou, the dukes of Zhou and Shao produced the *Luoyi tu* (Map of Luoyi) in connection with the establishment of the eastern capital Luoyi; this is the earliest recorded mention of a Chinese city map. However, the *Zhaoyu tu* (Map of a Mausoleum) from the Warring States period (475-221 B.C.), unearthed in 1977 at Pingshan county in Hebei province, is the earliest extant and original Chinese map. It is a plan of a royal mausoleum engraved on a bronze plate and inlaid with gold-leaf and silver-leaf; from the configuration of the plan and its annotations, it is clear that there was a fixed scale and orientation. In ancient China, maps functioned as the territorial emblems of a state and provided concrete proof of territorial rights, and they occupied a hallowed spiritual position. During the Zhou dynasty (11th century B.C.-771 B.C.), whenever a king enfeoffed princes and dukes, he would present them with maps of the corresponding territories, with the understanding that if any disputes were to occur they could be resolved with the relevant maps. Maps have also been utilized from an early date for military purposes; there are no less than nine *juan* of maps in the *Sunzi bing fa* (Sunzi's Art of War) written by the famous ancient Chinese military strategist Sun Wu, and four *juan* of maps may be found appended to the *Sun Bin bing fa* (Sun Bin's Art of War) by Sun Bin, another writer on military strategy. After the establishment of centralized political authority by the first emperor of the Qin in 221 B.C., maps of the entire empire began to be made, and because these were based on regional cartographic information, a system whereby maps were made for presentation to the court gradually evolved. Beginning with the Eastern Han (A.D. 25-220), regional and local maps were submitted to the throne on an annual basis. This tradition continued through the Tang and Song dynasties, but during the Ming the policy was amended so that maps were submitted once every three years. It was during the Ming that Luo Hongxian (1504-1564) produced the *Guang yu tu* (Enlarged Terrestrial Atlas), a work containing forty-four maps which significantly influenced later cartographic compilations. After the arrival of Matteo Ricci and other Jesuit missionaries in 1582, cartographic projections, surveying of longitudes and latitudes, and other Western mapmaking methods were introduced. During the Qing dynasty, large-scale surveying of longitudes and latitudes as well as trigonometrical surveys were carried out across the whole empire, resulting in the Kangxi-period *Huang yu quanlan tu* (Map of a Complete View of Imperial Territory) of 1708-1718 and the Qianlong-period *Neifu yu tu* (Terrestrial Atlas of the Inner Prefectures) of 1760-1762, which together marked a new development in the history of Chinese cartography.

The National Library of China possesses about 30,000 ancient Chinese maps. The *Yu ji tu* (Map of the Tracks of Yu) of 1136, featuring a cartographic grid with squares representing fixed ground distances (*ji li hua fang*) has attained classic significance in the history of cartography. The silk-based, 7-meter-square *Fujian yu tu* (Map of Fujian) made during the Kangxi period of the Qing dynasty is monumental in manner and luxuriously adorned, and is one of the finest of Chinese maps. It is particularly notable and valuable in showing for the first time how the island of Taiwan was designated a prefecture with three counties following the Qing conquest. Also of great research value are nearly 10,000 Qing maps of a typological or stylized variety (*yangshi lei*) obtained during the 1930s, which systematically present the layouts of imperial gardens, mausolea, and other buildings.

The *Pingjiang tu* (Map of the Prefectural City of Pingjiang) shown in this exhibition utilizes a joint planimetric and pictorial system to depict more than 640 man-made elements and natural features in the city of Suzhou, including the inner and outer city walls, streets and avenues, government seats and offices, temples, rivers, and bridges. It is not only one of the few surviving Song dynasty maps, but also the largest and most complete ancient city map engraved on stone. As such it has immense value for the study of the overall layouts of ancient Chinese cities, not to mention the economic and cultural conditions as well as standards of cartography during the Song period. Another exhibited item, the *Jiangxi quan sheng tushuo* (Atlas of Jiangxi Province, with Accompanying Descriptions), contains thirty-seven maps drawn in the manner of traditional Chinese pictorial maps, depicting mountains and ridges, rivers, lakes, city walls and moats, shrines and temples, villages and encampments, and other features within the various prefectures and counties of Jiangxi province in clear and vibrant colors. It is an important reference document for the study of the historical evolution of ancient regional and provincial travel routes, geographical features, and the social economy. The *Shengchao qi sheng yang tu* (Coastal Map of the Seven Maritime Provinces of the Illustrious Dynasty) is a representative map showing coastal features, and follows the convention of coastal defense maps. Beautifully drawn, it depicts coastal features from China's northeast all the way to Hainan, with particularly fine renditions of shoals, reefs, and archipelagoes. This very striking map is supplemented by a map of Taiwan, a map of the rear mountains of Taiwan, a map of the Pescadores (Penghu liedao), and a map of Qiongzhou prefecture (the island of Hainan). Even the ther Portuguese colony of Macao (Aomen) is shown with its city walls and a number of buildings.

Texts and illustrations from China's ethnic minorities

China is a unified nation of many peoples where the different ethnic groups have each contributed to the establishment of a splendid and brilliant civilization. The number of ancient scripts, rich in subject matter and diverse in formal appearance, has yet to be fully tallied, but there are close to thirty. Kharoshthi, for example, had already been introduced to China before the time of Christ; Sogdian is represented by inscriptions from the second and third centuries; Karashahr-Kucha script may be seen in documents of the fifth century; ancient Tibetan, Turkic, Uighur, Khitan, Tangut, Dai, and other scripts have histories exceeding a thousand years or close to that length of time. These different writing systems may be found in a wealth of texts and documents, and may be divided into several categories based on their formal characteristics: (1) Books, including various types of treatises, reference works, works from religious canons, etc.; (2) Archival documents, including official despatches, written contracts, personal correspondences, etc.; (3) Inscriptions on metal and stone, including engraved stelae, grave epitaphs, official seals, coins, etc.; and (4) Inscriptions and records, including inscriptions on wall paintings, calligraphy in ink on stone walls, etc. These formally diverse ancient documents have an important scholarly value, primarily in the fields of language, philology, philosophy, religion, literature, art, history, archaeology, astronomy, calendrical studies, and medicine, etc.

The National Library of China is the greatest repository of texts and documents from China's ethnic minorities, with very large holdings and extremely valuable editions. The "Dongba illustrations" and "Dongba texts" displayed in this exhibition are from the Naxi people of the Lijiang area in Yunnan province. The ancient pictographic script contained within the texts is part of a treasure trove of research materials on traditional Naxi culture. The color-illustrated *Chuangshi ji* (Annals of Creation) in the pictographic script of the Dongba is of great scholarly value because it records how the Naxi people perceived the formation of the world as well as legends pertaining to the emergence of the human race. The palm-leaf manuscripts of the Dai people are inscribed with metal styluses on the surfaces of pattra leaves. A dozen or so leaves are bound together to make a volume, while several, or even as many as twenty, such volumes make up a bundle. Bamboo or wooden boards are used to secure them at the top and bottom, producing a binding that is simple yet elegant. Black lacquer or gold flecks have been applied to the sides, thus making them more refined and beautiful. The principal contents of the palm-leaf scriptures are Buddhist scriptures, which preserve not only the form of earlier Theravada Buddhist texts, but also contain much material on the local history, geography, language, and literature of the Dai people. The *Sheli jisong* (Narrative Verses of Sariputta) exhibited here is part of the Buddhist canon's *Abhidhamma-pitaka*; the Dai script of the text was transliterated from the Pali and inscribed around the end of the nineteenth century. During the eleventh century, there was an ethnic minority in northwestern China called the Dangxiang who invented their own script, known as Tangut (*Xi Xia wen* in Chinese). Since this script long ago fell out of use, the several thousand volumes of texts and documents in Tangut script that have been recovered to date are precious materials for the study of the social aspects of ethnic minorities in the northwestern region. The content of Xi Xia documents includes Buddhist scriptures, Confucian texts, legal despatches, economic archives, and inscriptions engraved on stone stelae. The 10-*juan Liang huang baochan* (Precious Confessional of Emperor Wu of Liang), of which the ninth *juan* is displayed here, was translated from the Chinese version of the Buddhist canon, taking from it passages for the compilation of a work of confessional literature.

The Manchus, who established the last imperial line in China–the Qing–created their own script in 1599. During the three centuries that followed, Manchu and Chinese scripts literally co-existed side by side as the key official languages. The National Library of China possesses several million books and many thousands of bilingual rubbings in Manchu and Chinese, and houses the largest collection of Manchu books in the country. Two documents with parallel Manchu and Chinese texts, both belonging to the category of archival materials, are shown in this exhibition. One is a palace memorial from the Qianlong period, while the other is an imperial patent of nobility of the type conferred by the emperor upon high officials of the fifth rank and above as well as upon their parents and wives. Made from silk embroidered in five colors, it is not only valuable as documentary material, but is also an exquisite cultural relic rich in ornamental quality.

* * *

This United States exhibition of ancient Chinese books and documents from the National Library of China is a important event in cultural relations between the two countries. China is an ancient and civilized country with an extremely long history; the rich and varied forms of her ancient cultural records are an important aspect of ancient Chinese civilization. It is our sincere hope that through an exhibition of this nature, Americans will be better able to understand the circumstances under which ancient Chinese culture developed, and that they will also be better equipped to observe and understand the conditions for building up the modern Chinese nation.

Translated from the Chinese by Philip K. Hu

Catalogue essays

展品説明

Compiled and edited by Philip K. Hu

胡廣俊編著

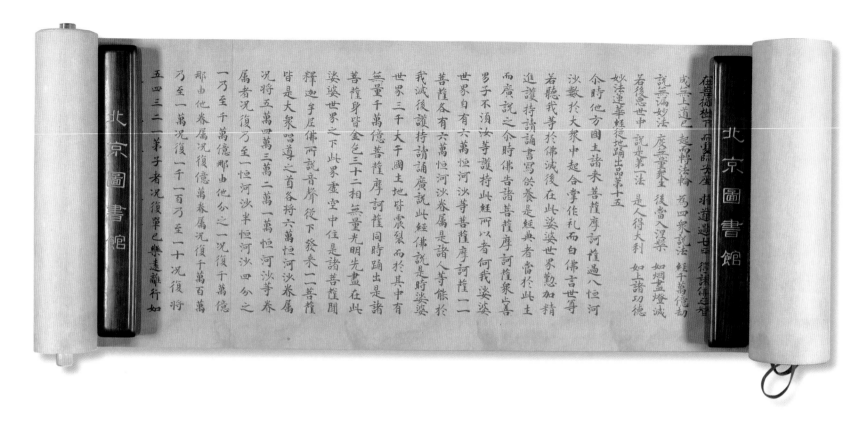

1

Dunhuang xie jing: Miaofa lianhua jing (7 juan)

Sutra of the Lotus of the Wonderful Law (*Saddharmapundarika-sutra*), 7 *juan*, Manuscript from Dunhuang

Tang dynasty (618-907), Zhengsheng period (695), dated 695
Translated from the Sanskrit by Kumarajiva (344-413)
From the Mogao Caves, Dunhuang, Gansu province
Handscroll containing *juan* 5 (*pin* 14-17), ink on 23 joined sheets of dyed yellow paper, 24.6 x 986.6 cm; height of first sheet: 19.6 cm

Xin 029

This scroll is one of more than 20,000 religious and secular manuscripts on paper dated between A.D. 406 and 996 that were recovered in 1900 from a sealed library among the Mogao Caves at Dunhuang. Large portions of the finds were subsequently acquired by the British Library and the Bibliothèque Nationale in Paris, while holdings are also to be found in Japanese and Russian institutions. The National Library of China has a substantial collection of over 10,000 scrolls that was begun in 1910 when the scholar Luo Zhenyu (1866-1940) first arranged for the transfer of manuscripts from Dunhuang to Beijing.

The *Miaofa lianhua jing* (Sutra of the Lotus of the Wonderful Law), commonly known as the *Lotus Sutra*, is a profound Buddhist scripture consisting of twenty-eight chapters (*pin*) in seven volumes (*juan*) with more than 60,000 characters; it contains a wealth of details and stories which reveal Mahayana Buddhist doctrines, but with special attention paid to Avalokitesvara (Guanyin), the Bodhisattva of Compassion. Most of the chapters contain both prose and verse passages, the latter form (*gatha*) being an aid to readers in memorizing the sutra. First completed in the second century A.D. in northwestern India, it was introduced to China during the third century. There are three extant Chinese translations of the *Lotus Sutra*, but the finest is the one dated 406 by the Kucha monk Kumarajiva (344-413), who arrived in Chang'an in 401 and proceeded to translate no less than thirty-five sutras and treatises into Chinese. Kumarajiva's translation of the *Lotus Sutra* is also the most well known because of its accuracy as well as the elegance and style of its language; it is regarded by the Tiantai, a distinctively Chinese Buddhist sect, as the supreme utterance of the Buddha.

The twenty-three joined sheets of Tang-dynasty yellow paper on which this fifth *juan* of the *Lotus Sutra* is inscribed has a closely woven fiber texture that has stood the test of time remarkably well. There are altogether 570 columns of regular script, with the number of characters per column varying between sixteen and twenty. Featured in this copy of the sutra are certain distinctive characters that had been created during the reign of Empress Wu (624-705; r. 690-705). The four chapters contained in this scroll are chapter 14, "Peaceful Practices"; chapter 15, "Emerging from the Earth"; chapter 16, "The Life Span of the Thus Come One"; and chapter 17, "Distinctions between Merits.

1

敦煌寫經

妙法蓮華經 七卷

後秦鳩摩羅什譯。唐證聖元年（695年）寫本。1900年發現於甘肅省敦煌莫高窟。此卷為卷五（品十四至十七）。楷書五百七十行，行十六至二十字不等。染黃紙，計二十三紙。高二四·六厘米，長九八六·六厘米·首紙框版高一九·六厘米。卷軸裝。
新 029

敦煌遺書在清光緒二十六年（1900年）甘肅敦煌石窟（俗稱千佛洞）中發現以後，在1907至1908年間，先被英國學者斯坦因將九千種卷子及畫繡美術品運往倫敦的大英博物館和印度新德里博物院等處，後又被法國漢學者伯希和運了至少五千多件到法國，分藏於巴黎的法國國家圖書館、盧浮宮、集美博物館等處。1910年清學部才將剩下部份運至北京，但在押運途中和抵北京以後又遭到官僚地主分子李盛鐸等人的盜竊。1911至1912年，

學部將存下來的敦煌遺書移交京師圖書館，後為北京圖書館所藏。現分散世界各地的敦煌遺書，都是研究中國古代歷史、經濟、政治、法律、社會、宗教、醫藥、術數、語文、文學等方面之珍貴資料。

中國國家圖書館舊藏敦煌遺書八千六百七十多卷，陳垣先生曾編印《敦煌劫餘錄》，著錄極詳。該館續收一千多卷，現總共藏有一萬卷以上。其中大多數是佛經，其次是道經，并有少數的梵文和藏文的寫本。此選錄的《妙法蓮華經》卷五，係續收的敦煌遺書，故編號以「新」字表明。

《妙法蓮華經》，亦稱《法華經》、《蓮華經》，是一部義理融攝淵博，情節曲折豐富的大乘佛教經典，為釋尊出世的本懷。此經主要宣傳大乘的意義，為何要信大乘佛教，以及如何達到大乘的最高境界。以淺顯易懂的故事為例，以羊車譬喻聲聞乘，以鹿車譬喻緣覺乘，以牛車譬喻菩薩乘。羊車最小，衹能在很窄的路上行走，而牛車最寬大，可

在大路上行車，路會越走越寬。此經宣揚了達到大乘成佛境界，必須經過艱苦的修行，經中提出「六度」，即「布施」、「持戒」、「忍辱」、「精進」、「禪定」、「明度無極」。原典約於公元二世紀成經於印度西北部，公元三世紀傳入中國。現存的漢譯本有三種，而以406年鳩摩羅什所譯的《妙法蓮華經》，由於辭藻優美，譯意雅達，流通最廣。是經卷次釐析有七卷、八卷之分，但通行者多為七卷二十八品。

此卷為七卷本《妙法蓮花經》之卷第五（第十四至十七品），即「安樂行品」、「從地湧出品」、「如來壽量品」、「分別功德品」。卷尾有題記：「大周證聖元年，歲次乙未四月戊寅朔廿一日戊戌，弟子薛崇徽奉為尊長敬造」。

此卷為公元七世紀武則天時期寫本，書法極為工整秀麗，并使用新創字，非常珍貴。

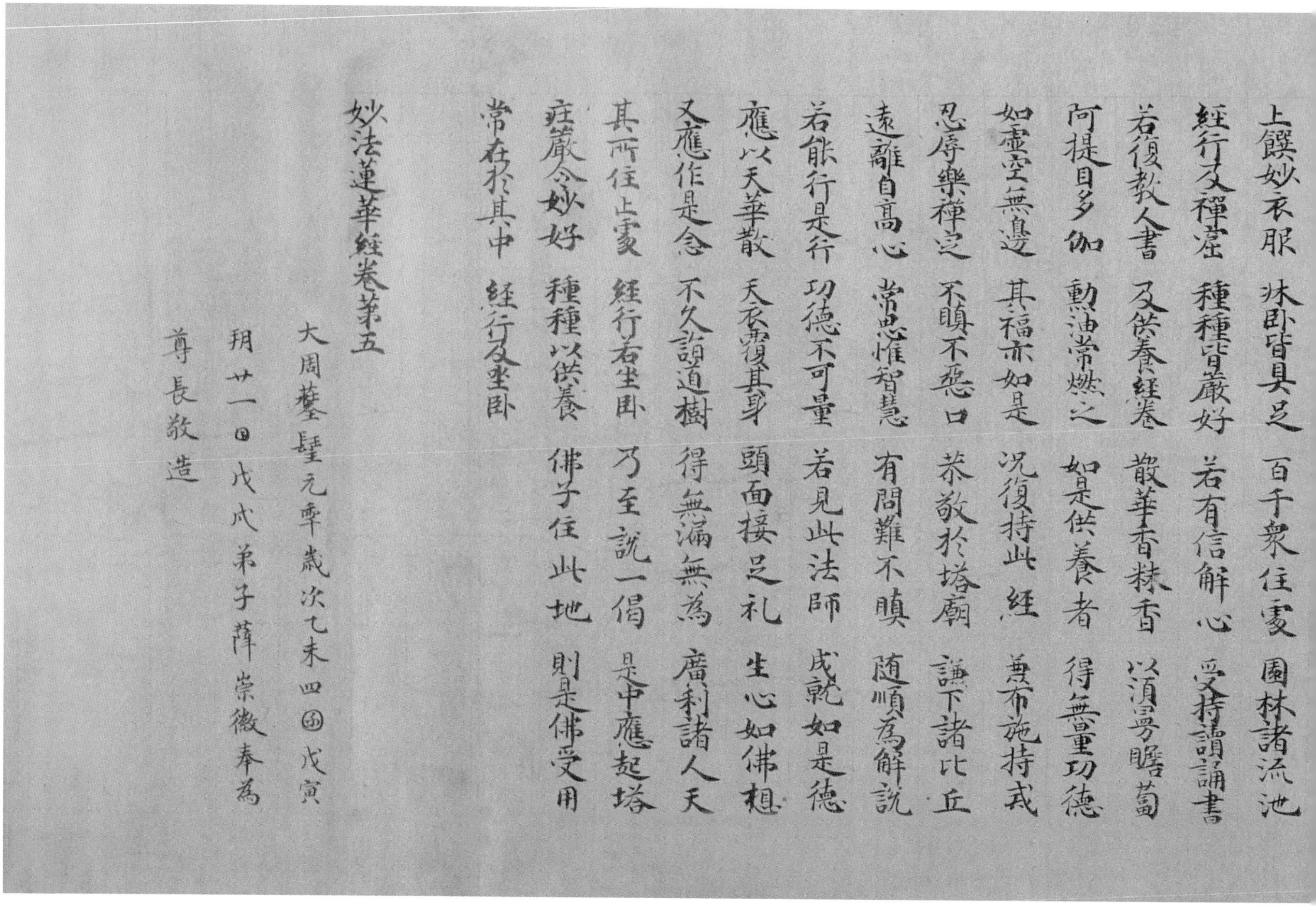

上饌妙衣服　沐卧皆具足　百千眾住處　園林諸流池

經行及禪窟　種種皆嚴好　若有信解心　受持讀誦書

若復教人書　及供養經卷　散華香抹香　以須曼瞻蔔

阿提目多伽　薰油常燃之　如是供養者　得無量功德

如虛空無邊　其福亦如是　況復持此經　兼布施持戒

忍辱樂禪之　不瞋不惡口　恭敬於塔廟　謙下諸比丘

遠離自高心　常思惟智慧　有問難不瞋　隨順為解說

若能行是行　功德不可量　若見此法師　成就如是德

應以天華散　天衣覆其身　頭面接足禮　生心如佛想

又應作是念　不久詣道樹　得無漏無為　廣利諸人天

其所住止處　經行若坐卧　乃至說一偈　是中應起塔

莊嚴令妙好　種種以供養　佛子住此地　則是佛受用

常在於其中　經行及坐卧

妙法蓮華經卷第五

大周葬聖元年歲次乙未四圓戊寅

朔廿一日戊戌弟子薛崇微奉為

尊長敬造

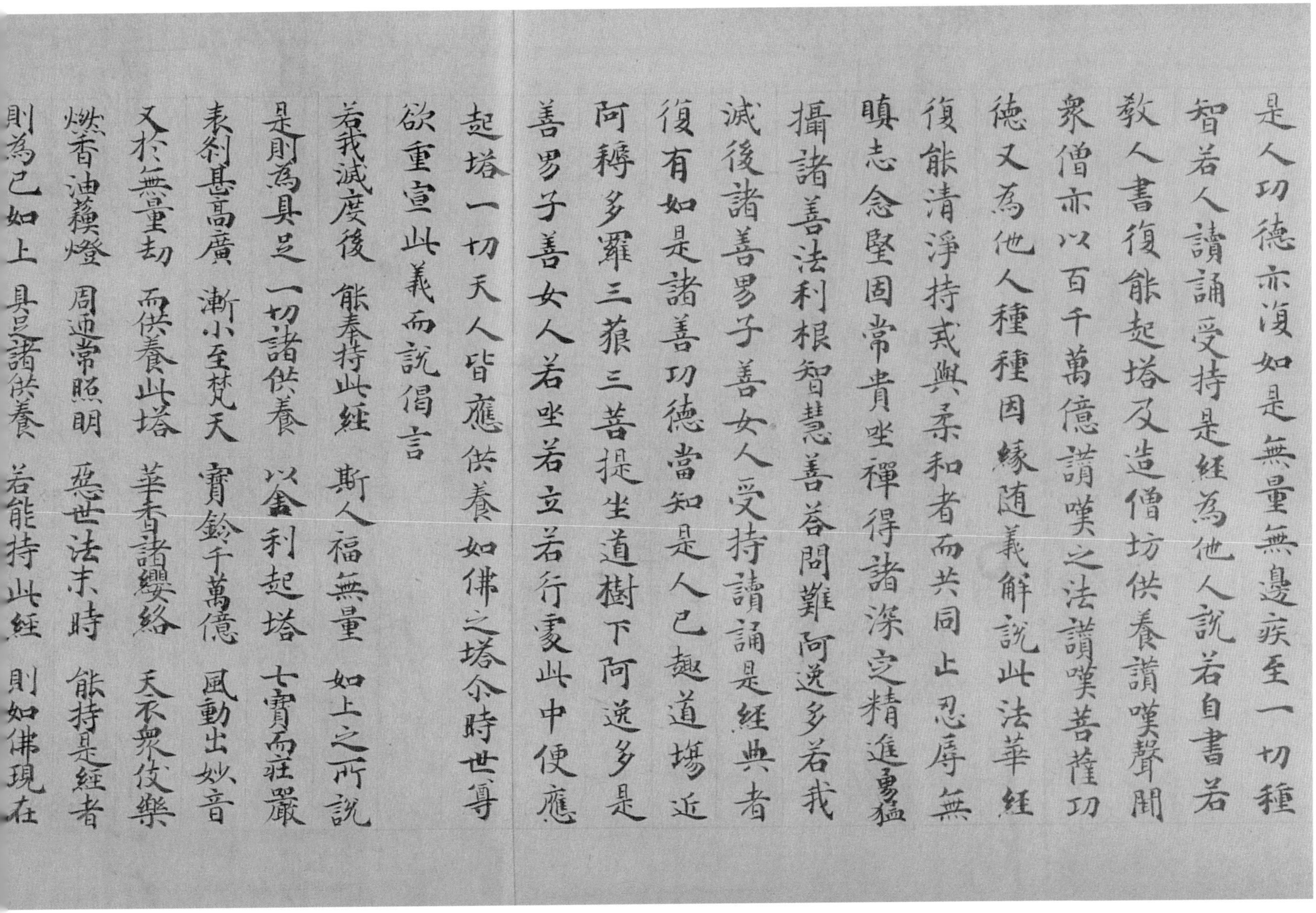

是人功德亦復如是無量無邊疾至一切種

智若人讀誦受持是經為他人說若自書若

教人書復能起塔及造僧坊供養讚嘆聲聞

眾僧亦以百千萬億讚嘆之法讚嘆菩薩功

德又為他人種種因緣隨義解說此法華經

復能清淨持戒與柔和者而共同止忍辱無

瞋志念堅固常貴坐禪得諸深定精進勇猛

攝諸善法利根智慧善荅問難阿逸多若我

滅後諸善男子善女人受持讀誦是經典者

復有如是諸善功德當知是人已趣道場近

阿耨多羅三藐三菩提坐道樹下阿逸多是

善男子善女人若坐若立若行豪此中便應

起塔一切天人皆應供養如佛之塔介時世尊

欲重宣此義而說偈言

若我滅度後　能奉持此經　斯人福無量　如上之所說

是則為具足　一切諸供養　以舍利起塔　七寶而莊嚴

表刹甚高廣　漸小至梵天　寶鈴千萬億　風動出妙音

又於無量劫　而供養此塔　華香諸瓔珞　天衣眾伎樂

燃香油蘇燈　周迊常照明　惡世法末時　能持是經者

則為已如上　具足諸供養　若能持此經　則如佛現在

2

Zhaocheng xian Guangsheng si ke Da Zang jing:

Da banruo boluo miduo jing (600 juan)

Greater Sutra of the Perfection of Transcendent Wisdom (*Mahaprajnaparamita-sutra*), 600 *juan*, from the Jin *Tripitaka* deposited at Guangsheng Temple, Zhaocheng County

Jin dynasty (1115-1234), Huangtong period (1141-1148) through Dading period (1161-1189), printed between 1149 and 1173

Translated from the Sanskrit by Xuanzang (602-664)

From the *Tripitaka* deposited at Guangsheng Temple, Zhaocheng county, Shanxi province

Handscroll containing *juan* 103, woodblock-printed ink on paper, 29.8 x 1320.0 cm; block size of illustrated frontispiece section: 26.1 x 38.7 cm; text section, height of blocks: 22.0 cm

0070

This Buddhist sutra is part of the renowned *Tripitaka* printed during the Jin dynasty (1115-1234) between 1149 and 1173. The sole surviving set, it was not mentioned in any old catalogues and was rediscovered only in the twentieth century. The blocks for this monumental undertaking are believed to have been engraved at the Tianning Temple in Jiezhou (now Jiexian in Shanxi province) under the sponsorship of a lay woman named Cui Fazhen. This particular set of the *Tripitaka* was originally stored at Guangsheng Temple in Shanxi's Zhaocheng county, hence it is popularly referred to as the "Zhaocheng *Tripitaka*" (Zhaocheng Zang), or simply as the "Jin *Tripitaka*." During the Jin dynasty, the engraving of woodblocks for printed works was centered around Pingshui in Shanxi, where high-quality paper was produced in large quantities; further to the north, ink-making factories were to be found in Taiyuan prefecture. Prior to the onslaught of warfare, printing and book production thrived in Shanxi.

Guangsheng Temple is located at the southern foot of Mount Huo, southeast of the town of Zhaocheng (now part of Hongdong county) and consists of the upper and lower temples as well as the Temple of the Water God (Shuishen miao). The Jin *Tripitaka* was originally kept in twelve wooden sutra cases in a hall in the upper temple. Sometime during September 1937, in the wake of the Japanese invasion of China, a Buddhist priest named Likong sealed all the priceless sutras within the uppermost storey of the Flying Rainbow Pagoda (Feihong ta) at Guangsheng Temple in order to safeguard them. Zhaocheng came under Japanese military occupation on February 26, 1938, following which there were repeated attempts to uncover the whereabouts of the Jin *Tripitaka*. In the spring of 1942, Zhaocheng county officials relayed an urgent telegram message from Chinese resistance forces based at Yan'an to the guerrilla chief Li Qilin, saying that a precious set of Buddhist sutras hidden in a pagoda at Guangsheng Temple was in imminent danger of being confiscated by Japanese troops. Under the protection of local guerrilla forces and cover of darkness, the entire set of sutras was removed from its hiding place in the early morning hours of April 27, 1942, and spirited to safety by soldiers of the Eighth Route Army. After being held for several years by the Chinese military administration at Taiyuan, the sutras were transferred to the special collections division of

Beijing Library (now the National Library of China) in 1949, where they were subsequently repaired, restored, and remounted.

The 682 satchels of the Jin *Tripitaka*, containing some 7,000 *juan*, were ordered with characters taken from the *Thousand-Character Essay* (*Qian zi wen*); the first satchel bearing the character *tian* and the last bearing the character *ji*. Only 4,800 or so *juan* have survived intact, with the rest either in a fragmentary state or lost. The National Library of China has in its possession 4,541 *juan* while the Shanxi Provincial Museum in Taiyuan has 1,025 *juan*; much smaller number of *juan* may be found in several other collections. The sutras are all in the form of handscrolls with yellow external backing papers and red rollers, but the lengths of scrolls vary considerably. The sutras are mostly printed on white mulberry-bark paper, with an occasional few printed on waxy yellow paper. The engraved woodblocks used for the *Tripitaka* generally measure approximately 22 cm high and 47 cm wide, but the printed characters are not of a uniform style throughout. These rare and valuable printed sutras reflect not only the well established state of Buddhism in northern China at this time, but also indicate the attainment of high standards of woodblock-engraving.

The scroll illustrated here contains *juan* 103 of the *Mahaprajnaparamita-sutra*, which may be translated as the "Greater Sutra of the Perfection of Wisdom" or as the "Great Sutra of the Wisdom That Reaches the Other Shore," an enormous 600-*juan* systematic exposition of the essential but difficult Mahayana Buddhist doctrinal concept of emptiness (*sunyata* in Sanskrit; *kong* in Chinese). It was translated from the Sanskrit by the Tang pilgrim monk Xuanzang (602-664) in 663. Each block contains twenty-three columns with fourteen

characters per column. Every sheet of paper in this section of the sutra contains the character *ying* taken from the *Thousand-Character Essay*. The beginning of each *juan*, as in this example, is embellished with an illustrated frontispiece (*fei hua*) which shows the Buddha, seated on a throne-platform, a halo surrounding his head, preaching the law. To the left and right are the Ten Disciples, one of whom faces the Buddha directly. At upper left and lower right there are two *vajra* (martial guardians) protecting the assembly. Sutra frontispieces such as this first emerged in the late Tang period; they functioned as pious embellishments of sacred scriptures and ensured that merit was accumulated by their sponsors. The earliest surviving woodblock-printed sutra frontispiece illustration is the British Museum's copy of the *Diamond Sutra* (*Jin'gang jing*) dated 868. The portrayal of the Buddha preaching to assembled beings became conventionalized and was applied with certain variations to sutra frontispieces for many centuries. In this instance, the composition and linework display many differences from woodblock illustrations of Song dynasty Buddhist texts, but the liveliness in the drawing and engraving is representative of Jin period engraved woodblock Buddhist images.

2

趙城縣廣勝寺刻大藏經

大般若波羅蜜多經六百卷

唐玄奘譯。金熙宗皇統九年至世宗大定十三年(1149-1173年)刻本。此為卷一百三，計二十四紙。每版二十三行，行十四字，上下單邊。卷高二九‧八厘米，長一三二〇厘米。扉畫版框高二六‧一厘米，寬三八‧七厘米。正文版框高二二厘米。卷軸裝。

0070

金代刻書以山西平水為中心，其地盛產紙張，質地堅韌，北有太原府「造墨場」，且未受戰爭影響，故刻書業極為發達。此經屬於著名的金刊佛教《大藏經》。《金藏》的刊印，據說總其成者為解州天寧寺開雕大藏經版會。因刻於金代，故稱《金藏》。因原來藏在廣勝寺內，故又稱《趙城廣勝寺藏》，也稱《趙城藏》、《趙城金藏》。廣勝寺位於山西省洪洞縣趙城鎮東南的霍山南麓，由上寺、下寺及水神廟組成。《金藏》原存於廣勝上寺的彌陀殿的十二個藏經木櫃中，不為人知。自一九三三年春，由中國著名高僧范成法師發現以來，平、津、滬、寧各報，相繼發表研究考證文章。《金藏》是中國現存最古老、最珍貴的《大藏經》版本，其發現是佛教文獻史及學術史上的一件大事。

一九三七年「七‧七」事變之後，日本侵略中國。力空法師為了保護此無價之法寶，在一九三七年九月將藏經封於廣勝寺飛虹塔的頂層。次年二月二十六日，日軍佔領趙城，此後日本人多次詢問《金藏》的藏處，欲以武力搶奪。一九四二年初春，山西趙城縣委通知游擊大隊政委李溪林說：接到上級轉來延安電報，有一部珍貴的佛經藏在趙城縣廣勝寺飛虹塔的二層上。據偵知日本侵略軍企圖搶走。幹部立即組織身強力壯的群眾，在游擊隊的掩護下，當年四月二十七日（壬午年三月十日）午夜零時許全部經卷由八路軍搶救出來，安全運出廣勝寺，前往太原軍區，才使這部佛經保存下來。一九四九年運交北京圖書館保存，將藏經裝訂修補珍藏起來。一九八四年至一九九六年間出版了一百零六冊的《中華大藏經（漢文部分）》，是以稀世珍本《趙城金藏》為影印底本的新版《大藏經》。

《趙城金藏》之藏經依千字文編帙，自「天」字至「幾」字，凡有六百八十二帙，約七千卷，現存四千八百卷，蓋已殘十分之三矣。中國國家圖書館藏四千八百一十三卷，而中國各地的圖書館、博物館亦有零星收藏，個別經卷還流落海外。據近年的調查，山西省博物館藏一百二十五卷；上海圖書館藏二十卷；北京大學圖書館藏六卷；南京博物館藏六卷；山西省廣勝寺藏三卷；廣西省博物館藏二卷；山西省圖書館藏一卷；山西省崇善寺藏一卷；北京故宮博物院藏一卷；台灣台北中央研究院藏一卷；德國慕尼黑圖書館藏一卷。

經皆卷子式，黃表赤軸，長短大小略有參差，大半用白桑皮紙印，偶見蠟黃紙印本。藏經中字體雖不一，但其刊刻反映了當時佛教在中國北方傳播的盛況和雕版技術的高超，是稀世瑰寶。《金藏》中有各種版式，大多為翻譯之經律論讚，版心高約二十二厘米，寬約四十七厘米。每卷前均鐫印卷首扉畫，描繪如來佛編祖正坐，頭肩圓光，妙相端然，與佛弟子說法。左右侍立弟子十人，一人仰首合什，聆聽佛法。其餘亦各具神態。兩角分別侍立一戎裝金剛，以示護衛。整個構圖和綫描嚴整有力，代表了北方雄渾豪放的風格。

《大般若波羅蜜多經》，亦稱《大般若經》，共六百卷，唐釋玄奘譯。此經內容是說，通過「般若」（智慧）才能把握佛教的「真理」，達到覺悟解脫。《趙城金藏》之《大般若波羅蜜多經》（天字帙至奈字帙）存三百五十九卷（內重出一卷），抄二十四卷。此展出為卷一百零三，題「三藏法師玄奘奉詔譯」。共二十四紙，每紙二十三行，行十四字。每紙首加注一小行，為經名、第幾卷、第幾紙，「盈字號」。此卷經文為「初分攝受品第二十九之五」以及「初分校量功德品第三十之一」。卷首附裝釋迦說法圖一幅，狀如廣勝寺上寺後殿造像，右端題「趙城縣廣勝寺」六字。此扉頁畫疏朗簡潔，繪刻者注意裝飾效果而又較為寫實，佛與弟子的刻劃具有個性，圖中袈裟以粗獷的黑綫條表現貼邊，使綫條有變化，增強衣紋轉折和立體感。

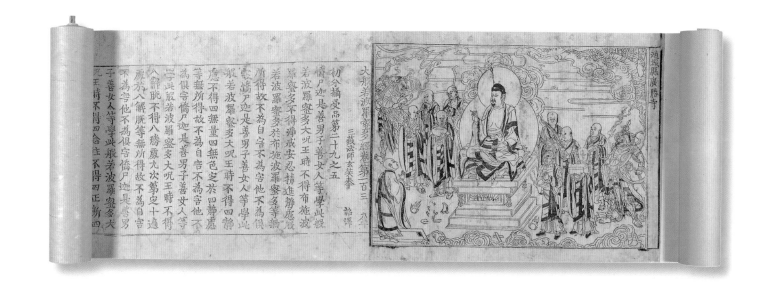

3

Ouyang Wenzhong gong ji (153 juan), fulu (5 juan)

Collected Works of Ouyang Xiu, 153 *juan*, with Supplement, 5 *juan*

Southern Song dynasty (1127-1279), Qingyuan period (1195-1200)

Compiled by Ouyang Xiu (1007-1072; *jinshi* of 1030); edited by Ouyang Fa et al.; proofread by Sun Qianyi; recompiled by Zhou Bida (1126-1204) et al.; engraved by Ye Yuan et al.

Jizhou, Jiangxi province: Zhou Bida, 1196

10 columns per half-folio; 16 characters per column; white folding margin at center of folio with double "fish-tails," number of engraved characters indicated at the top, and name of engraver at the bottom; double-line borders on left and right; single-line borders at top and bottom; overall dimensions of volumes: 36.7 x 23.5 cm; block sizes of text: approx. 21.1 x 15.5 cm; stitched binding

2392

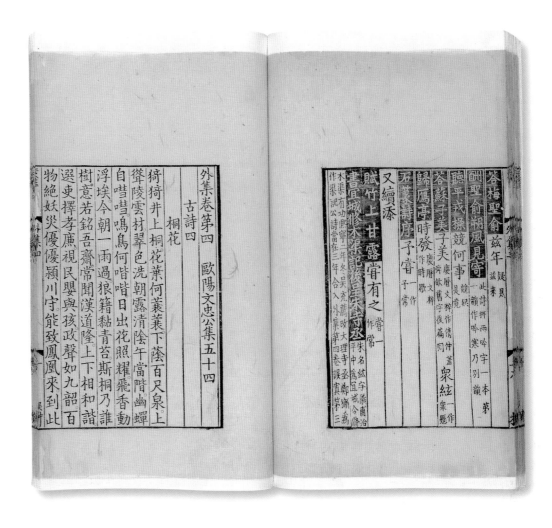

Ouyang Xiu (1007-1072; *jinshi* of 1030), a statesman, historian, epigrapher, essayist, and poet, was one of the leading cultural figures of the Northern Song dynasty. Heir to the "ancient style" (*guwen*) literary movement established in the Tang dynasty by Han Yu (768-824), he was the principal compiler of the *Xin Wu dai shi* (New History of the Five Dynasties) and the *Xin Tang shu* (New History of the Tang), as well as teacher to other great Song scholars including Su Shi (1037-1101). Among the official titles he held during his illustrious career were Vice Military Affairs Commissioner (*shumi fu shi*) and Participant in Determining Government Matters

or Vice Grand Councilor (*canzhi zhengshi*). He was finally permitted to withdraw from government service in 1071 and styled himself "Liu yi jushi" (The Retired Scholar of Six Ones).

Ouyang Xiu undertook the compilation of his own collected writings in the short period before his death in 1072. His son Ouyang Fa took over as editor after 1072, and another son, Ouyang Fei, invited Su Shi to write a preface to the 50-*juan Jushi ji* (Collected Works of the Retired Scholar) in 1091. A century later in 1191, Zhou Bida (1126-1204) and other

scholars from Ouyang Xiu's ancestral hometown of Luling, Jiangxi, began compiling the 153-*juan Ouyang Wenzhong gong ji* (Collected Works of Ouyang Xiu) which was printed in 1196 and in which the *Jushi ji* reappears as the first 50 *juan*. A 25-*juan* supplement to the literary collection (*wai ji*) contains some of the material left out by Ouyang Xiu in the *Jushi ji*; shown here is the opening section of one *juan* in the *wai ji*. In the remaining 28 *juan* are three collections of memorials and edicts drafted by Ouyang Xiu, his colophons on ancient epigraphical material, his annotations on books held by the imperial library, his *Shi hua* (Remarks on Poetry), his miscellaneous collection of court anecdotes, and his songs.

There are no longer any complete sets of the 1196 Zhou Bida edition of the *Ouyang Wenzhong gong ji* to be found. The National Library of China possesses several fragmentary sets from which this volume is taken. The so-called "butterfly binding" (*hudie zhuang*) used was a common bookbinding style during the Song and Yuan dynasties. The printed side of the sheet is folded in on itself with the text facing inward and with margins on all four sides; separate sheets are then bound together with glue along the center fold.

校，成為歐集的最佳版本，付吉州刻版。吉州即今江西省吉安，世傳吉州本歐集，指此。後世刊刻、整理歐集，都依據周必大刊本。周必大是江西最有名的刻家，除了刻印此書以外，還刊刻了《文苑英華》一千卷與《周益文忠公集》二百卷，於慶元二年（1196年）和開禧二年（1206年）間完成，三大部書皆刻鏤精湛，世稱「廬陵三絕」。

周必大吉州本《歐陽文忠公集》一百五十三卷，即〈居士集〉五十卷、〈外集〉二十五卷、〈易童子問〉三卷、〈外制集〉三卷、〈內制集〉八卷、〈表奏書啟六集〉七卷、〈奏議集〉十八卷、〈雜著述〉十九卷、〈集古錄跋尾〉十卷、〈書簡〉十卷，後附錄五卷。歐陽修之詩文，惟《居士集》五十卷為所自定，其餘皆他人掇拾所編。

此本刻印俱佳，與其他本不同者，布字間隔較遠，上下字無交插者。書寫娟秀又顯樸拙，本書為南宋時期江西刻本，反映了十二世紀江西地區刻

書的特點和風格。稍後江西地區又據此本翻版二次，行款版式悉同，世亦誤認為吉州本。明代諸本多從此本出，此本行，宋時歐集其他州郡刻本均散佚不傳。周必大本現存一百三十三卷，餘卷明人精寫補全。

每卷尾題後有「熙寧五年秋七男發等編定，紹熙二年三月郡人孫謙益校正」等二行，後附刻校記。版心上記字數，下記刻工，如葉源、上官通（或官通）、官達、陳全、鄧仁、劉文、陳元、程成、葉懋、忠、發、振、俊、仲、臻等等。宋諱玄、殷、穎、讓、朂、完、慎、敦字缺筆。按鐵琴銅劍樓藏書目錄及書影，日本宮內省圖書寮漢籍善本書目，寒瘦山房鬻存善本書目、雙鑑樓善本書目、文祿堂訪書記均曾著錄。茲選照外集卷三末半葉以及卷四首半葉。

3

歐陽文忠公集一百五十三卷附錄五卷

北宋歐陽修撰。南宋慶元二年（1196年）江西吉州（今吉安）周必大刻本。半葉十行，行十六字，校註小字雙行，左右雙邊，版心白口，雙魚尾。版心上記大小字數，下記刻工名。框高二一‧一厘米，寬一五‧五厘米。綫裝。

2396

歐陽修，字永叔，自號醉翁，晚號六一居士，江西廬陵吉水人。北宋天聖八年（1030年）舉進士甲科，官至樞密副使、參知正事。因議新法，與王安石不合，致仕，退居潁州，卒諡文忠。歐陽修一生博覽群書，以文章著名。編著有《新唐書》、《新五代史》、《毛詩本義》、《集古錄》、《歸田錄》、《洛陽牡丹記》、《試筆》、《居士集》、《六一詩話》、《六一詞》等。

歐陽修聲名顯赫，其文集屢經刊刻，此前已有汴京、浙、閩、蜀等多種刊本，遂致去取不一，文句互異，皆有錯訛。南宋慶元二年（1196年）周必大倩門客胡柯、彭叔夏等取諸本之長，重加編

4

Dade chongjiao Sheng ji zonglu (200 juan)

Comprehensive Record of Imperially Sanctioned Remedies Revised during the Dade Reign Period, 200 *juan*

Yuan dynasty (1279-1368), Dade period (1297-1307)

Originally compiled under the command of Emperor Huizong (1082-1135; r. 1101-1125) by eleven members of the Imperial Academy of Medicine between 1111 and 1118; revised; engraved by Chen Song et al.

Hangzhou, Zhejiang province: N.p. [government printing facility], 1299-1300

8 columns per half-folio; 17 characters per column; fine black folding margin at center of folio; double-line borders; overall dimensions of volumes: 29.9 x 22.9 cm; block sizes of text: approx. 23.5 x 19.1-19.2 cm; butterfly binding

No inventory number

The *Sheng ji zonglu*, which translates literally as "General Collection of Imperial Reliefs," was compiled under the command of Emperor Huizong (1082-1135; r. 1101-1125) by eleven members of the Imperial Academy of Medicine (*Tai yi yuan*) between 1111 and 1118. It concerns medical theories, *yunqi* (theory of the connection between diseases and seasonal changes), and treatment of diseases of various systems. The original Northern Song compilation of this monumental work con-

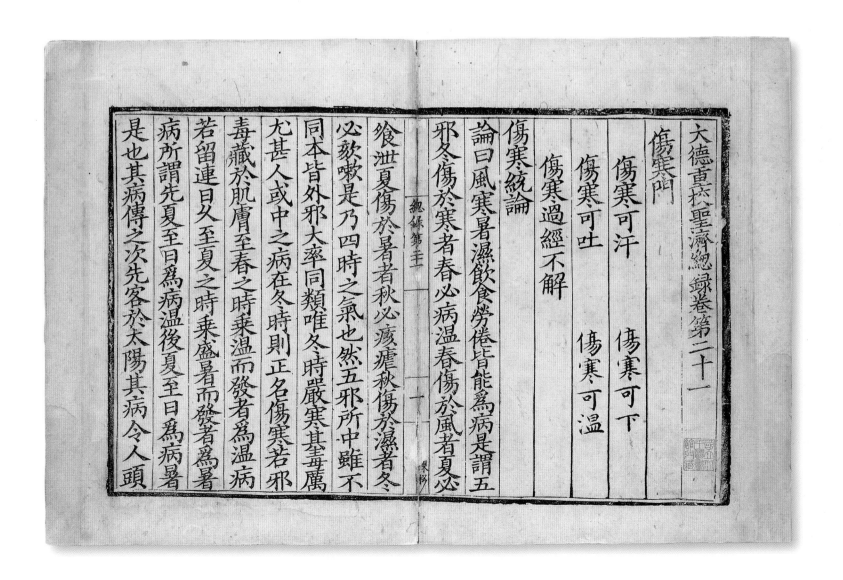

tained 200 *juan*, of which only 26 are extant. Covered within are numerous aspects of the art of healing, such as internal medicine, gynaecology, paediatrics, acupuncture, dieting, charms, and even the so-called "elixir of life." Also recorded are about 20,000 medicinal recipes.

This Yuan-dynasty volume is one of several in the National Library of China belonging to the revised edition of the encyclopaedia, also in 200 *juan*, but, like the original, the set is incomplete. It contains a preface by Jiao Yangzhi, a senior member of the Imperial Academy of Medicine. The colophon at the end of the final *juan* of this work indicates that printing was undertaken by the branch secretariat (*xing zhongshu sheng*) of Zhejiang province (located in Hangzhou) in the third year (1299) of the Dade reign period and was completed the following year in 1300; the names of the numerous supervisors (*tidiao guan*) of this project are recorded in six columns.

Shown here are the first and last folios of *juan* 21, which contains part of the encyclopaedia entitled *Shanghan men* (Section on Febrile Diseases Caused by Cold) which deals with the symptoms and management of typhus and typhoid fever; it includes much information gleaned from the Han-dynasty medical text *Shanghan lun* (Treatise on Febrile Diseases Caused by Cold; 10 *juan*) written by Zhang Ji (150-219).

4

大德重校聖濟總錄二百卷

元太醫院重修。元焦養直大德四年（1300年）序。元大德三年至
四年（1299–1300年）江浙等處行中書省刻本。杭州。框高二三

・五厘米，寬一九．一厘米。半葉八行，行十七字，四周雙邊，
版心細黑口，上記大小字數，下記刻工姓名。蝴蝶裝。

無號

《聖濟總錄》二百卷，宋徽宗政和年間（1111–1118年）敕廷臣修纂。北宋時重醫學，徽宗趙佶尤甚。本書是征集當時民間及醫家所獻醫方，搜古今秘笈，無有鉅細，結合內府所藏的秘方經整理匯編而成。全書共二百卷，載方兩萬多首，內容異常豐富，是集治療學之大成。首詳運氣之微，次備六淫之變，七方十劑，三因並舉，以後自「諸風」起至「神仙服餌」止，共分六十六門。每門之中，又分若干病癥；每一病癥先論病因病理，次列方藥治療。綜合全書所載病癥，概有內、外、婦、兒、五官、針灸諸科以及其他雜治、養生之類，既有理論，又有經驗，內容極其豐富，堪稱宋代的醫學全書。

宋版《政和聖濟總錄》早已泯沒無存。本書較早的兩次重刊，一為金大定年間（1161–1189年），一為元大德三年至四年（1299至1300年）。自茲以後，流傳漸少。《大德重校聖濟總錄》卷末題江浙等處行中書省大德三年（1299年）九月刊

造，至四年（1300年）二月畢工，又有提調官銜名六行，知此書實係大德間杭州官版。焦養直序末署「大德四年二月一日，集賢學士、嘉議大夫、典瑞少監，臣焦養直謹序」，及與議版行醫愈郎諸路醫學副提舉申甫等十二銜名。次載政和原序云，卷凡二百，方幾二萬，以病分門，門各有論，而敘統附焉。

此書紙墨瑩潔，幅廣行疏，字畫方整，頗似宋時浙本風格，是元代官刻本中的精品。元代很多官刻書是奉詔下杭州刻板，傳世元太醫院刻本除《大德重校聖濟總錄》以外，還有《危氏世醫得效方》、《傷寒論》等。中國國家圖書館所藏的幾部《大德重校聖濟總錄》屬於傳世最早版本，惜只存殘卷。日本文化十三年（1814年）東都醫學活字印本，即依此版本排印。

此展出卷二十一，即「傷寒門」，共四十二葉，所選照的為首葉及末葉。本卷版心下所錄刻工姓名有陳松、徐永、史、沈祥、陶、占、五、時中、金、孫、柳、茅化龍、茅文龍、徐文、王文佑、謝官保、謝拱之、齊明、陳新、高、允成、劉仁、劉、仲、王回、孫武、陳仁。此雖為殘本，但尚保存蝴蝶裝原式，紙幅寬廣，無修補版，彌足珍貴。

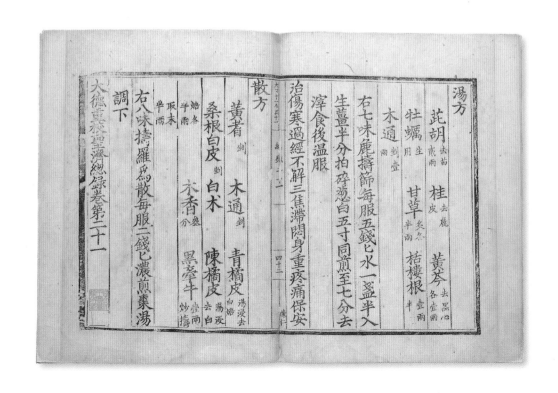

5

Xin bian Mulian jiu mu quan shan xiwen (3 juan)

New Compilation of the Text to the Play about Mulian Rescuing His Mother and Exhorting the World to Goodness, 3 *juan*

Ming dynasty (1368-1644), Wanli period (1573-1619)

Compiled by Zheng Zhizhen (1518-1595); proofread by Ye Zongtai; engraved by Huang Ting, Huang Bang (b. 1545), et al.

Xin'an, Anhui province: Zheng shi Gaoshi shanfang, 1582

10 columns per half-folio; 24 characters per column; small characters in half-columns; 24 characters per half-column; white folding margin at center of folio with single white "fish-tail"; single-line borders; overall dimensions of volumes: 25.8 x 16.7 cm; block sizes of text: approx. 20.2 x 13.4 cm; stitched binding

12430

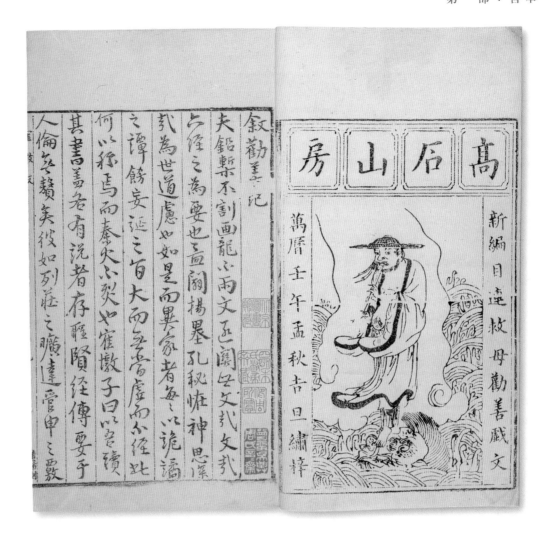

Mulian (Maudgalyayana in Sanskrit) was one of the ten disciples of the Sakyamuni Buddha and a key figure in Chinese Buddhist accounts. His mother apparently became "addicted" to meat and was condemned to hell as a starving ghost, and her subsequent rescue by Mulian is portrayed as a model of compassion. The story, transformed later into a play, is derived in part from the *Foshuo Yulan pen jing* (Sutra of the Sacrificial Feast for Hungry Ghosts Spoken by the Buddha; *Ullambana-sutra* in Sanskrit) and may also be found in a genre of literature called *bianwen* ("transformation texts") from Dunhuang. Vast productions of this play are staged in China, particularly in Anhui province, dur-

ing the *Yulan hui* (Festival of All Souls) which falls on the fifteenth day of the seventh lunar month.

The *Xin bian Mulian jiu mu quan shan xiwen* (New Compilation of the Text to the Play about Mulian Rescuing His Mother and Exhorting Her to Goodness), with a total of 100 acts (*hui*) divided between 3 *juan*, is the earliest extant edition of stage scripts (*tai ben*) for plays with the Mulian theme. It was compiled by Zheng Zhizhen, a native of Huizhou in Anhui province, and appeared in 1582 under the imprint of Zheng's own "Gaoshi shanfang" (Mountain Dwelling of the Lofty

Rocks).

This edition of 1582 contains fifty-seven illustrations. Although the illustrator is not known for certain, it was most probably Huang Ting or Huang Bang, who were responsible for the engraving of the woodblocks, as this was common practice during the early Wanli period. Huang Ting, the most senior member of the Huang clan of master artisans from Qiu village (in Shexian, Anhui) who is recorded in documents, once lived far from home in Beijing, a sign of the demand upon his services. This book is also one of the first works for which the names of the engravers are known.

The illustrations here are early examples of the Huizhou woodblock engraving school, with lively and expressive figures as well as high contrast between black-ink areas and blank spaces. The subject matter, composition, and engraving style are not only reminiscent of early Ming woodblock illustrations from Jian'an, Fujian province, but also exhibit the influence of Song and Yuan illustrated editions.

The original woodblocks used to print this book have been preserved and are now in the collection of the Anhui Provincial Museum in Hefei. Many later impressions of this book were made from the original blocks; this copy from the National Library of China is probably one such example. The first reproduction here shows the illustrated cover page from the first volume which provides the full title of the book along the right edge, the date of the engraving along the left, and the name of the publishing concern in large characters along the top. Facing this cover page is the beginning of one of the prefaces. The other reproduction, taken from the same volume, shows the start of *juan* 1 of the theatrical text and the first illustration related to the script.

目連救母故事濫觴於晉時流傳的《佛說盂蘭盆經》，從晉至唐元和年間，它主要憑借經文與宗教風俗活動盂蘭盆會得以傳播，然到了唐元和末年產生了變文之後，它的主要載體很快換成了變文。目連戲的初始劇宋雜劇《目連救母》就是由它派生出來的。雖然後世的戲劇與說唱文學故事進行了擴充，但在救母這一核心情節上一直依憑着它搭起的框架。

鄭之珍所撰、刻《新編目連救母勸善戲文》是現存最早的目連戲台本。鄭之珍，字子玉、汝席，號高石，別號高石山人，徽州（今安徽歙縣）祁門清溪人。明諸生。屢困場屋，遊心方外。喜談詩，兼習吳歙。生卒年均未詳，約明萬曆中前後在世。

《新編目連救母勸善戲文》之前有大型的目連戲，鄭本就是根據當時的台本改編而成的。此戲文全劇冗漫至百另二折，分上卷三十三折，中卷三十五折，下卷三十四折，以目連、目連父母和益利等為戲劇的主要人物，始終登場。上卷寫傅相虔誠奉佛，博施濟貧。因而感動了上蒼，得善報而升天界。中卷寫劉氏不信佛教、殺牲開葷，毀僧罵道，因而激怒鬼神，得惡報而下地獄。下卷寫傅羅卜為救母出離地獄，西行見佛，後在佛的幫助下超度母親升天。每卷皆有敷演場目與開場，而各有其終局，若釐而為三，又能具其獨立形式，可知此戲傾向於實演。

每卷內封面均在粗黑版框內鐫雕個別的牌記。上卷牌記上橫格鐫「高石山房」，右直格鐫「新編目連救母勸善戲文」，左直格鐫「萬曆壬午孟秋吉旦繡梓」。中、下卷內封面牌記左直格的文字與上卷不一，在此不錄。每卷均有目錄。上卷正文卷端題「新安高石山人鄭之珍編，館甥葉宗泰校」。上卷前有萬曆己卯葉宗春序、萬曆壬午陳昭祥序、萬曆壬午鄭之珍自序、萬曆癸未倪道賢序，後有萬曆壬午胡元祿跋。此版片原存祁門，現藏安徽省博物館，後印版甚多。此書雖為原刻本，但非初印本。

此書插圖代表了徽州早期版畫的風格。插圖共五十七幅，單雙面不一，畫風大膽活潑，綫條粗實有力，陰刻與陽刻互用，綫面結合，變化多端，尚不失古版畫作風。刻工黃鋌，生平不詳，卒於京師，可能是在北京國子監擔任了一定的職務。黃鋌，新安人，後遷居婺源（今屬江西省），常署名鈇，刻有《國朝明公尺牘》、《戰國策鈔》等書。徽派版畫以《新編目連救母勸善戲文》中的插圖為分水嶺，自此以後，版畫作風轉向工細纖巧。茲選照上卷內封面牌記與〈敘勸善記〉敘文上半葉，以及上卷正文上半葉與第一幅插圖。

此書另有鄭氏高石山房翻刻萬曆十年本、萬曆年間金陵唐氏富春堂刊本、清種福堂刊本、清會文堂刊本、清光緒十年（1884年）江津敬古堂刊本，圖亦大同小異。另有《行孝道目連救母》，本事同出《佛說盂蘭盆經》，云：「佛大弟子目犍連尊者」，神通第一。浙江紹興舊時七月十五中元節酬神戲，仍有《目連》劇演出，敷以燈彩，分上中下三本，於三宵演竣。

5

新編目連救母勸善戲文三卷

明鄭之珍撰。明葉宗泰校。明黃鋌、黃鈇刻。明萬曆十年（1582年）新安鄭氏高石山房原刻本。半葉十行，行二十四字，小字雙行，半行二十四字。四周單邊，單白魚尾，版心白口。框高二〇・二厘米，寬一三・四厘米。綫裝。

12430

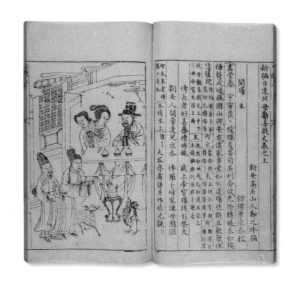

6

Yangzheng tujie

Illustrations and Explanations on Correct Cultivation

Ming dynasty (1368-1644), Wanli period (1573-1619)
Compiled by Jiao Hong (1541-1620; *jinshi* of 1589);
explanatory text by Wu Jixu; illustrated by Ding
Yunpeng (1547-ca. 1628); engraved by Huang Qi
Nanjing, Jiangsu province: Kuibi zhai, 1594
10 columns per half-folio; 20 or 21 characters per
column; white folding margin at center of folio; single-
line borders; overall dimensions of volumes: 30.1 x 19.
5 cm; block sizes of text: approx. 24.0 x 16.3 cm;
stitched binding

16750

Jiao Hong (1541-1620; *jinshi* of 1589) was a disciple of Geng Dingxiang (1524-1596) and a student of Luo Rufang (1515-1588), both prominent members of the Taizhou school of Neo-Confucian philosophy. After obtaining his metropolitan *jinshi* degree in 1589, Jiao became a Hanlin compiler (*Hanlin yuan bianxiu*) and in 1593 was appointed as one of the lecturers (*jiangguan*) to Zhu Changluo (1582-1620), the eldest son and eventual heir apparent of the Wanli emperor (r. 1573-1619). Jiao was a prolific author who wrote, compiled, or edited more than forty books, including the *Guochao xianzheng lu* (A Record of Worthies of the Reigning Dynasty), the *Ershi jiu zi pinhui shiping* (An Annotated Anthology of Twenty-Nine Philosophers), the *Guo shi jingji zhi* (Bibliographical Treatise of the State History), the *Yi quan* (An Aid to the Book of Changes), the *Yu gong jie* (An Elucidation of the Yu gong Chapter of the Book of History), and the *Jiao shi bi cheng* (Notebook

of Master Jiao).

The *Yangzheng tujie*, an illustrated compendium of sixty maxims and exemplary deeds of imperial heirs apparent drawn from history, was expressly compiled for Zhu Changluo's moral instruction. It was pre-

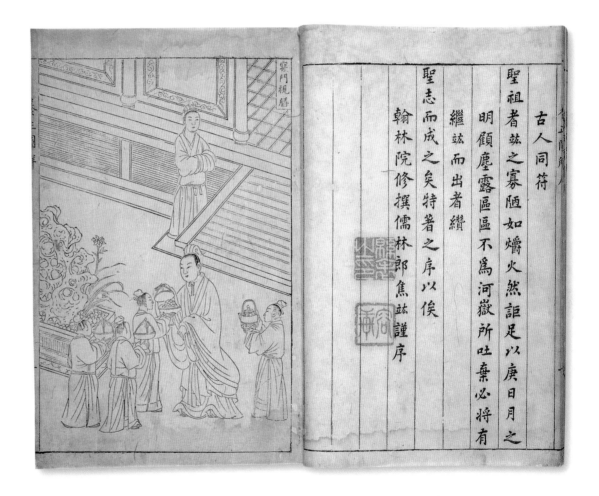

sented to the throne in 1597 but was never actually used by the prince due to the jealousy and opposition of Jiao's fellow lecturers, who believed that he had compiled the book in order to curry favor at court. However, when Jiao died in 1620 of old age after a full

and energetic retirement, the Tianqi emperor (r. 1621-1627) honored him posthumously with the position of Mentor (*Yu de*) in recognition of his service as lecturer to his father Zhu Changluo, who reigned all too briefly in 1620 as the Taichang emperor.

The *Yangzheng tujie* was printed twice in close succession during the Wanli period, using in both cases pictorial compositions of the renowned figure painter Ding Yunpeng (1547-ca. 1628), who had been specially invited to Nanjing to participate in this book project. The first edition of 1593 was made by Wang Yunpeng's "Wanhu xuan" in Xin'an Anhui; the engraver is identified as Huang Lin. The copy from the National Library of China shown here, formerly in the collection of Zheng Zhenduo (1898-1958), was published the following year in 1594 by the "Kuibi zhai" belonging to the bookseller Zheng Siming in Nanjing, with the engravings done by Huang Qi. These late Ming editions were not divided into *juan*, but when the book was republished in 1669 by the "Gaigong tang," it was reorganized by Cao Fen into 2 *juan* and the text reset in type. A Qing imperial palace edition, undivided into *juan* and containing poems by the Qianlong emperor (r. 1736-1795) as well as eulogizing verses by the Jiaqing emperor (r. 1796-1820) was belatedly printed at the Hall of Military Glory (Wuying dian) in 1895.

The full-page woodblock pictures of the 1593 "Wanhu xuan" edition are of a uniformly high quality in terms of composition, delineation, and engraving; they represent the most complex and sophisticated examples of Chinese book illustrations up to this time. As is appropriate for a work of this nature, figures are given considerable prominence and distinctive personalities in all the pictures, but many of the architectural details, interior furnishings, and landscape elements are also rendered with great care and accuracy. Figures and objects are juxtaposed so that spatial volumes are convincingly depicted, and all the illustrations are provided with a caption title. In contrast, the illustrations of the 1594 "Kuibi zhai" edition shown here are not quite as detailed or finely engraved as its immediate predecessor. The relative proportions of figures, objects, and architectural elements have been altered and intricate decorative patterns in several areas

have been left out altogether, clearly demonstrating that Huang Qi's skills as a copyist and engraver were not as well developed as those of Huang Lin, or perhaps that the exigencies of time prevented him from lavishing more care on the woodblock engravings. It also suggests that this Nanjing edition might have been intended for the "lower-end" of the market, printed with some haste for a more popular readership.

The pictures selected here are anecdotes from the lives of the two founders of the Zhou dynasty, Chang, the Duke of Zhou (ca. 1231-ca. 1135 B.C.) who was canonized as King Wen (*Wen wang*; "Cultivated King"), and his son Fa (ca. 1169-ca. 1116 B.C.), the first sovereign of the Zhou dynasty (ca. 1100-256 B.C.) who was canonized as King Wu (*Wu wang*; "Martial King"); their biographies may be found in the Zhou section of the *benji* (Basic Annals) in Sima Qian's *Shi ji* (Records of the Grand Historian). Jiao Hong's preface is followed immediately by the book's first illustration, "Inspecting Delicacies at the Main Entrance of the Inner Apartments of the Palace" (*Qin men shi shan*), where the very filial King Wen is seen inspecting delicacies prepared for his father. The other reproduction shows part of the text corresponding to the previous picture and the book's second illustration, "Sending Dried Fish Away from the Delicacies" (*Shan chi baoyu*), in which a youthful Fa, future King Wu, is informed by the bearded royal tutor Taigong Wang that his craving for a certain type of dried fish (*bao yu*) was inappropriate for someone of his status and that he was to follow the decorum laid out for the consumption of proper kinds of food.

6

養正圖解不分卷

明焦竑撰。明吳繼序解說。明丁雲鵬繪。明黃奇刻。明萬曆二十二年（1594 年）金陵奎璧齋刊本。半葉十行，行二十或二十一字，四周單邊，版心白口。框高二四厘米，寬一六‧三厘米。綫裝。
16750

焦竑，字弱侯，號澹園，衛籍日照人，住金陵（今南京）。明萬曆十七年（1589 年）進士第一名，官翰林院修撰。博覽群書，善為古文，典正訓雅，為明代著名文人。萬曆四十八年（1620 年）卒，年八十。熹宗時以先朝講讀恩復官，贈諭德，謚文端。編著有《國朝獻徵錄》、《二十九子品彙釋評》、《國史經籍誌》、《易筌》、《禹貢解》、《焦氏筆乘》等。

明萬曆間，焦竑在皇子講官時，為勸導皇長子朱常洛承續封建道統而采錄編撰進呈《養正圖解》。是書前有焦氏自序：「高皇帝開建鴻業，更立三才，為帝者首，乃海內甫定，即垂意根本至計，博選耆艾魁壘之士從太子諸王以遊，已命諸臣講讀經書暇，開陳明君良相、孝子忠臣諸故事，及時政沿革、民間疾苦之類，已又命繪農業艱難與古孝行圖以進，蓋其為教可謂本末具舉，蔑以復加矣。歲甲午，皇上命皇長子出閣講學，竑以職事叨從勸講之後，竊愧空疏，靡所自效，獨念四子五經，理之淵海，窮年講習，未易殫明，我聖祖顧於遺文故事，拳拳不置，良緣理涉虛而難見，事徵實而易知，故今古以通之、圖繪以象之，朝誦夕披而觀省備焉也。竑誠不自揆，仰遵祖訓，采古言行可資勸誡者著為圖說，名曰《養正圖解》，輒錄上塵以俟裁定。夫聖須學也，學須正也，而功必始於蒙養。古者八歲而就外傳，學小藝焉、履小節焉；束髮而入大學，學大藝焉、履大節焉。教之《春秋》而為之聳善而抑惡，教之故志使知廢興焉而戒懼，教之訓典使知族類而比義，蓋積習見聞，納之軌物，故成材易也。皇上範型在上，不肅而嚴，諭教條章，直有方駕古人、同符聖祖者，竑之寡陋如爝火然，詎足以庚日月之明？顧塵露區區，不為河嶽所吐棄，必將有繼竑而出者纘聖志而成之矣。特著之序以俟。翰林院修撰、儒林郎，焦竑謹序」。

正文有解說六十則，每則各附單面方式圖一

幅，以圖解形式通過歷史典故、古人事跡，宣講封建倫理道德及論行為規範。在解說中，作者借題發揮，明理析義，借古喻今，竭力闡述了儒家的綱常觀念及仁、義、禮、智、信的五德思想，宣揚了修、齊、治、平的為君之道。勸勉皇子務從細微瑣事修身養性，以達到治國平天下的目的。

《養正圖解》之六十插圖繪刻精細，古趣滿紙。繪者丁雲鵬，字南羽，號聖華居士，安徽休寧人。擅畫白描佛像、山水、人物，無不精妙。蘇州集雅齋所刻《唐詩五畫譜》之插圖，也是丁氏的作品。

據杜信孚纂輯的《明代版刻綜錄》，《養正圖解》的版本甚多，僅是晚明就有萬曆二十一年（1593年）安徽新安玩虎軒刊本（刻工為黃鏻）、萬曆二十二年（1594年）新安吳懷讓（字少逸）刊本與金陵書林鄭思鳴奎璧齋刊本，以及萬曆年間祝世祿刊本（祝世祿，字延之，號無功，德興縣人。萬曆十七年進士，休寧縣令、南京御史，歷尚寶寺卿）。以上的萬曆本均不分卷。後有清康熙己酉（1669年）曹鈖刪正，蓋公堂重刊，分上下二卷，圖式、字型與明本同出一版。此書作為培養封建統治繼承人的教材，受到清代統治者的賞識和推崇。乾隆帝為其作詩，嘉慶帝為其作贊，至光緒二十一年（年）載湉下達諭旨，書與御製詩贊一並武英殿不分卷刊刻頒行。

此本《養正圖解》為明萬曆二十二年（1594年）金陵奎璧齋刊本。齋主鄭思鳴，字元美，歙縣人。該本不分卷，圖繪刻亦精，刻工為黃奇，為鄭振鐸先生舊藏。茲選照焦竑自序末半葉以及第一幅插圖，題「寢門視膳」、第一則「寢門視膳」正文以及第二插圖，題「膳斥鮑魚」。

第一則，即「寢門視膳」，焦撰正文云：「文王之為世子，朝於王季，日三。雞初鳴而衣服，至於寢門外，問內豎之御者曰『今日安否何如？』內豎曰：『安』，文王乃喜。及日中又至，亦如之。及暮又至，亦如之。其有不安節，則內豎以告文王，文王色憂，行不能正履。王季復膳，然後亦復初。食上必在，視寒煖之節。食下，問所膳。命膳宰曰：『末有原』。應曰：『諾』，然後退」。

第二則，即「膳斥鮑魚」，焦撰正文云：「文王使太公望，傅太子發。太子嗜鮑魚，公不與曰『鮑魚不登於俎。豈有非禮而可養太子哉！』」其後為解說，以下全錄：「太公姓呂名望。發，是武王名。武王為太子時，文王使太公為傅。一切起居飲

食有不中節處，無不救正。武王好食鮑魚，太公不肯與，說道鮑魚一向不登俎豆，是非禮所當食也。豈非非禮之食，而可以養太子哉！一飲食之小，必教以正道，不肯苟從如此。況所非正言，所行非正事，所親非正人，其相匡救又當何如也。北齊廚宰進太子食，中有邪蒿。助教邢峙方授經，遽令止之曰：『此菜有不正之名，非太子所宜食』。文宣聞而大喜之。此事猶有古人之遺風也。」

這兩則以周文王、周武王的故事說明古之君子善修其身者，動息節宜以養生、飲食衣服以養禮、威儀

行義以養德，是故周公之制禮也，天子之起居、衣服、飲食各有其官，皆統於冢宰，蓋慎之至也。兩則後各附有吳繼序解說，因其文較長，在此不錄。

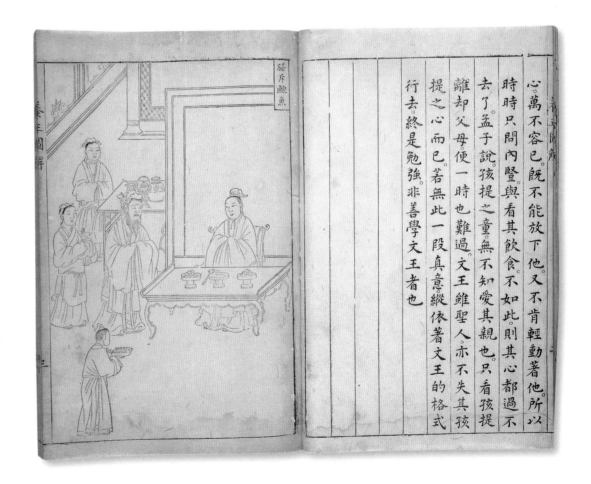

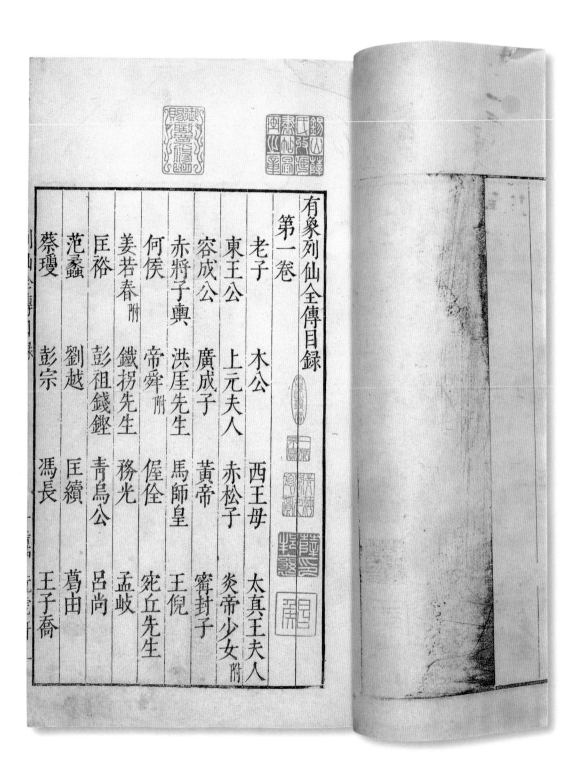

7

You xiang Liexian quan zhuan (9 juan)

Complete and Illustrated Biographies of Transcendents, 9 *juan*

Ming dynasty (1368-1644), Wanli period (1573-1619)
Compiled by Wang Shizhen (1526-1593; *jinshi* of 1547), with supplement by Wang Yunpeng (fl. 1600); proofread and edited by Wang Yunpeng (fl. 1600); engraved by Huang Yimu (1586-1641)
Xin'an, Anhui province: Wanhu xuan, 1600
11 columns per half-folio; 22 characters per column; white folding margin at center of folio; single-line borders; overall dimensions of volumes: 27.9-28.0 x 16.4-16.5 cm; block sizes of text: approx. 20.3-20.4 x 12.8-13.0 cm; stitched binding

16741

The *You xiang Liexian quan zhuan* is a woodblock-illustrated collection of 581 brief hagiographies of Daoist masters and adepts who were believed to have achieved immortality in one form or another; some entries have appended references to additional figures, bringing the total number to 640. It is based on the *Liexian zhuan* (Biographies of Transcendents) attributed to Liu Xiang (77-ca. 6 B.C.) which contained seventy such accounts. Although the late Ming compendium bears the name of the great literatus Wang Shizhen (1526-1593) as compiler and has a preface by Li Panlong (1514-1570), it would appear that both had little to do with the book, if anything at all, since both had died before publication. It is far more probable that Wang Yunpeng, who nominally provided the ninth and final *juan* as a "supplement," was the person responsible for the entire work, including the "Li Panlong" preface.

Selected for inclusion in this work were mythological as well as historical figures. Beginning with Laozi (ca. 6th century B.C.), readers are provided with information on the exemplary lives and fantastic exploits of all the celebrated Daoists, including the sage Zhuangzi (ca. 369-286 B.C.), Dongfang Shuo (154-93 B.C.), Guo Pu (276-324), the alchemist and theoretician Ge Hong (284-364), the scholar, physician, and polymath Tao Hongjing (456-536), the great Tang poets Li Bo (701-762), Bo Juyi (772-846), and Li He (791-817), the Yuan painter Huang Gongwang (1269-1354), and ending with Leng Qian and other immortals of the Ming dynasty.

The woodblocks employed for printing this work were finely engraved with a regularized standard script (*kaishu*) featuring somewhat elongated characters. The very thin and delicate horizontal strokes are counterbalanced by considerably thicker ones, and modulation in width is exhibited only in the diagonal strokes. The overall layout is simple but executed in a formal manner. This is typical in late Ming publications, in marked contrast to the more informal style used for the printing of popular literature in earlier periods. The dignified folios not only convey the authority of the text but also the vast erudition of its supposed compiler Wang Shizhen and the good taste of the actual compiler Wang Yunpeng.

There are altogether 203 woodblock illustrations in the *You xiang Liexian quan zhuan*: thirty-seven each in *juan* 1 and *juan* 2 (Warring States through late Han), twenty-two in *juan* 3 (late Han through the Three Kingdoms period), nineteen in *juan* 4 (Six Dynasties), twenty-four in *juan* 5 (through the Tang dynasty), seventeen in *juan* 6 (early Tang dynasty), twenty-nine in *juan* 7 (late Tang through Song), and eighteen in *juan* 8 (through the early Ming period). The nine "supplementary" *juan* devoted to Ming immortals through the late fifteenth century do not contain any illustrations. The figures are portrayed in a highly stylized manner typical of book illustrations by Wanli-period Huizhou engravers. The immortals are variously depicted as wearing straw raincoats,

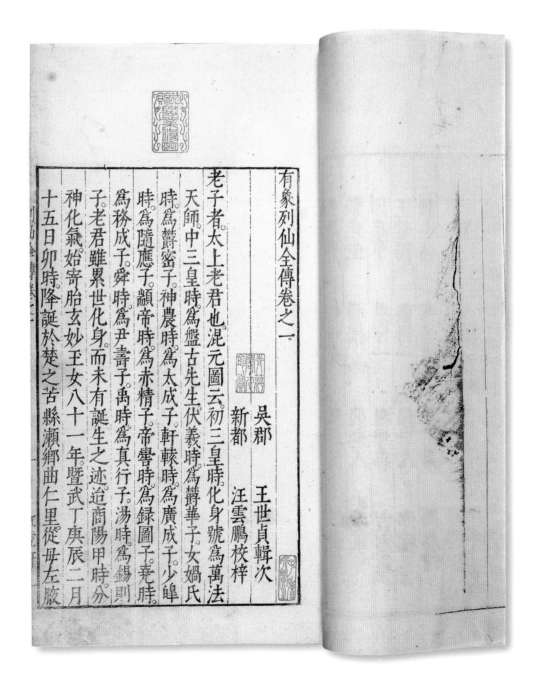

feathered capes, riding on clouds, moving across water, and mounted on some animal, bird, fish, mythical beast, or auspicious creature. Dragons, phoenixes, and clouds in particular are understood as efficient vehicles for transporting the immortals to celestial realms.

The first two reproductions taken from this copy owned by Zheng Zhenduo (1898-1958) are the table of contents for *juan* 1 and the opening folio of *juan* 1. Next is the illustration of Xi wang mu (Queen Mother of the West) and part of the accompanying text (*juan* 1, folios 4b and 5a). This ancient hybrid spirit who reigns over the Western Paradise is accompanied by two maidens, one of whom bears the coveted "peaches of immortality" (*shou tao*) from her celestial garden. The last illustration (from *juan* 2, folios 17b and 18a) is a depiction of She Zheng, a figure from the Western Jin dynasty (265-316) who could walk with his eyes shut and who was known as the "Four Hundred-Year-Old Child." He is represented with flames shooting from his eyes, after his disciple had pleaded with him to open them. Part of his biographical sketch appears on the facing half-folio.

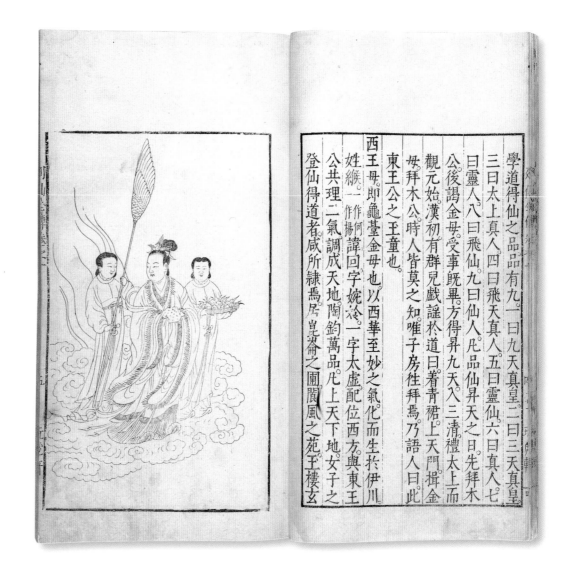

7

有象列仙全傳九卷

明王世貞輯。明汪雲鵬補。明黃 一木鐫。明萬曆二十八年(1600年)安徽新安汪雲鵬玩虎軒刻本。半葉十一行，行二十二字，四周單邊，版心白口，無魚尾。框二〇・三至二〇・四厘米，寬十三厘米。綫裝。

16741

　　中國的神仙傳記，以題名漢劉向撰《列仙傳》二卷為最早，此後相繼有不少類似撰述，如晉干寶所撰而後重編的《新編連相搜神廣記》，刊於元至正(1341–1360年)間，明嘉靖年間翻刻版，書名署《三教源流搜神大全》，又如明萬曆元年(1573年)金陵富春堂刻的《新刻出像增補搜神記大全》。

　　《有象列仙全傳》為晚明一部著名的神仙傳記，刊刻於萬曆二十八年(1600年)。全書九卷，起自上古，迄於明代弘治末年，在現存同類書籍中，當為內容最豐富的一種。卷一至卷八正文卷端題「吳郡王世貞輯次，新都汪雲鵬校梓」，共收四百九十七人。卷九正文卷端題「新都後學汪雲鵬輯

「補」，增八十四人，總共五百八十一人。前有《列仙全傳序》，題「濟南李攀龍撰。……新都汪雲鵬書」，序尾刻「黃一木鐫」。後有序，題「萬曆庚子夏日汪雲鵬序并書」。書口下間刻「玩虎軒」。

汪雲鵬，字光華，歙縣人，徽州地區著名版刻技工及出版家。其書坊玩虎軒為萬曆間新安名肆之一，刊通俗戲曲圖書以及有精美插圖的書籍不少，所刻版畫富麗精工，是徽州版畫中的上品。

此書乃汪雲鵬據明張文介萬曆十一年（1583年）刊刻的《廣列仙傳》七卷增補而成。前八卷署「吳郡王世貞輯次」，而李攀龍序文又說是他自己「乃搜群書……合而梓之」的，有所矛盾。所謂李序和王輯，皆非事實，而是書賈的故弄玄虛，作偽者可能就是本書的刊行者汪雲鵬。汪氏說合而梓之只是飾說之辭，根本就是據以《廣列仙傳》改編成八卷，其中有調整次序，也有補充及刪落，然後託於王世貞的名下；同時也將張文介的序略加更易數字，就署名李攀龍撰。汪氏所補遺的最末一卷，也是按時代先後而列。

書內有單面方式的插圖，未題畫人名氏。畫面變化不多，佈局稍嫌呆板。人物造型雖然比較一般，個性不夠突出，與刻工未能相稱，但在表現神仙的怡然自得的神態上也很有特色。刻工姓名見於書中的有黃一木。黃氏，號二水，生於萬曆十四年（1586年），刻《有象列仙全傳》時，年僅十五歲。刻工所刻雋雅秀麗，精密細巧，為最上乘徽派木刻畫作品。

中國國家圖書館所藏此部《有象列仙全傳》為最初白綿紙印本，神采奕奕，初為無錫薛氏青萍閣所藏，後為鄭振鐸先生珍藏，鈐有「長樂鄭振鐸西諦藏書」朱文方印、「長樂鄭氏匯書之印」朱文長方印。茲選照卷一目錄首葉上半葉、卷一正文首葉上半葉、卷一之「西王母」圖與文以及卷二之「涉正」圖與文。晉人涉正錄於此書的傳記為「涉正，字玄真，巴東人。漢末，說秦始皇時事了了。從二十弟子入吳，而正常閉目，雖行不開也。弟子隨之二十年，莫有見其開目者。有一弟子固請之，正乃為開目。開時，有聲如霹靂，有光如火電，弟子皆不覺伏地。良久乃能起，正已復還閉目。後道成仙去，其所眠食施行，并授諸弟子，皆以行氣絕房室及服石腦小丹。時李八百呼正為『四百歲兒』」。

《有象列仙全傳》一出，圖文并茂，所輯的神仙內容豐富，時代也最近，故成為現存同類書籍中流傳最廣的一種，有多種刊本行世，因而影響後世神仙傳記集的編撰也最大。此書別有刻工曾章刊圖本，圖與此本大同小異，然非同本。另有日本慶安三年（清順治七年；1650年）藤田莊右衛門復刻活字本，但其插圖對玩虎軒原本插圖并未照本翻刻，帶有較明顯的日本風格。

8

Lidai minggong hua pu

Manual of Paintings by Famous Masters of Successive Periods

Ming dynasty (1368-1644), Wanli period (1573-1619)

Compiled by Gu Bing (fl. 1594-1603); proofread and edited by Xu Shuhui; engraved by Liu Guangxin

Hulin [Hangzhou], Zhejiang province: Shuanggui tang, 1603

White folding margin at center of folio; single-line borders; overall dimensions of volumes: 33.4 x 22.7 cm; block sizes of text: approx. 27.1 x 19.2 cm; block sizes of illustrations irregular; stitched binding

01471

This book, popularly known as the *Gu shi hua pu* (Master Gu's Manual of Painting), is a collection of painting compositions by famous artists of successive dynasties copied by Gu Bing. Gu's family was from the area around the West Lake near Hangzhou, and he trained as an artist under Zhou Zhimian (act. ca. 1580-1610), a master of bird-and-flower painting in the Ming period. Gu Bing served briefly at the imperial court beginning in 1599.

The *Lidai minggong hua pu* was first published in Hangzhou by the "Shanggui tang" (Double Cassia Hall; most probably Gu Bing's own publishing concern) in 1603, and subsequently reprinted in 1613 and perhaps also in 1619. It was conceptually modeled after illustrated compendia such as the *Xuanhe Bogu tu* (Illustrations of Antiquities of the Xuanhe Reign Period) by Wang Fu (1079-1126), a pictorial catalogue of ancient bronzes

and other antiquities in the Northern Song palace collection; the *Tuhui baojian* (Precious Mirror for Drawing and Painting) of 1365 by Xia Wenyan (act. mid fourteenth century); and the *Tuhui baojian xu bian* (Supplement to the Precious Mirror for Drawing and Painting) of 1519 by Han Ang (act. early sixteenth century) for a selection of artists (and the texts of their biographies) through the mid fourteenth century.

Gu Bing's manual is in fact an illustrated history of Chinese painting narrated through the works of 106 artists, each of whom is represented by a single selection engraved on woodblocks by Liu Guangxin from Anhui. The first volume contains eighteen artists from the Jin dynasty (317-420) through the Five Dynasties period (907-960), while the second volume features thirty-one painters of the Song dynasty (960-1279). Fifteen masters of the Yuan dynasty (1279-1368) and sixteen from the earlier part of the Ming dynasty (1368-1644) give a total of thirty-one artists for the third volume. Finally, twenty-six painters of the middle and later Ming (1368-1644) complete the compendium. Only one woman painter is included: Guan Daosheng (1262-1319), wife of the Yuan scholar-official Zhao Mengfu (1254-1322). The subjects covered are broad in scope, and include landscapes (fifty-one examples), bird and flower paintings (thirty-eight), as well as figural compositions (seventeen). As a rule, pictures appear on the recto of folios while accompanying inscriptions (brief biographies and background information on the artists in the form of colophons) are placed on the verso. The various scales and formats found in Chinese painting are standardized to fit within the uniform rectangular dimensions of the woodblocks. In two exceptional instances, however, the illustrations of a horizontal

scroll composition of narcissus by the Southern Song artist Zhao Mengjian (1199-1264 or 1267) and a landscape by the Yuan painter Ni Zan (1301-1374) continue across the folded edge onto part of the reverse side of the folio.

The *Lidai minggong hua pu* represents the first fully illustrated art-historical compendium in China. It contains a number of misattributed works among the pre-Yuan selections, but the Yuan and Ming compositions by and large convey the main stylistic characteristics of the original paintings or those works which purported to be authentic. Gu Bing's pictorial manual appealed to professional as well as amateur artists as a handy reference of painting styles and compositions from many centuries and became so popular that it spawned a number of similar compendia during the late Ming period. It continues to be reprinted in the late twentieth century, attesting to its usefulness for those beginning the art of Chinese painting. The original edition of Gu Bing's work has become extremely scarce; the National Library of China has the distinction of possessing two copies, along with one copy of the second edition.

The first illustration here shows the cover page (*fengmian ye*) of the manual giving the formal title and publishing house as well as the beginning of the first preface. This is followed by another double-spread; on the right side are the inscription and seals of the late Ming official Xiao Yunju complementing the preceding figure painting by the Northern Song Emperor Renzong (1010-1063; r. 1023-1063), and on the left is a woodblock rendition of a composition with a melon, grasses, autumn vines, and two crickets attributed to Emperor Gaozong (1107-1187; r. 1127-1162) of the Southern Song. The artistic Gaozong was the founding ruler of the Southern Song dynasty (1127-1279) and also a notable calligrapher.

8

歷代名公畫譜

一名《顧氏畫譜》。明顧炳輯，明徐叔回校刊，明劉光信鐫。明萬曆三十一年（1603年）虎林（今杭州）雙桂堂刻本。四周單邊，版心白口。框高二七·一厘米，寬一九·二厘米。前有余玄洲、朱之蕃等序，并顧炳譜例六則。 綫裝。
01471

顧炳，字黯然，號懷泉，武林（今杭州）人。花鳥宗周之冕，畫山水，曾結茅吳山，技日益進。

傳摹晉唐，存其梗概。

顧炳《歷代名公畫譜》即是供人學畫人物畫的範本，也是一部有圖有文的繪畫簡史。顧氏按照夏文彥於元至正二十五年（1365年）編著的《圖繪寶鑒》以及韓昂於明正德十四年（1519年）編著的《圖繪寶鑒續編》的體例，以時代為序，輯錄了自晉至明著名畫家的優秀作品，縮小尺幅，仿佛筆意而成，可謂細摹精刻，頗費經營。

畫譜計一百零六家，共有插圖一百零六幅。山水、人物、花鳥俱全，形態生動，自然傳神，綫條流利，工致精麗，如觀名跡。刻法精堅，刀鋒犀利，粗拙有筆，細巧有力，實畫譜中神品。本書卷首有余玄洲序，對摹刻宗旨和工作的艱難情況作了詳細的敘述。另有譜例六則，係顧炳所撰寫，對本書的編輯體例和選摹標準有所説明。

畫譜不分卷，全四册。第一册六朝至五代十八位畫家，即晉顧愷之；宋陸探微；梁張僧繇；陳顧野王；唐閻立德、閻立本、吳道玄、鄭虔、李思訓、李昭道、王維、荊浩、韓幹、戴嵩、邊鸞；五代關仝、黃筌、黃居寶。

第二册宋代三十一位畫家，即宋仁宗皇帝、高宗皇帝、李公麟、顧德謙、郭忠恕、董源、范寬、李成、郭熙、趙昌、蘇軾、米芾、趙令穰、趙伯駒、巨然、趙孟堅、米友仁、楊補之、馬和之、李唐、陳容、楊士賢、李迪、蘇漢臣、蕭照、劉松年、李嵩、夏珪、馬遠、馬麟、陳居中。

第三册元代至明代中期三十一位畫家，即元趙孟頫、管夫人、魯宗貴、柯九思、趙雍、王淵、黃公望、錢選、吳鎮、倪瓚、王蒙、高克恭、吳瓘、盛懋、方方壺；國朝[明]商喜、邊景昭、王紱、李在、戴進、夏日永、孫龍、林良、杜堇、沈周、陶成、吳偉、呂紀、鍾欽禮、周臣。

第四册明代中期至明萬曆年間二十六位畫家，即唐寅、文徵明、姜隱、謝時臣、王穀祥、陳淳、文伯仁、仇英、朱貞孚、蔣嵩、朱端、張路、陸治、魯治、王一清、錢穀、張珍、沈仕、文嘉、莫雲卿、陳栝、周之冕、董其昌、范叔成、孫克弘、王廷策。

每幅畫後，都有名人書傳題跋，其中不乏佳作，可以幫助讀者領會畫意，熟悉畫家，引人入勝。名人包括顧起元、陳子龍、陶望齡、米萬鍾、焦竑、徐光啟、黃汝亨、陶允嘉等等。

茲選照第一册之封面葉（鐫「《歷代名公畫譜》。虎林雙桂堂藏板」）和余玄州《畫譜序》之

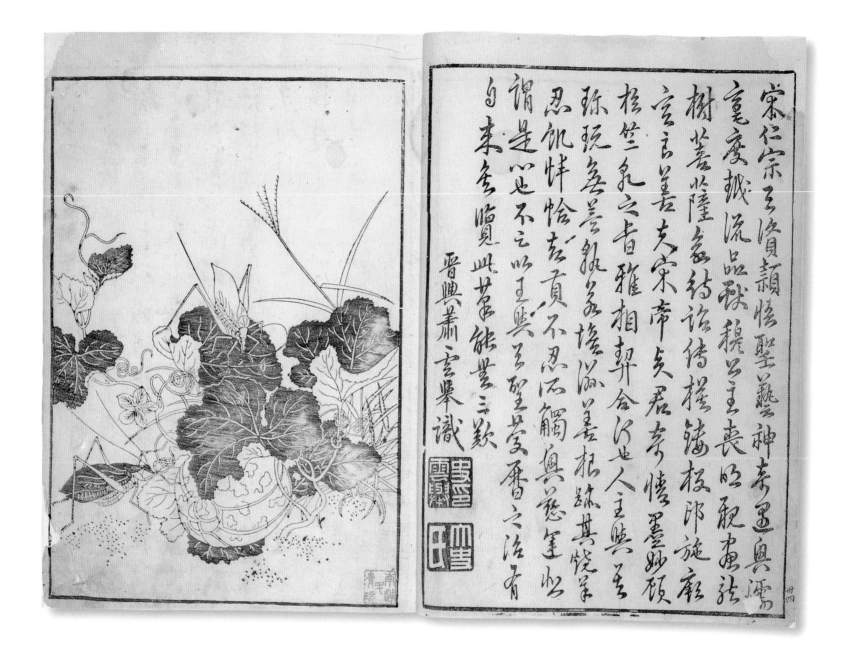

上半葉，以及第二冊之第一幅圖後明蕭雲舉題宋仁宗畫道釋和第二幅圖，摹宋高宗繪的「草蟲瓜實」。此圖摘得秋瓜一枚，橫置地上。畫上有絡緯一雙，草蟲畫中的吉祥題材，最常見者是螽斯，絡緯是螽斯科的一種。瓜果多子，瓜葉瓜鬚綿延，所

謂「瓜瓞綿綿」也。這也是農業社會祝福多子多孫的象徵。此幅為一吉祥題意作品，其後（即下半葉）有崔邦亮題字。

畫譜萬曆三十一年（1603年）杭州雙桂堂初刻刊行。初印本刊行後，顧氏哲嗣三聘、三錫增加

校訂後印行，北京大學圖書館所藏的為此本。萬曆四十一年（1613年）又經龔國彥重編刊行。以後在光緒十四年（1888年）上海鴻文書局據顧氏重印本，影石縮印，流傳很廣。原刻本現在已極為罕見。

9

Cheng shi mo yuan (12 juan), fulu Renwen jueli (9 juan)

Ink Garden of the Cheng Family, 12 *juan*, with Supplement of Writings by Various Personalities, 8 *juan*

Ming dynasty (1368-1644), Wanli period (1573-1619)
Compiled and edited by Cheng Dayue (1541-ca. 1616); illustrated by Ding Yunpeng (1547-ca. 1628), Wu Tingyu (act. 1573-1620), et al.; engraved by Huang Lin (b. 1564), Huang Yingdao (1578-1655), Huang Yingtai (1582-1662), Huang Yibin (b. 1586), et al.
Xinian, Anhui province: Zilan tang, 1606
White folding margin at center of folio; single-line borders; overall dimensions of volumes: 31.3 x 18.3 cm; block sizes of illustrations and texts vary; stitched binding
16212

Thanks to the availability of high-grade black soot from the pine forests and pauwlonia groves of Mount Huang, the making of inksticks and inkcakes became one of the hallmark trades of the Huizhou area, especially Shexian [county], in Anhui province. The selected designs, often adapted from existing or historical pictorial works but at times specially commissioned, were engraved by highly skilled craftsmen onto wooden molds that were used to shape the inksticks and inkcakes.

Catalogues of inkstick and inkcake designs were compiled and printed both as a record of the images used and also as a practical means of advertising the decorative products to an élite market of scholars and connoisseurs. In time, these catalogues became collectors' items, as much appreciated as the exquisitely manufactured blocks of ink. Many Ming catalogues of inks have survived, such as the *Mo fa ji yao* (Essentials of Inkmaking) of 1398 by Shen Jisun (act. late 14th century), the *Fang shi mo pu* (Ink Manual of the Fang Family) of 1588 by Fang Yulu (ca. 1541-1608), the *Cheng shi mo yuan* (Ink Garden of the Cheng Family) of 1606 by Cheng Dayue (1541-ca. 1616), the *Mo ping* (A Critique on Ink) of 1612 by Pan Fangkai, the *Mo hai* (Extensive Collection of Writings on Ink) of 1620 by Fang Ruisheng, the *Mo zhi* (A Record of Ink) of ca. 1644 by Ma Sanheng, and the *Mo biao* (A Chronology of Ink) published between 1628 and 1644 by Wan Shouqi (1603-1652). The Wanli period compendia by the rivals Fang Yulu and Cheng Dayue are recognized as the most important, not only

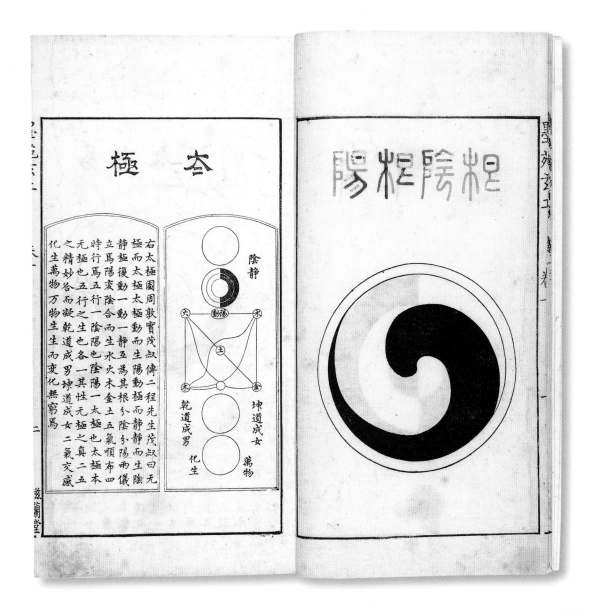

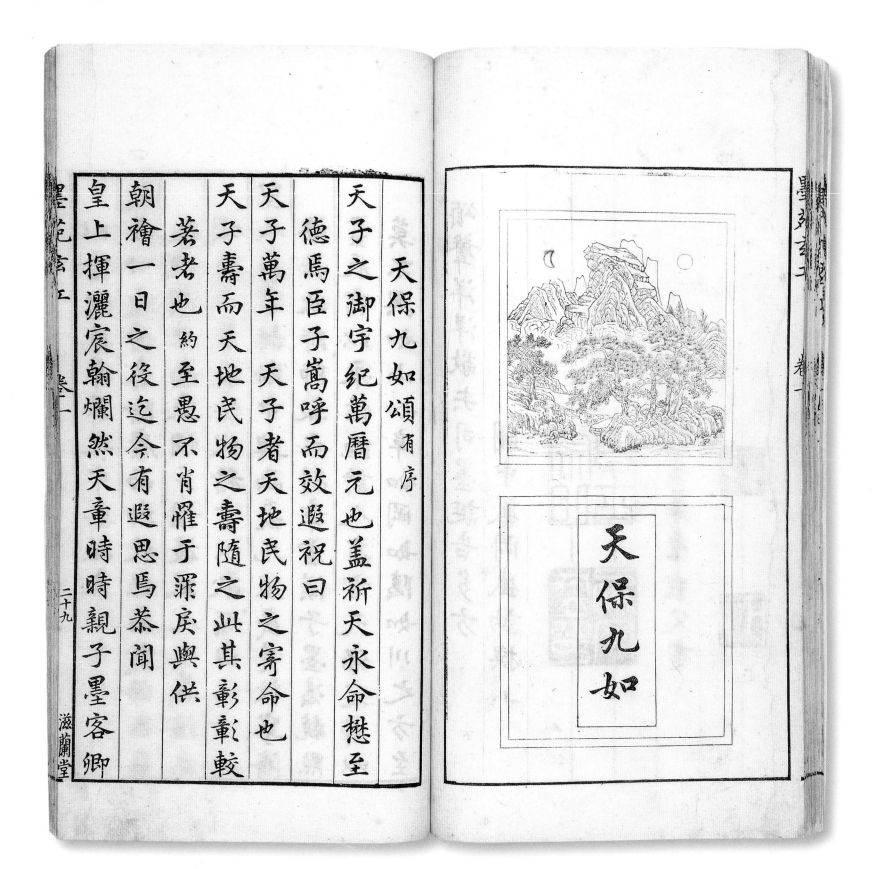

天保九如頌有序

天子之御宇紀萬曆元也蓋祈天永命懋至

德焉臣子嵩呼而效遐祝曰

天子萬年天子者天地民物之寄命也

天子壽而天地民物之壽隨之此其彰彰較

著者也約至愚不肖罹于罪戾興供

朝禣一日之後迄今有遐思焉恭聞

皇上揮灑宸翰爛然天章時時親子墨客卿

墨花吟二　卷一　二十九　滋蘭堂

for the astonishing range of inksticks and inkcakes presented (389 and more than 500 respectively), but because the catalogues themselves are remarkable for having achieved a very high quality of illustration, engraving, and printing.

The *Cheng shi mo yuan*, like the *Fang shi mo pu*, was printed in numerous editions, as and when there was demand and whenever a significant number of new inkstick and inkcake designs were produced. Cheng Dayue's ink catalogue may be found in editions of twelve *juan* or fourteen *juan*, while fifteen-*juan* editions have also been recorded. The appended portion which contains the writings of various famous personalities (*Renwen jueli*, "Cultivated Humanists and Ranked Officials from One's Native Place") comes in either eight or nine *juan*. While most of Cheng's catalogues were printed in monochrome black, there exist a number of rare sets notable for containing some of the very first multicolored prints to be made (for instance, the copy with blue, brown, and black ink at the Percival David Foundation of Chinese Art, University of London). However, as any given block was brushed with different colors in the desired areas prior to each pull, the resulting prints would often suffer from smudging and other less than satisfactory effects.

For certain editions of his encyclopaedic compendium, Cheng included three images from the Gospels accompanied by descriptive titles in Chinese and romanized Latin scripts. These pictures were taken from the *Evangelicae historiae imagines* of Geronimo Nadal (1507-1580) and others (Antwerp: Martin Nutius, 1593-1596), a book that had been brought to China by the Jesuit missionary Matteo Ricci (1552-1610). A fourth picture, of a "Madonna and Child," was a version of the miraculous Nuestra Señora de Antigua

in Seville Cathedral, produced at Arima in Japan under Jesuit auspices in 1597. Cheng had met Ricci in Nanjing in early 1606, where the latter presented him with the European compositions. The rarest of all the *Cheng shi mo yuan* editions, however, are those that contain eight rectangular illustrations based on the Song-dynasty tale *Zhongshan lang zhuan* (Story of the Wolf at Zhongshan).

This multicolor-printed twenty-*juan* set of the *Cheng shi mo yuan* in the National Library of China consists of twelve *juan* of the catalogue proper divided into six major classes of subject matter, followed by eight *juan* of collected writings. *Juan* 1-2 come under the heading of *Xuangong* ("Works of Natural Forces"); *juan* 3-4, *Yutu* ("Earthly Illustrations"); *juan* 5-6, *Renguan* ("People and Officials"); *juan* 7-8, *Wuhua* ("The Essence of Things"); *juan* 9-10, *Ruzang* ("Confucian Repository"); and *juan* 11-12, *Zihuang* ("Buddhist and Daoist Priests").

Among the reproductions here are designs and texts drawn from the *Classic of Changes* (*Yi jing*). *Gen yin gen yang* ("Foundations of Yin and Yang," in *juan* 1, folio 1b) and *Taiji* ("The Supreme Ultimate," in *juan* 1, folio 2a), for example, are seminal representations of Daoist cosmology which during the Ming period were invested with Neo-Confucian interpretations; they impart a sense of primordial *gravitas* to the manual. Also presented on facing half-folios are illustrations entitled *Tian bao jiu ru* ("May the Heavens Protect the Nine Similitudes," in *juan* 1, folio 28b) and *Tian bao jiu ru song* ("Ode to 'May the Heavens Protect the Nine Similitudes'," in *juan* 1, folio 29a), attractive yet dignified compositions for the obverse and reverse sides of an inkcake that were inspired by a piece in the *Xiao ya* section of the ancient *Classic of Poetry* (*Shi jing*); this particular pair of

designs can also be found in the *Fang shi mo pu* and therefore may have been commissioned when Fang and Cheng were collaborators prior to 1588. Judging from the accompanying ode, it is possible that inkcakes made according to this particular design were destined for presentation to the imperial court. Another substantial pair of inkcake designs entitled *Fei long zai tian* ("Flying Dragon in the Heavens," *juan* 2, folio 1a) and *Tian lao dui ting* ("Phoenixes Facing Each Other in the Court," *juan* 2, folio 5b) printed in vermilion and imperial yellow, were undoubtedly created with the palace in mind. Although it is unlikely that the 500-plus marvelous designs for inksticks and inkcakes failed to impress customers and rivals, Cheng seems to have left nothing to chance. He assembled more than 170 laudatory inscriptions and endorsements by a panoply of famous late Ming personalities and printed them in the eight-*juan* section following the catalogue proper.

9

程氏墨苑十二卷附錄人文爵里八卷

明程大約編。明丁雲鵬、吳廷羽等繪。明黃鏻、黃應泰、黃應道、黃一彬等鐫。明萬曆間（約1605年）安徽新安程氏滋蘭堂原刻彩色套印本。圖文並列。四周單邊，版心白口，下方刻「滋蘭堂」。框高二四‧五厘米，寬一四‧九厘米。綫裝。

16212

　　明代墨書、墨譜甚多，如洪武三十一年沈繼孫《墨法集要》、約萬曆十六年方于魯《方氏墨譜》、約萬曆三十四年程大約《程氏墨苑》、約萬曆四十年潘方凱《墨評》、約泰昌元年方瑞生《墨海》十二卷、崇禎末年麻三衡《墨志》、崇禎年間萬壽祺《墨表》。其中最為著名的是《方氏墨譜》與《程氏墨苑》。

　　此展出的《程氏墨苑》，是中國明代萬曆年間徽州版畫的代表作，並是研究墨史的重要著作。其編者程大約，字幼博，別字君房，號筱野，又號玄玄子、守玄居士、墨隱道人、獨醒客、鴻濛氏、郎山放民、紫宸近侍，安徽歙縣岩鎮人，太學生，善古文，曾仕鴻臚寺序班，有《程幼博集》六卷。其人好蓄墨，精墨法，有墨坊「還樸齋」（後更名為「寶墨齋」）販製其墨，所製墨曾貢入宮中。

　　《程氏墨苑》內容包羅萬有，精選奇擇。其繪刻、印製都極講究，無論畫面構成、黑白處理及刀法運用都有特點。該譜墨樣五百十九種之多，墨形有圓形、方形、長方形、圭形、不規則的雜珮式等。題材範圍包括山川景物、草木禽獸、佛道祥瑞、是珍貴的圖案資料，書中倩名家刻繪書畫皆美的墨樣。參與的畫家有丁雲鵬、江世會、鄭一桂等，而丁氏提供的畫樣頗多，其中「侑座之器」、「金人圖」、「五瑞四岳」、「十有二牧」與丁氏所繪於《養正圖解》的圖同為一規範。刻工黃鏻、黃應道、黃應泰均歙縣虬村名匠。良紙佳墨刊印成書，是當時出版界的盛事。程氏編此書是為了推銷產品，因此請當代百餘名家題辭銘贊，放在各個不相同的墨匣裡面。題跋文字自我揄揚，貶抑他人，充滿商業性宣傳謀利的意味。

　　此書印行先後有所不同，內容、篇頁常有出入。先印者內容少，後印者漸增加若干新的事物進去。圖錄有十二至十四卷本，附錄《人文爵里》有

八或九卷本。除此以外，程氏還翻刻天主教傳教士利瑪竇取自歐洲拿達爾於一五九五年出版的《福音歷史圖像》的三幅宣傳畫，即「信而步海，疑而即沉」、「二徒聞實，即捨空虛」以及「淫色穢氣，自速天火」。另有一幅「天主像」，為日本神學院據西洋銅版畫原稿及壁畫刻成，後為利瑪竇所得，於南京持贈程大約。程氏將這四幅圖加以翻刻，并附以羅馬注音，解釋圖畫的內容。又有附《中山狼傳》八幅圖與《續中山狼傳》的，也畫得有風趣之至。這兩部份，在早印本的《程氏墨苑》均沒有，附《中山狼傳》印本更為罕見，中國國家圖書館藏有一部。

世稱彩印本《程氏墨苑》也其為罕見。最早的彩印本刊於萬曆二十二年（1594年），其彩色木刻畫是應用相當原始及複雜的印刷方法。程氏在所刻的木板上，按照應該渲染的色彩塗刷上各種顏色，然後加以刷印，所用的都是同一塊木版。總計全書用彩色印刷的只有五十多幅，多半四色、五色印者，其中較精善的不過十多幅。此書初印本彩色各圖間有用不同顏色塗在一版上印刷或用餖版套印者，如「玄工」類之「昂宿圖」，衣作淺碧色，花作絳色。「人官」類之「蔽芾甘棠圖」，碧樹朱欄，別饒詩意。「廿八宿圖贊」，右列各符皆朱印。另有全部墨色印本，傳世尚多，但多不完整。

中國國家圖書館所藏此部《程氏墨苑》為彩印本，內含彩色印圖五十五幅。卷首目錄題《程幼博墨苑》，書分墨譜十二卷（原為六卷，每卷分上下，目錄作十二卷），共「玄工」（天）、「輿圖」（地）、「人官」（人）、「物華」（物）、「儒藏」（儒）、「緇黃」（道、釋）六類。附錄詩文共八卷。

茲選照卷一（玄工上）用藍、黃、棕三色套印的「根陰根陽圖」；墨印的「太極圖」；用綠、黃色套印的「天保九如圖」；墨印的「天保九如頌」。「天保九如」題材取自《詩經・小雅》中的「天保」，指連用九「如」字，祝頌福壽綿長，後遂以「天保九如」為祝壽頌詞。此外也選照卷二（玄工下）用紅、黃色套印的「飛龍在天圖」以及「天老對庭圖」，尤為精麗動人。「天老」，相傳為黃帝輔臣。

10

Zuoyin xiansheng jingding jiejing yi pu (2 juan)

Manual of *Weiqi* Strategies Carefully Edited by the Gentleman Zuoyin, 2 *juan*

Ming dynasty (1368-1644), Wanli period (1573-1619)
Compiled by Wang Tingna (ca. 1569-after 1628); proofread and edited by Zhan Guoli; illustrated by Wang
Geng (1573-1620); engraved by Huang Yingzu (1563
or 1573-1644)
Xin'an, Anhui province: Wang shi Huancui tang, 1609
Number of columns and characters per column per half-
folio irregular; white folding margin at center of folio;
single-line borders; overall dimensions of volumes:
27.9-28.0 x 29.9 cm; block sizes of texts and
illustrations: approx. 24.1-25.5 x 27.5-28.3 cm;
wrapped-back binding

16827

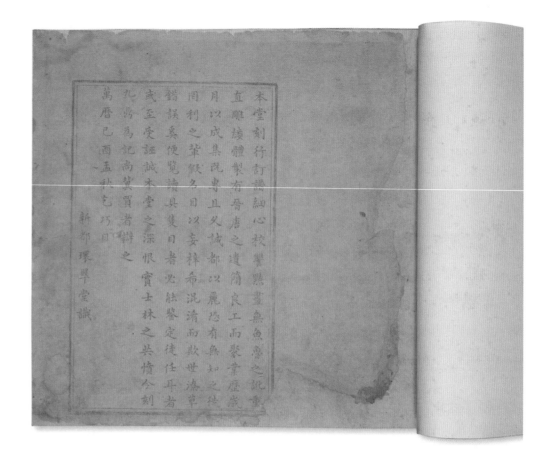

The ancient Chinese game of *weiqi*, also known as *yi*, was supposedly invented by Emperor Shun (2255-2206 B.C.) to strengthen the mental faculties of his son. It was certainly a well known game by the tenth century B.C., but truly flourished between A.D. 200 and 600. It spread to Japan in the mid eighth century, where it is known as *go*. As observers of *weiqi* have long noted, it is a distinctly modern military game whose objective is territorial conquest and capture of hostile men by encirclement. *Weiqi* is played by two contestants on a square board with 19 equidistant lines in the vertical and horizontal directions intersecting at 361 crosspoints. The 361 circular "stones" (*qi shi*) for placing on the crosspoints are convex on both sides; the 181 black ones are traditionally made of

slate and the 180 white ones made from shells. Like the game's equipment, the rules for *weiqi* are few and quite simple, with the goal of surrounding as many of the opponent's "stones" as possible, but there are a myriad possibilities for play and only the more strategic player will eventually win the game.

Weiqi was considered one of the four gentlemanly and scholarly accomplishments and consequently was taken very seriously. Many manuals were written by and for *weiqi* enthusiasts from the Tang dynasty onwards, such as the *Wangyou qingle ji* compiled by Li Yimin in the twelfth century at the beginning

of the Southern Song, the *Xuanxuan qi pu* (6 *juan*) compiled by Yan Defu and Yan Tianzhang around 1349, and the *Shishi xianji* (5 *juan*) compiled by Xu Gu in the sixteenth century during the Ming dynasty. During the Wanli period (1573-1619), there were numerous literati and famous personalities who wrote about *weiqi* at some length, including Wu Cheng'en (ca. 1500-1582) in his *Xiyou ji* (Journey to the West), Feng Yuanzhong (dates unknown) in his *Yi dan ping* (Commentary on the Origins of Weiqi), Xie Zhaozhe (1567-1624) in his *Wu za zu* (Five Assorted Offerings), and Wang Tingna (ca. 1569-after 1628) in his *Zuoyin xiansheng jingding jiejing yi pu* (Manual of Weiqi Strategies Carefully Edited by the Gentleman Zuoyin). In his celebrated *Wu za zu*, Xie Zhaozhe lists Wang Tingna as one of the premier *weiqi* players in the late Ming.

The *Zuoyin xiansheng jingding jiejing yi pu* is a fine example of a *weiqi* manual from the late Ming period. Wang Tingna, the compiler, was the scion of a well-to-do merchant family from Xiuning, Anhui province, and was thoroughly schooled in the classics. He sat for the civil service examinations in 1597 but failed to gain an advanced degree. Nevertheless, he was later appointed as a Salt Distribution Supervisor (*yan tiju* or *yanke tiju*), a position that may well have been obtained by purchase and which contributed greatly to his wealth and social networking. Wang, who relocated to Jinling (present-day Nanjing), was known by many style-names (*zi*) and sobriquets (*hao*), among them "Zuoyin xiansheng" [literally "The Gentleman Who Sits in Reclusion," but more accurately "The Gentleman Who Plays *Weiqi*," as the term *zuoyin* was originally used in the *Shishuo xinyu* (A New Account of Tales of the World) of Liu Yiqing (403-444). In addition to his skills in the literary arts and interest in garden design, Wang was one of the major printers and publishers of the Wanli period whose books, many of them illustrated with exquisite Huizhou-style woodcuts, all bear the imprint "Huancui tang" ("Hall Surrounded by Jade"). Wang's passion and skill in the board game of *yi* or *weiqi*, as noted in Xie Zhaozhe's *Wu za zu*, made him particularly qualified to compile this manual.

The *Zuoyin xiansheng jingding jiejing yi pu* (2 *juan*) forms the first of four parts of a larger 18-*juan* work known as the *Zuoyin xiansheng dingpu quanji* (Complete Collection of Manuals Edited by the Gentleman Zuoyin). It is followed by 3 *juan* of colophons and other laudatory texts, the *Zuoyin xiansheng ji* (Collected Works of the Gentleman Zuoyin), and the *Zuoyin xiansheng yuan xi tu* (Illustration of the Garden of the Gentleman Zuoyin) in 1 *juan*. The eighteen *juan* in the complete collection are divided into eight sections identified by the characters *jin*, *shi*, *tu*, *ge*, *si*, *mu*, *pao*, and *zhu* (or *jin*, *shi*, *si*, *zhu*, *pao*, *tu*, *ge*, and *mu*). Among the *Zuoyin xiansheng jingding jiejing yi pu*'s notable features is the nearly square format of the volumes, undoubtedly inspired and necessitated by the *weiqi* boards that form the bulk of its contents. However, the book is most celebrated for its

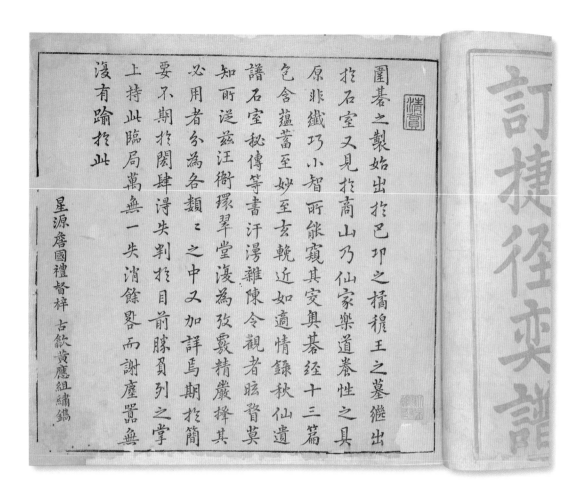

extraordinary six-paneled illustrated tableau, which is placed in the first volume after numerous prefaces and introductions.

This copy of Wang's *weiqi* manual in the National Library of China is from the renowned collection of Zheng Zhenduo (1898-1958). It is incomplete, consisting of two volumes that represents only part of the first *juan* belonging to the *jin* section. However, the original "cover page" (*fengmian ye*) of the book is perfectly preserved and mounted at the beginning of the first volume. The texts on both sides of the folded sheet are finely printed in a pale shade of red ink (a copy with the identical texts printed in blue ink recently came to light). The recto is an advertisement for the entire 18-*juan* collection, boldly claiming, among other things, that the whole enterprise was undertaken with much attention paid to the editing and collation so that it is completely free of typographical errors, that it was the result of many years of labor, and that it rises above the inferior editions put out by contemporary publishers. The text on the verso is tailored for the *weiqi* manual, with the full title printed in large characters and small characters stating the nature of the manual, alerting the reader to the fact that it contains numerous prefaces, poems, and lyrics by famous men whose various script styles are reproduced in calligraphic facsimile, and advising buy-ers to check that their copy has all the 593 printed folios. The second unpaginated folio, printed in black ink, functioned as the "inner cover page" (*nei fengmian ye*) of the book. Its recto contains an essay that traces in rapid sucession the origins of *weiqi*, the advent of *weiqi* manuals, and the special features of this particular edition by the "Huancui tang"; a certain Zhan Guoli is credited with supervising the engraving of the blocks while Huang Yingzu is identified as the master engraver. The verso is graced with decorative floral designs inset with a box containing two large seal-script characters for "Zuoyin," the compiler and publisher's sobriquet that alludes directly to the contents of the manual.

All subsequent folios are marked in the center folding margin with the characters *jin bu* (*jin* section), the folio number, and the publisher's imprint "Huancui tang." The folios in the first volume run continuously from 1 through 44, while the second volume contains folios 45 through 89. The amount of prefatory material in this work far exceeds that found in the majority of traditional Chinese publications and warrants special attention for the light it sheds upon Wang Tingna's personality as well as his impressive social and political connections. Folio 1 contains yet another frontispiece with "Zuoyin" in large seal-script characters as well as the date. Folio 2a features an illustration of nine bronze tripod vessels (*Jiu ding tu*), and a dedicatory inscription by the scholar-official Zhu Zhifan (1548-1626; *jinshi* of 1595) with four enormous characters and a signatory line spread over the next five half-folios. Folios 5a-22a are filled with prefaces by the late Ming officials Jiao Hong (1541-1620, *jinshi* of 1589), Guo Zizhang (1543-1618), Cheng Chaojing, Yuan Fuzheng, Jin Jizhen, and Li Zifang. Wang Tingna's own preface is found on folios 23a-25b, while his biography as composed by Gu Qiyuan (1565-1628) appears on folios 26a-29a. This is followed by two additional biographical accounts written by Lin Shiji and Mei Dingzuo (1549-1615) (folios 29b-31b), and a prefaced eulogy by Zhu Zhifan (folios 32a-34a).

The pictorial composition for which this work is famous is called the *Zuoyin tu* (a clever title which may be variously translated as "Illustration of the Zuoyin Garden," "Illustration of a Game of *Weiqi*," or "Illustration of Sitting in Reclusion"), and this is preceded by a text on folio 34a eulogizing it by the official Yao Lüsu. The illustration is spread over three double-spreads between folios 34b and 37a. In the first two panels (folios 34b-35a), four attendants and a pair of cranes are seen in a part of the estate that has a stone bridge over a small stream and garden stools placed under shady trees. The third panel (folio 35b) shows a couple of attendants peering out from behind garden rocks while four gentlemen are clustered around a flat-topped stone table as a game of *weiqi* is being played. One of the two seated contestants has just made a move on the board while the other reaches into a container for "stones" in preparation for his turn. Wang Tingna is presumably the player seen at the far right of the group, while the other three are clearly marked by their dress as a Confucian scholar, a Daoist practitioner, and a Buddhist priest. As the host and the commissioner of the illustration, Wang accords himself the privilege of making another appearance in the fourth panel as the tall figure emerging from a pavilion in the presence of attendants bearing a fan and a bundle of scrolls. The title, *Zuoyin tu* ("Illustration of Gentlemen Who Sit in Reclusion" or "Illustration of Gentlemen Playing *Weiqi*"), as well as the names of the

artist Wang Geng and the engraver Huang Yingzu, are unobtrusively placed and yet clearly visible within the representational space of a garden rock at the upper left of the fourth panel (folio 36a). In the last two panels (folios 36b-37a), five more attendants are seen preparing tea for the host and his guests, while across a stretch of water a box of books is being fetched from or replaced in a pavilion on stilts.

This composition, divided into three consecutive, generously proportioned double-spreads, is widely regarded as one of the finest examples of Huizhou-style woodblock illustration and engraving. Wang Geng, who was also responsible for all the illustrations in the *chuanqi* ("tales of the miraculous," a southern-style literary form) published by Wang Tingna, had a very distinctive pictorial sensibility; his slightly elongated figures, for example, project a dignified demeanor. The "stipple effect" on many areas of the compositions, particularly in the fantastically shaped garden rocks, is the result of Huang Yingzu's skillful, flawless, but nevertheless painstaking engraving of the blocks; the high contrast between light and dark areas thus achieved enhances the visual drama of the narrative. The illustration is followed by a colophon of the prefect of Changzhou, Ouyang Dongfeng, on folio 37b and a colophon by Lu Yunqing on folios 38a-39b. Another preface by Wang Tingna appears on folios 40a-43b, followed by a text entitled "Zuoyin xiansheng qi jing huicui" ("Fine Selections of *Weiqi* Classics by the Gentleman Zuoyin"), unsigned but printed with three of Wang's seals on folio 44a-b, thus concluding the first volume.

The second volume opens with a table of contents for the *weiqi* manual (*jin bu*, folio 45a-b) detailing a wide range of *weiqi* moves

and strategies found in the two *juan*. Only the first seventeen strategies, all part of *juan* 1, are to be found in the remaining folios, 46a through 89b, in this volume. Each half-folio shows between two to four exemplary moves (*bian*), with the name of the strategy and sequence of moves indicated in vertical columns of text on either the left or right margins. These two volumes appear to have been rebound with a little trimming of the free edges. They are remnants of a complete set that would have included several more volumes.

According to the table of contents in the *weiqi* manual, there would have been another printed illustration at the very end of the book bearing the title "Huancui tu." This unknown composition may have been a work much like the so-called "Huancui tang yuanjing tu" ("Illustration of Scenes in the Garden of the Hall Surrounded by Jade") which was printed as a series of sheets with block heights of approximately 24 cm and with a horizontal dimension totalling some 1,486 cm. Although the present whereabouts of the only known copy of this illustration (mounted as a handscroll) is unknown, it may be studied via a facsimile reproduction; this illustration, were it to be presented like the six-panel tableau above, would have taken up an astonishing fifty half-folios in the format of the *weiqi* manual, with enough sheets to warrant an entire bound volume by itself. The Zuoyin Garden (Zuoyin yuan), Wang Tingna's country estate near his hometown of Xiuning, was begun in 1600 and is known to have featured more than a hundred evocatively named structures and pleasure spots with Buddhist, Daoist, or Confucian associations, including an extensive man-made lake more than two meters deep. Tantalizing glimpses of this late Ming

landscape inspired by religious and philosophical syncretism, and made possible by combining profits from a lucrative official position and an in-house publishing concern, are afforded in the pictures from the *Zuoyin xiansheng jingding jiejing yi pu* that now also grace the covers of the present catalogue.

10
坐隱先生精訂捷徑奕譜二卷

簡稱《坐隱棋譜》、《坐隱先生訂棋譜》，一作《坐隱先生訂碁譜》。明汪廷訥編。明詹國禮督梓。明汪耕繪。明黃應組鐫。明萬曆三十七年（1609年）安徽新安汪氏環翠堂刻《坐隱先生全集》本。有圖。圖、文框大小不一，高約二四・一至二五・五厘米，寬約二七・五至二八・三厘米。包背裝。
16827

　　圍棋是中國一種古老的文化遺產，歷經兩千多年滄桑而始終不衰。圍棋，在古代稱「奕」，在日本寫作「碁」。奕棋的規則簡單，棋具簡單。但是，黑白兩色棋子在縱橫各十九路棋盤的三百六十一個交叉點上，卻能生出許許多多的變化。有關中國圍棋的書籍，從古到今，出了不少，主要是些棋藝書籍。現存著名的棋譜不少，如宋代御書院棋待詔李逸民編撰的《忘憂清樂集》，約成書於十二世紀南宋初；元嚴德甫、宴天章編著的《玄玄碁經》六卷，約成書於元至正九年（1349年）；以及明許穀編輯的《石室仙機》五卷，成書於十六世紀，即明正德、嘉靖年間。

　　明萬曆年間的名士，如吳承恩、湯顯祖、凌

濛初、馮元仲、謝肇淛、汪廷訥等都愛奕。各有作品為吳氏的《西遊記》、馮氏的《奕旦評》、謝氏的《五雜俎》，以及汪氏的《坐隱先生訂碁譜》。「坐隱」，為下圍棋的別稱。南朝宋劉義慶《世說新語》曰：「王中郎以圍棋為坐隱，支公以圍棋為手談」。宋李石《續博物志》曰：「王中郎以圍棋為坐隱，或亦謂之為手談，又謂之為棋聖」。謝肇淛於其《五雜俎》記有以下一段：「近代名手，弇州論之略備矣。以余耳目所見，新安有方生、呂生、汪生；閩中有蔡生，一時稱國手，而方於諸子，有白眉之譽。其後六合有王生，足跡遍天下，幾無橫敵。時方已入貲為大官，承談詩書，不復與角。而汪、呂諸生，皆為王所困，名震華夏」。

　　汪廷訥，原字去泰，後改字昌朝，一字無如，別號無無居士、無悶道人、全一真人、清癡叟、坐隱先生，安徽休寧汪村人。自幼出繼於同宗的富商為養子，為吳江沈詞隱弟子。生卒年不詳，大約二十二歲前後進入南京的文人圈子，又出錢取得南京國子監生員的資格。三十歲時，捐貲當上鹽課副提舉，從七品，駐蕪湖（鳩茲）。品級雖低，富商由此而成為朝廷命官，身份大為提高。汪氏以官鹽運使致富，甚好事，喜作曲，尚工樂府，善刻書。萬曆二十八年（1600年）在家鄉松夢山下大興土木，始修建坐隱園和環翠堂，次年開挖深七尺許

的昌湖，布置了一百多景點，日為詩酒之會。汪氏把富商的家業改造成為文人隱居的莊園，并自設印書局發行家刻本。環翠堂萬曆年間刊本現存有《關尹子文始真經注》九卷、《元本出相西廂記》二卷、《人鏡陽秋》二十二卷、《坐隱先生精訂王西樓樂府》一卷、《坐隱先生精訂金伯嶼爽齋樂府》一卷、《坐隱先生精訂梁少伯江東白苧》一卷、《文壇列俎》十卷、《坐隱先生精訂馮海浮山堂詞稿》四卷、《彩舟記》二卷、《投桃記》二卷、《義烈記》二卷、《環翠堂樂府獅吼記》二卷、《環翠堂華集》二卷、《無如子贅言》一卷《贅言續》一卷等。汪氏環翠堂刻本插圖雖有部分刊於金陵，但全體是典型、上乘的徽派版畫，幾條細若毫髮，一絲不苟，些衣紋折疊、花飾圖案和山石的點刻，再也沒有誰家能與之匹比的了。人物造型也具有非凡的功力，可惜臉型稍微定型化，山石結構、水浪波紋亦欠實感，這些均代表徽派版畫特點，可說是優點，也可評為缺點。

《坐隱先生精訂捷徑奕譜》二卷，有單行本、全集本。中國國家圖書館所藏本屬於《坐隱先生訂譜全集》。全集四種十八卷，分「金」、「石」、「土」、「革」、「絲」、「木」、「匏」、「竹」八部，首為《坐隱先生精訂捷徑奕譜》二卷、再次題贈三卷，後附《坐隱先生集》十二卷，後又有《坐

隱先生園戲圖》一卷（一作《坐隱園戲墨》，一作《坐隱園清賞》）。

《坐隱先生精訂捷徑奕譜》為全集八部之第一部。中國國家圖書館藏本現存二冊，版心上方記部別均題「金部」，下方記葉次，再下方記堂名「環翠堂」。此部書為鄭振鐸先生舊藏，鈐有「長樂鄭振鐸西諦藏書」朱文方印、「長樂鄭氏藏書之印」朱文長方印等藏書印。

第一冊內封面葉上下兩半葉均朱印，上半葉題：「本堂刻行《訂譜》，細心校讎，點畫無魚魯之訛，重直雕鏤，體製有晉唐之遺。簡良工而聚業，歷歲月以成集，既專且久，誠都以麗。恐有無知之徒，罔利之輩，假名目以妄梓，希混淆而欺世，潦草錯誤，奚便覽讀。具雙目者，必能鑒定；從任耳者，或至受誣。誠本堂之深恨，實士林之共憤。今刻『九鼎』為記，尚冀買者辯之。萬曆己酉孟秋乞巧日，新都環翠堂識。」下半葉即牌記有大字分左右兩行題「坐隱先生精訂捷徑奕譜」，其間以四行小字題「訂譜全書乃活套分類局棋譜，并海內名公贈、詩詞、歌賦，真、草、篆、隸，無不備具。共伍百玖拾參張，買者須查足數方為全玩。徽郡汪衙環翠堂識。」

朱印內封面葉後均為墨印葉，首為此文：「圍棋之製，始出於巴邛之橘、穆王之墓，繼出於石

室，又見於商山，乃仙家樂道養性之具。原非纖巧小智所能窺其奧奧。《碁經》十三篇，包含「蘊蓄」至「妙」至「玄輓」，近如《適情錄》、《秋仙遺譜》、《石室秘傳》等書，汗漫雜陳，令觀者眩瞀，莫知所從。茲汪衙環翠堂復為攷覈精嚴，擇其必用者分為各類，類之中又加詳焉。期於簡要，不期於閎肆。得失判於目前，勝負運之掌上；持此臨局，萬無一失；消餘嗒而謝塵囂，無復有踰於此。星源詹國禮督梓，古歙黃應組繡鐫」。此篇後有「坐隱」大篆二字，四周有花紋。

金部第一葉再題「坐隱」大篆二字并記年月。第二葉上半葉有「九鼎圖」，末署「心手同玄。金陵友人朱之蕃題贈昌朝詞丈」，四大字各半葉，款識半葉。再次有焦竑、郭子章、程朝京、袁福徵、金繼震、李自芳序。焦竑〈坐隱先生譜集敘〉云：「顧不名仕而名隱，不隱於他而隱于奕也」，末署「萬曆己酉歲六月，琅琊焦竑書於所居之恬愉館中」。郭子章〈坐隱先生訂譜全集序〉，末署「萬曆戊申仲春之吉，賜進士出身，資政大夫、巡撫貴州兼督湖北川東、提督軍務、右都御史兼兵部右侍郎，青螺郭子章拜撰。門人阮汝鳴書」。程朝京〈汪齭使坐隱訂譜全集序〉，末署「萬曆三十七年歲在屠維作噩春二月花朝日，賜進士，第亞中大夫、福建承宣布政使、司分守漳南道左參政、前

朝鮮，賜一品服，金陵友弟朱之蕃書，時萬曆三十五年二月日偕屬丁未，并此紀事」。再次為姚履素〈坐隱圖贊〉，末署「賜進士出、奉直大夫、刑部湖廣清史司郎中，友人姚履素頓首拜贊」。

接下為「坐隱圖」連式六幅（共三開，每開二幅），汪耕繪，黃應組刻，繪刻精致。汪耕，字于田，汪廷訥之好友或門客之一，善於繪寫人物山水，細致秀麗，為前人所未有。第四幅左上部石上以小字鎸「坐隱圖。汪耕寫」。黃應組，號仰川，擅刻書中插圖，刻書多種，為歙西虹村黃氏刻書名手之一。圖中描繪了汪氏坐隱園雅集情景，以第三幅為圖之重點，有兩人在臺上松陰石桌下棋，另有兩人在旁觀看。下棋的一位很可能就是圍棋高手汪廷訥本人，其他三客從服裝可知是儒家、佛教及道家的代表人物。第四幅有一人在園中行走，說不定是以園主份再次描繪汪廷訥本人。

圖後有歐陽東鳳〈坐隱圖跋〉，跋文以下全錄：「夫簡策有圖，非徒工繪事也。蓋記所未備者，可按圖而窮其勝；記所已備者，可因圖而索其精，圖為貢幽闡邃之具也。海陽汪坐隱先生青雲其跡而煙霞其心，有《坐隱集》行於世而弁圖於首。其山、亭、池、館，儼是輞川、竹塢、柳堤宛然曲水。此中置一坐隱先生，所謂『景中人者』非耶。千載而下當與蘭亭金並傳也。潛江友人歐陽東鳳」。歐陽跋文後有陸雲卿撰〈書坐隱圖後〉。再次為陸雲卿〈書坐隱圖後〉，末署「雲臺外史陸雲卿」。再次為汪廷訥〈訂譜小敘〉，末署「萬曆戊申暮春月上浣，坐隱先生纂于環翠堂。後學黃常吉謹書」。再次為〈坐隱先生棋經彙粹〉，後刻有「廷訥」朱文長方印、「昌朝」白文方印、「全一真人」白文方印。第一冊至此完畢，末葉葉次記「金部」第四十四葉。

第二冊前有〈坐隱先生訂棋譜目錄〉，首葉葉次記「金部」第四十五葉。據目錄，棋譜上卷有「超好手套，三十二變。釣竿套，八變。立仁套，六變。大套，十四變。小角套，十變。壓梁套，三十一變。鎮神套，二十九變。垂簾套，十七變。金井欄套，七變。捲簾套，九變。六四套，九變。七三套，九變。八三套，十二變。九三套，十八變。十三套，四變。十四套，十三變。雙飛套，八變。空花套，七變。十字套，八變。侵分套，五十變」，下卷有「敵手，二十六局。二子，六局。三子，一局。四子，七局。長生類。赫眼類。點眼類。造劫類。獨立類。過渡類。脫骨類。征枷類。撲跌類。聚點類。連環類。斷殺類。雜類。環翠圖」。此部

系禮、刑二部郎中，邑人程朝京撰。姻氏王尚哲鏡遠書」。袁福徵〈坐隱先生訂譜題辭〉，末署「賜進士，第比部郎，歷三州牧雲間，通家侍生袁福徵頓首拜撰。洪士英女吟甫書」。金繼震〈敘汪飺使坐隱先生訂譜〉，末署「賜進士，奉議大夫、刑部四川清吏司郎中、前奉敕審錄山東等處，通家眷侍生金繼震頓首拜撰。金汝誠書」。李自芳〈坐隱先生訂譜序〉，末署「賜進士，中憲大夫、知福建汀州府事，通家友人李自芳頓首拜撰。祝純一書」。

再次為汪廷訥〈自敘〉，云：「竊有志聖賢之學，盡斂生平俠氣而軌之中和。居常好游揚人，而人多毀我；好緩急人，而人多負我；好赴人之難，而人多中傷我。以此返照，大求懺悔。安分知機，

不與俗競。由是世外之情熱，丘壑之興濃，道義之念篤，是非之心淡……余自了悟指心，純陽示夢之後……」，末署「明萬曆己酉春三月戊子，清癡叟汪廷訥序」。汪序後為顧起元〈坐隱先生傳〉，末署「萬曆丁未仲秋月幾望，賜進士及第、翰林院國史編修、文林郎、記注起居、編纂章奏，江寧友人顧起元頓首拜撰。秣陵魏之璜書」。再次為林世吉〈題坐隱先生傳後〉，末署「閩中林世吉頓首纂」。再次為梅鼎祚〈書坐隱先生傳後〉，末署「萬曆戊申長至日戊戌，宣城梅鼎祚撰」。再次為朱之蕃〈坐隱先生贊，有序〉，末署「賜進士及第、奉議大夫、右春坊、右諭德、掌南京翰林院事、前翰林院脩撰、編纂章奏、記注起居、管理制敕、正使

現存的第二冊只含有棋譜上卷的「超好手套，三十二變」至「雙飛套，八變」，末葉葉次記「金部」第八十九葉。按朱印內封面葉所計，棋譜總共應有五百九十三葉，此部現存只有六至七分之一左右。

〈坐隱先生訂碁譜目錄〉末所標「環翠圖」之樣式不詳，但從諸文字記錄可知坐隱園內「三教合一」的建築與景點包括儒家傳統的蘭臺、蘭亭遺勝等，佛教的半偈庵、紫竹林等，道教的百鶴樓、全一龕等。景點另有白雲扉、嘉樹庭、五老峰、鶴巢、松院、羽化橋、憑夢閣、沖天泉、洗心池、萬花叢、長林、石幾、觀空洞、棋盤石、眺瞻臺、解嘲亭、憑閣軒、菊徑、秘閣、空花巷、懸榻齋、東壁、洗硯坡、嚶鳴館、曲霞藏、無如書舍、青蓮窟、玄津橋、朗悟臺、天花壇、達生臺、昌公湖、隱鱗潭、萬錦堤、六橋、浮家一葉、湖心亭、滄洲趣、面壁岩、釣鼇臺、砥柱、鴻寶關、茶丘藥圃、玄莊、雲區煙道、無無居、仁壽山、笑塵岩、天放亭等處。關於坐隱園，可參閱「環翠堂園景圖」一卷，足以考見汪氏庭園之全景。此圖為明錢貢畫，黃應組刻，萬曆年間（約1610年前後）汪廷訥環翠堂刊本。此長卷框高二四厘米，長約一四八六厘米，圖繪汪氏莊園景色，精工秀麗，洵國寶也。此卷為傅惜華先生舊藏，今不知流落何處，但有北京人民美術出版社一九八一年《環翠堂園景圖》玻璃版影印本可參考。

茲選照內封面葉上半葉、內封面葉下半葉、《坐隱圖》連式六幅（金部第三十四葉下半葉至第三十七葉上半葉）、棋譜之「垂簾套」第十六變二十二着以及第十七變二十二着（金部第七十四葉下半葉）、「金井欄活套」第一變二十四着、第二變二十着、第三變十八着以及第四變二十七着（金部第七十五葉上半葉）。

此棋譜藏者極罕，洵為珍品。日本國立公文書館藏有《坐隱先生訂譜全集》八卷。1995年五月十日「中國嘉德春季古籍善本拍賣會」以及1996年九月十四日「中國書店歷代稀見書刊資料拍賣會」均有此書出現。

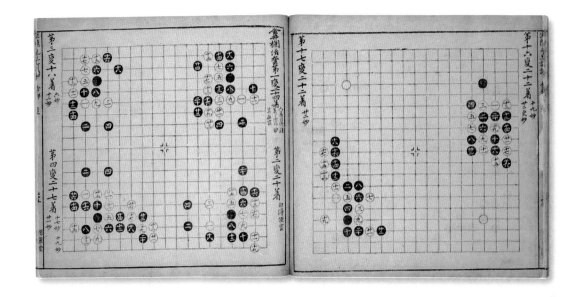

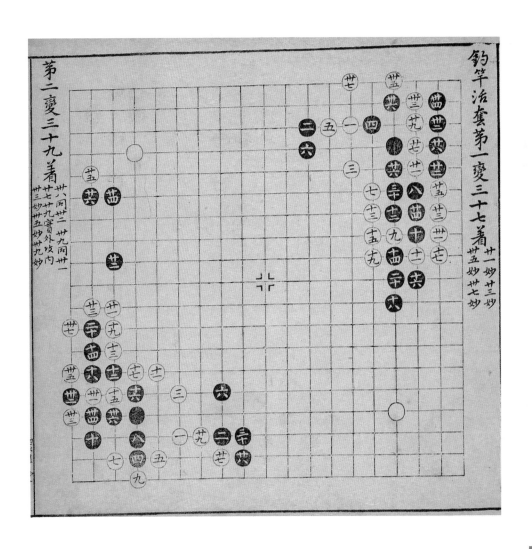

11

Xin jiaozhu guben Xixiang ji (6 juan)

Newly Annotated Edition of the Story of the Western Wing, Based on Classic Editions, 6 *juan*

Ming dynasty (1368-1644), Wanli period (1573-1619)

By Wang Dexin [also known as Wang Shifu (fl. 1295-1307)]; edited and annotated by Wang Jide (ca. 1542-1623); illustrated by Ru Wenshu (fl. early 17th century) based on the designs of Qian Gu (1508-ca. 1578); engraved by Huang Yingzu (1563 or 1573-1644) and Huang Yingguang (b. 1593)

Shanyin, Zhejiang province: Wang shi Xiangxue ju, 1614

10 columns per half-folio; 20 characters per column; white folding margin at center of folio; single-line borders; overall dimensions of volumes: 27.0 x 17.2 cm; block sizes of text: approx. 21.5 x 14.3 cm; stitched binding

16229

The *Xixiang ji* (Story of the Western Wing) is widely acknowledged as not only the masterpiece of Yuan northern-style *zaju* (drama; literally "variety show"), but also as the greatest Chinese drama of any period. Based on the *Yingying zhuan* (Story of Yingying) by the Tang dynasty writer Yuan Zhen (779-831) and the *Xixiang ji zhugong diao* (Story of the Western Wing in All Keys and Modes) by the Jin dynasty dramatist Dong Jieyuan (fl. 1190-1208), it tells the story of the love between a promising young student, Zhang Junrui, and the lovely but unfortunately already betrothed Cui Yingying. Through the clever machinations of Yingying's maidservant,

Hongniang, and in spite of the stern old Madame Cui's objections and a military revolt, the lovers are eventually united.

Numerous editions and annotated versions of this dramatic work were printed in the Ming and Qing periods in response to its great popularity. During the Ming alone there were no less than sixty editions, and many publishers included woodblock illustrations in an effort to make it even more attractive to potential readers, such as the Wang Jide edition of 1614 in the collection of the National Library of China. This edition features two sizes of printed characters: larger ones are used for the main text while smaller ones are used for the annotations. It also contains forty-three half-folios of illustrations, all but one of which are accompanied by identifying labels. With the exception of the first picture depicting Cui Yingying, all the other illustrations are in the double-paneled format, so that readers are treated to twenty-one finely engraved panoramic scenes and intimate vignettes. The identity of the engraver, Huang Yingguang (b. 1593), is given on the lower left border of the opening illustration; his signature is discreetly placed within the carved woodblocks of scenes 3-5 and 16-21. The illustration shown is from folios 1b and 2a of *juan* 1; it is the first of the double-page illustrations and offers a panoramic view of the Monastery of Universal Salvation (Pujiu si) in Puzhou, with its main Buddha hall, acroteria, gateways, and covered verandahs, as well as the monks' quarters at the rear. This is the setting in which the story's protagonists, Yingying and Student Zhang, meet for the first time.

This book was formerly in the collection of Zheng Zhenduo (1898-1958), the renowned scholar and connoisseur of Chinese woodblock printing and illustration.

11

新校注古本西廂記六卷

元王德信（記王實甫）撰。明王驥德校注。明錢穀繪圖。明汝文淑摹。明黃應組、黃應光刻。明萬曆四十二年（1614年）山陰王氏香雪居刻本。半葉十行，行二十字，四周單邊，版心白口，下方記「香雪居」。框高二一‧五厘米，寬一四‧三厘米。綫裝。
16229

　　《西廂記》天下奪魁，詞曲如花間美人，是中國古典戲曲文學作品中的瑰寶。歷代刻本甚多，僅明代刊本有六十多種，現存有四十種左右。

　　此本為王驥德校注《西廂記》。王驥德，字伯良，別號方諸生、秦樓外史、香雪居主人，浙江會稽（今紹興）人。當出生於嘉靖二十一年（1542年）。深通音律，能撰曲。著有的《南詞正韻》、《聲韻分合圖》、《方諸館集》，以及《離魂》、《救友》、《雙鬟》、《招魂》等雜劇已失傳；現僅存其《曲律》和《題紅記》傳奇、《男王后》雜劇，以及《新校注古本西廂記》。王驥德與其老師徐渭是鄰居，兩家只隔一道短牆，這肯定有助於王氏成為越中曲家群的曲學名家。卒於天啟三年（1623年），享年八十二歲。

　　在「凡例」第一條中，王氏便說明了用碧筠齋本、朱石津本、徐文長本、金在衡本、顧玄緯本、徐士范本以及一些「坊本」、「俗本」進行校勘的，但實際上他用以校勘曲文的本子還不止這些。王氏比其他校注者多做了一項工作，用董解元《西廂記諸宮調》和《新校注古本西廂記》作從頭至尾的全面對照比勘。

　　此書卷首有明人序，末署「萬曆歲在癸丑重陽日吳郡粲花館主人書」。次為王驥德〈新校注古本西廂記自序〉云：「……余自童年輒有聲律之癖。每讀其詞，便能拈所紕繆，復摭摩而恨，故為盲瞽學究妄誇箋釋，不啻嘔哂而欲付之烈炬也。既覓得碧筠齋若朱石津氏兩古本。序碧筠齋者稱淮于逸史首署，疏注僅數千，頗多破的。朱石津不知何許人，視碧筠齋大較相同。關中杜逢霖序，朱沒而其友吳厚邱氏手書以刻者。並屬前元舊文，世不多見。餘刻紛紛，殆數十種，僅毘陵徐士範、秣陵金在衡、錫山顧玄緯三本稍稱彼善。徐本間詮數語，偶窺一斑。金本時更字句，亦寡中竅。獨顧本類輯他書，似較該洽，恨去取弗精，疵繆間出，然總之

影響俗本，於古文無當也。故師徐文長先生說曲，大能解頤，亦嘗訂存別本，口授筆記，積有歲年。余往暨周生讀書湖上，攜一青衣，故善肉聲。鈆槧之暇，酒後耳熱時，令手紅牙，曼引一曲，桃花墮，而堤善柳若為按拍也。輒手丹鈆，為訂其謁者，芟其蕪者，補其闕者，務割正以還故吾。余家藏元人雜劇可數百種許，閒有所會，時疏數語。又雜采他傳記若諸劇語之相印證者，漫署上方。久之，遂盈卷帙。既又并微之本傳若王性之氏辯證及顧本所錄諸引，篇章有繫本記者，別為攷證一卷，附之簡末，稍為崔氏及實甫一伸沉冤。蓋實甫之詞稍難詮解者，在用意宛委，遣辭引帶，及隱語方言，不易疆合。憶余入燕，故元大都，實甫枌榆鄉也。舉詢其人，已瘖不能解，故余為釋句，其微辭隱義，類以意逆。而一二方，不敢漫為揣摩，必雜證諸劇，以當左契。大氐取碧筠齋古注十之二，取徐師新釋亦十之二。今之詞家吳郡詞隱先生，定稱指南，復函請參訂，先生謬假賞與，凡再易稿，始克成編。……萬曆甲寅春日大越琅邪生方諸偃史伯良氏書」。

接下為周公瑕署書四大字、例三十六則、標目、引證書目、目錄、單面式插圖一幅（即「崔孃遺照」，左下方記「新安黃應光鐫」）、雙面連式插圖二十二幅。卷一至五之正文卷端均題「元大都王實甫編，明會稽方諸生校注，明山陰徐渭附解，吳江詞隱生評，古虞謝伯美、山陰朱朝鼎同校」。卷六為〈新校注古本西廂記考〉，正文卷端題「明會稽方諸生彙考，古虞謝伯美、山陰朱朝鼎同校」。

《新校注古本西廂記》分五本，每本四折不標目，但每折用兩字標目，即「遇艷」、「投禪」、「賡句」、「附齋」、「解圍」、「邀謝」、「負盟」、「寫怨」、「傳書」、「省簡」、「踰垣」、「訂約」、「就歡」、「說合」、「傷離」、「入夢」、「報第」、「酬械」、「拒婚」及「完配」，共二十折。根據現在各種明刊本《西廂記》，全劇分五本，每本分四折，每折以兩字標出目的，實以王驥德為第一人。

本書配有精美動人的版畫，繪者為錢穀。錢穀，字叔寶，一字府卿，別號磬室、龍泓，江蘇吳縣人。工書善畫，遊文徵明門下。山水爽朗可愛，蘭竹兼妙。所作《西廂記》二十一幅插圖，靈氣盈紙，尤注重景致之刻劃，可惜圖畫原作尚未發現。臨摹錢穀原作的汝文淑，一作汝太君，吳江縣人。

毛休文之母。《玉臺畫史》則稱她為汝太君。工畫，所畫扇十八面，山水、草蟲無不臻妙，三百年中大方名筆，可與頡頏者不過二三而已，在女畫家中是出類拔萃的人物。刻工黃應組，號仰川，新安人。刻有汪耕繪《坐隱先生精訂捷徑奕譜》等。刻工黃應光，新安人，遷居杭州。有盛譽，所刻均為武林版畫的重要作品，如《元曲選》、容與堂本《李卓吾先生批評忠義水滸傳》等書插圖。

中國國家圖書館所藏此部《新校注古本西廂記》，為鄭振鐸先生舊藏，鈐有「長樂鄭振鐸西諦藏書」朱文方印。茲選照第一本第一折之插圖，描繪蒲州普救寺的全景，也是劇中小生張珙（字君瑞）與大家千金崔鶯鶯首次相見的情景。圖右下刻標目「遇艷」，左上刻題「長州錢穀叔寶寫，吳江汝氏文淑摹」。

此版本有民國十八年北平富晉書社、東來閣書店兩家影印本，名《高明本繪圖新校注古本西廂記六卷》。

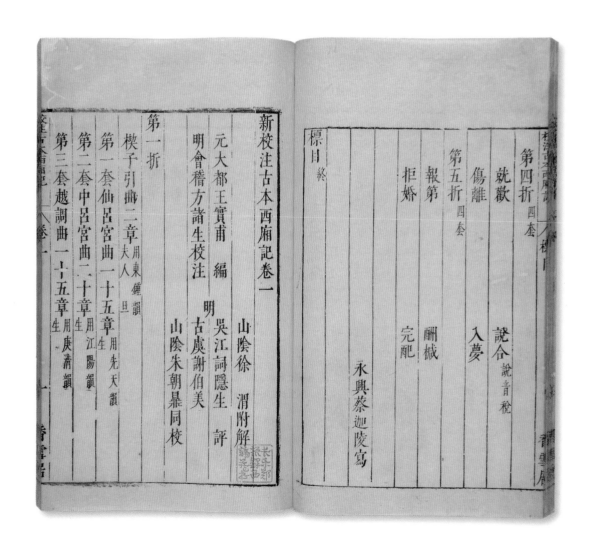

12

Li Zhuowu xiansheng piping Zhongyi Shuihu zhuan

(100 juan), yinshou (1 juan)

Outlaws of the Marsh from the Hall of Loyalty and Righteousness, with Commentaries by the Gentleman Li Zhuowu, 100 *juan*, with Introduction, 1 *juan*

Ming dynasty (1368-1644), Wanli period (1573-1619)
Compilation attributed to Shi Naiían (ca. 1290-ca. 1365); revision attributed to Luo Guanzhong (ca. 1330-ca. 1400); commentary attributed to Li Zhi (1527-1602); engraved by Wu Fengtai

Hulin [Hangzhou]: Rongyu tang, n.d. [ca. 1615]
11 columns per half-folio; 22 characters per column; white folding margin at center of folio; single-line borders; overall dimensions of volumes: 29.1 x 17.4 cm; block sizes of text: approx. 21.3 x 14.4 cm; stitched binding

17358

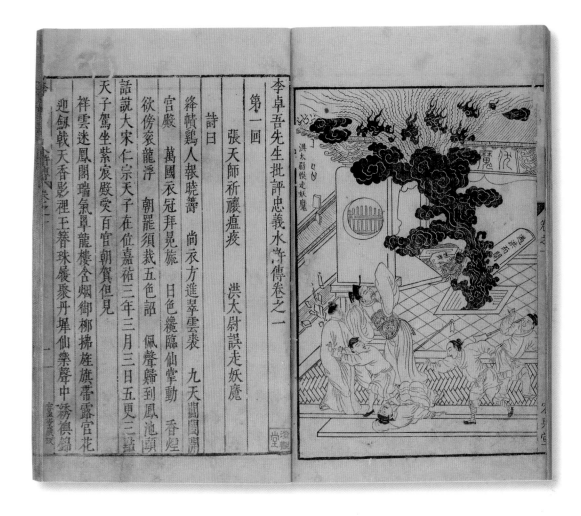

The *Shuihu zhuan* is among the most well known and beloved of Chinese picaresque novels. This quasi-historical prose epic has an episodic structure and is set around a marsh-girt mountain in Shandong province during the closing years of the reign of Emperor Huizong (1082-1135; r. 1101-1125). Song Jiang (fl. 1119-1121) and 107 other colorful, daredevil men and women (thirty-six major chiefs and seventy-two lesser ones) became the heroic leaders of a rebel army of thousands who robbed the rich and fought against the powerful and tyrannical government. Their lair was known as the Hall of Loyalty and Righteousness (Zhongyi tang), from which part of the book's title is derived. Long attributed to either Shi Nai'an or Luo Guanzhong, or to both, there is still no consensus on the actual authorship; indeed, this major work has engendered much literary scholarship and countless studies to date. The novel, one of the first to be written in vernacular Chinese, has been translated into a number of foreign languages; it is also well known in English as *The Water Margin, All Men Are Brothers*, or *Brigands of the Marsh*.

There are numerous editions of the *Shuihu zhuan*, with the number of chapters ranging between 71 and 124, making it the most textually diverse of Chinese novels. This Wanli-period edition published by Rongyu tang is one of the two versions with commentaries attributed to Li Zhi (1527-1602). It contains 100 chapters (*hui*), each of which has two corresponding woodblock illustrations at the head of the text. The two hundred finely engraved pictures were sometimes grouped together and printed as a separate volume. The episodes depicted are in most cases the most exciting or dramatic ones in the chapters, and many of the enormous cast of characters are portrayed with distinctive personalities. Although he was among the most important intellectual and literary figures of the late Ming period, Li Zhi was not the actual person responsible for many of the so-called "Li Zhuowu" commentaries, including this one; the principal forger is believed to be a certain Ye Zhou.

Reproduced here are the illustrations and opening pages from the first and second chapters (*hui*), respectively titled "The Commander Hong in Heedlessness Frees the Spirits" and "Jiu Wenlong Makes a Mighty Turmoil at the Village of the Shi Family."

12

李卓吾先生批評忠義水滸傳一百卷引首一卷

元施耐庵集撰。元羅貫中纂修。明李贄評。明吳鳳臺刻。明萬曆間（1573–1620；約1615年）虎林（今杭州）容與堂刻本。半葉十一行，行二十二字，四周單邊，版心白口。框高二一‧三厘米，寬一四‧四厘米。綫裝。

17358

《水滸傳》是中國古典長篇小説四大奇書之一。故事是在話本、雜劇的基礎上發展而成。明施耐庵創作，羅貫中編纂，寫梁山泊宋江等一百零八位好漢替天行道之義舉。

《水滸傳》的版本情況相當複雜，有繁本、簡本兩大系統。繁本有七十回本、百回本、百二十回本三種，其中百回本的成書早於百二十回本和七十回本。百回本中，以刻於明萬曆十七年（1589年）前有「天都外臣」（即汪道昆）序的本子為最早，但它缺佚甚多，所缺篇頁，是據清康熙間石渠閣本補綴的。另一個百回本即是容與堂本，它的成書雖然較天都外臣序本稍晚（在萬曆三十年前後），但內容完整無缺。《水滸傳》各種不同版本中出現過許多精美的插圖。現存版本的「水滸」插圖，大抵可以分成兩種，一是根據「水滸」回目內容作的故事插圖；一是依照故事發展作的圖文對照、有連續性、在形式上接近連環圖畫的插圖。

容與堂刻百回本《李卓吾先生批評忠義水滸傳》是《水滸傳》流傳過程中一個十分重要的本子。容與堂是明代虎林（今杭州）著名書坊，所刻書籍以小説、戲曲為主，多配有精美的版畫插圖。容與堂於萬曆年間刊刻所謂「李卓吾先生批評」本有《李卓吾先生批評幽閨記》二卷、《李卓吾先生批評紅拂記》二卷、《李卓吾先生批評玉合記》二卷、《李卓吾先生批評琵琶記》二卷四十二齣、《李卓吾先生批評西廂記》二卷等。此本雖名為《李卓吾先生批評忠義水滸傳》，但研究者早已懷疑其評語並非出於李贄（號卓吾），而係後人假托。此本的評語當出於無錫人葉晝（字文通）之手。此書雖非李贄所批，但其評語也頗有值得注意之處，已引起研究明代文學批評者的重視。此本不但是現存繁本《水滸傳》的最早的完整的本子，也是現存百回本的唯一完整的萬曆刻本，對研究《水滸傳》具有重大價值。

容與堂本每回前各以兩句回目為題，配有兩幅單面方式的插圖。均予保留，仍置於各回前。唯圖上所書回目，間有與正文回目不同處，或顛倒處。吳鳳臺所鐫刻的插圖繪刻精工，人物虎虎有生氣，背景從略，表現了梁山英雄人物不同的階級出，不同的社會地位、思想意識和精神面貌，描寫了他們對於人民的愛和對於統治階級的恨，以及他們不屈不撓進行革命鬥爭的樂觀主義精神。

茲選照第一回之第二幅插圖（「洪太尉誤走妖魔」）與其正文上半葉，以及第二回之第二幅插圖（「九紋龍大鬧史家村」）與其正文上半葉。

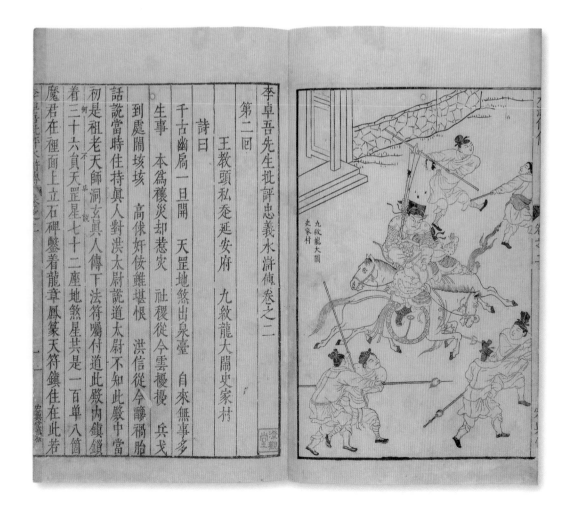

13

Yuan qu xuan tu (1 juan)

Illustrations from Selected Yuan Dramas, 1 *juan*

Ming dynasty (1368-1644), Wanli period (1573-1619)
Compiled and edited by Zang Maoxun (1550-1620; *jinshi* of 1580); engraved by Huang Yingguang (b. 1593), Huang Liqing, Huang Duanfu, et al.
Hangzhou, Zhejiang province: Diaochong guan, 1616
White folding margin at center of folio, with black "fishtail"; single-line borders; overall dimensions of volume: 25.7 x 16.2 cm; block sizes of illustrations: approx. 20.3 x 13.7 cm; stitched binding

16215

The *Yuan qu xuan* (Selected Yuan Dramas) is a collection of one hundred dramas (*zaju*), of which ninety-four works belong to the Yuan (1279-1368) and six to the early Ming period. Zang Maoxun (1550-1620; *jinshi* of 1580), the compiler and editor, made many changes to the original dramatic texts, adding or subtracting arias at will, often changing the focus of the plays, and altering the quality of the originals. Nevertheless, it is the most commonly used edition of Yuan plays and is extremely significant because it has preserved no less than two-thirds of all exant dramatic compositions from this period, many of which were produced for the imperial court or for very small, private audiences, and which may otherwise not have survived.

This work was originally printed in a handsome edition, which may have accounted for its popularity. The one hundred volumes of the complete work were divided into ten series of ten volumes each and printed in two batches. The first, in 1615, contained the *jia* through *wu* (first through fifth) series in fifty volumes, while the second containing the remaining *ji* through *gui* (sixth through tenth) series was published in 1616.

The 224 illustrations in the full set are all of a very fine quality and constitute the single highest concentration of images in any extant collection of Chinese dramatic works. Each drama in the compendium is accompanied by at least two illustrations, and some by as many as four. There was evidently a market for special editions containing only the illustrated folios that have a separate pagination, as is the case with the present example. This copy in the National Library of China formerly belonged to Zheng Zhenduo (1898-1958), who authored a number of works related to Yuan dramas and their pictorial illustration.

The three woodblock illustrations reproduced here are: "Chen hei jiang ming fei qing zhong hen" from the four-act tragedy *Po youmeng gu yan Han gong qiu* (Autumn in the Han Palace), the best work of Ma Zhiyuan (ca. 1260-ca. 1325), the most outstanding dramatist of the Yuan period (folio 1a); "Dongtang lao quan pojia zidi" from *Dongtang lao quan po jia zidi* (The Old Master Dongtang Admonishes the Prodigal Son) by Qin Jianfu (act. ca. 1330-1333) of the later Yuan dynasty (folio 13b); and "Liang Shanbo, Song Jiang jiangling" ("General Orders from Liang Shanbo and Song Jiang") from *Tongle yuan Yan Qing bo yu* (Yan Qing of the Tongle Hall Bets on a Fish) by the early Yuan dramatist Li Wenwei (folio 14a).

13

元曲選圖一卷

取自《元曲選一百種一百卷》。明臧懋循編訂。明黃應光、黃禮卿、黃端甫等刻。明萬曆四十四年 (1616年) 杭州臧氏雕蟲館刊本。計二百二十四圖。左右雙邊，版心白口，單魚尾。框高二〇‧三厘米，寬一三‧七厘米。線裝。

16215

臧懋循，字晉叔，號顧渚、顧渚山人，浙江長興縣人，家住太湖之濱，顧渚山之南。出生於明嘉靖二十九年 (1550年)，萬曆八年 (1580年) 進士，次年出任荆州府學教授。萬曆十年，委派為應天 (南京) 鄉試的同考官，事畢，調任夷陵 (今湖北宜昌) 知縣。次年任命為南京國子監博士。後被劾罷官，隱於顧渚山中，寄情于山林水涯，於天啟元年 (1620年) 病逝。臧氏精通音律，為明代著名戲劇家，著有《負苞堂集》等。刻有《古逸詞》、《古詩所》、《唐詩所》、《元曲選》、《校正古本荆釵記》、《玉茗堂四夢》、《改定曇花記》、彈詞《仙遊錄》等三種，總字數不少於三百萬。其中《元曲選》一百種最負盛名，影響最大。臧氏以家藏雜劇秘本與麻城劉承禧 (號延伯) 所藏錄之御戲監本參互校訂，摘其佳者，編定成書。

《元曲選》全書十集，每集十卷，共收錄九十四種元人作品、六種明初人作品。有自序二，分別署「萬曆旃蒙單閼之歲春上巳日書於西湖僧舍」及「萬曆丙春上巳日若下人臧晉叔書」，因知此書分兩批刊印，前批五十種刊於萬曆四十三年 (1615年)，後批五十種刊於萬曆四十四年 (1616年)，并知刻書地點在浙江杭州。序後「臧晉叔印」下有「雕蟲館」印，當為臧氏室名，故有「雕蟲館校定」之說。此書另有萬曆四十三年 (1615年) 羊城書林周時泰博古堂刻本，卷首冠圖，單面方式。

劇本大多經過臧氏加工整理，科白完整，并附音注。在數量上，擁有現存元人雜劇之三分之二，在質量上，乃從眾多雜劇秘本及宮廷內府本互相校訂選出，為收羅最富、影響最大之元人雜劇選集。一般研究元雜劇者多以此書為依據，流傳較廣。此書配有婉麗纖細的版畫插圖，反映出萬曆後期徽州版畫的風格。

《元曲選》插圖，單面方式，共二百二十四幅，每劇有圖二幅，有時多至四幅。圖右上標圖 (曲) 目。恣意運用古代各家之不同畫法，表現一

百部內容複雜異常的雜劇故事，抓住緊要關節，將其情景傳達出來。為現存曲類圖書中插圖最多的一種，另編為《元曲選圖》一卷，集中成一冊，有明萬曆臧氏雕蟲館刻本。

中國國家圖書館所藏此部《元曲選圖》，為鄭振鐸先生舊藏，鈐有「長樂鄭振鐸西諦藏書」朱文方印。祇存圖，無序、論與曲文。圖原位於卷首，葉碼以圖序單獨排列。圖單面方式，每劇圖兩幅或四幅不等，共二百二十四幅。刻版精細，刷印秀美。畫面所展示的故事情節，能抓住緊要關節，對該劇的內容極具概括性，同時又是十分具體而生動的。畫面構圖也極少雷同。作者還善於利用環境的描繪，烘托氣氛，表達感情。

茲選照圖三幅，為馬致遠《破幽夢孤雁漢宮秋雜劇》第二幅圖「沉黑江明妃青塚恨」、秦簡夫《東堂老勸破家子弟雜劇》第二幅圖「東堂老勸破家子弟」、李文蔚《同樂院燕青博魚雜劇》第一幅「梁山泊宋江將令」。

14

Tang shi yan yi pin

Exemplars of the Beautiful and the Refined in Tang Poetry

Ming dynasty (1368-1644), Tianqi period (1621-1627)
Compiled and edited by Yang Zhaozhi (17th century)
Wucheng, Zhejiang province: Wucheng Min Yishi, 1621
8 columns per half-folio; 18 characters per column;
columns not ruled; white folding margin at center of
folio; single-line borders; printed in black and red ink;
overall dimensions of volumes: 30.0 x 18.2 cm; block
sizes of text: approx. 20.5-20.7 x 14.3-14.4 cm; stitched
binding

18666

The earliest surviving example of two-color printing in black and red is the *Diamond Sutra* printed in 1340 at the Zifu Temple of Zhongxin Circuit, now in the National Central Library, Taibei. The main text of the sutra was printed in black, while the accompanying commentary and illustration (*Lingzhi tu*) were printed in red. This technique, however, did not reach its apogée until the late sixteenth and early seventeenth century.

Multiple-block printing of books became widespread in the late Ming, usually featuring rigid Song-style characters (*ying ti Song zi*) developed during the mid-Ming period for the main body of text and more fluid, calligraphic characters for the accompanying commentaries and annotations. Examples from the first half of the seventeenth century are plentiful, but the most famous ones are those printed by Min Qiji (1575-after 1656), Ling Mengchu (1580-1644), and their family members in the city of Wucheng (also called

Wuxing) in Huzhou prefecture, Zhejiang province. Their multiple-block editions, of which about 146 titles are known through a list compiled by the collector Tao Xiang (1871-1940), ranged between two colors (black and red; *zhumo taoyin*) and five colors (black, red, yellow, blue, and purple; *wu se taoyin*), encompassing a broad spectrum of classical texts, illustrated novels, dramatic works, and medical writings. These editions were renowned across China and are often referred to in Chinese bibliographic literature simply as "Min woodblock editions" (*Min ke ben*) and "Ling woodblock editions" (*Ling ke ben*). Multiple-block and multiple-color printing fell out of favor after the mid seventeenth century; only a few notable works of this type would be produced during the Qing dynasty (1644-1911), such as the four- and five-color *Yu zhi Guwen yuanjian* (Imperially Commissioned Profound Mirror of Ancient Essays) of 1685 (and later printings) and the six-color *Du Gongbu ji* (Collected Literary Works of Du Fu) editions of 1749 and 1834.

The *Tang shi yan yi pin* (Exemplars of the Beautiful and the Refined in Tang Poetry) illustrated here was printed by Min Yishi in 1621. It is a fine example of a late Ming *zhumo taoyin* edition, with the main texts printed in black and commentaries and punctuation in red, which appear all the more attractive on the bright white paper. Another distinctive feature is the use of a single-lined border around the text with no linear columnar divisions, so as to make room for the red-printed items. The compiler, a certain Yang Zhaozhi, was a native of Wulin (present-day Hangzhou) who was active during the Wanli period (1573-1619). Yang was particularly fond of Tang poems featuring beautiful women and courtesans as their principal subject, and poems of the period that employ

floral imagery as metaphors for pretty ladies.

The first edition of Yang's anthology was printed in 1618 by Li Qianyu's "Shengyun ge" (Shengyun Pavilion), but the 360 or so selections were not arranged in any particular order and were accompanied only by punctuation marks and no commentaries of any sort. Min Yishi's edition of 1621, however, contains an additional ten poems as well as a plethora of commentaries garnered from numerous critics of poetry. It also categorized the poems into structural groups under the headings five-character quatrains (*wu yan jue ju*), seven-character quatrains (*qi yan jue ju*), five-character regulated verses (*wu yan lü shi*), seven-character regulated verses (*qi yan lü shi*), five-character regulated verses with repeated quatrains (*wu yan pai lü*), old-style poetry (*gu feng*), and miscellaneous forms (*za ti*). In addition, characters erroneously printed in the earlier edition were corrected.

This work is not divided into *juan* but is made up of four *ji* ("collections"), with a general preface by the original compiler Yang Zhaozhi and general explanatory remarks (*zong fanli*) by the editor and printer Min Yishi. The preface refers to the separate collections as "four classes of Tang poetry" in the following order: *Tang shi ming yuan ji* (Collection of Renowned Beauties in Tang Poetry), *Tang shi xiang lian ji* (Collection of Fragrant Trousseaux in Tang Poetry), *Tang shi guan ji ji* (Collection of Gazing at Courtesans in Tang Poetry), and *Tang shi ming hua ji* (Collection of Famous Flowers in Tang Poetry). Each *ji* makes up a volume, and each has its own set of explanatory remarks (*fanli*) by Yang Zhaozhi preceding the poetic selections.

In his edition of the anthology, Min Yishi added commentaries on the poems by nu-

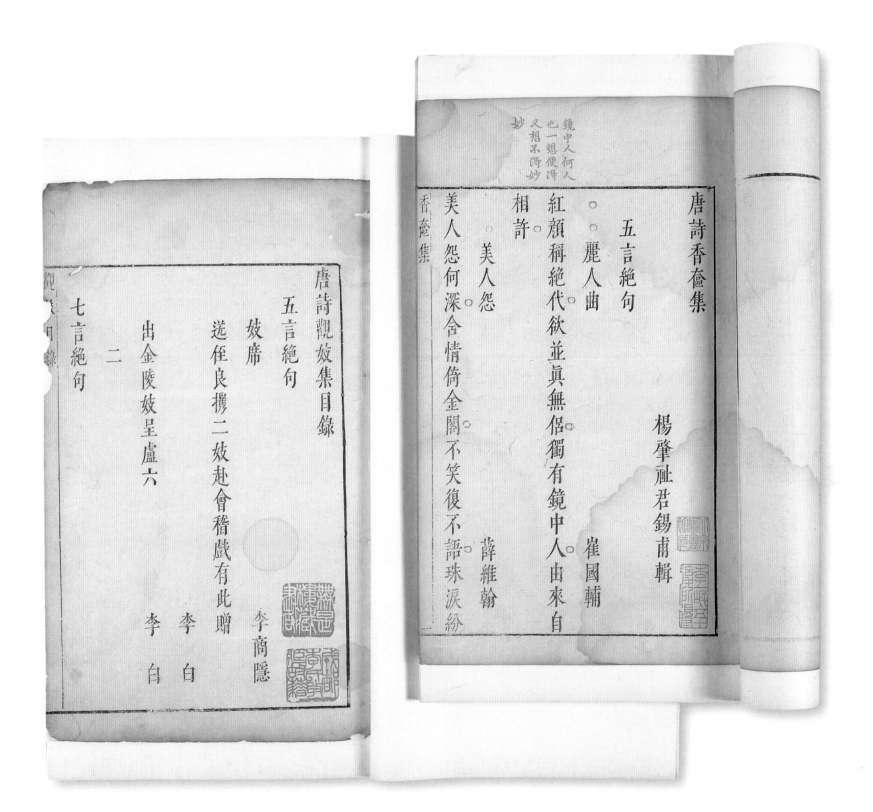

唐詩香奩集

五言絕句

楊肇祉君錫甫輯

○麗人曲　　　　　崔國輔

紅顏稱絕代欲並真無侶獨有鏡中人由來自
相許

○美人怨　　　　　薛維翰

美人怨何深含情倚金闕不笑復不語珠淚紛

鏡中人何人
也一想便得
又想不得妙
妙

merous eminent Tang, Song, and Yuan literary critics (most of whom were also poets in their own right), for example the monk Wuke (fl. 825-835), Zhou Bi (12th-13th century), the monk Tianyin, Guo (styled Decheng), Liu Zhenweng (1232-1297), Qin Guan (1049-1100), Wang Anshi (1021-1086), Mei Yaochen (1002-1060), Su Shi (1037-1101), Huang Tingjian (1045-1105), Mi Fu (1051-1107), Zhu Xi (1130-1200), Xie Fangde (1226-1289), Yu Ji (1272-1348), Satula (b. 1272 or b. 1308), and Zhao Fang (1319-1369). Literary critics of the Ming dynasty through the Tianqi period were by no means left out; included in the anthology are the critical voices of Yang Shen (1488-1559), Tang Yin (1470-1524), Jiao Hong (1541-1620), Li Mengyang (1473-1529), Ao Ying (*jinshi* of 1521), Li Panlong (1514-1570), Wang Shizhen (1526-1590), Zong Chen (1525-1560), Xu Zhongxing (1517-1578), Hu Yinglin (1551-1602), Li Weizhen (1547-1626), Jiang Yikui (17th century), Gu Lin (1476-1545), Li Zhi (1527-1602), Tang Xianzu (1550-1617), Yuan Hongdao (1568-1610), Wang Zhideng (1535-1612), Zhong Xing (1574-1624), and Tan Yuanchun (ca. 1585-1637). In addition to commentaries written by members of his family and personal acquaintances, Min Yishi also added remarks made by two of his illustrious ancestors, namely Min Gui (1430-1511; *jinshi* of 1464), one-time Minister of Punishments (*xing bu shangshu*), and Min Rulin (1503-1559; *jinshi* of 1532), who had been Minister of Rites (*li bu shangshu*) at the secondary imperial capital of Nanjing. The commentaries by these two high officials were taken from their respective literary collections, the *Min Zhuangyi ji* and the *Wutang ji*.

Min Yishi makes clear to the reader that Yang Zhaozhi had included in his compilation literary, romantically-themed works composed by Emperor Jianwen of the Liang dynasty (Liang Jianwen di; Xiao Gang; 503-551; r. 550-551), the last sovereign of the Chen dynasty (Chen Shubao; 553-604; r. 583-589), and other rulers of the Southern Dynasties. Although such pieces predate the period covered by the anthology, Min decided to retain them in his 1621 edition because of their historical relationship to (and implied influence on) this genre of Tang poetry.

Originally issued as four volumes, the present set from the collection of Li Yimang (1903-1990) contains only volumes 2 and 3. The second volume, *Tang shi xiang lian ji*, contains poems in all seven formal categories by Cui Guofu, Xue Weihan, Li Bo (701-762), Liu Shang, Yang Shidao, Zhang Wengong, Han Wo (844-923; *jinshi* of 889), Yuan Hui, Lu Lun (ca. 737-ca. 798), Yu Gu, Cui Dan, Zheng Renbiao, Du Shenyan (d. 708), Xue Boxing, Cen Shen (715-770; *jinshi* of 744), Wang Changling (ca. 690-ca. 756; *jinshi* of 727), Bo Juyi (772-846), Wang Biao, Zheng Gu, Zhang Ji (ca. 776-ca. 829), Rong Yu, Dai Shulun (732-789), anonymous, Yang Heng, Zhu Qingyu (b. 791; *jinshi* of 826), Liu Deren, Zhu Jiang, Liu Fangping, Luo Binwang (before 640-684), Cui Ying, Li Duan (d. ca. 787), Hu Lingneng, Meng Haoran (689-740), Liang Huang, Qu Tongxian, Cui Hao (*jinshi* of 723; d. 754), Zhang Jinghui, Yu Xuanji (ca. 844-868), Li Jiao (*jinshi* of 735), Cui Gui, Yang Ronghua, Fang Gan, Li Qunyu, Qin Taoyu, Liu Yuxi (772-842), Wang Xun, Liu Zun, Xu Xianfei, Liu Zhangqing (ca. 710-after 787; *jinshi* of 733), Liu Xiyi, Emperor Jianwen of the Liang (Xiao Gang), the last emperor of the Chen (Chen Shubao), Wang Wei (701-761), Zhang Bi, Li He (791-817), Yan Chaoyin, and Du Fu (712-770).

The third volume, *Tang shi guan ji ji*, contains poems from the first six formal catego-

ries by Li Shangyin (ca. 813-858), Li Bo, Sikong Shu (fl. 788), Wang Jian (751-ca. 830), Gu Kuang (ca. 725-ca. 814; *jinshi* of 757), Sun Qi (fl. 880), Rong Yu, Yang Shi'e, Zhang Youxin, Ping Kangji, Guan Xixi, Wang Bo (649-676), Chu Guangxi (707-ca. 760), Wen Tingyun (ca. 812-870), Zhang Wei, Liu Zhangqing, Cui Hao, Chen Ziliang, Li Jiao (*jinshi* of 735), Wang Zhenbo, Shen Junyou, Du Fu, Zheng Haigu, anonymous, Wan Chu, Zhang You, Xue Neng, Cui Zhongrong, Meng Haoran (689-740), Liu Zun, Wang Xun, Emperor Xiaoyuan of the Liang, Zhang Yue (667-731), Shen Quanqi (ca. 650-713), and Bo Juyi. A complete list of all the poets included in the four parts of this anthology would show that the overwhelming majority of the voices are male, with only a handful belonging to women, among them the courtesan-hostess Xue Tao (768-831) who is regarded as the most eminent of female poets of the Tang; the courtesan, concubine, and eventual Daoist nun Yu Xuanji; the imperial concubine Yang Guifei (d. 756); and the so-called Lady Flower Pistil (Huarui furen), who may be either Little Concubine Xu (Xiao Xu fei), consort of Wang Jian of the Former Shu of the Five Dynasties, or the Lady Fei, consort of Meng Chang, king of the Latter Shu of the Five Dynasties).

Pictured here are the recto of folio 1 of the main text of the *Tang shi xiang lian ji* and the recto of folio 1 of the table of contents of the *Tang shi guan ji ji*, together with a double-page spread from folios 3b and 4a of the latter.

14

唐詩豔逸品

亦名《唐詩四種》。明楊肇祉選輯并序。明天啟元年（1621年）烏程閔一栻刻朱墨套印本。半葉八行，行十八字，四周單邊，版心白口，無魚尾。框高二〇・五至二〇・七厘米，寬一四・三至一四・四厘米。線裝。

18666

現存最早的朱墨套印本為元代刊印的《金剛般若波羅密經》冠圖「靈芝圖」及注釋，但用顏色套印方法刷印古籍，到晚明時期被廣泛應用，盛於清道光、咸豐以後。潘承弼、顧廷龍《明代版本圖錄初編》卷十印：「朱墨套印肇自天啟、崇禎年間吳興望族閔氏、凌氏。……大抵套印諸書專事評語時復臆改其內容，實不取而面目別具。兩家居同閈，風趣自近，所刻遂似。或以委之閔氏一家督造，未敢置信，雖蟄蚑支流宜無偏廢焉。」

套印本通常正文採用明中葉發展出來的硬體宋字；評語則刻軟體字（書寫體）。其刻印既多流傳又廣，而著稱於世的，應推萬曆天啟間（1573年至1627年）的吳興閔齊伋和凌濛初兩家，以刻朱墨印本而聞名海內，所刻之書世稱「閔刻本」和「凌刻本」。武進套印本收藏家陶湘所編的《明吳興閔板書目》中有「閔刻本」與「凌刻本」，總記一百十八部一百四十六種，包括經類十五部十七種、史類七部七種、子類二十四部四十三種、集類六十四部六十九種，以及另外七部九種。

此展出烏程閔一栻所刻的《唐詩豔逸品》，評點採用紅色套印，色彩、字體互相輝映，真是賞心悅目，又便於區別，頗為藏書家所珍愛。閔氏家族為明末吳興著名出版家，所刻書籍紙質瑩潔，朱墨燦然，使讀者賞心悅目。《唐詩豔逸品》的輯者楊肇祉，字錫甫，武林人，活躍於明萬曆時期，生卒年不詳。楊氏閑居無事，諷詠唐詩，覺關於唐代女子之詩千芳萬卉，選其豔逸之品，就其詩之所詠者，故編《唐詩豔逸品》，為晚明唐詩總集的一種。楊氏輯的《唐詩豔逸品》四集為李乾宇盛芸閣刊刻於萬曆四十六年（1618年），原詩三百六十餘首，詩次凌亂，僅有圈點而無評語。至明天啟元年（1621年）又有烏程閔一栻刻套印本，增詩十首，乃廣搜名家評語，又以五七律絕、排律、古風、雜體等分體編排，對原刻訛謬處均予校正，足資參考。此書是典型的朱墨套印本，墨印原文，朱印評點，紙質潔白，朱墨斑斕。其版式為四周單邊，無豎直界格，以便行字旁套印朱色的評點批注。

此書序題「唐詩四種」，無卷數，內分四集，為〈唐詩名媛集〉、〈唐詩香奩集〉、〈唐詩觀妓集〉、〈唐詩名花集〉，每集一冊，皆各有凡例。每冊正文卷端題「楊肇祉君錫甫輯」。楊肇祉〈唐詩豔逸品敘〉曰：「品唐詩者，類以初、盛、晚三變為定品；三變之品，時也，非品也。作詩者不一人，諸品具標；品詩者不一人，雙眼各別，有如俎一陳，水陸畢備，滿前珍錯，下箸為難。余椎魯無能，不解風人之旨，而晴窗靜几，諷詠唐詩，于名媛、香奩、觀妓、名花諸篇，偶有所得，非獨鍾情於佳人、佚女、麗草、疏花也，以唐詩之豔逸者，首此四種。『豔』，如千芳絢綵，萬卉爭妍，明滅雲華，飄搖枝露，青林鬱楚，丹蠟蔥蒨，而一段巧綴英蕤，姿態醒目。『逸』，如湖頭孤嶼，山上清泓，鶴立松陰，蟬翳蘿幌，碧柯翹秀，翠篠修織，而一種天然意致，機趣動人，此余《豔逸品》所由刻也。若謂豔逸非所以品唐詩，余亦甘之矣。楊肇祉君錫甫題」。

〈唐詩豔逸品總凡例〉五則：

一、是集也，出自君錫選定，極其精矣。不佞實深
　　愛之，可謂千同心。故略為次，先後加批評

而無棄取。

一、原刻詩次雜亂，今特以五言絶、七言絶、五言律、七言律、排律、古風、雜體諸項分編，而各項之中或以朝代之先後，或以四時之早晚，序庶覺類聚群分。若謂如此，恐觀者反厭，則非所以論唐詩之妙矣。

一、原本祇有圈點而無評語，今特廣搜名家，如釋無可、周伯弼、釋天隱、國成德、劉會孟、秦少游、王介甫、梅聖俞、蘇東坡、黃山、米元章、朱晦菴、謝疊山、虞伯生、薩天錫、趙子常、楊用修、唐六如、焦弱侯、李崆峒、敧清江、李于鱗、王元美、宗方城、徐子與、胡元瑞、李本寧、蔣仲舒、顧華玉、李卓吾、湯若士、袁中郎、王百穀、鍾伯敬、譚友夏等，表表在如，耳目無論已。又如我先莊懿暨宗伯午塘公，有《二尚書詩集》行於世。又如故兄景倩、侄以平、故友莊若等，皆以詩名於三吳者，其評語大都悉當博採擇焉，雖有一二與君錫圈點相矛盾，而議論可採者亦錄，唯浮不切者不錄。

一、集中所載梁簡文帝、陳後主諸歌，本非唐詩，似宜刪去。然亦近唐詩，今姑仍原本，讀者幸無以淆入罪我也。原本訛謬其的差者，悉已改正；其兩可者，悉已註明。他如同一詩也，前後兩載；同一人也，而名字迭書；同一人之詩也，而句字略異，此其關係猶小，故不復改。若夫《名媛集》王昌齡「阿嬌」怨第一絶，復於《香奩集》刻。李白「美人」怨《香奩集》薛維翰「春女」怨，復於《名花集》刻。薛濤「梅詩」，又《名媛集》「長信」、「秋詞」二絶，卻係王昌齡，而誤刻崔國輔。《觀妓集》「燕子樓」詩第七絶，已於《名媛集》刻「樂天詠盼盼」者矣，乃其後又總係之關盼盼。《香奩集》劉商「怨婦」第二絶，有刻崔國輔古意者。《名花集》盧綸「白牡丹」絶，萬首詩中原作開元名公，不著姓氏，而他本有刻裴鄰者。楊渾「海棠」律，有刻鄰者。諸如此項，姑仍原本各各註明，而觀者玩其詩不必辨其人矣。

一、各集凡例係君錫所著，今仍分刻於前，使君錫選輯之意不至埋没云。

天啟元年巧日，烏程後學閔一栻謹識。

〈名媛集凡例〉五則：

一、所記名妃、淑姬、聲妓、孷姿，凡寫其志凜、秋霜、心盟、匪石、遯密、傳蹤者，咸載焉。

一、宮怨閨情，多有以傳寂寞之情，寫現在之景，令讀之不能起豔逸之思，適增離索之悲者，不載。

一、幽禁中自有一種丰姿，落寞中另有一種妖冶，此所謂益悲憤而益堪憐者，斯載。

一、有從味美人，不紀其生平之蹤跡，但寫一之丰韻者，自有《香奩集》可載，不入於此。

一、名妓列具行藏者，傳青樓煙館之跡者，不載。

〈唐詩名媛集目錄〉分編五言絶句、七言絶句、五言律詩、七言律詩、五言排律、古風、雜體。此集詩人為劉長卿、王維、令狐楚、東方虬、李白、崔國輔、郭元振、皇甫冉、趙象、賈至、羅隱、王昌齡、劉阜、裴交泰、女郎劉媛、劉言史、白居易、李商隱、儲光華、楊凌、李成用、王之渙、張祐、李涉、楊炎、鄭史、孫棨、于鵠、胡曾、李昌符、崔郊、楊巨源、羅虬、薛宜僚、王貞白、岑參、董思恭、駱賓王、張文琮、宋之問、常非月、李賀、陳標、錢起、韓偓、庾信、崔顥、劉禹錫、溫庭筠、畢耀。

〈香奩集凡例〉三則：

一、香奩以紀閨閣中事，有事跡不傳，而但詠其窈窕之資，以兼閨閣之用者，載焉，非不入名媛之訛。

一、閨詩甚夥，多以摹寫時景傳紀幽思，不悉閨婦之體態者，不入。

一、採蓮等詩以蓮上起典者，不載；若太白，若邪溪畔等詞，蓋傳女郎之態度者，咸載焉。

〈唐詩香奩集目錄〉分編五言絶句、七言絶句、五言律詩、七言律詩、五言排律、古風、雜體。此集詩人為崔國輔、薛維翰、李白、劉商、楊師道、張文恭、韓偓、袁暉、盧綸、于鵠、崔澹、鄭仁表、杜審、薛伯行、岑參、王昌齡、白居易、王表、鄭、張藉、戎昱、戴叔倫、無名氏、楊衡、朱慶餘、劉得仁、朱絳、劉方平、駱賓王、崔膺、李端、胡令能、孟浩然、梁鍠、屈同仙、崔顥、張敬徵、魚玄機、李嶠、崔珏、楊容華、方干、李群玉、秦韜玉、劉禹錫、王訓、劉遵、徐賢妃、劉長卿、劉希夷、簡文帝、陳後主、王維、張碧、李賀、閻朝隱、杜甫。

〈觀妓集凡例〉四則：

一、觀者以我觀之也，若徒列妓之品題，則於觀者何裨也。故必嬌歌艷舞，足以起人之幽懷，發人之贊賞者，斯載。

一、古宦宅妓非青樓比也，故贊美者則載，談情者不入。

一、高朋滿座，群妓笙簧亦以暢其胸次者，載。

一、不必評妓之臧否，而觀之者，有豔逸之思者，亦載。

〈唐詩觀妓集目錄〉分編五言絶句、七言絶句、五言律詩、七言律詩、五言排律、古風。此集詩人為李商隱、李白、司空曙、王建、顧況、孫棨、戎昱、羊士諤、張又新、平康妓、關盼盼、王勃、儲光義、溫庭筠、張謂、劉長卿、崔灝、陳子良、李嶠、王貞白、沈君攸、杜甫、鄭還古、無名氏、萬楚、張祐、薛能、崔仲容、孟浩然、劉遵、王訓、梁孝元帝、張說、沈佺期、白居易。

〈名花集凡例〉三則：

一、詠花者多以花之代謝寓意於人事之浮沉，則於花無當也，不入。

一、花有以豔名者，有以逸名者，有以香與色名者，則載。無一於此，不入。

一、觀花有感與攜觴共賞者，皆具一時之樂事，非以花之精神也，不入。

〈唐詩名花集目錄〉分編五言絶句、七言絶句、五言律詩、七言律詩。此集詩人為溫庭筠、元微之、丘為、皇甫冉、白居易、王維、雍裕之、崔興宗、梁宣帝、孟浩然、孔紹、無名氏、弘執恭、張文姬、王摩詰、盧僎、賈島、李白、劉禹錫、劉長卿、韓愈、庾肩吾、孔德紹、杜甫、戎昱、元載妻、薛濤、翁承贊、崔護、王建、鄭、陸龜蒙、楊貴妃、花蕊夫人、趙嘏、李紳、盧綸、張又新、李益、裴度、章孝標、張祐、陳標、薛能、李商隱、陳陶、李嘉佑、元禎、杜荀鶴、僧齊已、杜牧、盧照鄰、唐太宗、李嶠、王貞白、魏彥深、崔涯、辛德源、駱賓王、釋無可、許棠、楊渾、薛逢、薛濤、魚玄機、方干。

中國國家圖書館所藏這一部《唐詩豔逸品》為故國務院古籍出版規劃小組組長李一氓先生舊藏，存二集各一冊。書函題簽記「閔刻唐詩香奩、觀妓兩集，缺名媛、名花兩集。天啟本」。茲選照《唐詩香奩集》正文首半葉與《唐詩觀妓集》目錄首半葉，以及《唐詩觀妓集》之第三葉下半葉與第四葉上半葉。

15

Shizhu zhai shuhua pu (8 juan)

The Ten Bamboo Studio Manual of Calligraphy and Painting, 8 *juan*

Ming dynasty (1368-1644), Chongzhen period (1628-1644)

Compiled and selected by Hu Zhengyan (1584-1674); edited [and illustrated] by Gao Yang, Ling Yunhan, Wu Shiguan, Wei Zhihuang, Wei Zhike, Hu Zongzhi, Gao You, Xingyi heshang, et al.

Nanjing, Jiangsu province: Hu shi Shizhu zhai, 1644

Illustrations printed in 5 colors (including black); overall dimensions of volumes: 29.4 x 17.2 cm; each folded-leaf of illustration or text, approx. 28.9-29.2 x 25.8-26.0 cm; butterfly binding

17768

Hu Zhengyan (1584-1674), originally from Xiuning in Huizhou, Anhui province, established a residence in the vibrant metropolis of Nanjing where he ran a bookstore. His private garden contained several stands of verdant bamboo, from which was derived the name of the Ten Bamboo Studio and his sobriquet (*hao*), Master of the Ten Bamboo Studio (Shizhu zhai zhuren). This talented gentleman, accomplished in inkmaking, papermaking, seal-carving, and painting, is best known for his role in the compilation and production of the *Shizhu zhai jian pu* (The Ten Bamboo Studio Manual of Decorative Writing Papers) and the *Shizhu zhai shuhua pu* (The Ten Bamboo Manual of Calligraphy and Painting), the earliest painting manual in China to be printed in color and the first to include isolated illustrations of subject mat-

ter from nature, such as plants and flowers, fruits, and birds.

Apart from using examples of his own calligraphy and painting, Hu Zhengyan selected works by historical and contemporary artists including Zhao Mengfu (1254-1322), Shen Zhou (1427-1509), Wen Zhengming (1470-1559), Tang Yin (1470-1523), Lu Zhi (1496-1576), Chen Chun (1483-1544), Wu Bin (fl. ca. 1591-1626), Wu Shiguan (act. first half of 17th century), Qiu Ying (ca. 1494-ca. 1552), Wei Zhihuang (1568-1647), Wei Zhike (active first half of 17th century), Mi Wanzhong (1570-1628), Wen Zhenheng (1585-1645), Gao You (act. first half of 17th century), Gao Yang (act.

first half of 17th century), and others. By repeatedly studying and copying the models, Hu not only developed an acute sense of each artist's characteristic brush manner and compositional style for transfer onto woodblocks, he was also able to determine the appropriate color palettes and nuances of shading for every potential print.

Engraving of the woodblocks for the *Shizhu zhai shuhua pu*, entrusted to a team of the best artisans from Huizhou but supervised by Hu himself, began in 1619 and was not fully completed until 1633. A separate block was made for each color in a technique known as *taoban* ("set of blocks" or "overlaid

den Manual of Painting), but the superb quality of this late Ming exemplar would remain unsurpassed in the history of color wodblock-printing in imperial China. Hu Zhengyan's technical masterpiece would later exert considerable influence on the development of Japanese woodblock-printing compositions and engraving techniques.

The *Shizhu zhai shuhua pu* has eight *juan* individually named and arranged according to subject matter, which were probably first published in the following order based on the dates of the latest prefaces: *Shuhua pu* (Volume of Exemplars of Calligraphy and Painting; 1619), *Zhu pu* (Manual on Bamboo; 1622), *Mo hua pu* (Volume of Ink Masterpieces; 1624), *Shi pu* (Manual on Rocks; 1625), *Lingmao pu* (Manual on Birds; 1627), *Mei pu* (Manual on Prunus; undated), *Lan pu* (Manual on Orchids; undated), and *Guo pu* (Manual on Fruits; undated). Each illustration is given a double-page spread with a fold along the center, and is matched with a text or poem on an adjacent double-page. There is no known correct sequence of the eight sections, and the individual leaves within each volume also vary between editions. No less than twenty editions of this pictorial work have been identified; many later reprints are inferior in quality due to the use of newly cut, carelessly matched blocks and a lack of attention paid to color gradation.

These butterfly-bound volumes in the collection of the National Library of China are from one of the earlier and finer sets printed in 1644; they were part of the distinguished collection of Zheng Zhengduo (1898-1958). Illustrated here are four examples of early seventeenth-century compositions found in two volumes. From the frameless rectangular pieces in the *Shuhua pu* are Gao Yang's "Water-caltrops, Lotus Root, and Lotus Pods"

blocks") or *douban* ("assembled blocks" or "decorative blocks"). The most luxurious editions of this manual incorporated the *gonghua* ("embossed design" or "arched pattern"; known in the West as *gauffrage*) or *gongban* ("embossed blocks" or "arched blocks") method, a blind-stamping technique whereby illustrations with exquisite low-relief designs were produced by pressing the paper firmly against a dry, uninked engraved woodblock. The *douban* technique was especially time-consuming as numerous individual woodblocks were required for a single print. In addition, matching plates carved in intaglio and in relief were combined to produce the *gonghua* effect. The readied blocks

were then placed in exactly the right positions and colors applied according to the hues and gradations in the model. Finally, the images were printed onto flattened, slightly moistened paper in temperature- and humidity-controlled workshops; the best editions were printed on very high-quality *langgan* ("pearled") paper produced by Hu Zhengyan.

The engraving was so skillfully done that virtually no stray marks from or outlines of the cut blocks are to be seen in finely printed editions of the manual. As a result, illustrations in the *Shizhu zhai shuahua pu* appear as though painted by hand. The *douban* method was adopted in Qing-dynasty works such as the *Jiezi yuan hua zhuan* (Mustard Gar-

(*Ling ou lian shi*), with the seal "Gao Yang zhi yin" and two other seals; and Ling Yunhan's "Begonia, Grasses, and Asters" (*Qiu haitang deng huacao*), with a seal "Wuyun." From the round-fan compositions in the *Mohua pu* are Gao You's "Magnolia and Crab-apple Blossoms" (*Yulan haitang*), with the signature "Gao You" and a seal "Gao You zhi yin"; and lastly, the Daoist plant of immortality depicted in Hu Zhengyan's own "*Lingzhi* Fungus amidst Grass and Rocks" (*Lingzhi caoshi*), signed "Hu Zhengyan xie" and sealed "Yuecong."

15
十竹齋書畫譜八卷

明胡正言輯選。明高陽、凌雲翰、吳士冠、魏之璜、魏之克、胡宗智、高友及行一和尚等同校。胡正言、汪楷等刻。明崇禎十七年 (1644年) 南京胡氏十竹齋刻彩色套印本。每冊外高二九・四厘米，寬一七・二厘米。每圖雙面，紙高二八・九至二九・二厘米，寬二五・八至二六厘米。蝴蝶裝。
17768

　　胡正言，字曰從，別號十竹主人、默庵老人，室名十竹齋，安徽休寧人，三十歲後移居金陵 (今江蘇南京)。生於明萬曆十二年 (1584)，卒於清康熙十三年 (1674年)，經歷了明萬曆、泰昌、天啟、崇禎、清順治、康熙六代。胡氏壽高命長，博學多聞，精研六書，擅篆刻、繪畫、制墨諸

藝，喜藏書、刻書。曾官中書舍人，棄官後遂隱居不出，專心從事藝術工作。胡氏築室南京雞籠山側，庭院種竹十餘竿，故名其室曰「十竹齋」。編著有《十竹齋印存》、《胡氏篆草》、《十竹齋箋譜》等。《十竹齋書畫譜》與《十竹齋箋譜》可稱雙絕，在中國木刻畫史上有最高的地位。

　　《十竹齋書畫譜》共八卷，分裝十六冊，開化紙，蝴蝶裝，書中畫稿署名下皆鈐印。全譜分〈書畫冊〉、〈石譜〉、〈翎毛譜〉、〈竹譜〉、〈墨華冊〉、〈梅譜〉、〈果譜〉、〈蘭譜〉各一卷。每類四十幅，一圖一文，可對照以觀。寫形既妙，雕鏤亦巧，設色尤工。圖有胡正自己畫的，也有當代名家幾十人，如高友、高陽、周之冕、吳彬、吳士冠、凌雲翰、趙備、歸世昌、魏之克、米萬鍾、文震亨、倪瑛等所畫的，還有一些為摹以前名家的，如趙孟頫、沈周、唐寅、文徵明、陸治、陳淳等人的作品。參與胡氏校書的畫家，大都屬於賣畫

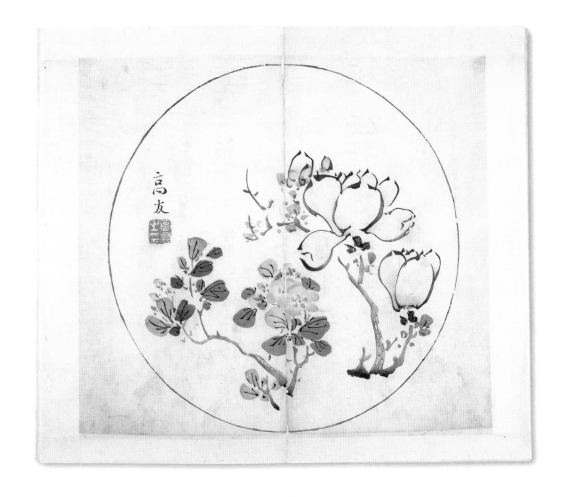

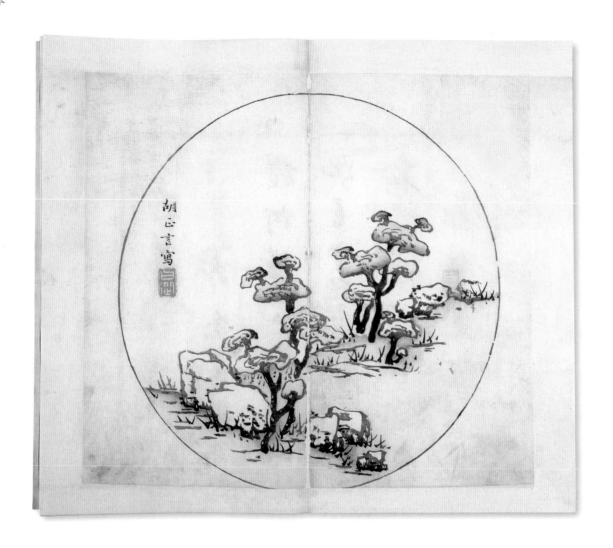

為生的職業畫家；胡氏無疑是他們的贊助人，而這種贊助關係是以同道、朋友的形式出現。

胡正言早在明萬曆四十七年（1619 年）已經開始從事《十竹齋書畫譜》繪制刻印的工作。〈翎毛譜〉有天啟七年（1627 年）楊文驄序，〈書畫册〉有崇禎六年（1633 年）醒天居士序，因推知此書刻版當在天啟、崇禎年間。胡氏運用「餖版」、「拱花」二法編印《十竹齋書畫譜》。「餖版」是以色分版的套印方法，將彩色畫稿先行分開各種顏色，分別鉤摹下來，每色各刻成一塊塊小木版，然後逐色依次套印，有的一幅畫多至幾十塊版，分先後輕重印刷六七十次，一朵花或一片葉，都要分出顏色的濃淡深淺，陰陽向背，妍麗雅致，幾於原作無異。「拱花」和近代凸版相似，印時用紙壓在版面

上，所繪器物紋絡，禽類羽翅，花朵輪廓就凸現在紙面，潔白無色，卻落落大方，素雅可愛。「餖版」、「拱花」刊版套印之精，在版畫技術上達到了登峰造極的程度。

《十竹齋書畫譜》原版初印本特點是用開化紙，傳世極少，在古籍版本中居重要地位。此譜行世者，多為清代翻刻復製，以棉紙刊印本，如康熙五十四年（1715 年）重刊胡氏彩色套印本、乾隆年間重刊胡氏彩色套印本、嘉慶二十二年（1817 年）芥子園重刊胡氏彩色套印本、道光年間重刊胡氏彩色套印本、光緒五年（1879 年）元和邱氏重刊胡氏彩色套印本。其他坊間翻刻本、影印本不備列舉。

中國國家圖書館所藏這部《十竹齋書畫譜》為鄭振鐸先生舊藏，茲選照四幅。取自「書畫譜」二

幅為高陽「菱藕蓮實」，鈐有「高陽之印」白文方印及另外白文、朱文方印二方，以及凌雲翰「秋海棠等花草」，鈐有「五雲」朱文方印。取自「墨華譜」二幅為高友「玉蘭海棠」，款識「高友」，鈐有「高友之印」白文方印，以及胡正言「靈芝草石」，款識「胡正言寫」，鈐有「曰從」白文長方印。

16

Lingyan ge gongchen tu

Portraits of Meritorious Officials from the Lingyan Pavilion

Qing dynasty (1644-1911), Kangxi period (1662-1722)

Illustrated by Liu Yuan (fl. 1662-1668); engraved by Zhu Gui (ca. 1644-1717)

Suzhou, Jiangsu province: Zhuhu tang, 1668

No folding margin at center of folio; no borders; overall dimensions of volume: 30.6 x 18.5 cm; block sizes of illustrations and texts vary; stitched binding

03859

Emperor Taizong (ca. 600-649; r. 626-649), second ruler of the Tang dynasty, assembled a remarkable team of ministers and eminent officials who were loyal, yet unafraid to be critical of his policies if they fell out of accord with Confucian ideals of rulership. In recognition of their services, the emperor commissioned the famous artist Yan Liben (ca. 600-674) to paint portraits of twenty-four meritorious officials on the walls of the Lingyan Pavilion (Lingyan ge) in his palace. The portraits were later engraved on stone during the Song dynasty (960-1279).

The woodblocks for the *Lingyan ge gongchen tu* (Portraits of Meritorious Officials from the Lingyan Pavilion) were engraved by Zhu Gui, a master craftsman living in Suzhou who would later be employed at the Qing court and who is best remembered for his work on the *Yu zhi Gengzhi tu* (Imperially Commissioned Illustrations of Riziculture and Sericulture) drawn by Jiao Bingzhen in 1696, and the *Wanshou shengdian tu*

(Illustration of Imperial Ceremonies for the Sixtieth Birthday of the Kangxi Emperor) of 1713 by Song Junye (act. ca. 1700-1713) and Wang Yuanqi (1642-1715).

In his preface to the *Lingyan ge gongchen tu*, Liu Yuan states that he saw thirty-six figures from the *Shuihu zhuan* (Outlaws of the Marsh) drawn by the eminent figure painter of the late Ming Chen Hongshou (1598-1652) at the home of a certain Tong Shoumin. He was very much impressed by the dignity and

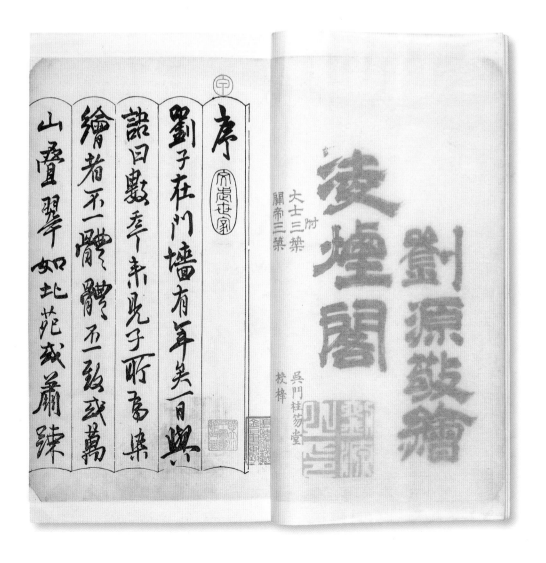

divinity of the figures, but lamented thus: "It is regrettable that Chen Hongshou painted no portraits of meritorious officials from the Lingyan Pavilion." Liu Yuan was not entirely right and may simply not have had the opportunity to see such works by the late Ming master; several painted portraits of the twenty-four meritorious officials attributed to Chen Hongshou have survived and have recently been published in a Japanese catalogue. In any case, to fill what he per-

ceived to be an artistic void, Liu Yuan made it clear that he based his illustrative style on that of Chen Hongshou.

The table of contents is unusually attractive with its "cracked-ice" design. The twenty-four historical figures illustrated by Liu Yuan, in the order that they appear in this book, are as follows: Emperor Taizong's brother-in-law, Zhangsun Wuji (ca. 600-659), minister of education (grand councilor), duke of the state of Zhao; Wang Xiaogong (act. 7th century), minister of works (grand councilor); the emperor's trusted advisor Du Ruhui (585-630), minister of works (grand councilor), duke of the state of Lai; Wei Zheng (580-643), minister of works (grand councilor), "Grand

Mentor of the Heir Apparent," duke of the state of Zheng; the emperor's personal secretary Fang Xuanling (578-648), minister of works (grand councilor), duke of the state of Liang; Gao Shilian (act. 7th century), minister of education (grand councilor), supervisor-in-chief of Bing prefecture, duke of the state of Shen; Weichi Jingde (585-658), minister of justice, "Commander Unequalled in Honor", duke of the state of E; Li Jing (571-649), "Lord Specially Advanced," duke of the state of Wei; Xiao Yu (late 6th-early 7th century), "Lord Specially Advanced," duke of the state of Song; Duan Zhihong (act. 7th century), "Bulwark-General of the State," duke of the state of Bao; Liu Hongji (act. 7th

century), "Bulwark-General of the State," duke of the state of Kui; Qu Tutong (act. 7th century), vice director imperial secretariat of the left, duke of the state of Jiang; Yin Kaishan (act. 7th century), vice director of the right of the branch department of state affairs of the Shandong circuit, duke of the state of Yun; Chai Shao (7th century), supervisor-in-chief of Jing prefecture, duke of the state of Qiao; Zhangsun Shunde (act. ca. 627-650), supervisor-in-chief of Jing prefecture, duke of the state of Pi; Zhang Liang (act. 7th century), supervisor-in-chief of Luo prefecture, duke of the state of Yun; Hou Junji (act. 7th century), minister of personnel, duke of the state of Chen; Zhang Gongjin (act. 7th century), "Courageous Guard of the Left," general-in-chief, duke of the state of Tan; Cheng Zhijie (act. 7th century), "Commandant of the Left," general-in-chief, duke of the state of Lu; the virtuous official Yu Shinan (558-638), minister of rites, duke of the commandery of Yongxing; Liu Zhenghui (act. 7th century), minister of revenue, duke of the state of Yu; Tang Jian (act. 7th century), minister of revenue, duke of the state of Ju; Li Shiji (act. 7th century), minister of war, duke of the state of Ying; and Qin Shubao (act. 7th century), "Militant Guard of the Left," general-in-chief, duke of the state of Hu.

Each of the twenty-four portraits above was accompanied by a column of text at the right giving the figure's name, official positions, and titles of nobility. On the verso of each folio was a short poem composed by Liu Yuan and written in various styles of calligraphy after famous Chinese masters from Wang Xizhi (ca. 307-ca. 365) of the Eastern Jin through to Wen Zhengming (1470-1559) of the mid Ming period. The striking calligraphic styles used by Liu were appropriate for heroic motifs and were meant to evoke the volume and dynamism of the variously posed figures.

These portraits of Tang officials are followed by three images of the Bodhisattva Guanyin (Avalokitesvara in Sanskrit) and three pictures of Guan Yu (162-220), a heroic field marshal of the Three Kingdoms who later became Emperor Guan (*Guan di*) and who, since the seventh century, has been regarded as a guardian spirit and the god of literature. All six appended images are also accompanied by inscriptions on the verso. The thirty pictures in the *Lingyan ge gongchen tu*, printed from variously sized blocks measuring between 21.5 and 25.3 cm in height and 14.0 to 15.5 cm in width, are fine examples of late seventeenth-century Chinese figural representations conveyed through woodblock engraving.

16

凌煙閣功臣圖不分卷

清劉源繪。清朱圭刻。清康熙七年（1668年）吳門柱笏堂刻本。外高三〇・六厘米，寬一八・五厘米。四周無框。線裝。
03859

劉源，字伴阮，號猿仙，河南洛陽人而寄居於江蘇蘇州。能詩善畫，時人有比之於王維者。劉氏《凌煙閣功臣圖》與同時的金古良《無雙譜》齊名，代表康熙時期的人物版畫的風格。朱圭，吳郡人，出書香門第，以木刻畫為業，康熙五十一年（1712年）成了皇家的木刻畫作者。朱氏有杰作存世，如焦秉貞繪的《御製耕織圖》、王原祁、宋駿業、冷枚等繪的《萬壽盛典圖》、《石濂和尚離六堂集》附圖，為康熙間吳中名匠，鐫圖以纖麗工緻著名。

此書以中國唐代歷史人物為題材。唐貞觀十七年（643年），唐太宗下詔，在當時長安凌煙閣畫上他的二十四位開國功臣之像。劉源繪此二十四功臣人像，意在頌揚功臣忠節。是書封面鐫「劉源敬繪凌煙閣，吳門柱笏堂授梓」，次為康熙年間佟彭年、蕭震等序，多為師友溢美之辭。再次為劉源〈自敘〉，謂受陳洪綬所畫「水滸」三十六人影響，而又出自機軸，乃作精心描繪。

圖前有目錄，以裂冰紋為背。圖之目次為「司徒趙國公長孫無忌」、「司空河間王孝恭」、「司空萊國公杜如晦」、「司空太子太師鄭國公魏徵」、「司空梁國公房玄齡」、「司徒并州都督申國公高士廉」、「開府儀同三司鄂國公尉遲敬德」、「特進衛國公李靖」、「特進宋國公蕭瑀」、「輔國大將軍襃國公段志宏」、「輔國大將軍夔國公劉弘基」、「尚書左僕射蔣國公屈突通」、「陝東道行臺右僕射鄖國公殷開山」、「荊州都督譙國公柴紹」、「荊州都督邳國公長孫順德」、「洛州都督鄖國公張亮」、「吏部尚書陳國公侯君集」、「左驍衛大將軍郯國公張公謹」、「左領軍大將軍盧國公程知節」、「禮部尚書永興郡公虞世南」、「戶部尚書渝國公劉政會」、「戶部尚書莒國公唐儉」、「兵部尚書英國公李世勣」、「左武衛大將軍胡國公秦叔寶」。末附「觀世音菩薩像」三尊、「關羽像」三尊，總共三十幅。

對於人物的布局章法，有許多別開生面之處，姿態生動活潑，變化豐富，筆法簡繁並用，能突出人物的重要特征。劉源的作風，接近陳洪綬的傳統，線條挺勁、結構緊煉，可稱上乘之作。插圖由吳中名匠朱圭刊刻，所鐫版畫纖麗工緻，精雅絕倫，頓時聲譽雀起，大為時人所重。圖像背面臨摹歷代書法家如鍾繇、王羲之、蔡邕、顏真卿、黃庭堅、杜甫、米芾、趙孟頫、文徵明、董其昌等各體法書題句為之贊。茲選照三開，前者為內封面葉及佟序首半葉，次者為目錄末半葉及第一幅圖（「司徒趙國公長孫無忌」），後者為第六幅圖背面題句及第七幅圖（「開府儀同三司鄂國公尉遲敬德」）。

17

Yu zhi Gengzhi tu

Imperially Commissioned Illustrations of Riziculture and Sericulture

Qing dynasty (1644-1911), Kangxi period (1662-1722)

Illustrated by Jiao Bingzhen (act. 1680-1720), with poetic inscriptions by the Kangxi emperor (1654-1722; r. 1661-1722) in upper margins; engraved by Zhu Gui (ca. 1644-1717) and Mei Yufeng (fl. 1696)

Beijing: Wuying dian, 1696

Album of 46 leaves, woodblock-printed on paper, mounted between wooden boards covered with brown patterned silk brocade; each leaf approx. 34.7 x 27.8 cm; block size of illustrations, approx. 24.4 x 24.4 cm

14921

The album entitled *Gengzhi tu* (Illustrations of Riziculture and Sericulture, or Illustrations of Tilling and Weaving) was based on the *Gengzhi shi* (Poems on Riziculture and Sericulture), a set of forty-five verses (twenty-one on rice cultivation, and twenty-four on rearing silkworms for the manufacture of silk) composed by the official Lou Shu (1090-1162; also variously rendered as Lou Shou and Lou Chou) for the Southern Song court around 1145. At that time, Lou Shu was serving as magistrate of Yuqian county, near the imperial capital Hangzhou. Sometime around 1210, Lou Shu's poems were engraved on stone by his grandsons Lou Hong and Lou Shen, with the support of their uncle the Grand Secretary Lou You. A quarter of a century or so later, in 1237, an edition of the poems was published with accompanying woodblock illustrations by Wang Gang, a prominent military officer from Jiangxi

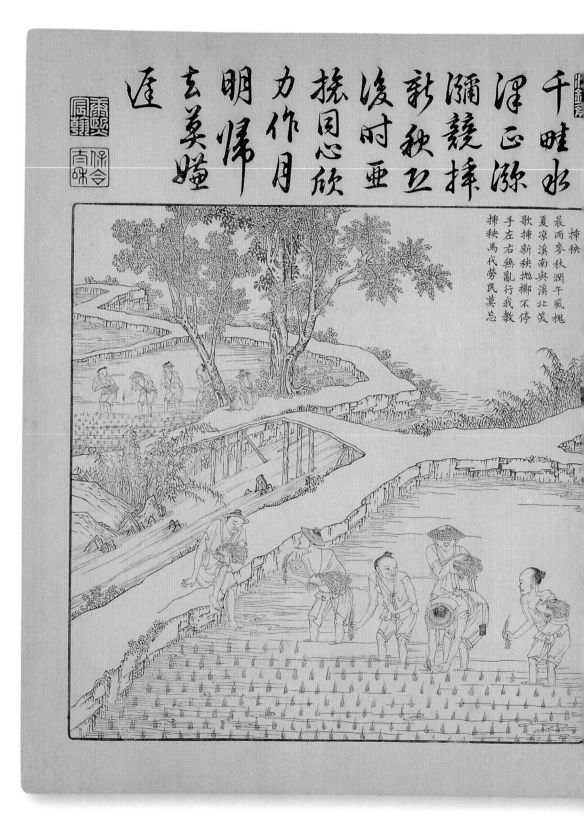

province. Although this too has not survived, it is widely believed to be the seminal illustrated edition.

The *Gengzhi tu* was certainly known during the Ming dynasty (1368-1644) by virtue of its having been copied in 1407 into the monumental *Yongle dadian* (Encyclopaedia of the Yongle Period), although that portion of the work is unfortunately now lost. The earliest extant *Gengzhi tu* is a Japanese edition of 1676 or a little earlier (*Kôshokuzu* in Japanese) that was rediscovered by Berthold Laufer in 1908; it bears the signature and seals of Kanô Einô (1631-1697), the third-generation head of the Kyô Kanô school. The forty-five pictures in this edition, based on a Chinese edition of 1462 commissioned by Song Zonglu, an official in Jiangxi province (with a preface by Wang Zengyou, an official from Guangxi province), not only match the number and sequence of Lou Shu's poems and paintings, but also appear to preserve much of the compositional structures and linework that would have been found in the original illustrations. It contains a preface composed in 1462 by Wang Zengyou, an official from Guangxi province, and a postface dated 1676.

This group of images depicting two of imperial China's most important economic activities entered a much heightened level of recension in the early Qing dynasty. During his "Southern Inspection Tour" of 1689, the Kangxi emperor was presented with a version of the *Gengzhi tu*. Duly impressed, he decided upon his return to Beijing to commission an updated set, for which he would contribute a preface and poems to accompany each picture. The artist selected for this task was Jiao Bingzhen (act. 1680-1720), who served as an official of the fifth rank in the Directorate of Astronomy (Qintian jian) during the period when it was headed by a

Jesuit missionary; he evidently acquired techniques of perspectival painting and *chiaschuro* from the Westerners at court. Taking as his model the *Gengzhi tu* version made available to him by the emperor, Jiao made certain adjustments that resulted in a total of forty-six pictures equally divided between the two sections. Apart from the original version or versions (on silk and on paper) produced by the artist, later copyists also produced numerous painted sets based on the printed edition. The Library of Congress owns a complete set of forty-six paintings in ink and color on silk mounted in four albums, while the National Museum of Chinese History in Beijing has recently published a number of album leaves in ink and light colors on paper. In the latter collection, each picture measures approximately 24.9 cm in height; the overall scale of the painted compositions is quite faithfully preserved in Zhu Gui's engraved version in which the blocks are approximately 24.4 cm high, or vice versa, if the pictures were copied from the printed set.

The initial printing of this revived *Gengzhi tu* did not take place until 1696, and thereafter several other printings were made. The preface of the Kangxi emperor was inscribed, and subsequently engraved, in forty-one columns of running script:

As I diligently labor day and night, examining [the principles of] rulership, I always remember that the most important thing for the people is food and clothing. I have read the chapters [entitled] *Bin feng* (Odes of the State of Bin) [from the *Shi jing* (Classic of Poetry)] and *Wu yi* (Against Luxurious Ease) [from the *Shu jing* (Book of Documents)], where there are detailed descriptions of sowing and reaping, [the rearing of] silkworms and mulberry trees, and [the process of making] fine silk embroidery. The ancients took these [descriptions] into [music made from] flutes and zithers and entered them into the corpus of classical literature. As for the one who is entrusted with a sovereign state under Heaven, he truly cannot afford not to think about these issues. In the proclamations and statutes of the Western Han [dynasty; 206 B.C.-A.D. 8], which are closest to those of antiquity, it is said: "Hunger stems from the decline of farming while cold results from the neglect of weaving." Furthermore it is said: "The elderly should pass away only after a long life; the young and the orphaned should [also] be able to live long." As one who wishes to see this come true, is it not my duty to not stop at this point?"

During each of my inspection tours to the provinces I listened to folk songs, and I was also happy to observe agricultural activities, the characteristics of lands in the north and south, the correct way of sowing seeds for millet and glutinous rice, the differences between the early and late seasonal breaks, and the method of catching and exterminating unfledged locusts. I often love to inquire about these things and to get to know about them all very clearly. When administering to affairs of state, I constantly speak about these things to all my statesmen and officers.

Ricefields have been established on the periphery of the Garden of Abundant Marshes (Fengze yuan), with many boundaries between the fields surrounded by streams of water. The crisscrossing paths between the ricefields fill one's gaze, and the sounds of well sweeps flood one's ears, and every year tens of *zhong* [an ancient unit of volumetric measure] of fine grain are harvested. Mulberry trees are planted along paths on the dikes, and beside them are sheds for silkworms, where cocoons are bathed and silk reeled from them, as is done under the eaves of thatch-roofed huts. The reason for building the "Studio for Knowing How to Sow" (Zhijia xuan) and the "Pavilion of Autumn Clouds" (Qiuyun ting) is to observe these activities at close range.

The ancients have this saying: "Those who dress in silken garments ought to think of the cold suffered by weaving women, and those who partake of grain ought to remember the hardship of farmers." I ponder these matters very carefully and attentively, and find them most profound and apposite. Therefore, the illustrations of riziculture and sericulture have been copied [by my order], each comprising twenty-three pictures. For each of these illustrations I composed a poem to sing the praises of laborious toil, and had them inscribed onto the pictures. The labor of farmers which causes them to have calloused hands and feet, as well as the distress of women who reel silk from co-coons and work the looms, are completely represented with great fidelity from the beginning to the end of the work.

Following precedents [of the Southern Song and later periods], woodblocks have been engraved for the purpose of preservation [of the illustrations], in order that they be shown to our descendants and subjects, so that they may all know that every single grain which they eat is the result of difficult work and every piece of cloth that they wear is not easily manufactured. It is said in the *Book of Documents* (*Shu jing*): "Only when one appreciates the products of the earth will his mind be in the right place"; therefore these pictures contain things which should stir the emotions. Only by teaching the people of the whole world to cherish their respective occupations, to be diligent and frugal, can ample food and clothing be ensured, so that all can enter the realms of peace, harmony, prosperity, and longevity. These, then, are my sincere good wishes for the well-being of the people!

Composed and inscribed on the day when one sacrifices to the god of the earth, during the second month of spring in the thirty-fifth year of the Kangxi reign.

The preface is followed by twenty-three illustrations of rice-planting activities, namely the soaking of seeds, ploughing, harrowing and leveling, smoothing, pressing with a roller, sowing, first seedlings, flooding, lifting seedlings, transplanting seedlings, first weeding, second weeding, third weeding, irrigating, harvesting, transportation to the threshing ground, threshing, husking, sieving, winnowing, milling, storing, and

offering a sacrifice. These are continued by twenty-three pictures of sericulture and weaving activities: the bathing of eggs, second moulting, third moulting, removing tiny silkworms, choosing mature silkworms, separating silkworms, picking mulberry leaves, cocooning, heating rearing trays, collecting cocoons, selecting cocoons, storing cocoons, reeling silk, moths emerging, offering a sacrifice, wefting, weaving, spooling, warping, dyeing, printing, cutting silk fabrics, and tailoring.

The pentasyllabic regulated verses originally composed by Lou Shu are all placed in blank areas within the woodblock frame of the illustrations, while the seven-character quatrains composed by the Kangxi emperor are superimposed on the wide upper margins. Although the poems for the illustrations of the "second moulting" and "choosing the mature silkworms" are apparently mismatched, and a number of faulty rhyming characters were used, there was no way that they could be explicitly corrected without offending the emperor. The imperial poetic compositions were actually transcribed on the original painted silk set of the *Gengzhi tu* by the scholar-official Yan Yudun (1650-1713), a descendant of the famous Ming literatus Wen Zhengming (1470-1559). Yan mimicked the large running-script calligraphy for which the emperor was known, as he did in much of the imperial literature that issued from the palace. Several versions of this 1696 edition exist, including those with duochromatic prints using red and black ink, and those later hand-tinted with watercolors to evoke Jiao Bingzhen's painted set.

The *Gengzhi tu* remained an important literary and pictorial work for the rest of the Qing dynasty. Following in the footsteps of his grandfather, the Qianlong emperor com-

missioned his own woodblock-printed version in 1739, with a fresh set of imperial poems and pictures believed to have been executed by the court painter Chen Mei (act. mid-18th century) and based on those by Jiao Bingzhen. In 1769, the Qianlong emperor ordered the pictures and poems on the *Gengzhi tu* by the Yuan-dynasty artist Cheng Qi (act. second half of 13th century) to be engraved on stone, from which rubbings could then be taken and widely disseminated. The broad appeal of this thematic set of words and images continued well into the nineteenth century, when still more editions of the *Gengzhi tu* appeared in both Japan (for example, the Kokodô edition printed in Himeji in 1808) and China (for example, the Dianshi zhai edition lithographed in Shanghai in 1886). It even transcended the medium of paintings and prints, finding great popularity in the decorative arts and as motifs for China's domestic and export porcelain industries, and even in numerous European prints, engravings, and watercolors.

17

御製耕織圖

又稱《佩文齋耕織圖》。清聖祖題詩。清焦秉貞繪。清朱圭、梅裕鳳刻。清康熙三十五年（1696年）內府刻本。計四十六圖。四周單邊，版心白口。每頁高三四・七厘米，寬二七・七厘米。圖框高二四・四厘米，寬二四・四厘米。冊頁裝。
14921

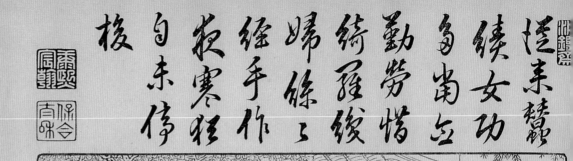

　　《耕織圖》是中國農桑生產最早的成套圖象資料。原作當在南宋時代，其繪者為樓璹。樓璹，字壽玉，一字國器，奉化（今浙江奉化）人，徙居鄞縣（今浙江寧波）。生於北宋元祐五年（1090年），卒於南宋紹興三十二年（1162年）。紹興（1131至1162年）中累官至朝議大夫。善繪事，除了《耕織圖》以外，還有《六逸圖》、《四隱圖》。卒年七十三。樓璹原為南宋高宗時於潛縣（今浙江省臨安縣）令，深念農夫蠶婦之辛苦，乃作耕、織二圖詩，根據圖與詩來顯示民間農業實況。樓璹於紹興十五年（1145年）撰繪《耕織圖》，乃是反映為政者之意見，蓋一欲挽救農村荒廢，二欲自江南豪強手中拯救被榨取之農民。圖、詩都能盡狀盡情，一時朝野傳誦，遂為高宗嘉獎。

　　南宋寧宗嘉定三年（1210年），樓璹之孫樓洪、樓深等，以之刻石傳於後世，此一事實，附於《知不齋叢書》「耕織圖詩」本文前後，此樓洪之跋文、樓璹姪樓鑰之後序及曾孫樓杓之跋文等，記載頗詳，可以一讀。南宋理宗嘉熙元年（1237年）有汪綱木刻復製品。宋以後，關於本書之記載，已不多見。元代有程棨之《耕織圖》四十五幅，亦是據樓本而繪。明代初期編的《永樂大典》曾收《耕織圖》，可惜已佚。明天順六年（1462年）有仿佛宋刻之摹本（附有王增祐跋），雖失傳，但有日本延寶四年（1676年）京都狩野永納據明天順本翻刻本，圖亦完全，現今一般均以狩野永納之《耕織圖》，作為樓璹《耕織圖》之代表。

　　清康熙二十八年（1689年），康熙帝南巡時，江南人士進獻藏書甚多，其中有「宋公重加考訂，壽諸梓以傳」的一種《耕織圖》。此圖包括耕圖共二十一幅；織圖共二十四幅；每圖均刻有樓　五詩。康熙帝命焦秉貞根據原意，另作耕圖、織圖各二十三幅。繪者焦秉貞，山東濟寧人，官欽天監五官正。工人物、山水、樓觀，其位置之自近而遠，

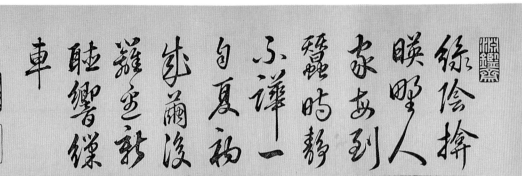

由大及小，不爽毫毛，蓋西洋法也。康熙中，祇候內廷。

　　焦秉貞奉詔繪制四十六幅圖，所作村落風景，田家作苦，典盡其致，深契聖衷，錫賚其厚，旋鏤板印。每圖加御製七言絕句，以之上梓，初印於康熙三十五年（1696年）。刻工為朱圭與梅裕鳳。朱圭，字上如，別署柱笏堂，江蘇蘇州人。其早期刻本有康熙八年（1669年）劉源繪圖本《凌煙閣功臣圖》、二十九年（1690年）石濂繪圖本《石濂和尚集》等。康熙三十年（1691年）前後入內府供職，五十六年（1717年）刻冷枚、宋駿業等繪內府本《萬壽盛典圖》。朱氏以《耕織圖》最聞名，翻刻本亦多。梅裕鳳，生平不詳，可能是吳郡派的名手之一。

　　焦秉貞所繪《耕織圖》，因沿襲樓璹圖摹繪，故究其題材基本上可以反映南宋以來江南農桑生產和農業技術的概貌。康熙《御製耕織圖》的內府刻本，在藝術上堪稱是清代殿版畫中的一部優秀作品。現在故宮博物院及中國國家圖書館等處均有珍藏。

　　中國國家圖書館所藏這部康熙《御製耕織圖》，紙質頗佳，版刻綫條流暢、細膩、鮮麗，稱善本，御製序文前後捺有朱色玉璽印，裝幀精緻。其卷首有康熙帝(愛新覺羅‧玄燁)自寫序文「〈御製耕織圖序〉。朕早夜勤毖，研求治理，念生民之本，以衣食為天。嘗讀《豳風》、《無逸》諸篇，其言稼穡蠶桑，纖悉具備，昔人以此被之管絃，列於典誥，有天下國家者，洵不可不留連三復於其際也。西漢詔令，最為近古，其曰：『農事傷，則饑之本也；女紅害，則寒之原也』。又曰：『老者以壽終，幼孤得遂長』。欲臻斯理者，舍本務其曷以哉？朕每巡省風謠，樂觀農事，於南北土疆之性，黍稷播種之宜，節候早晚之殊，蝗螟捕治之法，素愛諮詢，知此甚晰。聽政時恒與諸臣工之，於豐澤園之側，治田數畦，環以溪水，阡陌井然在目，桔槔之聲盈耳，歲收嘉禾數十鍾。隴畔樹桑，傍列蠶舍，浴蠶繅絲，恍然如茆簷蓽屋，因構『知稼軒』、『秋雲亭』以臨觀之。古人有：『衣帛當思織女之寒，食粟當念農夫之苦』。朕惓惓於此，至深且切也。爰臨耕織圖各二十三幅，朕於每幅，製詩一章，以吟詠其勤苦而書之於圖。自始事終事，農人胼手胝之勞，蠶女繭絲機杼之瘁，咸備極其情狀。復命鏤板流傳，用以示子孫臣庶，俾知粒食維艱，授衣匪易。《書》曰：『惟土物愛，厥心臧』。

庶於斯圖有所感發焉，且欲令寰宇之內，皆敦崇本業，勤以謀之，儉以積之，俾其衣食豐饒，以共躋於安和富壽之域，斯則朕嘉惠元元之至意也夫！康熙三十五年春二月社日題并書。」序行書，全四十一行，前有「佩文齋」白文長方印，後有「康熙宸翰」朱文方印、「稽古右文之章」白文方印。由此可見，康熙帝不僅對耕織生產的艱辛有所了解，而且深知農事好壞與經濟興衰，乃至政權恐固有極為密切的關係。

焦秉貞所繪《耕織圖》雖是依據南宋樓璹曾繪的《耕織圖》（或摹本）增減而成，但並非全部照搬，也有他自己的創見。如樓圖耕為二十一幅，織為二十四幅，耕織合計共四十五幅。焦圖在耕的部分增加了二幅，在織的部分卻刪去了三幅，增加了二幅，成耕二十三幅，織二十三幅，耕織合計共四十六幅。此外，焦圖之畫目次序也有所不同：耕圖有「浸種」、「耕」、「耕耨」、「耖」、「碌碡」、「布秧」、「初秧」、「淤蔭」、「拔秧」、「插秧」、「一耘」、「二耘」、「三耘」、「灌溉」、「收刈」、「登場」、「持穗」、「舂碓」、「篩」、「簸揚」、「礱」、「入倉」、「祭神」二十三幅；織圖有「浴蠶」、「二眠」、「三眠」、「大起」、「捉績」、「分箔」、「采桑」、「上簇」、「炙箔」、「下簇」、「擇繭」、「窖繭」、「練絲」、「蠶蛾」、「祀謝」、「緯」、「織」、「絡絲」、「經」、「染色」、「攀花」、「剪帛」、「成衣」

二十三幅。第四十六圖左下方刻「欽天監五官臣焦秉貞畫，鴻臚寺序班臣朱圭鐫」。在焦秉貞所繪之每幅上欄，刻有御製草書，樓璹之詩則嵌於繪畫上方空白欄中。茲選照四幅，即耕部「拔秧」、「插秧」二幅，織部「緯」、「織」二幅。

自十七世紀末年以來，《耕織圖》出現了種種不同版本，木刻本、繪本、石刻、墨本均行於世，例如康熙三十八年（1699年）張鵬翮刻本、康熙五十一年（1712年）內府刻本、康熙年間（約1710年與1722年間）雍親王胤禛（即未來的雍正帝）命院工設色絹底繪本五十二幅（其中重復六張，圖上亦無題詩）、康熙五十三年（1714年）歙縣汪希古恭摹刻於四十八墨板、乾隆七年（1742年）刻於《授時通考》本、乾隆三十四年（1769年）北京刻朱墨套印本（如鄭振鐸先生所舊藏本）、乾隆三十四年（1769年）高宗命畫院據元代程棨摹本作的《耕織圖》於北京皇家清漪園延賞齋左右廊壁嵌石刻（據元代程棨摹本）、乾隆年間（1770年前）徽州守臣摹刻於墨板、嘉慶十三年（1808年）《耕織圖詩》補刊本、光緒五年（1879年）上海點石齋《御製耕織圖》石印本、同治十一年（1872年）《耕織圖詩》刊本、光緒十一年（1885年）上海文瑞樓《御製耕織圖》、光緒十二年（1886年）上海點石齋《御製耕織圖》石印本。民國時期皆有多版，如1929年武進陶湘《耕織圖詩》。日本亦有翻刻本，如文化五年（1808年）重摹刊本。中國、日本以外，琉球、朝鮮亦均有《耕織圖》的翻刻本、臨摹本，見樓璹《耕織圖》影響之深。

18

Jiezi yuan hua zhuan er ji (8 juan), shou (1 juan), mo (1 juan)

The Mustard Seed Garden Manual of Painting, Second Series, 8 *juan*, with Introduction, 1 *juan*, and Postscript, 1 *juan*

Qing dynasty (1644-1911), Kangxi period (1662-1722)
Compiled by Wang Gai (1645-1707), Wang Shi (1649-1734), and Wang Nie (fl. late 17th-early 18th century)
Nanjing, Jiangsu province: Jiezi yuan sheng guan, 1701
Illustrations printed in color; 9 columns per half-folio of texts; 20 characters per column; white folding margin at center of folio; single-line borders; overall dimensions of volumes: 29.2 x 18.1 cm; block sizes of text: approx. 22.0 x 15.0 cm; stitched binding

15817

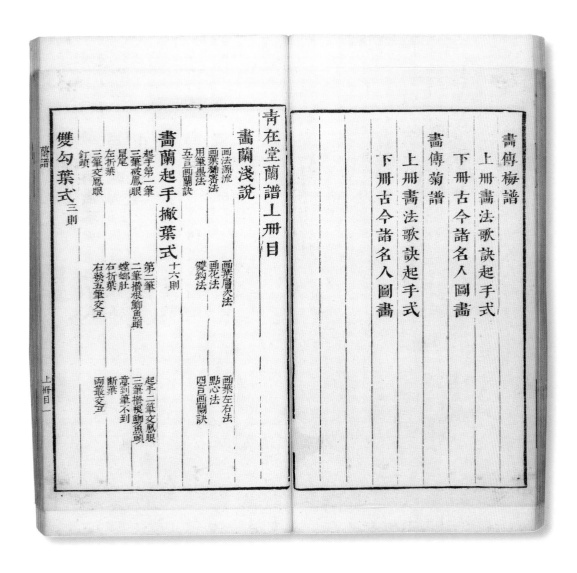

The initial series of the *Jiezi yuan hua zhuan* (The Mustard Seed Garden Manual of Painting) was compiled and edited by the artist Wang Gai (1645-1707), a native of Xiushui in Zhejiang. The preface was written by the renowned dramatist Li Yu (1611-ca. 1680), whose estate near Nanjing's southern gate was called the Jiezi yuan (Mustard Seed Garden). The manual was published in 1679 by Li Yu's son-in-law Shen Xinyou. This manual was undoubtedly inspired by the earlier *Shizhu zhai shuhua pu* (The Ten Bamboo Studio Manual of Calligraphy and Painting) printed by Hu Zhengyan (1584-1674), but the *Jiezi yuan hua zhuan* was designed to be much more of a pedagogical tool for aspiring painters than the *Shizhu zhai shuhua pu*. Wang Gai's manual contains a substantial amount of introductory text discussing the basic principles of Chinese painting, and subsequent sections break down the elements of landscape painting so that the figures, boats, trees, and rocks can be separately copied and mastered before the apprentice painter attempts his own composition from these elements. There is also considerably more use of calligraphic inscriptions and seals than in the *Shizhu zhai shuhua pu*, thereby making the compositions seem more like actual paintings.

The second and third series of 1701, with eight and four *juan* respectively, greatly augmented the original five which were limited to landscapes. These later series were also compiled and edited under the supervision of Wang Gai, but the work was principally undertaken by his two brothers Wang Shi (1649-1734) and Wang Nie (fl. late 17th-early 18th century), who in turn were assisted by the older painters Wang Zhi (act. late 17th century) and Zhu Sheng (1618-1690). The second series deals with orchids, bamboo, flowering prunus, and chrysanthemums, while the third series focuses on grasses, insects, flowering plants, and birds.

The National Library of China possesses various editions of all three series. The second series illustrated here is technically not divided into *juan*, but its four *pu* ("manuals") are each subdivided into two *ce* or "sections" (*shang* and *xia*), giving a total of eight *ce* which are called *juan* for the sake of convenience. The front of the first bound volume contains a long preface by Wang Gai printed in his calligraphy, a general table of contents covering all eight *juan*, and introductory remarks. Each *pu* has a separate, attractively designed inner cover page (*nei fengmian*), and its own table of contents; the *shang* sections are devoted to techniques and contain text and illustrations, while the *xia* sections are devoted to compositions and contain mostly pictures.

A spread from the first bound volume shows part of the general table of contents for the second series and part of the table of contents for the first volume itself. Two compositions, one of orchids among rocks from the "Manual on Orchids" (*Lan pu*, *xia ce*, folios 5b-6a), printed in black ink, brown ink, and two shades of green, and the other of new sprays of bamboo from the "Manual on Bamboo" (*Zhu pu*, *xia ce*, folios 4b-5a), printed in two graded shades of green, exemplify the high quality of illustration, engraving, and color-printing in many folios in the manual. From the "Manual on Blossoming Prunus" (*Mei pu*, *shang ce*, folios 7b-8a) are examples of double-petaled blossoms (half-folio at right) and examples of blossoms, stamens, pistils, and calyxes (half-folio at left). Taken from the "Manual on Chrysanthemums" (*Ju pu*, *shang ce*, folios 7b-8a) are models for "small flowers with delicate buds"

(half-folio at right), "a single flower on a cut stem" and "a pair of flowers on a cut stem" (half-folio at left).

The second series of the *Jiezi yuan hua zhuan* was enormously popular by virtue of its subject matter and superb visual quality. It continued to be printed from the old woodblocks in Nanjing by the same Wang family for at least a century; editions from 1782 and 1800 are known to exist. A publication identifying itself as the fourth series of the *Jiezi yuan hua zhuan* was printed in 1818; it is a completely separate work and is unrelated to the three series discussed here.

18

芥子園畫傳二集八卷首一卷末一卷

清王概、王蓍、王臬輯。清康熙四十年（1701年）南京芥子園甥館刻彩色套印本。全四册。四周單邊、版心白口。框高二二厘米，寬一五厘米。綫裝。
15817

《芥子園畫傳》共三集，專為中國畫津梁，初學畫者多習用之。初集山水譜五卷，為「畫學淺說」、「設色繪法」、「樹法葉法」、「石法皴法」、「點景人物」，康熙十八年（1679年）用開化紙五色套版印成。二集八卷，為〈蘭譜〉、〈竹譜〉、

〈梅譜〉、〈菊譜〉四部，各分上、下册。三集四
卷，為花卉、草蟲及花木、禽鳥兩譜，為王概、王
蓍、王臬編繪。王概，本名丏，字安節，秀水人，
寓居金陵，畫山水學龔賢，善作大幅。兄名蓍，本
名廣，字宓草，以花卉翎毛擅名，得黃筌遺法。弟
名臬，字司直，亦善畫。二、三集成於康熙四十年
（1701 年），也用木版彩色套印。「芥子園」為明
末戲曲家李漁于南京的別墅。題作「芥子園甥館」
的沈心友是李漁的女婿，並為此書的經營刻印者。

《芥子園畫傳二集》初由諸昇編畫竹、蘭，王
質編畫梅菊，後由王概、王蓍、王臬兄弟三人論
訂。每集首列畫法淺説，亦有畫法歌訣，次摹諸家
畫式，附簡要説明，末為摹仿名家畫譜。〈蘭譜〉
前有〈畫傳二集總目〉，題「繡水王安節、宓草、
司直摹古」。總目目次為：〈畫傳蘭譜〉，上册畫
法歌訣起手式，下册古今諸名人圖畫；〈畫傳竹
譜〉，上册畫法歌訣起手式，下册古今諸名人圖
畫；〈畫傳梅譜〉，上册畫法歌訣起手式，下册古
今諸名人圖畫；〈畫傳菊譜〉，上册畫法歌訣起手
式，下册古今諸名人圖畫。

關於畫師王質與諸昇，本書〈畫傳合集例〉第
二則云：「王蘊菴、諸曦菴，武林名宿也。聞畫傳
二集之請，兩先生白髮蕭蕭，欣然任事。三年乃
成。蘭竹二種俱曦菴所作。蘊菴佐之。蘊菴尤工花
卉，名冠兩浙。故花卉一叢，獨出蘊菴之手。昔先
大人雲將公喜植梅，至今抱青閣小園尚存百餘樹。
先叔穎良公喜栽菊，每至花放，觀者如堵。蘊菴兼
好之。值二花開時，凌霜踏雪，黎明而至夜分始
歸。自謂花之精神，莫妙於曉風承露，淡月籠煙。
故蘊菴於梅菊二種，得心應手，各為一
册。……」。末署「西冷沈心友因伯氏謹識。康熙
辛巳桂月芥子園甥館鐫藏」。

中國國家圖書館所藏這部《芥子園畫傳二
集》，套色準確精印，絢麗奪目，是清代版畫中的
代表作品。茲選照五開，為〈蘭譜〉上册中的〈畫
傳二集總目〉末半葉與〈青在堂蘭譜上册目〉首半
葉、〈蘭譜〉下册名人圖畫一幅（款識「蘊菴，質」，
以墨、黃、棕、深綠、淺綠色套印）、〈竹譜〉下
册名人圖畫一幅（題「新篁解籜」，以深綠、淺綠
色套印）、〈梅譜〉上册起手式一開（右半葉為「千
葉花式」，左半葉為「花鬚蕊蒂式」，均墨印）、
〈菊譜〉上册起手式一開（右半葉為「小花細蕊」，
左半葉為「單花折枝、雙頭折枝」，均墨印）。

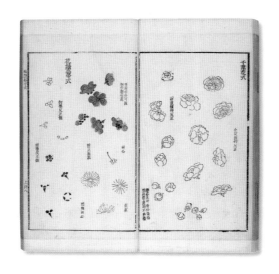

19

Yu zhi Guwen yuanjian (64 juan)

Imperially Commissioned Profound Mirror of Ancient Essays, 64 *juan*

Qing dynasty (1644-1911), Kangxi period (1662-1722)
Selected by the Kangxi emperor (1654-1722; r. 1661-1722); compiled and annotated by Xu Qianxue (1631-1711; *jinshi* of 1670); five-color edition printed with red, black, yellow, orange, and green inks
Beijing: Wuying dian, 1710
9 columns per half-folio; 20 characters per column; small characters in half-columns with varying number of characters per half-column; annotations in upper margins vary in number of columns, in number of characters per column, and in color of printing; no column lines in the main text sections; fine black folding margin at center of folio with double black "fish-tails"; single-line borders; overall dimensions of volumes: 31.7 x 17.3 cm; block sizes of text: approx. 19.4 x 14.2 cm; stitched binding; in original yellow silk covers

03308

The *Yu zhi Guwen yuanjian* (Imperially Commissioned Profound Mirror of Ancient Essays), also known as the *Yuanjian zhai guwen xuan* (Selected Ancient Essays from the Studio of the Profound Mirror) is a comprehensive anthology of classical prose literature compiled by the Minister of Justice (*xing bu shangshu*), Xu Qianxue (1631-1711) by order of the Kangxi emperor. It includes pieces from the ancient periods through the end of the Song dynasty in 1279. The original publication of this book by the palace printing bureau housed in the Hall of Military Glory (Wuying dian) took place in 1685. A Manchu

version, the *Gu wen yuwan giyan bithe*, was printed soon after, between December 26, 1685 and January 23, 1686. In 1746, a reduced size, five-color edition of the *Yu zhi Guwen yuanjian* was published as one of the nine titles forming the *Guxiang zhai xiuzhen ban shu*.

This particular set of the *Guwen yuanjian*, printed by the palace in 1710, is now missing its first volume which contains *juan* 1-4. The remaining 60 *juan* are bound in 23 volumes, all retaining their original yellow silk covers. Preceding the text in each volume is an additional page with the hand-painted design of two dragons amidst clouds. Shown here are the end of the table of contents and the beginning of the text of *juan* 6, which contains selections from the state of Zhou section in the *Guoyu* (Discourses of the States), written in the Warring States period and compiled during the early Western Han. Also illustrated is a double-page spread from *juan* 10, folios 6b and 7a showing selected essays from the Han dynasty. Punctuation marks in the text proper were printed in red, while upper marginal notes were printed in various colors. Comments made by the Kangxi emperor were printed in yellow, those by contemporary scholars in red, and those of earlier scholars in green or blue ink.

All editions of the *Guwen yuanjian* feature the marginal annotations and punctuation in red ink in the same places, but various combinations of colors were used for the other commentaries. Blue was often substituted for orange, and any given critic's commentary may appear in a different color from that found in another printed set. For example, complete sets held by the C.V. Starr East Asian Library of Columbia University in New York and by the East Asian Library at

the University of Minnesota Twin Cities campus in Minneapolis are printed in yellow, blue, red, green, and black. Different kinds of paper were also used, some inferior to others. This set from the National Library of China is printed on a very fine white paper. Although the *Guwen yuanjian* is much valued for its fine polychromatic printing, it does not represent the acme of this tradition; the greatest number of colors ever used for book-printing in imperial times is to be found in later works such as the twenty-*juan Du Gongbu ji* (Collected Literary Works of Du Fu) of 1749 in the National Museum of Chinese History (as well as another version of 1834), which is unmatched in the quality and scope of its six-color printing.

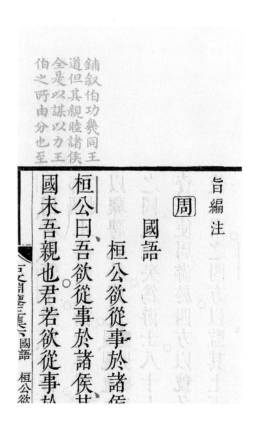

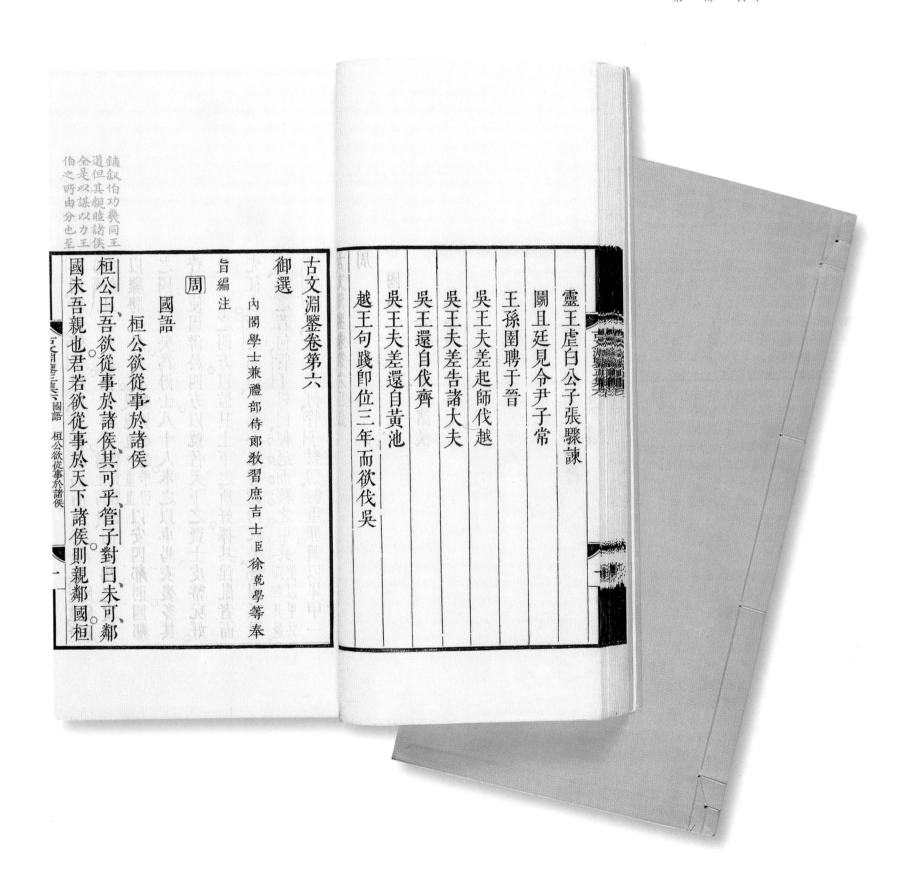

古文淵鑒卷第六

御選

　　內閣學士兼禮部侍郎教習庶吉士臣徐乾學等奉

旨編注

周

國語

　桓公欲從事於諸侯

國未吾親也君若欲從事於天下諸侯則親鄰國桓
桓公曰吾欲從事於諸侯其可乎管子對曰未可鄰

鋪叙伯功幾同王
道但其覩睦諸侯
全是以謀以力王
伯之所由分也至

靈王虐白公子張驟諫

鬬且廷見令尹子常

王孫圉聘于晉

吳王夫差起師伐越

吳王夫差告諸大夫

吳王還自伐齊

吳王夫差還自黃池

越王句踐即位三年而欲伐吳

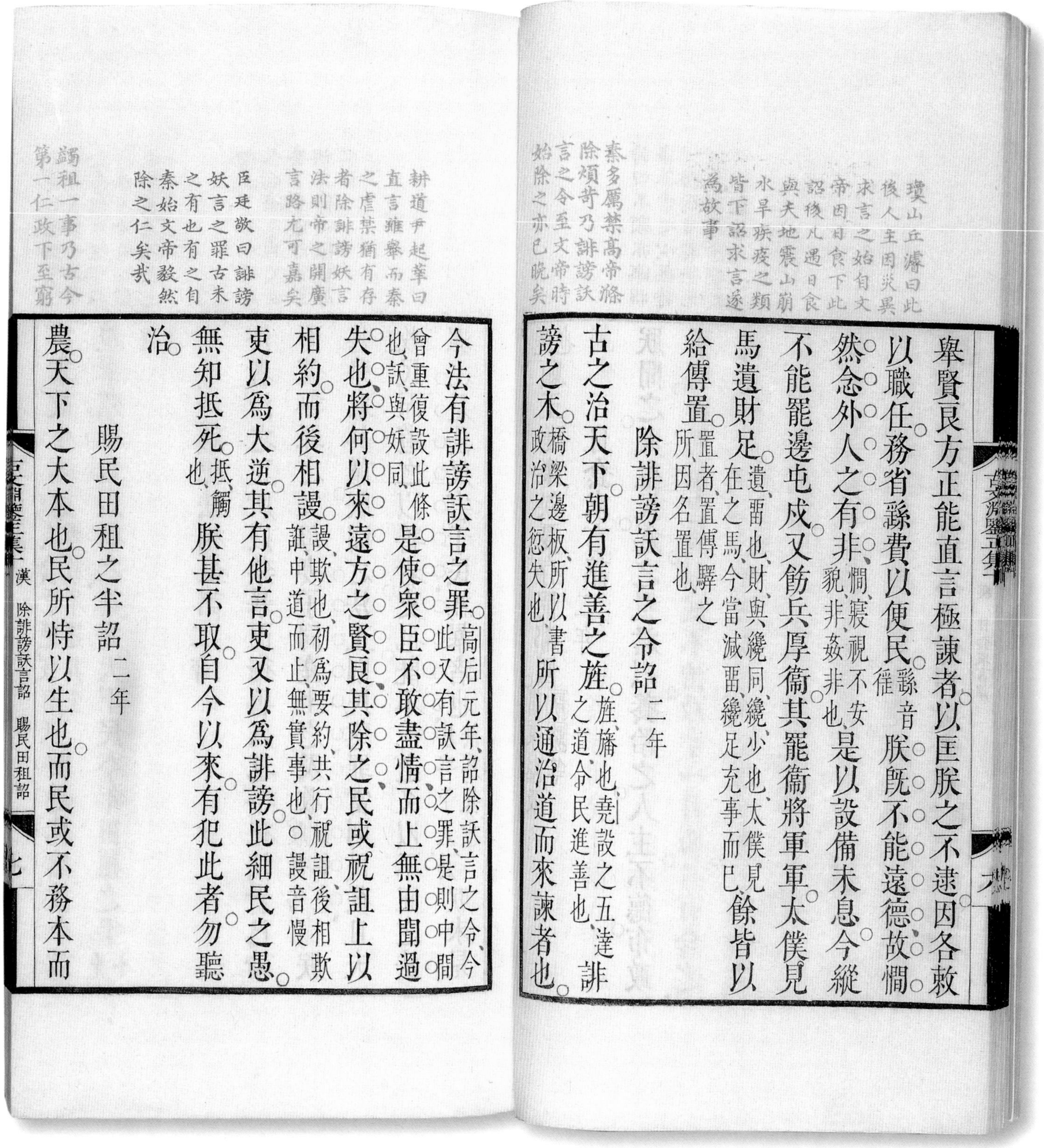
瓊山丘濬曰此後人主因災異求言之始自文帝因日食下此詔後凡遇日食與夫地震山崩水旱疾疫之類皆下詔求言遂爲故事
秦多厲禁高帝除除煩苛乃誹謗訞言之令至文帝時始除之亦已晚矣
舉賢良方正能直言極諫者以匡朕之不逮因各敕以職任務省繇費以便民繇音徭朕既不能遠德故憪然念外人之有非憪寢視不安貌非姦非也是以設備未息今縱不能罷邊屯戍又飭兵厚衛其罷衛將軍軍太僕見馬遺財足遺畱也財與纔同纔少也太僕見在之馬今當減畱纔足充事而已餘皆以給傳置置者置傳驛之所因名置也
除誹謗訞言之令詔 二年
古之治天下朝有進善之旌旌旛也堯設之五達之道令民進善也誹謗之木橋梁邊板所以書政治之愆失也所以通治道而來諫者也
耕道尹起莘曰直言雖舉而秦之虐禁猶有存者除誹謗妖言法則帝之開廣言路尤可嘉矣
臣廷敬曰誹謗妖言之罪古未之有也有之自秦始文帝毅然除之仁矣哉
蠲租一事乃古今第一仁政下至窮
今法有誹謗訞言之罪高后元年詔除訞言之令今此又有訞言之罪是則中間會重復設此條也訞與妖同是使衆臣不敢盡情而上無由聞過失也將何以來遠方之賢良其除之民或祝詛上以相約而後相謾謾欺也初爲要約共行祝詛後相欺誑中道而止無實事也謾音慢吏以爲大逆其有他言吏又以爲誹謗此細民之愚無知抵死抵觸也朕甚不取自今以來有犯此者勿聽治
賜民田租之半詔 二年
農天下之大本也民所恃以生也而民或不務本而

19

御製古文淵鑒六十四卷

亦稱《淵鑒齋古文選》。清聖祖玄燁選。清徐乾學等輯並註。清康熙四十九年（1710年）內府刻朱、黃、橙、深綠、淺綠五色套印本。半葉九行，行二十字，小字不等，正文無行格，四周單邊，雙黑魚尾，版心細黑口。框一九‧四厘米，寬一四‧二厘米。綫裝。

　　《御製古文淵鑒》匯集了從《春秋左傳》到宋代的中國古代文學名篇六百九十三種。文章體裁有《左傳》、《國語》、《國策》、《詔》、《表》、《書》、《議》、《奏》、《疏》、《論》、《序》等，擇其辭義精純可以鼓吹六經者彙為正集，瑰麗之篇列為別集，諸子列其要論以為外集。大旨以有裨世用者為主，所注考證，亦頗詳細。每卷前均有本卷目錄。正文用墨色，有朱筆圈點，注釋用朱、黃、橙、綠色分層套印，十分精致、美觀。前人評語蒐羅賅備，去取謹嚴，名物訓詁各有箋釋，前人評語在書的天頭，用黃、橙、綠色字標之，清朝評語則用朱色。正文內容及格式與康熙二十四年（1685年）內府四色套印本相同，惟朱、黃、深綠、淺綠外又加橙色成為五色，而四色套印本無橙色批語。此書另有朱、黃、綠、藍四色套印本。此書也有武英殿刊刻於康熙二十四年（1685年）的六十四卷三十六册滿文版，為清代大規模翻譯漢文散文的第一部集子。

　　此書輯者徐乾學，字原一，號健庵，江蘇昆山人。幼慧好讀，八歲能文。康熙九年（1670年）一甲三名進士，授翰林院編修，遷贊善，充日講起居注官，侍講學士，入直南書房，累官左都御史、刑部尚書、內閣學士兼禮部侍郎敎習庶吉士。嘗命總裁《大清一統志》、《清會典》、《明史》、纂輯《鑒古輯覽》、《古文淵鑒》等書。著有《通志堂經解》、《讀禮通考》、《澹園集》、《虞浦集》、《詞館集》、《碧山集》。藏書極富，有《傳是樓書目》行世。康熙五十年（1711年）四月卒於家，年七十有九。

　　中國國家圖書館所藏這部《御製古文淵鑒》，原六十四卷分裝二十四册，現存六十卷（卷五至六十四）二十三册。茲選照卷六目錄末半葉與正文前半葉（《國語‧周》部分），以及卷十第六葉下半葉與第七葉上半葉（漢代文章部分）。

　　此書為康熙年代彩色套印本的佳作之一。其後有類似而更精美的例子，如中國歷史博物館所藏一部《杜工部集》，以六種顏色刊刻於乾隆十四年（1749年），或道光十四年（1834年）涿州盧坤，以朱、墨、黃、綠、藍、紫六色套印的《杜工部集》二十五卷，斑斕彩色，娛目怡情。

20

Ju pu (1 juan)

Manual on Chrysanthemums, 1 *juan*

Qing dynasty (1644-1911), Qianlong period (1736-1795)

Compiled by Hongjiao (18th century); proofread and edited by Li Kai (1686-1755)

Beijing: Chunhui tang, 1757

10 columns per half-folio; 21 characters per column; white folding margin at center of folio; double-line borders; overall dimensions of volume: 25.1 x 15.5 cm; block sizes of text: approx. 18.4 x 13.0 cm; stitched binding

02753

Chrysanthemums (*ju*) are native to China, where they have been cultivated since 1000 B.C. or so, with improved forms appearing around 500 B.C. Their gorgeous autumnal blooms have long been celebrated in China, where they became the subject of countless poems, essays, and paintings. First introduced to Japan between 724 and 749 A.D., they found their way to continental Europe only in 1688, to England in 1764, and to the United States in 1798. Modern varieities of the garden chrysanthemum (*Chrysanthemum hortorum*) are mostly derived from *C. morifolium* and *C. indicum*, with the former tending to have larger blooms than the latter.

The chrysanthemum was already alluded to in ancient Chinese works such as the *Li ji* (Book of Rites) and the *Shi jing* (Classic of Poetry), but it was the Eastern Jin poet and recluse Tao Qian (ca. 365-427) who immortalized the plant in literature. Most early chrysanthemums had yellow flowers, but by the Tang there were varieties of white and purple chrysanthemums, while those with red flowers would appear later. Individual monographs and treatises or sections within larger compendia devoted to chrysanthemums have a long tradition in China, with works such as the pioneering *Ju pu* (Manual on Chrysanthemums) of 1104 by Liu Meng (fl. 1104) which identified 35 varieties, the *Ju pu* (Manual on Chrysanthemums; 1 *juan*) of 1175 by the governor at Nanjing Shi Zhengzhi (fl. mid- to late 12th century) which listed 28 types, the *Ju pu* (Manual on Chrysanthemums; 1 *juan*) of 1186 by Fan Chengda (1126-1193) with 36 forms of chrysanthemums in and around Suzhou, and the *Er'ru ting Qun fang pu* (Compendium of Clustered Fragrances from the Er'ru Pavilion; 28 *juan*, *juan shou*) of 1630 by Wang Xiangjin (1561-1653; *jinshi* of 1604), which records a staggering 270 varieties.

This Qing-dynasty manual on chrysanthemums was compiled by Hongjiao, the fourth son of Yinxiang (1686-1730), the first Prince Yi, and a grandson of the Kangxi emperor. In 1730, Hongjiao inherited the title "Prince of the Blood of the Second Degree" (*doroi junwang* in Manchu; *duolo junwang* in Chinese) and the fiefdom of the Ning commandery. The book, completed in 1746 but first printed only in 1757, contains prefaces by Hongjiao's uncle Yinxi (1711-1758), the twenty-first son of the Kangxi emperor known as Prince Shen; Hongyan (1733-1765), the sixth son of the Yongzheng emperor who became the second Prince Guo in 1738; Hongxiao (d. 1778), the second Prince Yi (signed as Bingyuzi); the editor Li Kai (1686-1755); Erong'an (*jinshi* of 1733; d. 1755), the earl of Xiangqin; Se'erhe (18th century); and Hongjiao himself.

One hundred types of chrysanthemums are listed and their salient features described. All of these horticultural varieties are supplied with picturesque and evocative names such as Powdery Butterfly, Honey Lotus, Purple Dragon Whiskers, White Phoenix, Silver Peony, Coral Snow, and Vermilion Platter, to mention only a few. The careful and detailed descriptions are warranted because the manual is not illustrated.

After the text proper are three colophons by Prince Shen, Prince Guo, and Prince Yi. A "Table of Chrysanthemums" (*Ju biao*) is appended at the end of the manual. Hongjiao divides the one hundred varieties of chrysanthemums into two categories, "upper" and "middle" (*shang* and *zhong*), each with three ranks, "upper," "middle," and "lower" (*shang*, *zhong*, and *xia*). Starting from the highest, these six classified ranks are as follows:

Class 1, "Divine Rank: Upper category, Upper rank" (*shen pin shang shang*): "Those which are so intoxicatingly abstruse that

the heavens are dazzled in an unimaginable way–they are called divine (*shen*)." The twenty-eight specimens in this category are: "National Beauty with a Natural Fragrance," "Container of Mist on a Brocaded Bed," "Light Contained within White Jade," "Pink Needles," "Purple Tassels," "Softly Branching Red Peaches," "Surpassing the Flute of Shi," "Dish of Seven Treasures," "Red Crystal Dish," "Yellow Octagonal Jade Rank Badge," "Camellia-colored Lotus," "Coral Branches," "The Two Qiao Sisters," "Golden Bandoline and Azure Waters," "Pine Needles," "Purple Needles," "Brilliance from a Jade Brush," "Sweet Lotus," "Crystal Ball," "Myriad Falling Red Petals," "Purple Shoots," "Chain of Jade Rings," "Snow on the Lotus Terrace," "Crape-myrtle Gentleman," "Egret's Neck, " "Amber Lotus," and "Purple Rushes."

Class 2, "Wonderful Rank: Upper Category, Middle Rank" (*miao pin shang zhong*): "Those which stand like phoenixes in a profoundly refined way, with aromas that are completely natural–they are called wonderful (*miao*)." The fifteen specimens in this category are: "Engraved Gold and Polished Gems," "Pink Crane Feathers," "Green Lotus Leaves," "Crimson-rouge Petals," "Carved Soft White Jade," "Golden Needles," "Purplish Rosy Goblet," "Golden Silk Belvedere," "Purple Lotus Leaves," "Coral Snow," "Purple Robes and Golden Belts," "Golden Phoenix Feathers," "Persian Cap," "Fir-cone Chrysanthemum," and "Brocade of the Weaving Maiden."

Class 3, "Untrammeled Rank: Upper category, Lower rank" (*yi pin shang xia*): "Those which are naturally unrestrained and solemnly tranquil, with delightful manners from on high–they are called untrammeled (*yi*)." The nine specimens in this

category are: "Golden Velvet," "Green Tunic and Yellow Skirt," "Made-up and Dressed-up Xizi," "Silver Embroidered Ball," "Waxed Dish," "White Shagreen," "Jade Cottonrose Hibiscus," "Purple Gauze Jacket," and "Silver Phoenix Feathers."

Class 4, "Outstanding Rank: Middle Category, Upper Rank" (*jun pin zhong shang*): "Those which are abstruse as though harking from distant antiquity, infused with purity and penetrated with serenity–they are called outstanding (*jun*)." The twelve specimens in this category are: "Cinnabar Bowl," "Silver Crane Feathers," "Yellow Oriole," "Purple Golden Dish," "Azure-hearted Jade," "Golden Ball Offered up by the Sea," "Purple Outfit," "Shower of Red Silk Trimmings," "Facing-the-Sun White," "Nourishing Apricot Blossoms," "Maiden's Radiant Flesh," and "Sandalwood Bowl."

Class 5, "Beautiful Rank: Middle Category, Middle Rank" (*yan pin zhong zhong*): "Those which are quiet and demure, meek and modest, but sprouting with loveliness and flaunting their seductiveness–they are called beautiful (*yan*)." The fifteen specimens in this category are: "White Phoenix," "Red Clouds over the Sea," "Pale Yellowish Powder," "Pink Twisted Threads," "Yellow Dye from the Zhe Tree," "Beautiful Flowering Grass," "Crimson Fuzhou Oranges," "Tiger-skin Lotus," "Embroidered-border Lotus," "Red Silken Jade," "Unloosened Entwined Silken Cords," "Pink and Azure," "Golden Twisted Threads," "Sandalwood Ball," and "Powdery Green Bamboo."

Class 6, "Harmonious rank: Middle Category, Lower Rank" (*yun pin zhong xia*): "Those which are like single branches recalling the *ruo* (a fabulous tree with luminous leaves), swaying in a placid and subtle way–they are called harmonious (*yun*)." The twenty-one specimens in this category are: "Golden Silk Lotus," "Golden Crab-apple," "Pink Butterfly," "Purple Azure Lotus," "Red Double-flowering Peaches," "Great Golden Wheel," "Silver Peony," "Azure Lotus," "Imperially Favored Yellow," "Concubine Yang in an Evening Outfit," "Yellow under Lamps," "Silver Twisted Threads," "Jade Pendant," "Golden Cottonrose Hibiscus," "Embroidered Cottonrose Hibiscus," "Pale Yellowish Purple," "Heart of Brocade and Mouth of Embroidery," "Pink Outfit," "Pink-hearted Lotus," "Yellow Citron," and "One Single Ball."

The one hundred varieties of chrysanthemums listed and classified in this book have names that range from those that are simply descriptive and based on color or shape, to those evoking other flowering plants, to those drawn from historical figures or literary sources. In the first and highest ranking category, for example, the chrysanthemum known as "Surpassing the Flute of Shi" (*Ying Shi guan*) makes little sense unless one extrapolates the name to mean "Surpassing the Music from the Flute of Shi Kuang," in which case the flower can be understood as being even more lovely than the singularly beautiful music that was produced by the ancient flautist Shi Kuang. Another specimen in the same group called the "Crape-myrtle Gentleman" (*Ziwei lang*) is not a botanical reference at all, but rather the title of an official position, "Secretariat Drafter from the Crape-myrtle Hall," which incorporates the name of the building in which the officer worked.

20

菊譜一卷

又名《東園菊譜》一卷，附《菊表》。清弘皎撰。清李鍇校。清乾隆二十二年（1757年）北京春暉堂刻本。半葉十行，行二十一字，四周雙邊，版心白口，下刻「春暉堂」，單魚尾。框高一八・四厘米，寬一三厘米。綫裝。

02753

菊花為中國十大名花之一，品種繁多，色彩豐富，花形多變，姿態萬千。菊花在中國有悠久的栽培歷史，在二千五百年前的古籍中，如《禮記》、《楚辭》等，已有關於菊花的記載。自晉代起，中國人將菊花作為觀賞對象，從陶淵明的詩句中可知菊花已開始在田園栽種。至唐代有幾種不同花色的品種先後出現。

宋代更有菊花品種的發展，同時藝菊專著也相繼問世，如劉蒙《菊譜》記號地之菊三十六品、史正志《菊譜》記吳門之菊二十八品、范成大《范村菊譜》記石湖之菊三十六品、沈競《菊譜》記菊五十八品、史鑄《百菊集譜》記菊一百六十多品。元代菊花專著較少，有楊維楨在《黃華傳》中記菊一百三十六種。明代有黃省曾《菊譜》記菊二百二十品、王象晉《群芳譜》記菊二百七十種、高濂《遵生八牋》記菊一百八十五種。清代的菊書、菊譜如雨後春筍，如陳淏子《花鏡》記菊一百五十三品、汪灝《廣群芳譜》記菊一百九十二種、陸廷燦《藝菊志》等等。

本書為清代許許多多的菊譜之一，記菊花形態色彩，列表評次，無圖。其撰者為清宗室愛新覺羅氏的弘皎，字鏡齋，號東園，自號秋明主人、鏡齋主人，室名春暉堂。弘皎是怡親王胤祥之四子，雍正中封多羅寧郡王。校者李鍇，字鐵君，號眉山，又號焦明子，晚號鳼青山人，遼東鐵嶺人。隸漢軍正黃旗，娶大學士索額圖女。一生致力經史，尤工詩詞。《清史列傳》卷七十一有傳。

弘皎《菊譜》原稿作於乾隆十一年（1746年），初刊刻於乾隆二十二年（1757年）。此書刻版字體為當時流行的一種字畫纖細，極秀麗的寫刻體，流暢自然，刻印精美，所用的紙墨俱佳，近似于清代內府刻書風格。封面頁題《菊譜》。秋明主人。鳼青李山校。正文前有慎親王胤禧丁丑（1757年）冬日〈序〉、果親王弘瞻乾隆丁丑長至前二日

〈秋明主人東園菊譜序〉、「冰玉子」（即怡親王弘曉）乾隆歲次著雍攝提格皋月下浣〈東園菊譜序〉、李鍇〈序〉、乾隆甲子（1744年）冬十月下澣鄂容安〈題辭〉、寒爾赫〈菊譜跋〉、乾隆甲子九月朔弘皎〈菊譜小引〉。

《菊譜》所記的百種菊為：「麯粉」、「柘枝黃」、「檀香毬」、「粉蝴蝶」、「紫薇郎」、「紅絲玉」、「銀鳳羽」、「瑛盤」、「燈下黃」、「蜜荷」、「松子菊」、「青心玉」、「綠衣黃裳」、「紫龍鬚」、「姑射肌」、「靚裝西子」、「繡芙蓉」、「大金輪」、「紫袍金帶」、「青蓮」、「含煙鋪錦」、「銀鶴毳」、「粉裝」、「紫羅襦」、「水精球」、「紫金盤」、「楊妃晚裝」、「檀香盤」、「麯紫」、「解環綠」、「雪蓮臺」、「珊瑚枝」、「紫茸」、「一粒球」、「玉毫光」、「銀撚線」、「天孫錦」、「玉連環」、「錦心繡口」、「白鮫綃」、「海紅蓮」、「粉鶴翎」、「金撚線」、「粉鍼」、「金膏水碧」、「琥珀蓮」、「紫霞觴」、「白鳳」、「六郎面」、「七寶盤」、「贏師管」、「金鳳羽」、「國色天香」、「金鍼」、「玉玲瓏」、「粉翠」、「落紅萬點」、「軟枝桃紅」、「金絲蓮」、「金剪絨」、「福橘紅」、「杏花頤」、「黃玉琼」、「紫裝」、「金海棠」、「銀牡丹」、「金芙蓉」、「佛手黃」、「白玉纏光」、「朝陽素」、「粉撚線」、「雨闌紅」、「金絲樓」、「鷺鷥管」、「截肪玉」、「玉芙蓉」、「粉心蓮」、「御愛黃」、「紫針」、「旨藟」、「海獻金球」、「松鍼」、「碧桃紅」、「粉菉竹」、「海雲紅」、「紫荷衣」、「虎皮蓮」、「二喬」、「波斯帽」、「紫纓」、「脂瓣」、「栗留黃」、「珊瑚雪」、「銀繡毬」、「綠荷衣」、「硃砂盤」、「紫翠蓮」、「蠟盤」、「錦邊蓮」、「追金琢玉」。

正文後有慎親王〈題東園菊譜銘〉、「經畬主人」（即果親王弘瞻）乾隆二十二年丁丑（1757年）長至前二日〈題東園菊譜後〉、怡親王乾隆歲次著雍攝提格薿實下浣〈題秋明四兄菊譜後〉。最後附弘皎所編的〈菊表〉，表前記：「景祐時有《冀王宮花品》，以牡丹五十種，分三等九品，班氏例也。當是時酌斟，求協商榷，命中諨信之權，不得以偏智任乎。花之靜閒者莫菊，若菊之為卉，秋榮後者讓也，抱芬不沐潔也，薄霜以秀貞也，三德若此而，肯後夫牡丹哉！東園所植菊，傀異，與常菊殊，是用程姿比態，析以品第，凡百種。花如解語，期於是微笑而已。斯表也，擇精釋蠡，陋劣者

卻妲己、褒姒，固不得與簡逖、陳豐同登於籍矣。下者不復次，作〈菊表〉六品。秋明主人再識。」列表評次百種菊，分以下二等六品：

「神品上上」：要眇奪天，不可思議，曰「神」：「國色天香」、「含煙鋪錦」、「白玉纏光」、「粉鍼」、「紫緹」、「軟枝桃紅」、「贏師管」、「七寶盤」、「六郎面」、「瑛盤」、「黃玉琮」、「海紅蓮」、「珊瑚枝」、「二喬」、「金膏水碧」、「松鍼」、「紫鍼」、「玉毫光」、「蜜荷」、「水精球」、「落紅萬點」、「紫茸」、「玉連環」、「雪蓮臺」、「紫薇郎」、「鷺鷥管」、「琥珀蓮」、「紫龍鬚」，共二十八種。

「妙品上中」：離立精湛，機趣自然，曰「妙」：「追金琢玉」、「粉鶴翎」、「綠荷衣」、「脂瓣」、「截肪玉」、「金鍼」、「紫霞觴」、「金絲樓」、「紫荷衣」、「珊瑚雪」、「紫袍金帶」、「金鳳羽」、「波斯帽」、「松子菊」、「天孫錦」，共十五種。

「逸品上下」：蕭散澹穆，灑然高從，曰「逸」：「金剪絨」、「綠衣黃裳」、「靚裝西子」、「銀繡球」、「蠟盤」、「白鮫綃」、「玉芙蓉」、「紫羅襦」、「銀鳳羽」，共九種。

「雋品中上」：邈如自遠，沖潔深靜，曰「雋」：「硃砂盤」、「銀鶴氅」、「栗留黃」、「紫金盤」、「青心玉」、「海獻金球」、「紫裝」、「雨闌紅」、「朝陽素」、「杏花頤」、「姑射肌」、「檀香盤」，共十二種。

「妍品中中」：姽嫿汋約，標穠逞媚，曰「妍」：「白鳳」、「海雲紅」、「麴粉」、「粉撚線」、「柘枝黃」、「旨藟」、「福橘紅」、「虎皮蓮」、「錦邊蓮」、「紅絲玉」、「解環縲」、「粉翠」、「金撚線」、「檀香球」、「粉粱竹」，共十五種。

「韻品中下」：孤標迴若，澹宕入微，曰「韻」：「金絲蓮」、「金海棠」、「粉蝴蝶」、「紫翠蓮」、「碧桃紅」、「大金輪」、「銀牡丹」、「青蓮」、「御愛黃」、「楊妃晚裝」、「燈下黃」、「銀撚線」、「玉玲瓏」、「金芙蓉」、「繡芙蓉」、「麴紫」、「錦心繡口」、「粉裝」、「粉心蓮」、「佛手黃」、「一粒球」，共二十一種。

茲選照二開，為內封面葉與慎親王胤禧〈序〉首半葉，以及弘皎〈菊譜小引〉末半葉與正文首半葉。

此書另有清光緒十五年（1889年）樂椒軒重刻本，題「懷古閣藏版」。

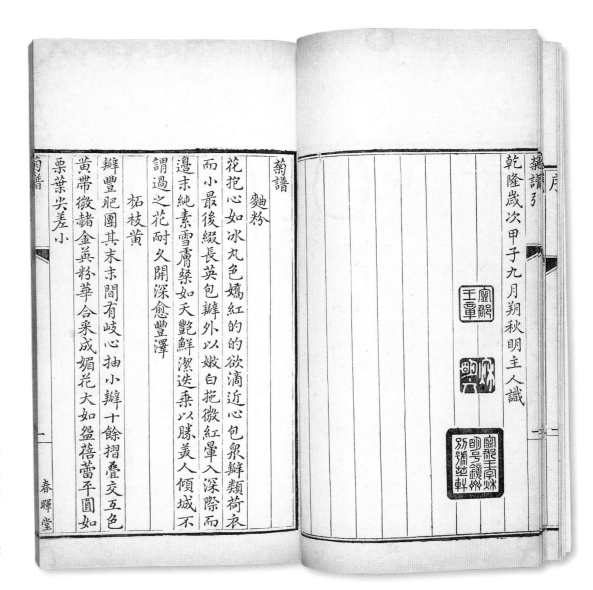

21

Jinyu tu pu

Illustrated Manual on Goldfish

Qing dynasty (1644-1911), Daoguang period (1821-1850)

Compiled by Gouqu shannong (act. mid-19th century)

N.p.: Yingxing shuwu, 1848

8 columns per half-folio of text; 20 characters per column; no folding margin at center of folio; inner single-line borders for text blocks; outer decorative borders for all blocks; overall dimensions of volume: 28.9 x 16.5 cm; block sizes of decorative borders, approx. 18.4 x 12.5 cm; block sizes of texts, approx. 13.0 x 9.5 cm; block sizes of illustrations, approx. 13.2 x 9.5 cm block; stitched binding

15899

Goldfish (*Carassius auratus*), domesticated descendants of the grayish or olive-colored crucian carp, are native to southeastern China and were mentioned in Chinese literature as early as the seventh century. When first discovered in significant numbers around Hangzhou and Jiaxing in Zhejiang province during the Northern Song dynasty (960-1127), they were considered sacred and left to breed naturally, but in the Southern Song period (1127-1279) they began to be raised in ponds by the imperial family, aristocrats, and scholar-officials as ornamental fish. Later, as the number of varieties multiplied, goldfish were kept in jars or tubs and became popular with people from all walks of life. They were introduced to Japan in 1502 and to Europe in the 1700s where they were much appreciated and illustrated.

Goldfish were mentioned in many Ming books, such as in *juan* 3 of the *Kaopan yushi* (4

juan) of 1592 by Tu Long (1542-1605) and the *Zhu sha yu pu* (Manual on Vermilion Fish) of 1596 by Zhang Qiande (Zhang Chou) (1577-1643?). The latter work, which existed only in manuscript form until its publication in 1914, dispenses advice such as the following: "The important thing is to keep as many kinds of goldfish as possible while their selection should be very strict. Buy several thousand at the fair each summer and raise

them in different jars. Get rid of undesirable ones until only one or two per cent remain. These are placed in two or three jars and bred with special care. In this way, you will be in possession of all sorts of marvelous fish."

The first comprehensive illustrated manuals on goldfish did not appear until the Qing dynasty (1644-1911). One such work is the National Library of China's *Jinyu tu pu* of 1848, the author of which is known only by the pseudonym "Gouqu shannong" (The Mountain Farmer Who is Crooked and Bent). In the preface, the author states that no ancient manuals on goldfish have survived, and that more recent ones, though well illustrated, are all too brief as far as descriptive and explanatory texts are concerned. In response to the situation, the author compiled the textual portion of this manual with information gleaned from encyclopaedic collections such as the *Bencao gangmu* (Classified Materia Medica) compiled by Li Shizhen (1518-1593), the *Qun fang pu* [also known as *Er'ru ting Qun fang pu*] (28 *juan, juan shou*) compiled by Wang Xiangjin (1561-1653; *jinshi* of 1604) in 1630, the *Hua jing* [also known as *Bi chuan Hua jing*] (6 *juan*) compiled by Chen Haozi (fl. 1688) in 1688, and the *Gezhi jingyuan* (100 *juan*) compiled by Chen Yuanlong (1652-1736) in 1735.

The eleven specific topics discussed in the text portion of the *Jinyu tu pu* of 1848 are as follows: the origins of goldfish, rearing goldfish in ponds, rearing goldfish in jars, selective mating, care of newly hatched fry, distinguishing colors and hues, recognizing certain attributes and characteristics, feeding, treatment of sick goldfish, distinguishing between genders, and ways of acquiring and admiring goldfish. One passage on mating provides the following counsel, "In selecting fish for mating, choose a male of excellent variety that complements the female in color, type, and size," emphasizing that careful and conscious efforts in artificial selection can enable breeders to raise fascinating varieties of goldfish with specific and desirable physical characteristics that appeal to the market. New types of goldfish included bizarre varieties with fan, fringe, or veil tails and sometimes with double or triple fins, and some with bulging telescopic eyes. Scaled gold-

fish have a metallic sheen of red, gold, white, silver, or black, while the rarer "scaleless" varieties actually have transparent scales and appear in bright red, blue, shades of purple, and calico patterns.

The illustrated portion, however, was based almost entirely on an earlier goldfish manual compiled by a person surnamed Xue, and depicted fifty-four types of goldfish. All of those are reproduced in this work, and two additional varieties not present in Xue's manual are appended at the end of the 1848 book. Here, the goldfish and water-plants are illustrated in various color combinations and hues of red, vermilion, yellow, black, brown, green, and blue.

Interestingly, one of the earliest extant ex-

amples of Chinese portrayals of goldfish may be found in a handscroll in the Musée National d'Histoire Naturelle in Paris. Painted in Beijing in 1772 by a Chinese Christian convert named Aloysius Ko, it depicts no less than ninety-two colorful goldfish in the manner of Western scientific illustration. The first European book about Chinese goldfish appeared soon after the scroll's arrival in Europe. Two illustrated editions (in quarto and octavo) of the *Histoire naturelle des dorades de la Chine* by Louis Edme Billardon de Sauvigny (1736-1812) were published in 1780 by Louis Jorry in Paris and feature fifty-six varieties of goldfish engraved by François Nicolas Martinet (b. 1731).

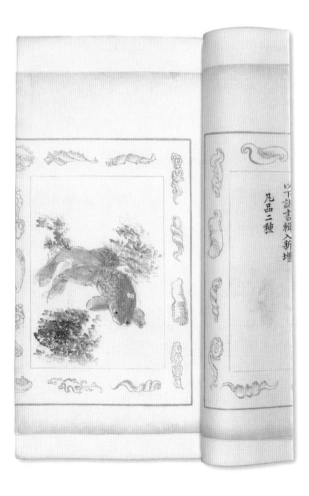

21

金魚圖譜不分卷

清句曲山農撰。清道光二十八年（1848年）景行書屋刻套印本。半葉八行，行二十字，小字雙行，版心白口，正文內框四周單邊，正文及圖外框四周花邊。花邊框高一八・四厘米，寬一二・五厘米。正文框高一三厘米，寬九・五厘米。圖框高一三・二米，寬九・五厘米。綫裝。

15899

　　金魚是中國人民樂於飼養的觀賞魚類。它身姿奇異，色彩絢麗，可說是一種天然的活的藝術品。根據史料的記載和近代科學實驗的資料，金魚起源於中國普通食用的野生鯽魚。它先由銀灰色的野生鯽魚變為紅黃色的金鯽魚，然後再經過不同時期的家養，由紅黃色金鯽魚逐漸演變成為各個不同品種的金魚。

　　金魚發現於晉朝（公元265至420年），其故鄉為浙江省嘉興、杭州兩地，自南宋開始家養。根據史料記載，1330年前後金魚已傳到鎮江和北京。到明正德年間（1506至1521年），北京皇宮的「南城」（即今北京市南池子附近）養有許多金魚。此後許多地方都用盆缸養育金魚。中國金魚傳到日本的最早記錄是1502年，傳到法國、英國是在十七世紀末葉，到十八世紀中葉，雙尾金魚已傳遍歐洲各國，傳到美國是在1874年。

　　現存有關中國古代金魚的專著書籍不多，其中明萬曆二十四年（1596年）蘇州人張謙德所著的《硃沙魚譜》，為描述金魚形態及飼養方法最詳盡最科學的古籍之一。

　　中國國家圖書館所藏的《金魚圖譜》，是現存最早附有彩圖的金魚專著。其內封面葉題「《金魚圖譜》。道光戊申，景行書屋」。撰者句曲山農，姓名不詳，其序文如下：「金魚譜舊無傳書。近人有譜，圖詳而說其略。今參取《本草綱目》、《群芳譜》、《格致鏡原》、《資生雜誌》、《培幼集》、《花鏡》諸書，薈錄為譜，以備譜錄之一。薛氏圖列魚五十四種，今附於後，樂間適性或有取焉。句曲山農識」。

　　此書正文部分有以下十一門：「原始」、「池畜」、「缸畜」、「配對」、「養苗」、「辨色」、「相品」、「飼食」、「療疾」、「識性」、「徵用」。撰者特別注重配對金魚，該門有此句：「咬

子時雄魚須擇佳品，與雌魚色類大小相稱」。可見在這個時期中國金魚的飼養已經進行有意識的人工選種。

　　本書文後附圖共五十六幅，以多色刊印。前五十四幅取自薛氏舊譜，其中有六種缺名。最後二幅，題「以下諸書輯入新增凡品二種」。本圖譜在繪畫技法中融入了西方透視的原理，畫面中的金魚有立體感，色彩鮮艷，栩栩如生。

　　茲選照內封面葉與序、正文首半葉、第一幅圖以及第五十六幅圖，後者上部印八行解說文字。

22

Shengping shu xiqu renwu hua ce

Albums of Beijing Opera Characters from the Shengping Bureau

Qing dynasty (1644-1911), undated, probably between Xianfeng period (1851-1861) and Tongzhi period (1862-1874)

Anonymous, attributed to the Qing palace painting atelier in Beijing, ca. 1851-1874

Set of 2 albums with a total of 97 leaves, ink, color, white pigment, and gold on silk; overall dimensions of each album: approx. 32.8-33.3 x 23.7-23.9 cm; each leaf, approx. 32.8 x 23.6 cm; each illustration, approx. 26.4 x 21.1 cm

17665

Beijing opera (*Jing ju*) has its origins in the regional musical and theatrical traditions of Hubei, Jiangxi, and Anhui provinces. It was first introduced to Beijing by visiting troupes from the southern provinces in 1790, became firmly established in the capital in the 1820s, and evolved into its mature form in the 1850s and 1860s when the *erhuang qiang* (from Jiangxi) and the *xipi qiang* (from Anhui) were combined. The resultant Beijing opera, therefore, is also known as *pihuang ju*. The costumes and facial make-up of all the characters are very elaborate and codified for the roles being played. Certain colors, for example, have specific associations or connotations: black is for loyalty, white for treachery, and red for bravery.

The Shengping Bureau (Shengping shu; "Bureau of Tranquillity and Peace") was the name of the court theatrical office established

in 1827 to replace the Southern Court (Nan fu), which had been in charge of theatrical performances by palace eunuchs since around 1740. The number of actors under the charge of the Shengping Bureau, a unit of the Office of Palace Ceremonial (Zhangyi si) in the Imperial Household Department (Neiwu fu), ranged between 60 and 110. They were responsible for staging regular dramatic productions twice a month (on the first and fifteenth days of the lunar calendar) and also on special occasions such as imperial birthdays and major festivals. Many of the actors

were court eunuchs and all performers received their professional training at the Shengping Bureau until 1860, when outsiders were for a brief time allowed to present their craft before the Xianfeng emperor (1831-1861; r. 1851-1861), and again from 1884 through 1910.

The characters featured in these albums are all actors in the *luantan* mode of Beijing opera. Vivid colors were applied onto the ivory-colored silk, with the sumptuous costumes and striking facial masks depicted in great detail. The actors are shown in various stances and with evocative gestures. All the parts being played are identified by small characters written in regular script at the upper right of each leaf. There are a number of mistakes in these identifications, reflecting the somewhat poor command of the Chinese language by

collection. The 97 leaves contained within these two albums are part of a much larger corpus of paintings of unknown number in the same format; numerous other leaves may be found elsewhere in Beijing among the collections of the Palace Museum and the

novel "Casual Talks on the Chou'e" about the notoriously wicked late Ming palace eunuch Wei Zhongxian (1568-1627). The characters depicted are the *zhuangyuan* ("Principal Graduate"), the *zhizhou* ("Department Magistrate"), Sun Wukong ("Monkey God"), and the *shui mu* ("Mother Jellyfish"). The opera tells of a mother jellyfish who inhabits an underwater crystal palace at Rainbow Bridge near the city of Sizhou in Anhui province. After spending a millennium in religious meditation, she has acquired supernatural powers but nevertheless yearns for the joys of secular life. She becomes enamored of the attractive and talented son of the department magistrate of Sizhou and marries him. He later flees from her with a pearl enabling him to travel safely through water, and she retaliates in fury by flooding Sizhou. Eventually Guanyin, the Bodhisattva of Compassion, arrives and saves the day by subduing the jellyfish. The other two leaves feature the characters Zhu Wen and Bian Yisui from the opera *Taiping qiao* ("The Bridge of Great Peace").

artisans working in the palace painting atelier. Leaves featuring the leading characters of the nine productions are not only inscribed with the title but also contain an additional column of text each at the lower middle right edges which were apparently added after the albums left the palace

Chinese Academy of Arts (Zhongguo yishu yanjiu suo).

Of the six leaves selected from one of the albums, the first four are from the opera *Sizhou cheng* ("The City of Sizhou"; also known as "Presenting a Pearl at Rainbow Bridge"), which is based on a story from the

22
昇平署戲曲人物畫册

清內府書畫處書畫人繪。無年月，應繪於清咸豐同治年間
(1815-1874年)。絹底彩繪本。二册，共九十七幅圖。每頁高三
二‧八厘米，寬二三‧六厘米。每圖高二六‧四厘米，寬二一‧
一厘米。册頁裝。
17665

昇平署位於北京市南長街南口路西，清初稱
為「南花園」，系宮廷種植花木、栽培盆景之處。
　　昇平署為內務府掌儀司的一部門，是清代掌
管宮廷專司戲班的機構。乾隆五年(1740年)設南
府，擢選內監，專司宮廷演戲事宜。道光七年
(1827年)改名為昇平署，改為戲劇機構後，隸屬
於內務府，對位置於西華門內的內務府而言，稱此
處為「南府」。直至清末，由內務府大臣統轄，除
了內廷以外，兼管民間戲班。人數則大見縮減，從
原來的兩千人，減少到四百人，後來不斷遞減，最
少時，只有六十餘人。宮廷內每逢朔望節令、喜慶
大典以及某些日常演出，大都由昇平署所屬演員承
應。演員有宮內太監，也有民間的職業演員。
　　《昇平署戲曲人物畫册》收集中國京劇人物扮
相寫真圖。畫册雖無文字載年代，應為清咸豐同治
間(1851-1874年)宮廷畫師作品。二册中有《泗
洲城》十二幅、《太平橋》八幅、《空城計》十幅、
《玉玲瓏》六幅、《落馬湖》十幅、《普天樂》二
十三幅、《千秋嶺》六幅、《蔡天化》十二幅以及
《反西涼》十幅，共九十七幅。每一出劇的劇中人
名下邊皆有一行小楷：「穿戴臉兒俱照此樣」。應
是從清宮流散以後，收買者所加上。故宮博物院所
藏若干幅、梅蘭芳舊藏若干幅與此畫册是同一來
源。
　　所畫全部劇目屬於「亂彈」劇種，即京劇。
「亂彈」名詞苦難索解。亂彈劇本，與彈詞頗近。
彈詞盛於南，為南方之民間文學，亂彈盛於北，為
北方之民間文學，一傳之於音樂，而其義更顯。
　　此畫册繪製非常精細，是屬於帝后所用之
「御賞物」，而並不是為演員以及管理戲箱員當備
忘錄。該譜具有很高的藝術和資料價值，是研究京
劇早期穿戴、臉譜的珍貴史料。
　　茲選照第一册六幅畫。前四幅為《泗洲城》之
「狀元」、「知州」、「孫悟空」與「水母」。泗

州城附近之虹橋，有水母娘娘，在水晶宮中，已修
煉千年，然貪戀紅塵，凡念未絕。一日見泗州太守
之子時廷芳，風度翩翩，心竊愛之。廷芳赴京趕
考，路過虹橋，水母施展法術，將時攝至水府，欲
偕伉儷。廷芳懼禍臨身，假意應充，後一夕，發現
水母衣襟之上，綴有避水珠一顆，乃向水母索取。
水母以愛公子心誠，欣然相贈。公子遂將水母灌
醉，懷珠而逃。及水母酒醒，不見公子，知已逃
去，不禁怒火中燒，率領族眾，水淹泗州，勒令太
守還珠並允與其子成親。太守求觀世音相救，觀世
音恐大水殃及百姓，召天神天將擒之。水母與之相
抗。菩薩幻化一老嫗，哭於道旁。水母問故，老嫗
言口中乾渴，心如火焚，是以啼哭。水母憐之，以
桶中清水相贈。正飲時，水母發現老嫗行跡可疑，
恐非凡人，急奪水桶。觀世音亦復原形，雙方爭
斗。觀世音復化作賣麵老嫗伺候道旁。水母與天神
天將爭斗良久，不意麵條化為鎖練，拴其肺腑，遂
被擒。此劇源出於神話傳說，《樵杌閑評》載其
事。元明雜劇有泗州大聖淹水母，為京劇泗州城藍
本。據《清代伶官傳》，此劇清咸豐十一年孫小六
始演於內廷。

後二幅為《太平橋》之「朱溫」與「卞宜隨」
(所題「卞宜隨」應指「卞應遂」)。晉王李克用與
梁王朱溫有宿怨。克用巡視河南，朱溫命其弟朱義
婉請李至汴梁赴宴，周德威諫阻，李不聽，竟偕部
將史敬思欣然前往。甫入席，朱溫托辭轉入內室。
朱妻王鸞英，原系皇室之女，朱溫初隨黃巢破京時
據為己妻，鸞英因恨朱溫謀篡，將設伏謀害之事乘
機向李透露。史敬思聞之，疾保克用乘機逃走。朱
溫據報立斬鸞英，并率從將追趕。史敬思護李克用
至太平橋，不意伏兵四起，為梁將卞應遂所乘，被
刺傷，史敬思立斬卞應遂，并裹傷再戰，因力不
敵，遂自刎。克用敗走，幸遇李存孝送糧至，始得
救。朱溫畏存孝之勇，追兵乃止。

23

Wenmei zhai Bai hua shi jian pu

The Hundred Flowers Poetry-Writing Paper from the Wenmei Studio

Qing dynasty (1644-1911), Xuantong period (1909-1911)

Illustrated by Zhang Zhaoxiang (fl. 1892-1907)

Tianjin: Wenmei zhai, 1911

No folding margin at center of folio; decorative borders; overall dimensions of volumes: 29.3 x 18.0 cm; block sizes of illustrations: approx. 23.7 x 15.0 cm; stitched binding

16218

The decorative "poetry-writing papers" (*shi jian pu*) produced by the Wenmei Studio in Tianjin continue the tradition of late Ming Nanjing productions of decorated stationery (*jian pu*) such as the *Luoxuan biangu jian pu* (The Wisteria Studio Album of Stationery Decorated with Ancient and Modern Designs) printed by Wu Faxiang (1579-1660) in 1626, and the *Shizhu zhai jian pu* (The Ten Bamboo Studio Manual Decorative Writing Papers) printed by Hu Zhengyan (1582-1673) in 1644.

The Tianjin-based artist Zhang Zhaoxiang's reputation as a painter of intimate garden vignettes featuring a wide variety of flowers, fruits, and plants was well established by the third quarter of the nineteenth century during the Tongzhi period (1862-1874). His work is represented by the exquisite illustrations for the multiple-color woodblock-printed *Bai hua tu pu* (Illustrated Manual of a Hundred Flowers). In addition to Chinese traditions of floral painting, Zhang

Zhaoxiang was almost certainly aware of important woodblock-illustrated scientific works such as the *Zhiwu mingshi tu kao* (Illustrated Study of the Names and Dispositions of Plants) compiled by Wu Qijun (1789-1874) and first printed in 1848, as well as botanical illustrations from the West which are known to have circulated during the late nineteenth and early twentieth centuries in cosmopolitan Tianjin. Although Zhang and the master of the Wenmei Studio did not name the specimens depicted, they are portrayed so well that for the most part they can be easily identified.

Many editions of this work exist, bearing the same title and preface but with different selections of illustrations and with different layouts. For example, certain editions are printed with flowers only on the recto of each folio with the verso left blank, while others contain illustrations on both recto and verso. The flowers depicted are not arranged in seaonal sequence or in any systematic way. This two-volume set from the National Library of China has title slips on the exterior of the front covers (pink on vol. 1, pale green on vol. 2); these and the preface were written by the calligrapher, painter, and

colors of [the paintings of] Mr. Yun has become all too difficult to encounter.

Mr. Zhang He'an [Zhang Zhaoxiang] of Xijin [Tianjin] is well versed in the Six Laws, and furthermore is skilled in [paintings of] cut branches of flowers and plants; there are no connoisseurs in China who do not consider him a reincarnation of Nantian [Yun Shouping]. The master of the Wenmei Studio has utilized the paintings of flowers and plants [by Zhang] for making a hundred examples of poetry-writing paper, engraving them onto woodblocks to promote their circulation; they are exact copies which perfectly match [the originals] and their dispositions are exceedingly beautiful. Is this not [reminiscent of] the statement "When Zhao Chang [ca. 960-after 1016, a Sichuanese painter known for his close studies of nature] paints flowers, he writes out their forms; when Xu Xi [d. before 975, the greatest bird-and-flower painter of antiquity] paints flowers, he gives fame to their spirits?"

Now that the engraving has been completed, I am writing down these words as a gift. It is presently the eighth month during the autumn of the *bingwu* year of the Guangxu reign period [1906]; written in the imperial capital by Zhang Zuyi from Tongcheng.

epigrapher Zhang Zuyi (1849-1917), a native of Tongcheng in Anhui who was later active in Shanghai. The preface is translated here in full:

The marvels of calligraphy and painting are attained through the heart and mind and cannot be easily sought through [mere] formal likeness. Critics of painting from the past considered "spirit resonance" (*shenyun*) as the highest quality and "formal likeness" (*jixiang*) as secondary. Nevertheless, one cannot omit either

"spirit resonance" or "formal likeness." Those from ancient and modern times who excelled in [paintings of] flowers and plants cannot be enumerated. During the present dynasty, Mr. Yun Nantian [Yun Shouping; 1633-1690] produced fine delicate drawings (*gongbi*) of nature, in which the spirit and disposition of the flowers were equally true to life; they can be said to be the most competent [of such paintings] in the artistic world. Since this time, the artistry exemplified by the [apparent] emitted fragrances and vivid

The "Six Laws" mentioned by Zhang Zuyi are those mentioned in the *Gu hua pin lu* (Old Record of the Classification of Painters) by the critic Xie He (act. ca. 500-535) of the Southern Qi dynasty (479-502), who listed them in the following order: *qiyun shengdong* (spirit resonance which means vitality); *gufa yongbi* (bone method, a way of using the brush); *yingwu xiangxing* (correspondence to the object which means the depicting of forms); *suilei fucai* (suitability to type which has to do with the laying on of colors); *jingying weizhi* (division and planning, i.e., placing and arrangement); and *chuanyi moxie* (transmission by copying, that is to say the copying of models).

The designs in this stationery catalogue were printed on individual sheets of ornamental paper, which in turn would have been stored in elegant stationery boxes. Because the designs were printed with vivid, multiple colors so as to make them appear as if they were paintings on paper, they would probably not have been written over as in the case of other kinds of decorated stationery printed with more delicate patterns in paler shades. By virtue of their short lines, poems would easily fit into the blank remaining spaces on the *Wenmei zhai Bai hua shi jian pu*. However, these papers were so exquisitely printed and finely embossed that they were often kept in pristine condition and not used even for the lofty purpose of inscribing poetry.

The first volume of this particular set contains large representations of various individual blossoms or sprays occupying the centers of the spaces framed by decorative borders; many of the designs do evoke the paintings of the great early Qing flower painter Yun Shouping, as rightly observed in the preface. The second volume has somewhat reduced floral and pictorial compositions (with animals or objects), some of which are placed asymmetrically along one side of the framed space. In addition, this volume features a number of embossed designs using the so-called *gonghua* technique (known in the West as *gauffrage*), which are so delicate that they can barely be discerned unless examined at very close range. There are no blank pages in either volume; both sides of

every folio are printed with illustrations.

In the first of the selected double-page spreads, there is a branch of the crape-myrtle (*ziwei* or *bai ri hong*; *Lagerstroemia indica*) to the right, while a single stalk of the polyanthus narcissus (*shui xian*; *Narcissus tazetta* var. *chinensis*) is juxtaposed against the nandina (*nan tian zhu* or *tian zhu*; *Nandina domestica*) at left. While there is no inherent relationship between the pictured plants, their placement on facing leaves demonstrates the artist's considerable aesthetic sense in balancing and contrasting colors, forms, and seasonal characteristics. In this particular case, the crinkly, pink-blossomed and oval-leaved crape-myrtle depicted by Zhang Zhaoxiang blooms outdoors with great aplomb in mid to late summer, while the narcissus buds in late winter and traditionally welcomes the spring with its pure white petals and yellow-orange cups; the bulbs are often grown indoors in basins during the lunar New Year. The nandina, which normally has dainty compound leaves that change color from pink to bronze to dark green to scarlet in the course of a year, is shown without foliage but with the attractive bright vermilion berries that adorn it for much of the winter season. The wide variety of flowers illustrated within this first volume are pictorially unified, since each composition occupies roughly the same amount of space on each leaf, and the subject is placed at the center but weighted towards the lower edge of the sheets, leaving more blank space at the top.

The other double-page spread is taken from the second volume. Shown at right are twin stalks of the anemone-centered chrysanthemum (*ju hua*; *Chrysanthemum indicum*) which flowers in autumn; it is paired with a branch of the purple-leaved amaranth (*san se xian* or *yan lai hong*; *Amaranthus tricolor*),

the unusual hue of which chromatically complements the simple yellow chrysanthemums. Illustrated on the facing leaf is the most exotic of all aquatic garden plants, the summer-blooming sacred lotus (*he hua*; *Nelumbo nucifera*); the gently curving stems of the rich pink blossom and the lotus leaves are wonderfully enhanced by a minimum number of brown reeds. The many subtleties found in this volume are further enhanced by exquisite *gonghua* embossing in very low relief, which is difficult to see except at very close range and in raking light. The one detail chosen here, also from the second volume, is Zhang Zhaoxiang's superb rendition of another flowering plant of the mid to late summer, the aconite or azure monkshood (also known as wolfsbane; *wutou*; *Aconitum carmichaelii*) with delicate *gonghua* embossing that adds a certain corporeality to the showy, deep blue helmet-like flowers borne on spikes.

23

文美齋百華詩箋譜不分卷

簡稱《百華詩箋譜》，一名《鄃庵百華詩箋》。清張兆祥繪。張祖翼序。清宣統三年（1911年）五月天津文美齋刻彩色套印本。四周花邊，外框二三・七厘米，寬一五・○厘米。綫裝。
16218

中國早期箋譜的佳作多出於金陵，如明天啟六年（1626年）吳發祥編印的《蘿軒變古箋譜》及南明弘光元年（1645年）胡正言編印《十竹齋箋譜》。吳氏與胡氏之箋譜均用「餖版」彩色套印，并以「拱花」技術無色凸板壓印，刊印傳世傑作箋譜。

天津文美齋所編印的《百華詩箋譜》，繼承晚明箋譜精工富麗的傳統．繪者張兆祥，號鄃庵，一作穌盦，河北天津人。善畫花鳥，尤長於折枝花卉，設色妍雅，備極工緻，多受清初畫家惲壽平的影響。文美齋主人將張氏所繪的圖加以梓版，採用餖版套印和拱花技術而刊印百幅圖，有牡丹、芍藥、蘭花、梅花、菊花、萬年青、紫丁香等等。圖皆秀麗生動、色彩鮮艷、詩意盎然，富有立體感，為晚清箋譜之佳作。

此箋譜有多種版本行世，如單純彩色套印本、彩色套印押花本、彩色套印橫幅本等。中國國家圖書館所藏此部《文美齋百華詩箋譜》二冊，其

中上冊為彩色套印本，下冊為彩色套印押花本。二冊各有張祖翼題簽，題「百華詩箋譜。光緒丙午中元，磊盦署」。上冊內封面葉上半葉題「文美齋詩箋譜。桐城張祖翼題」，下半葉題「宣統三年歲次辛亥五月刊成」。

詩箋譜前有張祖翼光緒三十二年（1906年）序：「書畫之妙，當以神會，難以形求。故世之評畫者，以神韻為上，跡象次之。然神韻、跡象缺一不可。古今工花卉者，不可勝數。至我朝，惲南田先生出以工筆寫生，花之精神與花之狀態，皆栩栩

欲活，可謂極藝林之能事矣。自是而後，術如惲先生之生香活色，夏戛其難之。柝津張穌盦先生精六法，尤工折枝花卉，海內賞鑒家莫不許為南田後身。文美齋主人以所畫花卉製為詩箋百幅，鑄版行世，侔色揣稱，盡態極妍，所謂『趙昌畫花寫花形，徐熙畫花名花神』者邪。鏤既竣，為書數語以贈。時光緒丙午秋八月，桐城張祖翼書於京師」。

茲選照詩箋譜五幅畫。其中選於上冊彩色套印本的相對一葉為「紫薇」及「水仙、南天竹」。紫薇（別名百日紅、滿堂紅、海棠樹等），花夏七月間開，叢生花於枝末，秋猶不落，世呼百日紅。水仙，一作水儒，是中國民間的清供佳品。其花純白色，副花冠亮黃色至深黃色，寒冬臘月開出素雅芳香的花朵，帶著生氣和春意。南天竹（別名天竺、萬壽子等），春花穗生白微紅，夏間開小白花，冬結子如豌豆正碧色，至冬色漸變如紅豆顆，朱紅纍纍如珊瑚，圓正可愛。木身上生小枝葉，葉相對而頗類竹。臘後始凋，世傳以為子碧如玉，南方人多植於庭檻之間。

選於下冊彩色套印押花本的相對一葉為「黃菊、通身紫色三色莧」及「荷花、水草」。黃菊為菊花中較古樸的品種之一，而三色莧（別名老少年、十樣錦、雁來紅）為觀葉植物，多種於園圃。荷花為水花之極大者，六月花開。最後為下冊一幅局部，描繪的是多年生草木「烏頭」（別名草烏、烏藥、鹽烏頭、奚毒、耿子等），春時莖初生有腦形似烏鳥之頭，故謂之烏頭。花期九、十月，花藍紫色。

滄浪亭印心石屋圖

Part 2: Epigraphical and pictorial rubbings

第 二 部 ：金 石

24a-b

Ke you wenzi de jiagu wen

Inscribed Oracle Bones

24a

Shang dynasty (ca. 1600-ca. 1100 B.C.), undated, from the reigns of the kings Zu Geng (ca. 1188-ca. 1178 B.C.) and Zu Jia (ca. 1177-ca. 1158 B.C.)

Turtle plastron fragments

Four fragments; dimensions vary (a: 5.8 x 7.1 cm; b: 7.0 x 5.5 cm; c: 6.5 x 6.3 cm; d: 5.9 x 4.5 cm)

Jiagu 5521, 5538, 5518, 6019

24b

Shang dynasty (ca. 1600-ca. 1100 B.C.), undated, from the reign of the king Wu Ding (ca. 1198-ca. 1189 B.C.)

Ox scapula fragments

Two fragments; dimensions vary (a: 4.8 x 7.5 cm; b: 27.7 x 15.2 cm)

Jiagu 5402, 5403

Royal divination was one of the central institutions of the Shang dynasty (ca. 1600-ca. 1100 B.C.) and the names of more than 120 Shang diviners, serving the last nine kings, are known to historians. Topics of divination ranged from the performance of the ancestral cult, apotropaic wishes for "no harm" in the next ten-day week, questions regarding the outcome of royal hunts, harvests, or childbirth, queries on impending disasters, enemy invasions, victory in battle, good fortune, or bad omens. Royal diviners obtained the scapulae (shoulder blades) of cattle and sheep that had been ritually sacrificed and turtle plastrons (ventral shells) or carapaces, and cracked them by applying hot metal rods or heated sticks of chaste wood to

hollows on the rough (back) sides so that T-shaped fissures would appear on the smooth (front) sides.

Although the diviners formulated the charges and oversaw the divinatory rituals, with few exceptions, only the king–who is sometimes referred to in the bones as "I, the one man" (*yu yi ren*)–had the prerogative to make pronouncements regarding the cracks, which could be interpreted as auspicious,

inauspicious, or neutral. The Shang king's monopoly of the critical act of interpretation may well be understood in terms of his kinship to the ancestors. After the king had made his forecast or interpretation, the number of each crack, along with the occasional "crack notation" about the good fortune of a particular crack, was incised beside it. A complete record of the divination, probably drafted on perishable material, was then incised into the bone or shell. The incised characters and the cracks were occasionally filled with vermilion or black pigments. After a certain period of time, whenever the usefulness of oracle bones had expired, they were buried in storage pits.

Oracle-bone inscriptions are the earliest form of recognizable writing in China. They are most commonly called *jiagu wen* ("writing on shell and bone"), which is short for *guijia shougu wenzi* ("writing on turtle shell and animal bone"), but are also known as *qi wen* ("inscribed script"), *zhenbu wenzi* ("oracular script"), or *Yinxu wenzi* ("script from the Yin ruins"), Yinxu being the name used since at least the Han dynasty for Yin, the final capital of the Shang, after its destruction. Variations exist in the structural configuration and size of the script, while the characters were written in many different ways. In general, however, the inscriptions are placed vertically in columns and read from top to bottom, with the arrangement of the characters depending on the shape of the turtle shell or animal bone used. Because thin strokes are predominant in oracle-bone inscriptions, the characters often appear to be written rather than incised.

Since their initial identification by the scholars Wang Yirong (1845-1900) and Liu E (1857-1909) in 1899, and the subsequent discovery by Luo Zhenyu (1866-1940) of their source at Xiaotun, Henan province, in 1908, more than 200,000 oracle bones or fragments of bones have been unearthed from Xiaotun alone; 50,000 of these bear decipherable inscriptions, and still more have been found elsewhere in China. Of the more than 3,000 graphs found on oracle bones, about 800 can be interpreted. The early finds of oracle bones allowed Luo's student Wang Guowei (1877-1927) to authenticate the names of

Shang kings listed in chapter 3 of Sima Qian's *Shi ji* (Records of the Grand Historian), and made it possible for the scholar Dong Zuobin (1895-1963) to establish a systematic chronology for the Shang.

The National Library of China has a very large collection of inscribed oracle bones, numbering 34,512 individual pieces. More than 28,000 of these are from the collection of Liu Tizhi (1879-1963), while 420 very fine specimens are from the collection of Luo Zhenyu. The library also possesses 70,677 sheets of rubbings taken from inscribed oracle bones. Most of these were published between 1978 and 1983 in the thirteen-volume *Jiagu wen he ji* compiled by the Chinese Academy of Social Sciences under the direction of Guo Moruo (1892-1978) and the editorship of Hu Houxuan (1911-1995).

24A-B

刻有文字的甲骨

24A

龜甲: 刻有商代（公元前十六世紀至公元前十一世紀）
祖庚、祖甲時祭祀祖先之卜辭。四片。
甲骨 *5521, 5538, 5518, 6019*

24B

獸骨: 刻有商代（公元前十六世紀至公元前十一世紀）武
丁時旬卜王事之卜辭。二片。
甲骨 *5402, 5403*

甲骨文，亦稱「契文」、「卜辭」、「龜甲文字」、「殷墟文字」、「貞卜文字」。因多鐫刻、書寫於龜甲、獸骨之上，故名。殷商時王朝占卜吉凶，常採用龜甲獸骨寫刻卜辭及與占卜有關的紀事文字。最初出土于河南省安陽小屯村之殷墟，當時不知是重要古物，或碾碎成粉作「刀尖藥」，或成批當作藥材中的「龍骨」。清光緒二十五年（1899年）為王懿榮、劉鶚等發現，二十九年（1903年）劉鶚著《鐵雲藏龜》，三十年（1904年）孫詒讓著《契文舉例》，始加以考釋。其後不斷發掘，約有十萬片以上。現知單字約近五千，有一千七百字左右可解讀，是中國目前最古文字，是研究當時社會歷史的重要資料。

甲骨文字是寫或刻在龜的腹骨、背骨，以及牛的肩胛骨上的文字。時間大約是從盤庚到帝辛滅亡前（相當公元前 1401 年至公元前 1122 年）。當時由於紙尚未發明，先民往往把所得的占卜之辭，刻在龜甲或獸骨上面。刻辭的內容，大都是殷王田獵、祭祀、求雨、詢問吉凶的紀事。

據甲骨學專家胡厚宣先生〈大陸現藏之甲骨文字〉發表一文，中國國家圖書館所藏較多的一批甲骨為劉體智先生舊藏，共二萬八千二百九十二片，裝楠木盒一百個。拓本題為《善齋所藏甲骨拓本》，共二十八本，一千三百四十一頁，其中缺號二，無字甲骨四，偽片一百十二，可以綴合者五十一，拼合成二十四版，實際劉氏藏二萬八千一百四十七片。所藏較早的一批為孟廣慧先生舊藏，有四百片，已選三百六十片著錄。所藏較精的一批為羅振玉先生舊藏，共三十二盒四百二十片，張仁蠡先生藏二百九十二片。抗戰期間的一批為胡厚宣先生

藏二千一百四十八片，其中一千九百片著錄於胡氏《戰後京津新獲甲骨集》。其他為羅伯昭、張珩、徐炳昶、郭若愚、何遂、曾毅公、邵伯炯及慶雲堂、通古齋、粹雅堂藏和文化部撥。所藏甲骨曾著錄於胡厚宣《戰後京津新獲甲骨集》、郭沫若《殷契粹編》、郭若愚《殷契拾掇》。據曾毅公先生所告，中國國家圖書館共藏三萬五千六百五十一片，除去偽片、無字等，實藏三萬四千五百十二片。

中國國家圖書館所藏甲骨拓片甚富，其中「善齋書契叢編甲骨拓本」收二萬八千一百九十四片，「北京圖書館所藏甲骨文字拓本全集」收三萬四千五百十二片，以及另外十項，總共十二項七萬六百七十七片。郭沫若主編、胡厚宣總編輯的《甲骨文合集》中收入了中國國家圖書館所藏甲骨拓本有十種之多，其中主要三種為「北京圖書館藏甲骨文字拓本」六冊，共五千四百零三片；「書契叢編」

十八冊四函，共二萬八千一百九十四片；「北京圖書館藏甲骨文字」，十三冊一函，共六百六十五片。

茲選祖庚、祖甲時祭祀祖先的龜甲四片及武丁時旬卜王事的獸骨二片，并附拓片，以便讀者分析甲骨上刻有的卜辭文字。

25

Quan Bo jia qingtong qi taben

Rubbings from the Inscribed Bronze Wine Vessel "Quan Bo" *Jia*

Shang dynasty (ca. 1600-ca. 1100 B.C.), undated
Hanging scroll, ink rubbed on paper, 132.8 x 53.1 cm;
height of rubbing of vessel: approx. 38.0 x 27.0 cm;
height of rubbing of inscription: approx. 9.0 x 3.0 cm
Date of rubbing not given; Qing dynasty (1644-1911),
late 19th-early 20th century

Biaozhou 512

Over the course of many decades, the National Library of China has assembled a collection of more than 3,000 rubbings taken from inscribed bronze vessels and instruments. The original artifacts were held in public or private collections, such as the Palace Museum in Beijing, the Baoyun lou collection, and collections which once belonged to Wu Shifen (1796-1856), Chen Jieqi (1813-1884), Duanfang (1861-1911), Luo Zhenyu (1866-1940), Liu Tizhi (1879-1963), Wang Chen (act. early 20th century), Chen Huaisheng, Zhang Zhihe, Zhang Wei, and others.

Some 2,000 of the rubbings are from vessels and instruments of the Shang, Zhou, and Warring States periods. A significant proportion of them are the so-called "full-figured rubbings" (*quanxing ta*) of bronze vessels. In making rubbings of this sort, the most ideal angle for recording the vessel must first be determined, followed by a careful sketch to take note of its overall shape, its surface curvatures, and its depth from front to rear. A graphite stylus is applied to sheets of

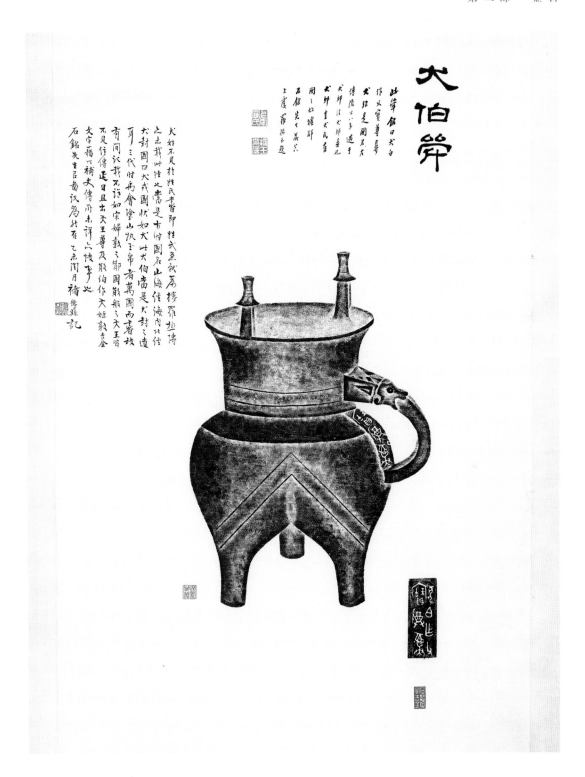

paper to make inverted "T" marks indicating the vessel's perpendicular points of reference. Height and width are indicated and a grid marked out. The finished perspective sketch is then transferred onto paper, which is moistened with "orchid liquid" and placed on the surface of the vessel. Only when the paper is almost dry is dark ink applied to the relief portions. This is repeated on as many different parts of a vessel as necessary and the resultant sheets are eventually joined to make a composite rubbing. Great skill, preferably acquired through training in perspective and draftsmanship, is required for making these kinds of rubbings on which proper gradations of dark and light ink bring out the three-dimensional aspects of the vessel. Although a considerable number of such rubbings were made after the Jiaqing period (1796-1820), not many have survived.

This "full-figured rubbing" was taken from a late Shang bronze vessel known from its inscription as the "Quan Bo" *jia*, the *jia* being a tripodal drinking vessel which also functioned as a ritual vessel used for storing and carrying wine. This type of vessel, produced between the late Shang and early Zhou periods, was consciously designed in a mannered way. It is similar to the *jue* in form but larger, with a rounded body that spreads at the lip and is surmounted by two capped columns, with a loop handle placed on one side of the body. A single or two character inscription placed on the inner surface of *jia* is typical of Shang period ritual bronzes and is probably the name of an ancestor or a clan. On later bronzes, however, the dedicatory inscriptions became much longer and more detailed. This "full-figured rubbing," mounted as a hanging scroll, was formerly in the collections of Luo Zhenyu and Chu Deyi (1871-1942), both eminent epigraphers

with significant collections of bronze vessels and rubbings.

The study of bronze inscriptions (*jin wen*) is of great importance for the dating, the determination of the identities of commissioners, and for establishing the specific function of a given object. Close examination of the form and decorative patterns can also be useful in deciphering and dating inscriptions. The large collection of such rubbings in the National Library of China has been used to correct errors present in standard epigraphical reference works such as Luo Zhenyu's *San dai jijin wencun* (Collection of Bronze Inscriptions from the Three Dynasties) of 1937.

25
犬伯斝青銅器拓本

原器商（公元前十六世紀至公元前十一世紀）時鑄。銘文七字，篆書。晚清拓本，年月不詳。全形拓。拓本紙高一三二・八厘米，寬五三・一厘米。拓片器高三八厘米，寬二七厘米；銘高九厘米，寬三厘米。立軸裝。

裱軸 512

中國國家圖書館幾十年間從公、私藏家手中收集了青銅器拓片三千餘件。拓片中原屬公藏的有故宮博物院藏器拓本以及寶蘊樓藏器拓本。原屬私藏的有陳介祺、劉體智、端方、孫壯、陳寶琛、羅振玉、王辰、吳式芬、陳淮生、張致和、張瑋等人所藏拓本。其中有相當一部分是青銅器全形拓本。全形拓，又稱器物拓、圖形拓、立體拓，出現約在清乾隆、嘉慶時代以後。全形拓的方法是：臨拓器物前先仔細揣摩所拓器物，選擇出更能代表該器物特徵的最佳角度，然後用鉛筆在準備好的綿連紙上畫出「⊥」形圖以表示器物的水平線和垂直綫，再

在「⊥」形圖上標出器物的高度、寬度點，并使兩點延伸呈示出器物的方格形，然後在方格中標畫出器物各部位的具體位置，并表示出近大遠小的器物透視關系。最後按圖上繪出的部位在所拓器物上若干次上紙上墨，完成全形拓。全形拓晚至清道光初年，嘉興馬傳巖，始從事於此。民國以來，當推金谿周希丁所拓為最佳。

此展出「犬伯斝」的青銅器全形拓。斝，音同「甲」。中國古代溫酒器，也用作祭祀時盛酒灌地的灌器。形如爵，但較大，有三足，兩柱，一鋬，圓口，平底，無流及尾。青銅斝主要盛行於商代。「犬伯斝」為低頸分襠式，侈口，頸圈甚矮，腹、深大，是商代晚期後段的典型式樣，僅器口之侈大不甚相同和柱式高低不甚相同而已。「犬伯斝」屬於商代晚期的青銅器，原器為張鈞衡舊藏。

此全形拓為羅振玉、褚德彝舊藏，有羅、褚題跋。羅振玉，字叔言、叔蘊，號雪堂，晚年更號貞松老人。江蘇淮安人，祖籍浙江上虞。清末奉召入京，任學部二等諮議官，後補參事官，兼京師大學堂農科監督。書法善篆、隸、楷、行，是創以甲骨文入書者之一。曾搜集和整理甲骨、銅器、簡牘、明器、佚書等考古資料，均有專集刊行。編著有《殷墟書契》、《殷墟書契菁華》、《三代吉金文存》等。褚德彝，原名德儀，避宣統諱更名德彝，字松窗、守隅等，號禮堂，又作里堂，別號漢威、舟枕山民等，浙江餘杭人。篆刻家，考古家，善書法。編著有《金石學續錄》、《竹人錄續》、《松窗遺印》等。

26

Ya 'qi' fu jia you qingtong qi taben

Rubbings from the Inscribed Bronze Wine Vessel "Ya 'Qi' Fu" Jia *You*

Shang dynasty (ca. 1600-ca. 1100 B.C.), undated
Hanging scroll, ink rubbed on paper, with inscribed colophons, ink on paper, 90.9 x 41.9 cm; sheet with rubbing, approx. 64.5 x 41.9 cm; sheet with colophons, approx. 26.3 x 41.9 cm; dimensions of vessel on rubbing: 36.0 x 27.0 cm; dimensions of rubbing of text on vessel: 7.0 x 4.0 cm; dimensions of rubbings of text on cover: 8.0 x 5.0 cm
Qing dynasty (1644-1911) rubbing, dated by inscription to 1887

Biaozhou 521

The *you*, a wine bucket or wine container, first appeared in the later part of the Shang dynasty (ca. 1600-ca. 1100 B.C.) and remained popular during the early period of the Western Zhou (ca. 1100-771 B.C.). It is shaped like a large oval-bodied *hu* vessel and has a swing handle and a lid. Its lower body is usually bellied and stands on a high, slightly spreading foot or on four bird feet. At the point at which it meets the body, the handle is surmounted by animal heads. By the late Western Zhou period there were no longer ritual vessels of the *you* type. Although a large number of *you* were cast with inscriptions, the texts do not provide a name for the vessel type; the present name *you* is taken from the Song dynasty (960-1279).

It has long been noted that Shang dynasty bronze inscriptions are routinely dedicated to ancestors identified by a generational tag, for example, *zu* ("grandfather") or *fu* ("father")

and by one of the ten "Heavenly Stems" (*tiangan*) used to designate the days in the Chinese week (i.e. *jia, yi, bing, ding*, etc.). The vessel shown in the rubbing bears a four-character dedicatory inscription; the first character is in the shape of the character *ya*, but the second does not correspond to any known character and is given here in approximation to the glyph for *qi*. This is followed by the generational tag *fu* and the prime sequential character *jia*. This particular *you* from the late Shang period is recorded in various catalogues such as the *San dai jijin wencun* (20 *juan*) compiled by Luo Zhenyu (1866-1940), the *Zhensong tang jigu yiwen* (16 *juan*, *buyi* 3 *juan*, *xu bian* 3 *juan*) compiled by Luo Zhenyu (1866-1940), and in the *Xu Yin wencun* compiled by Wang Chen (act. early 20th century). In the *San dai jijin wencun*, it is mistakenly identified as a vessel of the type *zhi*.

This "full-figured rubbing" was made in the seventh lunar month of 1887 and presented to the scholar, epigrapher, and collector Wang Yirong (1845-1900; *jinshi* of 1880) by Shanqi (also known as Longqin; 1863-1921), the last Prince Su whose lineage occupied fourth place among the "Eight Great Houses" of the Qing dynasty. The prince, an earnest student of epigraphy, respectfully dedicated the rubbing to "Elder Brother Liansheng" [Wang Yirong]. The other two inscriptions mounted above the rubbing are by Yuan Lizhun (1875-1936), and Zhu Yifan.

26

亞巽父甲卣青銅器拓本

原器商（公元前十六世紀至公元前十一世紀）時鑄。銘文四字，篆書。清光緒十三年（1887年）七月拓本。全形拓。拓片與題款，高九〇‧九厘米，寬四一‧九厘米。拓片紙高六四‧五厘米，寬四一‧九厘米。題款紙高二六‧三厘米，寬四一‧九厘米。器高三六厘米，寬二七厘米；蓋高七厘米，寬四厘米；蓋銘高八厘米，寬五厘米。立軸裝。

裱軸 *512*

卣，音同「有」。中國古代專用盛信香酒的酒器，是盛酒器中最重要的一類。橢圓口，深腹，圈，有蓋及提梁。主要盛行於商代和西周。此卣為橢圓體垂腹式，腹部橫截面呈扁方而圓，遂成橢圓形。器的側壁保持一定寬度的半圓面，腹部下垂甚低。蓋緣折邊。西周中期前段器。

此卣有銘文四字，曾著錄於羅振玉《三代吉金文存》、羅振玉《貞松堂集古遺文》、王辰《續殷文存》上冊等。《三代吉金文存》誤為觶。

此拓為王懿榮等舊藏，有肅親王隆勤（善耆）題款，附有袁勵准、朱益藩題跋。拓本有肅親王題：「光緒丁亥七月揭，奉廉生仁兄大人清賞。弟隆勤」。下鈐有「肅親王寶」朱文方印、「曦園主人」白文方印。拓本上方有袁勵准題款，云「此肅良親王贈王文敏公賜卣拓本也。…」，鈐有「中宮侍講」朱文方印、「高自標置」白文方印，以及朱益藩題款，鈐有「華心室」朱文長方印、「益藩長壽」白文方印。此拓以立軸裝裱，外題簽記「肅親王所贈賜卣拓本。日光堂」。

27

Jing Ren 'Nü' zhong qingtong qi taben

Rubbing from the Inscribed Bronze Bell "Jing Ren 'X'" *Zhong*

Late Western Zhou dynasty (ca. 1100-771 B.C.), un-dated

Hanging scroll, ink rubbed on paper, 108.0 x 58.4 cm; dimensions of vessel on rubbing, 74.1 x 43.0 cm

Date of rubbing not given; Qing dynasty (1644-1911), late 19th-early 20th century

Biaozhou 562

This is a "full-figured rubbing" of an inscribed *yongzhong*, the major chime-bell type of the Zhou dynasty. A chime-bell of this sort could have been made as part of a set of ritual vessels for presentation to a new lineage when it branched off from its principal lineage, or obtained as a gift of favor from one's superior, or made for the purposes of ancestor worship. Inscriptions were most frequently placed on the central *zheng* panel and on the *gu* portions of the *yongzhong*, which has an almond-shaped cross-section. The object from which this rubbing was taken bears a total of forty characters, with thirty-two on the central panel and eight on the lower register; seven of these forty characters are marked as repeating characters. The character for *Jing* is believed to be a place name, that for *Ren* is possibly the surname of the commissioner, while the unpronounceable character represented by the "X" is perhaps his given name.

The original *yongzhong*, once owned by the scholar-official Pan Zuyin (1830-1890; *jinshi*

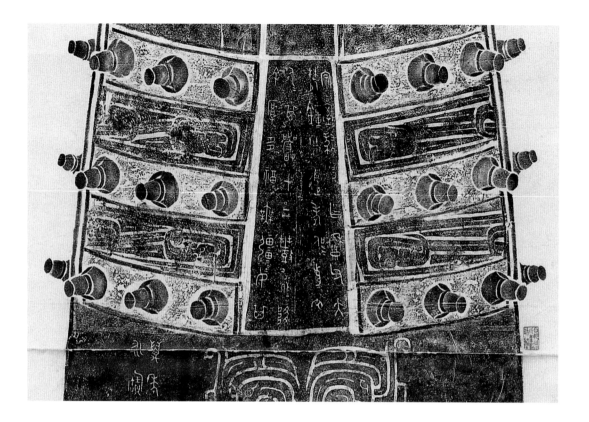

27

丼人女鐘青銅器拓本

原器西周（公元前十一世紀至公元前771年）晚期鑄。銘文四十字，又重文七字，篆書。晚清拓本，年月不詳。全形拓。拓片高七四・一厘米，寬四三厘米。紙高一〇八厘米，寬五八・四厘米。立軸裝。

裱軸 562

　　鐘，中國古代祭祀或宴饗時用的青銅樂器。最早的青銅鐘屬于西周時期。西周至春秋的多是所謂「甬鐘」，鐘頂有筒形的甬。厚重樸質，形制頗大，在傳世的西周後期鑄銘諸鐘中，是少見的巨製。

　　「丼人女鐘」，亦稱「丼人女鐘」、「丼人妖鐘」。「丼」、「丼」亦作「邢」。傳世有好幾枚：陳介祺舊藏一枚，現藏於日本京都市泉屋博古館；上海博物館藏一枚；1966年陝西省扶風縣齊鎮出土一枚，現藏於陝西省寶雞市博物館。此全形拓所拓之原器為潘祖蔭、端方舊藏，現藏於日本東京書道博物館。曾著錄於吳榮光《筠清館金文》、孫詒讓《古籀拾遺》、吳式芬《攈古錄金文》、鄒安《周金文存》、吳大澂《愙齋集古錄》、孫詒讓《古籀餘論》、郭沫若《兩周金文辭大系圖錄考釋》、方濬益《綴遺齋彝器款識考釋》、劉體智《小校經閣金文拓本》、羅振玉《三代吉金文存》等。

　　此鐘鼓面、舞上、篆間、甬幹各部均有銳利精巧的虺龍紋，鉦部中央及鼓左方有銘文。全形拓有端方清宣統元年（1909年）四月朔題款。

of 1852) and the Manchu-Chinese collector Duanfang (1861-1911), is an elegant object with a conventional design of reptiles and dragons on the lower portion of the body (*gu*), the shoulders (*wu*), the lined parts on the surface of the body (*zhuan*), and the handle (*yong*). This rubbing was made by Duanfang when the vessel was in his collection; the actual object is now preserved in the Museum of Calligraphy (Shodô hakubutsukan) in Tokyo. There are a number of vessels similar to this chime-bell, including one in the Shanghai Museum, one that was excavated at Fufeng county in Shaanxi province, and one in the Sumitomo Collection (Sen'oku hakkokan) in Kyoto which once belonged to the great collector Chen Jieqi (1813-1884). References to these vessels, and numerous rubbings taken from them, may be found in epigraphical compendia such as the *Yunqing guan jinwen* (5 *juan*) compiled by Wu Rongguang (1773-1843), the *Gu zhou shiyi* (3 *juan*) compiled by Sun Yirang (1848-1909), the *Chun gu lu jinwen* (3 *juan*) compiled by Wu Shifen (1796-1856), the *Zhou jinwen cun* (5 *juan*) compiled by Zou An (*jinshi* of 1903), the *Kezhai jigu lu* compiled by Wu Dacheng (1835-1902), the *Gu zhou yu lun* compiled by Sun Yirang (1848-1908), the *Liang Zhou jinwen ci daxi tulu kaoshi* compiled by Guo Moruo (1892-1973), the *Zhuiyi zhai yiqi kuanzhi kaoshi* (30 *juan*) compiled by Fang Junyi (1815-1889), and the *Xiaojiao jing ge jinwen taben* compiled by Liu Tizhi (1879-1963).

28

Zhong Yi fu xu qingtong qi taben

Rubbings from the Inscribed Bronze Vessel "Zhong Yi Fu" *Xu*

Late Western Zhou dynasty (ca. 1100-771 B.C.), undated

Hanging scroll, ink rubbed on paper, 148.8 x 42.6 cm (comprising sheet mounted above, 27.7 x 42.6 cm; sheet mounted at center with rubbings, 97.4 x 42.6 cm; and sheet mounted below, 23.7 x 42.6 cm); rubbing of vessel, approx. 18.2 x 29.6 cm; rubbing of inscription at upper right, approx. 11.9 x 6.0 cm; rubbing of inscription at upper left, approx. 11.9 x 6.0 cm

Date of rubbing not given; Qing dynasty (1644-1911), late 19th-early 20th century

Biaozhou 604

The *xu*, an oblong container for rice and sorghum that was also used as a grain-offering vessel in rituals, has a slightly flared mouth and a lid with appendages in the form of rectangles or small animals which enable it to function as a separate container when reversed. The vessel is also provided with handles and a foot-ring, and a small number of this type have been found with animal-feet supports. The *xu* closely resembles another bronze vessel type, the *gui*, in square or rectangular form, and certain inscriptions on *xu* even refer to them as *gui*. The *xu*, popular in the mid and late Western Zhou periods, was an immediate variation of the *gui*.

The *xu* shown in this fine "full-figured rubbing" bears an eleven-character inscription on the container and a ten-character inscription on the lid, which include reference to a certain "Zhong Yi Fu," from which the vessel

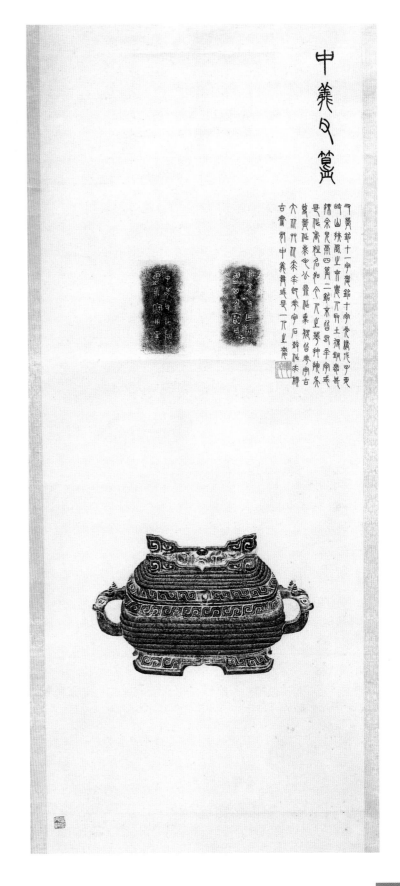

takes its name. Once owned by the collector Wu Dacheng (1835-1902), its present whereabouts is unknown. It is recorded in *San dai jijin wencun* (20 *juan*) compiled by Luo Zhenyu (1866-1940); *Zhensong tang jigu yiwen* (16 *juan*, *buyi* 3 *juan*, *xu bian* 3 *juan*) compiled by Luo Zhenyu (1866-1940); *Xigu lou jinshi cuibian* (10 *juan*) compiled by Liu Chenggan; and *Xiaojiao jing ge jinwen taben* compiled by Liu Tizhi (1879-1963). Vessels similar to this example have been excavated in Qishan county, Shaanxi province.

The rubbing carries a colophon by Han Huixun in one column of large seal script and seven columns of small seal script. Han's identification of the vessel as a *gui* is mistaken.

28

仲義父盨青銅器拓本

原器西周（公元前十一世紀至公元前 771 年）晚期鑄。銘文十一字，蓋十字，篆書。陝西岐山縣出土。晚清拓本，年月不詳。全形拓。裱軸全三紙，上下紙無拓片。中紙拓片器高一八・二厘米，寬二九・六厘米；銘高一一・九厘米，寬六厘米；蓋銘高一一・九厘米，寬六厘米。立軸裝。原題「仲義簋」，誤。

裱軸 604

盨，音同「須」。中國古代食器。用來盛黍、稷、稻、粱等飯食的器具。橢圓形，斂口，二耳，圈足，有蓋。出現於西周中期後段，主要流行於西周晚期，到春秋初期已基本消失。此器為獸首耳圈足，矩形蓋鈕式，橢方形，弇口鼓腹，獸首雙耳，圈下有「∩」形缺，蓋鈕作四矩形。西周晚期器。

此器有銘文十一字，其蓋有銘文十字。此器為吳大澂舊藏，曾著錄于羅振玉《三代吉金文存》、劉體智《小校經閣金文拓本》、《希古》（器）、羅振玉《貞松堂集古遺文》等，現藏處不詳。此拓本有韓惠洵篆書題跋，標題作「仲義父簋」，「簋」誤也。

29

Wadang ji ta

Collected Rubbings of Terminal Roof Tiles with Inscriptions and Animal Figures

Warring States period (475-221 B.C.), Qin dynasty (221-207 B.C.), and Han dynasty (206 B.C.-A.D. 220), variously dated and undated pieces

Set of 18 albums, ink rubbed on paper; each leaf approx. 34.5-35.3 x 23.5-23.9 cm; dimensions of individual rubbings vary; rough-edged binding

Date of rubbings not given, late Qing dynasty (1644-1911), Guangxu period (1875-1908)

Shanta 112

Terminal roof tiles (*wadang*) adorned with molded designs were manufactured during the late Zhou period (ca. 1100-256 B.C.), but the use of stylized characters as architectural ornaments appears to have developed in the state of Yan during the period of the Warring States (475-221 B.C.). The tradition flourished during the Qin (221-206 B.C.) and Han (206 B.C.-A.D. 220) dynasties. Western Han terminal roof tiles are typically divided into two or four sections; the winding, rope-like characters contained within are in relief and adapted to fit within the confines of circular forms. Large quantities of these terminal roof tiles, mostly in stylized small seal script, have survived. However, inscriptions on such tiles as well as those stamped on bricks, known collectively as *taowen* ("pottery inscriptions"), were long undervalued by scholars and collectors of epigraphy because the texts they bear are usually very short and deemed utilitarian. The longest known pottery inscription, a Qin-dynasty letter of investiture (*wa shu*), consists of only 119 characters.

Shown here are examples taken from two albums from a set of eighteen, which contain more than 900 rubbings of various terminal roof tiles from the Warring States through the Han. The circular tile (vertical diameter 17.3 cm, horizontal diameter 17.0 cm) bears a commonly used auspicious four-character inscription, *qian qiu wan sui* ("a thousand autumns and a myriad years"), which expresses a wish for prosperity and longevity. The two semicircular tiles are either from the Warring States or Qin periods; one depicts two animals under a tree (7.4 x 13.6 cm) while the other shows a dragon and a tiger (8.8 x 16.1 cm).

The albums were formerly in the collection of Chen Jieqi (1813-1884; *jinshi* of 1845), a native of Weixian in Shandong province. Chen was the most important connoisseur and collector of antiquities of the late Qing period; he amassed countless rubbings of objects within and outside his collection, and the rubbings he made personally are of an unmatched quality. Chen's contribution to Chinese archaeology lies primarily in his tireless assembling of inscribed pottery and bronze measuring vessels of the Qin dynasty; much of his work is documented in the voluminous correspondences he had with fellow epigraphers including Wu Shifen (1796-1856), Wu Yun (1811-1883), Pan Zuyin (1830-1890), and Wu Dacheng (1835-1902).

29

瓦當集拓

一名《陳簠齋藏瓦當拓本》。原物戰國、秦、漢（公元前 475 年
至公元 220 年）製。清陳介祺藏。清光緒年間（1875–1908 年）拓
本，計十八冊。拓本高三四‧五至三五‧三厘米，寬二三‧五至
二三‧九厘米。毛裝。

善拓 *112*

　　瓦當，覆於屋頂檐際的一種瓦件。瓦當銘文
中有自稱「瓦」的，也有自稱「當」的，還有自稱
「甍」的，并有自銘為「瓦當」的，後世則習稱之
為「瓦當」。瓦當本為實用建築材料，保護檐頭，
加固建築物，但經過古代匠師之銳意加工，則兼有
裝飾美觀之藝術作用。大致可分素面、文字文飾、
圖案文飾三種。

　　瓦當通常指半圓形或圓形之瓦頭。始見於周
代，秦漢已趨流行。陝西是秦漢都城所在地，出土
瓦當數量之多，居中國全國之首。特別能夠顯示其
時代特徵的是秦都雍城、咸陽，秦始皇陵，西漢京
師，漢長安城，漢長陵以及甘泉宮等遺址的瓦當。
在陝北的洛州、神木，陝西的商縣、安康等地也曾
有秦漢瓦當出土。戰國、秦、漢瓦當形狀多為圓
形，也有少數半圓形。

　　戰國、秦多為圖象瓦當，漢代以文字瓦當為
大宗，圖案瓦當貫穿於秦漢兩個時代。出土的圖象
瓦當有鹿紋、雙鹿紋、虎雁紋、斗獸紋、雙獾紋、
鳳紋、四獸紋、四鳥紋、燕樹紋、豹紋、夔鳳紋、
子母鳳紋、太陽紋、房屋建築紋等。圖案瓦當基本
圖案由當心及週邊紋飾組成，週邊多為葵紋、雲紋
等，當心多為樹枝紋、曲尺紋、方格紋、斜方格
紋、米字紋、四葉紋、乳釘等。文字瓦當在西漢時
期普遍出現，大多數為宮殿、官署、陵園等建築名
稱，還有一部份以吉祥語和其他為內容的文字瓦
當。瓦當文字多為陽文，字數不一，有一字、二
字、三字、四字，多至十六字者。字體豐潤美妙，
變化無窮，而以篆書為多，隸書次之，并有英芝
體、龜蛇體、蟲書體等多種。這些神態天真、氣韻
生動的圖象瓦當，結構優美的圖案瓦當以及奇妙古
拙的文字瓦當，是研究秦漢歷史與藝術不可多得的
實物資料。

　　此集拓為陳介祺舊藏，收戰國、秦、漢瓦當

九百余種。陳介祺，字壽卿，又字西生，號伯潛、
簠齋，山東濰縣（今濰坊）人。生於清嘉慶十八年
（1813 年），道光二十五年（1845 年）進士。授翰
林院編修，國史館協修，方略館分校。咸豐四年
（1854 年）辭官歸里，自號海濱病史、林下田間大
夫。賦詩志、治古器物、古文字學，為當代治金石
學之大師也。簠齋收藏之富，鑒別之精甲天下，僅
舉其有銘文者，商周銅器二百四十八件，秦漢銅器
九十七件，石刻一百一十九件，磚三百二十六件，
瓦當九百二十三件，銅鏡二百件，璽印七千餘方，
封泥五百四十八方，陶文五千片，泉鏡鏃各式范一

千件。陳氏於古文字學之貢獻，有鑑古、考古、釋
古、博古四方面，與吳式芬、吳雲、潘祖蔭、吳大
澂等，文字之交甚密。卒於光緒十年（1884 年），
享年七十二歲。

　　茲選照陳介祺所藏十八冊瓦當拓片中三件，
為第十冊第十一幅西漢「千秋萬歲」吉祥語圓形瓦
當（高一七‧三厘米，寬一七厘米）、第十七冊第
十九幅戰國或秦代雙獸樹紋半圓形瓦當（高七‧四
厘米，寬一三‧六厘米）以及第二十四幅戰國或秦
代龍虎紋半圓形瓦當（高八‧八厘米，寬一六‧一
厘米）。

30

Zhuan wen ji ta

Collected Rubbings of Stamped Bricks with Inscriptions

Qin dynasty (221-206 B.C.) through Six Dynasties (222-589), variously dated and undated pieces
Album of 28 leaves from a set of 7 albums, ink rubbed on paper; each leaf approx. 35.0 x 23.0 cm; dimensions of individual rubbings vary; rough-edged binding
Date of rubbings not given, late Qing dynasty (1644-1911), ca. second half of 19th century

Shanta 135

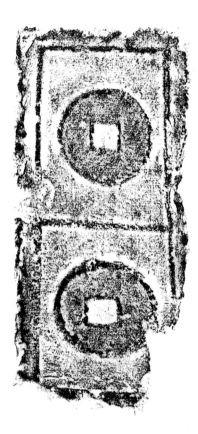

Bricks are a type of earthenware used in architectural construction to build and face walls as well as to pave floors. They are the principal materials used in ancient China for the building of houses, palaces, city walls, roads, and tombs. The oldest extant Chinese brick is a fragment from the late Western Zhou period (ca. 1100-771 B.C.) that was recovered from a pit of ashes at Yuntang in Fufeng county, Shaanxi province. This type of brick was not used for the erection of walls but rather attached to the faces of earthen walls for the dual purposes of protection and decoration. An industry that produced architectural earthenware developed rapidly during the Warring States period (475-221 B.C.). In addition to thin, narrow bricks and square bricks used for paving floors and facing walls, there appeared thick hollow bricks for the paving of foundations and construction of staircases. Around this time, such hollow bricks also began to replace wooden planks in the building of brick-vaulted chambers in tombs.

In the Qin dynasty (221-206 B.C.), the scale of brick manufacturing greatly expanded and firing techniques also underwent significant improvements. Paving bricks stamped with patterns of cords, coils, carpenters' squares, lozenges, square grids, parallel lines, suns, and flowers have been unearthed at the site of the imperial palace at Xianyang, the Qin capital. There are also many kinds of hollow bricks with a rich variety of designs not seen before this time, including those stamped with patterns of dragons and phoenixes. During the Western Han dynasty (206 B.C.-A. D. 8), bricks were widely used to pave the floors in large-scale buildings, while tombs

constructed with hollow bricks were very much in vogue. From the mid Western Han period onwards, there appeared tombs in which small, narrow bricks were used to adorn the faces of the walls and tally-shaped bricks were used to construct the arches. Only from around the time of the Eastern Han dynasty (A.D. 25-220), however, did bricks come to be widely used by the common people, who used them not only for paving floors but also to build walls and to construct houses, wells, and granaries.

The earliest bricks with inscriptions appeared during the Warring States period. In the initial period the majority of inscriptions on the bricks were stamped, with only a small number being manually incised. Because very few characters were used, as was the case with inscriptions on tiles and earthenware vessels from the same period, they were once all known as "inscriptions on earthenware" (*tao wen*). After the reign of Emperor Wudi of the Western Han, the content of inscriptions on bricks became increasingly rich; their formal appearance was also liberated from the constraints of the "carved-seal style" (*xi yin shi*) of earthenware inscriptions, allowing a unique artistic manner to be established.

In the Eastern Han period, bricks with inscriptions spread from the Shaanxi area to the North China Plain and the Jiangnan region; such bricks have been unearthed in Shaanxi, Henan, Inner Mongolia, Shanxi, Hebei, Liaoning, Shandong, Jiangsu, Hubei, Hunan, Zhejiang, Sichuan, and Guangdong. During the periods of the Wei, Jin, and Northern and Southern Dynasties (220-589), bricks with inscriptions flourished mainly in the areas around the middle and lower reaches of the Yangzi River. After the Sui (581-618) and Tang (618-907) periods, due to a variety of factors, bricks with inscriptions gradually fell out of use.

Bricks with inscriptions not only provide scholars of history, archaeology, epigraphy, and calligraphy with reliable and invaluable records, but also constitute a body of ancient inscribed sources as important as writings found on oracle bones, bronze vessels and instruments, carved seals, and stone surfaces. This album of rubbings of bricks with inscriptions once belonged to the collector Chen Jieqi (1813-1884). Shown here are two leaves from the first of the seven volumes in this set of rubbings. Both bricks in leaf 28 are dated the third year of the Ganlu reign era (A.D. 258) during the Three Kingdoms period (220-280); the one at right measures 27.2 x 6.1 cm while the other measures 12.7 x 5.9 cm. The rubbing mounted on leaf 34 is that of a somewhat larger (31.8 x 6.8 cm) and earlier brick stamped with an inscription and a pictorial representation; it is dated the sixth year of the Yongyuan reign era (A.D. 94) during the Eastern Han period.

30

磚文集拓

一名《陳氏藏磚拓本》。原磚秦（公元前221-206年）至六朝（公元222至589年）製。清陳介祺藏。清末（約十九世紀下半葉）拓本。全書計七冊一函，每頁約高三五厘米，寬二三厘米。拓片大小不一。毛裝。

善拓 *135*

　　磚屬於建築用陶，可以砌牆、貼壁、鋪地。是中國古代建造房屋、宮殿、城牆、道路、陵墓的主要材料。中國最早的磚是陝西扶風發現的一塊殘磚，出土於雲塘西周晚期灰坑中。此類的磚并不是用於築牆，而是貼砌於土牆的表面，對建築物有保護或裝飾的作用。戰國的建築陶業發展迅速，除了鋪地和貼壁的各種小型條磚、方磚外，還出現了鋪築踏步和台階的大型空心磚，在當時的陵墓中也開始用空心磚代替木板建造槨室。

　　到了秦代，磚的生產規模和燒造技術有了顯著的擴大和進步。秦都咸陽宮殿遺址出土有繩紋、迴紋、曲尺紋、菱形紋、方格紋、平行綫紋、太陽紋和花紋鋪地磚，還有龍紋、鳳紋空心磚，種類繁多、紋飾豐富，是前所未有的。西漢時期的大型建築已普遍用磚鋪地，空心磚墓十分盛行。西漢中期以後又出現了小磚室墓，除了使用小條磚砌墓壁外，還用楔形磚構築拱券。大約從東漢起磚在民間才真正被廣泛使用，當時居民不僅用磚鋪地，而且用磚築牆，建造了房屋、井壁和倉囷。

　　最早的磚文出現在戰國晚期。早期的磚文大多數為戳印，少數是刻劃的，字數很少，與同時期的瓦文、陶器銘文十分相似，所以過去的文獻將它們統稱為「陶文」。西漢武帝之後，磚文的內容不斷豐富，表現形式也從「璽印式」陶文的框框中解放出來，形成了自己獨特的藝術風格。

　　到了東漢，磚文由關中地區擴大到中原地區和江南地區，在陝西、河南、內蒙古、山西、河北、遼寧、山東、江蘇、湖北、湖南、浙江、四川、廣東均有出土。魏晉南北朝時期，磚文主要在長江中下游地區盛行。隋唐以後，由於種種原因，磚文才逐漸衰落下去。

　　磚文不僅為歷史、考古、古文字，以及書法史的研究提供了可靠的寶貴證據，而且是與甲骨文、金文、璽印文字、刻石文字同等重要的古代銘刻資料。此拓本為清陳介祺舊藏，收秦至六朝磚拓三百五十余種。茲選照第一冊第二十八頁雙件磚拓，為三國魏甘露三年（258年）的紀年磚與同年八月丁亥之「菱迴紋磚」，以及第三十四頁單件紀年磚拓，為東漢永元六年（94年）之「擊鼓出行圖磚」。

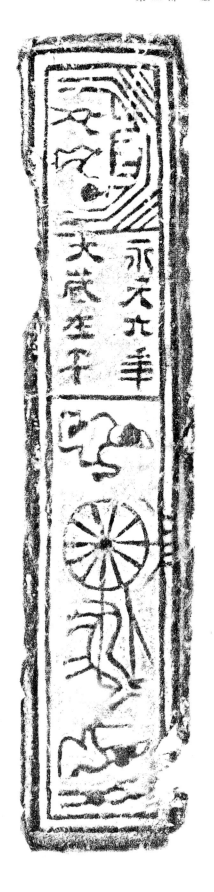

31

Jing ming ji ta

Collected Rubbings of Bronze Mirrors with Inscriptions

Han dynasty (206 B.C.-A.D. 220) through Sui dynasty (581-618), variously dated and undated pieces
Album of 28 leaves, ink rubbed on paper; each leaf approx. 32.7 x 26.8 cm; each sheet of rubbings approx. 22.5 x 22.8 cm; dimensions of individual rubbings vary
Date of rubbings not given, late Qing dynasty (1644-1911), ca. second half of 19th century

Shanta 207

Ancient Chinese bronze mirrors are mostly circular, and only a few are square. The reflective side is flat and highly polished, while the decorated reverse side bears a knob (*niu*) through which a fabric cord may be strung to aid in handling or hanging; only a very small number were made with handles.

Because of the deep roots of Daoism and Buddhism in Chinese culture, decorations on bronze mirrors include themes reflecting the desire for immortality, those expressing the hope that the Heavens will bestow blessings, those designed to ward off evil influences, or those containing prayers for good fortune.

Early Chinese mirrors attained an artistic apogée during the later Eastern Zhou (770-256 B.C.) and early Han (206 B.C.-A.D. 220) periods. Advances in bronze casting during the Han were accompanied by large-scale manufacture of mirrors with sophisticated decorative programs, most notably the "TLV" pattern (so named for the marks shaped like "T," "L," and "V" letters). Such mirrors are called *boju jing* in Chinese, meaning "*boju* gaming board mirrors"; also known as *guiju*

jing, "square-ruled mirrors" or "compass mirrors." Examples from the Western Han period (206 B.C.-A.D. 8) tend to be somewhat larger, heavier, and thicker in cross-section than their Eastern Zhou predecessors. They feature low relief decoration on finely patterned grounds emphasizing the four cardinal directions and are often accompanied by encircling laudatory inscriptions of auspicious phrases. Although the decorative layout of bronze mirrors during the Eastern Han (A.D. 25-220) continued to be based on the cardinal points, the subjects depicted increasingly turned to immortals and supernatural beings or auspicious birds and animals that were connected with Han astronomical and cosmological beliefs. Often animal symbols for east and west were reversed because mirrors were fixed to ceilings of burial chambers. The change in overall subject matter was also accompanied by a decorative style with modeling in high relief.

The 28 very fine rubbings mounted in this album were personally made by the late Qing collector and epigrapher Chen Jieqi (1813-1884), later coming into the possession of the scholar-statesman Liang Qichao (1873-1929). The mostly Han mirrors contain auspicious inscriptions as well as geometric and cosmic designs on their reverse sides, which can be very clearly seen and appreciated in the form of rubbings.

The two rubbings illustrated here are representative of the exquisite bronze mirror specimens collected and studied by Chen. The third rubbing in the album, was taken from a circular TLV mirror approximately 21 cm in diameter made by the Shangfang (Directorate for Imperial Manufactories) sometime between the late Western Han and early Eastern Han periods; it is decorated with TLV patterns, four divine beasts,

divinities, and animal designs in high relief (called *Shangfang si shen boju jing*), as well as a round knob with a quatrefoil base. The large square at the mirror's center encloses twelve nipples and a twelve-character inscription which lists the Twelve Earthly Branches. The outer band, diagonally hachured, features a fairly long inscription with 49 characters, reading "This is a fine mirror made by the Directorate for Imperial Manufactories [*Shangfang*] and it must be treated carefully lest it be damaged. The [blue] dragon on the left and the [white] tiger on the right forfend all evil. The vermilion bird [above] and the black turtle [below] accord with *yin* and *yang*. May you have many children and grandchildren so that you will be able to position yourself at the center. May both your parents be protected for a long time and be blessed with joy, wealth, and prosperity. May they wander at will on the renowned peaks plucking the Herb of Life. May you enjoy a long life exceeding that of metal and stone, as is fit for a nobleman or king." The rim has a design of auspicious flowing heavenly clouds with a raised sawtooth-patterned circle.

Another rubbing, mounted as the eighth leaf of the album, represents a genre of bronze mirrors with concentric circle designs and inscriptions known as *zhaoming lianhu mingdai jing* ("shine brightly"), which are typical of the Western Han period. This small circular mirror with a diameter of 11.6 cm contains an inscription of 21 characters which translates as: "The quality contained within [the mirror] is pure, because of which the mirror shines bright; its reflected light shines like the sun and moon. If the [state of one's] mind is sincere, then no steadfastness will be lost."

31

鏡銘集拓

一名《簠齋手拓鏡銘》。原鏡漢至隋（公元前206至公元617年）製。清陳介祺藏。清末（約十九世紀下半葉）拓本。全一册，計二十八幅。割裱本。每頁高三二‧七厘米，寬二六‧八厘米。拓片每紙高二二‧五厘米，寬二二‧八厘米。拓片大小不一。册頁裝。

善拓 207

　　中國古代的銅鏡形式，原則上以圓形為主。除正面必須平滑以外，鏡背則鑄有「鈕」，以便繫繩把持或懸掛，少數則帶有柄。由於中國文化與道教、佛教有密切關係，所以銅鏡上出現了求長生不老與昇天思想及天祿、辟邪、祈福之類造型。西漢銅鏡鏡身較厚，其文飾大多採用準確的四分法佈局，以陽刻細綫表現，有的還配上吉語銘文。到了東漢，其文飾雖仍採四分法佈局，題材則偏向神仙人物或吉祥禽獸等，並以高浮雕的形式出現。

　　此集拓為清陳介祺藏并手拓，收漢至隋銅鏡拓片。前附隋「董是洗」一幅，後均為漢鏡二十七幅。所拓銅鏡形神兼備，著墨均勻、凝重。此拓本為梁啟超舊藏，題簽記「陳簠齋手拓鏡銘。飲冰室藏本」。

　　茲選照拓片二幅。前者為本册第三幅東漢「尚方四神博局鏡」，徑二一厘米。圓形，圓鈕，蝙蝠形柿蒂紋鈕座。大方格內環列十二乳及十二地支銘。四方八極內青龍配一鸞一禽，白虎配獨角長毛獸及一禽，朱雀配一羽人騎獸奔馳及一禽鳥，玄武配一獨角長毛獸。外區銘文四十九字，為「尚方御竟大毋傷，左龍右虎辟不羊，朱鳥玄武調陰陽，子孫備具居中央，長保二親樂富昌，佻洄名山采神章，壽敝金石如侯王」。三角鋸齒及雲氣紋緣。後者為本册第八幅西漢「昭明連弧銘帶鏡」，徑一一‧六厘米。圓形，圓鈕，連弧形鈕座。座外一周連弧紋帶，連弧間有簡單的文飾。其外兩周短斜綫紋之間有銘文二十一字，為「內清質以昭明，光而象夫日月，心忽而忠，然而不泄乎」。字體較方整，素寬緣。

32

Han jun che huaxiang

Illustration of a Han Dynasty Procession

Eastern Han dynasty (25-220), undated, ca. mid- to late second century

Stone carved in low relief and engraved in clerical script; unearthed in 1882 at Linzi, Shandong province

Horizontal hanging scroll, cinnabar rubbed on paper; 94.3 x 151.6 cm; dimensions of stone slab in rubbing, 86.5 x 125.0 cm; colophon in ink on paper mounted beside left edge of rubbing, 94.3 x 16.1 cm

Date of rubbing not given, late Qing dynasty (1644-1911), between 1882 and 1909

Biaozhou 146

Rubbings of stones engraved with pictorial designs and inscriptions (*shike tapian*) have a long and distinguished tradition in China. Thin sheets of paper made from plant fibers such as bamboo or mulberry are normally employed for such purposes, while the ink or pigments to be used are mixed with measured drops of water on inkstones to produce the proper consistency. The paper is first affixed to the selected stone surface by coating it with a paste made from water and rich starch, then tamped all over with a round, ink-filled cloth pad, and finally peeled away to be air-dried. Using this method, all flat surfaces that come in contact with the tamping pad become inked or pigmented, and all incised or engraved areas of the stone retain the original color of the paper.

The National Library of China's immense collection of rubbings from engraved stones was begun in 1909, the same year the national library system was inaugurated. Over time, renowned collections such as those of Chen Jieqi (1813-1884), Gu Qianli (1766-1835), Qu Yong (d. 1846), Miao Jishan, Zhang Yu (1865-1937; *jinshi* of 1903), Ye Changchi (1849-1917; *jinshi* of 1889), Liang Qichao (1873-1929), Zhang Fang, Lu Hejiu (b. 1884), Tian Boying, and Wang Min were acquired. The collection now contains more than 40,000 items and over 100,000 individual sheets.

Illustrated here is a rubbing taken from one of the best known examples of ancient pictorial stones. Scenes of processions such as the one shown frequently appear in funerary carvings of the Han period (206 B.C.-A.D. 220). Many of the people for whom carved stone funerary monuments were constructed served as officials at the district or provincial level, and in these positions they functioned as representatives of both state and local interests, and as a link between the upper and lower echelons of society.

The bas-relief imagery on this striking cinnabar rubbing is believed to be from a funerary chamber in Shandong province. In the upper register, a lord or important official is seated in a canopied chariot and followed by three officials, the first of whom is identified by the cartouche as a *lingxia* (prefect, circuit general, or supervisor) and the second *menxia xiaoli* (minor headquarters clerk on the staff of the governor of a commandery). In the lower register are three other officials, the one at the front being a *menxia shuzuo* (palace clerk, one of low rank on the staff of the supervisor of the household of the heir apparent), the last a *zhubu* (recorder of an agency, normally handling the flow of documents in and out of their units; or assistant magistrate on the staff of various units of territorial administration, especially districts). The objects that resemble trees at the lower left and right are analogous to those found on other stones of the same period. The stone, which is also carved in relief on the reverse side, has yet to be identified with a specific monument.

This important fragment was formerly kept on the estate of the late Qing scholar and epigrapher Chen Jieqi, who built a pavilion for the sole purpose of protecting it, and whose family members made this fine cinnabar rubbing. However, even before the archaeologist Édouard Chavannes (1865-1918) published it for the first time in 1909, it had been purchased and shipped to France by the collector Adolphe-Adam Worch. Like the Chinese, the French valued not only the pictorial imagery but also the clerical-script inscriptions on the relief panel. The stone is believed to have subsequently entered a Parisian museum, as the attached colophon by Liang Qichao states with a palpable tone of regret.

32
漢君車畫像

東漢（公元 25 至 220 年）刻。無年月。原石清光緒八年
（1882年）出土於山東濰縣。畫像隸書題字存五處，共隸
書十四字。硃拓本。拓本紙高九四・三厘米，寬一五一
・六厘米。畫像拓片高八六・五厘米，寬一二五厘米。
梁啟超跋。紙高九四・三厘米，寬一六・一厘米。橫軸
裝。

裱軸 146

　　長期以來，中國國家圖書館一直重視石刻拓
本的搜集。自民國初年京師圖書館草創時期至今，
已有九十年的歷史。在此期間，通過各種方式，諸
如采訪、傳拓及社會名流捐贈等，搜集入藏了大量

的石刻拓本。大批名家收藏過的拓本源源不斷地歸
入館內。如清代著名學者顧千里、瞿鏞、繆繼珊、
章鈺、葉昌熾、梁啟超、張鈁、陸和九、田伯英、
王敏等人所藏拓本，都先後為館藏拓本的組成部
份。中國國家圖書館入藏的拓本所反映的時代久
遠，上起戰國秦漢，下至當代，綿延兩千餘載。此
外，所藏拓本種類繁多，數量龐大，已超過四萬多
種，十餘萬件。

　　畫像石的拓片，可視為最古老的石刻版畫。
此圖為漢君車出行圖，淺浮雕。原石出土後初歸山
東濰縣陳介祺，後流入法國，今藏於巴黎集美博物
館。

　　畫像分上下二層，上層之右一單騎有蓋輜
車，內坐二人，其右為御者執轡控一馬車，蓋前馬
上書有「君車」二字。後一騎者題「鈴下」二字。
其後一騎者題「門下小史」。下層前一似樹似芝，

旁一騎後題「門下書佐」，又二騎未刻字，其後又
一似樹似芝，上刻「主簿」，後殘缺。畫面上君車
出行，官吏侍從。浩浩蕩蕩，誇耀漢代官僚之權
勢。原石兩面刻畫，此係陽面畫像。

　　此硃墨初拓本為梁啟超舊藏并題簽、題跋。
跋文如下：「右石曾為濰縣陳簠齋所得，築亭護
之，曰『君車漢石亭』，自署『漢石亭長』。當時
拓片已不多見。此石為胡賈輦去在巴黎博物館中，
甋椎之事從茲絕矣。此本為簠翁家精拓，良可珍
秘。丁巳臘八，啟超題藏」。鈐「飲冰室藏金石圖
書」朱文方印、「任公」朱文方印、「新會梁啟超
印」白文方印。

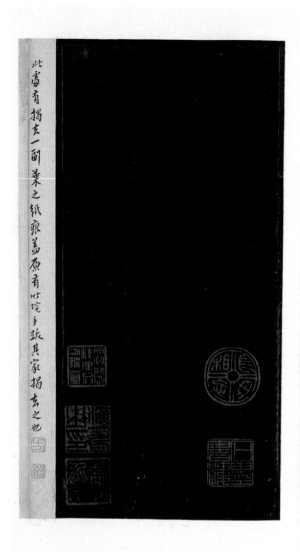

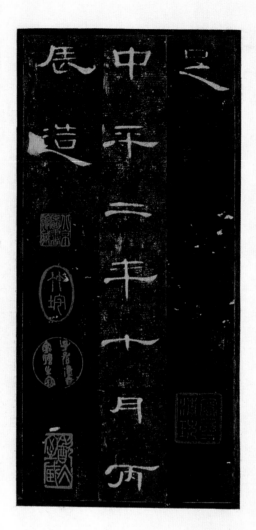

33

Han Geyang ling Cao Quan jigong bei

Commendatory Stele for Cao Quan, Magistrate of Geyang during the Han Dynasty

Eastern Han dynasty (25-220), Zhongping reign period (184-188), dated 185

Unearthed during the late Ming dynasty at Xinli village, Geyang county, Shaanxi province; stone engraved in clerical script; dimensions of original stele approx. 272.0 x 95.0 cm; stone now in the collection of the Forest of Stelae, Shaanxi Provincial Museum, Xi'an, Shaanxi province

Album of 42 leaves, ink rubbed on paper, accordion-style mounting between top and bottom wooden boards; overall dimensions of album, 31.5 x 15.9 cm; each leaf approx. 31.4 x 15.7 cm; each rubbing panel, approx. 25.0 x 11.5-11.6 cm, except first rubbing panel, 25.0 x 11.3 cm, and last rubbing panel, 24.8 x 12.1 cm

Date of rubbing not given, probably late Ming dynasty (1368-1644), between 1573 and 1644

Shanta 56

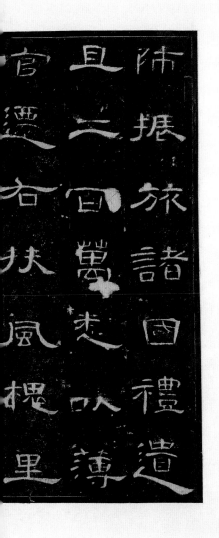

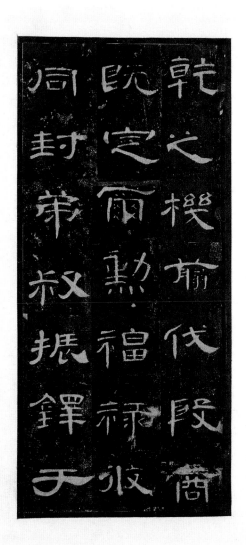

By the Eastern Han period (A.D. 25-220), and especially from the mid second century onwards, stelae were carved in profusion and bore lengthy inscriptions. Many of these stelae were erected to commemorate individuals. One such important stele records the achievements of Cao Quan, magistrate of Geyang. An example of *jigong bei* (stelae recording good and noble deeds), this is one of the best preserved stelae of the Han and exhibits excep-

tional finesse. The stele was discovered lying in tall grass during the late Ming (ca. 1573) by the official Li Yixuan (act. late 16th century); it was broken in two roughly equal sections and the seal cap was missing.

This stele was commissioned by sixty-one officials and residents of Geyang prefecture in what is now Shaanxi province to praise the virtues of the aristocratic Cao Quan and his clan. The eulogistic inscrip-

tion commends the official Cao Quan and informs the reader that he came from a long line of officials, worked as a minor official in Dunhuang and in the Liang inspector's offices, went on to serve in a military position in the Western Regions, took part in the suppression of the Yellow Turban Rebellion, and was a magistrate for two terms before retiring. The text includes a couplet describing Cao Quan's filial piety. Cao was excluded from office after 168, along with other relatives and subordinates of the partisans implicated in the unsuccessful coup against the eunuchs. The text also reveals why Cao Quan's former associates desired to establish a public monument that would redeem his character. Below is a translation of the text engraved on the stele's front side based on the rendering by Patricia Buckley Ebrey, with minor changes:

Our lord is named Quan, styled Jingyuan, and comes from Jiaogu in Dunhuang. His ancestors descended from the Zhou [ruling house]. When King Wu seized the opportunity and exterminated the Yin-Shang [dynasty], all shared in the benefits. [The king] enfeoffed his younger brother Shuzhenduo in the state of Cao and on this basis the lineage was started.

At the time of the transition from Qin to Han, Cao Can assisted the royal house. Shizong [Emperor Wu] expanded the territory. [Cao Can's] descendants moved to the area outside the region (*zhou*) of Yong [in Shaanxi and Gansu]. Dividing up, they settled in Youfufeng [commandery in Shaanxi], as well as in Anding, Wudu, Longxi, and Dunhuang [all commanderies in Gansu]. As the branches divided, the descendants were dispersed. Wherever they lived they were influential people.

Our lord's great-great-grandfather Min was recommended as "Filial and Incorrupt" (*xiaolian*, a reference to nomination by local officials for consideration at the capital for selection and appointment) and served as Chief Aide (*zhangshi*) of Wuwei [commandery in present-day Gansu province], Magistrate (*ling*) of Quren in Ba Commandery [Sichuan], and as Commandant (*duwei*) of Juyan [county] in Changyi [commandery in Gansu]. His great-grandfather Shu was [recommended as] "Filial and Incorrupt," becoming a Receptionist (*yezhe*), the Chief Aide of Jincheng [commandery in Gansu], Magistrate of Xiayang [Shaanxi], and Commandant of the Western Area in Shu commandery [Sichuan]. His grandfather Feng was [recommended as] "Filial and Incorrupt," becoming Assistant Commandant of the Dependent States (*duwei cheng*) in Changyi [Gansu], Administrator of the Marquisate (*houxiang*) of Shumi in Youfufeng [commandery in Shaanxi], Commandant of the Western Area of Jincheng [commandery in Gansu], and Governor (*taishou*) of Beidi [commandery in Gansu]. As a youth, his father Feng was well known in the region and commandery but unfortunately died young, and therefore his position did not match his merits.

When young our lord loved to study. He looked into the abstruse and was attentive to the details, there being no written works he did not investigate. A wise and filial nature took root in his heart. He supported his grandfather's concubine and respectfully served his stepmother, anticipating their thoughts and attending to their wishes. He omitted nothing in his reverence and ceremonies for the living and dead. For these reasons the villagers had a saying about him: "The one who has made two generations of relatives happy is Cao Jingyuan." Many generations will record his virtue; his name will not be lost.

With regard to his government service, in pureness [our lord] copied [Bo] Yi and [Shu] Qi, in straightforwardness he emulated Historian Yu. He served the commandery in several of the higher positions and was Administrator of Accounts (*shangji yuanshi*). Then he was appointed to minor official posts in the region (*zhou*) of Liang, including Vice Administrator (*zhizhong*) and Mounted Escort (*biejia*). He brought order to an area of ten thousand li, and the nobles did not go astray. When he went out to inspect the commanderies, he would bring charges against wrongdoers. The hearts of the greedy and violent were purified, his colleagues fell under the influence of his virtue, and [everyone from] far and near stood in awe.

In the second year of the Jianning reign era [169], [our lord] was recommended as "Filial and Incorrupt" and appointed as Gentleman of the Interior (*langzhong*, or palace secretary), then assigned as Divisional Major (*wubu sima*) of the Western Regions. At that time the King of Shule [Kashgar, modern Xinjiang], Hede, murdered his father, usurped the position, and would not offer tribute. Our lord raised an army to chastise him. He had the humanity to care for the wounded, the generosity to distribute the last of his provisions. As he attacked the cities and fought battles in the fields, his strategies gushed forth like a fountain and his stern demeanor stimulated the soldiers. Hede presented himself tied up and ready for death. [Our lord] brought back the army and comforted the troops. The gifts of the states [along the way] amounted to two million [cash], all of which he gave to the government.

[Next our lord] was promoted to Magistrate of Huaili [county] in Youfufeng [commandery in Shaanxi]. When his younger brother of the same mother died he quit his post. Then he was caught in the net of the ban [on the partisans], and stayed in seclusion at home for seven years. In the sixth year of the Guanghe reign era [183], he was again recommended as "Filial and Incorrupt." In the third month of the seventh year [184] he was appointed a Gentleman of the Interior (*langzhong*) and assigned as Magistrate of Lufu [county] in Jiuquan [commandery in Gansu].

When the heretical bandit Zhang Jue raised troops in You [northeast of Beijing] and Ji [Hebei, Shanxi, part of Henan and Manchuria], Yan [Shandong and part of Hebei], Yu [most of Henan, part of Hebei, Shandong, Anhui, and Hubei], Jing [Hunan, most of Hubei and part of Guizhou], and Yang [the Jiangnan region, including most of Jiangsu, Jiangxi, Zhejiang, and Fujian] simultaneously faced an emergency. At that time the Guo family and other commoners of our county started a revolt. They set fire to the government offices in the cities. The multitudes were in turmoil and everyone was anxious. Three commanderies declared emergencies, while orders to recruit soldiers repeatedly arrived [at the court]. At that point our sage ruler consulted with the officials who all said: "Our lord is the one! " He was transferred to the Magistracy of Geyang [county in Shaanxi]. He swept together the surviving embers and exterminated the remaining rebels, cutting them off at the roots. Afterwards, he paid calls on the elders and consulted with Wang Chang, Wang Bi, and other wise and superior people concerning the needs of the people. He brought comfort to the aged and cared for widows and widowers. His own money was used to buy grain to give to the infirm and blind. His eldest daughter Taofei and others made up medicine for

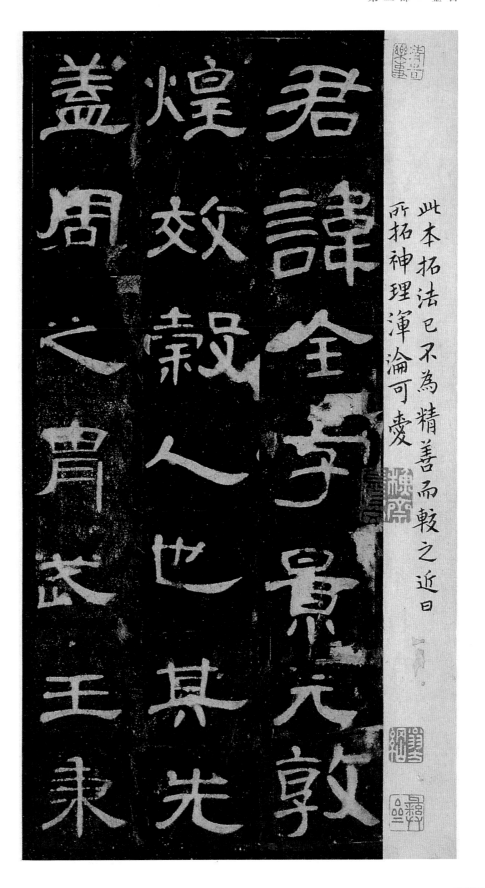

knife wounds and "divinely-illuminated" ointment, and personally went to the outlying hamlets. Wang Zai, Cheng Heng, and other minor officials supplied the ill [with medicine] to cure them and [clothes] to keep them warm. His benevolent rule spread faster than the courier network. The common people, carrying their children on their backs, converged like clouds. He had the walls and houses put in order and the market set up. [That year] the weather was seasonable and there was an abundant harvest. The farming men, weaving women, and artisans were respectful and grateful.

Earlier, in the first year of the Heping reign era [28 B.C.], the county had suffered a flood in Bomao Valley. After the disaster was over, in the *xu* and *hai* years [i.e., *wuxu* and *jihai*, 23-22 B.C.], an outer wall for the city was built. From that time on the old families and the gentlemen of cultivation did not rise into official positions. Our lord was troubled that the group of gentry was not succeeding. He opened a gate at the southern court so that the sacred peak of Mount Hua could be seen. The villages became enlightened and orderly. One result was that Li Ru, Luan Gui, Cheng Yin, and other scholars each received his due in the ranks conferred by men. [Our lord] expanded the courtrooms and extended the chambers of the bureaus. People were going up and down, bowing and giving way on the steps of the audience hall. The expenses did not come from the people nor was the labor service at the busy seasons.

The Palace Clerk (*menxia yuan*) Wang Chang, the Administrator of Records (*lushi yuan*) Wang Bi, the Recorder (*zhubu*) Wang Li, the Administrator of the Civil Affairs

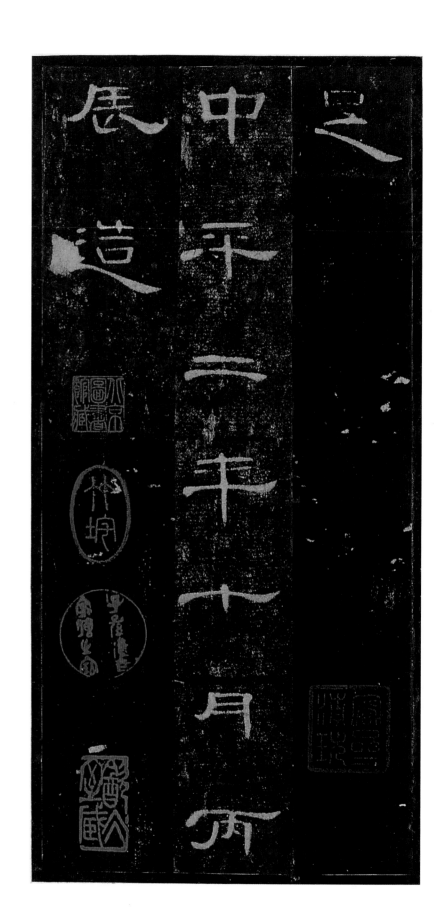

Section (*hucao yuan*) Qin Shang, the Scribe of the Labor Section (*gongcao shi*) Wang Zhuan, and others admired the excellence of this honorable person. Together they engraved a stone to record his merit, using these verses:

His exceptional wisdom was ample; his virtue and propriety were manifest.

Recommended to the royal court, he campaigned in the uncouth regions.

His authority blazing forth, he pacified the remote barbarians.

On returning with his army, he took charge of Huaili.

Because of his love for his brother, he retired to mourn him.

Angered by the rebels who burned the cities,

He took a commission to bring order to the ruins.

He suppressed the insubordinate, brought peace to the populace,

Repaired the official buildings, and opened the south gate

To make an opening toward the peaks and obtain a view of Mount Hua.

The countryside became enlightened and well ordered;

The officers liked his administration; the people had enough to eat.

Our lord is being promoted and will attain the highest posts.

Made on the *bingchen* day of the tenth month in the second year [185] of the Zhongping reign period.

The names and titles of fifty-six of the donors are listed in five columns on the reverse; these are written in slightly heavier script than the characters on the front face.

A significant change in the rendering of *bafen* ("eight-tenths"), the mature style of clerical script, is evident in this stele. The angularity and forcefulness in the brushwork of earlier clerical script appears to have given way to a fluid, more relaxed curvilinearity. There are twenty columns of characters, with forty-five characters in each column. The characters of this stele are elegant, elongated, and show more variation in the thickness and thinness of the various strokes within each character. Curved elements dominate the aesthetic, as seen in the increased number of bowed horizontal elements within the characters.

The rubbing of this stele, originally composed of one or more large sheets, was subsequently cut into strips and remounted in the present format. The album once belonged to the Qing scholar-officials Zhu Yizun (1629-1709; *boxue hongci* graduate of 1679) and Weng Fanggang (1733-1818; *jinshi* of 1752). According to one of the latter's nine inscriptions, Zhu Yizun's original colophon was removed from the album by the Zhu family for some reason. The album also contains two colophons by the late Qing-early Republican scholar-statesman Liang Qichao (1873-1929), and two short inscriptions by Zhao Huaiyu (1747-1823) and Li Yanzhang (1794-1836).

33

漢郃陽令曹全紀功碑

簡稱《曹全碑》。東漢靈帝中平二年（185年）十月刻立。無額，有碑陰題名。隸書，碑陽十九行，滿行四十五字。碑陰五列，第一列一行，第二列二十六行，第三列五行，第四列十七行，第五列四行。晚明拓本。割裱本，計二十一開。內高二五厘米，寬一二厘米。

善拓 *56*

《曹全碑》為著名漢碑之一，書法秀潤典麗，是漢隸中周圓筆的典型作品。係王敞等紀曹全功績而立。碑明萬曆（1573–1619年）初出土於陝西省郃陽縣舊城莘村，縣長李翼軒豐草中發現。篆額佚失不存。碑高二五三厘米，寬一二三厘米。出土時字畫完好，一字不缺。清康熙壬子（1672年）後，中有斷裂。出土後移存郃陽縣孔廟東門內，西向。一九六五年移置陝西省博物館碑林第三室。

碑陽文為：「君諱全，字景完，敦煌效穀人也。其先蓋周之胄。武王秉乾之機，翦伐殷商，既定爾勳，福祿攸同，封弟叔振鐸于曹國，因氏焉。秦漢之際，曹參夾輔王室，世宗廓土斥竟，子孫遷于雍州之郊，分址右扶風，或在安定，或處武都，或居隴西，或家敦煌。枝分葉布，所在為雄。君高祖父敏，舉孝廉，武威長史，巴郡胊忍令，張掖居延都尉。曾祖父述，孝廉，謁者，金城長史，夏陽令。祖父鳳，孝廉，張掖屬國都尉丞，右扶風孝隃廉侯相，金城西部都尉，北地大守。父琫，少貫名州郡，不幸早逝，是以位不副德。君童齔好學，甄極瑟緯，無文不綜。賢孝之性，根生於心。收養季祖母，供事繼母，先意承志，存亡之敬，禮無遺闕。是以鄉人為之諺曰：『重親致歡曹景完』。易世載德，不隕其名。及其從政，清擬夷齊，直慕史魚。歷郡右職，上計掾史，仍辟涼州，常為治中，別駕，紀綱萬，朱紫不謬。出典諸郡，彈枉糾邪，貪暴洗心，同僚服德，遠近憚威。建寧二年，舉孝廉，除郎中，拜西域戊部司馬。時疏勒國王和德，弒父篡位，不供職貢，君興師征討，有吮膿之仁，分醪之惠。攻城野戰，謀若涌泉，威牟諸賁，和德面縛而死。還師振旅，諸國禮遣且二百萬，悉以薄官。遷右扶風槐令，遭同產弟憂棄官，續遇禁罔。潛隱家巷七年。光和六年，復舉孝廉。七年三月，除郎中，拜酒泉祿福長。妖賊張角，起兵幽冀，兗豫荊楊，同時並動。而縣民郭家等復造逆亂，燔燒城寺，萬民騷擾，人裹不安。三郡告急，羽檄仍至。于時聖主諮諏，群僚咸曰：君哉！轉拜郃陽令，收合餘燼，芟夷殘迸，絕其本根，遂訪故老商量，俊乂王敞、王畢等，恤民之要，存慰高年，撫育鰥寡，以家錢糴米粟賜癃盲。大女桃妻等，合七首藥神明膏，親至離亭，部吏王宰、程橫等，賦與有疾者，咸蒙瘳悛。惠政之流，甚於置郵。百姓繦負，反者如雲。戢治廧屋，布肆列陳。風雨時節，歲獲豐年。農夫織婦，百工戴恩。縣，前以河平元年，遭白茅水災，害退於戌亥之間，興造城郭。是後，舊姓及修身之士，官位不登，君乃閔縉紳之徒不濟，開南寺門，承望華嶽，鄉明而治。庶使學者李儒、欒規、程寅等，各獲人爵之報。廓廣聽事官舍，廷曹廊閣，升降揖讓，朝覲之階，費不出民，役不干時。門下掾王敞、錄事掾王畢、主簿王歷、戶曹掾秦尚、功曹史王顓等，嘉慕奚斯、考甫之美，乃共刊石紀功。其辭曰：『懿明后，德義章。貢王庭，征鬼方。威布烈，安殊荒。還師旅，臨槐里。感孔懷，赴喪紀。嗟逆賊，燔城市。特受命，理殘圮。芟不臣，寧黔首。繕官寺，開南門。闕嵯峨，望華山。鄉明治，惠沾渥。吏樂政，民給足。君高升，極鼎足』。中平二年十月丙辰造』。碑陰之文，可參見《金石萃編》所錄，此從略。

《曹全碑》不僅有極高藝術價值，而且含有重要歷史價值。文中除記述曹全之生平、功績以及世系外，並記載漢代重大歷史事件，與文獻記載不同，可作為訂正歷史之參考。此碑文多別字，故後人疑為摹刻者，然就其端直樸茂而言，非漢人所不能。

此割裱本系清朱彝尊、翁方綱等舊藏之明拓「悉」字未損拓本。外題簽為梁啟超題：「朱竹垞舊藏本曹全碑，今歸飲冰室。乙丑正月題」。內題簽為翁方綱題：「曹全碑。曝書亭藏本」，并鈐「覃谿鑑藏」朱文長方印。有翁方綱、梁啟超跋，趙懷玉札，李彥章觀款四開。鈐有「彝齋」、「翁方綱」、「蘇齋金石文」、「容齋清玩」、「飲冰室藏」、「葉志詵審定記」等印。茲選照三開，即碑文首一開、「『悉』字未損」一開以及碑文末一開。

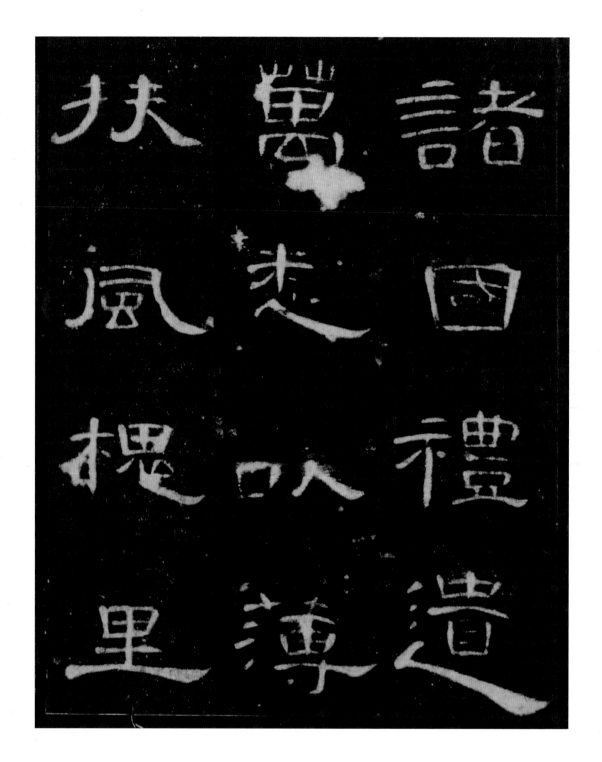

34

Han gu lingxiao Ba jun taishou Fan Min fujun bei

Epitaph of Fan Min, Governor of Ba Commandery during the Han Dynasty

Eastern Han dynasty (25-220), Jian'an reign period (196-219), dated 205

Inscribed in seal and clerical scripts by Liu Sheng and his son

From Lushan county, Yazhou, Sichuan province

Hanging scroll, ink rubbed on paper, 257.0 x 123.1 cm; dimensions of stele: 220.0 x 85.0 cm

Date of rubbing not given, probably late Ming dynasty (1368-1644) or early Qing dynasty (1644-1911)

Biaozhou 3

Fan Min (120-203) was a native of Fanjiaci in Lushan county, Sichuan, who served as the chief aide (*zhangshi*) of Yongchang commandery in present-day Yunnan. His final resting place lies in the village of Modong south of the county seat of Lushan in Sichuan province. After its collapse sometime during the Song dynasty (960-1279), the tomb chamber remained buried for more than a millennium until its excavation in 1958. One of the local legends of Yongchang commandery, "The Dragon Which Gave Issue to Nine Sons," is carved in stone on the doorway outside the tomb chamber.

Fan Min's epitaph had long been misattributed in records as the "Shoushan Epitaph of the Wei [period (220-265)]." After its rediscovery by Qiu Chang in the spring of 1102 during the Northern Song period, this epitaph was correctly renamed the *Fan Min*

bei (Epitaph of Fan Min). Qiu Chang and another man named Cheng Qin understood the historical value of this imposing late Eastern Han inscribed stone artifact and built a pavilion to protect it from the elements. Qiu and Cheng had their colophons engraved, in 1102 and 1159 respectively, on the reverse of the epitaph with one register above the other. Thereafter the epitaph was frequently recorded in epigraphical catalogues. However, after disparaging remarks about its authenticity were made by the renowned literatus Gu Yanwu (1613-1682), later scholars including Sun Xingyan (1753-1818) and Ouyang Fu joined the bandwagon, pronouncing for no good reason that the original stone had been lost or that the present stone had been recarved. Although the epitaph does contain several indecipherable characters, most of the text can be read. It documents the unstable social conditions as the Han neared its demise, with domestic troubles such as the Yellow Turban Rebellion of the peasants led by Zhang Jue and the activities of the Qiang people in the northwestern frontier region.

As seen from this rubbing, the *Epitaph of Fan Min* has a rounded head (*guishou*) with a pair of crouching dragons (*chilong*). The full title of the epitaph, in two columns of seal script totalling twelve characters, is placed just to the right of center of the head. A large circular hole pierces the stone just beneath the head. Laid out in twenty-two columns is the text of the epitaph, with the nineteenth and twenty-second columns left blank. The twenty remaining columns, with a maximum of twenty-nine characters per column, were engraved in closely spaced clerical script by a certain Liu Sheng and his son during the first ten days (*shangxun*) of the third month in the tenth year (205) of the Jian'an reign period.

This rubbing was most probably made during the mid-seventeenth century; it was successively owned by the Qing scholar Zha Sili (1653-1734; *jinshi* of 1700), Wang Jingmei, a certain person surnamed Jing (most probably the nineteenth-century collector Jing Qijun), and the late Qing-early Republican scholar-statesman Liang Qichao (1873-1929). In Liang's opinion, this is the finest example of a single-sheet rubbing. The three colophons are by the Ming collector Han Fengxi (1578-1653), Zha Sili, and Liang Qichao, with an additional three very short inscriptions written by Feng Hao (1719-1801), Yinglian (1707-1783), and Chen Jichang (fl. 1717).

34

漢故領校巴郡太守樊敏府君碑

簡稱《樊敏碑》。東漢靈帝建安十年（205年）三月上旬刻立，碑在四川雅州盧山。圭首上部有兩龍，中間有鳥向左立，額篆書二行，行十二字。碑文隸書，二十二行，行二十九字，第十九和第二十二行為空行，末行低十三字，刻歲月及書鐫人姓名。劉盛刻石，其子書丹。碑陰上截錄書十四行，行十字；下截正書，十四行，行十二字。碑四面有邊，中有界格，下有贔屭碑座。明末清初拓。整幅拓片，外高二五七厘米，寬一二三‧一厘米；內高二二〇厘米，寬八五厘米。掛軸裝。

裱軸3

樊敏，字升達，盧山縣樊家祠人，生於漢安帝永寧元年庚申（公元120年），卒於漢獻帝建安八年癸未（公元203年），卒年八十四歲。樊敏闕在四川盧山縣城南五華里沫東鄉，倒塌於宋代，埋藏地下有千餘年，一九五八年一月二十九日完成清理復原工作。據樊敏碑載，他曾任職永昌郡長史，故在他的墓前闕上雕刻了當地流傳的「龍生九子」的故事。

宋以前曾傳為《魏受禪碑》，北宋崇寧元年（1102年）三月，眉山邱常發現，考訂為《樊敏碑》。邱常和程勤二人曾建屋保護，并分別於崇寧壬午年1102年），紹興己卯（1159年）秋正書刻跋於碑陰，分兩截。上截，凡十四行，行十字。下截，凡十四行，行十二字。其後屢有著錄。後來顧亭林認為「濁惡或為贋鼎」，孫星衍、歐陽輔等說原石已佚，或翻刻，皆為臆說。《文物》一九六三年第十一期報道《樊敏碑》已復原，證明其碑未佚。碑文雖有漫漶，但文多可讀，從中可了解漢末動亂之狀，如內地有張角領導的黃巾農民運動的蓬勃發展，西北邊疆有羌族的活動。

樊敏碑高約二五〇厘米，寬約一一七厘米，上方微削，圓頂，圭首作二螭龍首向右抵於碑肩略似螭拱狀，碑首中稍偏右鐫「漢故領校巴郡太守樊府君碑」十二字，刻雙行，每行六字，篆書。其下有圓形穿眼，穿下方為碑文，空行二，刻二十行，行二十九字，計五百五十七字。

據宋洪适《隸釋》卷十一及清汪鋆《十二硯齋金石過眼錄》卷二所錄的「巴郡太守樊敏碑」碑文對照，此碑全文應如下：「君諱敏，字升達。肇祖

必戲，遺苗后稷，為堯種樹，舍潛于岐。天顧宣甫，乃萌昌發，周室衰微，霸伯匡弼。晉為韓魏，魯分為楊。充曜封邑，厥土河東。□漢之際，或居于□，或集于梁。君纘其緒，華南西疆，濱近聖禹，飲汶茹沔，總角好學。治《春秋》嚴氏經，貫穿道度，無文不睹。於是國君備禮招請，濯冕題□，傑立忠謇。有夷史之直，卓密之風。鄉黨見歸，察孝除郎。永昌長史，遷宕渠令。布化三載，遭離母憂，五五斷仁，大將軍辟。光和之末，京師擾穰，雄狐綏綏，冠履同□，投核長驅，畢志枕業，國復重察，辭病不就。再奉朝娉，十辟九臺，常為治中。從事，舉直錯柱。譚思舊制，彈饗糾貪。務鉏民穢，患苦施俗，喜怒作律，案罪殺人，不顧倡□，告子屬孫：敢若此者，不入墓門。州里僉然，號曰吏師。季世不詳，米巫凶虐，續蠢青羌，姦狡並起，陷附者眾，君執一心，賴無汚恥，復辟司徒，道隔不往，牧伯劉公，二世欽重，表授巴郡。後漢中，秋老乞身，以助義都尉，養疾閭里，又行褒義校尉。君仕不為人，祿不為己，桓桓大度，禮蹈其首。當窮台絙，松僑協軌，八十有四，歲在汁洽，絕驗期臻，奄忽藏形。凡百咸痛，士女涕泠。臣子褒術，刊石勒銘，其辭曰：『於戲与考，經德炳明。勞謙損益，耽古儉清。立朝正色，能無撓頗。威恩御下，持滿億盈。所歷見慕，遺歌景形。書載俊艾，股肱幹楨。有物有則，模楷後生。宜參鼎鉉，稽建皇靈。王路阪險，鬼方不庭。恒戢節足，輕寵賤榮。故□天選，而捐陪臣。晏嬰邸殿，留侯距齊。非辭福也，乃辟禍兮』。乿曰：『渾元垂像岳瀆淵仁兮，金精火佐寔生賢兮。□欲救民德彌大兮，遭偶陽九百六會兮。當□遯年兮遂逝兮，欹呼哀哉魂神往兮。建安十年三月上旬造，石工劉盛息悰書』」。

此拓本為查嗣瑮、王敬美、景氏、梁啟超遞藏，梁氏認為最佳的整幅卷軸拓本。有明代人韓逢禧、查氏、梁氏題跋考訂及馮浩、英廉、陳繼昌觀款六則，係明末清初拓本。鈐印有「逢禧」、「廉」、「嗣瑮」、「馮浩之印」、「蓮史」、「汝弼」、「馮浩之印」、「景氏秘藏」、「劍泉所得鴻寶」、「任公」、「壽如金石」、「飲冰室藏金石圖書印」、「梁啟超」、「寶佛庵主」、「王氏敬美」等印。

35

Biqiu Huicheng wei wang fu Luozhou chishi

Shiping gong zaoxiang tiji

Inscription for a Buddhist Image Constructed by the Monk Huicheng to Commemorate His Late Father, the Duke of Shiping and Regional Inspector of Luozhou

Northern Wei dynasty (386-534), Taihe reign period (477-499), dated 498

Text composed by Meng Guangda (act. late 5th century); calligraphy by Zhu Yizhang (act. late 5th century); overall dimensions: approx. 130 x 40 cm; head: 2 columns of regular script; 3 characters per column; text: 10 columns of regular script; maximum of 20 characters per column, each square containing characters averaging 4 x 4 cm

From the Guyang Cave, Longmen Grottoes, near Luoyang, Henan province

Hanging scroll, ink rubbed on paper with inscribed colophons, ink on paper, 104.7 x 54.0 cm; rubbing of engraved stele, approx. 89.9 x 41.2 cm

Date of rubbing not given, probably Qing dynasty (1644-1911)

Biaozhou 830

This rubbing was taken from the Guyang Cave, Longmen Grottoes, situated on the banks of the Yellow River near Luoyang in Henan province. It represents one of the most unique stone-carved Chinese inscriptions and was first recorded in 1787 by Bi Yuan (1730-1797) in his *Zhongzhou jinshi ji* (Bronze and Stone Inscriptions of Central China). Not

only is it counted among one of the "Twenty Outstanding Inscriptions of Longmen" (*Longmen ershi pin*), it has also been canonized as one of the "Four Exemplary Inscriptions of Longmen" (*Longmen si pin*).

The inscription on this rubbing was commissioned by the monk Huicheng to ensure the spiritual salvation of his deceased father, the gentleman Shiping, an aristocrat of the ruling Tuoba clan who had served as an official in several posts but whose name is absent from any other historical record of the Northern Wei dynasty (386-534). The engraved panel is situated at the outer edge of the upper tier of the cave's north wall, and is adjacent to a niche with a seated Buddha and two flanking attendants; it is dated the fourteenth day of the ninth month in the twenty-second year (498) of the Taihe reign period, and is of the finest possible quality in terms of design and workmanship.

Because he was a member of an imperial clan, Huicheng could well afford the services of the finest authors, calligraphers, and engravers for his dedicatory inscription. This is one of the rare instances in which both the names of the calligrapher and the engraver are supplied: Zhu Yizhang and Meng Dawen respectively. The angular calligraphic style with wedge-shaped dots and sharp-edged strokes is particularly notable, as are the many variant characters. This inscription and its chessboard grid is also remarkable for having been cut in relief rather than in the usual intaglio; rubbings taken from this object show the rare appearance of characters in black ink instead of the normal white reserve. The grid also enhances the individuality of each character and the experience of reading the text. The long, diagonal lines which extend across the surface of this rubbing reflect the actual damaged condition of the engraved stone; the

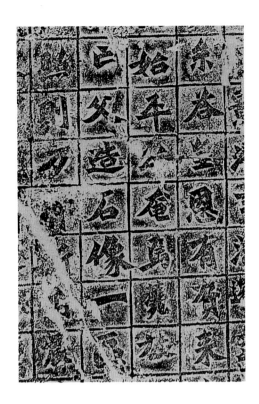

same cracks are visible in other rubbings as well as in published photographs of the object itself.

Judging from the well preserved imprints of several key characters in the text, this very fine early rubbing was most probably taken during the late Qianlong or Jiaqing periods. It is accompanied by an impressive number of colophons and stamped with many collectors' and connoisseurs' seals. The colophon at the upper right in large characters was composed by the Qing epigraphist and calligrapher Hu Zhen (1817-1862) and reads: "The characters vary in size like stars scattered in the heavens; their formal gestures glance around like fish splashing about in the water."

35

比丘慧成為亡父洛州刺史始平公造像題記

亦稱《始平公造像題記》、《慧成造像記》。北魏太和二十二年（498年）九月十四日刻立。石在河南省洛陽市龍門石窟古陽洞北壁上層。孟達撰文，朱義章書。陽文刻。額文正書六字。碑陽正書十行，行二十字，有方界格。清乾隆嘉慶年間（1736–1820年）拓本。縱九〇厘米，橫四〇厘米。立軸裝。

裱軸 *830*

《比丘慧成為亡父洛州刺史始平公造像》龕位於龍門石窟古陽洞北壁上層最外側。因是為統治者服務的比丘造像之一，肯定是有得到帝王的支持。比丘慧成造釋迦佛像，一是為了「答皇恩」，二是為其亡父能達到成佛的境界。比丘慧成的亡父爵衛為使持節、光祿大夫、洛州刺史、始平公，不見於史籍記載。

龕右（東）側造像碑，高一三〇厘米、寬四〇厘米。此碑之用棋子格陽文刻，為北魏石刻中所罕見，並是龍門石窟唯一的陽刻作品，極具藝術價值。此碑歷來奉其為「北魏造像中最佳者」、「北魏書法能品上」，被稱「龍門二十品」之一、「龍門四品」之一。後人因其陽文鐫刻較淺，鏟底挖深，遂傷字口。此為清代未經鏟底拓本，胡震舊藏。有胡震、錢松、孫文川、胡遠山、黃炳堃、周閑、吳鐵樵、王垕等人題跋十三款。鈐有「黃節讀碑」、「胡鼻山藏真印」、「錢松叔蓋印信宜長壽」等印。

題記文為：「始平公像一區。夫靈蹤□啟，則攀宗靡尋。容像不陳，則崇之必□。是以真顏□於上齡，遺形敷于下葉，暨于大代，茲功厥作。比丘慧成，自以影濯玄流，激逢昌運，率渴誠心，為國造石窟□（寺），□系答皇恩，有資來業。父使持節光祿大夫洛州刺史始平公奄焉喪，放仰慈顏，以攀躬□。匪烏在□，遂為亡父造像一區，願亡父神飛三□（智），□（五）周十地。□玄照，則萬□（有）斯明。震慧嚮，則大千斯□（曉）。元世師僧，父母眷屬，鳳翥道場，鸞騰兜率。若悟洛人間，三槐獨秀，九棘雲敷，五有群生，咸同斯願。太和□（廿）二年九月十四日訖。朱義章書。孟達文。」

36

Cao Wangxi zaoxiang ji

Inscription and Illustrated Panels for the Base of a Buddhist Image Constructed by Cao Wangxi

Northern Wei dynasty (386-534), Zhengguang reign period (519-524), dated 525

Hanging scroll, ink rubbed on paper, 127.9 x 65.3 cm; rubbing at uppermost register, approx. 27.0 x 62.5 cm; rubbing at upper middle register, approx. 26.0 x 62.5 cm; rubbing at lower middle register, approx. 26.0 x 63.3 cm; rubbing at lowermost register, approx. 25.5 x 61.5 cm

Date of rubbing not given, probably Qing dynasty (1644-1911)

Biaozhou 179

Cao Wangxi (act. early 6th century) was a native of Wei county in Wei commandery, which was part of Qi prefecture (in present-day Shandong province). During the late Northern Wei period (386-534), he served as general of Xiangcheng (in present-day Henan province) and district magistrate of Boren (near Tangshan in present-day Hebei province). The hanging scroll shown here contains four rubbings taken from all sides of the stone pedestal supporting a Buddhist image commissioned by Cao Wangxi. The principal panel depicts Maitreya (Sanskrit for "the Merciful One"), the Buddha of the Future, whose anticipated coming four thousand years after Sakyamuni Buddha's Nirvana, would presage the arrival of paradise on earth. Maitreya was among the most popularly worshipped and represented bodhisattvas during the Eastern Jin period (317-420) and the Northern and Southern Dynasties period (386-589).

The original Northern Wei stone pedestal, long detached from the statue it supported, had been stacked against a wall by villagers in Tonglin, Linzi county, Shandong province. It was subsequently acquired by the collector Chen Jieqi (1813-1884), and sold by his heirs sometime in 1921 to a museum in Paris. Prior to the stone's arrival at the Chen family estate, rubbings taken from it were rather ordinary. However, those taken between that time and its departure from China are of a much finer quality; the faces of the figures are rubbed with lighter tones of ink in order to highlight them, an effect that is evident in the separately taken rubbings mounted here as a hanging scroll. The set of rubbings once belonged to the scholar-statesman Liang Qichao (1873-1929), three of whose personal seals are impressed on either edge of the inscription.

The top panel with its centralized composition represents the front aspect of the pedestal. The Bodhisattva Maitreya, perched atop a lotus base, supports a lilypad and a censer in the shape of a "universal mountain" (*boshan lu*). On either side are crouching lions, while a pair of phoenixes are shown adjacent to the censer. The second panel represents one of the lateral sides of the pedestal, with movement taking place from right to left. It depicts a crowned royal personage dressed in court robes, holding a censer in his right hand, and flanked by two attendants who support him at the wrists. Following behind are other attendants, one raising up a tasseled canopy, another bearing a large fan carried in processions, and two others carrying ritual vessels. A young groom at right leads a noble steed, ornately turned out with an elaborate

saddle and guards to protect against mud or dirt attached to the saddle-flaps. In the third panel, where movement occurs from left to right, a royal consort or concubine carries a censer, flanked by two female attendants with double-chignon coiffures; their deportment parallels that of the group of three seen in the panel above. Behind them are three other female attendants carrying a wooden fan and ritual implements. Finally, there is a covered chariot with a propped-up awning drawn by an ox and led by an attendant. The dress, hairstyles, ritual implements, and modes of transport of the uppermost echelon of Northern Wei society are depicted in an exuberant though somewhat stylized manner, demonstrating the high level of pictorial representation achieved by stone engravers at this time.

The three pictorial sides of the pedestal were carved in relief with flowing, rhythmic lines, hence the images on the rubbing appear as positive rather than the usual negative forms. The inscription, on the other hand, was engraved in intaglio in twenty-two columns of regular script, with a maximum of nine characters per column. As with most Northern Wei inscriptions, there are a number of variant characters that do not have modern equivalents. In addition to the standard references to Buddhist notions of suffering and attainment of Nirvana, the inscription also supplies the precise day and month in the sixth year (525) of the Zhengguang reign period during the Northern Wei period that the image of Maitreya was dedicated, Cao Wangxi's official positions, and his purpose in commissioning the work. The complete text of the inscription is recorded in *juan* 6 of the *Shi'er yan zhai jinshi guoyan lu* compiled by the Qing epigrapher Wang Yun (1816-1879).

36
曹望憘造像記

北魏正光六年（525年）三月二十日刻。石在山東省臨淄縣桐林莊，原石現在法國巴黎博物館。拓本年月不詳。外高一二七‧九厘米，寬六五‧三厘米。拓本分四層，最上層高二七厘米，寬六二‧五厘米，中上層高二六厘米，寬六二‧五厘米，中下層高二六厘米，寬六三‧三厘米，最下層高二五‧五厘米，寬六一‧五厘米。立軸裝。

裱軸 179

　　曹望憘，北魏時為襄城將軍、柏仁令，齊州魏郡魏縣人。此為曹氏所造的彌勒造像佛座之石刻綫畫。彌勒菩薩是未來佛，據說釋迦牟尼曾預言，在他涅槃後四千年，彌勒將由兜率天下凡，在華林園的龍華樹下證道成佛，舉行三次法會，普度眾生，使數以億計的人成阿羅漢。彌勒是在東晉南北朝時代於民間流行很廣泛的一種佛教信仰。

　　石原在山東省臨淄縣桐林莊居民壘於牆間，

以後歸陳介祺所藏。1921年間，陳氏售于法國巴黎博物館。未歸陳氏前，拓工一般，歸陳氏則精拓，人面為淡墨。此拓本合四面為一幀，第一層（正面）中畫一蓮花結實，上生菩薩托一博山爐，左右各蹲坐一獅，上飛一對翔鳳。第二層畫一戴冠穿朝服的帝王模樣者，右手舉一博山爐，雙袖搭在身旁的侍者腕上，後有侍從擎一傘蓋，上飾流蘇；一執障扇者和二手捧禮器者相隨，最後一童子手牽高頭駿馬，馬披障泥寶鞍，裝備華麗。第三層畫一后妃托博山爐，旁有兩扎雙髻女侍，三人姿勢與上圖同，後有侍者擎障扇和舉荷花等禮器者；最後畫支棚方形轎，一牛駕轅，一侍女牽引。底層為題記。全圖形象地反映了北魏時期上層人物的衣裝髮式，牛馬轎，以及線描技藝的精湛水平。

　　座呈方形，三面為浮雕畫像，一面為造像記，正書二十二行，行九字，其文如下：「大魏正光六年歲次乙巳三月乙巳朔廿日甲子，夫法道初興，則十方趨一。釋迦啟建，則含生歸伏。然神潛涅槃，入於空境，形坐玄宮，使愚迷後軌。襄威將軍、柏仁令，齊州魏郡魏縣曹望＊Ｔ是以仰思三寶之蹤，恨未逢如來之際，減己家寶玄心獨拔，敬造彌勒下生石像一軀，□以建立之功，使津通之益仰為家

國、己、眷屬，永斷苦因。常與佛會，七世先亡，神昇淨境，親表內外，齊沐法澤，一切等類，共沾惠液。堂堂福林，蕩蕩難名，知財非己，竭家精成，佛潛己久，今方現形，匪直普潤，六合揚名」。末刻一「大」字。

　　本造像記曾著錄於汪鋆《十二硯齋金石過眼錄》第六卷。此拓本為梁啟超舊藏，右下有「飲冰室藏」朱文長方印，右下、左下有「芝閣所得」白文方印。

大魏正光六年歲次甲
正月□飛龍道已初興廿日次
三夫□釋迦初則十甲
□秋一□法道則仁□入合十
迷後麘州境休然□孫
歸軹襄□□□□
令空以魏襄郡威坐神潛達使
惛是麘思感玄容建
恨家□獨來三魏將玄潛□□
勒下生玄石心像□之際寶軍書柏使縣則仁
建立之功使□敬造顛□□孫巳乾□
斷苦家國□巳津一躯道益以孫
先丘日常身會春表七屬之永世益
外沿神亭淨法渾一切境親表等內世頒
共堂治惠林蕩蕩□佛
室堂福瑪家蕩□若名知
巳對非今已瑪精成鶊普菩
闡久合揚名形匜宜大
大普菩知

37

Ta menmei xiandiao

Finely Engraved Illustration in the Linear Manner on the Lintel of a Pagoda Doorway

Tang dynasty (618-907), undated

Provenance unknown

Hanging scroll, ink rubbed on paper, 126.9 x 135.6 cm; dimensions of lintel: 106 x 136 cm

Date of rubbing unknown, probably Qing dynasty (1644-1911)

Biaozhou 1

Stone-engraved illustrations in the linear manner (*shike xianhua*) represent a distinctly Chinese form of art. Talented artisans used sharp styluses to incise elaborate designs directly onto the smooth surfaces of stone. This type of illustration began in the Qin (221-206 B.C.) and developed through the Northern and Southern Dynasties (386-589), gradually encompassing a wide range of figural and narrative subjects. During the Tang dynasty (618-907) it continued to flourish and reached new heights. Representative examples of *shike xianhua* from the Tang include the illustration of women on a stone vault excavated south of Chang'an county in Shaanxi province; the illustration on the base of the stele of the Buddhist priest Daoyin; and the stele of the Duke of Bin. Most famous, however, are the the four pictorial stone lunettes or lintels (*menmei*) above doorways in the Great Wild Goose Pagoda at Ci'en Temple in Xi'an, executed during the Yonghui reign era (650-655).

This rubbing was taken from a semicircular stone lintel probably placed over the entrance of a vaulted corridor in a Tang-dynasty pagoda. Although the stone's origin cannot be identified, its style of illustration is characteristically Tang and is similar to that found in the northern, southern, and eastern doorways of the Great Wild Goose Pagoda. Despite uncertain provenances, incised illustrations of this kind constitute valuable materials for the study of pictorial style, stone engraving, and Buddhist architectural ornamentation during the Tang period.

A long and very densely inscribed colophon was placed at the lower center of the rubbing where a missing piece of stone translated into a corresponding blank space in the rubbing. The mass of very small characters was written by Yao Hua (1876-1930), an artist and devout Buddhist from Guizhou who resided at the Lotus Temple (Lianhua si) in Beijing. The stone lintel was already damaged by the time the rubbing was taken, and since it did not bear any kind of inscription and was of unknown origin, Yao was unable to ascribe a date to the work, nor could he concretely identify the Buddhist image at the center. However, he noted that the two small flanking figures are those of monks, the two figures with halos are bodhisattvas, and the two figures at either extremity are *vajras* (Buddhist temple guardians). The one to the right wields a "diamond club" (*jingang chu*) weighted at both ends to quell demons and is most probably a representation of the *vajra* Indra.

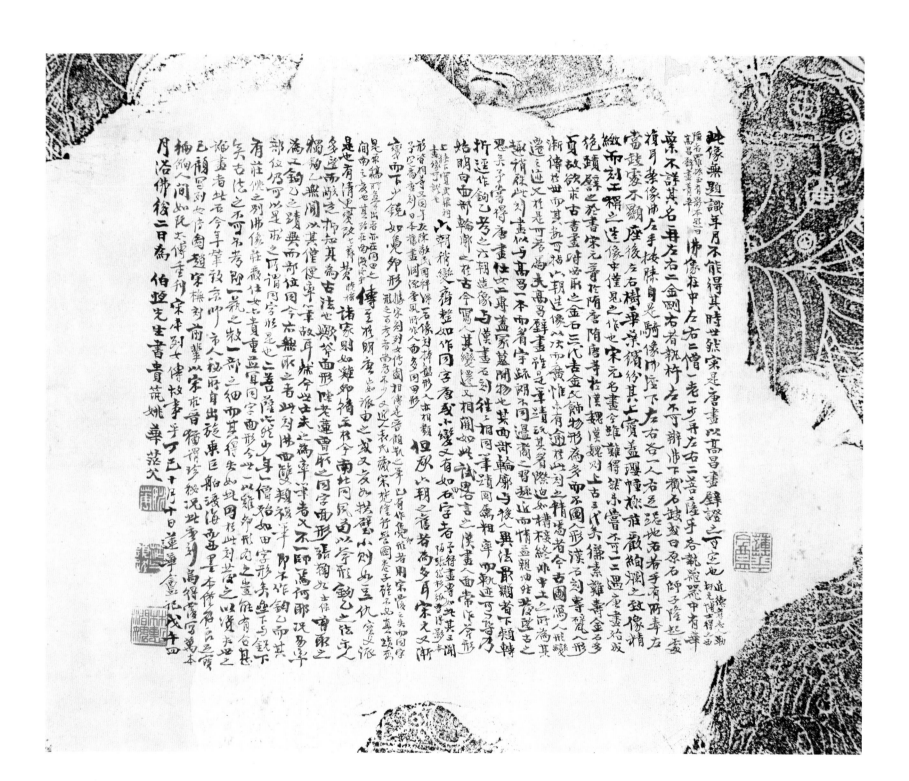

37
塔門楣綫雕

唐（618-907年）刻，無年月。來源不詳。約清（1644-
1911年）拓本。拓片外高一二六・九厘米，寬一三五・
六厘米。拓片內高一〇六厘米，寬一三六厘米。掛軸
裝。

裱軸 /

　　石刻綫畫是中國特有的民族藝術形式之一，
它是一種具有雕刻手法的陰刻綫畫，由富有才智
的匠師運用鋒利的「刀筆」直接畫在光滑的石面
上。中國石刻綫畫在秦、漢、晉、南北朝時代才
逐漸發展為整幅構圖的人物故事畫，至唐代更為興
盛。典型的唐代石刻綫畫有包括陝西省長安南郊
出土的韋頊石槨上的婦女畫像、西安慈恩寺大雁塔
的唐永徽年間（650至655年）綫雕東西南北四門
門楣、道因法師碑座綫刻、邠國公碑等。

　　此拓本來自唐代的古塔之一，所拓的是底層
券門或石門半圓形門楣上所雕的綫刻像，構圖充
實，造型豐滿，人物神態各異，畫面嚴謹，綫條
精美遒勁。雖不知此門楣的來源，但與西安大雁塔
的東、南、北三門門楣類似，是典型的唐代風範，
是研究唐代佛寺建築、雕刻、繪畫藝術的珍貴資
料。

　　此拓本為姚華舊藏并小字題跋。姚華，字重
光，號茫父，貴州貴筑人。於詩文詞曲、碑版古器
及考據音韻等，無不精通。書、畫則山水、花卉、
篆、隸、真、行，亦有高深造詣。姚氏久居北京蓮
花寺，因別署蓮花龕主，與文人書畫家陳師曾最
善，京師所製銅墨盒面圖畫，精者多出於其與師曾
手筆。晚年病臂，猶事揮毫。著有《弗堂類稿》。

　　據姚跋，「此像無題識，年月不能得。……
佛像在中，左右二僧，一老一少，再左右二菩
薩……再左右二金剛，右者執杵，左不可辨」。拓
片有「蓮華盦」朱文方印、「姚華」白文方印、「茫
父題跋」白文方印、「林漸澗樓」朱文方印。另有
兩方印，為「祝繼先金石文字之印」白文方印、「祝
氏續齋手拓」朱文長方印。

38

Guanyin xiang

Portrait of the Bodhisattva Guanyin

Purportedly Tang dynasty (618-907), undated

Woodcut illustration; traditionally attributed to Wu Daozi (689-759), probably Ming (1368-1644) or Qing dynasty (1644-1911)

Hanging scroll, ink rubbed on paper, 109.1 x 54.9 cm

Date of rubbing unknown, Qing dynasty (1644-1911)

Biaozhou 236

Guanyin (literally "Observer of Sounds"), the Bodhisattva of Compassion whose original appellation was Guanshiyin ("One Who Observes the Sounds of the World"), is by far the most popular bodhisattva in China. In Indian and early Chinese Buddhism, Guanyin (Avalokitesvara in Sanskrit) had been represented as a male figure, but during the Song dynasty he was transformed into a female deity, better known as the Goddess of Mercy–giver of comfort in the face of human suffering, provider of children, and protector of all who invoke her name. Guanyin's legendary abode is Mount Putuo, on an island off the coast of Zhejiang province.

Guanyin is believed to have no less than thirty-three manifestations (male or female, old or young, etc.) and has been depicted in numerous ways in Chinese iconography. In this rubbing taken from a woodcut, she is portrayed with the boy pilgrim Sudhana (Shancai in Chinese). According to the Garland Sutra (*Avatamsaka-sutra; Da fang guang fo Huayan jing*), Sudhana visits fifty-three teachers to learn the *Dharma*, and Guanyin is

the twenty-eighth one visited. Guanyin is shown here standing on a floating lotus leaf, her demeanor supremely serene amidst the billowing waves. Shancai, on the other hand, stands on the leaf of a water-lily, looking somewhat worried and hoping for safe passage. Though attributed at upper left to the famous Tang figure painter Wu Daozi (689-759), who used a highly linear and fluid style to render flowing robes to great advantage, this picture is probably of much later vintage.

38

觀音像

傳唐吳道子繪。無年月。木刻清 (1644–1911年) 拓本。
縱一〇九‧一厘米，橫五五厘米。掛軸裝。
裱軸 *236*

　　觀音，「觀世音」的略稱，因唐避太宗李世民諱，故略「世」字，稱「觀音」。與大勢至菩薩同為阿彌陀佛的左右協侍，稱「西方三聖」，是中國佛教的四大菩薩之一。佛典稱觀音為發大心以普救世人的大慈大悲菩薩。《妙法蓮華經》普門品説遇難眾生只要誦念其名號，他就能顯現三十三種化身尋聲往救。相傳顯靈説法的道場在浙江普陀山。中國寺院的觀音，早期塑像和圖像多作男像，唐代以後改作女像。

　　此圖描繪觀音和善財童子渡海的情形。洶湧的波濤上漂浮一荷花巨瓣，觀音立於其上，神色安詳；善財童子侍立於右側蓮葉上，而帶愁容，合十作祈拜狀，默禱風平浪靜，安抵彼岸，相比之下，益顯菩薩法力之無窮。此圖刀法嫻熟，筆道圓轉，應是高手所作。惟兩旁之松竹峭石鉤勒失度，左上題「吳道子筆」，顯然是後世人的附會。

39

Kongzi xiang

Portrait of Confucius

Purportedly Tang dynasty (618-907), undated

Attributed to Wu Daozi (689-759)

Hanging scroll, ink rubbed on 2 joined sheets of paper, 194.0 x 62.1 cm

Date of rubbing unknown

Biaozhou 138

Confucius (551-479 B.C.), whose actual name was Kong Qiu, was the preeminent thinker and political theorist of ancient China. He was born and raised near Qufu, capital of the small feudal state of Lu at the base of the Shandong peninsula, and made his living as a teacher and instructor in canonical texts. Distressed by the constant warfare between the Chinese states and by the venality and tyranny of the rulers, he urged a system of morality and statecraft that would preserve peace and provide people with stable and just government. He later became critical of Lu's government, which he regarded as having usurped the rightful authority of the Zhou dynasty, and achieved no political prominence during his lifetime. For some fourteen years, he traveled to several neighboring states, but was never successful in inducing any ruler to grant him high office so that he might introduce his reforms. Confucius is traditionally credited with the compilation of the *Lun yu* (Analects), in which he laid out his moral philosophies which emphasized exemplary government, education, and social ethics.

From the Han dynasty onwards, a number of canonical works associated with the Confucian cult were believed to have been compiled by Confucius, although the truth is uncertain. The Five Confucian Classics (*wu jing*) consist of the following: the *Book of Odes* or *Classic of Songs* (*Shi jing*) which contains poems dating from the tenth to the seventh century B.C.; the *Book of Changes* (*Yi jing*), a work on divination based on the eight trigrams and sixty-four hexagrams; the *Spring and Autumn Annals* (*Chunqiu*), or annals of Lu, the state in which Qufu lay; the *Book of Rites* (*Li ji*); and the *Book of Documents* (*Shu jing*), a collection of historical documents extending from the Shang dynasty to the late Zhou.

Two centuries after the death of Confucius, Emperor Wu of the Han dynasty (156-87 B.C.; r. 141-87 B.C.), acting on the advice of his trusted minister Dong Zhongshu (176-104 B.C.), made Confucianism the state ideology. From that time on, emperors of every dynasty conferred posthumous titles on the sage. The Northern Wei (386-534) emperors named him "Father Ni the Learned Sage"; emperors of the Tang (618-907) called him "Sage" and conferred upon him the title "Prince of Literary Excellence," which the Yuan dynasty (1279-1368) emperors expanded to "Prince of Literary Excellence and Sagely Accomplishment." The Ming (1368-1644) emperors named him "First Master of Sagely Accomplishment," and the Qing (1644-1911) rulers went even further and conferred princeships on the five generations of his immediate descendants.

This rubbing of a three-quarter-view, full-length portrait of Confucius is taken from one of thousands of iconic images that were engraved and placed in Confucian temples from at least the second century A.D. In this idealized and conventionalized portrait placed against a vacant backdrop, Confucius is depicted as an official dressed in flowing court robes, hands clasped together, and standing in a dignified manner. Although it bears the name of the great Tang dynasty painter Wu Daozi (689-759; known for his mastery of line), as do so many of this genre of portraits, the actual date of execution of this image is probably much later. The eulogy placed above the portrait is taken from a longer text composed by the Ming scholar-official Chen Fengwu (1475-1541; *jinshi* of 1496) and may be thus rendered: "His virtue is equal to Heaven and Earth; his way (*dao*) is the loftiest achieved in the past and in the present. He explained the Six Canonical Books and his statutes will endure for ten thousand generations." By virtue of the use of Chen Fengwu's eulogy, this portrait of Confucius was probably not executed before the Zhengde (1506-1521) or Jiajing (1522-1566) reign periods of the Ming dynasty.

39

孔子像

又名《孔丘像》、《夫子像》。無年月。傳唐吳道子繪。正書贊。拓片縱一九四厘米，橫六二‧一厘米。掛軸裝。

裱軸 *138*

孔子，名丘，字仲尼，春秋時期魯國陳邑昌平鄉（今山東省曲阜東南尼山附近）人，是中國歷史上偉大的思想家、政治家、教育家，儒家的創始人。孔子生於周靈王二十一年（公元前551年）冬十月庚子，生有異質，學無常師。嘗問禮於老子，學音樂於萇弘，學琴於師襄。聚徒講學，從事政治活動。年五十，攝魯國相事，其後不用，遂周游列國，十三年不見用，年六十八返魯，刪《詩》、《書》，定《禮》、《樂》，贊《周易》，修《春

秋》，以傳先王之道。弟子三千人，身通六藝者七十二人。卒於敬王四十一年（公元前479年）夏四月乙丑，年七十三。

孔子生前沒有被統治者所看重，他創立的儒家學說也未受到重視。但漢代以後，統治階級對孔子思想不斷改造，使孔子之道成為中國的正統思想，在各個朝代皆受到尊重。反映孔子事跡的畫像，最早的是東漢元嘉元年武梁祠石刻中的「孔子見老子圖」。在以後的朝代中也制作出有關孔子的單幅繪畫作品。為表達對孔子的崇敬、懷念，從漢代起，人民開始塑造能夠訴諸於視覺的孔子形象。北宋時，曲阜孔廟增加了臨摹的相傳晉代顧愷之繪孔子隨行像、唐代吳道子繪小影、行教像、司寇像石刻。元大德十一年（1307年），成宗加孔子號，曰：「大成至聖文宣王」。明正德十六年（1521年），孔子也被推崇為「大成至聖先師」。清康熙加封孔子為「萬世師表」。

此圖畫孔子素帶佩劍，手背翹外相握。石左下邊雖題「吳道子筆」，但顯然是後世人臨摹吳氏之原作。石右上部所題「德配天地，道冠古今，刪述六經，垂憲萬世」十六字，取自明陳鳳梧《孔子贊》，其文為「道冠古今，德配天地，刪述六經，垂憲萬世，統承羲皇，源啟洙泗，報功報德，百王崇祀」。由此可見，該圖繪制時代不早過明正德、嘉靖年間。

40

Zhao Songxue shu Taishang xuanyuan Daode jing

The *Daode jing* in the Calligraphy of Zhao Mengfu

Yuan dynasty (1279-1368), Yanyou reign period (1314-1320)

Calligraphy by Zhao Mengfu (1254-1322) in 18 or 19 small regular-script characters per column, dated 1316; text copied by Gu Xin (act. late 13th-early 14th century) and engraved by Wu Shichang (act. late 13th-early 14th century) in 1318

Album of 50 leaves, ink rubbed on yellow paper, accordion-style mounting between top and bottom wooden boards; overall dimensions of album, 31.7 x 17.0 x 2.6 cm; each leaf approx. 31.6 x 17.0 cm; each rubbing panel, approx. 23.9 x 12.9 cm

Date of rubbing not given, probably late Yuan dynasty (1279-1368)

Shanta 546

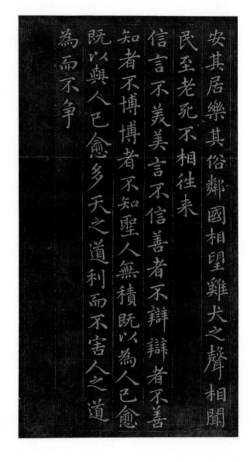

The *Daode jing* is one of the two principal canonical texts associated with philosphical Daoism, the other being the *Zhuangzi* (Sayings of Master Zhuang) of Zhuang Zhou (369-286 B.C.). The *Daode jing* (also known as the *Dedao jing* in silk manuscripts excavated at Mawangdui in 1973) is a relatively concise text with about 5,000 characters in eighty-one short aphoristic sections (*zhang*). Though traditionally attributed to Li Er (ca. 6th century B.C.), an older contemporary of Confucius (551-479 B.C.) and better known as Laozi, it is an anonymous text from around the fourth century B.C. and probably the product of composite authorship.

Zhao Mengfu (1254-1322), a member of the deposed Southern Song imperial clan, was summoned to the Mongol capital of Dadu in 1310 and quickly promoted to high office. He was also one of the preeminent calligraphers and painters of the Yuan dynasty, and is known to have made several complete transcriptions of the *Daode jing* in his exquisite small regular-script (*xiaokai*) calligraphy. The piece that he executed in the third year (1316) of the Yanyou reign period was traced by Zhao's good friend, the scholar-official Gu Xin, and engraved by Wu Shichang on a set of ten stone tablets two years later in 1318. These were housed in the White Cloud Monastery (*Baiyun guan*), the most significant Daoist abbey in Beijing, where the rubbings in this album were presumably made between 1318 and the fall of the Yuan dynasty in 1368. The stones incised with Zhao Mengfu's writing are of considerable epigraphical and historical importance since, as one of the eleven extant engravings of the *Daode jing* made between the early eighth and early fourteenth centuries, they can be used as comparative material with transmitted versions of this canonical text in other media.

The album of rubbings was once in the collection of the scholar and epigrapher Zhang Yu (1865-1937; *jinshi* of 1903) from Suzhou; after his death it was donated by his family to the national library (then known as the National Library of Peiping).

趙本《道德經》書於延祐三年（1316年），題「大德十一年歲在丁未十二月廿六日，吳興趙孟頫書」。趙氏時年六十三歲，字體工整秀麗，筆法穩健，獨具風格。書法繼承晉唐以來小楷的傳統，法度謹嚴，字形峭拔秀麗，結體妍媚舒展，筆法勁健圓潤。此帖是傳世趙書小楷法帖中的珍稀之本，全帖凡五千三百四十六字，首尾一致，無一懈筆。帖尾題「善夫顧信摹勒上石，姑蘇吳世昌鐫。延祐戊午十一月也」。摹勒者顧信，字善夫，江蘇昆山人，晚年號樂善處士。善書法，為趙孟頫之好友，得其書必鐫刻於石，曾刻《樂善堂帖》傳世。

此割裱本為章鈺舊藏之初拓本，拓工精良，拓本稀少。章鈺，字式之，別號茗移，江蘇長州人。清光緒二十九年（1903年）進士。著名的校勘學家和收藏家，對金石碑帖頗有研究，著有《讀書敏求記》、《四當齋集》。帖籤「趙松雪書太上玄元道德經」為章氏手題，旁書小字一行「元刻元搨，前人所謂親見仙人吹笛也。茗移秘笈」。茲選照二開，為首一開及末一開。

40

趙松雪書太上玄元道德經

簡稱《道德經》。東周老子（李耳）撰。元趙孟頫延祐三年（1316年）正書。元顧信摹。元吳世昌鐫。刻於元延祐五年（1318年）十一月。初拓割裱本，計二十五開。每半開刻烏絲欄七行，全拓凡三百四十二行，每行字數不等，共五千三百四十六字。內高二三‧九厘米，寬一二‧九厘米。經折裝。

善拓 546

《道德經》為道家學派的主要著作。相傳為春秋末李耳又名老聃所著。分上下篇，五千餘字，又稱《老子五千文》。上篇為《道經》，下篇為《德經》，故名。歷代關於《道經》、《德經》的次序真偽多有爭論。一九七三年長沙馬王堆漢墓出土帛書《老子》，《德經》在《道經》之前，為現存最古的《老子》抄本。書中用「道」來說明宇宙萬物的演變，提出了一個以道為核心的思想體系即「道生一，一生二，二生三，三生萬物」的觀點，為道教徒崇尚信仰，成為道教教義的理論基礎。

《趙松雪書太上玄元道德經》是趙孟頫小楷代表作之一。趙孟頫，字子昂，號松雪道人、別號甲寅人、水晶宮道人、敢死軍醫人、在家道人、太上弟子、三寶弟子。原籍大梁（今河南省開封），為宋太祖趙匡胤十世孫，因四世祖受賜居湖州，遂為吳興人。入元後，閑居里中，聲聞朝廷。後應召入仕，南北奔走。世祖時為官集賢直學士。仁宗時，拜翰林學士承旨，榮祿大夫。卒贈魏國公，諡文敏。趙氏是元代杰出書畫家，其書法以古人為法，博采眾家之長，各體皆精，篆、籀、分、隸、真、行、草，無不冠絕，小楷乃其最拿手之字體。

41

Lanting xiuxi tu

Illustration of the Spring Purification Gathering at the Orchid Pavilion

Ming dynasty (1368-1644), Yongle period (1403-1424), dated 1417

Original composition by Li Gonglin (ca. 1049-1106); copied by Zhu Youdun [Prince of Zhou] (1379-1439); engraved in 1417

Handscroll, ink rubbed on paper, 22.1 x 489.0 cm; illustration section, 17.9-18.1 x 329.1 cm

Date of rubbing not given, probably Qing dynasty (1644-1911)

Biaozhou 776

The "Preface to the Orchid Pavilion Preface" (*Lanting xu*) is one of the most famous essays in Chinese cultural history. Composed and written by the Eastern Jin literatus Wang Xizhi (ca. 307-ca. 365) in the mid-fourth century, it has long commanded canonical status as a prime example of fine Chinese calligraphy. The text of the preface is given in full below in a translation by Richard E. Strassberg:

In the ninth year of the Yonghe era in the beginning of the last month of spring when the calendar was in *guichou* [April 22, 353], we met at the Orchid Pavilion in Shanyin, Kuaiji, to celebrate the Purification Festival. All the worthy men assembled; the young and the senior gathered together. Here were lofty mountains and towering hills, thick groves and tall bamboo. And there was a clear, rapid stream, reflecting everything around it, which had been diverted in order to play the game of floating winecups along a winding course. We sat down in order of precedence. Though we had none of the magnificent sounds of strings and flutes, a cup of wine and then a poem were enough to stir our innermost feelings.

This was a day when the sky was bright and the air was pure. A gentle breeze warmed us. Upward we gazed to contemplate the immensity of the universe; downward we peered to scrutinize the abundance of living things. In this way, we let our eyes roam and our emotions become aroused so that we enjoyed to the fullest these sights and sounds. This was

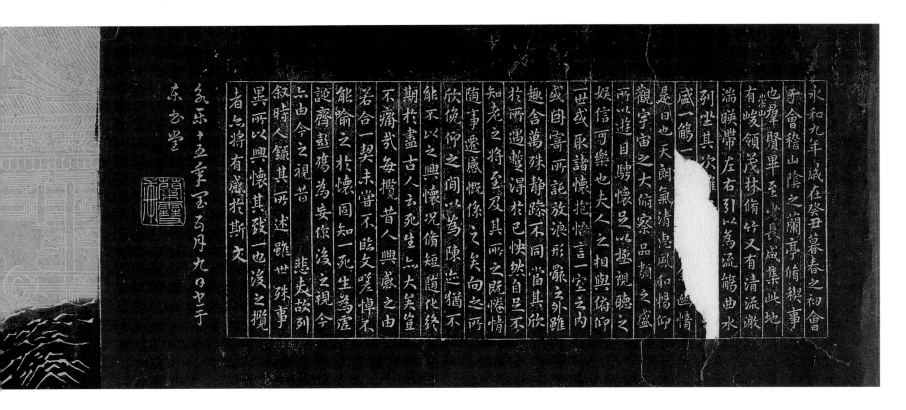

happiness, indeed!

Men meet as friends for but the brief span of their lives. Some are content to unburden their innermost feelings as they privately converse inside a chamber. Some are prompted to give rein to their desires and lead wild, unfettered lives. Although their preferences differ and their temperaments are unalike, yet both take pleasure from whatever they encounter, embracing it for but a while, happy and content, unaware that old age is fast approaching. And when they tire of something, they let their feelings change along with events as they experience a deep melancholy. What they had taken pleasure in has now passed away in an instant, so how can their hearts not give rise to longing Furthermore, longevity depends on Nature's

transformation: everything must come to an end. An ancient said, "Life and death are the greatest of matters, indeed!" Isn't this reason enough to be sad?

Whenever I read of the causes of melancholy felt by men of the past, it is like joining together two halves of a tally. I always feel sad when I read them, yet I cannot quite understand why. But I know that it is meaningless to say life and death are the same; and to equate the longevity of Pengzu with that of Shangzu is simply wrong. Future readers will look back on today just as we look back at the past. How sad it all is! Therefore, I have recorded my contemporaries and transcribed what they have written. Over distant generations and changing events, what gives rise to melancholy will be the same. Future readers

will also feel moved by these writings.

The original manuscript of the preface is lost, but the calligraphy has been preserved through a number of tracing copies, engraved stones, and rubbings. Of the many extant versions and recensions, the so-called "Dingwu" version is generally acknowledged to be the best and most faithful to the original. The effortlessly elegant running script employed by Wang Xizhi for the preface is all the more remarkable since it was supposed to have been executed while he was intoxicated. Throughout the centuries, Wang's preface and the event that it commemorated have also inspired many pictorial representations and commentaries; the compilation of scrolls and albums that combined various "Lanting" pieces became popu-

lar among collectors and connoisseurs.

This item from the National Library of China entitled *Lanting xiuxi tu* (Illustration of the Spring Purification Gathering at the Orchid Pavilion) is one such artifact in the history of "Lanting" compendia. The series of individual rubbings mounted as a handscroll opens with a rubbing of the "Dingwu" version of Wang Xizhi's preface in twenty-eight columns of running script. This particular rubbing is partly torn at the sixth and seventh columns, but all the missing characters here are known from other intact examples. The two-column inscription which follows is dated the ninth day of the intercalary fifth month in the fifteenth year of the Yongle period (corresponding to June 23, 1417); it was written by Zhu Youdun (1379-1439), son of Zhu Su (1361-1425), the Prince of Zhou, whose title he inherited in 1425.

The pictorial composition is attributed to

the Northern Song artist Li Gonglin (ca. 1049-1106). It was copied by Zhu Youdun, an accomplished painter, calligrapher, and dramatist in his own right who collected famous specimens of calligraphy, traced them, and had them engraved on stone; his renowned assemblage of rubbings was called the *Dongshu tang ji gu fatie* (Ancient Model Calligraphies Collected in the Dongshu Hall). Zhu's copy of Li's picture in the fine linear outline manner (*baimiao*) is just over 329 cm in length. It opens with the view of an elaborate waterside pavilion on stilts, with clumps of cymbidium orchids growing beside it on the bank. Within, an unidentified person, most probably Wang Xizhi, is flanked by two pages and sits at a table with a brush in one hand, gazing at the graceful curving necks of several swimming geese. Just beyond the gushing cascade is a group of young attendants preparing cups of wine and setting them adrift on lotus leaves. The winecups

float along a gently winding stream, on either bank of which Wang Xizhi (who appears again as the second seated figure), his guests, and family members are seated on mats. Each figure is accompanied by a cartouche indicating his official position and name, and, if he has been successful in composing one or more verses, the text(s) of his poetic composition(s). An arched stone bridge with carved balustrades signifies the conclusion of the long picture; five young attendants may be seen reaching into the water to retrieve the winecups. The two-column inscription placed at the end of the illustration dates it to the nineteenth day of the intercalary fifth month in the fifteenth year of the Yongle period (July 3, 1417) and states that it was "written [i.e., drawn and inscribed] at the Lanxue Studio" of Zhu Youdun. A large square intaglio seal belonging to Zhu accompanies the inscription.

The pictorial section of the handscroll is also notable for the two-tone technique in which the rubbing was made. Parts of the picture consist of white outlines on a black ground, as in conventional rubbings, while other areas feature outlines set against a pale brownish-beige tone. The first of the five sections illustrated here shows the opening of the handscroll with Wang Xizhi's preface. Next is the first part of the picture with Wang Xizhi watching geese, followed by a section depicting Xie An (320-385), Cao Mengzhi, Ren Ning, Sun Chuo (ca. 314-ca. 371), Yu Yun, Yang Mo, and two of Wang Xizhi's sons, Wang Xianzhi (344-386), and Wang Suzhi. The fourth picture shows the terminal section with the bridge and attendants retrieving winecups, while the fifth contains a section of the handscroll with colophons by Zhu Youdun.

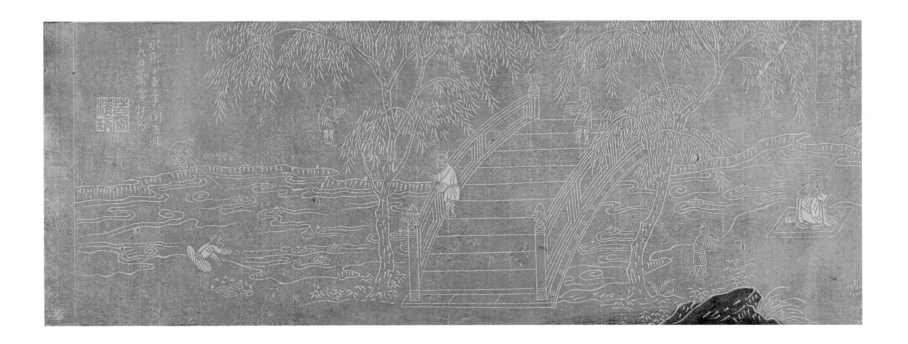

41

蘭亭脩禊圖

北宋李公麟製圖。明朱有燉摹。明永樂十五年（1417年）閏五月十九日刻。石久佚。清拓本。拓片高二二‧一厘米，長四八九厘米。圖高一七‧九至一八‧一厘米，長三二九‧一厘米。卷軸裝。

裱軸 776

王羲之，字逸少，琅琊（山東臨沂）人。東晉時，官至右軍將軍、會稽內史。永和九年（353年）三月上旬，與謝安、孫綽、郗曇、魏滂輩，及王凝之、渙之、獻之、立之等四十一人在會稽山陰（今浙江紹興）之蘭亭「脩禊」時飲酒賦詩，王羲之為之作並乘興書《蘭亭集序》。此圖繪刻這一故事的游樂詩會之情景。

圖前有王羲之《蘭亭集序》的摹本一幅，全行書二十八行。以下將序文全錄：「永和九年，歲在癸丑，暮春之初，會于會稽山陰之蘭亭，脩禊事也。群賢畢至，少長咸集。此地有崇山峻嶺，茂林脩竹，又有清流激湍，映帶左右，引以為流觴曲水，列坐其次。雖無絲竹管弦之盛，一觴一詠，亦足以暢敘幽情。是日也，天朗氣清，惠風和暢。仰

觀宇宙之大，俯察品類之盛，所以遊目騁懷，足以極視聽之娛，信可樂也。夫人之相與俯仰一世，或取諸懷抱，悟言一室之內，或因寄所託，放浪形骸之外，雖趣舍萬殊，靜躁不同，當其欣於所遇，暫得於己，快然自足，不知老之將至。及其所之既倦，情隨事遷，感慨係之矣。向之所欣，俛仰之間，以為陳迹，猶不能不以之興懷。況脩短隨化，終期於盡。古人云，死生亦大矣，豈不痛哉！每攬昔人興感之由，若合一契，未嘗不臨文嗟悼，不能喻之於懷。固知一死生為虛誕，齊彭殤為妄作。後之視今，亦由今之視昔，悲夫！故列敘時人，錄其所述。雖世殊事異，所以興懷。其致一也。後之攬者，亦將有感於斯文」。王序後刻朱有燉款識「永樂十五年閏五月九日書于蘭雪堂」以及「蘭雪軒」方印。

原圖傳為北宋李公麟作，明永樂十五年（1417年）以縷刻形式摹勒上石。卷首畫臨水廳榭，王羲之捻筆撫紙，構思其間，廳前疊泉奔流，白鵝嬉戲水中。圖中部描繪與會者四十二人（童僕不計），其中一十人詩兩篇成，十五人詩一篇成，十六人詩不成，各飲酒三觥。圖之末端畫一雕欄石橋，垂柳掩映，童子五人，三人在橋下打撈空杯覆盞，二童子在橋上，一扶欄，一捧食盒走來。表現詩人憩止於橋畔。童子收拾流觴往還上游浮杯處，全卷至此已是尾聲。摹此圖者為朱有燉，字誠齋，

號全陽子、老狂生、錦窠道人，鳳陽（今安徽鳳陽）人。周定王朱橚之長子，明洪熙初襲封周王。博學善書，為世子時編有《東書堂集古法帖》。尤工詞曲，著誠齋樂府傳奇若干種，著有《誠齋雜劇》、《誠齋樂府》等。卒諡憲，世稱周憲王。

此本用濃淡兩種墨色套拓而成，於拓本中最精彩。它以赭墨二色套拓後，在人物的頭臉鬚眉部分，更加重墨一一細拓，故人物神色畢現。類如這樣精拓本長卷，傳世者不多。原石舊存禁苑中，此卷可能為奉命特製者，異常可貴。

圖後有孫綽〈後序〉，行書十七行。再後有何延年《蘭亭記》、《尚書故實》并《唐野史》，有何子楚題語，全為朱有燉楷書，末署「永樂十五年閏五月十八日書于蘭雪軒」。最後為朱有燉行書題跋十六行，末署「永樂十五年閏五月十九日書」，刻印二，即「芸窗清玩」方印與「蘭雪軒」方印。

茲選照卷軸五段，為首題（王羲之〈蘭亭集序〉、朱有燉款識「永樂十五年閏五月九日書于蘭雪堂」）、圖第一段（王羲之於蘭亭執筆并觀鵝景）、圖中段之一（間有謝安、曹茂之、任凝、孫綽、庾蘊、楊模、王獻之、王宿之於溪兩旁賦詩飲酒景）、圖最後一段（橋梁下童僕收拾酒杯景）以及題跋最後一段。

42

Zhong Kui tu

Illustration of Zhong Kui the Demon Queller

Ming dynasty (1368-1644), Tianqi period (1621-1627)

dated 1624

Unmounted sheet comprising 3 joined sheets, ink rubbed on paper, 199.7 x 109.7 cm

Date of rubbing not given, Qing dynasty (1644-1911)

Huaxiang 1844

Zhong Kui is one the most Chinese popular folk icons. According to one of the legends about Zhong Kui, sometime during the Kaiyuan era (713-742) Emperor Xuanzong (685-762; r. 712-762) of the Tang fell ill and had a nightmare in which he was disturbed by Xu Hao, a small demon of destruction who stole his jade flute and his consort's perfume-bag. The little demon was subsequently captured and devoured by another imposing demon dressed in ragged clothes and black boots, who introduced himself to the emperor as Zhong Kui, a failed scholar who had committed suicide a century earlier and appointed himself as a spirit exorcist. When the emperor awoke from his dream, he commanded the court painter Wu Daozi (689-759) to paint a portrait of Zhong Kui.

It is believed that some Tang and Song emperors bestowed paintings of Zhong Kui upon court officials. From the ninth century onwards, portraits of Zhong Kui also became part of popular culture and were often painted at New Year as a means of chasing away demons. By the late Ming dynasty, an entire cult of Zhong Kui had been established,

and by the Qing period Zhong Kui had become associated with the exorcistic festival which took place on the fifth day of the fifth lunar month.

This portrait of Zhong Kui engraved on a large stone stele depicts him in the pose of a warrior. However, he carries a *qin* (zither) and a case of books. Based on the title slip on the case (*Jun tian guang yue*), this picture may be titled "Zhong Kui Listening to Heavenly Music." The two-columned inscription at upper left provides the name of Liang Jianting from Guanzhong (Shaanxi) who was a prefect (*taishou*) in Henan province, and a date in the early summer of the *jiazi* year of the Tianqi reign era, i.e., 1624. The other inscription at the middle left states that it was Liu Anxing, the district magistrate (*zhixian*) of Dengfeng county who was responsible for erecting the stone engraving. The original stone is now kept in the Shaolin Temple at Dengfeng in Henan province.

42

鍾馗圖

明天啟四年（1624 年）四月刻。石現在河南省登封市。
清（1644–1911 年）拓本。拓片紙高一九九‧七厘米，
寬一○九‧七厘米。

畫像 *1844*

　　鍾馗是中國民間傳說中驅妖逐邪之神。鍾馗
之說、鍾馗畫起源於何時都有種種說法。從現傳
古籍所記載的傳說看，鍾馗畫始於唐代。相傳唐
玄宗時期的大畫家吳道子是鍾馗的創始者，但吳
道子所畫的鍾馗圖，今已不可得。唐人題吳道子
畫鍾馗像，略云：明皇夢二鬼，一大一小。小者
竊太真紫香囊及明皇玉笛，繞殿而奔；大者捉其
小者，擘而啖之。上問何人，對曰：「臣鍾馗，即

武舉不捷之士也。誓與陛下除天下之妖孽」。後世
圖其形以除邪驅祟。

　　鍾馗題材的畫除了名家之作外，尚有不少民
間畫工繪制者。畫工之作大都刻版刷印，廣布城鄉
各地，印數既多，影響也大。雕版刷印鍾馗圖始於
北宋，其後民間藝術里，像石刻綫畫、木刻版畫
等鍾馗題材的作品，更是豐富多彩。

　　此圖刻鍾馗如武夫，攜琴一張，托書一函。
簽題「鈞天廣樂」。是圖以簡筆描法勾勒，刻法以
陰陽綫結合，筆姿雄健，形象生動。上題「大明天
啟甲子初夏河南太守關中梁建廷」和「登封縣知縣
劉安行立石」等字。原石現存登封少林寺中。

43

Sheng ji tu

Pictures of the Sage's Traces

Qing dynasty (1644-1911), Kangxi period (1662-1722), dated and engraved 1682

Illustrated by Chen Yin; eulogies and colophon composed by Lin Youfang; engraved by Zhu Bi

Album of 72 leaves (36 double-leaves), ink rubbed on paper; overall dimensions: 35.2 x 32.8 cm; each double-leaf approx. 30.8 x 61.4 cm

Date of rubbing not given, Qing dynasty (1644-1911)

Huaxiang 884

The life of Confucius (551-479 B.C.) is well chronicled, beginning with the *Shi ji* (Records of the Grand Historian) by Sima Qian (ca. 145-ca. 86 B.C.), in which the sage (with his disciples) is accorded an entire chapter covering his birth, journey to the state of Zhou to seek wisdom from Laozi, travel to the state of Qi, service as chief minister in the state of Lu, and his years of wandering among the various states, from Lu to Wey to Kuang to Pu, back to Wey, to Cao to Song to Zheng to Chen, again to Pu, again to Wey, to the Yellow River to Zou to Wei to Chen to Cai to She, back to Cai, to Chu to Wey, and back to Lu, as well as his editing of classical texts, discovery of a unicorn, lament for the death of his disciple Zilu, and finally his own death and burial.

The pictorial tradition of works bearing the title *Sheng ji tu* (Pictures of the Sage's Traces) dates back to the fifteenth century, though parts of the narrative had been visually represented as early as the Eastern Han period (A.D. 25-220). Since the earliest version of twenty-nine to thirty-four pictures commis-

sioned in 1444 by the censor Zhang Kai (1398-1460; jinshi of 1424), there have been a number of recensions and variations in terms of media (stone-engravings, prints, paintings, etc.), number of episodes (ranging between twenty-nine and 112 pictures), and formats (principally handscrolls or albums). Incised-stone versions of the illustrated biography, from which infinite sets of ink rubbings could potentially be made, appeared to be the preferred method of production. The morally instructive illustrations of the sage's life and travels, as distinct from the more familiar iconic portraits, were meant to assist ordinary people in visualizing and understanding Confucian teachings.

Although all the *Sheng ji* tu works consist of multiple episodes in the life of Confucius, they are nevertheless linked in a cohesive way internally by means of a chronological arrangement of scenes, and

in relation to each other by the successive borrowings and reworkings of a basic set of narrative images. Between 1444 and 1682, when the illustrations for the present album were engraved, other notable versions of the *Sheng ji tu* include those associated with He Tingrui (1497; 39 pictures; published in Hengzhou), Wu Jiamo [1589; *Sheng ji quan tu* (Complete Pictures of the Sage's Traces); 40 pictures], He Chuguang (1592; 112 pictures; at the Temple of Confucius, Qufu, Shandong province), and Ni Fuying (1609-1610; at the Temple of Confucius, Qingpu, Jiangsu province; now part of the municipality of Shanghai).

In 1682, Fang Zhengfan had incised stone tablets made in order to replace Ni Fuying's set from 1609-1610, which comprised thirty pictures purporting to reproduce Zhang Kai's early version. A total of thirty-six pictures, based on twenty-one of the surviving tablets, were drawn by Chen Yin, inscribed by Lin Youfang, and engraved by Zhu Bi of Suzhou.

The new tablets were kept at the seat of Qingpu county in Songjiang prefecture where a branch of Confucius' descendents had settled since the end of the Han period.

Without exception, all of Chen Yin's oblong compositions (the horizontal dimension being almost exactly twice that of the vertical) contain figures, but the scenes vary considerably between outdoor settings, interior architectural spaces, or a combination of both. In almost every picture a sense of dynamic asymmetry prevails, partly due to the fact that the text block occupies a significant amount of space at either the top right corner, top left corner, or somewhat further in but still suspended from the top edge, and partly because of the strong geometric lines used to delineate architectural elements or interior furnishings. A complete set of illustrations from the *Sheng ji tu* is reproduced in the *Kô Mô Seisekizu kan* published in 1940 by Baba Harukichi, a noted Japanese scholar of Confucianism. The pictures in this compilation are unnumbered, but are arranged chronologically according to the historical events depicted, beginning with the marriage of Confucius' parents and his birth, and concluding with a depiction of the sage's burial mound on the banks of the Si River surrounded by his mourning disciples.

This album of rubbings from the National Library of China contains only thirty-four of the thirty-six scenes that make up the whole work; the missing ones are the sixth (Confucius learning to play the zither from Shi Xiang in the state of Jin in 523 B.C.) and seventh (the meeting of Confucius and Laozi in 522 B.C.). In addition, a number of leaves in the Beijing album have been mounted out of sequence (1, 2, 3, 4, 5, 8, 9, 10, 11, 12, 24, 14, 15, 16, 17, 18, 20, 19, 21, 22, 23, 30, 13, 25, 27, 28, 29, 26, 31, 32, 33, 34, 35, and 36) when com-

pared to the complete set published in 1940.

The first illustration here shows the frontispiece with large characters giving the formal title of the work, *Dacheng zhisheng wenxuan xianshi zhou liu zhi tu* (Pictures of the Wanderings of the All-Encompassing Ultimate Sage and Cultivated First Teacher). Grandiose appellations were given from time to time throughout later Chinese history to honor the memory of Confucius. For example, in 739 during the Tang dynasty he was canonized as "Wenxuan wang" ("Prince of Cultivation"). The title used in the frontispiece, "Dacheng zhisheng wenxuan xianshi Kong zi" ("Confucius, the All-Encompassing Supreme Sage and Cultivated First Teacher") was conferred by the Shunzhi emperor in 1645 for use in Confucian temples; it was changed to "Zhisheng xianshi Kong zi" ("Confucius, Supreme Sage and First Teacher") in 1657.

All the pictorial compositions in the 1682 version of the *Sheng ji tu* include explanatory texts in prose, followed by eulogies (*zan*) in four-character verses composed by Lin Youfang, then serving as the district magistrate of Qingpu county in Songjiang prefecture. Of the two illustrated double-leaves selected, one depicts a setting from 509 B.C., in the first year of the reign of Duke Ding of Lu (r. 509-495 B.C.), concurrently the eleventh year in the reign of King Jing of Zhou (r. 519-476 B.C.). Confucius, then forty-three years old by Chinese reckoning, is seated at a table with writing implements spread out before him, surrounded by disciples, and looking outwards to the exterior. Six other figures, dwarfed by a massive garden rock and a cluster of plantains, are seen approaching the sage, presumably to seek instruction and wisdom. This particular picture is the twelfth in the complete cycle of thirty-six.

The second picture here (thirty-third in the full sequence) depicts a scene from 484 B.C., the eleventh year in the reign of Duke Ai of Lu (r. 494-468 B.C.), concurrently the thirty-sixth year in the reign of King Jing of Zhou. Confucius had returned to Lu from Wey, but was not offered a position in his home state as he had hoped. He devoted all his energies to the compilation and editing of classical texts, and amassed some three thousand followers. This scene shows the sage at the age of sixty-eight *sui*, seated at a low table, teaching from an open scroll, and surrounded by many of his seventy-two closest disciples.

The last double-leaf in the album, also shown here, consists of a long colophon by Lin Youfang engraved in thirty-five columns of regular script; it is dated the first day of the first lunar month in the *renxu* year (corresponding to February 7, 1682).

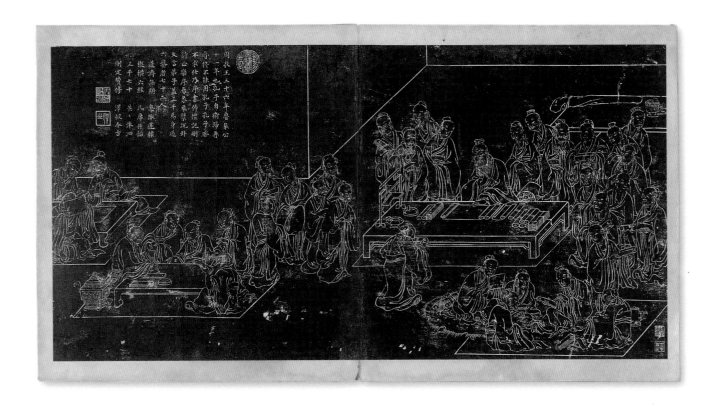

43

聖蹟圖

一名《至聖文宣先師周流之圖》。清康熙二十一年(1682年)正月十六日刻。石現在上海市。清陳尹繪。清蔺友芳正書傳贊并跋。清朱璧鐫。清(1644-1911年)烏金拓。割裱本。外高三五・二厘米，寬三二・八厘米，計三十六開，每開雙面圖高三〇・八厘米，寬六一・四厘米。冊頁裝。

畫像 *884*

宣傳孔子，由來已久。第一部編纂孔子言論行事的書是《論語》。漢司馬遷撰寫《史記》，有〈孔子世家〉一篇。特別是在理學大興之後，自宋、元、明以來，集聖蹟的書日漸增多，有用文字編年紀事的，如《孔子編年》；有附圖以表聖蹟的，如文圖并茂的插圖本《孔子家語》；有以圖為主的，如《聖蹟圖》，體裁雖各有不同，實質都是尊孔。《聖蹟圖》圖中所采擇的故事，材料多數來源於《論語》、《史記》這兩部書。

以圖畫來表現孔子一生的故事，不知始於何時，恐怕其來源是很早的。反映孔子行蹤《聖蹟之圖》約出現於明代，有彩繪本、木刻本、石刻本。舊有石刻的墨本，不知是否會較木刻本早些。山東曲阜孔廟中就有《聖蹟圖》的石刻，但其時代並不很早。今所知、所見的諸《聖蹟圖》，應以明正統九年(1444年)張楷(字式之)序刊的《聖蹟圖》木刻本為諸本之祖。其後有如明弘治十年(1497年)何珣(字廷瑞)跋刊《聖蹟圖》、明弘治年間的彩繪本、明正德元年鄧文質刊本(已失傳)、明嘉靖二十七年(1548年)瀋藩朱胤栘刻本《聖蹟圖》(一冊，明張楷撰，現藏中國國家圖書館)、明隆慶六年刊本、明萬曆十七年(1589年)武林吳嘉謨輯、序刊《孔聖家語圖》十一卷(現藏中國國家圖書館)，以及明萬曆二十年(1592年)山東巡按御史何出光(字兆文)石刻《聖蹟之圖》一百十二圖，拓本、序刊，石現存山東省曲阜孔子廟。

中國國家圖書館所藏這部《聖蹟圖》，原出現於清康熙二十一年(1682年)。繪者陳尹，字莘野，號雲樵，青浦(今屬上海市)人。學於華亭李藩，人物、山水、花鳥，初甚工細，後又疎老，有出藍之目。全套應有三十六幅圖，每圖有文有贊，但無題。圖首一開，隸書題「大成至聖文宣先師周流之圖」。唐開元二十七年(739年)，追謚「文宣王」。清順治二年(1645年)，定文廟謚號為「大成至聖文宣先師孔子」，十四年(1657年)，改稱「至聖先師孔子」。

此冊僅存三十四幅圖，不全。所缺二幅圖為全套之第六、第七幅。第六幅描繪周景王二十二年(公元前523年)孔子適晉學琴於師襄事跡，第七幅描繪周景王二十三年(公元前522年)孔子適周見老子事跡。除了有缺頁以外，此冊之圖裝裱次序有所混亂。全套三十六幅圖應是按照聖蹟編年以排列，讀者可參見日本學者馬場春吉所編著，由東京山東文化研究會發行於昭和十五年(1940年)的《孔孟聖蹟圖鑑》。中國國家圖書館藏本最後一開為蔺友芳石刻跋文，《孔孟聖蹟圖鑑》所引用的拓本卻未收。

茲選照《聖蹟圖》拓本四開，其中第一開為首題。第十一開描繪公元前509年的事跡，即所謂「退修詩書圖」(全套三十六幅圖按編年排列之第十二幅圖)，其右上題:「周敬王十一年，魯定公立。季氏僭公室，陪臣執國政，故孔子不仕，退而脩《詩》、《書》、《禮》、《樂》，以教弟子。弟子彌眾」。蔺友芳贊:「尼谿封沮，宗國政移。退而講學，禮樂詩書。函丈執業，群英濟濟。至教非私，無行不與」。贊後刻有「蔺友芳印」、「仲山」二印。左下刻有繪者陳尹二印，即「陳尹畫印」、「莘埜」。右下刻有「完璧堂珍藏」印。第三十二開描繪公元前484年的事跡，即所謂「杏壇禮樂圖」(全套三十六幅圖按編年排列之第三十三幅圖)，其左上題:「周敬王三十六年，魯哀公十一年也。孔子自衛歸魯，魯終不能用孔子。孔子亦不求仕，乃序《書》、傳《禮記》，刪《詩》，正《樂》，序《易・彖、象、繫、說卦、文言》。弟子蓋三千焉，身通六藝者七十二人」。蔺右芳贊:「道濟無期，息陬還轅。縱橫大經，几席丹鉛。三千七十，英英洙泗。刪定贊修，澤被今古」。贊前刻有「完璧堂珍藏」印。贊後刻有「蔺友芳印」、「仲山」二印。右下刻有繪者陳尹二印，即「陳尹畫印」、「莘埜」。第三十六開為蔺友芳題跋，全文楷書三十五行，末署「康熙二十一年，歲次壬戌孟春月甲子吉旦，江南松江府青浦縣知縣加一級蔺友芳謹識」。

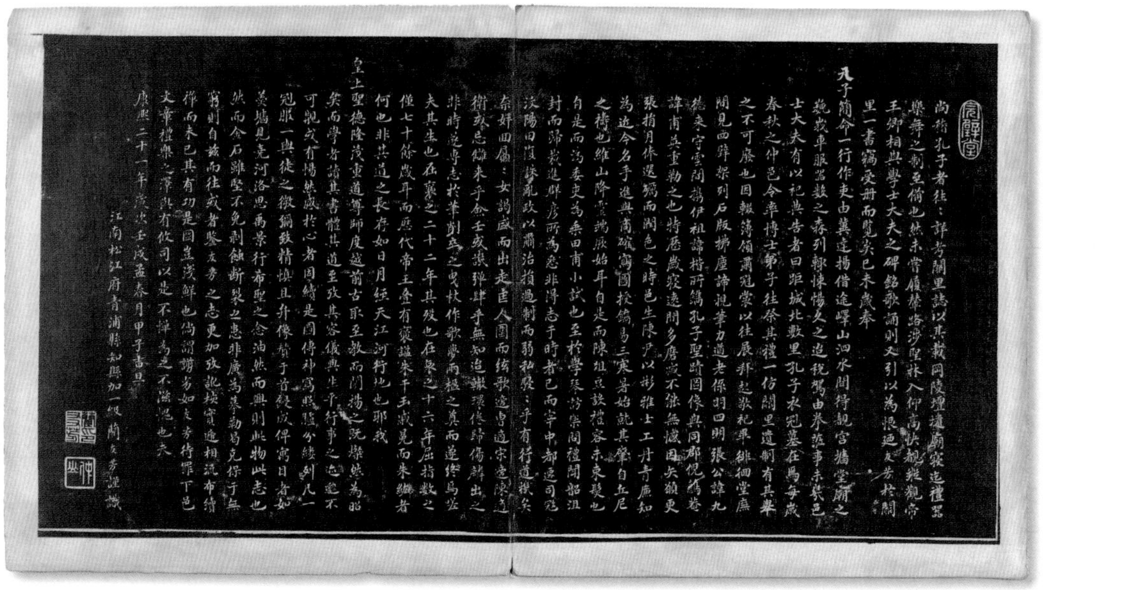

44

Yu ti Mianhua tu

Illustrations of Cotton Cultivation and Manufacture, with Imperial Inscriptions

Qing dynasty (1644-1911), Qianlong period (1736-1795), dated and engraved 1765

Compiled and edited by Fang Guancheng (1698-1768); inscription by the Qianlong emperor (1711-1799; r. 1736-1795); slabs engraved in regular, clerical, and running scripts

Album of 40 leaves, ink rubbed on paper; overall dimensions: approx. 30.5 x 29.8 cm; each leaf approx. 23.5 x 26.4 cm

Date of rubbing not given, probably late Qing dynasty (1644-1911), late 18th-19th century

Huaxiang 883

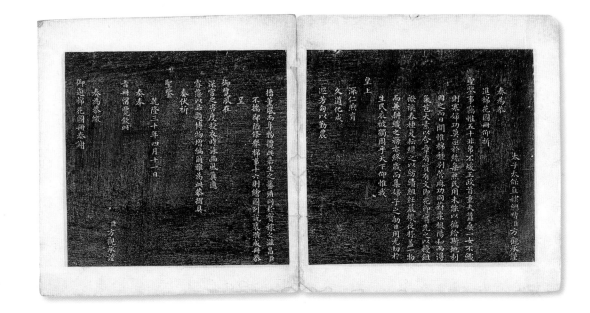

Cotton, a seed fiber plant imported from India, has been of great economic significance in China from the thirteenth century to the present. The two species found in China are *Gossypium herbaceum* and *Gossypium arboreum*, both belonging to the family *Malvaceae*. The plant is mentioned as early historical texts such as the *Hou Han shu* (History of the Later Han Dynasty), from which it is known that cotton fabric was used in Yunnan and Sichuan; the *Shi ji* (Records of the Grand Historian) refers to a cotton textile called *Shu bu* ("Sichuan cloth").

Between the Han and Song periods, cotton spread slowly from the southwest to Guangxi, Guangdong, and Fujian, and eventually to the lower Yangzi basin. By the early Yuan dynasty (1279-1368), the growing of

cotton and the manufacturing of cotton textiles became well enough established in Songjiang (now part of the Shanghai metropolitan area) to compete effectively with bast fiber products such as silk and ramie. By the Qing, cotton had grown into a major agricultural crop; during the Qianlong period it was said that every family in Pinghu, Zhejiang province, was engaged in spinning and weaving cotton textiles. Women would frequently work by candlelight late into the night so that the finished cloth could be taken to market early in the morning and exchanged for raw cotton.

In 1765, during the fourth of his six southern inspection tours (*nan xun*), the Qianlong emperor was presented with an album illustrating cotton cultivation by Fang Guancheng, who served as governor-general of Zhili (modern-day Hebei province) for eighteen years. Copies of the pictures were subsequently sent to be engraved in intaglio

on twelve heavy slabs of Duan stone (all measuring 118.5 cm in length, 73.5 cm in width, and 14.2 cm in thickness except for one which was 98 cm long, 41.5 wide, and 13.5 cm thick). These finely incised slabs have been preserved in pristine condition and are now in the collection of the Hebei Provincial Museum.

This album of rubbings taken from the original stone slabs opens with the text of two memorials submitted to the Qianlong emperor by Fang Guancheng, one in connection with the presentation of the illustrations and the other upon completion of the stone engravings; next are the governor-general's postscript to the "Illustrations of Cotton Cultivation" and the "Mumian fu" ("Prose-Poem on the Cotton Plant") composed by the Kangxi emperor (1654-1722; r. 1661-1722). Finally, there are sixteen square leaves of illustrations (with an explanatory text and a poem by Fang on the facing leaves) pertaining

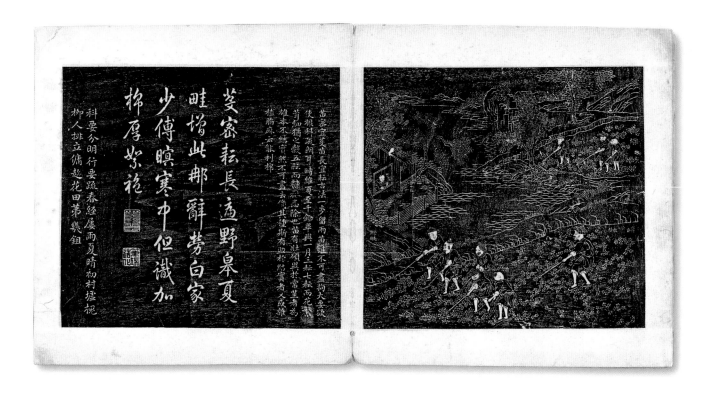

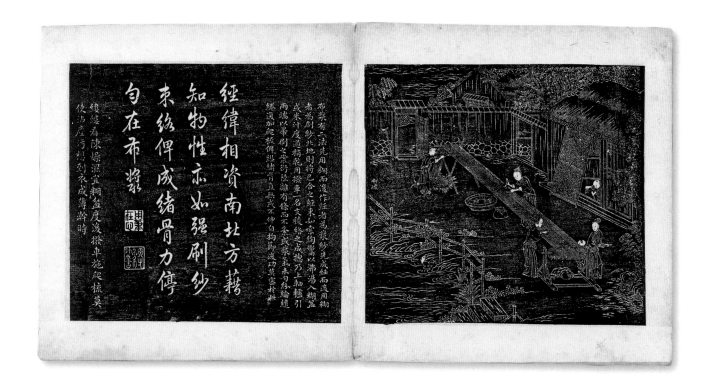

to the following activities: sowing, irrigation, weeding, topping, cotton picking, cotton sunning, cotton purchasing and selling, cotton ginning, cotton fluffing, making slivers, spinning, coiling threads, starching, warping, weaving (as well as oil extracting), and dyeing.

Each of the illustrations is accompanied by an explanatory text giving details of the technical aspects of cotton cultivation as well as related activities such as the spinning and weaving of cotton yarn. The three texts that accompany the illustration of "spinning" are here provided in full in the translation of Dieter Kuhn (with minor modifications). The detailed explanation written by Fang Guancheng in prose and engraved at far right of the slab in small regular script (*kaishu*) demonstrates the depth of his understanding of and interest in minute aspects of agricultural life:

To construct a [spindle-]wheel for spinning [two] upright posts are taken to harness the wheel and horizontally arranged [pieces of] wood [as bearings] to control the spindle (*ting*). The spinner is near to the spindle-wheel (*kuang*). The left hand of the spinner holds the cotton sliver (*miantiao*), the right hand turns the driving-wheel. The spindle follows the motion of the driving-belt. [In this way] the yarn is naturally drawn (on the spindle) as it is in reeling silk. This is called spinning yarn (*fang xian*). After four days of [drawing-out, *yin*], spinning a single yarn gives one *jin* [596.82 grams], [enough] to supply a weaving [loom] [for one day's work]. Combining two or three yarns [into one thread] supplies a [strong] sewing thread (*feng zhi*). The price of the twisted

thread is thirty percent higher than the value of the spun cotton. If the thread is even and there are no little hairs, the price increases by fifty percent. In the Wusong area [north of Shanghai] it is called *fang sha*, spinning yarn; the wheel is driven by foot and one hand spins three or five yarns [simultaneously in parallel]. It is an energy-saving [device].

Next is the Qianlong emperor's seven-character quatrain, engraved in large running-script characters at the center of the text panel:

In mutual harmony the yarn is spun as the
    spindle and wheel rotate;
As in silk reeling, they use enhanced
    techniques.
Hearsay has it that in Wusong the skill
    differs.
As soon as the wheel is driven the yarns
    are spun separately.

Finally, the seven-character quatrain by Fang Guancheng, using the same rhyme scheme as the emperor, appears at the far left:

In the sound of the spinning-wheel, the
    waterclock drips constantly deep in the
    night.
The yarn spins lightly and evenly like silk
    threads being reeled.
Under the eaves of the thatched house of
    the young bride–praised be the skill of
    her hands.
Her yarn fetches a price as high as that for
    silk threads.

The three double-leaves shown here are the text of Fang Guancheng's first memorial to the throne, followed by the third pair of pic-

ture and texts associated with "weeding" (*yun qi*) and the thirteenth pair of picture and texts related to "starching" (*bu jiang*).

Apart from the aesthetic quality of the engravings, Fang Guancheng's *Yu ti Mianhua tu* is a historical document and scientific record supplying useful information on an important component of agriculture and the textile industry during the Qing period. It is part of a body of imperially sponsored agricultural works and encyclopaedias compiled between the second half of the eighteenth century until the fall of the dynasty. Fang's work was reprinted in 1808 with additional notes under the title *Shou yi guang xun* (Instructions on Dressmaking) and under the editorship of Dong Gao (1740-1818; *jinshi* of 1763). The literary historian Yoshikawa Kôjirô (1904-1980) made a Japanese translation of the original work (*Gyodai Menkazu*) in 1937.

44

御題棉花圖

簡稱《棉花圖》。清乾隆三十年（1765 年）七月刻。石在河北省保定市。清方觀承正書說、詩。清高宗弘曆行書詩。清（1644-1911 年）拓。一冊，計二十開四十頁。外高三〇・五厘米，寬二九・八厘米。內高二三・五厘米，寬二六・四厘米。冊頁裝。

畫像 883

中國棉花是來自印度，傳入中國之路綫 似可分為兩路。一路由中亞細亞經新疆而至河西走廊，為草棉；然後向東傳播。另一路從緬甸、越南經雲南、廣西二省的河谷地帶，傳入中國南部，為木棉；其後之分佈自南向北。中國初期（六朝至唐代）之棉作，皆在西部和南部邊疆省份，元明兩代以後，才漸向中部推廣。元末明初陶宗儀著《南村輟耕錄》有云：「韃靼人跡跋中土，而木棉始移植於我國，閩、粵、關、陝，首得其利。元時乃傳至江南，江南又始於松江。有明以來，始適江北」。清乾隆時，在河北省虖沱河流域提倡植棉；北方的棉作漸盛。

《御題棉花圖》是清乾隆三十年（1765 年）直隸總督方觀承主持繪制的一套植棉、紡績直到織染成布整個過程的圖譜。方觀承，字遐，安徽桐城人，乾隆時任直隸總督達二十年之久。據《清史稿》記載，乾隆三十年「高宗南巡，觀承迎駕，……四月，條舉木棉事十六則，繪圖以進。」方觀承將原本進呈，摹本付刻於石上。刻石為十二塊端石，其中十一塊長一一八・五厘米，寬七三・五厘米，厚一四・二厘米；另一塊長九八厘米，寬四一・五厘米，厚一三・五厘米。圖為陰文綫刻，綫條極為工細謹密。畫面各具形象，如描繪壓着千斤重擔在作牛馬般的苦力勞動，既突出了主題，反映當時農村一般農民的艱苦情況，有濃厚的生活氣息。原石尚存在河北省保定市蓮池書院之壁間，歷經二百餘年，至今完好無損。

《棉花圖》共十六幅圖，目次如下：方觀承於乾隆三十年四月十一日向皇帝進呈《棉花圖》的奏文一章、方氏於乾隆三十年七月十六日《棉花圖》碑成後再次奏文一章、方氏《棉花圖》跋、刻題簽三條、清帝康熙《木棉賦》、《棉花圖》十六幅，分「布種」、「灌溉」、「耘畦」、「摘尖」、「采棉」、「揀曬」、「收販」、「軋核」（以上為治棉），「彈花」、「拘節」、「紡績」、「挽經」、「布漿」、「上機」、「織布」、「練染」（以上為紡織染整）。每圖除附有文字說明及方觀承的七言詩外，還有乾隆帝親題七言詩一首，故名《御題棉花圖》。

《棉花圖》的顯著特點是每圖後均有一段文字，簡明扼要地說明該項技術的要求。《棉花圖》以圖為主，圖文并茂，通俗易懂，是當時倡導和推廣植棉和棉紡技術的優秀科普作品。流傳至今仍是研究中國農業科技史，特別是植棉史、棉紡織史，以及清代前期冀中地區農業經濟的可貴資料。

《棉花圖》石刻本拓片中有墨、硃、藍拓本，而墨拓流傳較多。茲選照中國國家圖書館墨拓本三開，為方觀承第一篇奏文（第一開）、「耘畦」圖說詩（總第七開，圖第三）以及「布漿」圖說詩（總第十七開，圖第十三）。

乾隆《棉花圖》鐫刻後影響頗廣，嘉慶十三年（1808 年），內廷又據此翻刻成版畫，易名為《授衣廣訓》，分上下卷，其後有《喜詠軒叢書》本及 1949 年後影印本。在二十世紀三十年代，《棉花圖》還曾被譯成日文出版，在海外得到廣泛的流傳。

45

Jing qing Wei zhuo tu

Illustration of the Clear Jing River and the Muddy Wei River

Qing dynasty (1644-1911), Qianlong period (1736-1795), dated and engraved 1790

Illustration and text by Dong Gao (1740-1818; *jinshi* of 1763), with poetic inscriptions by the Qianlong emperor (1711-1799; r. 1736-1795)

Sheets of rubbings mounted as a handscroll, ink rubbed on paper, 29.0 x 351.0 cm; text section preceding illustration, 29.0 x 107 cm; illustration with added blue, pale brownish-orange, and green washes, 29.0 x 69.0 cm; text section following illustration, 29.0 x 175.0 cm

Date of rubbing not given, probably late Qing dynasty (1644-1911), 19th century

Biaozhou 350

Dong Gao (1740-1818) was a son of the eminent Qing official Dong Bangda (1699-1769; *jinshi* of 1733). The younger Dong obtained his *jinshi* degree in 1763 and served as a lecturer in the classics colloquium (*jingyan jiangguan*), Vice Minister of the Left in the Ministry of Revenue (*hu bu zuo shilang*), and Vice Minister in the Ministry of Personnel (*li bu shilang*), among many other senior positions in government. In 1809 he was appointed Grand Preceptor of the Heir Apparent (*taizi shaobao*). For the four decades that he served at court, he gained the trust and respect of both the Qianlong and Jiaqing emperors. Dong Gao was also an accomplished painter with many works entering the palace collection, and a skilled calligrapher who was responsible for many of the writings attributed to the Qianlong emperor

during his old age.

As demonstrated in this picture documenting geographical and ecological conditions in Shaanxi province, Dong Gao's artistic skills were well utilized in reporting a matter of concern to the imperial court. Historically, the Jing and Wei Rivers alternated between being clear and silted, and the site of their confluence near the provincial capital of Xi'an was such that the two streams of water would appear unmixed for a stretch after meeting. During the Spring and Autumn period (770-476 B.C.), the Jing was clear while the Wei was turbid, but this became reversed during the period between the Warring States (475-221 B.C.) and the early Western Jin (265-316). During the Northern and Southern Dynasties (386-589), the Jing once again became clear and the Wei carried the bulk of the silt, but after that, through the Sui (581-618) and Tang periods (618-907), there was another reversal of the waters' conditions. After the Tang dynasty, however, the situation became stable and the Jing remained clear while the Wei was murky.

The illustration is preceded by a poetic inscription by the Qianlong emperor, the rhyme of which was inspired by the reply to a memorial drafted by Qin Cheng'en, the provincial governor of Shaanxi. In addition, there is a text composed by Dong Gao explaining how he had actually inspected the confluence of the Jing and Wei rivers, and found that the water flowing in the Jing was indeed clear whereas that in the Wei was turbid. Thereafter he made this illustration and appended an explanatory text so that he could present it to the throne for inspection.

Dong Gao's striking picture combines the qualities of a map and a painting. The four cardinal directions are indicated at the center of each edge, with north at the top. The

Jing River is shown in blue wash entering the picture diagonally (southeastward) from the top left edge, and meeting the Wei River, which flows generally eastwards, at the center of the picture. The Wei continues further eastward until it empties into the Yellow River (Huang he), shown as the wide curving band with rushing currents at upper right. The region hemmed in by the three rivers contains ricefields (depicted with short green lines) irrigated by the Longdong Canal (Longdong qu). Prefectures and counties along the courses of the Jing and Wei are listed, and four blocks of text placed in the blank spaces explain the historical conditions of the rivers in some detail.

45

涇清渭濁圖

清乾隆五十五年（1790 年）三月刻。清董誥繪圖并正書說。清高宗弘曆行書記并詩。清（1644–1911 年）拓。縱二九厘米，橫三五一厘米。圖前部分縱二九厘米，橫一〇七厘米。圖部分縱二九厘米，橫六九厘米。圖後部分縱二九厘米，橫一七五厘米。卷軸裝。

裱軸 350

　　渭水是長安八水之一，也是黃河中游較大的支流。發源於甘肅渭源縣西鳥鼠山，東南流經隴西、武山、伏羌、天水、清水諸縣。入陝西境，東經寶雞、郿縣至長安縣南，納黑水潨河及豐、滈、潏、灞諸水，至高陵會涇水，橫貫渭水平原，東出潼關縣入黃河。渭水自古就是關中農田水利淵藪和水上交通要道，中下游築有灌溉工程，農業發達。

　　涇水，源出寧夏回族自治區南部六盤山東麓，流經甘肅省，東南流，又東，入陝西邠州長武縣界。馬嶺河上承泥水東南注之。又東，逕縣境北，陶林溝北注之。又南，東入邠州界。經淳化、醴泉至高陵縣入渭水。全長四百五十一公里。涇水是渭水最大的支流，在關中的農田灌溉事業中發揮着重要作用，古代曾經在涇水流域修築了著名的鄭國渠。

　　涇水和渭水自古以來就清濁不同。但歷史上涇渭清濁情況常有變化。據說春秋時期是渭清涇濁，南北朝時期是涇清渭濁。到了唐代，又是涇濁渭清。唐代以後至今又變成了涇清渭濁。現在，當春秋兩季沒有暴雨時，涇渭交匯處還可以看到這種奇特的自然現象。

　　此圖繪者董誥，字雅倫，一字西京，號蔗林、柘林，浙江富陽人。父達，官禮部尚書。乾隆二十八年（1763 年）進士，殿試進呈卷列第三，高宗因大臣子，改二甲第一。選庶吉士。三十一年散官，授編修。三十六年，入直南書房。初，董達善畫，受高宗知。董誥承家學，繼為侍從，書畫亦被宸賞，尤以奉職恪勤為上所眷注。累遷內閣學士。四十年，擢工部侍郎，調戶部，歷署吏、刑兩部侍郎，兼管樂部。充四庫館副總裁，接辦《全書薈要》，命輯《滿洲源流考》。四十四年，命為軍機大臣。五十二年，加太子少保，擢戶部尚書。五十四年，命管理稽察上諭事件處。五十五年十一月，加太子少保銜。乾隆五十六年（1791 年）十月刊石經於太學，以董誥充副總裁。台灣、廓爾喀先後底定，並列功臣，圖形紫光閣。嘉慶元年（1796 年），授東閣大學士，總理禮部，仍兼戶部事務。

嘉慶二十三年（1818年）十月病卒，贈太傅。諡文恭。工詩古文，善書畫。編著有《西巡盛典》、《授衣廣訓》等。

圖前有清高宗乾隆庚戌（1790年）季春御筆〈西安巡撫秦承恩覆奏涇清渭濁實據詩以誌事一韻二首〉。圖尾有「臣董誥恭畫」款識。圖後有董誥〈御製涇清渭濁紀實〉，題「…臣查看過涇渭二水合流處所實在涇清渭濁情形，謹繪圖貼說恭呈御覽謹奏。乾隆庚戌季春月。臣董誥奉敕敬書」。此圖刻於乾隆五十五年（1790年）三月，應是前一年董誥管理稽察上諭事件處時所繪。

茲選照卷軸三段。第一、二段為清高宗弘曆行書記并詩，第三段為董誥繪圖。

46

Yinxin shi wu tu shuo

Illustrations and Records of the Yinxin Stone Dwellings

Qing dynasty (1644-1911), Daoguang period (1821-1850), dated and engraved 1836

Illustrator(s) unknown; texts by Tao Shu (1778-1839; *jinshi* of 1802)

Album of 36 leaves (18 double-leaves), ink rubbed on paper, accordion-style mounting; each leaf approx. 39.2 x 25.1 cm

Date of rubbing not given, probably late Qing dynasty (1644-1911), between 1836 and 1911

Huaxiang 882

Tao Shu (also pronounced Tao Zhu; 1778-1839) was a native of Anhua in Hunan who claimed descent from the famous Eastern Jin poet and recluse Tao Qian (ca. 365-427). After Tao Shu obtained his metropolitan *jinshi* degree in 1802, he was appointed as a compiler in the Hanlin Academy (*Hanlin yuan bianxiu*) and moved steadily up the civil service ladder, becoming an assistant examiner in Sichuan in 1810, a censor in 1814, intendant of the Chuandong Circuit in Sichuan in 1819, provincial judge of Shanxi in 1821, and financial commissioner of Anhui between 1823 and 1825.

From 1825 to 1830, Tao Shu was the governor of Jiangsu, where he is remembered for the measures he took to transport tribute grain to the capital when parts of the Grand Canal were flooded. In 1826, he delivered by the sea route the quota of rice for that year, using 1,562 junks from Shanghai to Tianjin, but this route was abandoned the following year due to opposition from corrupt officials

who profited by the use of the Grand Canal. In 1830, Tao Shu was appointed the governor-general of Jiangsu, Jiangxi, and Anhui provinces, a post he held for nine years. When the office of the censor supervising the Liang-Huai salt administration was abolished in early 1831 and given concurrently to the governor-general at Nanjing, Tao Shu became the first such candidate to take responsibility for this important charge. Many improvements in the administration of the salt revenue may be credited to Tao Shu, who resigned from office in March 1839 due to illness and died four months later.

In 1835, when he was governor-general at Nanjing, Tao Shu was presented with a plaque with four large characters in the calligraphy of the Daoguang emperor (r. 1821-1850) which read "Yinxin Stone Dwelling." Tao Shu adopted this name for his study, but it was also used to name structures at a variety of historical sites and scenic spots in Jiangsu province that he visited during the course of his governorship between 1825 and 1830.

This album from the National Library of China opens with a frontispiece (dated 1836) in large clerical-script characters by Ruan Yuan (1764-1849), the governor of Zhejiang, a major reformer of the early nineteenth century who sought moral and intellectual regeneration through classical studies. This is followed by four illustrations commissioned by Tao Shu, showing the placement of pavilions bearing the name "Yinxin Stone Dwelling" in the cities of Nanjing, Suzhou, Yangzhou, and Qingjiang or their environs. Each picture, identified by a horizontally written title in clerical script along the top edge, takes up two full leaves; each accompanying descriptive text, engraved in neat columns of small regular script, occupies

only part of the adjoining leaf. The album features a special technique of making rubbings from engraved stones, the so-called "black gold rubbings" (*wujin ta*) made with lustrous black ink on thick paper and burnished with a polishing shell. The very fine quality of the resultant rubbings further enhances the carefully detailed drawings as well as the expert engraving of the designs on stone slabs.

The illustrations from the album presented here are the first two, namely the Nanjing and Suzhou scenes. In the first picture at Jinling (Nanjing), the Yinxin Stone Dwelling is situated near the summit of Mount Bo; it is the square pavilion just to the right of center. The Yinxin Stone Dwelling at the Surging Waves Pavilion (Canglang ting) in Suzhou is a double-storied pavilion also placed just right of center. In the other two illustrations not shown, the Yinxin Stone Dwelling at Yangzhou is a circular pavilion at one corner of the Fajing Temple complex, to the east of the famous Pingshan Hall (Pingshan tang) and overlooking the riverbank. The remaining Yinxin Stone Dwelling in this album is that at Qingjiang (also called Qingjiangpu or Qinghe) near Huaiyin, Jiangsu province; it is set on a raised platform, next to the Terrace of King Yu (Yu wang tai) just to the right of center.

Immediately following the pictures and explanations is a series of poetic inscriptions by several of Tao Shu's contemporaries, namely Dong Guohua in eighteen columns of regular script, Zhu Lun (act. 1810-1877) in seventeen columns of regular script, Shilin in thirty-one columns of clerical script, and Huang Shoufeng, the renowned seal-carver and a son of the famous bibliophile Huang Peilie (1763-1825), in thirty-seven columns of seal script and two columns of regular script.

There is also a long colophon by Yao Ying (1785-1853), who served as the district magistrate of Wujin, Suzhou, and Yizheng in Jiangsu province, in fifty-four columns of regular script and dated the second lunar month of 1836.

The National Library of China has another album of rubbings with the same name which contains an additional six locales with Yinxin Stone Dwellings, namely "Yinxin shiwu shanshui quan tu," "Yinxin shiwu Nanya zhi tu," "Yinxin shiwu Beiya zhi tu," "Yueli Yinxin shiwu tu," "Jinshan Yinxin shiwu tu," and "Jiaoshan Yinxin shiwu tu." These were also commissioned by Tao Shu and engraved the following year in 1837.

46

印心石屋圖説

清道光十六年（1836年）刻。石在江蘇鎮江焦山。陶澍正書説，首阮元隸書橫題。清（1644-1911年）烏金精拓本一冊，計十八開。高三九・二厘米，寬二五・一厘米。經折裝。

畫像 882

　　陶澍，字子霖，號雲汀、桃花魚叟，湖南安化人。清嘉慶七年（1802年）進士，改翰林院庶吉士，嘉慶十年（1805年）散官，授職編修。道光元年（1821年）調福建按察使、安徽布政使。三年（1823年）授安徽巡撫。五年（1825年），因洪澤湖決口，漕運阻淺，特調任江蘇巡撫，親至上海主持漕糧海運，雇沙船一千五百餘艘，運蘇、松、

常、鎮、太五府州漕糧一百六十餘萬石至天津，為清代大規模海運漕糧之始，十年（1830年），升兩江總督兼管兩淮鹽政。任內力圖整頓淮鹽積弊，裁省浮費，嚴核庫款，緝禁私鹽，以保淮鹽行銷。又於淮北試行票鹽，後推及淮南。勇於任事、力革時弊，為朝野所重。十五年（1835年）入覲，賜御書「印心石屋」匾額。其他若治皖之荒疏，在吳之三江水利，亦稱名績。官至宮保尚書、太子少保。工書近北碑。道光十九年（1839年）六月卒，謚文毅。著有《印心石屋文集》、《奏議》七十六卷、《陶桓公年譜》、《淵明集輯注》、《靖節年譜》、《蜀軺日記》。

　　此冊係《印心石屋圖》之一，圖繪綫刻南京、蘇州、揚州、杭州之名勝，陶澍説，用烏金精拓。「印心石屋」之名為皇上所取而賜給陶澍，其書屋稱「印心石屋」。本冊圖、説前有五面隸書題「御

題印心石屋圖」七大字，末署「道光十六年，阮元題」，并刻「雲台」長方印、「阮元伯元」方印以及「節性齋」方印。圖、説即「金陵印心石屋圖」、「金陵印心石屋圖説」、「滄浪亭印心石屋圖」、「滄浪亭印心石屋圖説」、「蜀岡印心石屋圖」、「蜀岡印心石屋圖説」、「清河印心石屋圖」、「清河印心石屋圖説」，各為一開。

　　「金陵印心石屋圖説」記：「謹按：金陵城西清涼山前，突起山阜，曰：『博山』，岡巒秀特，群山環繞。冶城案其前，牛首山、獻花巖峙其南，三山二水綠其西，蔣山、青龍山障其東，石頭城、雞籠山、雨花臺與青溪、秦淮諸水前後盤互映帶，儼如圖畫。茲搆屋博山之陽，勒石恭奉宸翰，龍光煥奕。遠望天印山，即方山，在數十里外，蒼翠欲浮，如卿雲之拱日焉」。

「滄浪亭印心石屋圖說」記：「謹按：滄浪亭在蘇州府學之東，宋臣蘇舜欽所構，坊題『滄浪勝跡』。積水彌數畝。上有小山，高下曲折，與水相縈帶。前松後竹，澄流碧莎，光影會合於户牖之間。前撫臣宋犖續修，頃復重葺亭崞小山頂，虛敞而臨高。城外靈巖、天平、支硎諸山蒼翠吐欲，若浮於檐際。南禪寺在其西，循北麓稍折而東有軒曰『自勝』。迤西十餘步有屋三，檻前三互土。岡後環清澔，曰『觀魚處』。南廊敬鑴列聖南巡時御賜諸臣句聯。今於江南臨水建屋，恭奉御書印心石屋石刻，俾三吳之士同遂瞻仰焉」。

「蜀岡印心石屋圖說」記：「謹按：蜀岡在揚州城西北四里許，一名昆岡。鮑照賦所謂『軸以昆岡』者，此也。岡前曲水縈洄，竟川含綠。東南有橋，五亭翼然覆於其上，是名蓮花橋。西有塔有寺，厥名蓮性。岡上萬松疊翠。迤東最高處為功德林。岡之中為平山堂，宋歐陽修守揚州時所建。以南望，京口諸山恰與檻平也。我聖祖仁皇帝南巡時重修，賜『賢守清風』額。堂西第五泉。堂東有寺，舊名棲靈。乾隆三十年賜名法净寺。東為平遠樓，俯臨河上，壁刻『淮東第一觀』五字。茲擇樓前爽塏處建亭勒石，恭摹御書，俾維揚士庶得申欽仰奉公之忱云」。

「清江印心石屋圖說」記：「謹按：清江浦有元帝山，乾隆三十七年移奉禹王聖像於此，因以臺名。碧瓦丹楹，高出雲表。登臺覽勝，則見運河前橫，帆檣往來如織。其東廣衢修巷，市廛輻輳，慈雲寺、朱公橋，巋然在望。臺之後為普應寺，唐貞觀五年建，有玉帶河繞之。其西為龍池，綠藻紅蕖，光景蒨絢。又西為長堤，柳影參差，遙隄而外，煙波浩淼，則洪澤湖也。臺上恭懸高宗純皇帝『平成永賴』額、仁宗睿皇帝『功成漸暨』額。茲謹就臺左構屋，恭奉御書『印心石屋』石刻，並將浦上投贈諸作環嵌壁間，寶翰騰輝直與河出榮光同昭麻應云」。

圖和圖說後有董國華、朱檱、石麟、黃壽鳳題詩，以及姚瑩題跋。董國華正書十八行，末署「道光丙申仲夏奉題宮保大人祖雲翁大前輩大人御題印心石屋圖冊，謹用題字為韻成七言四章錄請鈞誨。館後學吳縣董國華呈稿」，并刻二印。朱檱正書十七行，末署「印心石屋詩三章，用東坡次文潞

公超然臺韻，謹求宮保老夫子大人誨正……受業朱檱敬呈」，并刻一印。石麟隸書三十一行，末署「吳縣石麟敬呈」，并刻三印。黃壽鳳篆書三十七行、正書二行，末署「黃壽鳳呈稿」，并刻二印。

姚瑩五十四行正書題跋，以下全錄：「皇上御極之十有五年，宮保尚書、兩江總督兼鹽政，安化陶公述職至京師，上以公督兩江地方、軍政漕河鹺務庶績，咸懋褒嘉之，所以慰勞公者殊厚。既詢公家世，公悉以對。且請一月假省先墓，蒙俞可。上復詢所居，公對：『在安化東北東鄉資江之濱。幼從父讀書，江上兩岸石壁屹立如門。潭心一石高出水面，四方如印』。上對讀書所，因以『印心石屋』名其室，上欣然親作四字以賜。字方八寸許，前有可師可法壁中書，引章後有小璽，曰『虛心實行』。公入謝，且當謹勒石垂不朽。上曰：『豈摩崖耶？若爾則所書尚小，當更作擘窠字』。翼日，御書復賜大字，方徑尺只有六寸，遒勁整嚴，乾端坤倪，宸翰昭回，超邁夐古。公再入謝，上問：『前此有之乎？』公對：『聖祖時嘗書賜近臣，惟宋犖巡撫江蘇得之。乾隆中純皇帝書「清愛」二字，賜劉墉以名其堂。今臣少賤讀書之所，兩荷璇毫，實向來未有。』上頷之，天容甚霽。方鑿務之。初改也，中外紛然，疑謗四起，乃斷出宸衷。特命大臣及公求窮變通久之道。公行之五年，成效大著。天語屢贊，謂公一心堅定，能不撓，至以子産治鄭執殺，誰嗣為比，寵光所自，厥有由來，此同寅協恭，諸臣所咸為感動者也。己丑、庚寅之間，淮商疲敝，幾於渙散，庫貯蕩然。公受命設施，不數年跛癱頓起。眾商感戴皇仁，浹髓淪肌，緬昔全盛之時，翠華屢幸維揚，山川草木悉被榮光，御筆留題所在，為烈睿皇帝暨今天子，軫念東南疊更災歉，不肯以供億之事稍耗物力。數十年來閭閻望幸，雖殷率無由，就瞻雲日，商庶之情，莫能自申。眾商乃請於公，恭奉御書勒石茲土，公許之，謹擇平山堂、金焦二山各鑴一石俾，億兆咸得仰觀，以遂其愛慕之誠焉。於戲，海寧黔黎食被天朝深仁厚澤二百年矣。聖學天縱炳燿至於累葉，然皆念關民瘼覆幬而噢咻之，匪但以文物聲名遠軼百代也。惟公忠誠，上契聖心，乃成茲一德之美，汪濊所流，被及兩淮者如此，則公之歸勒於資江也。湖南北士庶爭覩御書，其歡欣鼓舞，更當如何也。瑩隨公相度金山勒石處，既定，乃奉命為記。賜進士、出身護理、兩淮鹽運使、司鹽運使、淮南監掣同知，臣姚瑩恭譔。道光十六年二月□日」。

茲選照「金陵印心石屋圖」及「滄浪亭印心石屋圖」二開，左面圖說空虛部分未照。中國國家圖書館另藏一册《印心石屋圖》，亦陶澍正書說，首隸書橫題，道光十七年（1837年）正月刻，共六幅，為「印心石屋山水全圖」、「印心石屋南崖之圖」、「印心石屋北崖之圖」、「嶽麓印心石屋圖」、「金山印心石屋圖」，以及「焦山印心石屋圖」。

47

Zhuili tu [Dili tu]

Geographical Map

Southern Song dynasty (1127-1279), undated

Drawn by Huang Chang (1146-1194), ca. 1190; engraved on stone stele by Wang Zhiyuan (1193-1257) in the Chunyou period (1241-1252), dated 1247

Dimensions of original stele: 202.3 x 105.0 cm, 108.8 cm at the base

Hanging scroll, ink rubbed on paper, approx. 183.9-184.2 x 101.0 cm

Date of rubbing not given, Republican period (1911-1949)

2/1187/2/5022

Chinese maps which contain substantial amounts of text often provide useful information on roads, waterways, landmarks, distances, but they are also a source of important cultural data. The *Zhuili tu* [*Dili tu*] (Geographical Map), engraved on stone and represented here by a rubbing, is a good example of such a map.

The scholar and imperial tutor Huang Chang (1146-1194) drew up the map around the year 1190 as one of eight cartographic works presented to Zhao Kuo, the prince of Jia, who subsequently ascended the throne as the Southern Song Emperor Ningzong (1168-1224; r. 1195-1224). The map shows the circuits (*lu*), superior prefectures (*fu*), military prefectures (*jun*), and ordinary prefectures (*zhou*) in the Southern Song territories. On the one hand, the map was produced as a didactic tool to illustrate the loss of large territories to the Jurchens who established the Jin dynasty (1115-1234), including the Northern Song capital of Kaifeng, the Yellow River

basin, the Great Wall, and "a vast forest stretching several thousands of *li*". On the other hand, it was designed to impress upon the future sovereign that he had a responsibility to reclaim those lands for the Chinese empire.

The lengthy colophon incised below the map addresses the historical difficulties in unifying China, noting that "only one out of every ten [rulers] has been able to bring unity to all under Heaven." In the text, moral rectitude is portrayed as the key ingredient for successful administration, as illustrated both by positive and negative examples. The sage-rulers who established the great Shang (ca. 1600-ca. 1100 B.C.) and Zhou (ca. 1100-256 B.C.) dynasties began with fairly modest lands (not unlike the Southern Song with its significantly reduced territories), while the mid-eighth century An Lushan rebellion which nearly splintered the Tang empire and the Khitan invasions of the early tenth century are given as examples of how the country is most vulnerable when its rulers become complacent.

The original map, which is no longer extant, had been obtained in Sichuan by Wang Zhiyuan (1193-1257), a native of Yongjia county in Zhejiang province. In 1247, when Wang served as judicial commissioner of the western circuit of Jiangsu and Zhejiang provinces (*Liang Jiang xi lu tidian xingyu gongshi*), he had the map, as well as three others originally presented to Zhao Kuo, engraved on stone in Suzhou, where it has been preserved at the Confucian temple. The first character of the map's elegantly engraved title at the top is pronounced *zhui*; it is an archaic version of the character *di*.

47

墜理圖

南宋光宗紹熙年間（1190年至1194年；約1190年）黃裳繪。南宋理宗淳祐七年（1247年）刻石。石現存蘇州市碑刻博物館（文廟）。碑高二〇二‧三厘米，上寬一〇五厘米，下寬一〇八厘米。圖縱一八三‧九至一八四‧二厘米，橫一〇一厘米。民國年間（1911年至1949年）拓本。掛軸裝，修。

2/1187/2/5022

《墜理圖》名之「墜」字，為古代籀文（大篆）「地」字的寫法。此圖為南宋全國性的輿地圖，原為黃裳向嘉王趙擴（後為宋寧宗）進呈的八幅圖之一，約繪於南宋紹熙元年（1190年）。

圖中所繪為兩宋疆域，繪制并進獻此圖的目的是為了使嘉王披圖則思祖宗境土半陷於异域而未歸。原圖後來為浙江永嘉縣人王致遠在四川獲得，淳祐七年（1247年）王致遠任兩浙西路提典刑獄公事時，于蘇州刻石，「以永其傳」。

全圖無畫方，但可推算出比例尺為1:2500000。該圖北到黑龍江、長白山，西至玉門關，南到海南島，東達海。圖上表示南宋之路、府、軍、州。所有府、州名刻成陰字，均加方框。路名刻成陽字。西南少數民族地區地名不加框。山脈采用傳統寫景法繪畫，森林和長城以形象符號表示，有的地區還繪有樹林符號，并加注「平地松林廣數千」。所有州名、山名都加上長方形的框，所有水名皆有橢圓形圈，以資醒目。河流和海岸綫輪廓比較簡略。所有河名都注在河流的源頭，并加橢圓外框。

圖下有王致遠的跋文與附記，約占總碑長的四分之一，共三十二行。全文六百四十六字，實存五百六十六字，補進六十四字，共六百三十字，其余十六字由于嚴重磨損而空缺。

48

Pingjiang tu

Map of the Prefectural City of Pingjiang

Southern Song dynasty (1127-1279), Shaoding period (1228-1233), engraved 1229

Drawn by Li Shoupeng, engraved by Lu Ting and Zhang Yucheng

Size of the original stele: approx. 279.0 x 142.0 cm

Re-engraved in 1917

Hanging scroll, ink rubbed on paper, 253.4 x 141.5 cm

Date of rubbing not given, Republican period, between 1917 and 1949

221.201/1229/1139

The *Pingjiang tu* is the oldest extant map depicting the city and superior prefecture of Pingjiang (corresponding to present-day Suzhou). It was made in the period between July 22 and August 20, 1229, under the supervision of Li Shoupeng, the prefect of Pingjiang who held office there for less than a year (January 24-November 14, 1229).

No scale is indicated on the map, but analyses indicate that different scales were used. The scale along the north-south axis of the outer city, which had walls totalling 32 *li*, is about 1:1500, while that along the east-west axis is around 1:2,300, thus giving an average scale of 1:2,000. As for the inner city (the administrative center), which had a circumference of 4 *li*, the north-south scale is 1:175 and the east-west 1:167, which averages out to 1:170. The four cardinal directions are indicated at the mid-points of each edge of the map; the north-south alignment is off by 7°54' to the south and east.

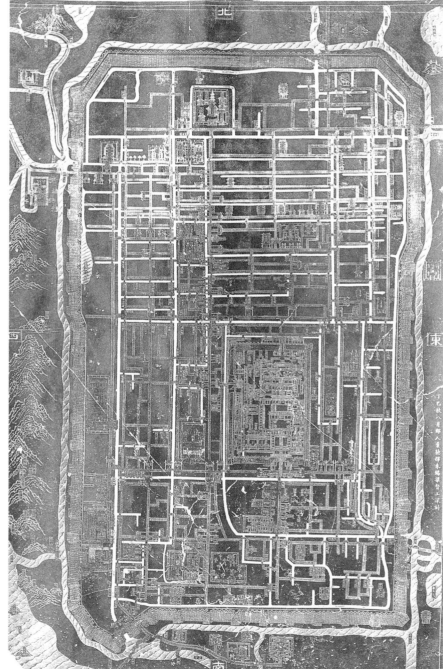

One of the special characteristics of this map is the use of uniform legends which include both pictorial and graphic types. There are no less than 614 vertical or horizontal annotations on the map engraved in regular script (*kai shu*) of varying sizes; nearly half of these are the names of bridges that span the canals of this water-borne city, while others give the names of squares, temples, monasteries and other locales. Natural geographical features are also shown, including ten types of water bodies and water networks such as canals, moats, rivers, lakes, river confluences, ponds, bays, and pools. Lake Tai and the Grand Canal are also indicated. Topographical elements like hills and mountains outside the city walls are named, while those within are generally not marked. However, parks and gardens both inside and outside the city are shown, reflecting the important place that they occupied in the landscape of Song dynasty Suzhou.

In terms of human geography, the map organizes the city into zones defined by the networks of water and land transportation. There are eight major north-south streets and six principal east-west thoroughfares, with more streets and canals running east-west than in the perpendicular direction. Pingjiang was the seat of the superior prefecture of Pingjiang, which had jurisdiction over Changzhou and Wu counties; the governmental apparatus for the two levels of administration, prefectural (*fu*) and county (*xian*), are reflected in the map, as are military installations. Religious buildings such as temples, monasteries, and shrines are also clearly shown.

There are remarkably few omissions and mistakes on the map, which is highly comprehensive and accurately depicts the city as it stood some fifty years before Marco Polo

(1254-1324) is believed to have visited it. The map was re-engraved in 1917 by Huang Weixuan under the supervision of Zhu Xiliang and the distinguished bibliophile Ye Dehui (1864-1927), both natives of Suzhou. Rather than recarving the map on a new slab of stone, the original stele was used. The incised lines and legends which had been worn away after centuries of rubbings were merely deepened, making possible the kind of clarity that is seen in this rubbing from the National Library of China. The stele itself is displayed at the Suzhou Municipal Museum of Inscribed Stelae (Suzhou shi beike bowu guan), within the compound of the Confucian temple (Wen miao) established in 1034.

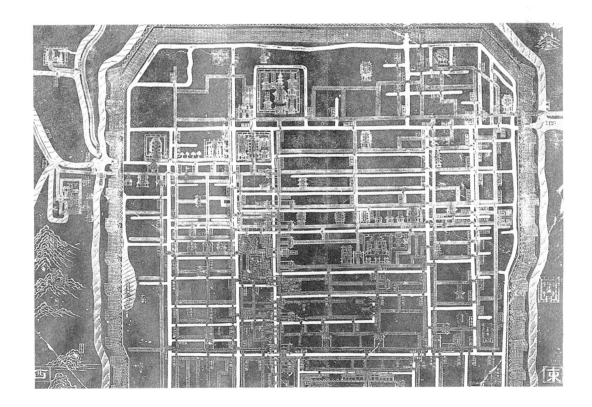

48

平江圖

南宋紹定二年（1229年）刻石。石現藏蘇州市碑刻博物
館（文廟）。碑高二七九厘米，寬一三八厘米。民國年間
墨拓本。圖縱二五三‧四厘米，橫一四二厘米。掛軸
裝。

221.201/1229/1139

　　此圖為宋代平江（今蘇州市）城市地圖。十
二、十三世紀之交平江知府李壽朋主持編繪，南宋
紹定二年（1229年）呂梃、張允成等刻石。城內比
例尺南北方向約為 1:2500，東西方向約 1:3000。
該圖繼承中國古代城市地圖的傳統畫法，并有所創
新，採用平面和三維立體、形象結合的方法，兼顧
地圖的平面精度和建築物的立體效果，詳細、清晰
地繪出了城廓、城廂、平江府衙、平江軍、吳縣等
軍政府署以及縱橫交錯的河流、街道、三百五座橋
梁、近二百五十座殿堂、廟宇、寺觀等建築群。平
江城、內城、宮城分別以不同符號表示。圖邊簡略
表示城郊一些名勝，如虎丘、天平山、姑蘇臺等。
此圖真實地反映了宋時平江府的城市概貌，為中國
傳世最大、最完整的古代碑刻城市地圖，也是世界
罕見的巨幅古代城市地圖。

　　圖右下邊題「丁巳秋八月郡人葉德輝、朱錫
梁督工深刻」。丁巳為民國六年（1917年），刻工
黃慰萱。

49

Yudi tu

Map of Imperial Territories

Originally drawn during the Ming dynasty (1368-1644), Jiajing period (1522-1566), dated 1526; postcript by Yang Ziqi (1458-1513)

Modern copy of original made in 1983

Hanging scroll, ink, color, and white pigment on 2 widths of silk stitched together, 160.2 x 182.6 cm

2/1526/19892

The *Yudi tu* (Map of Imperial Territories) is one of the finest extant examples of Ming maps showing political and administrative divisions. The original version of the map, drawn in color on silk around 1512 or 1513 during the Zhengde reign period of the Ming dynasty, has long since disappeared. A re-worked version based closely on the original was made in 1526 and bears a long colophon by Yang Ziqi (1458-1513); it is now in the collection of the Lüshun Museum. The National Library of China's hand-drawn copy of the 1526 map was made in 1983.

The *Yudi tu* provides at a glance the territorial scope and divisions of the Ming empire, whose external borders are demarcated by a red line, as are the provincial boundaries. Although the map does not possess an explicit scale, the shape of the coastline, courses of rivers, overall configurations of lakes, political subdivisions, and locations of administrative seats are relatively accurate, suggesting that some kind of scale must have been used to draft the original map. Using traditional Chinese cartographic conventions, the network of rivers and waterways is comprehen-

sively shown. The sources of a number of rivers are provided, the most notable of which being that of the Yellow River. Mountains, lakes, and other topographical features, as well as historic sites and scenic spots are all indicated pictorially. All in all, there are more than two thousand annotations on the map. Excepting some five hundred names of mountains and mountain ranges, the majority of named sites are those of human settlements; significantly populated areas are represented by geometric shapes like circles, squares, rectangles, or rhombuses. Cities and

towns are uniformly colored white, the provincial capitals are shown as red circles, while the imperial capital Shuntian (modern Beijing) and the secondary capital Yingtian (modern Nanjing) are prominently visible as the yellow octagons with red borders.

Yang Ziqi's colophon supplements the map by supplying not only a comprehensive list of names of the empire's two imperial capitals, thirteen provinces, superior prefectures, ordinary prefectures, counties, sub-counties, and their administrative seats, but also the appellations of neighboring

countries and regions. The colophon includes a separate legend for cities and towns, as well as information on how and why the map was made. The *Yudi tu* came to be a very influential cartographic work, for a great number of later maps of the Chinese empire were based upon it in concept and presentation.

In this map, the stylized representation of the waters off China's coast extends even to places where the borders should be terrestrial, such as the northeast corner where the Liaodong peninsula merges into the landmass of northeast Asia, and in the southwest where Guangdong, Guangxi, and Yunnan meet neighboring states in southeast Asia. With the Great Wall closing off the north and forbidding mountain ranges in the far west naturally shutting out Tibetan- and Mongol-held territories, the China projected in this map is a particularly insular one, reflecting a world view vastly different from that of a century before, when Chinese fleets under the command of Admiral Zheng He (1371-1433) reached the shores of East Africa.

49

輿地圖

又稱《楊子器跋輿地圖》。1983年據明嘉靖五年（1526年）重繪本摹繪。絹底彩繪本。圖縱一六一厘米，橫一八二・五厘米。掛軸裝。

2/1526/19892

原圖為絹底彩繪，約繪于明正德七年至八年（1512–1513年），已佚。明嘉靖五年（1526年）重繪，圖下方有楊子器題寫的跋文而取名。圖縱一六五厘米，橫一八〇厘米，現藏遼寧省旅順博物館。此為中國國家圖書館所藏重繪本摹本，繪制於年。

《輿地圖》是現存明代政區地圖的優秀代表作之一。圖上北下南，明代所轄範圍一覽圖中。主要繪出明代全國行政區域，用顯著的紅色線條勾繪各省行政界綫。圖面雖無畫方也未注比例，但海岸輪廓、河湖形狀、政區範圍、省府治所的地理位置等基本正確，説明他們是按一定比例和方位繪制的。

地圖內容的表示採用了中國古代地圖的傳統繪制方法，水系繪畫完整，部分河流注出河源，其中黃河源頭畫得最為出色。地物和地貌，如山脈和名勝古跡，皆用寫景法表示，畫工極精。居民地使用了規格化的圖形符號。圖中注記二千多個，除五百多座山脈名稱外，均為居民地名稱。為彌補地圖繪畫之不，圖下又用跋文及説明，詳細記載了當時兩京十三省之府、州、縣、衛、所以及週邊地區的具體數目與名稱，以及繪圖的參考資料和繪圖目的。應該特別指出，該圖下部特列「凡例」，用文字敍述的方式，將圖中所用的居民地符號一一列出，可謂地圖圖例之雛形。

楊子器跋《輿地圖》，是中國傳統制圖鼎盛時期的一幅具有代表性的地圖珍品。其後有很多地圖，無論是繪圖方法，還是內容、結構、形式，均受其影響。

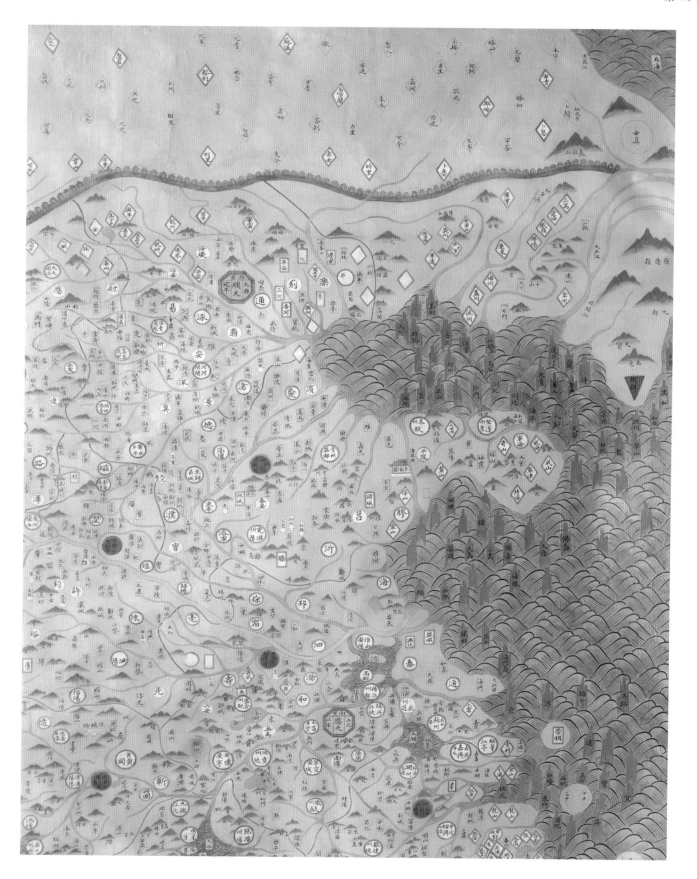

50

Jiangxi quan sheng tushuo

Atlas of Jiangxi Province, with Accompanying Descriptive Notes

Ming dynasty (1368-1644), Wanli period (1573-1619),
undated, ca. 1600
Album of 2 frontispiece leaves and 78 leaves of maps
and corresponding texts; overall dimensions of album,
35.2 x 30.0 cm; frontispiece leaves in ink on tangerine
gold-sprinkled paper, each leaf 28.8 x 26.6-26.9 cm;
map leaves in ink, color, white pigment, and gold on
silk; text leaves in ink on silk; each leaf approx. 35.0 x
30.0 cm; each map approx. 28.6-29.0 x 26.4-26.7 cm;
each text approx. 28.8-29.0 x 26.6-26.8 cm

224/1600/9055

Jiangxi ("east of the river"), a province in
southeastern China lying between the valleys
of the Yangzi and the Xi rivers, first grew
prosperous in the late eighth century A.D.
through tea cultivation, silver mining, and
control of the Gan River, a major north-south
trade and transportation route between the
lower Yangzi valley and Guangdong
province. It is primarily a land of mountains
and hills but has broad plains and fertile valleys along the lower reaches of its many
rivers, all of which flow into Lake Poyang,
the largest freshwater lake in China that
drains into the Yangzi.

This late Ming geographical work is the
oldest extant atlas of Jiangxi but is no longer
complete. Mounted as an album, it now contains thirty-seven maps, including a general
map of the province, six maps of the superior prefectures of Raozhou, Fuzhou,

Jianchang, Ganzhou, Ji'an, Yuanzhou, and individual maps of thirty counties. Names of built structures such as schools, temples, monasteries, and pagodas are written in ink within white-pigmented cartouches (mostly vertical but with a few horizontal ones), while natural landforms like mountains and peaks are indicated in gold ink set against rich mineral hues. The names of rivers and other water bodies are not given on any of the maps, but the more significant ones are mentioned in the descriptive notes, along with information pertaining to the history, topographical features, strategic establishments, and folk customs of each administrative unit.

The overall map of Jiangxi, spread across two facing leaves in the album, functions both as a highly schematic layout of the administrative divisions in the province as well as a kind of table of contents for the atlas, since each prefecture and county indicated would have had a more detailed single-leaf map and an accompanying descriptive text. The large settlement at the center represents the county and prefecture of Nanchang, within which the provincial capital of the same name was located. Lying on the right bank of the Gan River, the 2,500-year-old city of Nanchang has many historical buildings of great interest.

The county-level map illustrated here is that of Linchuan, part of Fuzhou prefecture in north central Jiangxi. The county seat of Linchuan is located on the banks of the Ru River, which doubles as the city's eastern moat and before flowing north to join the Yangzi. The city boasted an impressive cultural history with many illustrious figures who lived there, such as the great calligrapher Wang Xizhi (ca. 307-ca. 365) who served as an administrator (*nei shi*) in the city, the poet Xie Lingyun (385-433) and the great

Tang official and calligrapher Yan Zhenqing (709-785) who both served as prefects. Linchuan was also the childhood home of the Northern Song statesman Wang Anshi (1021-1086).

Also illustrated is one of the prefectural maps, that of Ji'an. Formerly called Luling and Jizhou, Ji'an prefecture has long been an important market center and a hub for both water and land transportation on the Gan River in south central Jiangxi. It was also the ancestral home of such famous Song dynasty scholars as Ouyang Xiu (1007-1072; *jinshi* of 1030) and Zhou Bida (1126-1204); a voluminous edition of Ouyang Xiu's complete collected works, the *Ouyang Wenzhong gong ji*, was printed there in 1192.

50
江西全省圖說

明萬曆年間（1573-1619年）絹地彩繪本。現殘存一冊，存圖三十七幅（總圖一幅，府、縣分圖三十六幅）。每頁縱三五厘米，橫三〇厘米。總圖縱二六厘米，橫五六・六厘米。府、縣分圖每幅縱二八・六至二九厘米，橫二六・四至二六・七厘米。冊頁裝。

224／1600／9055

《江西全省圖說》是明萬曆年間（1573-1619年）繪製的冊裝地圖，也是現存最早的一部江西省地圖集，輯錄了江西總圖一幅，饒州、撫州、建昌、贛州、吉安、袁州等府圖各一幅，縣圖三十幅。圖前篆書題「省方觀民」四大字，無款。此圖冊原為國立南京圖書館藏，後歸中國國家圖書館。

圖中採用中國古代地圖傳統的地物、地貌形象畫法繪制而成，精細的描繪了江西省、府、縣境內的地理情況，制圖者不僅將圖幅內的山嶺、河流、湖泊、樹木、城池、祠廟寺院、村寨、房屋等繪畫得形象逼真，並一一標注名稱，色彩艷麗，生動精美。除贛縣圖外，每圖皆配合楷書圖說，記述了歷史沿革、地理特徵、險要以及風俗等情況，是研究中國古代地圖及明代江西歷史地理的珍貴資料。

茲選照「江西全省圖」（第三開）、「臨川縣」（第十二開）、「吉安府」（第三十三開）。臨川縣圖上標順化門、布政司、撫州府、臨川縣、泰山等名。吉安府圖上標吉安府、廬陵縣、吉水縣、永豐縣、龍泉縣、萬安縣、太和縣、永新縣、永寧縣、安福縣、十九處巡司以及部分山名。

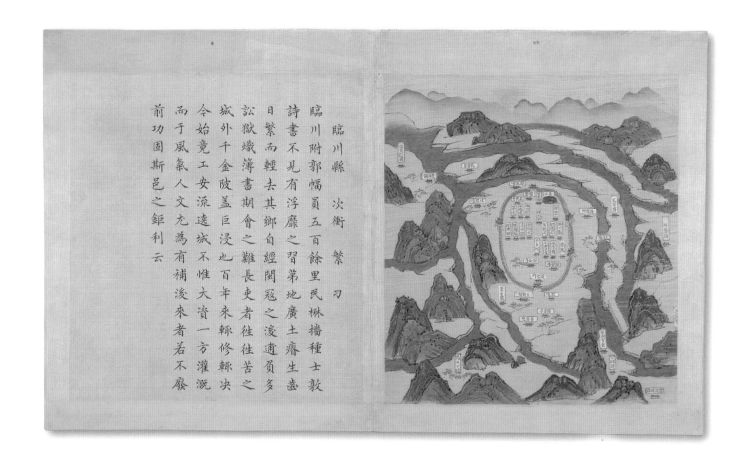

吉安府　景繁

吉安秦漢時九江廬陵郡屬南部都尉理兩
安城名肇三國唐以後號吉州今曰吉安府
府治據章江上流南接章貢北竟淦水東控臨
汝西驪袤桂規土二千餘里咽喉荆廣唇齒
淮浙神岡揖其前螺山歸其後江流廻合東
其下古所謂天作之邦文章節義鳴中國蓋
自顏魯公流風歐陽公八代飈舉文文山兩
間正氣逮

熙朝雅益翔翔匪秋文科第已耳顧歧旁比壤
劇驂俊俀會適館授蔡比比告困矣土瘠民稠
兩資身多業鄰都其俗尚氣君子重名小人
務訟無之軍民雜襲豪猾矜騰吏治鮮效廬
陵泰和景稱難理永寧龍泉稍稍易治云

51

Tianxia jiu bian fenye renji lucheng quan tu

Complete Map of Allotted Fields, Human Traces, and Travel Routes Within and Without the Nine Frontiers under Heaven

Ming dynasty (1368-1644), Chongzhen period (1628-1644), dated 1644

Drawn and printed by Cao Junyi in Nanjing

Hanging scroll, ink woodblock-printed on paper, 124.6 x 124.6 cm

1/1644/14526

From the late Ming period onwards, Chinese scholars experimented with a number of ways to combine cartographic knowledge dispensed by Jesuit missionaries with traditional Chinese mapping conventions. One such example is the *Tianxia jiu bian fenye renji lucheng quan tu* (Complete Map of Allotted Fields, Human Traces, and Travel Routes Within and Without the Nine Borders under Heaven). Drawn by Cao Junyi and printed in 1644, the year the Ming dynasty collapsed, this impressive map remained a principal model for Chinese cartographers during the Qing period (1644-1911).

This map showcases Ming dynasty China at the center and indicates its two imperial capitals of Beijing and Nanjing, thirteen provinces, the Great Wall, as well as significant mountains and rivers. The source of the Yellow River is drawn in the shape of a gourd while river courses and coastlines are somewhat distorted since the map was not drawn to scale. Using assorted legends, the map also

includes the superior prefectures (*fu*), ordinary prefectures (*zhou*), counties (*xian*) (which are provided with a brief account of their history), and administrative headquarters (*wei*) throughout the empire. In addition, the locations of "aboriginal offices" (*tusi*) in southern and southwestern China are indicated. The text at the top of the map gives the title and an explanation of the countries of the world. The text at the bottom describes the two capitals and thirteen provinces, including their names, population figures, production and taxation figures for commodities such as rice, wheat, raw silk, processed silk, cotton, linen, money, horse fodder, and salt; all the information is taken from the *Da Ming yitong zhi* (General Gazetteer of the Ming Dynasty). The texts on either side of the map list the twenty-nine strategic passes of the Nine Frontiers and thirty-three foreign countries.

Although Europe, Africa, the Middle East, and the Indian subcontinent are represented on the map, the two latter areas are shown primarily by means of cartouches. The African continent is dramatically reduced and is suspended along the map's left side. The European landmass is portrayed even more marginally and is almost unrecognizable in the upper left section. The names of several mythical countries depicted off China's southeastern coast come from the ancient *Shanhai jing* (Classic of Mountains and Oceans), but the majority of place names outside of China were clearly taken from Jesuit books, maps, and atlases. All of the information is taken from the General Gazetteer of the Ming Dynasty (*Da Ming yitong zhi*).

In his *Tianxia jiu bian fenye renji lucheng quan tu*, Cao Junyi makes the first Chinese attempt at cartographic accuracy by indicating thirty-six longitudinal lines (but without degree

markings); latitudes are given on both sides of the map. The estimated distances from the subsidiary Ming imperial capital at Nanjing to various "barbarian" countries are provided. Cao also includes by way of substantial commentaries a wealth of factual information and historical data on China's strategic rivers, lakes, mountains, and seas. By no means did he fully undertstand or accept the Western conception of the world, not only remaining conservative in his treatment of world geography but also employing the framework and terminologies of traditional Chinese cosmology and the Chinese tributary system. Another unscientific practice may be observed in his definition of "barbarian" peoples, where he does not make clear distinctions between actual foreign countries and the mythical places and inhabitants found in the *Shanhai jing*.

This map was privately printed in Nanjing, probably in considerable quantity and with commercial intentions in mind, but not many have survived; the British Library possesses another copy of this 1644 map. There are early Qing versions of Cao Junyi's *Tianxia jiu bian fenye renji lucheng quan tu*, such as the one printed in Suzhou by Wang Junfu in the second year of the Kangxi period (1663), and another version reprinted in Japan without the longitudes and latitudinal markings.

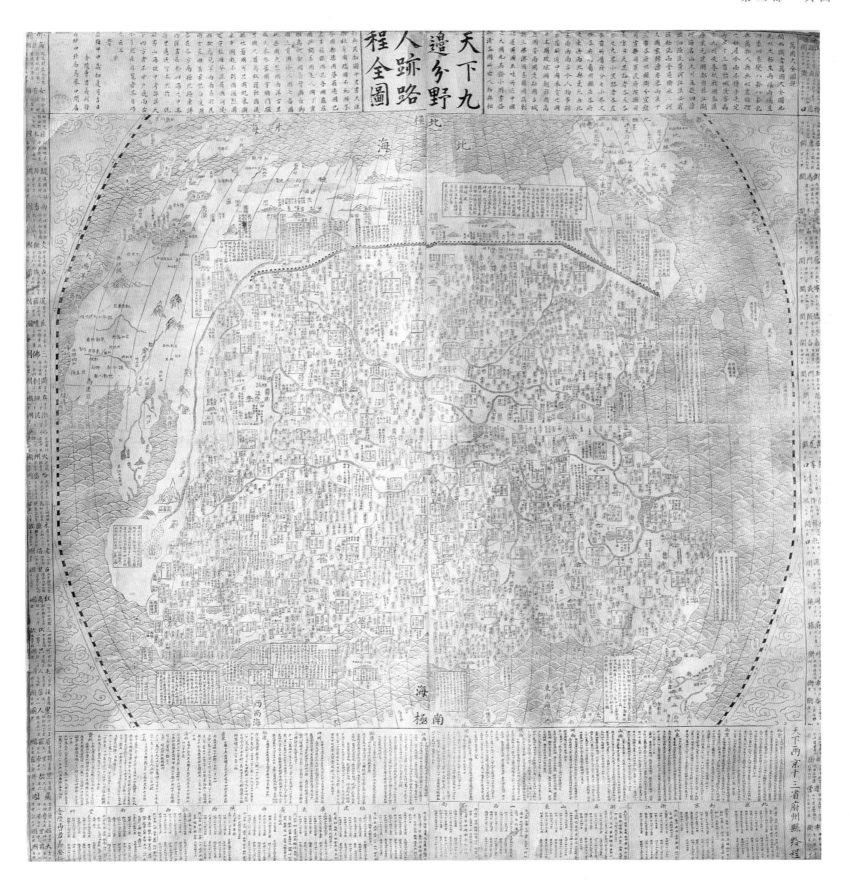

51

天下九邊分野人跡路程全圖

明崇禎十七年（1644年）金陵曹君義木刻印本。紙本。
圖縱一二四‧六厘米，橫一二四‧六厘米。單幅掛軸
裝。

1／1644／14526

《天下九邊分野人跡路程全圖》是中國民間出
版的一幅較早的世界地圖，明崇禎十七年（1644
年）曹君義刊印。此圖雖仍以明代中國為中心，但
已不再是用島嶼的形式羅列其他國家于四周來表示
「天下」的傳統中國式世界地圖，而是以圖、文相

兼的形式，展現明朝的疆域以外的歐洲、地中海、
非洲、南北美洲和南極洲。詳細刻繪明兩京十三省
的行政區劃；用不同符號表示府、州、縣、衛和土
司，并畫出府的轄境；用立面形象表示山脈和長
城，河流、湖泊與海洋均加繪波紋。重要的歷史人
物事跡和境外的介紹，分別用文字記注于相應的地
點。黃河在圖上十分突出，河源畫成葫蘆型；因未
采用計畫方水系、海岸綫的輪廓失真較大。中國
部份雖比較詳細，但國外部份較為粗略。歐、亞、
非洲及南北美洲一些國家的名稱亦有標注，但圖形
簡略、繪製粗糙，誤差很大。古巴置于右上，位置
失實。

圖的上緣為圖題及「萬國大全圖說」，下緣為
「天下兩京十三省府州縣路程」，左右兩側分別用
文字記述「九邊」二十九處關鎮至北京的里程，域
外三十三個國家的物產、習俗以及距北京或應天府

的里程。各省建置數目、里程、户口、米麥、絲
絹、棉麻、銀鈔、馬草、食鹽的數額資料均自《大
明一統志》。

其繪制手法與喻時《古今形勝之圖》、梁輈
《乾坤萬國全圖，古今人物事跡》相近。但是該圖
繪有三十六條未標經度的經綫；左右兩緣上下各
分成0-90緯度差，大致以非洲中南部及中國淮河
為上下分界。歐洲、地中海及非洲西南部的位置輪
廓基本屬實，南、北美洲分別置於右下、右上兩
隅。此圖法首見於傳統的中國全圖，顯然吸收了來
華耶穌會士繪繪的世界地圖資料，屬於坊間私刻售
賣品。

清康熙二年（1663年），姑蘇王君甫編印的
《大明九邊萬國，人跡路程全圖》應當是曹君義圖
的翻刻本。日人梅村彌白亦曾重梓，并删除了經
綫和緯度。

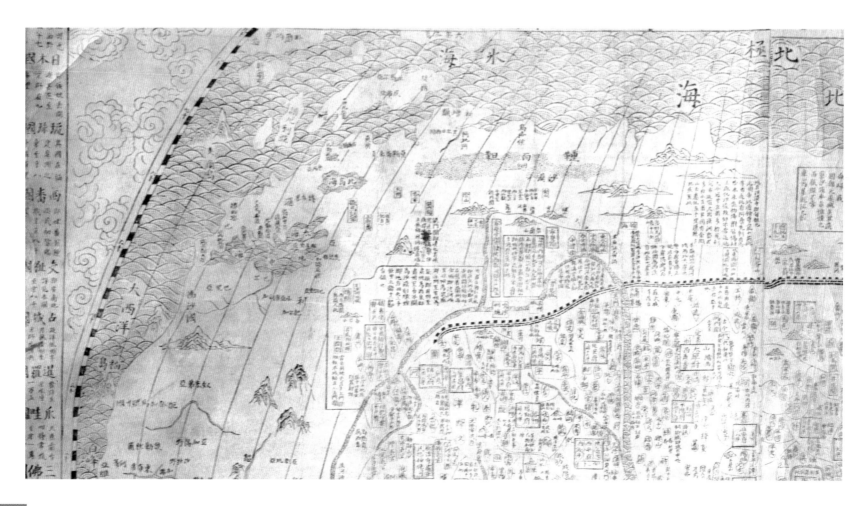

52

Xi hu xinggong tu

Map of the Detached Imperial Residence on the West Lake

Qing dynasty (1644-1911), Qianlong period (1736-1795), undated, ca. 1770

Album of 80 leaves, each leaf approx. 13.6-13.7 x 6.5 cm, with alternating sections of paintings and texts mounted as a handscroll; painting sections in ink and color on silk, text sections in ink on paper; overall dimensions: 13.6-13.7 x 520 cm

No inventory number

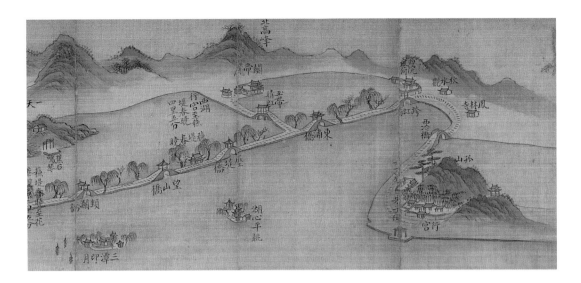

West Lake (Xi hu) has long been celebrated as one of the most beautiful places in all of China, a sight to behold in any season of the year. Situated just outside the western walls of Hangzhou and to the north of the Qiantang River in Zhejiang province, the lake and its environs have been immortalized in countless essays and poems, including a number by the Tang poet Bo Juyi (772-846) and the Song scholar-official Su Shi (1037-1101), after whom the Bo Causeway (Bo ti) and the Su Causeway (Su ti) at West Lake are named.

In addition to the detached palace situated within the city walls of Hangzhou (*nei xinggong*), a suburban imperial residence (*wai xinggong*) was built for the Kangxi emperor (1654-1722; r. 1661-1722) on Solitary Hill (Gu shan), a small island near the midsection of the lake's northwestern edge. This attractive location, accessed via the Su Causeway, was considered the finest for capturing views of the lake and its environs, including the ten most scenic sights or vantage points with

poetic names such as Thunder Peak Pagoda in the Sunset Glow (Lei feng xi zhao) and Nanping Hill Where the Evening Bell Resounds (Nanping wan zhong). The Qianlong emperor (1711-1799; r. 1736-1795) visited Hangzhou no less than six times on his southern inspection tours (in 1751, 1757, 1762, 1765, 1780, and 1784) and would always take the opportunity to enjoy the spectacular scenery and historic sites at West Lake. Solitary Hill was also chosen as the site for the Pavilion of Flourishing Literature (Wenlan ge), a repository for one of the enormous sets of the imperially sactioned *Siku quanshu* (Complete Books of the Four Treasuries).

This map, originally a compact accordion-style album of 80 leaves that was remounted as a handscroll, is an eighteenth-century guidebook made for the Qianlong emperor and his entourage while staying at West Lake. Five sightseeing intineraries from the detached imperial residence are included and rendered in alternating pictorial and texual sections, with the illustrations coming first

in each case.

The first section, comprising eight illustrated leaves and ten text leaves, details the route and distances from the imperial residence at West Lake to Spring Dawn on the Su Causeway (Su ti chun xiao), Viewing Fish at Huagang Pond (Huagang guan yu), Liuyu Mountain Dwelling (Liuyu shan ju), Fayun Monastery (Fayun si), Monastery Where the Tigers Ran Away (Hupao si), Cave of the Stone House (Shiwu dong), Li'an Monastery (Li'an si), Dragon Well Monastery (Longjing si), Chan Monastery of Pure Compassion (Jingci chan si), and other locales.

The next section has the same number of illustrated and text leaves and depicts the itinerary from the suburban imperial residence to Yeast Courtyard and Lotus Breezes (Qu yuan feng he), Jumping Fish at Jade Spring (Yu quan yu yue), Two Peaks Piercing the Clouds (Shuang feng cha yun), Cloud Forest Monastery (Yunlin si), and two other destinations.

The following two sections of the map are itineraries beginning from the detached

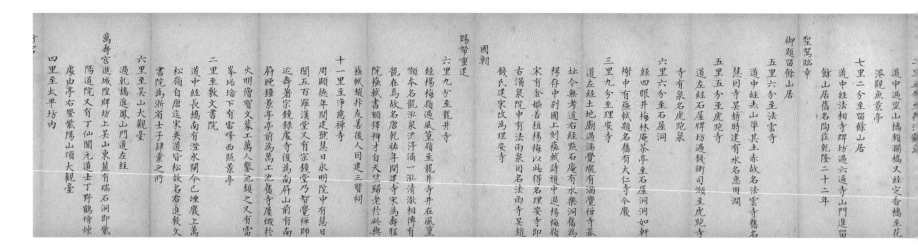

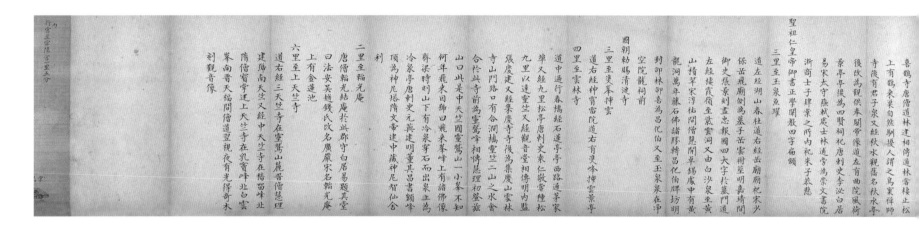

palace in the city of Hangzhou. The eight illustrated leaves and six text leaves of the third section cover the route from the urban palace to the Zongyang Palace, Lingering Snow on the Interrupted Bridge (Duan qiao can xue), Autumn Moon on the Calm Lake (Ping hu qiu yue), before returning to the imperial residence at West Lake. Section 4 contains the longest visual narrative with twelve illustrated leaves followed by eight leaves of text. Among the sights mentioned here are the Gate for Awaiting the Hangzhou Bore (Hou chaomen), Phoenix Hill (Fenghuang shan), Temple of the Song Emperor Taizu), Temple of the Earth (Tudi miao), White Pagoda Hill (Baita ling), Kaihua Temple (Kaihua si), Pagoda of Six Harmonies (Liu he ta), Xu Village (Xu cun), Pavilion of the Five-Cloud Mountain (Wuyun shan ting), Monastery of the Seven Buddhas (Qi fo si), and Yunqi Monastery (Yunqi si).

The fifth and last section of the scroll is also much shorter, with four painted and six descriptive leaves. This itinerary goes from the imperial residence at West Lake to such sights as Listening to Orioles amidst the Willows and Waves (Liu lang wen ying), Three Pools That Mirror the Moon (San tan yin yue), Mid-Lake Pavilion (Hu xin ting), Spring Dawn on the Su Causeway (Su ti chun xiao), and eventually back to the imperial residence on Solitary Hill.

52

西湖行宮圖

清乾隆（1736–1795 年）年間（約1770 年）繪製。繪圖
部份絹底彩繪本，文字部份紙底墨寫本。原經折裝，共
八十面，每面縱一三‧六至一三‧七厘米，橫六‧五厘
米。圖、文總縱一三‧六至一三‧七厘米，橫五二〇厘
米。卷軸裝。
無號

　　西湖在浙江省杭州市區西，為中國著名遊覽
勝地。西湖自然景色絢麗多采，湖光山色，相映成
趣。其歷史悠久，文物繁盛。西湖不僅有如畫的自
然風光可供遊賞，更有數不清的古蹟名勝供尋訪。
著名的「西湖十景」，即「蘇堤春曉」、「花港觀

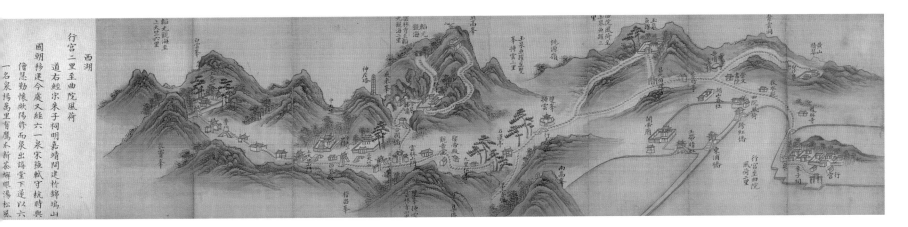

魚」、「柳浪聞鶯」、「曲院風荷」、「雷峰夕照」、「平湖秋月」、「三潭印月」、「斷橋殘雪」、「南屏晚鐘」和「雙峰插雲」。

《西湖行宮圖》是一套道里圖說，繪制了十八世紀中國乾隆皇帝南巡時設於西湖湖區的各處行宮及十八景等名勝。乾隆帝曾先後六次南巡，於乾隆十六年（1751年）、二十二年（1757年）、二十七年（1762年）、三十年（1765年）、四十五年（1780年）、四十九年（1784年）到杭州，整頓軍旅、巡視書院、遍訪西湖名勝，遣官致祭岳飛。乾隆四十七年（1782年）將孤山行宮玉蘭館改建為文瀾閣，庋藏《四庫全書》。

清內務府造辦處輿圖房曾繪制不少杭州與西湖行宮圖，如《杭州城內行宮圖》一卷、《浙江杭州西湖外行宮圖》一卷、《西湖行宮正殿圖》一冊等。此本《西湖行宮圖》繪制精美，是典型的官本地圖。此圖未著撰人，原十幀地圖連同圖說裱裝成

十折冊，後重裱裝成卷軸。用鳥瞰圖的形式描繪了圍繞杭州城和西湖的皇帝出遊的綫路。每折圖說詳細記錄了遊覽綫路的各個景點與相互的距離，以下依次簡錄：

第一段道里圖八面、說十面，記西湖行宮四里五分至蘇堤春曉，二里五分至花港觀魚，七里二分至留餘山居，五里六分至法雲寺，五里五分至虎跑寺，六里六分至石屋洞，三里九分至理安寺，六里九分至龍井寺，十一里至淨慈禪寺，二里至敷文書院，六里至吳山觀臺，四里至太平坊內。

第二段道里圖八面、說十面，記西湖行宮二里至曲院風荷，三里至玉泉魚躍，三里至雙峰插雲，四里至雲林寺，二里至韜光庵，六里至上天竺寺。

第三段道里圖八面、說六面，記杭州省城內行宮一里五分至宗陽宮，九里至教場，四里至斷橋殘雪，一里至平湖秋月，一里至西湖行宮。

第四段道里圖十二面、說八面，記杭州省城內行宮四里五分至候潮門，三里至浙江秋濤，四里至鳳凰山，二里至宋太祖廟，二里至都土地廟，二里至白塔嶺，二里至開化寺六和塔，二里至徐村，二里至五雲山亭，三里至雲棲下院，三里至七佛寺，二里至三聚亭，一里至雲棲寺。

第五段道里圖四面、說六面，記西湖行宮登舟六里至柳浪聞鶯，四里至三潭印月，二里至湖心亭，一里至蘇堤春曉，二里至一天山，四里至西湖行宮。

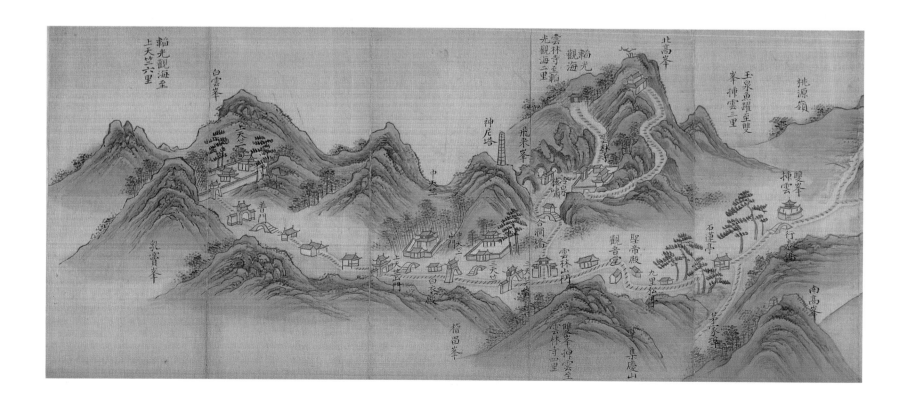

53

Taiwan ditu

Map of Taiwan

Qing dynasty (1644-1911), Qianlong period (1736-1795), undated, 1787 or earlier

Handscroll, ink and color on paper, approx. 40.5-40.6 x 437.9 cm

232/1784-2/3638

The island of Taiwan, separated from the Chinese mainland by a 160-km wide strait, was named Ilha Formosa ("Beautiful Island") by the Portuguese in 1590. In 1624, the Dutch, under the aegis of the East India Company, founded forts in the southwest at the site of present-day Tainan. The Spanish established bases in the north, but were expelled by the Dutch in 1641 who assumed complete control of the island. They in turn were forced to abandon Taiwan in 1662 when the loyalist Ming general Koxinga (Zheng Chenggong; 1624-1662), fleeing from the Manchus, seized Taiwan and established a kingdom; this too was short-lived as the Manchus finally conquered the island in 1683. With increased Chinese immigration from Fujian and Guangdong provinces, rice and tea cultivation were introduced to Taiwan. The aboriginal population, which lived on hunting, fishing, and shifting agriculture, was gradually pushed into the interior highlands.

This undated map of Taiwan in the handscroll format is one of the earliest surviving hand-painted maps of the island. It was produced during the Qianlong period (1736-1795) but no later than 1787, roughly a century after the Qing conquest. As land is depicted on the upper portion of the map and water is shown below (as though it were being viewed from Fujian province across the strait), the scroll begins with the southernmost point of Taiwan and terminates with the northern end, covering a distance of approximately 400 km.

The title given to this map is somewhat

misleading, since only the western half of Taiwan is depicted. The broad coastal plain which features largely in this map has always supported most of the island's population; the locations of various counties, harbors, cities, towns, settlements, and minority mountain communities are indicated. Taiwan's rugged anticlinal mountain ranges, with some forty-eight peaks over 3,000 meters high, are depicted in pictorial elevation using heavy mineral colors along the entire length of the map, while rivers flowing westward, cutting successive terraces along their descent and building up alluvial plains that slope gently toward the sea, are also represented. From 1683 to 1895, Taiwan was administered as part of Fujian province; the island's capital Taiwan fu (at the site of present-day Tainan), had the status of a prefectural seat and is clearly represented on the map. Also shown is the archipelago known as the Pescadores (Penghu liedao) in the Taiwan Strait. The numerous artillery stations and barracks represented on the island suggest that this map may have been used for military purposes.

Three short sections of the handscroll reproduced here show the southern tip of Taiwan with Mount Shamajitou and offshore islands; the west central part of the island centered on Zhuluo county (known as Jiayi county after 1787) and its seat; and the northern extremity with Mount Jilong and the city of Jilong, which would later become the major port of Keelung. In this richly colored map, the insular nature of Taiwan is emphasized through the exquisite rendering of gigantic waves, and the distinctions between cartography and art are decidedly blurred.

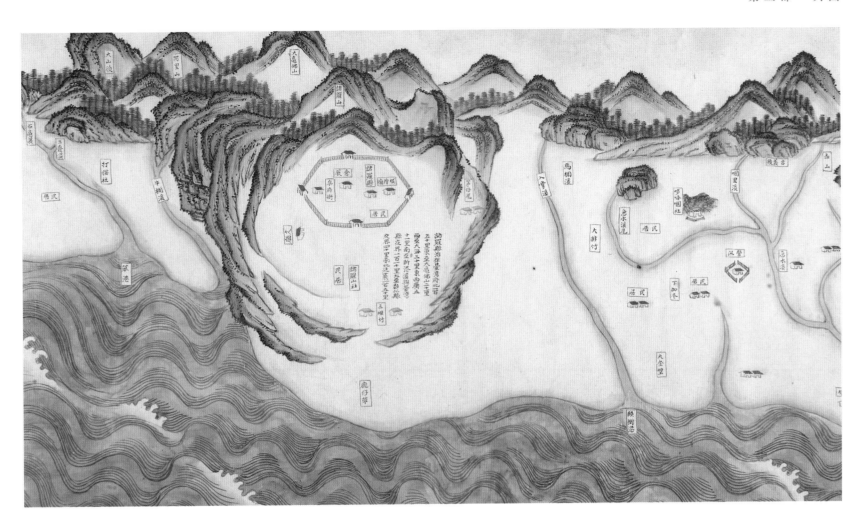

53
臺灣地圖

清乾隆二十八年（1763年）題簽，繪製年代下限為乾隆
五十二年(1787年)。紙底彩繪本。圖縱四〇‧五厘米，
橫四四〇厘米。卷軸裝。

232/1784-2/3638

　　台灣府於清康熙二十三年（1684年）便隸屬
於福建省。本圖為清乾隆年間繪本，故又稱為《福
建台灣地理全圖》。據圖中嘉義縣仍稱「諸羅縣」
推斷，其繪製年代下限為乾隆五十二年（1787
年），為中國現存最早的手繪台灣地圖之一。

　　本圖繪畫遵循陸上海在下的原則，故地圖方
位為上東下西。圖繪內容自台灣島北端的雞籠山和
雞籠城（今基隆市）至島南端的沙馬磯頭山、紅頭
嶼和小琉球山（今高雄之南琉球嶼），西至澎湖列
島。此圖內容重點表示台灣島西部山川、平原的地
形地物，水系和居民地，包括府、縣和台灣最早興
起的港口城鎮，以及山區少數民族番社住地。山地
採用重彩形象繪畫，雄偉奇秀。圖中畫出的大小河
流，自東向西流入大海。海水用大波浪花紋表示。
此外，圖上還表示了炮台等兵要內容，使地圖兼有
軍事用途。

54

Shengchao qi sheng yang tu

Coastal Map of the Seven Maritime Provinces of the Illustrious Dynasty

Qing dynasty (1644-1911), Jiaqing period (1796-1820), dated 1798

Handscroll, ink, color, and gold on paper, 29.2 x 888.9 cm

068.2/(2)/1798/6798

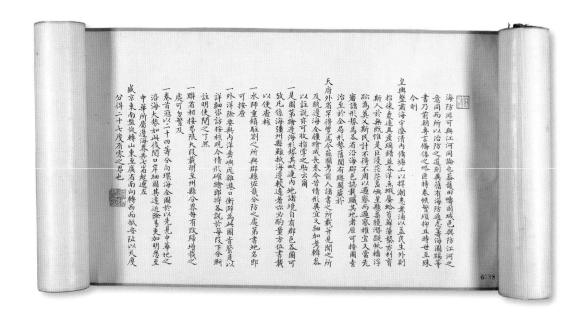

The seven maritime provinces referred to in the title of this map are Shengjing (roughly corresponding to modern-day Liaoning), Zhili (modern Hebei), Shandong, Jiangsu, Zhejiang, Fujian, and Guangdong provinces. This 1798 map is one of many based on the *Yanhai quan tu* (Complete Coastal Map of the Seven Maritime Provinces) drawn by Chen Lunjiong in the early Yongzheng period between 1723 and 1730. Chen's map had six sections: a map of the eastern hemisphere, a coastal map of China, a map of Taiwan, a map of the inner mountains of Taiwan, map of the Pescadores (Penghu liedao), and a map of Qiongzhou (Hainan).

The handscroll opens with an explanatory narrative with five main points listed separately at the end of the text. The circular map depicts the eastern hemisphere with Japan and most of the Russian Far East at upper right, part of Antarctica at lower right, England at the upper left, the entire African continent at left, and a number of archipelagos in the South Atlantic Ocean at lower left. Not surprisingly, China occupies a central position and its territory is greatly exaggerated in relation to other countries; all its prov-

inces as well as the imperial capital are listed by name. The didactic purpose of this map was clearly to reinforce China's pride during the height of its territorial expansion and its self-perception as a world power.

The main portion of the map shows the coastline and immediate hinterland of the seven maritime provinces, beginning with Shengjing in the north and continuing through Guangdong in the south but oriented in a horizontal fashion for the handscroll format. Detailed geographical and narrative descriptions are inscribed in neat blocks of texts in varying lengths within the blank spaces of the map. The first section depicting the Gulf of Bohai as well the Liaodong and Shandong peninsulas is particularly detailed, with names provided for a great number of cities, towns, ports, and rivers. The Great Wall is shown with its eastern terminus at Shanhaiguan, and the subsidiary Manchurian capital of Fengtian

(Mukden; modern Shenyang) is the first city encountered on the map.

Another section of interest is the rugged coast of Fujian province with its numerous bays, inlets, and sheltered harbors. The entire west coast of Taiwan, lying some 160 km across the strategic Taiwan Strait, is shown along the lower edge of the scroll between the provincial capital of Fuzhou and Zhao'an county; the island of Taiwan and the Pescadores are shown separately in a subsequent section. The island of Qiongzhou ("Rose-Jeweled Kingdom"; later called Hainan), administered during the Qing as part of Guangdong province, is also treated with great detail. This tropical frontier island had been a place of exile for centuries and from the late Ming onwards a target of Sino-Vietnamese piracy in the Gulf of Tonkin. Qiongzhou later became important as a southern military outpost for the Manchus and as a trading zone between China and

Jiaozhi (northern Vietnam). On this map, the round island is crammed with the names of its rivers and mountains, ports, and human settlements written in many orientations; an extensive description to its left provides even more information.

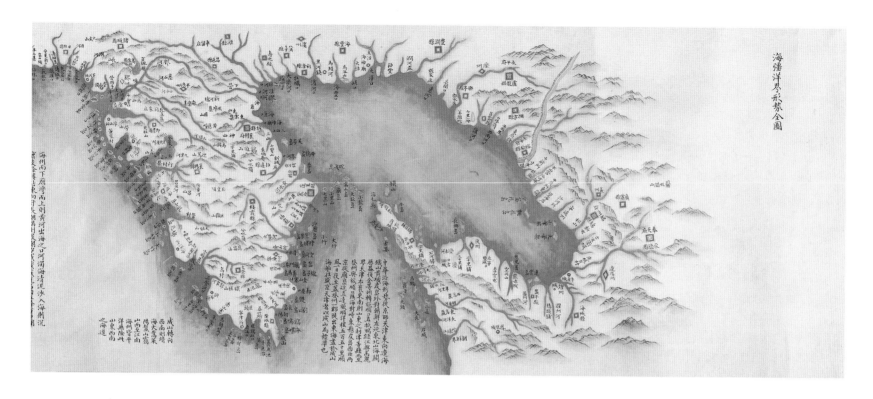

54

盛朝七省沿海圖

清嘉慶三年（1798年）紙底彩繪本。圖縱二九・二厘米，
橫八八八・九厘米。卷軸裝。

08.2／（2）／1798／6798

　　傳世的《七省沿海圖》摹繪本較多，流傳亦廣。此圖名《盛朝七省沿海圖》，為清嘉慶三年（1798年）繪制。圖為自右至左「一」字形開展式，從鴨綠江、遼東半島繪至與交趾（今越南）分界處，包括沿海的盛京（今遼寧）、直隸（河北）、山東、江蘇、浙江、福建和廣東七省，故名七省沿海圖。此圖是以陳倫炯於雍正初年（1723–1730年）繪制的沿海全圖為藍本，再進行某些補充修改而

成。陳倫炯的沿海全圖計有六幅，即四海總圖、沿海全圖、台灣圖、台灣後山圖、澎湖圖和瓊州府圖（今海南島），因此此圖亦由以上圖類似組成。

　　《盛朝七省沿海圖》首列環海全圖，次為海疆洋界全圖，後附瓊州、澎湖、台灣前後山等圖。圖前有解說并附五則，其中第五則題「卷首冠以二十四籌分向環海全圖於以先見中華地之沿海大勢如此。後閱口岸細圖，其遠近險易更加明悉至中華所屬邊海界共七省。起遼左盛京，東南盤旋轉山東至廣省南向轉西而抵安阯以天度得得二十七度有零之界也」。圖最後注出「嘉慶戊午孟夏下浣重校圖本」字樣。

　　此圖以上方為陸，下方為海。繪畫方法極為精致，表現中國東部七省沿海的山川地形、島嶼暗礁、村鎮民宅的分布位置，是中國古代海圖的代表作之一。

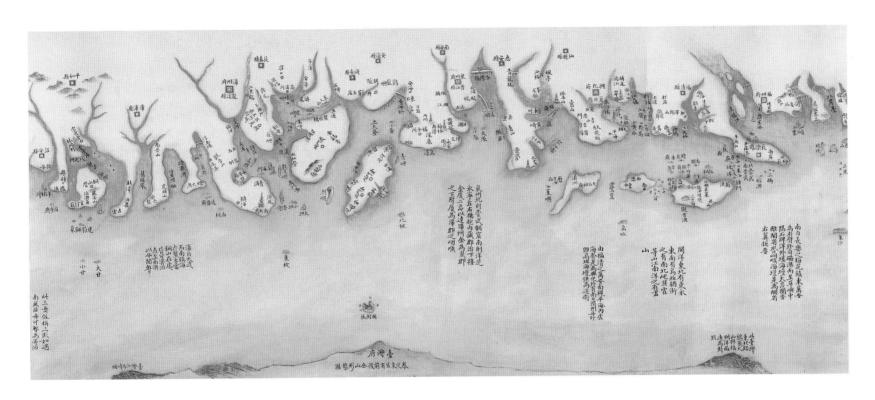

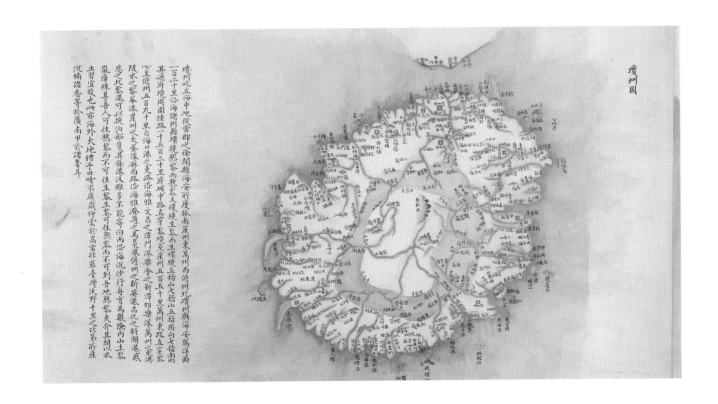

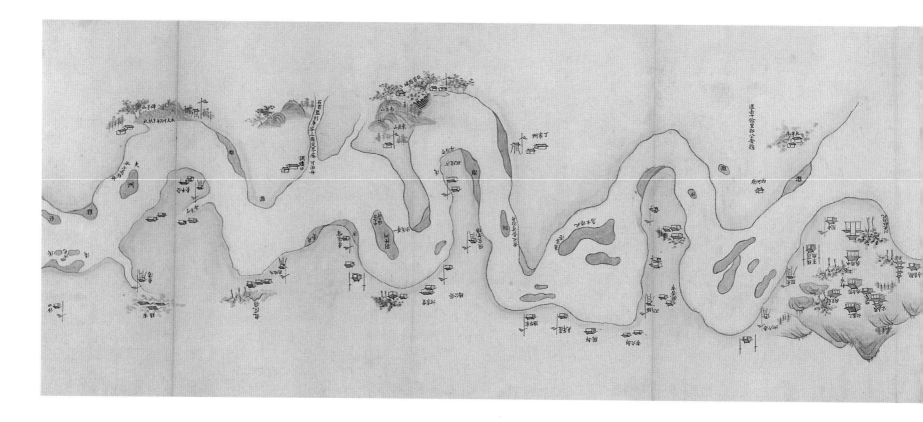

55

Changjiang mingsheng tu

Map of Scenic Attractions along the Yangzi River

Qing dynasty (1644-1911), undated, dated 1867

Illustrated by Feng Shiji

Album of 68 leaves mounted as a handscroll; first frontispiece section by Ouyang Zibin in ink on pale pink paper, 25.3 x 60.3 cm; second frontispiece section by Feng Shiji in ink on paper, 25.3 x 30.3 cm; map section in ink and light color on paper, 25.3 x 1120.6 cm; colophon section by Feng Shiji in ink on paper, 25.3 x 592.8 cm

074.2/(22)/1867/7474

The Yangzi River is the longest river in China and in all Asia, and the third-longest in the world. 5,550 km long, it rises in the highlands between Tibet and Qinghai and flows generally eastwards through Tibet, Sichuan, Yunnan, Hubei, Hunan, Jiangxi, Anhui, and Jiangsu provinces before discharging into the East China Sea at Chongming Island near Shanghai. Because it is navigable all the way to Yichang, its scenery has long been enjoyed by visitors on boats.

This unique sightseeing map of the river was painted in pale, subtle colors by Feng Shiji of Shanyin during the mid-autumn of 1867. Originally folded accordion-style into a convenient size, its sixty-eight leaves are now stretched out as a very long handscroll, graced with a frontispiece inscription in large characters by Ouyang Zibin. It covers the middle and lower reaches of the Yangzi River from Shishou county, Hubei province, in the west to Jiangyin county, Jiangsu province, in the east. This heavily populated section of the river has a great number of significant historic and scenic sites along its banks.

Unrolling the handscroll from right to left, the south bank of the river is at the top and north bank at the bottom. Just as the river's scenery can be enjoyed from both sides of a boat, the map can be read from either the top or bottom edge, depending on whether the user was going upstream or downstream,

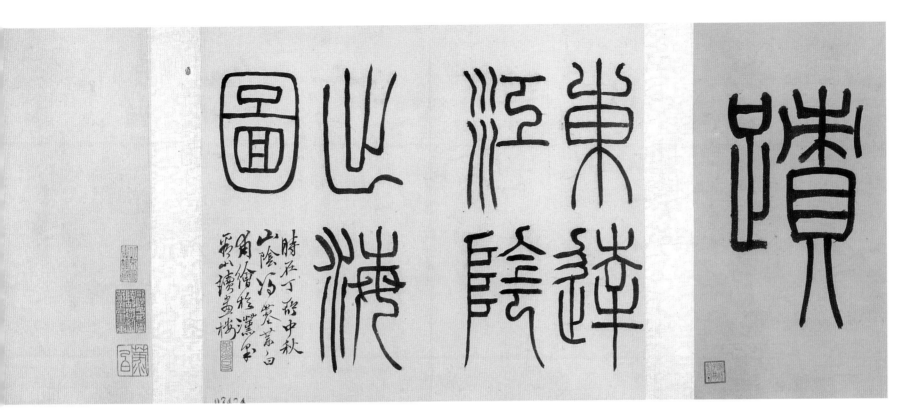

and which side of the river was being observed at the time. In addition to drawing the map, Feng Shiji also contributed one of the two frontispieces and a long colophon text which he called the *Changjiang yantu kao ji* (A Study of Sites along the Banks of the Yangzi River). The colophon provides detailed descriptions of many of the scenic attractions and historical relics identified on the map.

The two selected sections of the map illustrated here show the river as it traverses the major cities of Wuchang in Hubei (located 1,010 km from the sea), and Nanjing in Jiangsu. Wuchang is actually a conglomeration of three cities—Wuchang, Hanyang, and Hankou—at the confluence of the Han, Xiang, and Yangzi Rivers. Wuchang, capital of the state of Wu in the third century A.D., is on the right bank of the Yangzi River, while Hanyang and Hankou are on the left bank. In 1858, less than a decade before this map was made, the Treaty of Tianjin had secured the opening of four ports along the Yangzi–Hankou, Jiujiang, Nanjing, and Zhenjiang–to foreign trade and development as well as foreign tourism.

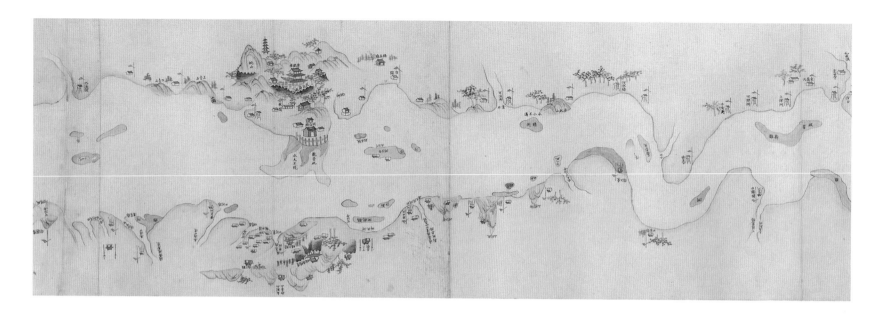

55
長江名勝圖

清同治六年（1867年）馮世基繪製。紙底彩繪本。原經
折裝，共六十八面。圖總縱二五・三厘米，橫一一二〇
・六厘米。卷軸裝。

074.2 ／（22）／1867／7474

　　長江是中國第一大江，出自青海，流經西
藏、四川、雲南、湖北、湖南、江西、安徽、江
蘇諸省。長江流域人文歷史悠久，自然風光壯
麗，有豐富而獨特的旅遊景點。

　　該圖上南下北，主要描繪長江兩岸的風景名

勝、文化古跡等。西起湖北省石首縣，東至江蘇省
江陰縣。圖中各要素均採用透視符號表示，并借用
中國傳統的山水畫表現手段，形象逼真，是現存較
早的江河名勝遊覽圖。所繪長江兩岸各類地物要素
均朝向河流中心綫，給人以站在船頭、隨船行進，
一路觀覽長江兩岸自然景色之感受。這種「對景
法」的表現形式，常見於中國古代的江圖、河圖和
航海圖，有獨到的功用。該圖色彩和諧，清秀雅
典，不愧為一幅藝術佳作。

　　此圖原是經折裝，共六十八面，後改卷軸
裝。圖前有歐陽子彬題「長江勝蹟」四大字，并有
繪者山陰馮世基丁卯（1867年）中秋題「東達江陰
之海圖」。圖後有馮世基行書「長江沿途攷蹟」，
共三十九面。

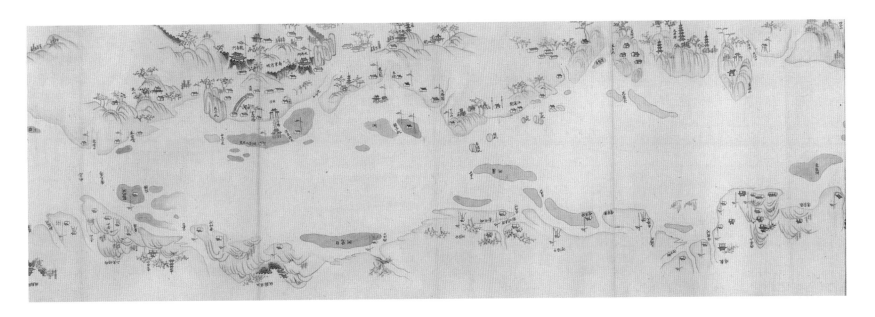

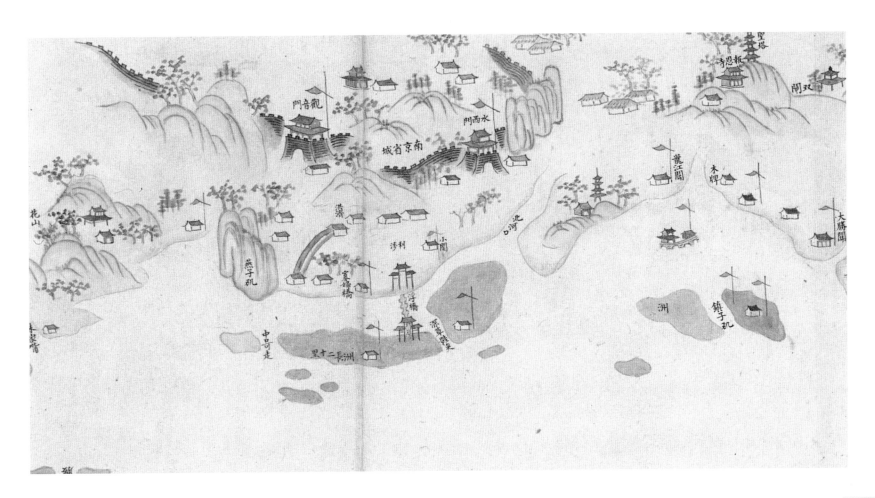

56

Bishu shanzhuang quantu

Complete Map of the Mountain Retreat forEscaping Summer's Heat

Qing dynasty (1644-1911), Guangxu period (1875-1908), undated, ca. 1900

Horizontal hanging scroll, ink, color, and white pigment on paper (with identification labels in ink on red paper affixed to†scroll), 212.0 x 382.5 cm

074.45/(211.911)/1900-2

The Mountain Retreat for Escaping Summer's Heat (Bishu shanzhuang) is located about 250 km northeast of Beijing in the town of Rehe (Jehol; modern-day Chengde). The palatial retreat enclosed by a long wall was begun in 1703 by the Kangxi emperor (1654-1722; r. 1661-1722) and was later expanded by the Qianlong emperor (1711-1799; r. 1736-1795) through 1792. Nominally a summer retreat, it actually functioned as a secondary capital for the Qing court which spent parts of every summer and autumn there. Although the palace complex proper contained mostly Chinese-style buildings and gardens laid out in the traditional Chinese manner, the preferred architectural language for the monumental structures was Tibetan. In 1767, the Putuozongsheng Temple, a scaled-down replica of the Potala Palace in Lhasa was built in honor of the empress dowager's eightieth birthday and the Qianlong emperor's sixtieth. In 1780, a replica of Tashilhunpo monastery, seat of the Panchen Lama at Shigatse, was constructed in time for the visit of the Sixth Panchen Lama, Pelden Yeshe (1738-1780). All

in all eleven Lamaist temples were built between 1713 and 1780 on the hills east and west of the retreat complex, though they are referred to as the Eight Outlying Temples (*wai ba miao*).

This massive map was drawn during the Guangxu period (1875-1908), around the turn of the century, as Manchu rule in China was drawing to a close. It adopts the manner of traditional Chinese landscape painting to feature the imperial retreat, the Eight Outlying Temples, and the scenic landscape of the surrounding hills. The thirty-six scenic spots with four-character names bestowed by the Kangxi emperor and the other thirty-six scenic locales with three-character names by the Qianlong emperor are labeled in ink on red paper and mounted individually on the surface of the map. These named areas evoked the scenery in different regions of the Chinese empire and, along with the outlying temples and monasteries, were part of a microcosm of the vast realm controlled by Qing rulers.

56
避暑山莊全圖

清光緒（1875-1908）年間（約1900年）繪製。紙底彩繪本。圖縱二一二厘米，橫三八二‧五厘米。橫軸裝。
074.45／（211.911）／1900-2

　　避暑山莊，亦稱「承德離宮」或「熱河離宮」。在今河北省承德市區北部山區。清朝康熙皇帝在平定中國南部三藩之亂後，根據政治上的需要，便將注意力轉向北方，決定在古北口外建立圍場，每歲行圍，以便習武。熱河行宮始建于康熙四十二年（1703年），康熙四十七年（1708年）初具規模，

至乾隆五十七年（1792年）陸續建成。佔地面積約五‧六四平方千米，周圍宮牆長達十公。

　　山莊分宮殿區和苑景區兩大部份，既有天設地造的山水草木之秀，又有人工建築的殿閣亭榭之美。由康熙、乾隆二帝分別欽定的七十二景點遍布其內。山莊群山環抱，夏季氣候宜人。從康熙帝後期始，直到咸豐（1851-1861年）年間，清帝于每年夏季都到山莊避暑巡幸，并處理朝政。因此，避暑山莊成為清代北京皇宮之外的又一處政治活動中心。山莊以外，于北面、東面先後建有十一座不同風格的寺廟，為少數民族首領朝觀時的住所。現僅存八座，俗稱「外八廟」。這些寺廟環繞在避暑山

莊的周圍，形似眾星捧月，把滿、漢、蒙、回、藏、維各民族間感情與文化融在一起。山莊周圍有遠近不同的許多奇峰怪石，各呈體態，維妙維肖，饒有趣味，與避暑山莊和外八廟融合成一區優美的風景勝地。現為全國重點文物保護單位。

　　《避暑山莊全圖》是一幅清皇家園林專題地圖，是中國古代同類地圖中的精品。採用傳統形象畫法，生動地描繪了承德離宮、外八廟及附近山水勝景全貌。以紅色貼簽分別標示出康熙四字題名的三十六景和乾隆三字題名的三十六景。全圖內容豐富，畫工精巧，色彩絢麗，圖象逼真，立體感強。

57

Zi Dajianlu zhi qianhou Zang tucheng tu

Map of the Routes from Dajianlu to Anterior and Posterior Tsang

Qing dynasty (1644-1911), Guangxu period (1875-1908), dated 1901

Illustrated by An Cheng

Handscroll, ink and color on silk, 41.4 x 316.3 cm

057.63/(227.003)/1901/0146

During the Qing period, Tibet occupied a land mass considerably larger than its present size and comprised four regions from east to west, namely Chams, Ü, Tsang, and Ngari. The vastness of Tibet's territory and the great navigational difficulties it presented for travelers made good route maps indispensable items. This hand-drawn map from the National Library of China is an excellent example of a Chinese route map covering the distance between western Sichuan and the far west of Tibet, even though its title suggests that it does not extend beyond the borders of Tsang.

Cham (Khams in Tibetan; Kang in Chinese), easternmost of the traditional Tibetan provinces, has more than its fair share of spectacular topography. Here, the Himalayas extend north to south rather than east to west through Cham, obstructing the main routes between Tibet and China. The land is further disrupted by heavily forested valleys and gorges cut by the three great rivers that run through the area—the Salween, Mekong, and Yangzi. The Chinese equivalent for Ü (Dbus, pronounced "u") is Wei but the province was commonly called Qian

Zang (Anterior Tsang), comprising the Kyichu valley and the Lhokha region to its south, with the capital at Lhasa. Tsang (Gtsang in Tibetan; Zang in Chinese), with its capital at Shigatse (Gzhis-ka-rtse), was known as Hou Zang (Posterior Tsang) and occupied the areas north and south of the Brahmaputra to the west of its confluence with the Kyichu, including the fertile valley of the Nyangchu River. These two central Tibetan provinces were also collectively known as Ütsang (Dbus-gstang). In ancient and medieval times, the far west of Tibet (from the highland region of Lato to the watersheds of the Indus and Sutlej Rivers) formed a separate administrative region known as Mar yul or Ngari Korsum, but this largely unpopulated area was later incorporated within Ütsang and known in the late Qing simply as Ngari (Ali in Chinese).

Dajianlu (Dartsedo or Dar-rtse-mdo in Tibetan; later renamed Kangding by the Chinese) was a walled town some 400 km southwest of Chengdu, lay within a deep gorge at the confluence of the Zheduo (Cheto) and Yakra (Yala) tributaries which form the Dadu (Dardo) River. Formerly the capital of the Chakla kingdom, it prospered as a frontier town between China and Tibet. From 1696, Dajianlu was the one place where Tibetans were allowed by the Dalai Lama to carry on trade and to purchase bricks of tea-leaves from growers in western Sichuan province; the town was also the center of Sichuan's thriving logging industry. Towering south of Dajianlu is the mighty peak of Mount Gongga (Minya Konka in Tibetan; 7,556 meters above sea level), while northwest of the town lay the Tagong Grasslands, a vast expanse of green meadow surrounded by snow-capped peaks and dotted with Tibetan herdsmen and tents. The Tagong Lamasery there dates back to the Qing dynasty.

An inscription near the beginning of the map provides the following succinct account:

There are altogether three routes to Tsang which originate at Dajianlu—the northern, central, and southern routes. The northern route begins from the nothern entrance of the gorge at Dajianlu, cuts across grassy plains, and thus is the most expedient means of reaching Posterior and Anterior Tsang. The central route starts from the southern entrance of the gorge at Dajianlu and then heads north to Chamdo; this is also the route taken by Tibetan tea traders. The southern route goes via Litang, Batang, and Drayab, the same as that taken by [Chinese] officials stationed in Tibet as well as by government troops and mounted postal couriers. Because the southern route has a warmer climate and is more densely inhabited, it is easier to change from porters and horses to yak caravans along this route. However, because of the many bends to be negotiated along the way, it is far more circuitous than the other two routes.

Of the three routes indicated on the map by short black parallel lines, the northern one reaches farthest and terminates in Ngari. The central route ends at Kyirong (Jilong in Chinese) and the southernmost route terminates at Nyalam (Nielamu in Chinese). A bold red line indicates the border of Sichuan province, while borders with Yunnan province, Nepal, Sikkim, Bhutan, Vietnam, Siam, the territory of Xinjiang, and Russia are also indicated on the map. Rivers and mountains are rendered in green while plains and grasslands are shown in yellow.

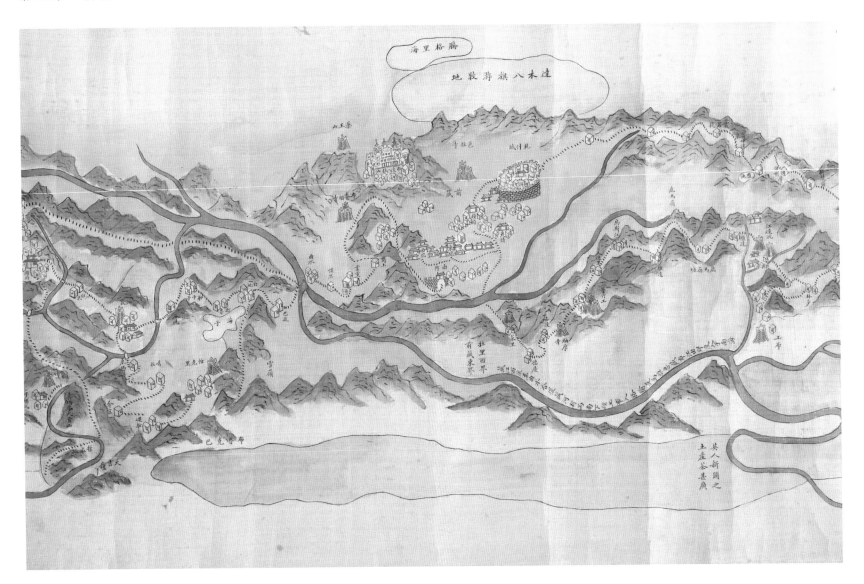

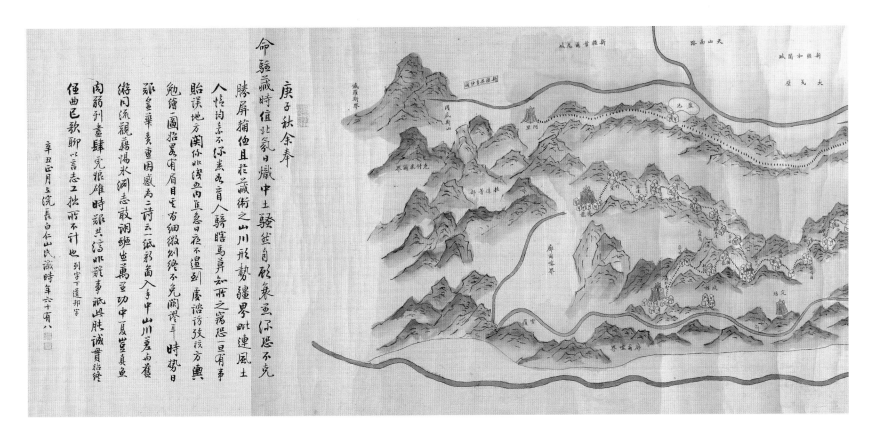

57
自打箭鑪至前後藏途程圖

清光緒二十七年（1901年）安成繪。絹底彩繪本。圖縱四一・四厘米，橫三一六・三厘米。卷軸裝。
057.63 ／（227.003）／1901 ／0146

　　此圖以黑色虛線分別表示自四川省打箭爐（圖上作打箭鑪）經前藏赴後藏阿、濟龍、聶拉木之北、中、南三條路綫。

　　打箭爐，一作打箭鑪，本明正土司地，俗傳。以武候南征，遣將郭達，安爐造箭之地，故名。清屬四川，後改康定府。地據大雪山高處，為自藏入蜀之第一要道。前藏即烏斯藏也，蕃字烏加斯字，切音，作衛，故又名衛（或危），一名喇薩，又作拉撒，華佛地也。位於今西藏中南部。東界舊西康，南界印度，西界後藏，北界新疆、青

海，以拉薩為首府。達賴喇嘛居於此。後藏以日喀則為首府，在唐亦吐蕃地。有寺曰札什倫布，乃班禪喇嘛坐床之所。後藏人敬禮班禪與前藏奉達賴喇嘛等。

　　圖右下部題：「由鑪出口赴藏共有北、中、南三道。北道出鑪關北門，由草地直達前後藏，最為捷徑。中道出南關偏北赴察木多，皆番商茶路。南道由裏、巴、察拉各台行走，駐藏大臣暨各官兵馳驛所經。因南路天氣較暖，居民稠密，易於催辦夫馬替換烏拉，然彎曲如弓，道路折耳」。圖後有題跋，款「辛丑正月上浣長白仁山氏識，時年六十有六」。

　　此圖無比例又無標程距離。但從清代不少附有圖的川藏、西藏路程譜，如成書於嘉慶三年（1798年）的松筠《西招圖略》及鑴於光緒丙戌（1886年）的黃沛翹《西藏圖考》，可知川藏各地點之間的站數及距離極大。例如自打箭鑪至塘八站共計程六百八十五里，自塘至巴塘六站共計程五百四十五里，自巴塘至察木多十四站共計程一千四百五十里，

自打箭鑪由霍爾德革草地至察木多三十九站共計程一千八百八十五里，自前藏喇薩西南行九日八站至後藏八站共計程九百里，自後藏至聶拉木二十九站共計程二千八百五十一里。

　　此圖金沙江、雅礱江、瀾滄江、雅魯藏布江等分別注出流向。採用形象畫法，較詳細地繪出了昌都、拉、拉薩、日喀則等城廓，以及土司寨、寺廟、村落、山脈等，并生動地表現出作者途中所見西藏正教要地，如達賴喇嘛在拉薩的布達拉宮、班禪喇嘛在日喀則的札什倫布寺，是現存較早的入藏道路圖。

58

Nan yue quan tu

Complete Map of the Sacred Peak of the South

Qing dynasty (1644-1911), undated, ca. 1908

Handscroll, ink and color on paper, 31.8 x 210.0 cm

074.3/(226.51)/1908/2882

The Sacred Peak of the South refers to Mount Heng (Heng shan) in south central Hunan province, the other four sacred peaks or marchmounts (*yue*) in China being Mount Tai (Tai shan or Dong yue; "Sacred Peak of the East"; in Shandong), Mount Song (Song shan or Zhong yue; "Sacred Peak of the Center"; in Henan), Mount Hua (Hua shan or Xi yue; "Sacred Peak of the West; in Shaanxi), and Mount Heng (Heng shan or Bei yue; "Sacred Peak of the North"; in Shanxi). The five sacred peaks were associated with the birthplaces and graves of the five mythical emperors of Chinese antiquity.

The Sacred Peak of the South, was first mentioned in the *Shun dian* and *Yu gong* chapters of the *Shu jing* (Book of Documents) and in the *Zhifang shi* chapter of the *Zhou li* (Rites of Zhou). Mount Heng is actually a 400-km-long range, said to contain some seventy-two granite peaks stretching between Hengyang in the south and Changsha in the north, towering above the low-lying valley of the Xiang River. The highest of these, the Blessed Fire Peak (Zhurong feng), reaches an elevation of 1,298 meters above sea level.

This handscroll map, produced during the last years of the Qing dynasty, takes the form of traditional Chinese landscape painting. Stretching from right to left (north to south)

are the provincial capital of Changsha, the county seat of Xiangtan, and and prefectural seal of Hengzhou. Among the scenic spots identified on the map are the Yuelu Peak across the Xiang River from Changsha, Shibing Peak, the city of Xiangtan, Tianzhu Peak, the main cluster of peaks culminating in the Blessed Fire Peak, the Mid-Mountain Pavilion (Banshan ting), the Temple of Offerings (Shang feng si), the South Terrace Monastery (Nantai si) first built in the sixth century, the Water Curtain Cave (Shuilian dong), the Guanyin Peak with a cave temple dedicated to Guanyin, and the Nine Transcendents Monastery (Jiu xian guan). The most prominent architectural feature of the map is the Temple of the Sacred Peak of the South (Nan yue miao), one of the most magnificent in all of China. First built during the Tang dynasty in 725 and expanded through the Song, Yuan, and Ming periods, it was destroyed by fire in the late Ming. It was rebuilt in 1708 but once again succumbed to flames during the Tongzhi period (1862-1874). The temple complex in the map depicts it after the last rebuilding of 1882. At the end of the scroll is the prefectural seat of Hengzhou; a three-character inscription on the lower edge denotes the eastern bank, reminding the viewer that the peaks of Mount Heng lie on the western side of the Xiang River.

58

南岳全圖

清末（約1908年）繪製。紙底彩繪本。圖縱三一‧八厘米，橫二一○厘米。卷軸裝。

074.3 ／（266.51）／19098／2882

　　南岳即衡山，又名岣嶁山，是中國五岳之一，譽有「五岳獨秀」之稱。位於湖南省中南部衡山縣城西，立於湘江之西濱。衡山俯瞰湘江，群峰巍聳，山勢雄偉，著名山峰有七十二座，其中以祝融、天柱、芙蓉、紫蓋、石廩五峰最著名。主峰祝融海拔一千二百九十八米，為最高點。南以衡陽回雁峰為首，北以長沙岳麓山為，綿延四百公里。

　　按照古代帝王留下的傳統，南岳是天子巡狩和祭祀必到的地方之一。衡山歷來為遊覽、祀禮之

地，山上文物古跡、歷代碑刻甚多。衡山全七十二峰，有「天下南岳」牌樓、大廟、祝聖寺、藏經殿、方廣寺、上封寺、祝融殿、南臺寺、福嚴寺、高臺寺、萬壽宮、三生塔、九仙觀、開雲亭、南天門、半山亭等古跡。所謂「衡山四絕」，即祝融峰之高，方廣寺之深，藏經殿之秀，水帘洞之奇。南岳廟坐落於衡山腳下，它是中國五岳中規模最大，總體布局最完整的古建築群之一。南岳大廟始建於唐開元十三年（725年），宋、元、明代加以擴建，明末毀於戰火。清康熙四十七年（1708年）復建。雍正、乾隆、嘉慶時期幾經修葺，同治年間再毀，光緒八年（1882年）重建。

　　此圖為清末期彩繪，採用傳統的山水畫畫法，以水平方向自右向左形象生動地描繪了長沙省城、湘潭縣城、衡山縣城、衡州府城等省府縣城池，以及寺廟名勝、古塔古木，以至江中行船等，表現得尤為詳盡細緻，雄偉壯觀。全圖繪畫精美，色彩艷麗，形象逼真，使觀者如入其境。

Part 4: Texts and illustrations from China's ethnic minorities

第四部：少數民族語文

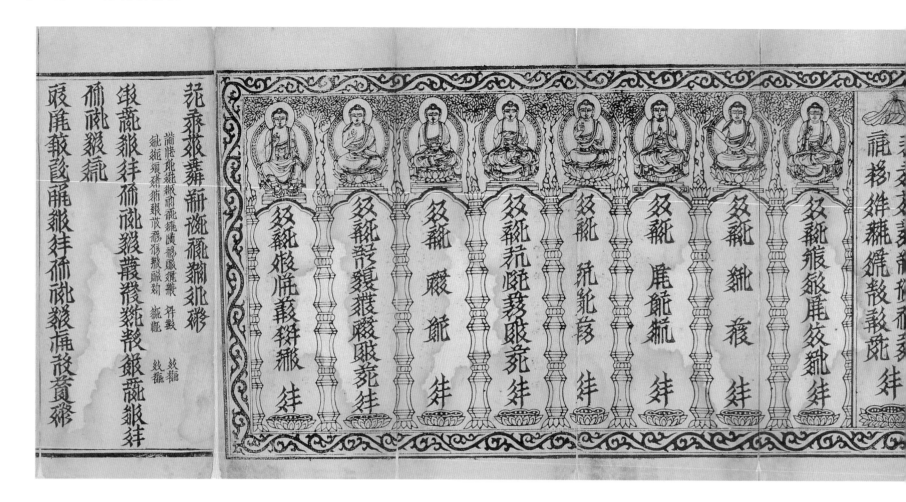

59

Xi Xia wen Cibei daochang chanfa (Liang huang baochan) (10 juan)

Rules for Confession in the Place of the Merciful and Compassionate One (Precious Confessional of Emperor Wu of Liang), 10 *juan*, in Tangut Script

Yuan dynasty (1279-1368), Dade reign period (1297-1307), undated, ca. 1300

105 leaves folded accordion-style between top and bottom boards; each board, approx. 32.7 x 13.2 cm; each leaf, approx. 32.5 x 13.1 cm; block size of first illustrated frontispiece of 4 leaves, approx. 26.9 x 51. 5 cm; block size of second illustrated section of 4 leaves, approx. 27.2 x 51.7 cm; height of block of main text of 97 leaves, approx. 26.9 cm

No inventory number

The *Cibei daochang chanfa* (Rules for Confession in the Place of the Merciful and Compassionate One) is a late-fifth century apocryphal work thought to have been compiled either by a prince of the Southern Qi (479-502) or by Emperor Wu of Liang [Xiao Yan; (464-549; r. 502-549)] between 483 and 493. Because the attribution to the emperor is better known and more widely accepted, this text is popularly called the *Liang huang baochan* (Precious Confessional of Emperor Wu of Liang). According to legend, his wife, the Empress Xi, died after committing murder in a fit of jealous anger and was reincarnated as a lowly snake. In order to save her from such a terrible and undignified fate, the emperor had this ritual penance text composed at his court as an offering of merit

which was eventually accepted, whereupon the deceased empress was accorded karmic status better suited to her exalted earthly position. If this attribution is correct, then it represents the earliest extant ritual text of the Pure Land (*Jingtu*) sect of Chinese Buddhism; *chanfa* ("rules for confession") such as this were used in "confessional ceremonies."

The Tangut version of the *Cibei daochang chanfa* was translated from the Chinese sometime between between 1049 and 1139. It contains undated prefaces by Emperor Huizong (r. 1068-1086) and his mother, the empress dowager Liang (d. 1099). The prefaces, which claim credit for the translation, may have

been composed in the early 1070s at the beginning of Huizong's reign when the empress dowager wielded power as regent following the demise of Emperor Yizong in 1086 and when she exercised a pivotal role in the centralization of the Buddhist establishment. The text, a suitable expression of the throne's concern for the spiritual welfare of its subjects, may also have been utilized during ceremonies in 1094 celebrating the repairing of the Gantong stupa at Liangzhou.

Tangut is a logographic writing system of about 6,600 characters modeled upon Chinese and Khitan scripts. It was devised and promulgated by the Xi Xia state (1032-1227;

centered in the region of present-day Ningxia province) in 1036, and very soon after was used for the translation of the Buddhist *Tripitaka* from Sanskrit, Chinese, Tibetan, and Uighur, a monumental undertaking that was likely completed by the end of the twelfth century. Special sets of Tangut letters were developed for the transcription of Sanskrit syllables and Chinese characters; there are altogether 348 character elements which may be joined in forty-four different combinations.

This ritual text of the *Cibei daochang chanfa*, however, was printed only around 1300 or during the early years of the fourteenth century by Yuan authorities, along with the rest of the Tangut *Tripitaka*, long after the destruction of the Xi Xia empire by the troops of Genghis Khan in 1227. Tangut remained in use for some time after 1227 because of its important role in Mongol-Tibetan relations; in 1302, the printing of a 3,620-*juan* Tangut edition of the *Tripitaka* was completed at the Wanshou Temple in Hangzhou, presumably for distribution in formerly Xi Xia lands. The printing of this Tangut edition of the *Cibei daochang chanfa*, therefore, may have been part of this great project of the Yuan dynasty. However, by the later sixteenth century the Tangut language and its unique script finally ceased being used altogether. The Xi Xia script can be translated into other languages, such as Chinese, but as yet no widely accepted system of transcription has been developed.

This copy of the Tangut *Cibei daochang chanfa* in the National Library of China is one of only two known to have survived, the other being held by the Tenri Library in Japan. The Tenri copy has *juan* 9 as well and a number of fragments, while the Beijing copy is nearly complete, containing most parts of the full 10 *juan*. Each *juan* contains an illustrated frontispiece, depictions of Buddhas, and a prefatory text.

The right half of the illustration here shows the title slip of *juan* 9 printed on yellow paper, followed immediately by the four-fold frontispiece which depicts Emperor Wu of Liang conducting a repentance ceremony, with a large serpent on the ground in front of his raised throne, while the seated Buddha is seen at right surrounded by his close disciples. The name of the engraver, Yu Sheng, is indicated in Chinese characters at the lower middle right edge of the picture. The left half of the illustration features the

next five folds in *juan* 9, where eight Buddhas occupy the upper register in four of the folds, with their names given in corresponding columns of text underneath; this decorative columnar format has a counterpart in the Chinese version of the *Cibei daochang chanfa* printed around 980 during the reign of the Northern Song emperor Taizong. The preface to *juan* 9 follows, with the names of the empress dowager Liang and Emperor Huizong given in the two columns of smaller characters.

59

西夏文慈悲道場懺法（梁皇寶懺）十卷

傳梁武帝撰。元大德年間（約1300年）杭州路刻本。此為卷九。上下夾板高三二‧七厘米，寬一三‧二厘米。每面高三二‧五厘米，寬一三‧一厘米。卷首扉畫四面，框高二六‧九厘米，寬五一‧五厘米。扉畫後圖四面，框高二七‧二厘米，寬五一‧七厘米。經文框高二六‧九厘米。經文每面五行，行十五字。經折裝。

無號

西夏王朝建立於1032年，其境土之大，奄有今甘肅大部，寧夏全部，陝西北部和青海、內蒙古的部分地區。西夏文是1036年模仿漢字創制的文字，以偏旁、部首組合而成，并有獨特的語法結構，被西夏王朝廣泛使用。

西夏時期大力推行用西夏文字翻譯各種漢文經史典籍及佛經。西夏王朝於乾定四年（1226年）至寶義元年（1227年）間被成吉思汗的蒙古軍毀滅亡以後，西夏文字尚流行河西一代。元朝的統治階級曾於元大德六年（1302年），在杭州路大萬壽寺雕印西夏文《大藏經》三千六百餘卷。考古材料證明，西夏文在個別地方還一直延續到明代晚期，河北省保定市近年還出土了晚至弘治十五年（1502年）用西夏文字雕寫的石經幢。

《慈悲道場懺法》，俗稱《梁皇寶懺》，傳六世紀梁皇為夫人郗氏除罪生福而著的經卷。中國國

家圖書館所藏《慈悲道場懺法》十卷，基本上保存完整。每卷前有「懺法本事圖」一幅四面，即「梁皇寶懺圖」，後四面中記佛名。後有序三面，題名譯文為「天生全能祿蕃式法正國皇太后梁氏御譯，救德主世增福正民大明皇帝寬名御譯」。後有傳七面。經背有墨書西夏文一行，譯文為「有此典者痴移慧增」。

「梁皇寶懺圖」中實分為幾幅，與序言中所敘故事情節相合。序言大意是：梁武帝妃郗氏狠毒，死後變為一蟒，她托夢訴于武帝，望其救拔于痛苦之中，於是武帝請人集《慈悲道場懺悔法》十卷，郗氏得以由蟒蛇化為天人。此圖中有西夏文題款兩處。一為六字，漢文對譯應是「郗氏蛇為處」，可譯為「郗氏變蛇處」。此題款恰在一大蟒蛇之旁，顯然它是這部份圖畫的文字注解。另一處五字，漢譯文應是「郗氏天生處」。此題款在一天人之旁，亦當為這部份圖的注釋。圖右側還有一漢文題款，僅三字，為「俞聲刊」。俞聲精於雕刊圖像又能刻寫西夏文和漢文的漢人，曾補修宋刻本《禮記正義》、《爾雅疏》，乃元時杭州名匠。此書與西夏文《大藏經》同為大德間杭州路刻本。茲選第九卷，全一百零五面，文字部份計九十七面。

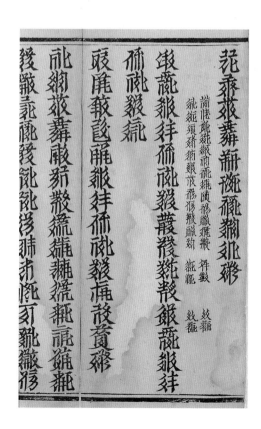

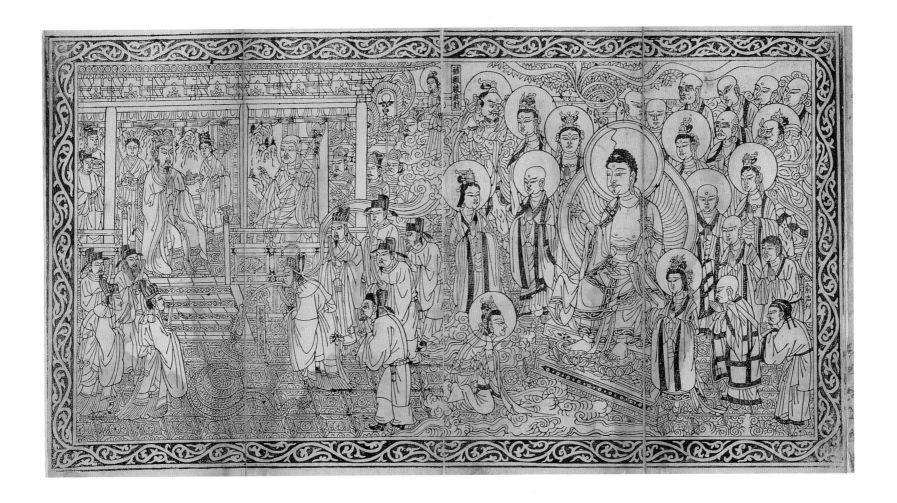

60

Meng wen Jin guangming zuisheng wang jing (10 juan)

Sutra of the Golden Radiance of the Most Victorious Kings (*Suvarnaprabhasottamaraja-sutra; Qutuγ-tu degedü altan gerel-tü sudur nuγud-un qaγan nere-tü yeke kölgen sudur*), 10 *juan*, in Mongolian Script

Qing dynasty (1644-1911), undated, ca. 18th century
Translated from the Tibetan version by Sesrab Senge
(act. ca. 1323-1367)
150 loose folios between top and bottom sutra covers,
and between top and bottom carved wood covers; overall dimensions of ensemble: approx. 17.0 x 63.7 x
13.7 cm; top carved wood cover with inscription in
Lentsa (an ornamental form of Devanagari script) and
decorative designs in relief over gilt ground, carved on
both ends, flat on inside surface, 17.0 x 63.7 x 2.2 cm;

top sutra cover covered in polychrome silk brocade with
design of *shou* character roundels, bats, and clouds,
17.2 x 61.2 x 1.4 cm; recessed panel on inner side of
top sutra cover, 11.0 x 51.8 cm, with illuminated panel
protected by 3 layers of silk guards in various color
combinations; sutra folios, texts inscribed in gold on
black varnished ground and enclosed by double lines,
with borders in indigo, each approx. 16.9 x 61.0 cm;
bottom sutra cover covered in polychrome silk brocade with design of *shou* character roundels, bats, and
clouds, 17.2 x 61.2 x 1.4 cm; recessed panel on inner
side of bottom sutra cover, 11.1 x 52.0 cm, with illuminated panel protected by 3 layers of silk guards in
various color combinations; bottom carved wood cover,
with decorative designs in relief over gilt ground, carved
on both ends, flat on inside surface, 17.2 x 63.6 x 2.3
cm

0299

The *Suvarnaprabhasottamaraja-sutra* (Sutra of
the Golden Radiance of the Most Victorious
Kings) is one of the most important and
popular Mahayana scriptures; it is often ab-
breviated as the *Suvarnaprabhasa-sutra* (Sutra
of the Golden Radiance). The "most victorious kings" in the full title refers to the *deva*
kings who came to pay homage to the
Buddha. It is the one sutra where a number
of sensitive topics, such as the relationship
between the state and Buddhism, or the re-
sponsibilities of rulers, are addressed in several of its nineteen chapters, but accomplished in a manner at once aesthetic,
appealing, and impressive. For instance, an
entire chapter is devoted to medicine and
healing, in which the connection between
medical and religious practices is reinforced.
In the chapter on laws, the sutra makes it clear
that religion and government are joined by
the Buddhist *Dharma*.

There exists four Tibetan translations of
this sutra, five in Chinese [the most well
known being the elegant translation by the
monk Yijing (635-713)], one each in Uighur,

Mongolian, Tangut, Kalmuck, Manchu, and Japanese, as well as fragments in Sogdian, Khotanese, and other languages. This sutra had a tremendous impact on Japan (after being translated from the Chinese as the *Konkômyô saishôôkyô*), where it was instrumental in the establishment of Buddhism as a state religion. Its influence there remained undiminished for many centuries and festivals of the *Sutra of the Golden Radiance* were held annually to protect the country. In addition, the *Suvarnaprabhasottamaraja-sutra* is also one of the nine canonical writings of Nepalese Buddhism.

The Mongolian version, first translated from the Tibetan by the Saskya monk Sesrab Senge (also written as Sirab Sengge; act. ca. 1323-1367), is known in full as the *Qutuγ-tu degedü altan gerel-tü sudur nuγud-un qaγan nere-tü yeke kölgen sudur* but is often simply called the *Altan gerel* ("Golden Radiance"). Classic Mongolian is the language of Buddhist scriptures as translated from the Tibetan, since Buddhism in Mongolia had been introduced from Tibet, and Mongolians have long considered it the classical language of Buddhism. Mongolian script, written downwards in vertical columns, is derived from the Uighur which in turn was borrowed from the Sogdian and the Aramaic.

This part of the *Suvarnaprabhasottamaraja-sutra* in the National Library of China is richly presented in a large *pothi*-sized book format kept between unconnected carved *zitan* covers, in a manner derived from the palm-leaf *pothi* of Indian Buddhist literature. The top cover contains a single line in Lentsa, an ornamental form of Devanagari script, flanked on the left by the letter representing *ga* (the third consonant) and on the right by a letter conventionally used in mantras. Recessed panels on the inner sides of both top

and bottom wooden covers have silk guards in various colors and are decorated with illuminated miniatures of Lamaistic gods.

The sutra consists of 150 loose folios beginning with the one numbered "two," the first folio in the sequence having been embedded as the inner side of the top sutra cover. The loose oblong folios have inscriptions on both recto and verso, except the final leaf which is inscribed on only one side and has two Buddhist icons flanking the text. Each folio has surrounding margins in indigo, while the text panels have inscriptions in gold on black ground, with a double border (thick on the outer edge and thin on the inner edge) in yellowish pigment. Each inscription has thirty-eight to forty columns of text. Pagination of each leaf is indicated in gold on the indigo paper surface along the left edge of the text or image panel. The bottom sutra cover is similar to the top one except that it has an illuminated panel with five icons (instead of three). The lavishness of this sutra ensemble is an embodiment of religious wisdom, while the great care taken in making it was believed to bring merit to the commissioner and to all those involved in its production.

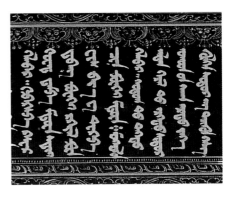

60

蒙文金光明最勝王經十卷

元希儒僧格由藏文版翻譯。清（1644–1911年）代（約十八世紀）磁青紙黑色字心內泥金寫本。此經寬一七厘米，長六三·七厘米，厚一三·七厘米。長方形散頁兩面書寫，總計一百五十一頁，每頁寬一六·九厘米，長六一厘米。雙欄。貝葉夾裝，上下各一塊紫檀護經板。上護經板寬一七厘米，長六三·七厘米，厚二·二厘米，外刻梵文並以金粉填充。上夾板外側有雲頭花紋，內側呈凹形，寬一一厘米，長五一·八厘米，彩繪佛像三尊，並覆蓋五色經卯三層。下護經板寬一七·二厘米，長六三·六厘米，厚二·三厘米，外亦刻梵文並以金粉填充。下夾板外側有雲頭花紋，內側亦呈凹形，寬一一·一厘米，長五二厘米，彩繪佛像五尊，並覆蓋五色經卯三層。

0229

《金光明最勝王經》為《金光明經》三譯中最後出而最完備者，常簡稱《最勝王經》。據稱是佛說於王舍城耆闍崛，天台大師將此經歸屬大乘、方等部，兼別圓二教的通教。此經系統地論述了佛教的基本理論、儀規、咒語等。在日本，此經亦與《妙法蓮華經》、《仁王般若經》同被推尊崇為護國三部經，在全國的國分寺誦讀。

蒙文《金光明最勝王經》為元代蒙古族著名翻譯家希儒僧格（亦作相哥寔立、相闍實理、相哥實立、穎哥識律、僧格實哩；字世瀅，號靜庵，高昌人）由藏文版翻譯。蒙古文創制於十三世紀，歷史上用蒙古文翻譯過大量佛教經典。本件佛經以蒙文抄寫於十八世紀左右。

經板分為內外兩層，外層上下各一塊有精細雕刻的木質經板，其正面有梵文字。內層上下各一塊木質經板，反面各以凹形木板為之。內層上經板凹入部份既是經文第一面，兩側各彩繪佛像一尊，并覆以三層絲綢，絲綢外面為黃、藍或紅色，面均為綠色。內層下經板凹入部份彩繪佛像五尊，其絲綢顏色以內層上經板相同。

本經用泥金在特製的磁青紙上寫成，有雙欄。內畫框廓，由左而右，豎寫經文。左上有蒙文書寫卷頁次，右側則書以漢譯經目。全冊一百五十一頁，字體工整，裝飾華麗，是專作供奉用的藝術品。

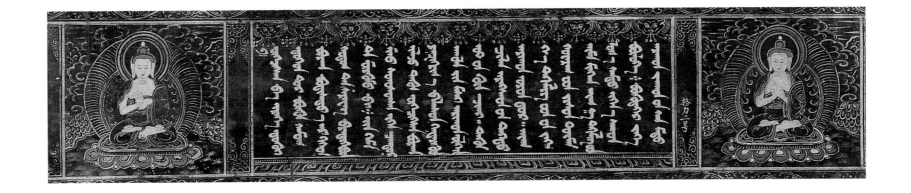

61

Fan, Zang, Han san ti hebi Sheng Miaojixiang zhenshi ming jing (1 juan)

Sutra of Reciting the True Names of the Noble Manjusri (*Aryamanjusrinamasangiti; 'Phags-pa 'Jam-dpal-gyi-mtshan-ya'n-dag-par-brjod-pa; Sheng Miaojixiang zhenshi ming jing*) in Sanskrit, Tibetan, and Chinese Scripts

Qing dynasty (1644-1911), undated, ca. 18th century 43 loose folios between top and bottom sutra covers; each folio approx. 10.2 x 41.1 cm; top sutra cover, approx. 10.3 x 41.1 x 1.7 cm; recessed panel on outer side of top sutra cover, 4.1 x 18.2 cm; recessed panel on inner side of top sutra cover, 7.0 x 34.0 cm; bottom sutra cover, approx. 10.3 x 41.1 x 1.7 cm; recessed panel on inner side of bottom sutra cover, 6.6 x 33.5 cm

No inventory number

Sanskrit, the linguistic parent of all Indo-Aryan languages, is an ancient language that was used for the translation of Buddhist scriptures from the original Pali. The Sanskrit title of this sutra is transliterated as *Aryamanjusrisatyanama-sutra*, but it is properly translated as *Aryamanjusrinamasangiti* (Sutra of Reciting the True Names of the Noble Manjusri) and known either as such, or simply as the *Manjusrinamasangiti*, in bibliographic references. The fullest Sanskrit title of this work appears in the *tantra* section of the *Kanjur* as *Manjusrijnanasattvasya paramarthanamasangiti* (Rehearsal of the Supreme Names of Manjusri the Knowledge-Being). Tibetan is a Sino-Tibetan language first written down in the seventh century; a Sanskrit-Tibetan dictionary was compiled in the ninth century. The Tibetan title for this sutra is *'Phags-pa 'Jam-dpal-gyi-mtshan-ya'n-dag-par-brjod-pa*, and it was the Tibetan version which was translated into Chinese by the monk Zhihui during the Yuan dynasty before being admitted into the Chinese Mahayana canon.

The 160 verses (*gatha*) and some mantra sentences of the *Aryamanjusrinamasangiti* are not only replete with early Buddhist and later Mahayana lore but also contains vestiges of Hindu religious concepts. The very fine original Tibetan translation of the *Aryamanjusrinamasangiti* by Rin-chen-bzan-po was among the most revered and recited texts among all the Tibetan Buddhist sects. There exists a plethora of commentaries and expository literature on this text, which once enjoyed tremendous importance in Mahayana Buddhism, particularly for those aspiring to bodhisattvahood, but it has now become less popular with Tibetan lamas than with Nepalese Buddhists.

Generally ascribed to the tenth century or thereabouts, the text may well date back to the fifth century, if not earlier. Though tantric in nature, it is not specifically titled as a tantra; it is more in the genre of a litany in which enumerates the "names" and laudatory epithets of Manjusri. Although the text itself has no discrete chapters, it is often divided into thirteen sections in the numerous commentaries. The string of epithets applied to Manjusri is found beginning with the fifth section ("The Great Mandala of Vajradhatu") and concludes with the tenth section ("Procedure-of-Duty Wisdom"). The "names" recited in these six sections of the text are not what Manjusri is called, in the sense of the grammatical vocative, but rather in the nominative, intending, "You, Manjusri, are" thus and thus; they are names in the sense of characteristic. For instance, in the third verse of the eighth section ("Discriminative Widsom"), Manjusri is "formless, of lovely form, and foremost; multiform and made of mind, glorious appearance of all forms, bearing no end of reflected images."

This very handsome copy of the *Aryamanjusrinamasangiti* from the National Library of China was probably made sometime in the eighteenth century. It is kept in a woven cloth wrapper with a grid of floral designs and a polychrome silk tie-cord. The top sutra cover is covered with gold and red silk brocade with a simple floral pattern superimposed on a ground of chevrons. The recessed panel contains the sutra's trilingual title inscribed in gold on a plain black ground in three rows: the Sanksrit title in Devanagari script at the top, Tibetan in the center, and Chinese at the bottom. Following Sanskrit and Tibetan conventions, the Chinese characters are read left to right instead of the usual

right to left.

The inner side of the top sutra cover contains an illuminated panel with three icons finely drawn in colors, gold, and white pigment. The slightly recessed panel is protected by a silk curtain with a woven design of blossoming plants on the exterior and a royal blue damask on the interior. The bottom sutra cover is likewise embellished with an illuminated panel (with five icons) and a protective curtain, except that its outer side, upon which the ensemble rests, does not have a recessed panel like its top counterpart.

Forty-three individual folios of the sutra were dyed purplish blue, with the text written in gold upon black-painted central panels. The parallel Sanskrit, Tibetan, and Chinese texts are divided into two registers while foliation is supplied within vertical columns on either side of the text panels (Tibetan on the left, Chinese on the right). Since the top sutra cover with the three icons is embedded with the first folio, the top purplish blue folio pictured is technically the second and is numbered accordingly. The text on it constitutes the first verse of the first section ("Asking for Instruction") of the *Aryamanjusrinamasangiti* and reads in translation as "Now Vajradhara, srimat, supreme tamer of those hard to tame, the hero, victorious over the three worlds, lord of secrets, the adamantine lord."

61

梵、藏、漢三體合璧聖妙吉祥真實名經一卷

清（1644–1911年）代（約十八世紀）磁青紙黑色字心泥金寫本。全書長方形散頁兩面書寫，總計四十三頁，每頁寬一○・二厘米，長四一・一厘米。上下有夾板。貝葉夾裝，上下各一夾板，錦緞貼面。上夾板寬一○・三厘米，長四一・一厘米，厚一・七厘米。上夾板外側三體經名呈凹形，寬四・一厘米，長一八・二厘米。上夾板內側呈凹形單綫彩繪佛像三尊，寬七厘米，長三四厘米。下夾板寬一○・三厘米，長四一・一厘米，厚一・七厘米。下夾板內側呈凹形彩繪佛像五尊，寬六・六厘米，長三三・五厘米。有彩色錦緞夾簾遮護。

無號

此為一部用梵文、藏文、漢文書寫的《聖妙吉祥真實名經》，為文殊菩薩發菩薩心之願文，中明五智勇識之真實名。後有文殊之一百八名讚等。此佛經先以梵文翻譯成藏文，元代釋智慧自藏文翻譯成漢文。

上夾板內外均有凹入部分，外面為經名，內面為彩繪佛像三尊。下夾板內面有彩繪護法神五尊，但其外面無凹入部分。彩繪佛像、護法神均配以色彩鮮艷的絲綢。

經文用泥金繕寫在特制的磁青紙，每散頁上下面以梵、藏、漢文由左至右橫寫二行，頁數載於每頁兩旁的豎行（左邊為藏文頁數，右邊為漢文頁數）。第一張散頁即經文第二頁，其漢文部分繕寫：「唐聖妙吉祥真實名經。敬禮孺童相妙吉祥。復次吉祥持金剛，難調伏中勝調伏，勇猛超出三界內，自在金剛密中勝」。字體工整，制作精美。此三體合璧的佛經大約成書於十八世紀，是一件不可多得的佛教藝術品。

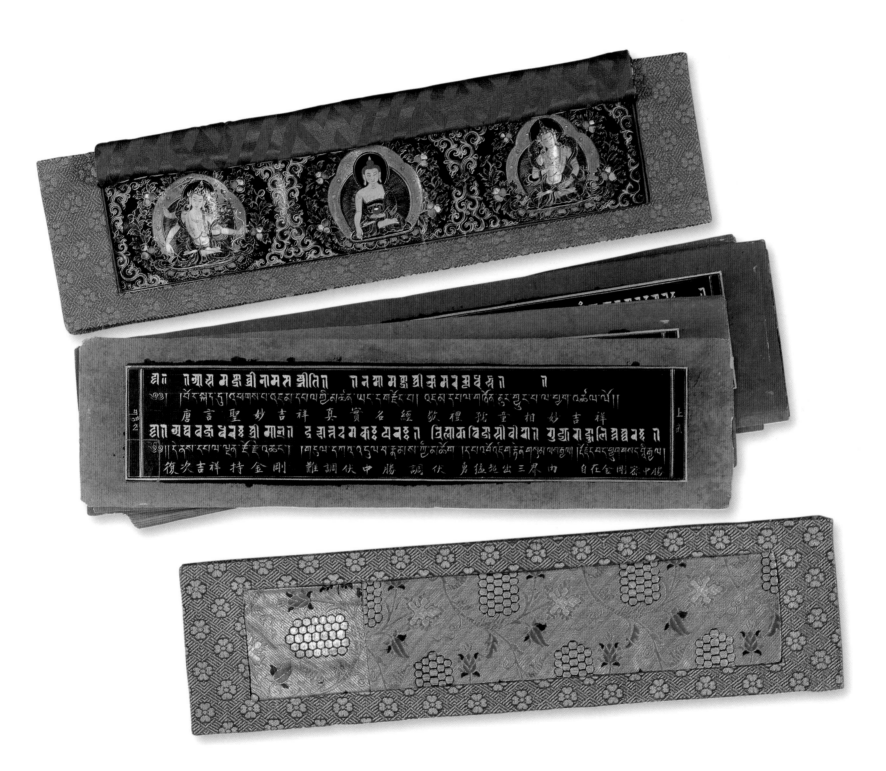

62

Zang chuan fo jiao San bai foxiang tu

Three Hundred Icons of Tibetan Buddhism

Qing dynasty (1644-1911), Qianlong period (1736-1795), undated

Attributed to Lcan-skya Qutuɤtu Rol-p'ai-rdo-rje (1717-1786)

Beijing: Songzhu si, n.d. [between 1736 and 1795]

110 folios with two perforations along top edge of each folio for binding with string; each folio approx. 9.0 x 23.3 cm; height of complete stack, 2.2 cm; block sizes of 10 folios with prefatory text, approx. 5.6-5.9 x 17.1-17.2 cm; block sizes of 100 folios with illustrations on the recto, approx. 5.6-5.7 x 17.2-17.6 cm; block sizes of 100 folios with explanatory texts on the verso, approx. 5.7-5.9 x 17.5-17.6 cm

No inventoy number

The full Tibetan title of this extremely important iconographic collection is transliterated as *Bla-ma-yi-dam-mchog-gsum-bkah-sdod-dan-bcas-pahi-tshogs-zhin-gi-sku-brnan-gsum-brgyahi-grans-tshan-ba;* its Chinese equivalent reads as *Shangshi, benzun, sanbao, hufa deng ziliang tian: Sanbai foxiang ji.* Though undated and unsigned, it was xylographed (printed with woodblocks) in Beijing during the Qianlong period and can be attributed with great certainty to Lcan-skya Qutuɤtu Rol-p'ai-rdo-rje (also known as Lalitavajra in Sanskrit; respectively Jangjia Ruobiduoji or Youxi jin'gang in Chinese).

Rol-p'ai-rdo-rje was born in 1717 at Liangzhou, Gansu, and at the age of three (four by Chinese reckoning) was installed as the reincarnation of the Gelugpa (Dge-lugs-pa) hierarch. In 1724, he was rescued from a life-threatening invasion of Youning Temple in Qinghai and escorted to Beijing the following year under the special protection of the Yongzheng emperor (1678-1735; r. 1723-1735). Later he was appointed Grand Lama and became head of Songzhu Temple, the chief Lamaist establishment in Beijing.

As a young man Rol-p'ai-rdo-rje studied with the imperial prince Hongli, the future Qianlong emperor; he mastered Chinese, Sanskrit, Mongolian, and Manchu with little effort and was responsible for the editing of the Manchu-language *Tripitaka,* the compilation and editing of the imperial polyglot version of the *Tripitaka* (in Manchu, Chinese, Mongolian, and Sanskrit), the translation of the Mongolian version of the *Tanjur* (Translation of Treatises), and editing the Mongolian version of the *Kanjur* (Translation of the Revealed Scriptures), amongst many other contributions to the corpus of Buddhist works. Apart from his religious role, however, Rol-p'ai-rdo-rje was the Qianlong emperor's *de facto* political advisor on all matters pertaining to Mongolia and Tibet; he served as the emperor's personal emissary to Tibet and also acted as intermediary and translator for the emperor in his dealings with the Dalai Lama and the Pachen Lama.

Prior to this illustrated work, there were no authoritative representations of the bewildering number of Tibetan Buddhist icons in pictorial form, nor was there a truly systematic compilation of their proper Sanskrit and Tibetan names. Only someone of Rol-p'ai-rdo-rje's supreme authority and great erudition could have compiled so thorough a pantheon of three hundred icons. Although a very modestly scaled publication, it encapsulates the entire range of Tibetan Buddhist iconography. Such albums are extremely important when studying *thangkas* and other paintings in which the representations of deities are not specifically identified. Gods and goddesses may be rendered in many different aspects, such as in the appeased (*santa*) or wrathful states (*krodha*). Most likely xylographed in Beijing at the Songzhu Temple during the mid- or late Qianlong period for the benefit of lamas-in-training, it is representative of Tibetan-style woodblock engraving and printing, and remains to this day the principal source used by scholars in describing Tibetan iconography.

The first ten folios contain the text of the preface in Tibetan and Mongolian, with foliation in Tibetan and Chinese (on the left and right margins respectively). This work is referred to as *sku-brnan brgya-phrag-gsum* on the verso of the second preface folio and as *sku-brnan sumbrgya* on the verso of the eighth preface folio, the latter being the title by which this iconographic collection is known in Mongolia. According to the preface, the pantheon includes spiritual masters (*bla-ma*), tutelary deities (*yi-dam*), Buddhas, bodhisattvas, sravakas and pratyekabuddhas (*nan-ran*), viras (*dpah-bo*) and dakinis (*mkhah-hgro*), dharmapalas (*chos-skyon*) and other guardian deities (*bsrun tshogs*). Each of the following one hundred illustrated folios has three icons arranged hierarchically with the central figure being the first, the one at right the second, and the one at left the third; their Tibetan names are given below.

Illustrated here are the first three of the one hundred folios seen from the recto and verso. Of the hundred folios, folio 1 (top row) is unquestionably the most important one, with Rgyal-ba-sakya-thub-pa-la-na-mo [Jina Sakyamuni (6th century B.C.); the historical Buddha] at the center, Rje-btsun-'jam-dpal-dbyangs-la-na-mo [Bhattaraka Manjughosa;

Manjusri, eminent disciple of the historical Buddha; Bodhisattva of Wisdom] at right, and Rje-btsun-byams-pa-la-na-mo [Bhattaraka Maitreya (270-350); Maitreya, the Future Buddha, a founder of the Yogacara school] at left. Folio 2 (middle row) features Dpal-mgon-klu-sgrub-la-na-mo [Srinatha Nagarjuna (A.D. 2nd century); founder of the Madhyamika philosophical school of Buddhist thought], Rje-btsun-thogs-med-la-na-mo [Bhattaraka Asanga (ca. 375-430); Teacher of the *Dharma* and a founder of the Yogacara school], and Rje-btsun-arya-de-ba-la-na-mo [Bhattaraka Aryadeva]. In folio 3 (bottom row) are Rje-btsun-phyogs-glang-la-na-mo [Bhattaraka Dinnaga; disciple of Vasubandhu and a Buddhist logician], Rje-btsun-chos-grags-la-na-mo [Bhattaraka Dharmakirti (7th century); a Buddhist logician], and Rje-btsun-dbyig-gnyen-la-na-mo [Bhattaraka Vasubandhu (4th century, or ca. 400-480); younger brother of Asanga and a founder of the Yogacara school and greatest systemizer of the *Abhidharma* type of Buddhist philosophy]. The icons in the second and third folios are known as the "Six Jewels of India" (*rgyan drug*). The *dharanis* (magical formulae believed to protect its writers and reciters) which correspond to each of these icons appear on the verso of each folio and are reproduced in a matching order; they are an important part of this collection not only because they are useful for ritual and meditation but because the Sanskrit names of all the icons are embedded within them.

62

藏傳佛教三百佛像圖

全稱《上師、本尊、三寶、護法等資糧田—三百佛像集》。傳章嘉・若必多吉（章嘉・呼圖克圖三世活佛）編制。乾隆年間（1736-1795年）北京嵩祝寺木刻刊行本。葉夾裝，無夾板。全一百頁（序十頁上下刊印，圖一百頁上下刊印）。每頁高九厘米，寬二三・三厘米。整疊高二・二厘米。序頁匡高五・六至五・九厘米，寬一七・一至一七・二厘米。圖上頁框高五・六至五・七厘米，寬一七・二至一七・六厘米。圖下頁框高五・七至五・九厘米，寬一七・五至一七・六厘米。

無號

三世章嘉，即章嘉・呼圖克圖三世活佛，名章嘉・若必多吉，譯游戲金剛，是清乾隆年間藏傳佛教的領導人。康熙五十六年（1717年）生於甘肅涼州西蓮寺附近，四歲時被認定為二世章嘉活佛的轉世，迎入青海的佑寧寺。雍正三年（1725年）送往北京，與皇四子弘曆（未來的乾隆皇帝）一同讀書。三世活佛有極高深的知識，博聞強記，除佛學外，還通曉漢、蒙、滿等民族文字。雍正十二年（1734年）被皇帝封為「灌頂普慧廣慈大國師」，頒發詔書，并賜金印等。後來也得到乾隆帝的尊崇與信任，乾隆元年（1743年）被賞賜管理京師寺廟喇嘛札薩克達喇嘛印，乾隆八年（1736年）賜御用金龍黃傘，乾隆）十六年（1751年）賜「振興黃教大國師」。

章嘉活佛熱心教務，曾編印過不少佛教典籍，如《首楞嚴經》譯本之編校、《滿文藏經》之整理、《御製滿文蒙古西番合璧大藏全咒》之編纂、《欽定同文韻統》之纂修、《蒙譯甘珠爾》之校正、《蒙譯丹珠爾》之翻譯、《金剛經藏譯》之指導、《造像度量經》之釐定以及《諸佛菩薩聖像贊》之編纂。

章嘉・若必多吉編制《上師、本尊、三寶、護法等資糧田—三百佛像集》，是為了使藏傳佛教的喇嘛能夠辨識大批的佛、菩薩、護法諸位尊神的形象。此圖集描繪了藏傳佛教諸佛像共三百幅，圖前有章嘉活佛寫的序十頁，用藏文後蒙古文刻印。圖一百頁，每頁正面有三尊以及藏文佛名，背面分上下兩部份，上半部份有梵、藏兩種文字，下半部為「十二因緣咒」，咒文音譯為「葉哈達喇嘛阿呵都巴喇拔幹阿呵都納得卡阿納答塔阿噶多哈鴉拔達答得卡阿鴉尼雜岳囉哈達厄拔嘛拔阿低伊嘛哈阿

沙喇嘛斯」。每頁正背面的圖與文都有按照次序排列，以中央一尊為首，次為右邊一尊，最後為左邊一尊。

編制此圖集的主要原因是普及知識，所以刻印并不特別考究，圖像繪制也頗簡單，只具體畫出了形象，在像的下面注上名稱，以便學習者能看圖識象。圖像背面每一尊像都印有「心咒」或「十二因緣咒」，說明這是經過加持，一定要珍重地供奉，不可褻瀆。

《三百佛像圖》雖然已經流傳了二百多年，但由于它是藏傳佛像，沒受到應有的重視，因之在漢族地區保存頗少，現在已經是難得的珍貴書籍。同版有朱印本或墨印本，中國佛教圖書文物館有初版朱印本，此選錄為中國國家圖書館所藏初版墨印本。

茲選照圖集前三頁的正面和背面。第一頁的三尊（以中、右、左次序）為「釋迦能仁（釋迦牟尼佛）」、「至尊妙音聲（文殊菩薩）」及「至尊慈氏（彌勒菩薩）」。第二頁的三尊為「吉祥怙主龍樹」、「至尊無著」及「至尊聖天」。第三頁的三尊為「至尊陳」、「至尊法稱」及「至尊世親」。

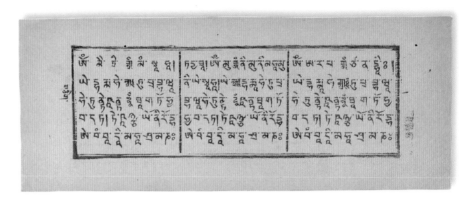

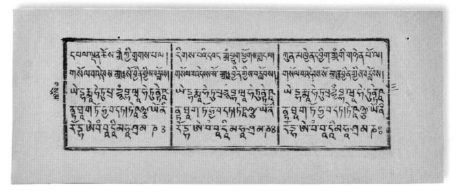

63

Man Han hebi zouzhe

Palace Memorial in Manchu and Chinese Scripts

Qing dynasty (1644-1911), Qianlong period (1736-1795), dated 1760

Composed by Zhuang Yougong (*jinshi* of 1739; d. 1767)

Document with 21 folds; folded in accordion-style; overall dimensions of document completely unfolded, 23.5 x 247.8 cm; each leaf approx. 23.5 x 11.8 cm

1143

Original palace memorials (*zouzhe* in Chinese, *bukdari* in Manchu, literally "memorial written on folded paper"; also known in Chinese as *tiben*, "routine memorial") are very important archival documents for the study of Qing history. Their contents tend to be very specific and are considered authentic and reliable sources of regional and local data, providing a wide range of information such as rainfall or drought conditions, prices of commodities, examination scandals, politicking among high officials, peasant uprisings, etc. After reading the memorials, the emperor would give his endorsement, issue instructions, or reply by inscribing them with a vermilion brush. Palace memorials are often the most direct records of how certain historical affairs developed and their subsequent management by the bureaucracy and the court.

During the Qing dynasty, most, if not all, documents of any consequence to the state were written either exclusively in Manchu or in Manchu and Chinese. One of the principal advantages of using the Manchu language is the ease with which secrecy could be maintained vis à vis the Chinese populace at large and even with respect to those serving at court. Manchu belongs to the Tungusic group of languages in the Altaic family and its script is adapted from Mongol with the addition of certain diacritics. Mongol orthography was first employed for Manchu around 1599, and by 1632 a more distinctive writing system was in place. Manchu has a syllabary of 1,441 syllabic graphs.

In the Kangxi period (1662-1772), the format of memorials was not standardized. However, from the Qianlong period (1736-1795) onwards until the end of the dynasty in 1911, the number of columns and characters per column were prescribed to be six columns per folded leaf and eighteen characters per column, not including the two or three characters that sit above above the main body of the text for honorary elevation. In 1651, it was decreed that references in a memorial to the imperial palaces should be raised by one character while references to the emperor raised by two characters. In addition, references to heaven and earth, ancestral temples, imperial tombs, temple names of emperors, as well as edicts and rescripts of imperial ancestors were to be raised by three characters above the main text of the memorial.

This bilingual palace memorial was submitted by the official Zhuang Youguang (*jinshi* of 1739; d. 1767) to the Qianlong emperor in 1760. Zhuang was the top-ranking graduate of the 1739 metropolitan *jinshi* examinations; he was appointed to a series of important posts: Academician of the Grand Secretariat (*neige xueshi*), Vice Minister of Revenue (*hu bu shilang*); he also served as governor of Jiangsu, Zhejiang, and Fujian provinces. According to Qing biographical sources, Zhuang was unfairly implicated in scandals by fellow high-ranking officials on a number of occasions and twice narrowly escaped execution.

The Manchu portion of the memorial, read from left to right, has a total of six leaves with six columns per fold except for the final leaf which has only four columns of text. Some of the leaves in the Manchu section had torn loose from the rest of the document, as seen in the photograph taken prior to its restoration. The Chinese portion, read right to left, is written in very small, delicately inked, and stylized regular script (*kaishu*) over thirteen folds. The cover fold on the Chinese end is inscribed in red ink and stamped with an imposing tall rectangular official seal impression with its legend in relief. Another such seal is found at the end of the Chinese text following Zhuang Yougong's signature. One fold, between the Manchu and Chinese texts, is left blank.

63

滿漢合璧奏摺

清乾隆二十五年（1760年）莊有恭書寫。紙本，計二十一面，每面高二三・五厘米，寬一一・八厘米。滿文部份六面，漢文部份十四面，中間空一面。單面高二三・五厘米，寬一一・八厘米。二十一面高二三・五厘米，長二四七厘米。折裝。

1143

　　奏摺，一作奏折，并稱題本。從清代康熙時期開始，臣工直接向皇帝陳述意見，報告政務與私事，或提出請求時之一種公文書，關於國家施政，皆可於其中窺知，故為研究史實之直接資料。奏摺內容，不受公私事件的限制，文武大員對於地方利弊，施政得失，民情風俗，無論鉅細，凡有開見，必得據實奏聞，各報各的，彼此不能相商。奏摺的格式，字數行數，在康熙年間，尚未劃一，自高宗以後宣宗末年，奏摺行數與字數，則有明確規定，

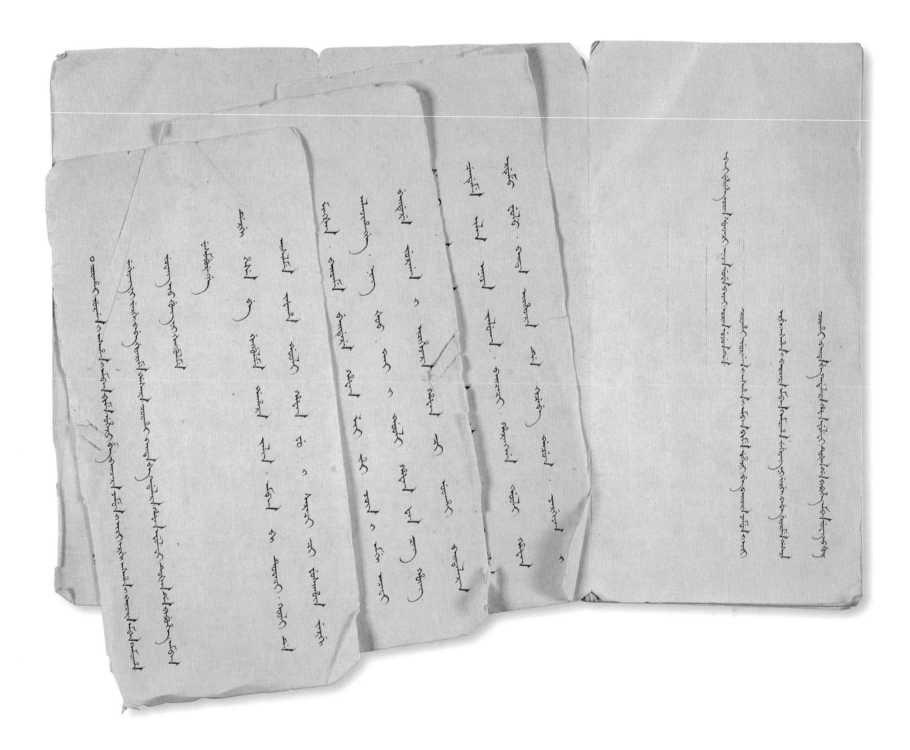

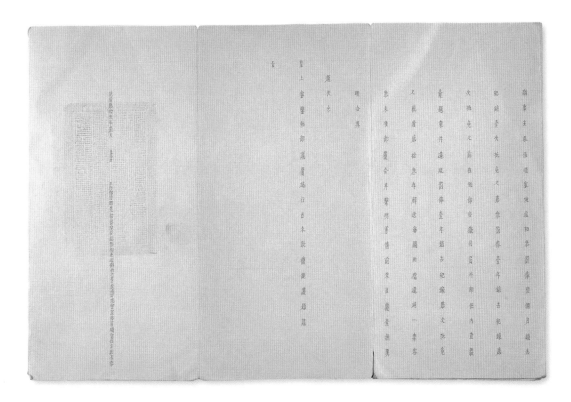

即每面六行，每行應二十或二十一字，抬頭二字或三字，平行寫十八字。

中國國家圖書館所藏的宮中檔歷朝滿漢文奏摺甚多，都是珍貴的第一手史料。本件係乾隆二十五年（1760年）二月二十九日高級官員莊有恭向皇帝奏事的滿漢奏摺文書，用奏摺紙（即毛邊紙）繕寫，共計二十一面。

莊有恭，字容可，號滋圃，廣東番禺人。乾隆四年（1739年），一甲一名進士。授修撰，命在尚書房行走。乾隆五年（1740年），充日講起居注官。累遷侍講學士。九年，遷光祿寺卿。尋丁父憂，十一年，特擢內閣學士。十三年，提督江蘇學政。十五年正月，授戶部侍郎，尋充江南鄉試正考官，八月，仍提督江蘇學政。十六年，授江蘇巡撫。二十四年，調浙江巡撫。二十五年（1760年）二月，劾署杭州將軍伊領阿、副都統劉揚達違例咨取轎役工食，經臣駁回，伊領阿等，仍自乘用，命革伊領阿劉揚達職，有恭交部議敘紀錄一次。有恭所至有善政，坐事兩遭顛躓，均詔原之。歷官刑部尚書，協辦大學士罷，復官至福建巡撫。乾隆三十二年（1767年）七月卒。

奏摺滿文部分每面六行，最後一面四行。漢文部份用極細小楷書寫，每面六行，行十八至二十一字，前題「兵部侍郎兼都察院右副都御史巡撫浙江等處地方提督軍務革職留住臣莊有恭謹題為欽奉⋯」，後款「乾隆貳拾伍年貳月貳拾玖日兵部侍郎兼都察院右副都御史巡撫浙江等處地方提督軍務革職留住臣莊有恭。」首面有乾隆帝朱批「該部議奏」四字。此奏摺用滿漢兩種文字書寫，字體工整，格式規範，有重要的文物價值和史料價值。

64

Man Han hebi gaoming

Imperial Patent of Nobility in Manchu and Chinese Scripts

Qing dynasty (1644-1911), Jiaqing period (1796-1820), dated 1799

Presented to the parents of Yulin (*jinshi* of 1795; d. 1833)

Handscroll, ink, color, and white pigment on 5 contiguous sections of silk brocade, 30.4-30.7 x 181.5 cm (from left to right, beginning with Manchu section: section 1, peach, 30.6-30.7 x 41.4 cm; section 2, cream, 30.7-30.8 x 31.9 cm; section 3, gold, 30.6-30.7 x 32.3 cm; section 4, vermilion, 30.4-30.5 x 32.1 cm; section 5, olive green, 30.4-30.5 x 43.8 cm)

80319

Documents known as *gaoming* (variously translated as "patent of nobility" or "patent by ordinance") were used by the emperor to confer a variety of lower nobility ranks and hereditary ranks inheritable in perpetuity upon officials of the fifth rank or above. The Manchus also granted honorary titles to single officials and members of their families for special merits, called *tan'en* ("great graces"). These were not inheritable and were mere titles with less practical significance than the hereditary ranks. The character *shou* in a patent means that an honorary title was granted to the official himself, while *feng* indicates that the honorary title or titles were granted to his wife or living parents and other relatives. The character *zeng* was used when honorary titles were posthumously conferred upon the official's deceased progenitors. The purchase of titles is first mentioned in a palace memorial from the fifth year of the Jiaqing period (1800), just at the beginning of the downfall of the dynasty.

During the early Qing period, the texts of patents were artistically woven from pure silk, but later on they were made of thick paper covered with a layer of silk-threads in various colors–red, blue, black, white, yellow, etc. Dragons in blue, red, green, or white were painted on the upper and lower rim as well as on the two ends, but no characters are printed or woven into them. Most patents were in Manchu and Chinese, or only in Manchu, but there are instances with Mongolian and Tibetan scripts. The exterior of patent scrolls were usually covered with red

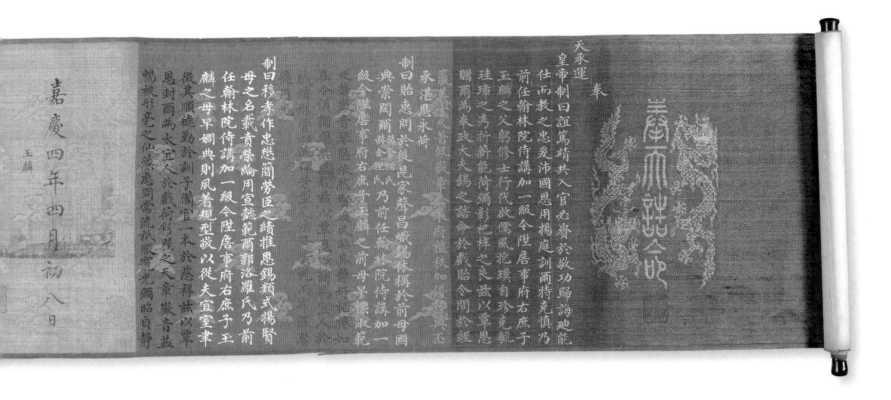

silk brocade with a design of golden flowers, while the rollers were frequently made of jade.

This patent was presented to ennoble the parents of Yulin (*jinshi* of 1795; d. 1833), a Manchu Plain Yellow bannerman, scholar, and military leader, in recognition of his distinguished service to the Qing state during one of its expansionist phases in the far west. Later in the dynasty, during the Daoguang period (1821-1850), Yulin was appointed as a general in charge of the strategically important region centered on the city of Ili (Yining; Ghuljia) in northwestern Xinjiang.

The patent was given on the eighth day of the fourth lunar month in 1799, at the time when Yulin received a prestigious appointment as junior compiler (*bianxiu guan*) in the

True Records Institute (*Shi lu guan*), where he would participate in historiographic and other compilations made under imperial sponsorship; this post was traditionally a stepping stone to high levels in the civil service. The scroll is handwritten, using multiple colors on different bands of colored silk brocade, in vertical columns of Manchu and Chinese. The Manchu text is read from left to right, while the Chinese is read from the opposite direction. The Chinese end contains the phrase *Feng tian gaoming* ("Patent by Ordinance [of the Emperor, who is] entrusted by Heaven") in large seal-script characters flanked by twin dragons; its counterpart in Manchu, *Abkai hesei g'aoming*, may be seen at the opposite end. The Chinese text of the patent begins with the phrase *feng tian*

cheng yun ("entrusted by heaven with the care of the empire").

64

滿漢合璧誥命

清嘉慶四年（1799年）滿漢文書寫於五色織錦。高三〇‧七厘米，長一八一‧五厘米。卷軸裝。

80319

誥命是中國古代皇帝給高級官員及其先代和妻室賜爵或授官的詔令。清代的誥命用五色絲織品制作，用滿漢兩種文字書寫，再鈐以皇帝專門的印鑒，制作精美典雅。本件是清嘉慶四年（1799年）頒發給玉麟父母的誥命。

玉麟，滿洲正黃旗人，姓哈達納喇氏，字子振，一字厚齋，號研農，一號小湖。乾隆六十年乙卯（1795年）進士，改翰林院庶吉士。嘉慶元年（1769年），散官，授編修。二年（1797年）四月，充玉牒館纂修官，五月，充日講起居注官。嘉慶三年（1798年），升侍講。四年（1799年）四月，

充實錄館纂修官，七月，升右春坊右庶子，十二月，升國子監祭酒，仍兼實錄館行走。道光元年（1821年）八月，授左翼總兵，尋調鑲白旗漢軍副都統，十二月，授兵部左侍郎。二年（1822年）五月，調刑部左侍郎，六月，授都察院左都御史，十一月，署禮部尚書兼管太常寺鴻臚寺事務，尋授禮部尚書三年二月，署吏部尚書，四月，調兵部尚書，八月，署步軍統領。道光八年（1828年）正月，重定回疆，晉加太子太保銜，以軍機大臣繪像紫光閣，御為製贊。道光九年（1829年）三月，充會試副考官，六月，授伊犁將軍。官至兵部尚書。道光十三年（1833年）三月回京，行至陝西長安縣，病卒。加恩晉贈太保，諡文恭，入祀賢良祠。

以下錄此誥命漢文部份全文：「奉天承運，皇帝制曰：誼篤靖共，入官必資於敬。功歸海迪，能仕而教之忠，爰沛國恩，用揚庭訓。爾，特克慎乃前任翰林院侍講加一級，今陞詹事府右庶子玉麟之父，躬修士行，代啟儒風，抱璞自珍，克毓珪璋之秀，折薪能荷，彌彰杞梓之良。茲以覃恩，贈爾為

奉政大夫錫之誥命。於戲。貽令問於經籀，義方久著，佩徽章於策府，禮秩加優，茂典丕承，湛恩永荷。制曰：貽惠問於後昆，家聲昌熾，錫休稱於前母，國典崇閎。爾，赫舍理氏，赫舍理氏，乃前任翰林院侍講加一級，今陞詹事府右庶子玉麟之前母，早標淑範，久著徽音，琴瑟依然，賢媛凰昭其靜好，栖棬如在，令儀猶想其風規。茲以覃恩，贈爾為宜人。於戲。煒彤管以流，輝芳型足法，降紫泥而布，澤潛德用光。制曰：移孝作忠，懋簡勞臣之績，推恩錫類，式揚賢母之名，載賁榮編，用宣懿範。爾，郭洛羅氏，乃前任翰林院侍講加一級，今陞詹事府右庶子玉麟之母，早嫻典則，凰著規型，敬以從夫，宜室，聿徵其順德，勤於訓子備官，一本於慈祥。茲以覃恩，封爾為太宜人。於戲。荷彩瞿之天章，徽音益暢，被彤毫之仙藻，惠問常流。祇服寵光，彌昭貞靜。嘉慶四年四月初八日」。後題「玉麟」二字。

依據以上簡略傳記，可知此誥命應是玉麟充實錄館纂修官時賞賜。

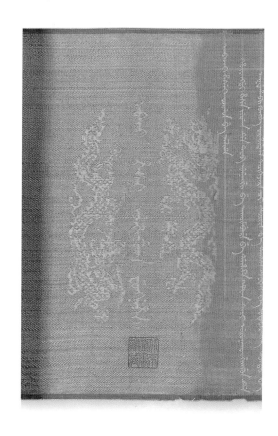

65

Yi wen Liu zu shi

History of the Six Ancestors in Yi Script

Qing dynasty (1644-1911), Jiaqing period (1796-1820), dated 1814

Manuscript copied by Shu Gejiao, ink on paper; 7 columns per page read from right to left, with varying numbers of characters per column; some pages of text missing or partially missing; 12 illustrations appended

From Wuding, Yunnan province

Overall dimensions of volume, 26.7 x 18.8 cm; stitch-bound on right edge

452

The Yi people, also known in the past as the Lolo, are one of the largest national minority groups in China. Primarily farmers, they now number around 6.5 million, and live mostly in the southwestern provinces of Yunnan, Sichuan, and Guizhou, as well as in Guangxi. While their history can be traced with certainty through actual texts for the last five hundred years, the Yi may well have been in existence for several thousand years.

Yi is a Tibeto-Burman language with an indigenous logographic script, in which every letter represents a syllable that is also a morpheme. The characters are written in vertical columns, usually from left to right, but sometimes from right to left. There are altogether eight to ten thousand characters in extant Yi records, though only a little more than a thousand were frequently used. The corpus of Yi texts includes works on history, literature, medicine, health, astronomy, geography, language, writing, agriculture, religion, and other subjects. Books in Yi script are mostly bound with goatskin, locally made cloth, or linen, but there are also certain books written on paper that are stitch-bound in the traditional Chinese manner. The texts are mostly composed in the form of five-character verses.

Traditional Yi script is now obsolescent, having been replaced by a fairly recently invented mode of writing. The National Library of China's collection of texts in traditional Yi script are mostly from the Wuding area in Yunnan province. The text featured here, known in translation as *History of the Six Ancestors*, is an invaluable genealogical work which contains both matrilineal and patrilineal records. This manuscript copy was made in 1814 and is written in vertical columns from right to left. Five-character verses are predominant, with a number of long and short phrases interspersed throughout. The text tells the story of the founding Yi ancestor Dumu, who went to Mount Luoni seeking refuge from a flood and ended up marrying the daughters of three important clans. Six sons–Mu'aqie, Mu'aku, Mu'are, Mu'awo, Mu'ake, and Mu'aqi–issued from these unions; they went on to establish the six principal lineages of the Yi people, respectively the Wu, Zha, Ni, Heng, Bu, and Mo. Although the text is a historical one, it is written with great literary flourish and is executed in a fine calligraphic style.

65

彝文六祖史

清嘉慶十九年（1814年）七月舒閣焦抄寫于雲南武定。一册，原四十七頁，缺四頁，每頁七行，行字數不等，有十二屬圖。高二六‧七厘米，寬一八‧八厘米。右邊綫裝。
452

彝族是文化豐富的古老民族，也是中國西南地區人口最多的土著居民，主要分布在雲南、四川、貴州三省和廣西壯族自治區。

彝文是一種古老的音節文字，一個字形代表一個意義，其文字總數達一萬餘個，但經常使用的只有一千多個。彝文有象形、會意、指事等造字方法，也有同音假借現象。獨體字多，合體字少。彝文古籍卷帙浩繁，涉及歷史、文學、醫藥、衛生、天文地理、語文字、農業技術和宗教經典等方面。

彝文古籍大多是用羊皮、土布、麻布包背裝，但也有紙本綫裝的書籍。書寫大多是五言詩的形式寫成，從右往左豎行寫和從左往右豎行寫的兩種方法。用「、」、「。」、「△」符號段句。

中國國家圖書館所藏的彝文典籍絕大部份是從雲南武定彝區收集來的。此部彝文典籍是著名的《六祖史》（原文音譯為《睒竇権濮》，中文意稱《古代六祖》、《夏代六祖》，中文亦稱《六祖經緯史》、《六祖輝煌史》），是彝族的歷史文獻之一。彝族母系、父系都有記載在內，不僅有濃厚的文學色彩，而且具有一定的史料價值。本書抄寫於清嘉慶十九年（1814年），從右往左豎行書寫。書中以五言詩句為主，兼和長短句，主要記載彝族始祖篤慕因洪水泛濫在洛尼山避難，并與雲貴三大部落聯姻的歷史故事。篤慕的六子後來分宗立室，即慕阿且成為武氏之祖，慕阿枯成為乍氏之祖，慕阿熱成為尼氏之祖，慕阿卧成為恒氏之祖，慕阿克成為布氏之祖，慕阿齊成為默氏之祖。此故事後來發展成為彝族六大支系的歷史。

238

66

Dai wen ke xie Lun Zang Sheli jisong beiye jing

Palm-Leaf Manuscripts Written in Dai Script with *Narrative Verses of Sariputta* from the *Abhidhamma-pitaka*

Qing dynasty (1644-1911), undated, ca. 19th century
Translated from the Pali *Abhidhamma-pitaka*
From Xishuangbanna, Yunnan province
4 bundles of palm-leaves, each leaf approx. 6.4 x 48.9 cm; height of stacked bundles, approx. 4.6 cm

No inventory number

The Dai people constitute one of the main ethnic and linguistic groups among China's fifty-five national minority groups. There are more than a million Dai living in the southwestern province of Yunnan, mainly in the Xishuangbanna Autonomous District (Prefecture) of the Dai people. Xishuangbanna is the Chinese translation of Sip Sawng Panna, the Dai name for the region meaning "twelve rice-growing districts." The Dai in Yunnan are closely related to the Dai in Thailand, Myanmar (Burma), Vietnam, and Laos; the latter three countries have common borders with Yunnan. The Dai language is strongly monosyllabic, but disyllables also exist, especially for borrowed words from Sanskrit and probably some Austro-Asiatic languages. Their writing system resembles those used in northern Thailand, Laos, and Myanmar, and four regionally based scripts known as the Na (used in Dehong), Le (used in Xishuangbanna), Beng (used in Ruili and Menglian), and Hao (used in Jinping) are employed.

The Dai people practice Theravada Buddhism, which is dominant in Southeast Asia but not in China. The Dai-Le script of Xishuangbanna is the one used for the recording of Theravada scriptures, including an 84,000-volume set of the *Tripitaka*. Characteristic of Dai culture are Buddhist texts in the form of palm-leaf manuscripts (*pothi* in Sanskrit), an ancient medium for writing which originated in India, where leaves of two principal varieties of palm trees were used, namely the palmyra palm (*Borassus flabellifer Linn*), whose leaves are thicker and stiffer, and the talipot palm (*Coryoha umbraculifera Linn*), which has softer and more flexible leaves. The leaves used by the Dai people come from abundant palm trees in the tropical and subtropical forests around Xishuangbanna. There is a story, called the *Green-Leaf Letters* (*Lü ye xin* in Chinese), on the discovery and early use of plantain leaves for writing prior to the use of palm-leaves.

The making of palm-leaf manuscripts is a time-consuming process. Harvested leaves are first trimmed with a sharp knife into a uniform size, bundled together in stacks of three to five leaves, and put into a cooking vessel to be boiled. Leaves must be submerged completely in water, and lime or lemon is added so that the leaves will be bleached into a very pale greenish-white tone. After removal from the cooking vessel, the leaves are taken to nearby rivers and scrubbed with fine sand particles. Then they are dried and pressed flat, aired for a period of time, and bound together to await inscription. Fifty to a hundred leaves make up one volume, and five to six hundred leaves make up one bundle. Each leaf is approximately 60 cm long and 10 cm wide, though smaller sizes also exist. Pierced holes made about 15 cm away from one end of each

leaf allow cords to be strung through to secure the palm-leaves, which are stored flat between two wooden boards.

Palm-leaf inscriptions may be made by incision with a pointed iron stylus, or written with a pen or brush. In the case of incision with a stylus, a light grid is first marked on the leaf's surface; the grid may be five-lined, six-lined, or eight-lined, the last of which being the most common. The finished text is then varnished with a plant emulsion, which brings out the outlines of the inscribed text. After being bound into volumes, the sides of the bundled texts are applied with a layer of gilding and with red or black lacquer as an added protection and decoration. Most palm-leaf manuscripts of Buddhist works are stored in temples and monasteries, where there are special rooms to prevent the ill effects of excessive humidity and insects. Apart from Theravada scriptures, palm-leaf manuscripts were also used for writing literary and historical works, as well as texts on medicine, mathematics, literature, music, dance, painting, astronomy, and calendrical studies (the Dai calendar was begun in A.D. 638).

These palm-leaf manuscripts from the National Library of China written in Dai script contain the *Narrative Verses of Sariputta* (*Sheli jisong*). They are from the *Abhidhamma-pitaka* (*Abhidharma-pitaka* in Sanskrit; *Lun Zang* in Chinese; Thesaurus of Discourses), one of the three divisions of the Buddhist *Tripitaka* which contains the philosophical works and provides exegeses of Buddhist doctrine, as presented in a genre of texts that systematically elaborate and analyze the doctrines expounded in the discourses (*sutta*). The narrative verses (*gatha*) contained within these palm-leaves are composed of stanzas or songs that are created in high tension with spiritual and uplifting insight. It should be

mentioned, however, that some of the *gatha* attributed to Sariputta are not traceable in the Pali Canon.

66
傣文刻寫論藏舍利偈頌貝葉經

貝葉經。一册分四扎，每葉高六・四厘米，寬四八・九厘米，整册厚約四・六厘米。清刻寫本，十九世紀刻寫。收集於雲南省西雙版納傣族地區，經文以傣仿文拼寫巴利語。

無號

　　中國傣族主要分布在雲南省西南部西雙版納地區。傣族全民信仰的小乘佛教，是從印度經緬甸、泰國傳進傣族地區，已有一千多年歷史。傣文是拼音文字，是由佛經采取梵文（巴利文）字母而創造出來的。它的創立，最初是適應宗教需要，為記錄經文而創立的。傣族使用四種文字，為傣文（德宏傣文）、傣泐文（西雙版納傣文）、傣崩文（瑞麗、孟連傣文）以及傣毫文（金平傣文）。其中傣泐文的符號體系及字母順序均與巴利文相同，只是傣文為正確反映傣語實際又增加了十五個字母。用於書寫佛經書的是傣泐文，除中國大部份傣族地區流行外，在泰國、老撾、緬甸北部也使用這種文字。

　　傣族信仰的小乘佛教具有前期佛教即原始佛教的特點，廣泛深入地滲透于傣族政治、社會、經濟、文學、文化和精神深處。傣族的佛教經典繁富，卷帙浩瀚，大部份經書藏于佛寺，所譯之《三藏》經典聲稱有八萬四千部，其中《經藏》五大類二萬一千部，《律藏》五大類二萬一千部，《論藏》七大類四萬二千部。此外也有一部五卷本的貝葉經名為《別悶西板酤》專門講述這八萬四千部佛經的由來傳說。

　　貝葉是一種生產于熱帶、亞熱帶地區的貝多羅樹葉子，屬棕櫚類，在傣族西雙版納地區的熱帶森林有這種樹生長。將貝葉製作成書寫材料，有它獨特的工藝程序。砍下葉樹的貝葉片，用快刀將貝葉一片一片割整齊，三至五卷成一卷梱好，放入鍋煮。煮時，鍋水位要超出貝葉，而且還要加酸或檸檬，以便使貝葉變成淡綠白色，然後才從鍋里將它取出來，拿到河邊用細沙搓洗乾淨，而後將貝葉曬

乾壓平，先收起來，讓它通一段時間的風，準備訂成匣。

　　傣泐文字的貝葉經是用鐵筆在貝多羅樹葉上刻寫的。貝葉經多以十餘頁線裝成册，數册或一二十册成套，裝幀優雅古樸，有的在邊沿上塗黑漆或金粉，精致美觀。貝葉經大多不注明著者和寫作年代，只能根據其內容反映的時代特點和文字上反映的語情況來推測或考定其寫作年代。此選傣族刻寫於貝葉經的《舍利偈頌》，為《論藏》界論之一，約成書於十九世紀。《論藏》就釋尊說示的教法（經）加以問答、註釋，作有系統地整理而成的一部經典。

　　貝葉經除小乘佛教經典外，還有許多文學作品、歷史記載，以及天文、歷法、地理、法律、倫理等方面的經書。貝葉重疊，上下以板相夾，用繩串結，故稱梵夾裝。此種裝幀形式隨佛教而流傳，對中國藏、回紇、蒙古、滿等民族的佛教典籍影響巨大。

67A-B

Naxi zu Geba wen, xiangxing wen Dongba jing er

zhong

Two Dongba Texts of the Naxi People in Geba and Pictographic Scripts

67A

Qing dynasty (1644-1911), undated, ca. 18th-19th centuries

Dongba Text in Geba script

Booklet of 14 folios (including top and bottom covers), ink on paper; each folio, approx. 9.4 x 28.6 cm

0026

67B

People's Republic (1949-present), dated 1950

Annals of Creation in Pictographic Script, with Accompanying Translation in Chinese

Manuscript of 18 double-leaves, ink and color on paper, stitch-bound on left side; each leaf approx. 20.1 x 28.0 cm

Naxi pictographic script on upper register of each leaf, divided into 4 horizontal rows; each row is subdivided at irregular intervals with single or double lines; Chinese translation on lower register in 5 to 8 horizontal rows

227055

Nestled in the valleys of northwestern Yunnan province beneath the majestic snow-capped peaks around Jade Dragon Mountain, the Naxi kingdom flourished from the eighth century until 1723 when it came under Chinese control. The Naxi people, who now number around 278,000 and have their capital at Lijiang (at the first great bend of the Jinsha River), speak a Tibeto-Burman language which is monosyllabic. They possess the only living pictographic script in the world, in addition to a phonetic script called Geba; some texts are written in a combination of both scripts.

Geba script is drawn from three sources: Chinese characters, "indigenous" graphs, and simplified pictographs. The phonetic values of Geba script are not fixed; each *dongba* tends to prefer one set of symbols over another, and symbols can have various phonetic values, or a phonetic value can be signified by a number of graphs. Whereas the pictographs are a universal Naxi script, Geba is not widely distributed and is found only in the southern part of Naxi territory, in Lijiang town and surrounding plain region, and in the Judian-Weixi area.

Naxi pictographic script, said to have been invented by King Moubao Azong in the thirteenth century, is made up of tiny stylized drawings of people, animals, plants, etc. Like Tibetan, it is written horizontally and is read from left to right. The script was invented for exclusive use by the *dongba* (derived from the Tibetan *tön-pa*, meaning priest) as aids in the recitation of ritual texts during funeral rites, religious ceremonies, and shamanistic practices as it did not have the tonal shortcomings of the earlier phonetic script. Most elements in the script are associated with a concept, not a sound, and not every single word has to be written down, only as much as is needed to remind the reader of the text's contents. Although the indigeneous pictographic script may appear naïve to untrained eyes, it is far from primitive and is as sophisticated a form of writing as ancient scripts such as Mayan and Egyptian hieroglyphics. Scholars have shown how Naxi pictographs are linguistically specific icons, and the pictographs have also proven to be sufficiently systematized that a computer program could be devised for inputting and retrieving the script's components by isolating radicals (*bushou*) in imitation of Chinese.

Naxi pictographic books are not a recent invention. There is reasonable evidence that the Naxi were already producing pictographic texts during the Mongol period (1253-1381). The Mongols undoubtedly made a profound impression on the Dongba tradition, since it is clear that certain pictographs could not have come into the Dongba repertoire if the Naxi people had not had significant contacts with the Mongols. Zhu Baotian, a leading specialist of Naxi language and culture, has classified Dongba texts into thirteen major categories: sacrifice to the highest deity; sacrifice to the serpent king; romance and love-related ceremonies; prayers for longevity; aspiration for wisdom; sacrifice to the god of bravery and victory; ancestral worship; repelling sickness; casting out evil spirits; blocking malicious ghosts; prayers for a better reincarnation; divination; and miscellaneous ceremonies.

There are more than a thousand types of Naxi scriptures and texts in existence, covering an encyclopaedic range of subjects such as religion, customs, language, writing, history, geography, literature, art, philosophy, astronomy, and calendrical studies. From an anthropological standpoint, these pictographic texts are of unique importance because they represent the complete ritual corpus of a single tribe, providing a wealth of information on the religious beliefs and world-view of the Naxi people.

The physical corpus of Dongba scriptures is quite sizable. The texts are written on locally produced paper and resemble Tibetan books in shape but are stitch-bound along the left side except for divinatory texts, which are stitched along the upper edge. About 20,000 volumes of Naxi texts are extant, half of which are kept in major repositories such as the Lijiang Library, the Yunnan Provincial Library in Kunming, the Nanjing Library, and the National Library of China in Beijing. Smaller but significant collections of Naxi pictographic texts in the West may be found at institutions such as the Library of Congress, the Harvard-Yenching Library at Harvard University, and the Staatsbibliothek in Berlin.

The National Library of China's Naxi collection consists of more than four thousand manuscripts, most of which was assembled in 1942 when the scholar Fu Sinian (1896-1950), assisted by Zhou Rucheng, went to Lijiang to acquire Dongba texts. The booklet shown here is a representative piece from the collection; it is made up of fourteen stiffened folios (including the titled and illustrated top cover as well as the blank bottom cover) made by the Naxi from tree bark. It is in the standard form of a long rectangle and stitch-bound along the left side. The twelve inner folios are inscribed on both sides and each folio is divided into four rows of fourteen or fifteen Geba "characters." Geba and Tibetan books have in common the shape of the manuscripts (with leaves stitched on the left side), the reading sequence from left to right, and the fact that both are syllabic.

The Naxi people possess three great epic poems (the historical poem *The Post-Ancestor Deluge* or the *Annals of Creation*, the heroic poem *The Struggle between the Black and the White*, and the elegaic poem with an untranslatable title rendered in transliteration as *Lvbberlvssaq*, which relates the tragic fate of a young couple). These poems, along with other myths and legends, also occur in the Dongba scriptures. The pictographic text shown here is the *Annals of Creation* (known as *Chuangshi jing* or *Chuangshi ji* in Chinese), a Naxi creation myth that is above all a ritual text. It is best comprehended as a magic formula where the power of the Word replays and consequently recreates the origins of the world, reproducing the good things of life (such as the Naxi people) and keeping the evil ones at bay (such as ghosts and demons). In its basic form, the *Annals of Creation* is a wonderful epic poem recited in five-syllable verses which tells not only of the things in the Creation but of all human feelings, power, desire, fear and hope, and combines moments of majestic drama with pathos, suspense, and humor.

67A-B

納西族哥巴文、象形文東巴經二種

67A

哥巴文東巴經。無寫作年代和作者姓名。用竹制蘸水筆寫在本地特制厚棉紙上。一冊，計十四頁。外縱九‧四厘米，橫二八‧六厘米。左邊綫裝。

0026

67B

象形文《創世經》。又稱《創世記》、《創始紀》。東巴象形文彩繪、漢文墨寫合璧本。紙底抄本。一冊，計十八頁。外縱二〇‧一厘米，橫二八厘米。左邊綫裝。

227055

納西族有近三十萬人，主要分布在中國西南部滇、川、藏交界的橫斷山脈地區，其中大約有百分之七十的人口聚居在雲南省麗江納西族自治縣境內。東巴文化是中國珍貴文化遺產之一，在國內外早負盛名。

「東巴」，意為「智者」，是納西族原始社會沿襲下來的巫師和祭司。納西族東巴教經書，大多用納西族象形文字寫成。這種文字比原始的圖畫文字進步，但又比能系統記錄語的表意文字落後，約產生於公元七世紀左右，是世界上稀有的「活着的象形文字」。東巴經內容豐富，涉及納西族從原始社會、奴隸社會到初期封建社會的歷史、哲學、宗教、文字、藝術、農牧業以及天文、曆法等，是研究古代納西族的百科全書。納西族的象形文經典，現存總計約二萬餘冊，中國內外約各占一半。中國國家圖書館和麗江納西族自治縣圖書館最多，其次為北京中央民族學院、雲南省圖書館和雲南省社會科學院東巴文化研究室（麗江）。台灣台北國立故宮博物院也藏不少的東巴文典籍。國外以美國國會圖書館最多，其次為哈佛大學哈佛燕京圖書館、德國柏林國立圖書館和英國倫敦大英博物館等。

納西族的形象文典籍可依照內容分類，如祭東巴什羅、祭龍王、祭風、求壽、祭賢、勝利神、祭家神、替生、除穢、闢死門、祭死者、占卜、零雜經等。此選兩部東巴經，其中一部以哥巴文書寫。哥巴文的「哥巴」一詞，意為「弟子」，說明這種文字是由後世弟子們所創制。哥巴文中有大量象形文的縮寫字并借用不少漢字，說明哥巴文的產

生晚於東巴文。哥巴文屬音節文字，筆畫簡單，一個字表示一個音。但標音不標調，難區別詞義。又有一音數字和異義同字，難確解其義。流行範圍和寫下的經書數量，遠不及東巴。

東巴文是象形文字（也有認為是圖畫文字），它比原始記事的圖畫文字進步，但又比能系統記錄語的表意文字原始。東巴文由象形符號、表音符號和附加符號構成，以象形符號為主。在象形符號中包括象形、會意、合體、轉意、指事等字符；表音符號包括假借字和形聲字；附加符號是各種點、綫等不能單獨成字的符號。

創世神話是納西古典神話的本源，主要反映的是自然的形成（開天辟地）和人類的起源及遷徙繁衍，幾乎大部份東巴經神話的開頭，毫無例外地以「太古時候」來講起，詳略不等地要敘述一段天地日月、山川木石以及某個特定的人、神的出現和形成。此部象形文《創世經》是東巴文文獻中的代表作，1950年在雲南所得。其封面有象形文、漢文標題以及彩圖，經文上方四排為墨書象形文并加以五彩，下方五至八排配有墨書漢文譯文，尾題「…歲次庚寅九月二十四日譯成。麗江周汝誠持贈與中央民族訪問團夏康農團長以為紀念」。

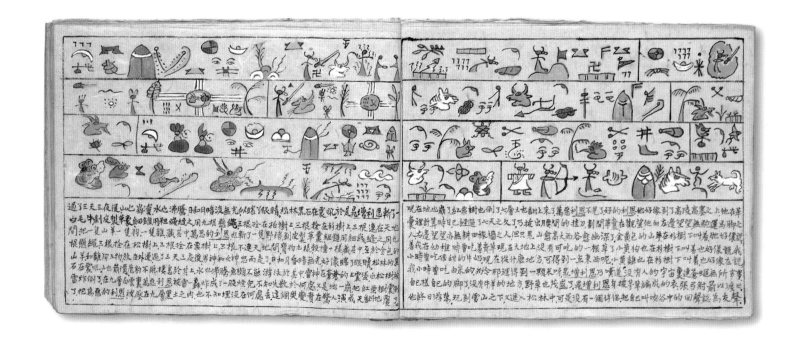

68A-C

Naxi zu Dongba tu san zhong

Three Dongba Illustrations from the Naxi People

68A

Qing dynasty (1644-1911) or Republican period (1912-1949), undated, 1930s or earlier

Illustration of Deities and Demons

2 linen panels stitched together to form 1 panel; unmounted; approx. 102.0 x 62.0 cm

111 bao-1

68B

Qing dynasty (1644-1911) or Republican period (1912-1949), undated, 1930s or earlier

Illustration of the Spirit Way

Vertical handscroll, color and white pigment on linen; approx. 1475.0 x 28.0 cm

111 bao-2

68C

Qing dynasty (1644-1911) or Republican period (1912-1949), undated, 1930s or earlier

Illustration of the Spirit Way

Vertical handscroll, color and white pigment on paper; approx. 1125.0 x 30.0 cm

111 bao-3

Naxi beliefs grew out of the shamanistic Bon religion of pre-Buddhist Tibet; they were also later influenced by and incorporated elements of Daoism and Tibetan Buddhism. The dongba (derived from the Tibetan *tön-pa*, meaning priest) imitate Bon monks in dress and actions; they are often also accomplished shamans, medicine men, scholars, artists,

craftsmen, dancers, and singers. The Naxi believe that their dead proceed automatically and directly to hell. The souls of the deceased must therefore be led back out from the infernal depths towards heaven by the *dongba* or ritual specialists during the performance of elaborate funeral rites, and pictorial illustrations are an integral part of these ritual occasions.

The "Illustration of Deities and Demons" shown here is divided into four registers, the topmost of which contains a triad of benevolent deities within what appears to be a celestial realm. The seated and haloed principal deity in the second register is flanked by a scribe and a demon holding a banner an ambiguous phrase in Chinese characters, *shan e fei ming*, which may be translated as "good and evil cannot be discerned" or "good and evil are not [necessarily] clear"; a winged serpent and a winged dragon-like beast hover at the upper corners. The third register has five animal-headed, human-bodied creatures portrayed in stylized stances. Finally, the lowermost register shows a pair of human figures perched above flames and accompanied by two horses. The composition is both fascinating and well structured, while the limited palette of blues, yellows, and reds is accented with white pigment throughout. Such a picture would probably have been hung during religious ceremonies conducted by the *dongba* and rolled up after each use.

Pictures known as *shenlu tu* ("illustrations of the spirit way" or "illustrations of the spirit road") are visualizations of journeys from the underworld to celestial realms, reflecting both ancestral Naxi and Tibetan Buddhist notions of life and death. Vertically oriented and extending between fifteen and twenty meters in length, they are mostly drawn on locally produced linen or other cloths which are treated with a paste of white powder; a smaller number are executed on paper. These illustrations are composed of more than a hundred individual and continuous sections divided into three major narrative groups: thirty-three strata of spirit lands, human figures dwelling on earth, and eighteen demonic lands. Hell is always shown in the lowermost sections, the human realm in the middle segments, and heaven in the topmost ones; the entire imagined sequence that the deceased person's soul has to traverse is replicated.

The two very long painted scrolls shown here were used during Naxi funeral services. One of them is on linen, the other on paper, are both applied with bright mineral pigments. In each instance, the gods, figures, and demons number no less than 360, while seventy to eighty kinds of fabulous winged creatures and beasts are depicted. There is no shortage of gruesome scenes in the lower sections of the scrolls to remind the living that no stay in the infernal lands should last very long if possible. The contents of these scrolls are complex yet organized, the linework employed simple and bold but executed with flair and fluidity, and though somewhat primitive in appearance, the illustrations capture the spirit of a unique culture.

68A-C

納西族東巴圖三種

68A

《東巴神軸畫》。清代（1644–1911年）或民國初期。麻布底彩繪圖。一張。縱一〇二厘米，橫六二厘米。第111包之一

68B

《東巴長卷畫神路圖》。清代（1644–1911年）或民國初期。麻布底彩繪卷軸。一卷。縱一四七五厘米，橫二八厘米。第111包之二

68C

《東巴長卷畫神路圖》。清（1644–1911年）或民國初期。紙底彩繪卷軸。一卷。縱一一二五厘米，橫三〇厘米。第111包之三

　　中國雲南省納西族信奉的東巴教是一種原始宗教，信仰多神，崇拜日月星辰、山水風火等自然現象和自然物，奉神話人物丁巴什羅為始祖。七世紀以後，因與吐蕃接觸頻繁，受西藏苯教影響較大。該教的巫師叫「東巴」，意為「智者」。出自東巴教的各種藝術作品包括木牌畫、畫譜、東巴經書、竹筆畫與經書封面、占卜經、紙牌畫、卷軸畫、神路畫等。茲選三幅東巴圖，是三十年代采集於納西族地區。第一幅為「神軸畫」，第二、第三幅為「神路圖」。

　　「神軸畫」是東巴用礦物質顏料繪於布質卷軸上的各種神像畫，掛在東巴作法道場時的臨時擺設的經堂之中，當是接受藏傳佛教和內地佛教之後的產物，納西語稱「普老幛」、「普老」即神，「幛」是漢語借詞。神軸畫早期用麻布，近代多用白布，還有少數是用紙畫的。其數量眾多，是東巴繪畫藝術逐步跨入發達階段而趨於精熟的標志。其中畫祖師的像較多，因為舉行各種道場時都要掛祖師像於經堂中心。此選一幅彩繪《東巴神軸畫》所用的是麻布，圖分四橫段，右邊一像上并標有「善惡非明」四漢字。

　　另有一部分神軸畫，主要繪一尊大神或護法

神，不同儀式所掛的神像不盡相同；每幅表現的是某個神祇及其所居的神界。在結構和布局上，主神居中，四周畫戰神、神明東巴、鵬、龍、獅、白髦牛、紅虎及各種東巴教的吉祥符號，內容比較豐富。東巴神軸畫在納西族傳統藝術風格的基礎上，吸收融合了漢傳佛教、道教和藏傳佛教的畫風藝術，特別是受元、明以來藏傳佛教「唐卡」神軸畫的影響較為明顯，因此它對研究納西東巴文化的形成及其與漢、藏文化的交流，具有重要的學術價值。

「神路圖」，納西語叫「恒日」，用於喪儀和超度亡靈儀式，因該圖旨在導引死者步入神靈之路，故謂之「神路圖」。它是東巴繪畫藝術中傑出

的煌煌巨作。全長約十五至二十米左右，寬三十厘米左右，多用本地土布或麻布抹上白粉漿後繪制而成，亦有少數繪制在紙上的。神路圖是由百餘幅片斷組成的連續畫，內容結構大體可分為三部份：三十三界神地、人間和十八個鬼域。在這長幅巨作中，畫有三百六十多個栩栩如生的不同人物，包括端詳莊坐的神佛，作法跳舞之東巴，奇形怪狀之鬼怪，及七十餘種奇禽異獸。它用連環式的畫面，及貫寓其中的神話故事和教諭，反映了納西先民的生命意識，這種意識融匯了納西族傳統的和受藏傳佛教影響的生死觀，認為人死後靈魂不滅，而亡靈又會被十八層鬼域和各種鬼怪所阻，只有通過東巴的超度導引，才能到達祖先靈魂的居住地，與祖先團

聚，然後送到三十三界神地，使之受到神的庇佑。透過神鬼紗幕，畫卷表達的卻是納西人民追求光明福境的願望和懲惡揚善、完善人生的倫理美學。

茲選《東巴長卷畫神路圖》二幅，內容各分三段，以下往上為地獄、人間、佛地。此神路圖場面宏大，氣勢壯觀，呈現出高超獨特的畫技藝風：看構思，錯綜紛紜而不亂；看設色，七彩艷抹而不雜；看筆法，浪漫豪放而不散；看線條，粗獷簡約而流暢；看造型，古拙率真而傳神。統卷格調平和渾樸，不僅是納西族的藝術瑰寶，也是中華民族藝術寶庫中的珍品。

Sources, references, and related readings

引用文獻資料及主要參考書籍

1

Sutra of the Lotus of the Wonderful Law (*Saddharmapundarika-sutra*), 7 *juan*, Manuscript from Dunhuang

敦煌寫經

妙法蓮華經七卷

Nanjio Bunyiu [Nanjô Bun'yû], *A Catalogue of the Chinese Translation of the Buddhist Tripitaka, the Sacred Canon of the Buddhists in China and Japan, Compiled by Order of the Secretary of State for India* (Oxford: Clarendon Press, 1883. Reprint. Tokyo: Nanjô hakushi kinen kankôkai, 1929), p. 44, no. 134; *Dunhuang jie yu lu (An Analytical List of the Tun-huang Manuscripts in the National Library of Peiping)*, compiled and edited by Chen Yuan, Guoli zhongyang yanjiu yuan lishi yuyan yanjiu suo zhuankan, no. 4 [Beiping: Guoli zhongyang yanjiu yuan lishi yuyan yanjiu suo (The National Research Institute of History and Philology of Academia Sinica), 1931], vol. 4, pp. 270a-357b; Dong Zuobin, "Guanyu Dunhuang Tang xieben Miaofa lianhua jing," *Dalu zazhi (The Continent Magazine)* 7, no. 12 (December 31, 1953), p. 36; Lionel Giles, *Descriptive Catalogue of the Chinese Manuscripts from Tunhuang in the British Museum* (London: Published by the Trustees of the British Museum, 1957); Zhang Tiexian, "Dunhuang gu xieben congtan," *Wenwu*, no. 149 (1963, no. 3) (March 1963), pp. 7-11; *The Sutra of the Lotus Flower of the Wonderful Law*, translated from Kumarajiva's version of the Saddharmapundarika-sutra by Senchu Murano (Tokyo: Nichiren Shu Headquarters, 1974), pp. 190-237; Mizuno Kôgen, *Buddhist Sutras: Origin, Development, Transmission* (Tokyo: Kôsei Publishing Co., 1982); *Scripture of the Lotus Blossom of the Fine Dharma (The Lotus Sutra)*, translated from the Chinese of Kumarajiva by Leon Hurvitz (New York: Columbia University Press, 1976. Reprint. New York: Columbia University Press, 1982), pp. 208-257; *Dunhuang yishu zongmu suoyin*, compiled and edited by Shangwu yinshu guan, new ed. (Beijing: Zhonghua shuju, 1983); Shi Anchang, "Guanyu Wu Zetian zao zi de wushi yu jiegou," *Gugong bowu yuan yuankan (Palace Museum Journal)*, no. 26 (1984, no. 4), pp. 84-90; Shi Anchang, "Dunhuang xie jing duandai fafan, jian lundi bian zi qun de guilü," *Gugong bowu yuan yuankan (Palace Museum Journal)*, no. 30 (1985, no. 4), pp. 58-66; *Dunhuang yishu zuixin mulu*, edited by Huang Yongwu (Taibei: Xinwenfeng chuban she, 1986), pp. 505-514; John C. Huntington, "A Note on Dunhuang Cave 17, 'The Library,' or Hong Bian's Reliquary Chamber," *Ars Orientalis* 16 (1986), pp. 93-101; Jean-Pierre Drège, "Quelques collections 'nouvelles' de manuscrits de Dunhuang," *Cahiers d'Extrême-Asie*, no. 3 (1987), pp. 113-129; Jean-Pierre Drège, "The Dunhuang and Central Asian Manuscripts and the History of Books," in *Chinese Studies: Papers Presented at a Colloquium at the School of Oriental and African Studies, University of London, 24-26 August 1987*, edited by Frances Wood (London: The British Library, 1988), pp. 171-174; Monique Cohen and Nathalie Monnet, *Impressions de Chine* (Paris: Bibliothèque Nationale, 1992), p. 30, cat. no. 11 [color; selected section of handscroll illustrated]; *The Lotus Sutra*, translated by Burton Watson (New York: Columbia University Press, 1993), esp. pp. ix-xxii [translator's introduction], and pp. 196-244 [chapters 14-17]; *Miaofa lianhua jing tulu (A Special Exhibition of Illustrations of the "Lotus Sutra")*, compiled and edited by Guoli gugong bowu yuan bianji weiyuan hui (Taibei: Guoli gugong bowu yuan, 1995), Chinese text, pp. 2-5 and pp. 143-145; Du Weisheng, "The Restoration of the *Dunhuang Manuscripts in the National Library of China*," in *Dunhuang and Turfan: Contents and Conservation of Ancient Documents from Central Asia*, edited by Susan Whitfield and Frances Wood (London: The British Library, 1996), pp. 29-31; Jiao Mingchen, *Dunhuang xie juan shufa yanjiu* (Taibei: Wen shi zhe chuban she, 1997), esp. pp. 117-173, pp. 308-315, and figs. 42 and 43.

2

Greater Sutra of the Perfection of Transcendent Wisdom (*Mahaprajnaparamita-sutra*), 600 *juan*, from the Jin Tripitaka deposited at Guangsheng Temple, Zhaocheng County

趙城縣廣勝寺刻大藏經

大般若波羅蜜多經六百卷

Nanjio Bunyiu [Nanjô Bun'yû], *A Catalogue of the Chinese Translation of the Buddhist Tripitaka, the Sacred Canon of the Buddhists in China and Japan, Compiled by Order of the Secretary of State for India* (Oxford: Clarendon Press, 1883. Reprint. Tokyo: Nanjô hakushi kinen kankôkai, 1929), pp. 1-4, no. 1; Jiang Weixin, "Jin Zang diaoyin shimo kao, fu Guangsheng si Da Zang jing jianmu," in *Song Zang yizhen xu mu* [N.p. (Shanghai): N.p. (Yingyin Song ban Zang jing hui), n.d. (1936)], *fulu* 1a-42b; Ye Gongchuo, "Lidai Zang jing kao lüe," in *Zhang Jusheng xiansheng qishi shengri jinian lunwen ji*, compiled and edited by Cai Yuanpei, Hu Shi, and Wang Yunwu (Shanghai: Shangwu yinshu guan, 1937), pp. 25-42, 20 unnumbered pages of illustrations, and pl. 2 (*jia, yi, bing, ding,* and *wu*); *Zhongguo banhua shi tulu* (Shanghai: Zhongguo banhua shi she, 1940-1942), in vol. 1; K.T. Wu, "Chinese Printing under Four Alien Dynasties (916-1368 A.D.)," *Harvard Journal of Asiatic Studies* 13, nos. 3-4 (December 1950), pp. 456-457, and pl. 4 [halftone; selected woodblock-printed frontispiece illustrated]; *Zhongguo yinben shuji zhanlan mulu*, compiled and edited by Beijing tushu guan (Beijing: Zhongyang renmin zhengfu wenhua bu shehui wenhua shiye guanli ju, 1952), p. 47, nos. 246 and 247; L. Carrington Goodrich, "Earliest Printed

Editions of the Tripitaka," *The Visvabharati Quarterly* 19, no. 3 (Winter 1953-1954), pp. 215-220; *Zhongguo banke tulu*, compiled and edited by Beijing tushu guan, 2d rev. ed. (Beijing: Wenwu chuban she, 1961), vol. 1, p. 84, and vol. 4, pls. 253 and 254; Guo Weiqu, *Zhongguo banhua shi lüe* (Beijing: Zhaohua meishu chuban she, 1962), p. 31 and fig. 10; Hu Zhenqi, "Shanxi sheng bowu guan suo cang Zhaocheng Zang," *Wenwu*, nos. 138-139 (1962, nos. 4-5) (May 1962), p. 92; Zhang Xiulan, "Ji Zhaocheng Zang lingben," *Wenwu*, no. 331 (1983, no. 12) (December 1983), pp. 88-89; *Zhonghua Da zang jing (Han wen bufen)*, compiled and edited by Zhonghua Da zang jing bianji ju, vol. 2 (Beijing: Zhonghua shuju, 1984), pp. 19-27; *Zhongguo gudai banhua bai tu*, compiled and edited by Zhou Wu (Beijing: Renmin meishu chuban she, 1984), no. 8; *Zhongguo gudai muke hua xuan ji*, compiled and edited by Zheng Zhenduo (Beijing: Renmin meishu chuban she, 1985), vol. 1 [unpaginated; halftone; 1 selected frontispiece illustrated]; *Zhongguo meishu quanji: Huihua bian*, vol. 20, *Banhua*, compiled by Zhongguo meishu quanji bianji weiyuan hui (Shanghai: Shanghai renmin meishu chuban she, 1988), illustrations section, p. 16, no. 16 [halftone; selected frontispiece illustrated], text section, p. 7, no. 16 [catalogue entry in Chinese by Li Zhitan]; *Chûgoku kodai hanga ten: Machida shisei 30-shûnen kinen, Nitchû heiwa yûkô jôyaku teiketsu 10-shûnen kinen*, Chûgoku hanga 2000-nen ten, dai 3 bu, compiled by Machida shiritsu kokusai hanga bijutsukan [and] Takimoto Hiroyuki (Machida, Japan: Machida shiritsu kokusai hanga bijutsukan, 1988), p. 87, cat. no. 3.12; Li Fuhua, "'Zhaocheng Jin Zang' yanjiu," *Shijie zongjiao yanjiu (Studies in World Religions)*, no. 46 (1991, no. 4), pp. 1-18; Hu Shixiang, "Ba lu jun jiuhu 'Zhaocheng Jin Zang' jishi," *Fojiao wenhua (The Culture of Buddhism)*, no. 5 (1993, no. 1), pp. 24-26; Kobayashi Hiromitsu, *Chûgoku no hanga: Tôdai kara Shindai made (Chinese Woodblock Illustrations from the Tang through the Qing Dynasty)* (Tokyo: Tôshindô , 1995), p. 18, and p. 19, fig. 014; Yao Tao-chung, "Buddhism and Taoism under the Chin," in *China under Jurchen Rule: Essays on Chin Intellectual and Cultural History*, edited by Hoyt Cleveland Tillman and Stephen H. West, SUNY Series in Chinese Philosophy and Culture, edited by David L. Hall and Roger T. Ames (Albany, N.Y.: State University of New York Press, 1995), p. 174; Li Ping, "Jiuhu 'Zhaocheng Jin Zang' de cehua zhe Likong fashi xinglüe–yi 'Huoshan zhi' he Likong fashi zi zhuan de nianpu wei ti," *Wenxian*, no. 64 (1995, no. 2), pp. 109-132; Li Ping, "Likong fashi jiuhu 'Zhaocheng Jin Zang' wenti kaoshi," *Wenxian*, no. 65 (1995, no. 3), pp. 94-103; Li Zhizhong, *Gu shu banben jianding* (Beijing: Wenwu chuban she, 1997), pp. 44-45, and fig. 9 [halftone; 1 selected frontispiece illustrated]; *Zhongguo gudai yinshua shi tuce (An Illustrated History of Printing in Ancient China)*, compiled by Zhongguo yinshua bowu guan (The Printing Museum of China) [Hong Kong: Xianggang chengshi daxue chuban she (City University of Hong Kong Press); Beijing: Wenwu chuban she (Cultural Relics Publishing House), 1998], p. 64 [bottom]; Zhou Xinhui, "Zhongguo fojiao *banhua* shi zonglun," in *Zhongguo gudai fojiao banhua ji*, chief editor: Zhou Xinhui, co-editors: Chen Jian and Ma Wenda (Beijing: Xueyuan chuban she, 1998), vol. 1, introductory text section, p. 35, and vol. 1, illustrations section, p. 103; *Zhongguo guojia tushu guan guji zhenpin tulu*, edited by Ren Jiyu (Beijing: Beijing tushu guan chuban she, 1999), pp. 112-113, cat. no. 118 [selected section of another scroll from the Jin-dynasty *Tripitaka* illustrated].

3

Collected Works of Ouyang Xiu, 153 *juan*, with Supplement, 5 *juan*

歐陽文忠公集一百五十三卷附錄五卷

Zhongguo yinben shuji zhanlan mulu, compiled and edited by Beijing tushu guan (Beijing: Zhongyang renmin zhengfu wenhua bu shehui wenhua shiye guanli ju, 1952), p. 31, no. 89; *Guoli zhongyang tushu guan Song ben tulu*, compiled and edited by Guoli zhongyang tushu guan (Taibei: Zhonghua congshu weiyuan hui, 1958), pp. 287-288, fig. 132 [halftone; 1 selected half-folio illustrated]; *Zhongguo banke tulu*, compiled and edited by Beijing tushu guan, 2d rev. ed. (Beijing: Wenwu chuban she, 1961), vol. 1, p. 32, and vol. 3, pl. 143; Su Bai, "Nan Song de diaoban yinshua," *Wenwu*, no. 135 (1962, no. 1) (January 1962), pp. 15-28; *A Sung Bibliography (Bibliographie des Sung)*, initiated by Étienne Balazs, edited by Yves Hervouet (Hong Kong: The Chinese University Press, 1978), p. 492 [bibliographic entry by James T.C. Liu (Liu Zijian)]; Ronald C. Egan, *The Literary Works of Ou-yang Hsiu (1007-72)* (Cambridge and New York: Cambridge University Press, 1984), esp. pp. 1-11 [introduction]; Rainer von Franz, "Ou-yang Hsiu," in *The Indiana Companion to Traditional Chinese Literature*, edited and compiled by William H. Nienhauser, Jr. (Bloomington, Ind. and Indianapolis: Indiana University Press, 1986-1998), vol. 1, pp. 639-641, and vol. 2, pp. 386-387; *Beijing tushu guan guji shanben shumu*, compiled by Beijing tushu guan [Beijing: Shumu wenxian chuban she, n.d. (1987)], vol. 4, pp. 2123-2124; *Guoli zhongyang tushu guan tecang xuan lu*, compiled and edited by Guoli zhongyang tushu guan tecang zu, rev. ed. (Taibei: Guoli zhongyang tushu guan, 1989), p. 25, fig. 18 [color; 1 selected leaf (*juan* 43/1a) illustrated]; J. Sören Edgren, "Southern Song Printing at Hangzhou," *Bulletin of the Museum of Far Eastern Antiquities* 61 (1989), p. 124, Bibliography B, no. 083; Susan Cherniack, "Book Culture and Textual Transmission in Sung China," *Harvard Journal of Asiatic Studies* 54, no. 1 (June 1994), pp. 5-102; Jean-Pierre Drège, "Des effets de l'imprimerie en Chine sous la dynastie des Song," *Journal asiatique* 282, no. 2 (1994), pp. 409-442, accompanied by summary in English, p. 442; Yang Yanping, "Song dai de Jiangxi ke shu," *Wenxian*, no. 69 (1996, no. 3), pp. 186-187; *Zhongguo guojia tushu guan guji zhenpin tulu*, edited by Ren Jiyu (Beijing: Beijing tushu guan chuban she, 1999), pp. 42-43, cat. no. 46 [2 selected half-folios showing general table of contents and the beginning of *juan* 1, and 2 cases containing 12 other stitch-bound volumes of this work].

4

Comprehensive Record of Imperially Sanctioned Remedies Revised during the Dade Reign Period, 200 *juan*

大德重校聖濟總錄二百卷

Zhongguo yinben shuji zhanlan mulu, compiled and edited by Beijing tushu guan (Beijing: Zhongyang renmin zhengfu wenhua bu shehui wenhua shiye guanli ju, 1952), p. 50, no. 267; *Zhongguo banke tulu*, compiled and edited by Beijing tushu guan, 2d rev. ed. (Beijing: Wenwu chuban she, 1961), vol. 1, p. 52, and vol. 4, pls. 274 and 275; *Guoli zhongyang tushu guan Jin Yuan ben tulu*, compiled and edited by Guoli zhongyang tushu guan (Taibei: Zhonghua congshu bianshen weiyuan hui, 1961), pp. 209-210, fig. 90 [1 selected half-folio illustrated]; *Sheng ji zonglu*, compiled by Zhao Ji [Emperor Huizong (1082-1135;

r. 1101-1125) and eleven members of the Imperial College of Physicians between 1111 and 1118] [Beijing: Renmin weisheng chuban she, 1962 (2d printing, 1982)], vols. 1-2, esp. vol. 1, pp. 511-527; Yu Shenchu, *Zhongguo yi xue jianshi* (Fuzhou: Fujian kexue jishu chuban she, 1983), p. 129; *Si bu zonglu yiyao bian*, compiled and edited by Ding Fubao and Zhou Yunqing (Originally published by Shangwu yinshu guan, 1955. Reprint. Beijing: Wenwu chuban she, 1984), vol. 2, pp. 486a-487b; *Beijing tushu guan guji shanben shumu*, compiled by Beijing tushu guan [Beijing: Shumu wenxian chuban she, n.d. (1987)], vol. 3, p. 1258; *Zhongguo yi xue da cidian*, compiled and edited by Xie Guan et al., reprint [N.p. (Beijing): Zhongguo shudian, 1988], vol. 3, pp. 3573-3574; *Guoli zhongyang tushu guan tecang xuan lu*, compiled and edited by Guoli zhongyang tushu guan tecang zu, rev. ed. (Taibei: Guoli zhongyang tushu guan, 1989), p. 90, fig. 70 [color; 1 selected leaf (*juan* 50/1a) illustrated].

5

New Compilation of the Text to the Play about Mulian Rescuing His Mother and Exhorting the World to Goodness, 3 *juan*

新編目連救母勸善戲文三卷

Zhongguo banhua shi tulu, [compiled by Zheng Zhenduo] (Shanghai: Zhongguo banhua shi she, 1940-1942), in vol. 5; Guo Weiqu, *Zhongguo banhua shi lüe* (Beijing: Zhaohua meishu chuban she, 1962), pp. 65-70 and fig. 35; Fu Xihua, *Zhongguo banhua yanjiu zhongyao shumu*, in *Shuhua shulu tieti fukan* (Hong Kong: Xianggang Zhong Mei tushu gongsi, 1969), p. 14a, no. 1237; "The Great Maudgalyayana Rescues His Mother from Hell," translated by Eugene Eoyang, in *Traditional Chinese Stories: Themes and Variations*, edited by Y.W. Ma and Joseph S.M. Lau (New York: Columbia University Press, 1978), pp. 443-455; Sewall Jerome Oertling, II, "Ting Yün-p'eng: A Chinese Artist of the Late Ming Dynasty" (Ph.D. diss., The University of Michigan, 1980), pp. 396-397; László Lörincz, *Molon Toyin's Journey into the Hell: Altan Gerel's Translation* (Budapest: Akadémiai Kiadó, 1982), pt. 1, pp. 5-12; *Ming dai banke zonglu* (8 *juan*), compiled and edited by Du Xinfu; reviewed and corrected by Zhou Guangpei and Jiang Xiaoda (Yangzhou: Jiangsu Guangling guji keyin she, 1983), *juan* 4/5b (in vol. 4); *Mulian jiu mu quan shan xiwen* [compiled by Zheng Zhizhen (fl. 1582)], Quan Ming chuanqi, [no. 68], Zhongguo xiju yanjiu ziliao, ser. 1 [Taibei: Tianyi chuban she, n.d. (1983)], vols. 1-3; *Zhongguo gudai banhua bai tu*, compiled and edited by Zhou Wu (Beijing: Renmin meishu chuban she, 1984), no. 29; *Hui pai banhua shi lun ji*, compiled and edited by Zhou Wu (Hefei, Anhui: Anhui renmin chuban she, 1984), text section, p. 54, and illustrations section, p. 4, figs. 12-13 [3 selected half-folios illustrated]; *Zhongguo guben xiqu chatu xuan*, compiled and edited by Zhou Wu (Tianjin: Tianjin renmin meishu chuban she, 1985), pp. 108-109, no. 65 [2 selected half-folios illustrated]; *Zhongguo gudai muke hua xuan ji*, compiled and edited by Zheng Zhenduo (Beijing: Renmin meishu chuban she, 1985), vol. 3 [unpaginated; halftone; 2 selected leaves illustrated]; *Beijing tushu guan guji shanben shumu*, compiled by Beijing tushu guan [Beijing: Shumu wenxian chuban she, n.d. (1987)], vol. 4, pp. 3067-3068; *Zhongguo meishu quanji: Huihua bian*, vol. 20, *Banhua*, compiled by Zhongguo meishu quanji bianji weiyuan hui (Shanghai: Shanghai renmin meishu chuban she, 1988), illustrations section, p. 84, no. 79 [halftone; 2 selected leaves illustrated], text section, p. 30, no. 79 [catalogue entry in Chinese; *Chûgoku kodai hanga ten: Machida shisei 30-shûnen kinen, Nitchû heiwa yûkô jôyaku teiketsu 10-shûnen kinen*, Chûgoku hanga 2000-

nen ten, dai 3 bu, compiled by Machida shiritsu kokusai hanga bijutsukan [and] Takimoto Hiroyuki (Machida, Japan: Machida shiritsu kokusai hanga bijutsukan, 1988), p. 108, cat. no. 5.6; *Ritual Opera, Operatic Ritual: "Mu-lien Rescues His Mother" in Chinese Popular Culture: Papers from the International Workshop on the Mu-lien Operas*, with an additional contribution on the Woman Huang legend by Beata Grant, edited by David Johnson [N. p. (Berkeley, Calif.): N.p. (Chinese Popular Culture Project), 1989], pp. 1-45 (David Johnson, "Actions Speak Louder Than Words: The Cultural Significance of Chinese Ritual Opera"); pp. 191-223 (Stephen F. Teiser, "The Ritual Behind the Opera: A Fragmentary Ethnography of the Ghost Festival, A.D. 400-1900"); and pp. 312-324 (Yao Dajuin, "The Mu-lien Operas: A Selective Bibliography"); *Ming dai banhua yishu tushu tezhan zhuanji (Exhibition of Graphic Art in Printed Books of the Ming Dynasty)*, edited by Guoli zhongyang tushu guan (National Central Library) [Taibei: Guoli zhongyang tushu guan (National Central Library), 1989], p. 329 [catalogue entry in Chinese and English]; Zhu Hengfu, "Ming Qing Mulian xi taiben liubian kao," *Wenxian*, no. 52 (1992, no. 2), pp. 42-58; Zhu Hengfu, "Mulian gushi zai shuochang wenxue zhong zhi liubian kao," *Wenxian*, no. 56 (1993, no. 2), pp. 27-47; Nancy Berliner, "Wang Tingna and Illustrated Book Publishing in Huizhou," *Orientations* 25, no. 1 (January 1994), pp. 68-69, and fig. 3; Liao Ben, *Zhongguo xiju tushi* (Zhengzhou, Henan: Henan jiaoyu chuban she, 1996), pp. 210-211, nos. 3-92 and 3-93 [halftone; 2 selected leaves illustrated], and p. 395, nos. 3-616 through 3-620 [halftone; 1 selected double-leaf and 4 selected photographs of woodblocks illustrated]; *Guben xiqu shi da mingzhu banhua quanbian*, compiled and edited by Shoudu tushu guan (Beijing: Xianzhuang shuju, 1996), vol. 1, pp. 406-427; *Zhongguo gudai fojiao banhua ji*, chief editor: Zhou Xinhui, co-editors: Chen Jian and Ma Wenda (Beijing: Xueyuan chuban she, 1998), vol. 2, illustrations section, pp. 104-106 [2 selected half-folios and 1 selected folio illustrated].

6

Illustrations and Explanations on Correct Cultivation

養正圖解不分卷

Zhongguo renming da cidian, compiled and edited by Zang Lihe et al. (Hong Kong: Taixing shuju, 1931), pp. 1175; *Zhongguo banhua shi tulu*, [compiled by Zheng Zhenduo] (Shanghai: Zhongguo banhua shi she, 1940-1942), in vol. 6; Tu Lien-chê, "Chiao Hung," in *Eminent Chinese of the Ch'ing Period (1644-1912)*, edited by Arthur W. Hummel, vol. 1 (Washington, D.C.: The Library of Congress; Washington, D.C.: United States Government Printing Office, 1943), pp. 145-146; Guo Weiqu, *Zhongguo banhua shi lüe* (Beijing: Zhaohua meishu chuban she, 1962), pp. 77-78; *Xidi shumu*, [6 *juan* (5 *juan*, *tiba* 1 *juan*)], compiled and edited by Beijing tushu guan [N.p. (Beijing): Wenwu chuban she, 1963], *juan* 1/20a (in vol. 1); Fu Xihua, *Zhongguo banhua yanjiu zhongyao shumu*, in *Shuhua shulu tieti fukan* (Hong Kong: Xianggang Zhong Mei tushu gongsi, 1969), p. 5b, no. 953; Sewall Jerome Oertling, II, "Ting Y̲n-p'eng: A Chinese Artist of the Late Ming Dynasty" (Ph.D. diss., The University of Michigan, 1980), pp. 396-403; *Ming dai banke zonglu* (8 *juan*), compiled and edited by Du Xinfu; reviewed and corrected by Zhou Guangpei and Jiang Xiaoda (Yangzhou: Jiangsu Guangling guji keyin she, 1983), *juan* 2/42b (in vol. 2), *juan* 3/3b (in vol. 3), *juan* 3/26a (in vol. 3), and *juan* 3/35a (in vol. 3); *Hui pai banhua shi lun ji*, compiled and edited by Zhou Wu (Hefei, Anhui: Anhui renmin chuban she, 1984), text section, pp. 55-56, and illustrations section, p. 7, figs. 22-23 [2 selected half-folios, 1 each from 2 editions, illustrated]; *Zhongguo gudai muke hua xuan ji*, compiled and edited by Zheng Zhenduo (Beijing: Renmin meishu chuban she, 1985), vol. 3 [unpaginated; halftone; 1

selected leaf illustrated]; Edward T. Ch'ien, *Chiao Hung and the Restructuring of Neo-Confucianism in the Late Ming*, Neo-Confucian Studies, sponsored by The Regional Seminar in Neo-Confucian Studies, Columbia University (New York: Columbia University Press, 1986), pp. 50-52, and p. 287, no. 37; *Chûgoku Min Shin no ehon* (Osaka: Ôsaka shiritsu bijutsukan, 1987), p. 79, cat. no. 154 [illustration], p. 124, cat. no. 154 [catalogue entry]; *Beijing tushu guan guji shanben shumu*, compiled by Beijing tushu guan [Beijing: Shumu wenxian chuban she, n.d. (1987)], vol. 2, p. 407; *Zhongguo meishu quanji: Huihua bian*, vol. 20, *Banhua*, compiled by Zhongguo meishu quanji bianji weiyuan hui (Shanghai: Shanghai renmin meishu chuban she, 1988), illustrations section, p. 47, no. 44 [halftone; 1 selected leaf illustrated], text section, p. 18, no. 44 [catalogue entry in Chinese]; *Chûgoku kodai hanga ten: Machida shisei 30-shûnen kinen, Nitchû heiwa yûkô jôyaku teiketsu 10-shûnen kinen*, Chûgoku hanga 2000-nen ten, dai 3 bu, compiled by Machida shiritsu kokusai hanga bijutsukan [and] Takimoto Hiroyuki (Machida, Japan: Machida shiritsu kokusai hanga bijutsukan, 1988), p. 189, cat. no. 6.74; *Yangzheng tujie* (2 *juan*), compiled by Jiao Hong, explanatory text by Wu Jixu, Wanwei biecang, vol. 62 [N.p. (Nanjing): Jiangsu guji chuban she, 1988]; *Ming dai banhua yishu tushu tezhan zhuanji (Exhibition of Graphic Art in Printed Books of the Ming Dynasty)*, edited by Guoli zhongyang tushu guan (National Central Library) [Taibei: Guoli zhongyang tushu guan (National Central Library), 1989], p. 54-57 [2 selected leaves illustrated], and p. 308 [catalogue entry in Chinese and English]; *Jinling gu banhua (Ancient Woodblock Prints in Jinling)*, compiled and edited by Zhou Wu (Nanjing: Jiangsu meishu chuban she, 1993), p. 314; Xia Wei, "The Huizhou Style of Woodcut Illustration," *Orientations* 25, no. 1 (January 1994), p. 65; Nancy Berliner, "Wang Tingna and Illustrated Book Publishing in Huizhou," *Orientations* 25, no. 1 (January 1994), pp. 69-71, and figs. 5-6; *Qing dai neifu ke shu mulu jieti*, compiled and edited by Gugong bowu yuan tushu guan and Liaoning sheng tushu guan (Beijing: Zijin cheng chuban she, 1995), pp. 290-291; Kobayashi Hiromitsu, *Chûgoku no hanga: Tôdai kara Shindai made (Chinese Woodblock Illustrations from the Tang through the Qing Dynasty)* (Tokyo: Tôshindô, 1995), p. 56, and p. 58, fig. 060; *Jiaye tang cang shu zhi*, compiled by Miao Quansun, Wu Changshou, and Dong Kang, reorganized and punctuated by Wu Ge (Shanghai: Fudan daxue chuban she, 1997), p. 400.

7

Complete and Illustrated Biographies of Transcendents, 9 *juan*

有象列仙全傳九卷

Exposition d'ouvrages illustrés de la dynastie Ming (Ming dai banhua shuji zhanlan hui mulu), [preface by Du Boqiu (Jean-Pierre Dubosc); introduction by Fu Xihua (Fou Hsi-houa)], [Beijing: Centre franco-chinois d'études sinologiques (Zhong Fa Han xue yanjiu suo), 1944], pp. 42-43, cat. no. 43 [catalogue entries in Chinese and French], and p. 145, no. 16 [caption to illustration in Chinese and French], and pl. 6, no. 16 [halftone; 1 selected leaf illustrated]; *Zhongguo yinben shuji zhanlan mulu*, compiled and edited by Beijing tushu guan (Beijing: Zhongyang renmin zhengfu wenhua bu shehui wenhua shiye guanli ju, 1952), p. 77, no. 512; Fu Xihua, *Zhongguo banhua yanjiu zhongyao shumu*, in *Shuhua shulu tieti fukan* (Hong Kong: Xianggang Zhong Mei tushu gongsi, 1969), p. 5a, no. 932; *Zhongguo gudian wenxue banhua xuanji*, edited by Fu Xihua (Shanghai: Shanghai renmin meishu chuban she, 1981), vol. 1, pp. 288-291, nos. 187-190 [4 selected leaves illustrated]; *Ming dai banke zonglu* (8 *juan*), compiled and edited by Du Xinfu; reviewed and corrected by

Zhou Guangpei and Jiang Xiaoda (Yangzhou: Jiangsu Guangling guji keyin she, 1983), *juan* 3/3b (in vol. 3); *Hui pai banhua shi lun ji*, compiled and edited by Zhou Wu (Hefei, Anhui: Anhui renmin chuban she, 1984), text section, p. 56, and illustrations section, p. 9, figs. 28-29 [2 selected half-folios illustrated]; *Zhongguo gudai muke hua xuan ji*, compiled and edited by Zheng Zhenduo (Beijing: Renmin meishu chuban she, 1985), vol. 3 [unpaginated; halftone; 4 selected leaves illustrated]; *Zhongguo shenhua chuanshuo cidian*, compiled and edited by Yuan Ke (Shanghai: Shanghai cishu chuban she, 1985); Stephen W. Durrant, "Lieh-hsien chuan," in *The Indiana Companion to Traditional Chinese Literature*, edited and compiled by William H. Nienhauser et al. (Bloomington, Ind.: Indiana University Press, 1986; reissued in 1998 as vol. 1 of 2), pp. 566-567; *Chûgoku Min Shin no ehon* (Osaka: Ôsaka shiritsu bijutsukan, 1987), p. 43, cat. no. 81 [illustration], p. 43, cat. no. 81 [catalogue entry]; *Beijing tushu guan guji shanben shumu*, compiled by Beijing tushu guan [Beijing: Shumu wenxian chuban she, n.d. (1987)], vol. 3, p. 1669; Kobayashi Hiromitsu, "Figure Compositions in Seventeenth-Century Chinese Prints and Their Influences on Edo-Period Japanese Painting Manuals" (Ph.D. diss., University of California, Berkeley, 1987), pp. 25-35; *Liexian quan zhuan*, reprinted in *Zhongguo gudai banhua congkan*, compiled and edited by Zheng Zhenduo (Shanghai: Shanghai guji chuban she, 1988), vol. 3, pp. 3-328, with postscript by Shanghai guji chuban she; *Zhongguo minjian xinyang ziliao huibian*, ser. 1, edited by Wang Qiugui and Li Fengmao (Taibei: Taiwan Xuesheng shuju, 1989), vol. 1, tiyao, pp. 7-9 [introductory text by Li Fengmao]; *You xiang Liexian quan zhuan*, [compiled and edited by Wang Yunpeng], *Zhongguo minjian xinyang ziliao huibian*, edited by Wang Qiugui and Li Fengmao, ser. 1, vol. 6. Zheng bian, no. 5 (Taibei: Taiwan Xuesheng shuju, 1989); *Zhonghua shenmi wenhua cidian*, edited by Wu Kang et al. (Haikou, Hainan: Hainan chuban she, 1993); Anne Birrell, *Chinese Mythology: An Introduction* (Baltimore and London: The Johns Hopkins University Press, 1993), esp. pp. 1-22 [introduction]; Suzanne E. Cahill, *Transcendence and Divine Passion: The Queen Mother of the West in Medieval China* (Stanford, Calif.: Stanford University Press, 1993); Kobayashi Hiromitsu, *Chûgoku no hanga: Tôdai kara Shindai made (Chinese Woodblock Illustrations from the Tang through the Qing Dynasty)* (Tokyo: Tôshindô, 1995), p. 43, and p. 46, fig. 043; *Guben xiaoshuo banhua tulu*, compiled and edited by Shoudu tushu guan (Beijing: Xianzhuang shuju, 1996), vol. 7, figs. 391-398 [8 selected leaves illustrated]; *Zhongguo shenxian huaxiang ji*, compiled and edited by Cheng Yin (Shanghai: Shanghai guji chuban she, 1996); *Liexian quan zhuan* (Shijiazhuang, Hebei: Hebei meishu chuban she, 1996); Ingrid Fischer-Schreiber, *The Shambhala Dictionary of Taoism*, translated [from the German] by Werner Wˌnsche (Boston: Shambhala Publications, Inc., 1996), pp. 49-51, and pp. 54-55; *In Search of the Supernatural: The Written Record*, translated by Kenneth J. DeWoskin and J.I. Crump, Jr. (Stanford, Calif.: Stanford University Press, 1996), pp. xxiii-xxxvi; Stephen R. Bokenkamp, *Early Daoist Scriptures*, with a contribution by Peter Nickerson (Berkeley and Los Angeles: University of California Press, 1997), pp. 21-23; Shen Jin, *Meiguo Hafo daxue Hafo Yanjing tushu guan Zhongwen shanben shu zhi* (Shanghai: Shanghai cishu chuban she, 1999), p. 518, cat. no. 0921.

8

Manual of Paintings by Famous Masters of Successive Periods

歷代名公畫譜

Zhongguo yinben shuji zhanlan mulu, compiled and edited by Beijing tushu guan (Beijing: Zhongyang renmin zhengfu wenhua bu shehui wenhua shiye guanli ju, 1952), p. 77, no. 523; *Zhongguo banke tulu*, compiled and edited by Beijing tushu guan, 2d rev. ed. (Beijing: Wenwu chuban she, 1961), vol. 1, p. 107, and vol. 8, pls. 672 and 673; Guo Weiqu, *Zhongguo banhua shi lüe* (Beijing: Zhaohua meishu chuban she, 1962), pp. 96-100 and fig. 47; Fu Xihua, *Zhongguo banhua yanjiu zhongyao shumu*, in *Shuhua shulu tieti fukan* (Hong Kong: Xianggang Zhong Mei tushu gongsi, 1969), p. 1a, no. 820; *Ming dai banke zonglu* (8 *juan*), compiled and edited by Du Xinfu; reviewed and corrected by Zhou Guangpei and Jiang Xiaoda (Yangzhou: Jiangsu Guangling guji keyin she, 1983), *juan* 7/20a (in vol. 7) and *juan* 8/6a (in vol. 7); *Hui pai banhua shi lun ji*, compiled and edited by Zhou Wu (Hefei, Anhui: Anhui renmin chuban she, 1984), text section, p. 65, and illustrations section, pp. 63-64, figs. 180-184 [6 selected half-folios from 5 editions illustrated]; *Zhongguo gudai banhua bai tu*, compiled and edited by Zhou Wu (Beijing: Renmin meishu chuban she, 1984), no. 43; *Zhongguo gudai muke hua xuan ji*, compiled and edited by Zheng Zhenduo (Beijing: Renmin meishu chuban she, 1985), vol. 3 [unpaginated; halftone; 1 selected leaf and 1 selected double-leaf illustrated]; Joseph Needham, *Science and Civilisation in China*, vol. 5, *Chemistry and Chemical Technology*, pt. 1, *Paper and Printing*, by Tsien Tsuen-hsuin (Cambridge and New York: Cambridge University Press, 1985), pp. 264-265, and fig. 1175; *Chûgoku Min Shin no ehon* (Osaka: Ôsaka shiritsu bijutsukan, 1987), p. 63, cat. no. 120 [illustration], p. 121, cat. no. 120 [catalogue entry]; *Beijing tushu guan guji shanben shumu*, compiled by Beijing tushu guan [Beijing: Shumu wenxian chuban she, n.d. (1987)], vol. 3, p. 1353; Kobayashi Hiromitsu, "Figure Compositions in Seventeenth-Century Chinese Prints and Their Influences on Edo-Period Japanese Painting Manuals" (Ph.D. diss., University of California, Berkeley, 1987), pp. 160-163; *Zhongguo meishu quanji: Huihua bian*, vol. 20, *Banhua*, compiled by Zhongguo meishu quanji bianji weiyuan hui (Shanghai: Shanghai renmin meishu chuban she, 1988), illustrations section, p. 154, no. 149 [halftone; 1 selected leaf illustrated], text section, p. 54, no. 149 [catalogue entry in Chinese]; *Chûgoku kodai hanga ten: Machida shisei 30-shûnen kinen, Nitchû heiwa yûkô jôyaku teiketsu 10-shûnen kinen*, Chûgoku hanga 2000-nen ten, dai 3 bu, compiled by Machida shiritsu kokusai hanga bijutsukan [and] Takimoto Hiroyuki (Machida, Japan: Machida shiritsu kokusai hanga bijutsukan, 1988), p. 186, cat. nos. 6.72; *Gu shi hua pu*, reprinted in *Zhongguo gudai banhua congkan*, compiled and edited by Zheng Zhenduo (Shanghai: Shanghai guji chuban she, 1988), vol. 3, pp. 331-578, with postscript by Beijing daxue tushu guan; Kobayashi Hiromitsu, "Chûgoku kaigashi ni okeru hanga no igi: Ko shi gafu (1603-nen kan) ni miru rekidai meiga fukusei o megutte," *Bijutsushi*, no. 128 (vol. 39, no. 2) (March 1990): pp. 123-135 [accompanied by résumé in English, "Significances of Pictorial Printing in the History of Chinese Painting–A Study of the 1603 'Gushi huapu' Painting Manual," résumé section, reverse pagination, pp. 1-2]; *Kinsei Nihon kaiga to gafu, edehon ten: Meiga o unda hanga*, compiled and edited by Machida shiritsu kokusai hanga bijutsukan (Machida, Japan: Machida shiritsu kokusai hanga bijutsukan, 1990), vol. 2, pp. 18-19, cat. no. 3 (3-1, 3-2, 3-3, 3-4, 3-5, 3-6, 3-7, 3-8) [halftone; 8 selected double-leaves from 2 copies of the 1603 edition recompiled by Gu Sanxi and Gu Sanpin illustrated], and vol. 2, p. 179, cat. no. 3 [captions in Japanese]; Kobayashi Hiromitsu, *Chûgoku no hanga: Tôdai kara Shindai made (Chinese Woodblock Illustrations from the Tang through the Qing Dynasty)* (Tokyo: Tôshindô, 1995), p. 63, and p. 64, fig. 068, pp. 65, 91, 94, and 99, and p. 101, fig. 109, and p. 102, figs. 110, 111, and p. 104, fig. 113, and pp. 105 and 108; Michela Bussotti, "The 'Gushi huapu,' a Ming Dynasty Wood-Block Printing Masterpiece in the Naples National Library," *Ming Qing yanjiu* 4 (1995), pp. 11-44; Julia K. Murray, "Gaozong," in *The Dictionary of Art*, edited by Jane Turner (New York: Grove's Dictionaries, Inc., 1996), vol. 12, p. 52; Craig Clunas, *Pictures and Visuality in Early Modern China* (Princeton: Princeton University Press, 1997), pp. 138-148 [text], and figs. 74-76 [3 selected leaves illustrated], and pp. 201-202 [notes]; *Zhongguo gudai fojiao banhua ji*, chief editor: Zhou Xinhui, co-editors: Chen Jian and Ma Wenda (Beijing: Xueyuan chuban she, 1998), vol. 2, illustrations section, pp. 123-126 [4 selected half-folios illustrated].

9

Ink Garden of the Cheng Family, 12 *juan*, with Supplement of Writings by Various Personalities, 8 *juan*

程氏墨苑十二卷附錄人文爵里八卷

Zhongguo banhua shi tulu, [compiled by Zheng Zhenduo] (Shanghai: Zhongguo banhua shi she, 1940-1942), in vol. 7; *Exposition d'ouvrages illustrés de la dynastie Ming (Ming dai banhua shuji zhanlan hui mulu)*, [preface by Du Boqiu (Jean-Pierre Dubosc); introduction by Fu Xihua (Fou Hsi-houa)], [Beijing: Centre franco-chinois d'études sinologiques (Zhong Fa Han xue yanjiu suo), 1944], pp. 16-17, cat. no. 17 [catalogue entries in Chinese and French]; Zhao Wanli, "Cheng shi mo yuan za kao," *Zhong Fa Han xue yanjiu suo tushu guan guankan (Scripta Sinica: Bulletin bibliographique du Centre franco-chinois d'études sinologiques)*, no. 2 (1946), pp. 1-9 [accompanied by résumé in French, Tchao Wan-li, "À propos du Mouo yuan de Tch'eng Ta-yue," ii-iii]; *Zhongguo yinben shuji zhanlan mulu*, compiled and edited by Beijing tushu guan (Beijing: Zhongyang renmin zhengfu wenhua bu shehui wenhua shiye guanli ju, 1952), p. 77, no. 526; *Zhongguo banke tulu*, compiled and edited by Beijing tushu guan, 2d rev. ed. (Beijing: Wenwu chuban she, 1961), vol. 1, p. 108, and vol. 8, pl. 675; Guo Weiqu, *Zhongguo banhua shi lüe* (Beijing: Zhaohua meishu chuban she, 1962), pp. 108-110 and fig. 50; *Chinese Art: Painting, Calligraphy, Stone Rubbing, Wood Engraving*, by Werner Speiser, Roger Goepper, and Jean Fribourg, translated by Diana Imber (New York: Universe Books, Inc., 1964), pp. 280-281, no. 130; Fu Xihua, *Zhongguo banhua yanjiu zhongyao shumu*, in *Shuhua shulu tieti fukan* (Hong Kong: Xianggang Zhong Mei tushu gongsi, 1969), p. 3b, no. 874; K. T. Wu, "Ch'eng Ta-yüeh," in *Dictionary of Ming Biography, 1368-1644*, edited by L. Carrington Goodrich and Chaoying Fang (New York and London: Columbia University Press, 1976), vol. 1, pp. 212-215; Yu-ho Tseng Ecke, "Ting Yün-p'eng," in *Dictionary of Ming Biography, 1368-1644*, edited by L. Carrington Goodrich and Chaoying Fang (New York and London: Columbia University Press, 1976), vol. 2, pp. 1289-1290; Sewall Jerome Oertling, II, "Ting Yün-p'eng: A Chinese Artist of the Late Ming Dynasty" (Ph.D. diss., The University of Michigan, 1980), pp. 393-401, 403-404, 410-412; Yin Runsheng, "Pinglun Fang Yulu yu Cheng Junfang liang jia mo dian," *Gugong bowu yuan yuankan (Palace Museum Journal)*, no. 14 (1981, no. 4), pp.44-48; Zhou Wu, "Hui pai banhua," *Duoyun*, no. 4 (November 1982), pp. 142-143; *Ming dai banke zonglu* (8 *juan*), compiled and edited by Du Xinfu; reviewed and corrected by Zhou Guangpei and Jiang Xiaoda (Yangzhou: Jiangsu Guangling guji keyin she, 1983), *juan* 5/1b (in vol. 5); Wang Zhongmin, *Zhongguo shanben shu tiyao* (Shanghai: Shanghai guji chuban she, 1983), p. 305; *Hui pai banhua shi lun ji*, compiled and edited by Zhou Wu (Hefei, Anhui: Anhui renmin chuban she, 1984), text section, p. 57, and illustrations section, pp. 17-19, figs. 47-55 [10 selected half-folios illustrated]; J. Sören Edgren, *Chinese Rare Books in American Collections* (New York: China Institute in America, 1984), pp. 104-105, cat. no. 30; *Zhongguo gudai banhua bai tu*, compiled and edited by Zhou Wu (Beijing: Renmin meishu chuban she, 1984), no. 36; *Zhongguo gudai muke hua xuan ji*, compiled and edited by Zheng Zhenduo (Beijing: Renmin meishu chuban she, 1985), vol. 3 [unpaginated; halftone; 4 selected leaves illustrated]; Cai Hongru, "Ming dai zhi mo mingjia Cheng Junfang ji qi 'Mo yuan,'" *Wenwu*, no. 346 (1985, no. 3) (March 1985), pp. 33-35; Chûgoku Min Shin no ehon (Osaka: Ôsaka shiritsu bijutsukan, 1987), p. 67, cat. no. 130 [illustration], p. 122, cat. no. 130 [catalogue entry]; *Beijing tushu guan guji shanben shumu*, compiled by Beijing tushu guan [Beijing: Shumu wenxian chuban she, n.d. (1987)], vol. 3, p. 1371; *Chûgoku kodai hanga ten: Machida shisei 30-shûnen kinen, Nitchû heiwa yûkô jôyaku teiketsu 10-shûnen kinen*, Chûgoku hanga 2000-nen ten, dai 3 bu, compiled by Machida shiritsu kokusai hanga bijutsukan [and] Takimoto Hiroyuki (Machida, Japan: Machida shiritsu kokusai hanga bijutsukan, 1988), pp. 232-233, cat. nos. 9.1 and 9.2; *Ming dai banhua yishu tushu tezhan zhuanji (Exhibition of Graphic Art in Printed Books of the Ming Dynasty)*, edited by Guoli zhongyang tushu guan (National Central Library) [Taibei: Guoli zhongyang tushu guan (National Central Library), 1989], pp. 114-119 [6 selected leaves illustrated], p. 255, fig. 16 [1 selected leaf illustrated], p. 258, fig. 19 [1 selected leaf illustrated], p. 262, no. 4 [1 selected double-leaf illustrated], p. 265, fig. 13 [1 selectecd leaf illustrated], p. 286, fig. 5 [1 selected leaf illustrated], and p. 299, fig. 11 [1 selected double-leaf illustrated]; *Cheng shi mo yuan*, [compiled by Cheng Dayue], reprint, 12 vols. in 2 cases (Beijing: Zhongguo shudian, 1990); Monique Cohen and Nathalie Monnet, *Impressions de Chine* (Paris: Bibliothèque Nationale, 1992), pp. 101-102, cat. nô. 66 [halftone; 2 selected leaves illustrated]; Cai Meifen [Tsai Mei-fen], "Ming dai de mo yu mo shu (Inkcakes and Books on Ink during the Ming Dynasty)," in *Zhonghua minguo jianguo bashi nian Zhongguo yishu wenwu taolun hui: Lunwen ji: Qi wu (International Colloquium on Chinese Art History, 1991: Proceedings: Antiquities)*, compiled and edited by Guoli gugong bowu yuan bianji weiyuan hui [Taibei: Guoli gugong bowu yuan (National Palace Museum), 1992], pt. 2, pp. 681-725 [in Chinese; includes abstract in English, 683-687; see also 4 unnumbered pages of color plates with 7 illustrations at beginning of volume]; *Manmu linlang: Guoli zhongyang tushu guan shanben tecang (A Cornucopia of Rare Editions: The National Central Library's Rare Book Collection)*, compiled by Guoli zhongyang tushu guan (National Central Library) [Taibei: Guoli zhongyang tushu guan (National Central Library), 1993], pp. 120-121 [2 selected leaves illustrated], and p. 166 [catalogue entry in English]; Nancy Berliner, "Wang Tingna and Illustrated Book Publishing in Huizhou," *Orientations* 25, no. 1 (January 1994), p. 69; *Cheng shi mo yuan*, reprinted in *Zhongguo gudai banhua congkan er bian*, compiled and edited by Shanghai guji chuban she (Shanghai: Shanghai guji chuban she, 1994), vol. 6, pts. 1-2, with postscript by Li Zhitan; Kobayashi Hiromitsu, *Chûgoku no hanga: Tôdai kara Shindai made (Chinese Woodblock Illustrations from the Tang through the Qing Dynasty)* (Tokyo: Tôshindô, 1995), pp. 75-78, and figs. 080, 081, 082, 083, and 084; *The Dictionary of Art*, edited by Jane Turner (New York: Grove's Dictionaries, Inc., 1996), vol. 7, pp. 91-94, and fig. 310; Zheng Zhenduo, *Zheng Zhenduo shuhua*, edited by Jiang Deming, selected by Zheng Erkang (Beijing: Beijing chuban she, 1996), pp. 298-299; *Cong Beijing dao Fan'ersai: Zhong Fa meishu jiaoliu (From Beijing to Versailles: Artistic Relations between China and France)* [Hong Kong: Xianggang shizheng ju (Urban Council, Hong Kong), 1997], pp. 150-151, cat. no. 46; Craig Clunas, *Pictures and Visuality in Early Modern China* (Princeton: Princeton University Press, 1997), pp. 173-174 [text], and fig. 91 [1 selected leaf illustrated], and p. 204 [notes]; Wai-fong Anita Siu, "Ink-making in China," *Orientations* 28, no. 6 (June 1997), pp. 54-60; Lin Li-chiang, "The Proliferation of Images: The Ink-Stick Designs and the Printing of the 'Fang-shih mo-p'u' and the 'Ch'eng-shih mo-yüan'" (Ph.D. diss., Princeton University, 1998), vol. 1, pp. 1-229, and vol. 2, esp. figs. 2.1, 2.2, 2.3, 5.4, 5.5, and 5.6; *Zhongguo gudai fojiao banhua ji*, chief editor: Zhou Xinhui, co-editors: Chen Jian and Ma

Wenda (Beijing: Xueyuan chuban she, 1998), vol. 2, illustrations section, pp. 145-150 [6 selected half-folios illustrated]; James Cahill, "Chinese Painting: Innovation After 'Progress' Ends," *China: 5,000 Years: Innovation and Transformation in the Arts*, selected by Sherman Lee (New York: Guggenheim Museum Publications, 1998), pp. 186-187; *Zhongguo guojia tushu guan guji zhenpin tulu*, edited by Ren Jiyu (Beijing: Beijing tushu guan chuban she, 1999), p. 197, cat. no. 221 [1 selected half-folio from *juan 1, xia*, of another impression in the library's collection illustrated].

10

Manual of Weiqi Strategies Carefully Edited by the Gentleman Zuoyin, 2 *juan*

坐隱先生精訂捷徑奕譜二卷

Horace F. Cheshire, *Goh, or Wei Chi: A Handbook of the Game and Full Instruction for Play*, introduction & critical notes by T. Komatsubara (Hastings, Eng.: Horace F. Cheshire, 1911); *Zhongguo banhua shi tulu*, [compiled by Zheng Zhenduo] (Shanghai: Zhongguo banhua shi she, 1940-1942), in vol. 6; *Exposition d'ouvrages illustrés de la dynastie Ming (Ming dai banhua shuji zhanlan hui mulu)*, [preface by Du Boqiu (Jean-Pierre Dubosc); introduction by Fu Xihua (Fou Hsi-houa)], [Beijing: Centre franco-chinois d'études sinologiques (Zhong Fa Han xue yanjiu suo), 1944], pp. 22-23, cat. no. 23 [catalogue entries in Chinese and French], and p. 142, no. 8 [caption to illustration in Chinese and French], and pl. 3, no. 8 [halftone; 2 selected leaves illustrated]; Edward Lasker, *Modern Chess Strategy, with an Appendix on Go* (Philadelphia: David McKay Company, 1945), pp. 369-436 ["The Game of Go"]; Guo Weiqu, *Zhongguo banhua shi lüe* (Beijing: Zhaohua meishu chuban she, 1962), pp. 56-58; *Xidi shumu*, [6 juan (5 juan, tiba 1 juan)], compiled and edited by Beijing tushu guan [N.p. (Beijing): Wenwu chuban she, 1963], *juan 2/25b*, no. 10325 (in vol. 2); Fu Xihua, *Zhongguo banhua yanjiu zhongyao shumu*, in *Shuhua shulu tieti fukan* (Hong Kong: Xianggang Zhong Mei tushu gongsi, 1969), p. 4a, no. 890; *Huancui tang yuan jing tu* (Beijing: Renmin meishu chuban she, 1981); Zhou Wu, "Wang Tingna yu Hu Zhengyan: Ji Ming dai liang wei chuban jia," *Duoyun*, no. 2 (November 1981), pp. 154-156; Zhou Wu, "Hui pai banhua," *Duoyun*, no. 4 (November 1982), pp. 140-145, continued on p. 147; *Ming dai banke zonglu (8 juan)*, compiled and edited by Du Xinfu; reviewed and corrected by Zhou Guangpei and Jiang Xiaoda (Yangzhou: Jiangsu Guangling guji keyin she, 1983), *juan 7/11b* (in vol. 7); *Hui pai banhua shi lun ji*, compiled and edited by Zhou Wu (Hefei, Anhui: Anhui renmin chuban she, 1984), text section, pp. 16-18, 54, and 66, and illustrations section, pp. 68-69, fig. 193 (1-3) [3 selected sections of woodblock-printed handscroll illustrated], and pp. 74-76, fig. 203 (1-6) [6 half-folios illustrated]; *Zhongguo gudai muke hua xuan ji*, compiled and edited by Zheng Zhenduo (Beijing: Renmin meishu chuban she, 1985), vol. 4 [unpaginated; halftone; 2 selected sections illustrated]; *Zhongguo weiqi (Chûgoku no igo) (China Weiqi)*, edited by Liu Shancheng, proofread by Shurong qi yuan (Chengdu: Sichuan kexue jishu chuban she; Chengdu: Shurong qi yi chuban she, 1985), esp. pp. 1-406 and pp. 591-833; *Chûgoku Min Shin no ehon* (Osaka: Ôsaka shiritsu bijutsukan, 1987), p. 76, cat. no. 147 [illustration], p. 123, cat. no. 147 [catalogue entry]; *Beijing tushu guan guji shanben shumu*, compiled by Beijing tushu guan [Beijing: Shumu wenxian chuban she, n.d. (1987)], vol. 3, p. 1365; *Zhongguo meishu quanji: Huihua bian*, vol. 20, Banhua, compiled by Zhongguo meishu quanji bianji weiyuan hui (Shanghai: Shanghai renmin meishu chuban she, 1988), illustrations section, p. 66, no. 62 [halftone; 4 selected leaves illustrated], text section, p.

24, no. 62 [catalogue entry in Chinese]; *Chûgoku kodai hanga ten: Machida shisei 30-shûnen kinen, Nitchû heiwa yûkô jôyaku teiketsu 10-shûnen kinen*, Chûgoku hanga 2000-nen ten, dai 3 bu, compiled by Machida shiritsu kokusai hanga bijutsukan [and] Takimoto Hiroyuki (Machida, Japan: Machida shiritsu kokusai hanga bijutsukan, 1988), p. 143, cat. no. 5.89; *Jinling gu banhua (Ancient Woodblock Prints in Jinling)*, compiled and edited by Zhou Wu (Nanjing: Jiangsu meishu chuban she, 1993), pp. 262-265; Xu Shuofang, *Wan Ming qujia nianpu* (Hangzhou: Zhejiang guji chuban she, 1993), vol. 3, *Gan Wan juan*, pp. 505-545, esp. pp. 540-542; Nancy Berliner, "Wang Tingna and Illustrated Book Publishing in Huizhou," *Orientations* 25, no. 1 (January 1994), pp. 70-75, and fig. 11; Kobayashi Hiromitsu, *Chûgoku no hanga: Tôdai kara Shindai made (Chinese Woodblock Illustrations from the Tang through the Qing Dynasty)* (Tokyo: Tôshindô, 1995), p. 53, and p. 55, fig. 056, and pp. 56, 59, and 66; *Zhongguo Jiade '95 chun ji paimai hui: Guji shanben (China Guardian '95 Spring Auctions: Rare Books)* [Beijing: Zhongguo Jiade guoji paimai youxian gongsi (China Guardian Auctions Co., Ltd.), 1995], lot no. 455 [2 selected double-spreads illustrated; see also detail of illustrated folio on front cover]; *Lidai xijian shukan ziliao paimai hui* (Beijing: Zhongguo shudian, 1996), lot no. 77 [1 selected double-spread illustrated]; Robert E. Hegel, *Reading Illustrated Fiction in Late Imperial China* (Stanford, Calif.: Stanford University Press, 1998), pp. 145-146, and table 3.10.

11

Newly Annotated Edition of the Story of the Western Wing, Based on Classic Editions, 6 *juan*

新校注古本西廂記六卷

Gao Mingben huitu Xin jiaozhu guben Xixiang ji (6 *juan*), [by Wang Shifu; edited and annotated by Wang Jide; with additional commentaries by Xu Wei], reprint [originally published Shanyin: Wang shi Xiangxue ju, 1614] (Beiping: Fujin hushe; Beiping: Donglai shudian, 1929); Bo Songnian, "Tan Ming kanben Xixiang ji chatu," *Meishu yanjiu*, no. 8 (1958, no. 4), pp. 45-47 [see also 6 illustrations preceding text]; Guo Weiqu, *Zhongguo banhua shi lüe* (Beijing: Zhaohua meishu chuban she, 1962), pp. 72-73; *Xidi shumu*, [6 *juan* (5 *juan*, tiba 1 *juan*)], compiled and edited by Beijing tushu guan [N.p. (Beijing): Wenwu chuban she, 1963], juan 5/34b, no. 10609 (in vol. 5); Fu Xihua, *Zhongguo banhua yanjiu zhongyao shumu*, in *Shuhua shulu tieti fukan* (Hong Kong: Xianggang Zhong Mei tushu gongsi, 1969), p. 12b, no. 1176; *Koten hyakushu (One Hundred Classics in the Tenri Central Library)* [Tokyo: Tenri gyararî (Tenri Gallery), 1972], cat. no. 61; Thomas Lawton, "Ch'ien Ku," in *Dictionary of Ming Biography, 1368-1644*, edited by L. Carrington Goodrich and Chaoying Fang (New York and London: Columbia University Press, 1976), vol. 1, pp. 236-237; "The Story of Ying-ying," translated by James R. Hightower, in *Traditional Chinese Stories: Themes and Variations*, edited by Y.W. Ma and Joseph S.M. Lau (New York: Columbia University Press, 1978), pp. 139-145; *Zôtei Minkan Gen zatsugeki Seishôki mokuroku*, compiled and edited by Denda Akira (Tokyo: Kyôko shoin, 1979); Jiang Xingyu, *Ming kan ben Xixiang ji yanjiu* (Beijing: Zhongguo xiju chuban she, 1982), esp. pp. 128-162; *Ming dai banke zonglu* (8 *juan*), compiled and edited by Du Xinfu; reviewed and corrected by Zhou Guangpei and Jiang Xiaoda (Yangzhou: Jiangsu Guangling guji keyin she, 1983), juan 3/36b-37a (in vol. 3); Wang Zhongmin, *Zhongguo shanben shu tiyao* (Shanghai: Shanghai guji chuban she, 1983), p. 688; *Hui pai banhua shi lun ji*, compiled and edited by Zhou Wu (Hefei, Anhui: Anhui renmin chuban she, 1984), text section, p. 68, and illustrations section, pp. 90-91, figs. 232-234 [6 selected half-folios (3 double-

spreads) illustrated]; *Zhongguo guben xiqu chatu xuan*, compiled and edited by Zhou Wu (Tianjin: Tianjin renmin meishu chuban she, 1985), pp. 164-167, no. 88 [4 selected half-folios (2 double-spreads) illustrated]; *Zhongguo gudai muke hua xuan ji*, compiled and edited by Zheng Zhenduo (Beijing: Renmin meishu chuban she, 1985), vol. 4 [unpaginated; halftone; 2 selected facing leaves illustrated]; James M. Hargett, "Hsi-hsiang chi," in *The Indiana Companion to Traditional Chinese Literature*, edited and compiled by William H. Nienhauser et al. (Bloomington, Ind.: Indiana University Press, 1986; reissued in 1998 as vol. 1 of 2), pp. 407-409 [see also updated bibliography in vol. 2, pp. 320-321]; *Chûgoku Min Shin no ehon* (Osaka: Ôsaka shiritsu bijutsukan, 1987), p. 7, cat. no. 5 [illustration], p. 109, cat. no. 5 [catalogue entry]; *Beijing tushu guan guji shanben shumu*, compiled by Beijing tushu guan [Beijing: Shumu wenxian chuban she, n.d. (1987)], vol. 4, p. 3016; Jiang Xingyu, *Xixiang ji kaozheng* (Shanghai: Shanghai guji chuban she, 1988); *Zhongguo meishu quanji: Huihua bian*, vol. 20, *Banhua*, compiled by Zhongguo meishu quanji bianji weiyuan hui (Shanghai: Shanghai renmin meishu chuban she, 1988), illustrations section, p. 101, no. 96 [halftone; 2 selected leaves illustrated; figs. 15 and 16], text section, p. 36, no. 96 [catalogue entry in Chinese]; *Xixiang ji*, compiled and edited by Guoli gugong bowu yuan bianji weiyuan hui, Ming dai banhua congkan, no. 4. [facsimile reproduction of the copy of the 1614 edition of the *Xin jiaozhu guben Xixiang ji* published by Xiangxue ju in the possession of Guoli gugong bowu yuan (National Palace Museum)] (Taibei: Guoli gugong bowu yuan, 1988); *Xixiang ji jianshang cidian*, compiled and edited by He Xinhui and Zhu Jie [N.p. (Beijing): Zhongguo funü chuban she, 1990]; Wang Shifu, *The Moon and the Zither: "The Story of the Western Wing"*, edited and translated with an introduction by Stephen H. West and Wilt L. Idema, with a study of its woodblock illustrations by Yao Dajuin (Berkeley and Los Angeles: University of California Press, 1991), pp. 437-468, followed by 24 unnumbered pages of illustrations; see figs. 15, 16, 17, 38, and 62; Han Sheng, "'Xixiang ji' gujin banben mulu jiyao," in *Xixiang ji xin lun*, compiled and edited by Han Sheng, He Xinhui, and Fan Biao (Beijing: Zhongguo xiju chuban she, 1992), pp. 161-205; *"Seishôki to Mindai no sashiebon" ten*, compiled and edited by Machida shiritsu kokusai hanga bijutsukan [Machida City Museum of Graphic Arts] [Machida, Japan: Machida shiritsu kokusai hanga bijutsukan (Machida City Museum of Graphic Arts), 1993]; Xu Shuofang, *Wan Ming qujia nianpu* (Hangzhou: Zhejiang guji chuban she, 1993), vol. 2, *Zhejiang juan*, pp. 237-289, esp. pp. 280-281; Zhang Renhe, *"Xixiang ji" lunzheng* (Changchun, Jilin: Dongbei shifan daxue chuban she, 1995); *Guben xiqu shi da mingzhu banhua quanbian*, compiled and edited by Shoudu tushu guan (Beijing: Xianzhuang shuju, 1996), vol. 1, pp. 138-177.

12

Outlaws of the Marsh from the Hall of Loyalty and Righteousness, with Commentaries by the Gentleman Li Zhuowu, 100 *juan*, with Introduction, 1 *juan*

李卓吾先生批評忠義水滸傳一百卷引首一卷

All Men Are Brothers [Shui Hu Chuan], translated from the Chinese by Pearl S. Buck, 2 vols. (New York: The John Day Company, 1933. Reprint. 2 vols. New York: Grove Press, Inc., 1957); Richard Gregg Irwin, *The Evolution of a Chinese Novel: Shui-hu-chuan* (Cambridge, Mass.: Harvard University Press, 1953); *Shuihu yanjiu lunwen ji*, edited by Zuojia chuban she bianji bu (Beijing: Zuojia chuban she, 1957); Guo Weiqu, *Zhongguo banhua shi lüe* (Beijing: Zhaohua meishu chuban she, 1962), pp. 92-94 and fig. 41; *Ming*

Rongyu tang ke Shuihu zhuan tu, compiled and edited by Zhonghua shuju Shanghai bianji suo [facsimile reproduction of illustrations from the copy in the possession of the Beijing tushu guan] (Beijing: Zhonghua shuju, 1965); Fu Xihua, *Zhongguo banhua yanjiu zhongyao shumu*, in *Shuhua shulu tieti fukan* (Hong Kong: Xianggang Zhong Mei tushu gongsi, 1969), p. 10b, no. 1117; *Koten hyakushu (One Hundred Classics in the Tenri Central Library)* [Tokyo: Tenri gyararî (Tenri Gallery), 1972], cat. no. 64; K.C. Hsiao, "Li Chih," in *Dictionary of Ming Biography, 1368-1644*, edited by L. Carrington Goodrich and Chaoying Fang (New York and London: Columbia University Press, 1976), vol. 1, pp. 807-818; Winston L.Y. Yang, "Lo Kuan-chung," in *Dictionary of Ming Biography, 1368-1644*, edited by L. Carrington Goodrich and Chaoying Fang (New York and London: Columbia University Press, 1976), vol. 1, pp. 978-980; *Zhongguo gudian wenxue banhua xuanji*, edited by Fu Xihua (Shanghai: Shanghai renmin meishu chuban she, 1981), vol. 1, pp. 372-373, nos. 246-247 [2 selected leaves illustrated]; *Ming dai banke zonglu* (8 *juan*), compiled and edited by Du Xinfu; reviewed and corrected by Zhou Guangpei and Jiang Xiaoda (Yangzhou: Jiangsu Guangling guji keyin she, 1983), *juan* 4/2a (in vol. 4); *Hui pai banhua shi lun ji*, compiled and edited by Zhou Wu (Hefei, Anhui: Anhui renmin chuban she, 1984), text section, p. 67 and illustrations section, p. 80, figs. 211-212 [2 selected half-folios illustrated]; Anne Selina Farrer, "The 'Shui-hu chuan': A Study in the Development of Late Ming Woodblock Illustration" (Ph.D. thesis, University of London, 1984), vols. 1-2; *Zhongguo gudai muke hua xuan ji*, compiled and edited by Zheng Zhenduo (Beijing: Renmin meishu chuban she, 1985), vol. 4 [unpaginated; halftone; 2 selected leaves illustrated]; Y.W. Ma and Tai-loi Ma, "Shui-hu chuan," in *The Indiana Companion to Traditional Chinese Literature*, edited and compiled by William H. Nienhauser, Jr. (Bloomington, Ind. and Indianapolis: Indiana University Press, 1986-1998), vol. 1, pp. 712-716, and vol. 2, pp. 416-418; Shi Nai'an and Luo Guanzhong, *Outlaws of the Marsh: An Abridged Version*, translated by Sidney Shapiro [based on the unabridged version of *Outlaws of the Marsh* published by the Foreign Languages Press, Beijing, 1980] [Hong Kong: The Commercial Press (Hong Kong) Ltd., 1986; 4th impression, 1996]; *Chûgoku Min Shin no ehon* (Osaka: Ôsaka shiritsu bijutsukan, 1987), p. 37, cat. no. 69 [illustration], p. 116, cat. no. 69 [catalogue entry]; *Beijing tushu guan guji shanben shumu*, compiled by Beijing tushu guan [Beijing: Shumu wenxian chuban she, n.d. (1987)], vol. 4, p. 2909; Andrew H. Plaks, *The Four Masterworks of the Ming Novel* (Princeton: Princeton University Press, 1987), pp. 279-359, esp. pp. 288-289, and pp. 513-517; *Zhongguo meishu quanji: Huihua bian*, vol. 20, *Banhua*, compiled by Zhongguo meishu quanji bianji weiyuan hui (Shanghai: Shanghai renmin meishu chuban she, 1988), illustrations section, p. 134, no. 129 [halftone; 1 selected leaf illustrated], text section, p. 47, no. 129 [catalogue entry in Chinese]; Margaret Berry, *The Classic Chinese Novels: An Annotated Bibliography of Chiefly English-language Studies* (New York and London: Garland Publishing, Inc., 1988), pp. 91-125; Shi Nai'an and Luo Guanzhong, *Rongyu tang ben Shuihu zhuan*, edited and punctuated by Ling Geng, Heng He, and Diao Ning, 2 vols. (Shanghai: Shanghai guji chuban she, 1988); *The Broken Seals: Part One of "The Marshes of Mount Liang": A New Translation of the "Shuihu Zhuan" or "Water Margin" of Shi Nai'an and Luo Guanzhong*, translated by John Dent-Young and Alex Dent-Young (Hong Kong: The Chinese University Press, 1994), chapters 1-22 of the 120-chapter edition; Kobayashi Hiromitsu, *Chûgoku no hanga: Tôdai kara Shindai made* (Chinese Woodblock Illustrations from the Tang through the Qing Dynasty) (Tokyo: Tôshindô, 1995), p. 38, and fig. 033; *Guben xiaoshuo banhua tulu*, compiled and edited by Shoudu tushu guan (Beijing: Xianzhuang shuju, 1996), vol. 7, figs. 404-419 [16 selected leaves illustrated]; *The Tiger Killers: Part Two of "The Marshes of Mount Liang": A New Translation of the "Shuihu Zhuan" or "Water Margin" of Shi Nai'an and Luo Guanzhong*, translated by John Dent-Young and Alex Dent-Young (Hong Kong: The Chinese University Press, 1997), chapters 23-43 of the 120-chapter edition; Robert E. Hegel, *Reading Illustrated Fiction in Late Imperial China* (Stanford, Calif.: Stanford University Press, 1998), pp. 149-151, and fig. 3.11;

Zhongguo guojia tushu guan guji zhenpin tulu, edited by Ren Jiyu (Beijing: Beijing tushu guan chuban she, 1999), p. 171, cat. no. 188 [2 selected facing half-folios illustrated].

13

Illustrations from Selected Yuan Dramas, 1 *juan*
元曲選圖一卷

Zhongguo banhua shi tulu, [compiled by Zheng Zhenduo] (Shanghai: Zhongguo banhua shi she, 1940-1942), in vol. 6; *Exposition d'ouvrages illustrés de la dynastie Ming (Ming dai banhua shuji zhanlan hui mulu)*, [preface by Du Boqiu (Jean-Pierre Dubosc); introduction by Fu Xihua (Fou Hsi-houa)], [Beijing: Centre franco-chinois d'études sinologiques (Zhong Fa Han xue yanjiu suo), 1944], pp. 30-31, cat. no. 30 [catalogue entries in Chinese and French]; Guo Weiqu, *Zhongguo banhua shi lüe* (Beijing: Zhaohua meishu chuban she, 1962), p. 74 and fig. 38; *Xidi shumu*, [6 *juan* (5 *juan*, tiba 1 *juan*)], compiled and edited by Beijing tushu guan [N.p. (Beijing): Wenwu chuban she, 1963], *juan* 5/34a, no. 10521 (in vol. 5); Fu Xihua, *Zhongguo banhua yanjiu zhongyao shumu*, in *Shuhua shulu tieti fukan* (Hong Kong: Xianggang Zhong Mei tushu gongsi, 1969), p. 12a, no. 1166; Shih Chung-wen, *The Golden Age of Chinese Drama: Yüan "Tsa-chü"* (Princeton University Press, 1976); *Zhongguo gudian wenxue banhua xuanji*, edited by Fu Xihua (Shanghai: Shanghai renmin meishu chuban she, 1981), vol. 1, pp. 452-459, nos. 307-314 [8 selected leaves illustrated]; *Ming dai banke zonglu* (8 *juan*), compiled and edited by Du Xinfu; reviewed and corrected by Zhou Guangpei and Jiang Xiaoda (Yangzhou: Jiangsu Guangling guji keyin she, 1983), *juan* 5/13b (in vol. 5) and *juan* 6/15b (in vol. 6); *Hui pai banhua shi lun ji*, compiled and edited by Zhou Wu (Hefei, Anhui: Anhui renmin chuban she, 1984), text section, p. 68, and illustrations section, p. 94, figs. 240-241 [2 selected half-folios illustrated]; *Zhongguo guben xiqu chatu xuan*, compiled and edited by Zhou Wu (Tianjin: Tianjin renmin meishu chuban she, 1985), pp. 81-83, no. 52 [3 selected half-folios illustrated]; *Zhongguo gudai muke hua xuan ji*, compiled and edited by Zheng Zhenduo (Beijing: Renmin meishu chuban she, 1985), vol. 4 [unpaginated; halftone; 2 selected leaves illustrated]; Hsü Tao-Ching, *The Chinese Conception of the Theatre* (Seattle and London: University of Washington Press, 1985), pp. 255-265; *The Indiana Companion to Traditional Chinese Literature*, edited and compiled by William H. Nienhauser et al. (Bloomington, Ind.: Indiana University Press, 1986; reissued in 1998 as vol. 1 of 2), p. 780; *Chûgoku Min Shin no ehon* (Osaka: Ôsaka shiritsu bijutsukan, 1987), p. 20, cat. no. 15 [illustration], p. 110, cat. no. 15 [catalogue entry]; *Beijing tushu guan guji shanben shumu*, compiled by Beijing tushu guan [Beijing: Shumu wenxian chuban she, n.d. (1987)], vol. 4, p. 2999; *Chûgoku kodai hanga ten: Machida shisei 30-shûnen kinen, Nitchû heiwa yûkô jôyaku teiketsu 10-shûnen kinen*, Chûgoku hanga 2000-nen ten, dai 3 bu, compiled by Machida shiritsu kokusai hanga bijutsukan [and] Takimoto Hiroyuki (Machida, Japan: Machida shiritsu kokusai hanga bijutsukan, 1988), p. 121, cat. nos. 5.38 and 5.39; *Zhongguo meishu quanji: Huihua bian*, vol. 20, *Banhua*, compiled by Zhongguo meishu quanji bianji weiyuan hui (Shanghai: Shanghai renmin meishu chuban she, 1988), illustrations section, p. 107, no. 102 [halftone; 1 selected leaf illustrated], text section, p. 39, no. 102 [catalogue entry in Chinese]; *Ming dai banhua yishu tushu tezhan zhuanji (Exhibition of Graphic Art in Printed Books of the Ming Dynasty)*, edited by Guoli zhongyang tushu guan (National Central Library) [Taibei: Guoli zhongyang tushu guan (National Central Library), 1989], p. 288, fig.11 [1 selected leaf illustrated], p. 291, fig. 17 [1 selected leaf illustrated], and p. 329 [catalogue entry in Chinese and English]; Zheng Shangxian, "Zang Jinshu gaiding 'Yuan qu xuan' kao," *Wenxian*, no. 40 (1989, no. 2), pp. 50-56; Monique Cohen and Nathalie Monnet, *Impressions* de Chine (Paris: Bibliothèque Nationale, 1992), pp. 96-97, cat. no. 63 [halftone; 2 selected leaves from the Bogu tang edition illustrated]; Long Zhuangwei, "'Yuan qu xuan' 'yin shi' tanwei," *Wenxian*, no. 53 (1992, no. 3), pp. 40-49; *Jinling gu banhua (Ancient Woodblock Prints in Jinling)*, compiled and edited by Zhou Wu (Nanjing: Jiangsu meishu chuban she, 1993), pp. 309-311; Xu Shuofang, *Wan Ming qujia nianpu* (Hangzhou: Zhejiang guji chuban she, 1993), vol. 2, *Zhejiang juan*, pp. 441-485, esp. pp. 476-482; *Yuan qu xuan jiaozhu*, edited by Wang Xueqi (Shijiazhuang, Hebei: Hebei jiaoyu chuban she, 1994), vols. 1-4 in 8 pts.; *Yuan qu xuan tu*, reprinted in *Zhongguo gudai banhua congkan* er bian, compiled and edited by Shanghai guji chuban she (Shanghai: Shanghai guji chuban she, 1994), vol. 7, with postscript by Li Zhitan; Liao Ben, *Zhongguo xiju tushi* (Zhengzhou, Henan: Henan jiaoyu chuban she, 1996), pp. 356-357, nos. 3-518 through 3-520 [halftone; 3 selected leaves from the Bogu tang edition illustrated]; Shen Jin, *Meiguo Hafo daxue Hafo Yanjing tushu guan Zhongwen shanben shu zhi* (Shanghai: Shanghai cishu chuban she, 1999), pp. 776-779, cat. nos. 1360 and 1361.

14

Exemplars of the Beautiful and the Refined in Tang Poetry

唐詩艷逸品

Tao Xiang, "Ming Wuxing Min ban shumu," *Qinghe* 5, no. 13 (cumulative no. 109) (1937), pp. 1-10; *A Descriptive Catalog of Rare Chinese Books in the Library of Congress*, compiled by Wang Zhongmin, edited by T.L. Yuan (Washington, D.C.: Library of Congress, 1957), vol. 2, pp. 1061-1062; Zhang Zhongjiang, *Lidai jinü yu shige* [Taoyuan, Taiwan: Zhiquan chuban she, n.d. (1966)], pp. 14-76; *Ming dai banke zonglu (8 juan)*, compiled and edited by Du Xinfu; reviewed and corrected by Zhou Guangpei and Jiang Xiaoda (Yangzhou: Jiangsu Guangling guji keyin she, 1983), *juan* 4/51a (in vol. 4) and *juan* 5/16a (in vol. 5); Wang Zhongmin, *Zhongguo shanben shu tiyao* (Shanghai: Shanghai guji chuban she, 1983), p. 464; *Zhongguo gudai muke hua xuan ji*, compiled and edited by Zheng Zhenduo (Beijing: Renmin meishu chuban she, 1985), vol. 4 [unpaginated; halftone; 2 selected leaves illustrated]; *Chûgoku kodai hanga ten: Machida shisei 30-shûnen kinen, Nitchû heiwa yûkô jôyaku teiketsu 10-shûnen kinen*, Chûgoku hanga 2000-nen ten, dai 3 bu, compiled by Machida shiritsu kokusai hanga bijutsukan [and] Takimoto Hiroyuki (Machida, Japan: Machida shiritsu kokusai hanga bijutsukan, 1988), p. 153, cat. no. 6.7; *Tang shi shu lu*, compiled and edited by Chen Bohai and Zhu Yi'an (Ji'nan, Shandong: Qi Lu shu she, 1988), p. 66; *Tang shi da cidian*, edited by Zhou Xunchu [N.p. (Nanjing): Jiangsu guji chuban she, 1990], p. 623; *Zhongguo shudian 1998 nian chun ji shukan ziliao paimai hui* (Beijing: Beijing Haiwang cun paimai youxian zeren gongsi, 1998), lot no. 66 [2 volumes from complete set of 4 volumes of the 1621 edition illustrated]; Shen Jin, *Meiguo Hafo daxue Hafo Yanjing tushu guan Zhongwen shanben shu zhi* (Shanghai: Shanghai cishu chuban she, 1999), p. 522, cat. no. 0928.

15

The Ten Bamboo Studio Manual of Calligraphy and Painting, 8 *juan*

十竹齋書畫譜八卷

Robert Treat Paine, Jr., "The Ten Bamboo Studio: Its Early Editions, Pictures, and Artists, " *Archives of the Chinese Art Society of America* 5 (1951), pp. 39-54; *Zhongguo yinben shuji zhanlan mulu*, compiled and edited by Beijing tushu guan (Beijing: Zhongyang renmin zhengfu wenhua bu shehui wenhua shiye guanli ju, 1952), p. 80, no. 568, and p. 81 [halftone; 1 selected double-leaf illustrated]; *A Descriptive Catalog of Rare Chinese Books in the Library of Congress*, compiled by Wang Zhongmin, edited by T.L. Yuan (Washington, D.C.: Library of Congress, 1957), vol. 1, pp. 596-597; *Zhongguo banke tulu*, compiled and edited by Beijing tushu guan, 2d rev. ed. (Beijing: Wenwu chuban she, 1961), vol. 1, p. 111, and vol. 8, pl. 707; Guo Weiqu, *Zhongguo banhua shi lüe* (Beijing: Zhaohua meishu chuban she, 1962), pp. 110-113 and fig. 51; *Xidi shumu*, [6 *juan* (5 *juan*, tiba 1 *juan*)], compiled and edited by Beijing tushu guan [N.p. (Beijing): Wenwu chuban she, 1963], *juan* 2/23a, no. 10503 (in vol. 2); *Chinese Art: Painting, Calligraphy, Stone Rubbing, Wood Engraving*, by Werner Speiser, Roger Goepper, and Jean Fribourg, translated by Diana Imber (New York: Universe Books, Inc., 1964), pp. 298-299, no. 139, and pp. 304-319, nos. 142-150, and pp. 344-351, nos. 164-169, and pp. 358-359, no. 174; Fu Xihua, *Zhongguo banhua yanjiu zhongyao shumu*, in *Shuhua shulu tieti fukan* (Hong Kong: Xianggang Zhong Mei tushu gongsi, 1969), p. 2a, no. 837; Jan Tschichold, *Chinese Color Prints from the Ten Bamboo Studio*, translated by Katherine Watson (London: Lund Humphries, 1972); *The Prints of the Ten Bamboo Studio, Followed by Plates from the Kaempfer Series and Perfect Harmony*, presentation and Commentary by Joseph Vedlich (N.p.: Crescent Books, a division of Crown Publishers, Inc., 1979); Dawn Ho Delbanco, "Illustrated Books of the Ming Dynasty," *Orientations* 12, no. 11 (November 1981), pp. 33-36, and figs. 12 and 12a [color; 2 selected double-leaves illustrated]; Zhou Wu, "Wang Tingna yu Hu Zhengyan: Ji Ming dai liang wei chuban jia," *Duoyun*, no. 2 (November 1981), pp. 154-156; Zhou Wu, "Hui pai banhua," *Duoyun*, no. 4 (November 1982), pp. 143-144; *Ming dai banke zonglu (8 juan)*, compiled and edited by Du Xinfu; reviewed and corrected by Zhou Guangpei and Jiang Xiaoda (Yangzhou: Jiangsu Guangling guji keyin she, 1983), *juan* 1/2b (in vol. 1); Wang Zhongmin, *Zhongguo shanben shu tiyao* (Shanghai: Shanghai guji chuban she, 1983), p. 296; *Hui pai banhua shi lun ji*, compiled and edited by Zhou Wu (Hefei, Anhui: Anhui renmin chuban she, 1984), text section, pp. 73-74, and illustrations section, pp. 127-129, figs. 327-333 [14 selected half-folios (7 double-spreads) illustrated]; J. Sören Edgren, *Chinese Rare Books in American Collections* (New York: China Institute in America, 1984), pp. 114-155, cat. no. 35; Joseph Needham, *Science and Civilisation in China*, vol. 5, *Chemistry and Chemical Technology*, pt. 1, *Paper and Printing*, by Tsien Tsuen-hsuin (Cambridge and New York: Cambridge University Press, 1985), pp. 283-286, and fig. 1190; *Zhonghua minguo chuantong banhua yishu (The Traditional Art of Chinese Woodblock Prints)*, organized by Xingzheng yuan wenhua jianshe weiyuan hui (Council for Cultural Planning and Development, Executive Yuan) [Taibei: Xingzheng yuan wenhua jianshe weiyuan hui (Council for Cultural Planning and Development, Executive Yuan), 1986], pp. 28-43 [16 selected double-leaves illustrated]; *Chûgoku Min Shin no ehon* (Osaka: Ôsaka shiritsu bijutsukan, 1987), p. 65, cat. no. 121 [illustration], p. 121, cat. no. 121 [catalogue entry]; *Shizhu zhai yanjiu wenji: "Shizhu zhai shuhua pu" kanxing sanbai liushi nian jinian*, compiled by Shizhu zhai yishu yanjiu bu (Nanjing: Shizhu zhai yishu yanjiu bu, 1987), pp. 2-9 [article by Wang Bomin] , pp. 10-13 [article by Wei Yinru] , pp. 14-17 [article by Zeng Jingchu] , pp. 28-29 [article by Zhou Wu] , pp. 41-47 [article by Huang Hongyi] , pp. 48-

52 [article by Hua Rende] , pp. 57-59 [article by Wu Junfa] , pp. 63-65 [article by Mu Xiaotian] , pp. 70-74 [article by Zhang Erbin] , pp. 75-78 [article by Xiao Ping] , pp. 90-93 [article by Zhang Guobiao] , pp. 100-112 [article by Hu Yi] [for full citations to the above articles, see bibliography under each author]; *Beijing tushu guan guji shanben shumu*, compiled by Beijing tushu guan [Beijing: Shumu wenxian chuban she, n.d. (1987)], vol. 3, pp. 1354-1355; *Zhongguo meishu quanji: Huihua bian*, vol. 20, *Banhua*, compiled by Zhongguo meishu quanji bianji weiyuan hui (Shanghai: Shanghai renmin meishu chuban she, 1988), illustrations section, p. 160, no. 155 [halftone; 1 selected double-leaf illustrated], text section, p. 56, no. 155 [catalogue entry in Chinese]; *Chûgoku kodai hanga ten: Machida shisei 30-shûnen kinen, Nitchû heiwa yûkô jôyaku teiketsu 10-shûnen kinen*, Chûgoku hanga 2000-nen ten, dai 3 bu, compiled by Machida shiritsu kokusai hanga bijutsukan [and] Takimoto Hiroyuki (Machida, Japan: Machida shiritsu kokusai hanga bijutsukan, 1988), pp. 239-240, cat. nos. 9.7 and 9.8; Pan Yuanshi, "Shizhu zhai shuhua pu," in *Ming dai banhua yishu tushu tezhan zhuanji (Exhibition of Graphic Art in Printed Books of the Ming Dynasty)*, edited by Guoli zhongyang tushu guan (National Central Library) [Taibei: Guoli zhongyang tushu guan (National Central Library), 1989], pp. 230-247, accompanied by abstract in English, "The Graphic Art Album Shih Chu Chai Shu-hua P'u" [translated from the Chinese by Andrew Morton], pp. 340-341, and also pp. 104-107 [2 selected leaves illustrated], and p. 316 [catalogue entry in Chinese and English]; *Kinsei Nihon kaiga to gafu, edehon ten: Meiga o unda hanga*, compiled and edited by Machida shiritsu kokusai hanga bijutsukan (Machida, Japan: Machida shiritsu kokusai hanga bijutsukan, 1990), vol. 2, p. 28, cat. no. 12 (12-1, 12-2, 12-3, 12-4, 12-5, 12-6) [halftone; 6 selected double-leaves illustrated], and vol. 2, p. 179, cat. no. 12 [captions in Japanese]; Monique Cohen and Nathalie Monnet, *Impressions de Chine* (Paris: Bibliothèque Nationale, 1992), pp. 154-156, cat. nos. 95-97 [color; 3 selected double-leaves illustrated]; *Manmu linlang: Guoli zhongyang tushu guan shanben tecang (A Cornucopia of Rare Editions: The National Central Library's Rare Book Collection)*, compiled by Guoli zhongyang tushu guan (National Central Library) [Taibei: Guoli zhongyang tushu guan (National Central Library), 1993], pp. 102-103 [2 selected leaves illustrated], p. 149 [catalogue entry in Chinese], and p. 168 [catalogue entry in English]; *Jinling gu banhua*, compiled and edited by Zhou Wu (Nanjing: Jiangsu meishu chuban she, 1993), pp. 364-365; Kobayashi Hiromitsu, *Chûgoku no hanga: Tôdai kara Shindai made (Chinese Woodblock Illustrations from the Tang through the Qing Dynasty)* (Tokyo: Tôshindô, 1995), p. 70, and pp. 105-107, and fig. 115, and p. 145; Li Zhizhong, *Gu shu banben jianding* (Beijing: Wenwu chuban she, 1997), pp. 37-38, and fig. 8 [halftone; 1 selected double-leaf illustrated]; Nancy Berliner, "The Diverse Roles of Rocks as Revealed in Wood-block Prints," *Orientations* 28, no. 6 (June 1997), pp. 67-68, and fig. 15; *East Asian Books*, Catalogue 19 (London: Sam Fogg Rare Books and Manuscripts, 1998), pp. 60, 62-65, cat. nos. 54 and 59; *Zhongguo gudai yinshua shi tuce (An Illustrated History of Printing in Ancient China)*, compiled by Zhongguo yinshua bowu guan (The Printing Museum of China) [Hong Kong: Xianggang chengshi daxue chuban she (City University of Hong Kong Press); Beijing: Wenwu chuban she (Cultural Relics Publishing House), 1998], p. 83 [bottom]; James Cahill, "Chinese Painting: Innovation After 'Progress' Ends," in *China: 5,000 Years: Innovation and Transformation in the Arts*, selected by Sherman Lee (New York: Guggenheim Museum Publications, 1998), p. 187, see also cat. no. 201 [color; 10 selected double-leaves illustrated]; *Zhongguo guojia tushu guan guji zhenpin tulu*, edited by Ren Jiyu (Beijing: Beijing tushu guan chuban she, 1999), p. 198, cat. no. 224 [1 selected double-leaf from another impression in the library's collection illustrated].

16

Portraits of Meritorious Officials from the Lingyan Pavilion

凌煙閣功臣圖不分卷

Zhongguo banhua shi tulu, [compiled by Zheng Zhenduo] (Shanghai: Zhongguo banhua shi she, 1940-1942), in vol. 17; *Zhongguo yinben shuji zhanlan mulu*, compiled and edited by Beijing tushu guan (Beijing: Zhongyang renmin zhengfu wenhua bu shehui wenhua shiye guanli ju, 1952), p. 84, no. 587; *Zhongguo banke tulu*, compiled and edited by Beijing tushu guan, 2d rev. ed. (Beijing: Wenwu chuban she, 1961), vol. 1, pp. 112-113, and vol. 8, pl. 713; Guo Weiqu, *Zhongguo banhua shi lüe* (Beijing: Zhaohua meishu chuban she, 1962), pp. 151-153; Jin *Weinuo*, "'Bunian tu' yu 'Lingyan ge gongchen tu,'" *Wenwu*, no. 144 (1962, no. 10) (October 1962), pp. 13-16; Fu Xihua, *Zhongguo banhua yanjiu zhongyao shumu*, in *Shuhua shulu tieti fukan* (Hong Kong: Xianggang Zhong Mei tushu gongsi, 1969), p. 4a, no. 904; *The Cambridge History of China*, edited by Denis Twittchett and John K. Fairbank, vol. 3, *Sui and T'ang China, 589-906*, Part I, edited by Denis Twitchett (Cambridge and New York: Cambridge University Press, 1979), pp. 193-200; *Zhongguo gudai banhua bai tu*, compiled and edited by Zhou Wu (Beijing: Renmin meishu chuban she, 1984), no. 87; *Zhongguo gudai muke hua xuan ji*, compiled and edited by Zheng Zhenduo (Beijing: Renmin meishu chuban she, 1985), vol. 6 [unpaginated; halftone; 1 selected leaf illustrated]; *Chûgoku Min Shin no ehon* (Osaka: Ôsaka shiritsu bijutsukan, 1987), p. 66, cat. no. 128 [illustration], p. 122, cat. no. 128 [catalogue entry]; *Beijing tushu guan guji shanben shumu*, compiled by Beijing tushu guan [Beijing: Shumu wenxian chuban she, n.d. (1987)], vol. 3, pp. 1353-1354; Kobayashi Hiromitsu, "Figure Compositions in Seventeenth-Century Chinese Prints and Their Influences on Edo-Period Japanese Painting Manuals" (Ph.D. diss., University of California, Berkeley, 1987), pp. 116-119; *Zhongguo meishu quanji: Huihua bian*, vol. 20, Banhua, compiled by Zhongguo meishu quanji bianji weiyuan hui (Shanghai: Shanghai renmin meishu chuban she, 1988), illustrations section, p. 165, no. 160 [halftone; 1 selected leaf illustrated], text section, p. 58, no. 160 [catalogue entry in Chinese]; *Chûgoku kodai hanga ten: Machida shisei 30-shûnen kinen, Nitchû heiwa yûkô jôyaku teiketsu 10-shûnen kinen*, Chûgoku hanga 2000-nen ten, dai 3 bu, compiled by Machida shiritsu kokusai hanga bijutsukan [and] Takimoto Hiroyuki (Machida, Japan: Machida shiritsu kokusai hanga bijutsukan, 1988), p. 205, cat. no. 7.21; *Lingyan ge gongchen tu*, reprinted in *Zhongguo gudai banhua congkan*, compiled and edited by Zheng Zhenduo (Shanghai: Shanghai guji chuban she, 1988), vol. 4, pp. 275-366, with postscript by Shanghai guji chuban she; *Kinsei Nihon kaiga to gafu, edehon ten: Meiga o unda hanga*, compiled and edited by Machida shiritsu kokusai hanga bijutsukan (Machida, Japan: Machida shiritsu kokusai hanga bijutsukan, 1990), vol. 1, p. 19, cat. no. 11 [color; 1 leaf by Chen Hongshou illustrated], and p. 148, cat. no. 11 [catalogue entry in Japanese]; *Lingyan ge gongchen tu* (Shijiazhuang, Hebei: Hebei meishu chuban she, 1996); *Zhongguo gudai fojiao banhua ji*, chief editor: Zhou Xinhui, co-editors: Chen Jian and Ma Wenda (Beijing: Xueyuan chuban she, 1998), vol. 3, illustrations section, pp. 24-27 [4 selected half-folios illustrated].

17

Imperially Commissioned Illustrations of Riziculture and Sericulture
御製耕織圖

Léon de Rosny, Catalogue de la bibliothèque japonaise de Nordenskiöld, coordonné, revu, annoté et publié par Léon de Rosny et précédé d'une introduction par le marquis d'Hervey de Saint-Denys (Paris: Imprimerie nationale, 1883), p. 254, cat. no. 677; *Yu zhi Gengzhi tu*, 2d lithographic ed. (Shanghai: Dianshi zhai, 1886); Friedrich Hirth, *Ueber fremde Einflüsse in der chinesischen Kunst* (Munich and Leipzig: G. Hirth's Verlag, 1896), pp. 57-60, and fig. 17; Berthold Laufer, "The Discovery of a Lost Book," *T'oung Pao* 13 (1912), pp. 97-106; Édouard Chavannes, review of *Kéng tschi t'u: Ackerbau und Seidengewinnung in China: Ein kaiserliches Lehr- und Mahn-Buch, aus dem Chinesischen übersetzt und mit Erklärungen Versehen von O. [Otto] Franke, mit 102 Tafeln und 57 Illustrationen im Text*, by Otto Franke, *T'oung Pao* 14 (1913), pp. 306-309; Paul Pelliot, "À propos du «Keng tche t'ou»," in *Mémoires concernant l'Asie Orientale, Inde, Asie Centrale, Extrême-Orient, publiés par l'Académie des Inscriptions et Belles-lettres*, tome 1, edited by Émile Senart et al. (Paris: E. Leroux, 1913), pp. 65-122; Otto Franke, *Kêng tschi t'u: Ackerbau und Seidengewinnung in China: Ein kaiserliches Lehr- und Mahn-Buch, aus dem Chinesischen übersetzt und mit Erklärungen Versehen von O. [Otto] Franke, mit 102 Tafeln und 57 Illustrationen im Text*, Abhandlungen des Hamburgischen Kolonialinstituts, Bd. 11 (Reihe B, Völkerkunde, Kultuegeschichte und Sprachen, Bd. 8) (Hamburg: L. Friederichsen & Co., 1913); Otto Franke, "Zur Geschichte des Kêng tschi t'u: Ein Beitrag zue chinesischen Kunstgeschichte und Kunstkritik," *Ostasiatische Zeitschrift* 3 (1914-1915), pp. 169-208; Arthur W. Hummel, "Accessions to the Division of Chinese Literature," *Report of the Librarian of Congress for the Fiscal Year Ending June 30, 1928* (1928), pp. 274-277 [under the marginal headings "The Keng Chih T'u or 'Tilling and Weaving Pictures'" and "The Discovery of a Lost Book"]; Arthur W. Hummel, "Chinese and Other East Asiatic Books Added to the Library of Congress, 1928-1929," *Report of the Librarian of Congress for the Fiscal Year Ending June 30, 1929* (1929), pp. 285-288 [under the marginal heading "Newly discovered 'Pictures on Tilling and Weaving'"]; Fritz Jäger, "Der angebliche Steindruck des »Kêng-tschi-t'u« vom Jahre 1210," *Ostasiatische Zeitschrift*, n.s. 9 (1933), pp. 1-4; Arthur W. Hummel, "Division of Orientalia," *Annual Report of the Librarian of Congress for the Fiscal Year Ended June 30, 1938* (1938), pp. 217-221 [under the sectional heading "Pictures on Tilling and Weaving"]; Arthur W. Hummel, "Division of Orientalia," *Annual Report of the Librarian of Congress for the Fiscal Year Ended June 30, 1940* (1940), pp. 165-166 [under the sectional heading "A Ming Encyclopaedia With Pictures on Tilling and Weaving and on Strange Countries"]; Gösta Montell, "Kêng chih t'u: 'Illustrations of Husbandry and Weaving,'" *Ethnos* 5, nos. 3-4 (1940), pp. 165-183; *Zhongguo banhua shi tulu*, [compiled by Zheng Zhenduo] (Shanghai: Zhongguo banhua shi she, 1940-1942), in vol. 17; Walter Fuchs, "Rare Ch'ing Editions of the Keng-chih-t'u," *Huaxi xiehe daxue Zhongguo wenhua yanjiu suo jikan (Studia Serica: Journal of the Chinese Cultural Studies Research Institute, West China Union University)* 6 (1947), pp. 149-157; Bernhard Karlgren, "The Book of Documents," *Bulletin of the Museum of Far Eastern Antiquities*, no. 22 (1950), pp. 56-59 [under the sectional heading "Wu yi"]; *Zhongguo yinben shuji zhanlan mulu*, compiled and edited by Beijing tushu guan (Beijing: Zhongyang renmin zhengfu wenhua bu shehui wenhua shiye guanli ju, 1952), p. 87, no. 617; *Zhongguo banke tulu*, compiled and edited by Beijing tushu guan, 2d rev. ed. (Beijing: Wenwu chuban she, 1961), vol. 1, p. 113, and vol. 8, pls. 716 and 717; Guo Weiqu, *Zhongguo banhua shi lüe* (Beijing: Zhaohua meishu chuban she, 1962), p. 135, pp. 140-142, and fig. 57; *Chinese Art: Painting, Calligraphy, Stone Rubbing, Wood Engraving,*

by Werner Speiser, Roger Goepper, and Jean Fribourg, translated by Diana Imber (New York: Universe Books, Inc., 1964), pp. 292-293, no. 136; *Yu zhi wen di er ji, juan 32/15a-17a*, reprinted in facsimile as *Kangxi di yu zhi wenji*, Zhongguo shi xue congshu, [no. 41], edited by Wu Xiangxiang (Taibei: Taiwan xuesheng shuju, 1966), vol. 2, pp. 1104-1105; Fu Xihua, *Zhongguo banhua yanjiu zhongyao shumu*, in *Shuhua shulu tieti fukan* (Hong Kong: Xianggang Zhong Mei tushu gongsi, 1969), p. 19a, no. 1414; Thomas Lawton, *Chinese Figure Painting* (Washington, D.C.: Smithsonian Institution, 1973), pp. 54-57, cat. nos. 7 and 8; Nakamura Kyûshirô, "Gengzhi tu zhong suo jian Song dai zhi fengsu yu Xiyang hua zhi yingxiang," translated from the Japanese by Zhao Yashu, *Shihuo yuekan (Shih-huo Monthly)* 3, no. 4 (July 1973), pp. 187-194; Otani Takeo, "Gengzhi tu zhi yanjiu, " translated from the Japanese by Zhao Yashu, *Shihuo yuekan (Shih-huo Monthly)* 3, no. 5 (August 1973), pp. 220-227; Zhao Yashu, "Gengzhi tu yu Gengzhi tu shi (yi)," *Shihuo yuekan (Shih-huo Monthly)* 3, no. 7 (October 1973), pp. 331-335; Zhao Yashu, "Gengzhi tu yu Gengzhi tu shi (er)," *Shihuo yuekan (Shih-huo Monthly)* 3, no. 9 (November 1973), pp. 409-426; Zhao Yashu, "Gengzhi tu yu Gengzhi tu shi (san)," *Shihuo yuekan (Shih-huo Monthly)* 3, no. 11 (February 1974), pp. 526-531; Zhao Yashu, "Gengzhi tu yu Gengzhi tu shi (si)," *Shihuo yuekan (Shih-huo Monthly)* 4, no. 5 (August 1974), pp. 192-201; Dieter Kuhn, "Die Darstellungen des 'Keng-chih-t'u' und ihre Wiedergabe in populär-enzyklopädischen Werken der Ming-Zeit," *Zeitschrift der Deutschen Morgenländischen Gesellschaft*, Bd. 126, Heft 2 (1976), pp. 336-367; *Trésors de Chine et de Haute Asie: Centième anniversaire de Paul Pelliot* (Paris: Bibliothèque nationale, 1979), pp. 89-92, cat. no. 167 [3 selected leaves illustrated]; J. Sören Edgren, *Catalogue of the Nordenskiöld Collection of Japanese Books in the Royal Library* [Stockholm: N.p. (Kungliga Biblioteket) 1980], p. 332, cat. no. 1029; Wang Zichun, "Sericulture," in *Ancient China's Technology and Science*, compiled by the Institute of the History of Natural Sciences, Chinese Academy of Sciences (Beijing: Foreign Languages Press, 1983), pp. 305-314; Gao Hanyu and Shi Bokui, "The Spinning Wheel and the Loom," in *Ancient China's Technology and Science*, compiled by the Institute of the History of Natural Sciences, Chinese Academy of Sciences (Beijing: Foreign Languages Press, 1983), pp. 504-519; Zhao Chengze, "Silk and Silk Textile Technology," in *Ancient China's Technology and Science*, compiled by the Institute of the History of Natural Sciences, Chinese Academy of Sciences (Beijing: Foreign Languages Press, 1983), pp. 520-533; Shiow-jyu Lu Shaw, *The Imperial Printing of Early Ch'ing China, 1644-1805* [N.p. (San Francisco): Chinese Materials Center, 1983]; Wen Xingzhen, "Kangxi yu nongye," *Gugong bowu yuan yuankan (Palace Museum Journal)*, no. 19 (1983, no. 1), pp. 20-30; J. Sören Edgren, *Chinese Rare Books in American Collections* (New York: China Institute in America, 1984), pp. 120-121, cat. no. 38; *Zhongguo gudai banhua bai tu*, compiled and edited by Zhou Wu (Beijing: Renmin meishu chuban she, 1984), no. 91; Joseph Needham, *Science and Civilisation in China*, vol. 6, *Biology and Biological Technology*, pt. 2, *Agriculture*, by Francesca Bray (Cambridge and New York: Cambridge University Press, 1984), pp. 49-50, 73, 234-236, 280-281, 295-296, 314, 352-358, and 599; Si Xi, "Xiuzhen xing de Gengzhi tu: Jian tan woguo xiri nonggeng fangshi," *Gugong wenwu yuekan (The National Palace Museum Monthly of Chinese Art)*, no. 13 (vol. 2, no. 1) (April 1984), pp. 11-17; *Zhongguo gudai muke hua xuan ji*, compiled and edited by Zheng Zhenduo (Beijing: Renmin meishu chuban she, 1985), vol. 6 [unpaginated; halftone; 2 selected leaves illustrated]; *Europa und die Kaiser von China, 1240-1816* (Frankfurt am Main: Insel Verlag, 1985), p. 300, cat. no. 10/9 [1696 edition], and pp. 300-301, cat. nos. 10/10 and 10/11 [1739 edition]; Ellen Johnston Laing, "Ch'ing Dynasty Pictorial Jades and Painting," *Ars Orientalis* 16 (1986), pp. 60-61, figs. 11-12 [2 sections of Yuan-dynasty painting by Cheng Qi], figs. 13-14 [2 leaves from the 1696 edition in the University of Oregon Museum of Art, Eugene, Ore.], fig. 15 [anonymous painting, 19th century], and figs. 16-17 [2 Kangxi-period jade screens in the Seattle Art Museum]; *Chûgoku Min Shin no ehon* (Osaka: Ôsaka shiritsu bijutsukan, 1987), p. 71, cat. no. 138 [illustration], p. 122, cat. no. 138 [catalogue entry]; *Beijing tushu guan guji shanben shumu*, compiled by Beijing tushu guan [Beijing: Shumu wenxian chuban she, n.d. (1987)], vol. 3, p. 1357; Joseph Needham, *Science and Civilisation in China*, vol. 5, *Chemistry and Chemical Technology*, pt. 9, *Textile Technology: Spinning and Reeling*, by Dieter Kuhn (Cambridge and New York: Cambridge University Press, 1988), pp. 180-182, 270-272, 314-315, 331-332, and 342-345; *Zhongguo meishu quanji: Huihua bian*, vol. 20, *Banhua*, compiled by Zhongguo meishu quanji bianji weiyuan hui (Shanghai: Shanghai renmin meishu chuban she, 1988), illustrations section, p. 176, no. 170 [halftone; 1 selected leaf illustrated], text section, p. 61, no. 170 [catalogue entry in Chinese]; *Chûgoku kodai hanga ten: Machida shisei 30-shûnen kinen, Nitchû heiwa yûkô jôyaku teiketsu 10-shûnen kinen*, Chûgoku hanga 2000-nen ten, dai 3 bu, compiled by Machida shiritsu kokusai hanga bijutsukan [and] Takimoto Hiroyuki (Machida, Japan: Machida shiritsu kokusai hanga bijutsukan, 1988), p. 209, cat. no. 7.23; *Gugong zhencang Kang Yong Qian ciqi tulu (Qing Porcelain of Kangxi, Yongzheng and Qianlong Periods from the Palace Museum Collection)*, edited by Li Yihua [Hong Kong: Liangmu chuban she (The Woods Publishing Co.); Beijing: Zijin cheng chuban she (Forbidden City Publishing House), 1989], p. 418, no. 100 [miniature album with painted ceramic leaves from the Qianlong period]; *Kinsei Nihon kaiga to gafu, edehon ten: Meiga o unda hanga*, compiled and edited by Machida shiritsu kokusai hanga bijutsukan (Machida, Japan: Machida shiritsu kokusai hanga bijutsukan, 1990), vol. 1, pp. 24-45, cat. nos. 13-22 [color; 10 Japanese treatments of theme illustrated], and vol. 1, pp. 149-150, cat. nos. 13-22 [catalogue entries in Japanese], and vol. 2, pp. 61-72, cat. nos. 23, 23a, and 24 [halftone; 6 leaves and 46 leaves from 2 copies of the 1696 Chinese edition illustrated, and 45 leaves from the 1676 Japanese edition illustrated], and vol. 2, p. 180, cat. nos. 23 [including 23a] and 24 [captions in Japanese]; Monique Cohen and Nathalie Monnet, *Impressions de Chine* (Paris: Bibliothèque Nationale, 1992), pp. 142-143, cat. no. 87 [color; 1 selected leaf illustrated]; Christine U. Karg, "Seidenspinner und Maulbeerbaum–Die Seidenerzeugung in China, " in *China, eine Wiege der Weltkultur: 5000 Jahre Erfindungen und Entdeckungen*, edited by Arne Eggebrecht (Mainz am Rhein, Germany: Verlag Philipp von Zabern, 1994), pp. 194-199, and Abb. 147-150 [color; 4 selected leaves of 1696 edition illustrated]; *Zhongguo gudai Gengzhi tu (Farming and Weaving Pictures in Ancient China)*, compiled by Zhongguo nongye bowu guan (China Agricultural Museum), edited by Wang Chaosheng [Beijing: Zhongguo nongye chuban she (China Agriculture Press), 1995], pp. 78-95; Kobayashi Hiromitsu, *Chûgoku no hanga: Tôdai kara Shindai made (Chinese Woodblock Illustrations from the Tang through the Qing Dynasty)* (Tokyo: Tôshindô, 1995), pp. 119-121, and fig. 131; *Zhongguo Jiade '95 chun ji paimai hui: Guji shanben (China Guardian '95 Spring Auctions: Rare Books)* [Beijing: Zhongguo Jiade guoji paimai youxian gongsi (China Guardian Auctions Co., Ltd.), 1995], lot no. 433 [4 selected leaves illustrated; this edition of 1696 contains seals impressed with cinnabar]; *Qing dai gongting huihua*, edited by Nie Chongzheng {Hong Kong: Shangwu yinshu guan [The Commercial Press (Hong Kong) Ltd.], 1996}, pp. 74-90, no. 11 [color; all 52 leaves of album depicting Yinzhen (the future Yongzheng emperor) and his consorts in tilling and weaving scenes illustrated]; *Mizuho no kuni Nihon: Shiki kôsakuzu no sekai*, by Reizei Tamehito, Kôno Michiaki, Iwasaki Takehito, [and Namiki Seishi] (Kyoto: Tankôsha, 1996), pp. 4-5 [essay by Iwasaki Takehito], pp. 24-25 [essay by Kôno Michiaki], and p. 98 [essay by Kôno Michiaki]; *Cong Beijing dao Fan'ersai: Zhong Fa meishu jiaoliu (From Beijing to Versailles: Artistic Relations between China and France)* [Hong Kong: Xianggang shizheng ju (Urban Council, Hong Kong), 1997], pp. 214-215, cat. no. 79 [color; 1 selected leaf illustrated]; *Qing dai banben tulu*, compiled and edited by Huang Yongnian and Jia Erqiang (Hangzhou: Zhejiang renmin chuban she, 1997), vol. 1, pp. 65-67 [2 selected leaves illustrated]; *A Journey into China's Antiquity: National Museum of Chinese History*, compiled by National Museum of Chinese History (Beijing: Morning Glory Publishers, 1997), vol. 4, pp. 209-210, nos. 192-1, 192-2, and 192-3 [color; 3 selected leaves illustrated]; *Zhongguo gudai yinshua shi tuce*

(An Illustrated History of Printing in Ancient China), compiled by Zhongguo yinshua bowu guan (The Printing Museum of China) [Hong Kong: Xianggang chengshi daxue chuban she (City University of Hong Kong Press); Beijing: Wenwu chuban she (Cultural Relics Publishing House), 1998], p. 89 [lower left corner]; *Yu zhi Gengzhi tu*, illustrated by Jiao Bingzhen (Beijing: Zhongguo shudian, 1998); *Zhongguo guojia tushu guan guji zhenpin tulu*, edited by Ren Jiyu (Beijing: Beijing tushu guan chuban she, 1999), p. 184, cat. no. 202 [1 selected leaf illustrated].

18

The Mustard Seed Garden Manual of Painting, Second Series, 8 *juan*, with Introduction, 1 *juan*, and Postscript, 1 *juan*

芥子園畫傳二集八卷首一卷末一卷

Le Kie tseu yuan houa tchouan: Traduit et commenté par R. Petrucci: Introduction générale, translation and commentary by Raphael Petrucci (Leiden: E.J. Brill, 1912); Alfred Kaiming Ch'iu, "The Chieh Tzu Yuan Hua Chuan (Mustard Seed Garden Painting Manual): Early Editions in American Collections," *Archives of the Chinese Art Society of America* 5 (1951), pp. 55-69; *Zhongguo yinben shuji zhanlan mulu*, compiled and edited by Beijing tushu guan (Beijing: Zhongyang renmin zhengfu wenhua bu shehui wenhua shiye guanli ju, 1952), p. 84, no. 597; *Chinese Color-Prints from the Painting Manual of the Mustard Seed Garden*, with an introduction by Jan Tschichold and sixteen facsimiles in the size of the originals (New York: The Beechhurst Press, 1953); Mai-mai Sze, *The Tao of Painting: A Study of the Ritual Disposition of Chinese Painting; with a Translation of the "Chieh Tzu Yüan Hua Chuan" or "Mustard Seed Garden Manual of Painting," 1679-1701* (New York: Pantheon Books Inc., 1956), vol. 2; *Zhongguo banke tulu*, compiled and edited by Beijing tushu guan, 2d rev. ed. (Beijing: Wenwu chuban she, 1961), vol. 1, p. 113, and vol. 8, pl. 718; Guo Weiqu, *Zhongguo banhua shi lüe* (Beijing: Zhaohua meishu chuban she, 1962), pp. 154-157 and fig. 59; Mai-mai Sze, *The Tao of Painting: A Study of the Ritual Disposition of Chinese Painting; with a Translation of the "Chieh Tzu Yüan Hua Chuan" or "Mustard Seed Garden Manual of Painting," 1679-1701*, 2d ed. (New York: Pantheon Books Inc., 1963); Fu Xihua, *Zhongguo banhua yanjiu zhongyao shumu*, in *Shuhua shulu tieti fukan* (Hong Kong: Xianggang Zhong Mei tushu gongsi, 1969), pp. 2a-b, nos. 838-840; Dawn Ho Delbanco, "Nanking and the Mustard Seed Garden Painting Manual" (Ph.D. diss., Harvard University, 1981), vol. 1 [text] and vol. 2 [illustrations]; J. Sören Edgren, *Chinese Rare Books in American Collections* (New York: China Institute in America, 1984), pp. 118-119, cat. no. 37; *Chûgoku Min Shin no ehon* (Osaka: Ôsaka shiritsu bijutsukan, 1987), p. 121, cat. no. 123 [catalogue entry]; *Beijing tushu guan guji shanben shumu*, compiled by Beijing tushu guan [Beijing: Shumu wenxian chuban she, n.d. (1987)], vol. 3, pp. 1356; *Zhongguo meishu quanji: Huihua bian*, vol. 20, *Banhua*, compiled by Zhongguo meishu quanji bianji weiyuan hui (Shanghai: Shanghai renmin meishu chuban she, 1988), illustrations section, pp. 214-215, no. 207 [1 halftone and 1 color; 2 selected pairs of facing leaves illustrated], text section, pp. 74-75, no. 207 [catalogue entry in Chinese]; *Chûgoku kodai hanga ten: Machida shisei 30-shûnen kinen, Nitchû heiwa yûkô jôyaku teiketsu 10-shûnen kinen*, Chûgoku hanga 2000-nen ten, dai 3 bu, compiled by Machida shiritsu kokusai hanga bijutsukan [and] Takimoto Hiroyuki (Machida, Japan: Machida shiritsu kokusai hanga bijutsukan, 1988), pp. 244, 245, 246, cat. no. 9.13; *Kinsei Nihon kaiga to gafu, edehon ten: Meiga o unda hanga*, compiled and edited by Machida shiritsu kokusai hanga bijutsukan (Machida, Japan: Machida shiritsu kokusai hanga bijutsukan, 1990), vol. 2, p. 11, cat. no. 15 (15-4, 15-5, and 15-6) [color; 3 selected double-leaves from 1701 edition of the second series illustrated], and vol. 2, p. 179, cat. no. 15 [captions in Japanese]; Monique Cohen and Nathalie Monnet, *Impressions de Chine* (Paris: Bibliothèque Nationale, 1992), pp. 157-158, cat. no. 98 [halftone and color; 2 selected double-leaves illustrated]; Kobayashi Hiromitsu, *Chûgoku no hanga: Tôdai kara Shindai made (Chinese Woodblock Illustrations from the Tang through the Qing Dynasty)* (Tokyo: Tôshindô, 1995), pp. 110-116, and figs. 120, 121, 123, 124, and p. 117; *East Asian Books*, Catalogue 19 (London: Sam Fogg Rare Books and Manuscripts, 1998), pp. 60, 62-65, cat. nos. 54, 55, 56, 57, and 58; Robert E. Hegel, *Reading Illustrated Fiction in Late Imperial China* (Stanford, Calif.: Stanford University Press, 1998), pp. 285-286; *Zhongguo gudai yinshua shi tuce (An Illustrated History of Printing in Ancient China)*, compiled by Zhongguo yinshua bowu guan (The Printing Museum of China) [Hong Kong: Xianggang chengshi daxue chuban she (City University of Hong Kong Press); Beijing: Wenwu chuban she (Cultural Relics Publishing House), 1998], p. 91 [bottom]; *Zhongguo guojia tushu guan guji zhenpin tulu*, edited by Ren Jiyu (Beijing: Beijing tushu guan chuban she, 1999), p. 201, cat. no. 228 [2 selected facing half-folios illustrated].

19

Imperially Commissioned Profound Mirror of Ancient Essays, 64 *juan*

御製古文淵鑒六十四卷

Tu Lien-chê, "Hsü Ch'ien-hsüeh," in *Eminent Chinese of the Ch'ing Period (1644-1912)*, edited by Arthur W. Hummel, vol. 1 (Washington, D.C.: The Library of Congress; Washington, D.C.: United States Government Printing Office, 1943), pp. 310-312; *Yu zhi wenji, juan* 19 / 15b-18b, reprinted in facsimile as *Kangxi di yu zhi wenji*, Zhongguo shi xue congshu, [no. 41], edited by Wu Xiangxiang (Taibei: Taiwan xuesheng shuju, 1966), vol. 1, pp. 310-311; *Die Kaiserliche Ku-wen-Anthologie von 1685/6 Ku-wen yüan-chien in mandjurische Übersetzung*, herausgegeben von Martin Gimm, Bd. 1, *Kap. 1-24 (Chou- bis Chin-Dynastie)* (Wiesbaden, Germany: Otto Harrassowitz, 1969), xli-lxvi; Walter Simon and Howard G.H. Nelson, *Manchu Books in London: A Union Catalogue* (London: Published for the British Library by British Museum Publications Limited, 1977), cat. nos. II.139.A-C, III.72, and III.73; *Qing shi liezhuan* (80 *juan*), compiled and edited by Taiwan Zhonghua shuju, 2d Taiwan ed. (Taibei: Taiwan Zhonghua shuju, 1983), *juan* 10 / 6b-11a (in vol. 2); Shiow-jyu Lu Shaw, *The Imperial Printing of Early Ch'ing China, 1644-1805* [N.p. (San Francisco): Chinese Materials Center, 1983], pp. 36-37, and pp. 41-42; *Beijing tushu guan guji shanben shumu*, compiled by Beijing tushu guan [Beijing: Shumu wenxian chuban she, n.d. (1987)], vol. 4, p. 2776; Monique Cohen and Nathalie Monnet, *Impressions de Chine* (Paris: Bibliothèque Nationale, 1992), p. 151, cat. no. 93 [color; 2 selected leaves illustrated]; *Qing dai neifu ke shu mulu jieti*, compiled and edited by Gugong bowu yuan tushu guan and Liaoning sheng tushu guan (Beijing: Zijin cheng chuban she, 1995), pp. 397-398; *Qing dai banben tulu*, compiled and edited by Huang Yongnian and Jia Erqiang (Hangzhou: Zhejiang renmin chuban she, 1997), vol. 1, pp. 48-50 [2 selected leaves illustrated]; *Artefacts of Ancient Chinese Science and Technology*, compiled by the Editorial Board of the Artefacts of Ancient Chinese Science and Technology (Beijing: Morning Glory Publishers, 1998), p. 36, fig. 3-16 [illustration of the *Du Gongbu ji* edition in the National Museum of Chinese History]; *Zhongguo shudian 1998 nian qiu ji shukan ziliao*

paimai hui (Beijing: Beijing Haiwang cun paimai youxian zeren gongsi, 1998), lot no. 48 [3 selected half-folios of 1685 palace edition illustrated]; *Duoyun xuan '99 qiu ji yishu pin paimai hui: Guji banben zhuanchang (Duo Yun Xuan '99 Autumn Auction of Art Works)* [Shanghai: Shanghai Duoyun xuan yishu pin paimai gongsi (Duo Yun Xuan Art Auctioneer's), 1999], lot no. 535 [illustration of a Daoguang-period edition of the *Du Gongbu ji* printed by the Yunye an], and lot no. 536 [illustration of a Guxiang zhai edition of the *Yu zhi Guwen yuanjian* printed in the Kangxi period].

20

Manual on Chrysanthemums, 1 *juan*

菊譜一卷

Qinding Gujin tushu jicheng, compiled by Chen Menglei et al., with editorial revisions by Jiang Tingxi et al. (Beijing: Wuying dian, 1726; reprint; Shanghai: Zhonghua shuju, 1934), *Bowu huibian, Caomu dian, juan* 87-91, *Ju bu*, in vol. 538, pp. 38a-62a; *Zhiwu mingshi tukao* (38 *juan*), *fu Zhiwu mingshi tukao changbian* (22 *juan*), by Wu Qijun, edited by Lu Yinggu (preface dated 1848; rev. ed., 1919; 2d rev. ed., 1933; reprint; Taibei: Taiwan Shangwu yinshu guan, 1965), *Zhiwu mingshi tukao* section, p. 241 (in *juan* 11); S.L. Emsweller, "The Chrysanthemum . . . Its Story Through the Ages," *Journal of the New York Botanical Garden* 48, no. 566 (February 1947), pp. 26-29; Li Hui-Lin, *The Garden Flowers of China* (New York: The Ronald Press Company, 1959), pp. 37-47; *Zhongguo banke tulu*, compiled and edited by Beijing tushu guan, 2d rev. ed. (Beijing: Wenwu chuban she, 1961), vol. 1, p. 87, and vol. 6, pl. 524; Joseph Needham, *Science and Civilisation in China*, vol. 6, *Biology and Biological Technology*, pt. 1, *Botany*, with the collaboration of Lu Gwei-djen and a special contribution by Huang Hsing-tsung (Cambridge and New York: Cambridge University Press, 1986), pp. 409-417; *Beijing tushu guan guji shanben shumu*, compiled by Beijing tushu guan [Beijing: Shumu wenxian chuban she, n.d. (1987)], vol. 3, p. 1381; *Zhongguo hua jing (China Floral Encyclopaedia)*, edited by Chen Junyu and Cheng Xuke (Shanghai: Shanghai wenhua chuban she, 1990), pp. 121-127.

21

Illustrated Manual on Goldfish

金魚圖譜不分卷

Tu Long, *Kaopan yu shi* (4 *juan*) [first published in 1592; reprint of typeset and punctuated edition], Congshu jicheng chubian, vol. 1559 (Beijing: Zhonghua shuju, 1985), p. 68; *Zhu sha yu pu*, compiled by Zhang Qiande [Zhang Zhao], manuscript dated 1596, typeset ed., in Meishu congshu (Taibei: Guangwen shuju, 1963), ser. 2, no. 10 [vol. 20], pp. 125-134; *Qinding Gujin tushu jicheng*, compiled by Chen Menglei et al., with editorial revisions by Jiang Tingxi et al. (Beijing: Wuying dian, 1726; reprint; Shanghai: Zhonghua shuju, 1934), *Bowu huibian, Qinchong dian, Yu bu, Jinyu bu*, in *juan* 145, in vol. 526, pp. 46a-47a; Louis Edme Billardon de Sauvigny, *Histoire naturelle des dorades de la Chine* [Paris: Louis Jorry, 1780 (2 editions, in quarto and in folio)]; A.C. Moule, "A Version of the Book of Vermilion Fish," *T'oung Pao* 39, livr. 1-3 (1949), pp. 1-82; George Hervey, *The Goldfish of China in the XVIII Century* (London: The China Society, 1950); *Der kleine Goldfischteich*

(Leipzig: Insel-Verlag, n.d.), pp. 25-42; Zhang Binglun, "Researches in Heredity and Breeding," in *Ancient China's Technology and Science*, compiled by the Institute of the History of Natural Sciences, Chinese Academy of Sciences (Beijing: Foreign Languages Press, 1983), pp. 285-286; Jin Zhang, *Hao liang zhi le ji* (Beijing: Wenwu chuban she, 1985), pp. 1-4; Zhang Shaohua, *Beijing jinyu*, 2d rev. ed. (Beijing: Beijing chuban she, 1987), pp. 1-4 and pp. 8-14; *Beijing tushu guan guji shanben shumu*, compiled by Beijing tushu guan [Beijing: Shumu wenxian chuban she, n.d. (1987)], vol. 3, p. 1383; *Chinese Goldfish*, [by Li Zhen] (Beijing: Foreign Languages Press, 1988), pp. 13-32, and pp. 65-99; Wang Chunyuan, *Zhongguo jinyu (Chinese Goldfish)* (Beijing: Jindun chuban she, 1994), pp. 1-7.

22

Album of Beijing Opera Characters from the Shengping Bureau

昇平暑戲曲人物畫册

Qing Shengping shu zhi lüe, compiled and edited by Wang Zhizhang [N.p. (Beiping): Guoli Beiping yanjiu yuan shi xue tanjiu hui, 1937], vol. 1, pp. 41-50, vol. 2, pp. 548-622; Zhang Bojin, *Guo ju yu lian pu* (Taibei: Mei Ya shuban gufen youxian gongsi, 1969); Colin P. Mackerras, *The Rise of the Peking Opera, 1770-1870: Social Aspects of the Theatre in Manchu China* (Oxford: Clarendon Press, 1972), pp. 116-124, pp. 154-161; Jacques Pimpaneau, *Promenade au Jardin des Poiriers: L'opéra chinois classique* (Paris: Musée Kwok On, 1983), esp. pp. 59-100; Charles O. Hucker, *A Dictionary of Official Titles in Imperial China* (Stanford, Calif.: Stanford University Press, 1985), p. 339, no. 4095 and p. 420, no. 5186; Li Tiyang, "Qing dai gongting xiju," in *Jing ju shi yanjiu: Xiqu lunhui (er) zhuanji*, texts supplied by Beijing Jing ju shi yanjiu hui, edited by Beijing shi xiqu yanjiu suo (Shanghai: Xuelin chuban she, 1985), pp. 61-73; Lang Xiuhua, "Qing dai Shengping shu yan'ge," *Gugong bowu yuan yuankan (Palace Museum Journal)*, no. 31 (1986, no. 1), pp. 13-18; J.D. Schmidt, "Ching chü," in *The Indiana Companion to Traditional Chinese Literature*, edited and compiled by William H. Nienhauser, Jr. (Bloomington, Ind. and Indianapolis: Indiana University Press, 1986; reissued in 1998 as vol. 1 of 2), vol. 1, pp. 316-318 [see also updated bibliography in vol. 2, p. 292]; *Zhongguo jing ju shi*, compiled and edited by Beijing shi yishu yanjiu suo and Shanghai yishu yanjiu suo (Beijing: Zhongguo xiju chuban she, 1990), vol. 1, pp. 210-238; Colin P. Mackerras, *Chinese Drama: A Historical Survey* (Beijing: New World Press, 1990), pp. 60-78; Jin Yaozhang, "Jing ju jingjiao lian pu de yanbian," in *Zhongguo xiju lian pu wenji*, compiled and edited by Huang Dianqi (Beijing: Zhongguo xiju chuban she, 1994), pp. 76-86; Liao Ben, *Zhongguo xiju tushi* (Zhengzhou, Henan: Henan jiaoyu chuban she, 1996), pp. 118-119, nos. 2-188 through 2-192 [color; 5 selected leaves illustrated], pp. 318-325, nos. 3-388 through 3-408 [color; 18 selected leaves illustrated]; *Beijing tushu guan cang Shengping shu xiqu renwu hua ce* (Beijing: Beijing tushu guan chuban she, 1997) [color; all 97 leaves illustrated]; *Zhongguo guojia tushu guan guji zhenpin tulu*, edited by Ren Jiyu (Beijing: Beijing tushu guan chuban she, 1999), p. 203, cat. no. 232 [1 selected leaf illustrated].

23

The Hundred Flowers Poetry-Writing Paper from the Wenmei Studio

文美齋百華詩箋譜不分卷

Li Hui-Lin, *The Garden Flowers of China* (New York: The Ronald Press Company, 1959); Shen Zhiyu, "Ba 'Luoxuan biangu jian pu,'" *Wenwu*, no. 165 (1964, no. 7) (July 1964), pp. 7-9, and pl. 1 [halftone; 4 selected sheets illustrated]; *Zhiwu mingshi tukao* (38 *juan*), *fu Zhiwu mingshi tukao changbian* (22 *juan*), by Wu Qijun, edited by Lu Yinggu (Reprint. Taibei: Taiwan Shangwu yinshu guan, 1965), *Zhiwu mingshi tukao* section, esp. pp. 280-281, p. 397, and pp. 610-612, and *Zhiwu mingshi tukao changbian* section, pp. 692-693; Fu Xihua, *Zhongguo banhua yanjiu zhongyao shumu*, in *Shuhua shulu tieti fukan* (Hong Kong: Xianggang Zhong Mei tushu gongsi, 1969), p. 3a, nos. 861-863; Yu Hailan, "Qing dai hua jian yishu," *Duoyun (Flowery Cloud)*, no. 7 (November 1984), pp. 158-159; *Zhongguo gudai muke hua xuan ji*, compiled and edited by Zheng Zhenduo (Beijing: Renmin meishu chuban she, 1985), vol. 7 [unpaginated; halftone; 1 selected leaf illustrated]; *Zhonghua minguo chuantong banhua yishu (The Traditional Art of Chinese Woodblock Prints)*, organized by Xingzheng yuan wenhua jianshe weiyuan hui (Council for Cultural Planning and Development, Executive Yuan) [Taibei: Xingzheng yuan wenhua jianshe weiyuan hui (Council for Cultural Planning and Development, Executive Yuan), 1986], pp. 22-27 [6 selected sheets illustrated], and pp. 44-53 [10 selected sheets illustrated]; Wang Qingzheng, "The Arts of Ming Woodblock-printed Images and Decorated Paper Albums," in *The Chinese Scholar's Studio: Artistic Life in the Late Ming Period: An Exhibition from the Shanghai Museum*, edited by Chu-tsing Li and James C.Y. Watt, pp. 58-60, pp. 96-97, cat. no. 27 [color and halftone; 4 selected half-folios illustrated], and p. 161, cat. no. 27 [catalogue entry by Robert D. Mowry] (New York: Thames and Hudson Inc., published in association with New York: The Asia Society Galleries, 1987); *Beijing tushu guan guji shanben shumu*, compiled by Beijing tushu guan [Beijing: Shumu wenxian chuban she, n.d. (1987)], vol. 3, p. 1358; *Zhongguo meishu quanji: Huihua bian*, vol. 20, *Banhua*, compiled by Zhongguo meishu quanji bianji weiyuan hui (Shanghai: Shanghai renmin meishu chuban she, 1988), illustrations section, p. 218, no. 210 [color; 2 selected leaves illustrated], text section, p. 76, no. 210 [catalogue entry in Chinese]; *Chûgoku kodai hanga ten: Machida shisei 30-shûnen kinen, Nitchû heiwa yûkô jôyaku teiketsu 10-shûnen kinen*, Chûgoku hanga 2000-nen ten, dai 3 bu, compiled by Machida shiritsu kokusai hanga bijutsukan [and] Takimoto Hiroyuki (Machida, Japan: Machida shiritsu kokusai hanga bijutsukan, 1988), p. 250, cat. no. 9.17; *Zhongguo hua jing (China Floral Encyclopaedia)*, edited by Chen Junyu and Cheng Xuke (Shanghai: Shanghai wenhua chuban she, 1990); *Wenmei zhai shi jian pu* [Originally published in Tianjin: Wenmei zhai, 1911. Reprint (facsimile reproduction). Beijing: Zhongguo shudian, 1992]; *Zhongguo Jiade '95 chun ji paimai hui: Guji shanben (China Guardian '95 Spring Auctions: Rare Books)* [Beijing: Zhongguo Jiade guoji paimai youxian gongsi (China Guardian Auctions Co., Ltd.), 1995], lot no. 446 [2 selected volumes illustrated; this edition has illustrations on the verso only]; *Botanica: The Illustrated A-Z of Over 10,000 Garden Plants and How to Cultivate Them* (Milsons Point, N.S.W., Australia: Mynah, an imprint of Random House Australia Pty Ltd., 1997); James Cahill, "Chinese Painting: Innovation After 'Progress' Ends," in *China: 5,000 Years: Innovation and Transformation in the Arts*, selected by Sherman Lee (New York: Guggenheim Museum Publications, 1998), p. 187, see also cat. no. 202 [color; 6 selected album-mounted sheets illustrated], and cat. no. 203 [color; 7 selected double-leaves illustrated]; *Zhongguo shudian 1998 nian chun ji shukan ziliao paimai hui* (Beijing: Beijing Haiwang cun paimai youxian zeren gongsi, 1998), lot no. 186 [2 selected half-folios from 2 volumes illustrated; this edition said to be printed in 1906]; Peter Valder, *The Garden Plants of China* (Balmain, N. S.W., Australia: Florilegium, 1999).

24A-B
Inscribed Oracle Bones
刻有文字的甲骨

Tsuen-hsuin Tsien, *Written on Bamboo and Silk: The Beginnings of Chinese Books and Inscriptions* (Chicago: The University of Chicago Press, 1962), pp. 19-37; Tung Tso-pin [Dong Zuobin], *Fifty Years of Studies in Oracle Inscriptions* (Tokyo: Centre for East Asian Cultural Studies, 1964); Hsü Chin-hsiung, *The Menzies Collection of Shang Dynasty Oracle Bones*, vol. 1, *A Catalogue* (Toronto: The Royal Ontario Museum, 1972); Christian Deydier, *Les Jiaguwen: Essai bibliographique et synthèse des études* (Paris: École française d'Extrême-Orient, 1976); Hsü Chin-hsiung, *The Menzies Collection of Shang Dynasty Oracle Bones*, vol. 2, *The Text* (Toronto: The Royal Ontario Museum, in cooperation with Hong Kong: The Chinese University of Hong Kong, 1977); David N. Keightley, *Sources of Shang History: The Oracle-Bone Inscriptions of Bronze Age China* (Berkeley and Los Angeles: University of California Press, 1978); *Jiagu wen he ji*, edited by Guo Moruo, compiled by Zhongguo shehui kexue yuan lishi yanjiu suo, vol. 3 [1978], p. 796, no. 5509 zheng, and p. 797, no. 5509 fan [*Jiagu* 5403]; vol. 6 [1979], p. 2298, no. 16886 [*Jiagu* 5402]; vol. 8 [1981], p. 2950, no. 22723 [*Jiagu* 5538, *Jiagu* 5518], and p. 3210, no. 25663 [*Jiagu* 6019] [N.p. (Beijing): Zhonghua shuju, 1978-1983]; Hsü Chin-hsiung, *Oracle Bones from the White and Other Collections* (Toronto: The Royal Ontario Museum, 1979); Wu Haokun and Pan You, *Zhongguo jiagu xue shi* (Shanghai: Shanghai renmin chuban she, 1985); William G. Boltz, *The Origin and Early Development of the Chinese Writing System* (New Haven, Conn.: American Oriental Society, 1994), pp. 31-72; David N. Keightley, "Sacred Characters," in *China: Ancient Culture, Modern Land*, edited by Robert E. Murowchick (Norman, Okla.: University of Oklahoma Press, 1994), p. 70-79; Hu Houxuan, "Dalu xian cang zhi jiagu wenzi," *Zhongyang yanjiu yuan Lishi yuyan yanjiu suo jikan (Bulletin of the Institute of History and Philology, Academia Sinica)* 67, pt. 4 (December 1996), pp. 815-876 [includes abstract in English, "The Collection of Oracle Bone Inscriptions on the Chinese Continent," p. 876; David N. Keightley, "Shang Oracle-Bone Inscriptions," in *New Sources of Early Chinese History: An Introduction to the Reading of Inscriptions and Manuscripts*, edited by Edward L. Shaughnessy [N.p. (Bethlehem, Pa.): The Society for the Study of Early China; Berkeley, Calif.: The Institute of East Asian Studies, University of California, Berkeley, 1997], pp. 15-55; Endymion Wilkinson, *Chinese History: A Manual* (Cambridge, Mass.: Harvard University Asia Center, 1998), pp. 377-396; Li Xueqin, "Jiagu xue yi bai nian de huigu yu qianzhan," *Wenwu*, no. 500 (1998, no. 1) (January 1998), pp. 33-36 [accompanied by abstract in English, "One Century of Study of Oracle Bone and Shell Inscriptions: Retrospective and Projection," p. 37]; David N. Keightley, "The Oracle-Bone Inscriptions of the Late Shang Dynasty," in *Sources of Chinese Tradition*, compiled by Wm. Theodore de Bary and Irene Bloom, 2d ed., vol. 1 (New York: Columbia University Press, 1999), pp. 3-23.

25
Rubbings from the Inscribed Bronze Wine Vessel "Quan Bo" *Jia*
犬伯罨青銅器拓本

John J. Bodor, *Rubbings and Textures: A Graphic Technique* (New York and Amsterdam: Reinhold Book Corporation, 1968), pp. 6-15 and pp. 49-54; *San dai jijin wencun*, compiled and edited by Luo Zhenyu [originally published 1937; reprint; 3 vols.; Beijing: Zhonghua shuju, 1983); Joseph Needham, *Science and Civilisation in China*, vol. 5, *Chemistry and Chemical Technology*, pt. 1, *Paper and Printing*, by Tsien Tsuen-hsuin (Cambridge and New York: Cambridge University Press, 1985), p. 144 and p. 145, and fig. 1107; Ma Chengyuan, *Ancient Chinese Bronzes*, edited by Hsio-yen Shih (Hong Kong and Oxford: Oxford University Press, 1986), pp. 195-196; Robert W. Bagley, *Shang Ritual Bronzes in the Arthur M. Sackler Collections* (Washington, D.C.: The Arthur M. Sackler Foundation; Cambridge, Mass.: Arthur M. Sackler Museum, Harvard University, 1987); *Beijing tushu guan cang qingtong qi quanxing tapian ji*, compiled and edited by Beijing tushu guan (Beijing: Beijing tushu guan chuban she, 1997), vol. 1, prefatory matter section, pp. 1-2 [preface by Jia Shuangxi], and vol. 3, catalogue section, pp. 59-60 [illustrations of rubbing and colophons; catalogue entry in Chinese].

26
Rubbings from the Inscribed Bronze Wine Vessel "Ya 'Qi' Fu" Jia *You*
亞龏父甲卣青銅器拓本

Tu Lien-chê, "Wang I-jung," in *Eminent Chinese of the Ch'ing Period (1644-1912)*, edited by Arthur W. Hummel, vol. 2 (Washington, D.C.: The Library of Congress; Washington, D. C.: United States Government Printing Office, 1944), pp. 826-828; Ma Chengyuan, *Ancient Chinese Bronzes*, edited by Hsio-yen Shih (Hong Kong and Oxford: Oxford University Press, 1986), pp. 198-199; Robert W. Bagley, *Shang Ritual Bronzes in the Arthur M. Sackler Collections* (Washington, D.C.: The Arthur M. Sackler Foundation; Cambridge, Mass.: Arthur M. Sackler Museum, Harvard University, 1987); *Yin Zhou jinwen jicheng*, compiled and edited by Zhongguo shehui kexue yuan kaogu yanjiu suo, vol. 10 [N.p. (Beijing): Zhonghua shuju, 1990], illustrations section, p. 143, nos. 5049.1, 5049.2; *Beijing tushu guan cang qingtong qi quanxing tapian ji*, compiled and edited by Beijing tushu guan (Beijing: Beijing tushu guan chuban she, 1997), vol. 3, catalogue section, pp. 24-25 [illustration of rubbings and colophons; catalogue entry in Chinese].

27

Rubbing from the Inscribed Bronze Bell "Jing Ren 'X'"

Zhong

井人女鐘青銅器拓本

Chin shi kyûzô jû shô: Sen'oku seishô besshû (Ten Bronze Bells Formerly in the Collection of Ch'ên Chieh-ch'i, being a Special Volume of the Senoku-seishô, or, The Collection of the Chinese Bronzes of Baron Sumitomo), explanatory notes by Hamada Kôsaku, 2d ed. [N.p. (Kyoto): N.p. (Sumitomo Kichizaemon), 1924], pagination for Japanese section, pp. 10-11, no. 1, and pagination for English section, p. 7, no. 1; Guo Moruo, *Liang Zhou jinwen ci daxi kaoshi* (Tokyo: Bunky°d shoten, 1935), vol. 2, pp. 149b-150b [text fully transcribed and explicated]; Hiromu Momose, "Tuan-fang," in *Eminent Chinese of the Ch'ing Period (1644-1912)*, edited by Arthur W. Hummel, vol. 2 (Washington, D.C.: The Library of Congress; Washington, D.C.: United States Government Printing Office, 1944), pp. 780-782; *Shanghai bowu guan cang qingtong qi*, compiled and edited by Shanghai bowu guan (Shanghai: Shanghai renmin meishu chuban she, 1964), vol. 1, no. 61 [color; front view illustrated], vol. 2, no. 61 [catalogue entry; text of inscription transcribed in full]; Noel Barnard [Ba Na] and Cheung Kwong-yue [Zhang Guangyu], *Zhong Ri Ou Mei Ao Niu suo jian suo ta suo mo jinwen huibian (Rubbings and Hand Copies of Bronze Inscriptions in Chinese, Japanese, European, American, and Australasian Collections)* (Taibei: Yee Wen Publishing Coy. Ltd., 1978), vol. 3, *Inscriptions Nos. 128-246*, pp. 239-240, nos. 157-158; *Yin Zhou jinwen jicheng*, compiled and edited by Zhongguo shehui kexue yuan kaogu yanjiu suo, vol. 1 [N.p. (Beijing): Zhonghua shuju, 1984], illustrations section, p. 99, no. 110, text section, p. 14, no. 110; Ma Chengyuan, *Ancient Chinese Bronzes*, edited by Hsio-yen Shih (Hong Kong and Oxford: Oxford University Press, 1986), pp. 203-204; *Shang Zhou qingtong qi mingwen xuan*, compiled by Shanghai bowu guan Shang Zhou qingtong qi mingwen xuan bianxie zu, vol. 1, *Shang, Xi Zhou qingtong qi mingwen* (Beijing: Wenwu chuban she, 1986), pp. 234-237, no. 396, and vol. 3, *Shang, Xi Zhou qingtong qi mingwen shiwen ji zhushi*, edited by Ma Chengyuan; compiled by Chen Peifen, Pan Jianming, Chen Jianmin, and Pu Maozuo (Beijing: Wenwu chuban she, 1988), p. 272, no. 396; Jessica Rawson, *Western Zhou Ritual Bronzes from the Arthur M. Sackler Collections* (Washington, D.C.: The Arthur M. Sackler Foundation; Cambridge, Mass.: Arthur M. Sackler Museum, Harvard University, 1990), vols. 1-2; Edward L. Shaughnessy, *Sources of Western Zhou History: Inscribed Bronze Vessels* (Berkeley and Los Angeles: University of California Press, 1991); Lothar von Falkenhausen, *Suspended Music: Chime-Bells in the Culture of Bronze Age China* (Berkeley and Los Angeles: University of California Press, 1993), pp. 40-46, pp. 151-157, and pp. 164-167; Edward L. Shaughnessy, "Western Zhou Bronze Inscriptions," in *New Sources of Early Chinese History: An Introduction to the Reading of Inscriptions and Manuscripts*, edited by Edward L. Shaughnessy [N.p. (Bethlehem, Pa.): The Society for the Study of Early China; Berkeley, Calif.: The Institute of East Asian Studies, University of California, Berkeley, 1997], pp. 57-84; *Beijing tushu guan cang qingtong qi quanxing tapian ji*, compiled and edited by Beijing tushu guan (Beijing: Beijing tushu guan chuban she, 1997), vol. 1, catalogue section, p. 11 [illustration of rubbing and colophon; catalogue entry in Chinese].

28

Rubbings from the Inscribed Bronze Vessel "Zhong Yi Fu"

Xu

仲義父盨青銅器拓本

Ma Chengyuan, *Ancient Chinese Bronzes*, edited by Hsio-yen Shih (Hong Kong and Oxford: Oxford University Press, 1986), p. 191; *Yin Zhou jinwen jicheng*, compiled and edited by Zhongguo shehui kexue yuan kaogu yanjiu suo, vol. 9 [N.p. (Beijing): Zhonghua shuju, 1988], illustrations section, pp. 30-31, nos. 4386.1, 4386.2, 4387.1, 4387.2, text section, p. 6, nos. 4386-4387; Edward L. Shaughnessy, *Sources of Western Zhou History: Inscribed Bronze Vessels* (Berkeley and Los Angeles: University of California Press, 1991); Edward L. Shaughnessy, "Western Zhou Bronze Inscriptions," in *New Sources of Early Chinese History: An Introduction to the Reading of Inscriptions and Manuscripts*, edited by Edward L. Shaughnessy [N.p. (Bethlehem, Pa.): The Society for the Study of Early China; Berkeley, Calif.: The Institute of East Asian Studies, University of California, Berkeley, 1997], pp. 57-84; *Beijing tushu guan cang qingtong qi quanxing tapian ji*, compiled and edited by Beijing tushu guan (Beijing: Beijing tushu guan chuban she, 1997), vol. 1, catalogue section, p. 190 [illustration of rubbings and colophon; catalogue entry in Chinese].

29

Collected Rubbings of Terminal Roof Tiles with Inscriptions and Animal Figures

瓦當集拓

Tseng Yu-ho Ecke, *Chinese Calligraphy* (Philadelphia: Philadelphia Museum of Art; Boston: Boston Book & Art, Publisher, 1971), cat. no. 5; *Qin Han wadang (Eave Tiles of the Qin and Han Dynasties)*, compiled and edited by Xi'an shi wenwu guanli weiyuan hui (Xian Municipal Administrative Commission for Cultural Relics) [N.p. (Xi'an): Shaanxi renmin meishu chuban she, (title page dated 1984) 1985], preface by Fu Jiayi in Chinese and English; *Xin bian Qin Han wadang tulu*, compiled and edited by Shaanxi sheng kaogu yanjiu suo Qin Han yanjiu shi (Xi'an: San Qin chuban she, 1986), pp. 1-12 and p. 391; *Wadang huibian*, compiled and edited by Qian Juntao, Zhang Xingyi, and Xu Mingnong (Shanghai: Shanghai renmin meishu chuban she, 1988), introductory text by Zhang Xingyi [unpaginated]; Xu Xitai, Lou Yudong, and Wei Jiaozu, *Zhou Qin Han wadang* (Beijing: Wenwu chuban she, 1988), esp. introductory text [unpaginated]; Chen Jieqi, Qin qian wenzi zhi yu, reorganized by Chen Jikui (Ji'nan, Shandong: Qi Lu shushe, 1991); *Zhongguo gudai yinshua shi tuce (An Illustrated History of Printing in Ancient China)*, compiled by Zhongguo yinshua bowu guan (The Printing Museum of China) [Hong Kong: Xianggang chengshi daxue chuban she (City University of Hong Kong Press); Beijing: Wenwu chuban she (Cultural Relics Publishing House), 1998], p. 33 [middle left].

30

Collected Rubbings of Stamped Bricks with Inscriptions

磚文集拓

Kandai no gazôsen [Exhibition: Figured Bricks in Han Dynasties (202 B.C.-220 A.D.) in the Collection of Tenri Univ. Sankôkan Museum], compiled and edited by Tenri sankôkan (Tokyo: Tenri gyararî (Tenri Gallery), 1987); *Zhongguo gudai zhuan wen*, compiled and edited by Wang Yong and Li Miao (Beijing: Zhishi chuban she, 1990), text section, pp. 1-31; *Zhongguo gudai yinshua shi tuce (An Illustrated History of Printing in Ancient China)*, compiled by Zhongguo yinshua bowu guan (The Printing Museum of China) [Hong Kong: Xianggang chengshi daxue chuban she (City University of Hong Kong Press); Beijing: Wenwu chuban she (Cultural Relics Publishing House), 1998], p. 33 [lower left and lower right corners].

31

Collected Rubbings of Bronze Mirrors with Inscriptions

鏡銘集拓

A. Bulling, *The Decoration of Mirrors of the Han Period: A Chronology* (Ascona, Switzerland: Artibus Asiae Publishers, 1960); Michael Loewe, *Ways to Paradise: The Chinese Quest for Immortality* (London and Boston: George Allen & Unwin Ltd., 1979), pp. 60-85 [chapter 3, "TLV Mirrors and Their Significance"], pp. 144-147 [notes to chapter 3], pp. 158-191 ["Classification and List of TLV Mirrors"], pp. 192-203 ["Select Inscriptions of TLV Mirrors"], and pls. 2-20, 22; Wong Yanchung, "Bronze Mirror Art of the Han Dynasty" [translated from the Chinese by Christopher Homfray], *Orientations* 19, no. 12 (December 1988), pp. 42-53; Kong Xiangxing, and Liu Yiman, *Zhongguo tong jing tudian* (Beijing: Wenwu chuban she, 1992), pp. 230-233, and pp. 268-273; *Bronze Mirrors from Ancient China: Donald H. Graham Jr. Collection*, preface, essay and catalogue by Toru Nakano, essays by Tseng Yuho Ecke and Suzanne Cahill [N.p. (Honolulu): N.p. (Donald H. Graham, Jr.), 1994], pp. 9-49 [essay by Nakano Tôru], and p. 82, cat. no. 12 through p. 205, cat. no. 73 [mirrors from Western Han through Sui or early Tang]; *Zhongguo guojia tushu guan guji zhenpin tulu*, edited by Ren Jiyu (Beijing: Beijing tushu guan chuban she, 1999), p. 262, cat. no. 286 [1 selected leaf illustrated].

32

Illustration of a Han Dynasty Procession

漢君車畫像

Édouard Chavannes, *Mission archéologique dans la Chine septentrionale: Planches* (Paris: Imprimerie nationale; Paris: Ernest Leroux, Éditeur, 1909), pt. 1, pl. LXII, no. 126 [halftone; entire rubbing illustrated]; Édouard Chavannes, *Mission archéologique dans la Chine septentrionale*, tome 1, pt. 1, *La sculpture à l'époque des Han* (Paris: Ernest Leroux, Éditeur,

1913), pp. 249-250; *Corpus des pierres sculptées Han (estampages), I (Han dai huaxiang quanji chu bian: Bali daxue Beijing Han xue yanjiu suo tu pu congkan zhi yi)*, [compiled by Fu Xihua] [Beijing: Centre d'études sinologiques, Pékin, Université de Paris (Bali daxue Beijing Han xue yanjiu suo), 1950], Chinese text, p. 29, no. 255 [catalogue entry in Chinese], and pl. 155 [halftone; entire rubbing illustrated]; R.H. van Gulik, *Chinese Pictorial Art as Viewed by the Connoisseur: Notes on the Means and Methods of Traditional Chinese Connoisseurship of Pictorial Art, Based upon a Study of the Art of Mounting Scrolls in China and Japan* (Rome: Istituto Italiano per il Medio ed Estremo Oriente, 1958), p. 88; John J. Bodor, *Rubbings and Textures: A Graphic Technique* (New York and Amsterdam: Reinhold Book Corporation, 1968), pp. 6-15 and pp. 49-54; Doi Yoshiko, *Kodai Chûgoku no gazôseki* (Tokyo: Dôhôsha, 1986), pp. 117-129, and pp. 207-213 [summary in English, "Ancient Chinese Stone Reliefs"]; Yang Boda, "Shi lun Shandong huaxiang shi de kefa," *Gugong bowu yuan yuankan (Palace Museum Journal)*, no. 38 (1987, no. 4), pp. 3-4, p. 13, pp. 15-16, and p. 24 n. 21 [see also 2 illustrations on inside front cover]; *Zhongguo meishu quanji: Huihua bian*, vol. 18, *Huaxiang shi huaxiang zhuan*, compiled by Zhongguo meishu quanji bianji weiyuan hui (Shanghai: Shanghai renmin meishu chuban she, 1988), illustrations section, p. 73, no. 87 [color; entire rubbing illustrated], text section, p. 30, no. 87 [catalogue entry in Chinese by Shen Kuiyi; inscriptions transcribed in full]; *Liang Qichao tiba moji shufa ji*, compiled and edited by Ji Yaping, Jia Shuangxi, et al. (Beijing: Rongbao zhai chuban she, 1995), p. 50, no. 34 [illustration], and p. 209 [transcription]; R. Thomas Berner, "The Ancient Chinese Process of Reprography," *Technology and Culture* 38, no. 2 (April 1997), pp. 424-431.

33

Commendatory Stele for Cao Quan, Magistrate of Geyang during the Han Dynasty

漢郃陽令曹全紀功碑

Shike tiba suoyin, edited by Yang Dianxun, rev. ed. (Shanghai: Shangwu yinshu guan, 1957), pp. 18-19; *Kan Sô Zen no hi*, Shoseki meihin sôkan, no. 5 [Tokyo: Nigensha, 1959 (18th printing, 1973)]; Patricia Buckley Ebrey, "Later Han Stone Inscriptions," *Harvard Journal of Asiatic Studies* 40, no. 2 (December 1980), pp. 325-353, esp. pp. 339-351; Gao Wen, *Han bei ji shi* (Kaifeng: Henan daxue chuban she, 1985), pp. 487-505, and fig. 15; Ma Ziyun, *Beitie jianding qianshuo* (Beijing: Zijin cheng chuban she, 1985), figs. 10-1 and 10-2; *Zhongguo meishu quanji: Shufa zhuanke bian*, vol. 1, *Shang Zhou zhi Qin Han shufa*, compiled by Zhongguo meishu quanji bianji weiyuan hui (Beijing: Renmin meishu chuban she, 1987), illustrations section, pp. 172-173, no. 100 [color; 3 selected leaves of album illustrated], text section, p. 82, no. 100 [catalogue entry in Chinese by Su Shishu]; *Sô Zen no hi: Gokan*, Chûgoku hôsho sen, no. 8 (Tokyo: Nigensha, 1988); *Guoli zhongyang tushu guan tecang xuan lu*, compiled and edited by Guoli zhongyang tushu guan tecang zu, rev. ed. (Taibei: Guoli zhongyang tushu guan, 1989), p. 49, fig. 40 [color; 1 selected leaf from album of rubbings illustrated]; Yuan Weichun, *Qin Han bei shu* (Beijing: Beijing gongyi meishu chuban she, 1990), pp. 534-555; *Liang Qichao tiba moji shufa ji*, compiled and edited by Ji Yaping, Jia Shuangxi, et al. (Beijing: Rongbao zhai chuban she, 1995), pp. 42-43, no. 27 [illustrations], and pp. 206-207 [transcriptions]; *An Siyuan cang shanben beitie xuan (The Chunhuage tie and Rare Rubbings from the Collection of Robert Hatfield Ellsworth)* (Beijing: Wenwu chuban she, 1996), pp. 92-95 [catalogue entry by Wang Jingxian]; *Cao Quan bei* (Beijing: Huaxia chuban she, 1999); *Zhongguo guojia tushu guan guji zhenpin tulu*, edited by Ren Jiyu (Beijing: Beijing tushu guan chuban she, 1999), p. 229, cat. no. 256 [2 selected facing leaves from album of rubbings illustrated].

34

Epitaph of Fan Min, Governor of Ba Commandery during the Han Dynasty

漢故領校巴郡太守樊敏府君碑

Li shi (27 *juan*), compiled by Hong Shi [preface dated 1167], [facsimile reproduction of the Ming Wanli-period edition], *juan* 11/9a-12b, in Sibu congkan san bian, vol. 30 (Shanghai: Shanghai shudian, 1985)]; *Shi'er yan zhai jinshi guoyan lu* (18 *juan*), compiled and edited by Wang Yun [preface by Wang Yun dated 1886], reprint ed. (Yangzhou: Chen Henghe shulin, 1931), *juan* 2/10a-13a, also reprinted in *Shike shiliao xin bian*, compiled by Xinwenfeng chuban gongsi bianji bu (Taibei: Xinwenfeng chuban gongsi, 1977), vol. 10; *Baqiong shi jinshi buzheng* (130 *juan*), compiled by Lu Zengxiang, edited by Liu Chenggan (Wuxing: Lu shi Xigu lou, 1925), *juan* 6/20a-33a, also reprinted in *Shike shiliao xin bian*, compiled by Xinwenfeng chuban gongsi bianji bu (Taibei: Xinwenfeng chuban gongsi, 1977), vol. 10, p. 4100-4107, and also reprinted as *Baqiong shi jinshi buzheng* (130 *juan*), fu *Jinshi zhaji*, *Jinshi quwei*, *Yuan jinshi ou can*, compiled by Lu Zengxiang (Beijing: Wenwu chuban she, 1985), pp. 31-34; *Shike tiba suoyin*, edited by Yang Dianxun, rev. ed. (Shanghai: Shangwu yinshu guan, 1957), pp. 20-21, and p. 113; Cao Dan, "Lushan xian Han Fan Min que qingli fuyuan," *Wenwu*, no. 157 (1963, no. 11) (November 1963), pp. 65-66 [see also figs. 1-3 following text]; *Catalogue of Chinese Rubbings from Field Museum* (Chicago: Field Museum of Natural History, 1981), pp. 73-74, cat. no. 292; *Li shi, Li xu* [*Li shi* (27 *juan*); *Li xu* (21 *juan*)], compiled by Hong Shi [preface to *Li shi* dated 1167; reprint, facsmile reproduction of the Hong shi Huimu zhai edition of 1872] (Beijing: Zhonghua shuju, 1985), pp. 128-129, and pp. 315-318; *Beijing tushu guan cang shike xu lu*, edited by Xu Ziqiang (Beijing: Shumu wenxian chuban she, 1988), pp. 43-44, no. 32; *Beijing tushu guan cang Zhongguo lidai shike taben huibian*, compiled and edited by Beijing tushu guan jinshi zu, vol. 1 (Zhengzhou, Henan: Zhongzhou guji chuban she, 1989), p. 187; Yuan Weichun, *Qin Han bei shu* (Beijing: Beijing gongyi meishu chuban she, 1990), pp. 577-588; *Liang Qichao tiba moji shufa ji*, compiled and edited by Ji Yaping, Jia Shuangxi, et al. (Beijing: Rongbao zhai chuban she, 1995), p. 47, no. 31 [illustration], and p. 208 [transcriptions].

35

Inscription for a Buddhist Image Constructed by the Monk Huicheng to Commemorate His Late Father, the Duke of Shiping and Regional Inspector of Luozhou

比丘慧成為亡父洛州刺史始平公造像題記

Bi Yuan, *Zhongzhou jinshi ji* (5 *juan*) [first published 1787], Congshu jicheng chu bian, compiled and edited by Wang Yunwu (Shanghai: Shangwu yinshu guan, 1936), p. 11 (in *juan* 1); *Shike tiba suoyin*, edited by Yang Dianxun, rev. ed. (Shanghai: Shangwu yinshu

guan, 1957), pp. 264-265; Joseph Needham, *Science and Civilisation in China*, vol. 5, *Chemistry and Chemical Technology*, pt. 1, *Paper and Printing*, by Tsien Tsuen-hsuin (Cambridge and New York: Cambridge University Press, 1985), pp. 141-142, and fig. 1105; Ma Ziyun, *Beitie jianding qianshuo* (Beijing: Zijin cheng chuban she, 1985), fig. 29; *Zhongguo meishu quanji: Shufa zhuanke bian*, vol. 2, *Wei Jin Nanbei chao shufa*, compiled by Zhongguo meishu quanji bianji weiyuan hui (Beijing: Renmin meishu chuban she, 1986), illustrations section, pp. 162-163, no. 89 [entire rubbing and colophons illustrated in color, and detail of inscription in halftone], and text section, pp. 56-57, no. 89 [catalogue in Chinese by Xu Zhiqiang]; *Beijing tushu guan cang shike xu lu*, edited by Xu Ziqiang (Beijing: Shumu wenxian chuban she, 1988), pp. 117-118, no. 3; *Zhongguo meishu quanji: Diaosu bian*, compiled by Zhongguo meishu quanji bianji weiyuan hui, vol. 11, *Longmen shiku diaoke* (Shanghai: Shanghai renmin meishu chuban she, 1988), illustrations section, p. 12, no. 11 [color], text section, p. 4, no. 11 [catalogue entry in Chinese]; *Beijing tushu guan cang Zhongguo lidai shike taben huibian*, compiled and edited by Beijing tushu guan jinshi zu, vol. 3 (Zhengzhou, Henan: Zhongzhou guji chuban she, 1989), p. 33; Amy McNair, "Engraved Calligraphy in China: Recension and Reception," *The Art Bulletin* 77, no. 1 (March 1995), pp. 109-113, and figs. 2-3 [halftone; entire rubbing and colophons, and selected detail of rubbing, illustrated]; *Longmen ershi pin: Beike yu zaoxiang yishu*, edited by Liu Jinglong [Beijing: Zhongguo shijie yu chuban she (China Esperanto Press), 1995], no. 4 [unpaginated; 12 pages of text, drawings, and photographs]; Wang Renbo, "Shi lun Yungang, Longmen shiku Bei Wei zhuyao zaoxiang ticai yu fojiao shi zhu wenti, " in *Shanghai bowu guan jikan*, no. 7 (Shanghai: Shanghai shuhua chuban she, 1996), pp. 276-277; *Zhongguo gudai yinshua shi tuce (An Illustrated History of Printing in Ancient China)*, compiled by Zhongguo yinshua bowu guan (The Printing Museum of China) [Hong Kong: Xianggang chengshi daxue chuban she (City University of Hong Kong Press); Beijing: Wenwu chuban she (Cultural Relics Publishing House), 1998], p. 31 [upper left corner]; Lu Huiwen, "Calligraphy of Stone Engravings in Northern Wei Loyang," in *Character & Context in Chinese Calligraphy*, edited by Cary Y. Liu, Dora C.Y. Ching, and Judith G. Smith (Princeton, N.J.: The Art Museum, Princeton University, 1999), pp. 78-103; *Zhongguo guojia tushu guan guji zhenpin tulu*, edited by Ren Jiyu (Beijing: Beijing tushu guan chuban she, 1999), pp. 232-233, cat. no. 260 [entire rubbing and colophons illustrated].

36

Inscription and Illustrated Panels for the Base of a Buddhist Image Constructed by Cao Wangxi

曹望憘造像記

Shi'er yan zhai jinshi guoyan lu (18 *juan*), compiled and edited by Wang Yun [preface by Wang Yun dated 1886], reprint ed. (Yangzhou: Chen Henghe shulin, 1931), *juan* 6/13b-14b, also reprinted in *Shike shiliao xin bian*, compiled by Xinwenfeng chuban gongsi bianji bu (Taibei: Xinwenfeng chuban gongsi, 1977), vol. 10, p. 7843; *Shike tiba suoyin*, edited by Yang Dianxun, rev. ed. (Shanghai: Shangwu yinshu guan, 1957), p. 269; *Zhongguo meishu quanji: Huihua bian*, vol. 19, *Shike xianhua*, compiled by Zhongguo meishu quanji bianji weiyuan hui (Shanghai: Shanghai renmin meishu chuban she, 1988), illustrations section, p. 3, no. 3 [color; entire sheet comprising 4 rubbings illustrated], text section, p. 1, no. 3 [catalogue entry in Chinese]; *Beijing tushu guan cang Zhongguo lidai shike taben huibian*, compiled and edited by Beijing tushu guan jinshi zu, vol. 4 (Zhengzhou, Henan:

Zhongzhou guji chuban she, 1989), p. 181; Ma Ziyun and Shi Anchang, *Beitie jianding* (Guilin, Guangxi: Guangxi shifan daxue chuban she, 1993), p. 175-176, and fig. 87 [halftone; entire sheet comprising 4 rubbings illustrated].

37

Finely Engraved Illustration in the Linear Manner on the Lintel of a Pagoda Doorway

塔門楣線雕

Wang Ziyun, "Tang dai de shike xianhua," *Wenwu cankao ziliao*, no. 68 (1956, no. 4) (April 1956), pp. 29-33 [see also illustration on p. 28]; *Beijing tushu guan cang huaxiang taben huibian*, compiled by Beijing tushu guan shanben bu jinshi zu (Beijing: Shumu wenxian chuban she, 1993), vol. 9, p. 221; Luo Zhewen, *Ancient Pagodas in China* (Beijing: Foreign Languages Press, 1994), p. 133 [text], and p. 136 [illustration]; Luo Zhewen, *Zhongguo gu ta* (Beijing: Waiwen chuban she, 1994), p. 133 [text], and p. 136 [illustration]; Xia Zhifeng and Zhang Binyuan, *Zhongguo gu ta* (Hangzhou: Zhejiang renmin chuban she, 1996), pp. 73-84, pp. 92-101, and pp. 158-160.

38

Portrait of the Bodhisattva Guanyin

觀音像

C.N. Tay, "Kuan-Yin: The Cult of Half Asia," *History of Religions* 16, no. 2 (November 1976), pp. 147-177; *Zhongguo meishu quanji: Huihua bian*, vol. 19, *Shike xianhua*, compiled by Zhongguo meishu quanji bianji weiyuan hui (Shanghai: Shanghai renmin meishu chuban she, 1988), illustrations section, p. 153, no. 141 [color; entire rubbing illustrated], text section, p. 52, no. 141 [catalogue entry in Chinese]; Latika Lahiri, " Kuan-Shih-Yin, Avalokitesvara in Chinese Buddhism," in *Buddhist Iconography* (New Delhi: Tibet House, 1989), pp. 142-148; Yü Chün-fang, " Feminine Images of Kuan-yin in Post-Tang China," *Journal of Chinese Religions*, no. 18 (Fall 1990), pp. 61-89; *Beijing tushu guan cang huaxiang taben huibian*, compiled by Beijing tushu guan shanben bu jinshi zu (Beijing: Shumu wenxian chuban she, 1993), vol. 9, p. 220 (zhou 236); Yü Chün-fang, "Guanyin: The Chinese Transformation of Avalokiteshvara," in *Latter Days of the Law: Images of Chinese Buddhism, 850-1850*, edited by Marsha Weidner (Lawrence, Kan.: Spencer Museum of Art, The University of Kansas, in association with Honolulu: University of Hawaii Press, 1994), pp. 151-181.

39

Portrait of Confucius

孔子像

Baba Harukichi, *Kôshi seisekishi* (Tokyo: Daitô bunka kyôkai, 1934), pp. 162-163, no. 7; Baba Harukichi, *Kô Mô Seisekizu kan* (Tokyo: Santô bunka kenkyûkai, 1940), section on portraits, p. 46, lower right corner [halftone; entire rubbing illustrated; inscription transcribed in full]; Liu Wu-Chi, *Confucius, His Life and Time* (New York: Philosophical Library, Inc., 1955. Reprint. Westport, Conn.: Greenwood Press, Publishers, 1972); Kong Demao and Ke Lan, *The House of Confucius*, translated [from the Chinese] by Rosemary Roberts, edited and with an introduction by Frances Wood (London and Sydney: Hodder & Stoughton Limited, 1988), pp. 7-9; *Confucius: The Analects ("Lun yü")*, translated by D. C. Lau, 2d ed. (Hong Kong: The Chinese University Press, 1992), pp. ix-liii [introduction]; *Beijing tushu guan cang huaxiang taben huibian*, compiled by Beijing tushu guan shanben bu jinshi zu (Beijing: Shumu wenxian chuban she, 1993), vol. 6, p. 170; John E. Wills, Jr., *Mountain of Fame: Portraits in Chinese History* (Princeton: Princeton University Press, 1994), pp. 11-32; David Shepherd Nivison, "The Classical Philosophical Writings," in *The Cambridge History of Ancient China: From the Origins of Civilization to 221 B.C.*, edited by Michael Loewe and Edward L. Shaughnessy (Cambridge and New York: Cambridge University Press, 1998), pp. 752-759.

40

The *Daode jing* in the Calligraphy of Zhao Mengfu

趙松雪書太上玄元道德經

Gao Heng and Chi Xichao, "Shi tan Mawangdui Han mu zhong de boshu 'Laozi,'" *Wenwu*, no. 222 (1974, no. 11) (November 1974), pp. 1-7; Mawangdui Han mu boshu zhengli xiaozu, "Mawangdui Han mu chutu 'Laozi' shiwen," *Wenwu*, no. 222 (1974, no. 11) (November 1974), pp. 8-20; *Yuan dai huajia shiliao*, compiled and edited by Chen Gaohua (Shanghai: Shanghai renmin meishu chuban she, 1980), pp. 30-99; Ren Daobin, *Zhao Mengfu xinian* [N.p. (Zhengzhou, Henan): Henan renmin chuban she, 1984]; *Zhao Mengfu xiaokai Daode jing zhenji*, [compiled and edited by Shanghai shuhua chuban she] [Shanghai: Shanghai shuhua chuban she, 1986 (6th printing, 1999)]; Dai Lizhu, *Zhao Mengfu wenxue yu yishu zhi yanjiu* (Taibei: Xuehai chuban she, 1986), p. 142; *Zhongguo meishu quanji: Shufa zhuanke bian*, vol. 4, *Song Jin Yuan shufa*, compiled by Zhongguo meishu quanji bianji weiyuan hui, edited by Shen Peng (Beijing: Renmin meishu chuban she, 1986), illustrations section, p. 147, no. 89 [color; selected section of handscroll illustrated], text section, pp. 71-72, no. 89 [catalogue entry in Chinese by Li Fengxia]; *Lao-tzu: Te-tao ching: A New Translation Based on the Recently Discovered Ma-wang-tui Texts*, translated, with an introduction and commentary, by Robert G. Henricks (New York: Ballantine Books, 1989); Lu Renlong, "Zhao Mengfu yu daojiao: Jian shu Song mo Yuan chu daojiao fazhan de yixie tezhi," *Shijie zongjiao yanjiu (Studies in World Religions)*, no. 45 (1991, no. 3), pp. 24-34; Livia Kohn, *Early Chinese Mysticism: Philosophy and Soteriology in the Taoist Tradition* (Princeton: Princeton University Press, 1992), pp. 40-80; Michael LaFargue, *The Tao of the Tao Te Ching: A Translation and Commentary* (Albany, N.Y.: State University of New York Press, 1992), pp. 1-185; William G. Boltz, "Lao tzu Tao te ching, " in Early Chinese Texts: A Bibliographical Guide, edited by Michael Loewe (N.p.: The

Society for the Study of Early China; Berkeley, Calif.: The Institute of East Asian Studies, University of California, Berkeley, 1993), pp. 269-292, esp. p. 286, no. 10; *Zhongguo kaishu ming tie jinghua*, compiled and edited by Ouyang Zhongshi (Beijing: Beijing chuban she, 1994), vol. 3, pp. 414-454 [halftone; entire set of rubbings illustrated]; Wang Lianqi, "Zhao Mengfu shufa yishu jian lun," in *Zhao Mengfu yanjiu lunwen ji*, edited by Shanghai shuhua chuban she (Shanghai: Shanghai shuhua chuban she, 1995), pp. 777-806; Ingrid Fischer-Schreiber, *The Shambhala Dictionary of Taoism*, translated [from the German] by Werner Wünsche (Boston: Shambhala Publications, Inc., 1996), pp. 88-90, and pp. 174-176; David Shepherd Nivison, "The Classical Philosophical Writings," in *The Cambridge History of Ancient China: From the Origins of Civilization to 221 B.C.*, edited by Michael Loewe and Edward L. Shaughnessy (Cambridge and New York: Cambridge University Press, 1998), pp. 802-805; Donald Harper, "Warring States Natural Philosophy and Occult Thought," in *The Cambridge History of Ancient China: From the Origins of Civilization to 221 B.C.*, edited by Michael Loewe and Edward L. Shaughnessy (Cambridge and New York: Cambridge University Press, 1998), pp. 881-882; Richard John Lynn, *The Classic of the Way and Virtue: A New Translation of the 'Tao-te ching' of Laozi as Interpreted by Wang Bi* (New York: Columbia University Press, 1999); Sun Zhixin, "A Quest for the Imperishable: Chao Meng-fu's Calligraphy for Stele Inscriptions," in *The Embodied Image: Chinese Calligraphy from the John B. Elliott Collection*, by Robert E. Harrist, Jr. and Wen C. Fong, with contributions by Qianshen Bai et al. (Princeton, N.J.: The Art Museum, Princeton University, 1999), pp. 302-319; *Zhongguo guojia tushu guan guji zhenpin tulu*, edited by Ren Jiyu (Beijing: Beijing tushu guan chuban she, 1999), p. 258, cat. no. 283 [2 selected facing leaves from album of rubbings illustrated].

41

Illustration of the Spring Purification Gathering at the Orchid Pavilion

蘭亭脩禊圖

Chinese Art: Painting, Calligraphy, Stone Rubbing, Wood Engraving, by Werner Speiser, Roger Goepper, and Jean Fribourg, translated by Diana Imber (New York: Universe Books, Inc., 1964), pp. 254-255, no. 119a-b; *Chinese Connoisseurship: The Ko Ku Yao Lun, The Essential Criteria of Antiquities*, translated and edited by Sir Percival David (London: Faber and Faber, 1971), pp. 38-68; *Lanting chenlie pin mulu* [Hong Kong: Xianggang Zhongwen daxue Zhongguo wenhua yanjiu suo wenwu guan (Art Gallery, Institute of Chinese Studies, Chinese University of Hong Kong), n.d. (1973)], esp. cat. nos. 159-160, and fig. 160; D.R. Jonker, "Chu Yu-tun," in *Dictionary of Ming Biography, 1368-1644*, edited by L. Carrington Goodrich and Chaoying Fang (New York and London: Columbia University Press, 1976), vol. 1, pp. 380-381; Guo Moruo, "You Wang Xie muzhi de chutu lun dao Lanting xu de zhenwei" [originally published in *Wenwu* (1965, no. 6)], reprinted in *Lanting lun bian*, compiled by Wenwu chuban she (Beijing: Wenwu chuban she, 1977), pp. 5-32; *Emperor, Scholar, Artisan, Monk: The Creative Personality in Chinese Works of Art*, catalogue by Paul Moss (London: Syndey L. Moss Ltd., 1984), catalogue volume, pp. 31-35, cat. no. 6, and plate B, *Prince I's Lan-t'ing Ink Rubbing Compilation (1592)*; *Zhongguo meishu quanji: Shufa zhuanke bian*, vol. 2, *Wei Jin Nanbei chao shufa*, compiled by Zhongguo meishu quanji bianji weiyuan hui (Beijing: Renmin meishu chuban she, 1986), illustrations section, pp. 92-93, no. 55 [halftone], and text section, p. 35, no. 55 [catalogue in Chinese by Ai Zhigao]; *Zhongguo meishu quanji: Huihua bian*, vol. 19, *Shike xianhua*, compiled by

Zhongguo meishu quanji bianji weiyuan hui (Shanghai: Shanghai renmin meishu chuban she, 1988), illustrations section, pp. 88-89, nos. 75-78 [color; 4 selected sections of handscroll illustrated], and text section, pp. 26-28, nos. 75-78 [catalogue entry in Chinese]; *Beijing tushu guan cang Zhongguo lidai shike taben huibian*, compiled and edited by Beijing tushu guan jinshi zu, vol. 51 (Zhengzhou, Henan: Zhongzhou guji chuban she, 1990), pp. 40-42; *Inscribed Landscapes: Travel Writing from Imperial China*, translated with annotations and an introduction by Richard E. Strassberg (Berkeley and Los Angeles: University of California Press, 1994), pp. 63-66, and fig. 9; *East Asian Books*, Catalogue 19 (London: Sam Fogg Rare Books and Manuscripts, 1998), pp. 66-68, cat. nos. 60 and 61; and p. 166, cat. no. 179; *Zhongguo guojia tushu guan guji zhenpin tulu*, edited by Ren Jiyu (Beijing: Beijing tushu guan chuban she, 1999), pp. 260-261, cat. no. 285 [selected section of handscroll illustrated, showing text of preface composed by Wang Xizhi, inscription by Zhu Youdun, and the opening and closing sections of the pictorial composition (which have been digitally "joined" in the reproduction)]; *Duoyun xuan '99 qiu ji yishu pin paimai hui: Guji banben zhuanchang (Duo Yun Xuan '99 Autumn Auction of Art Works)* [Shanghai: Shanghai Duoyun xuan yishu pin paimai gongsi (Duo Yun Xuan Art Auctioneer's), 1999], lot no. 667 [2 selected sections of handscroll with rubbings of the Wanli-period engraving illustrated].

42

Illustration of Zhong Kui the Demon Queller

鍾馗圖

Lidai Zhong Kui hua yanjiu, compiled and edited by Wang Zhende and Li Tianxiu (Tianjin: Tianjin renmin meishu chuban she, 1985), pp. 1-42; Stephen L. Little, "The Demon Queller and the Art of Qiu Ying (Ch'iu Ying)," *Artibus Asiae* 46, nos. 1-2 (1985), pp. 22-41; *Zhong Kui bai tu*, edited by Wang Lanxi and co-edited by Wang Shucun (Guangzhou: Lingnan meishu chuban she, 1990), 95, no. 79; Chia Chi Jason Wang, "The Iconography of Zhong Kui in Chinese Painting" (Master's thesis, University of California, Berkeley, 1991); *Beijing tushu guan cang huaxiang taben huibian*, compiled by Beijing tushu guan shanben bu jinshi zu (Beijing: Shumu wenxian chuban she, 1993), vol. 7, p. 38; *Ying sui ji fu: Yuan cang Zhong Kui ming hua tezhan (Blessings for the New Year: Catalogue to the Special Exhibition of Paintings of Chung K'uei)*, compiled and edited by Guoli gugong bowu yuan bianji weiyuan hui [Taibei: Guoli gugong bowu yuan (National Palace Museum), 1997].

43

Pictures of the Sage's Traces

聖蹟圖

Baba Harukichi, *Kôshi seisekishi* (Tokyo: Daitô bunka kyôkai, 1934); Baba Harukichi, *Kô Mô Seisekizu kan* (Tokyo: Santô bunka kenkyûkai, 1940), section on documentary records, pp. 1-7, section on portraits, pp. 1-37 [halftone; frontispiece and all 36 rubbings illustrated; all inscriptions transcribed in full]; Liu Wu-Chi, *Confucius, His Life and Time* (New York: Philosophical Library, Inc., 1955. Reprint. Westport, Conn.: Greenwood Press, Publishers, 1972); Kaji Nobuyuki, *Kôshi gaden: Seisekizu ni miru Kôshi rur no shôgai to oshie* (Tokyo:

Shûeisha, 1991), pp. 160-165; Satô Kazuyoshi, "'Seisekizu' no rekishi," in *Kôshi gaden: Seisekizu ni miru Kôshi rur no shôgai to oshie*, by Kaji Nobuyuki (Tokyo: Shûeisha, 1991), pp. 160-165; *Confucius: The Analects ("Lun yü")*, translated by D.C. Lau, 2d ed. (Hong Kong: The Chinese University Press, 1992), pp. 209-240 [Appendix 1], and pp. 241-262 [Appendix 2]; *Beijing tushu guan cang huaxiang taben huibian*, compiled by Beijing tushu guan shanben bu jinshi zu (Beijing: Shumu wenxian chuban she, 1993), vol. 1, pp. 136-170; John E. Wills, Jr., *Mountain of Fame: Portraits in Chinese History* (Princeton: Princeton University Press, 1994), pp. 11-32; *Sheng ji tu*, compiled and edited by Gong Fada and Xiao Yu (Wuhan: Hubei jiaoyu chuban she, 1994), preface by Xu Xiaomi, unpaginated; Thomas A. Wilson, *Genealogy of the Way: The Construction and Uses of the Confucian Tradition in Late Imperial China* (Stanford, Calif.: Stanford University Press, 1995); Julia K. Murray, "Illustrations of the Life of Confucius: Their Evolution, Functions, and Significance in Late Ming China," *Artibus Asiae* 62, nos. 1-2 (1997), pp. 73-134, esp. p. 108, fig. 26 [halftone; selected section illustrated], and p. 125, no. A-13; Craig Clunas, *Pictures and Visuality in Early Modern China* (Princeton: Princeton University Press, 1997), pp. 49-51 [text], and p. 194 [notes]; Grant Hardy, *Worlds of Bronze and Bamboo: Sima Qian's Conquest of History* (New York: Columbia University Press, 1999), pp. 153-168.

44

Illustrations of Cotton Cultivation and Manufacture, with Imperial Inscriptions

御題棉花圖

Mian ye tushuo (8 *juan*) (Beijing: Nong gongshang bu, 1911), *juan* 1-4; *Gyodai Menkazu*, compiled and written by Fang Guancheng (1698-1768), selected text in the original Chinese, translation by Yoshikawa Kôjirô (Originally prepared and published by N.p.: Mansh menka kyôkai, 1937. Reprint. Beijing: Kahoku menzan kaishinkai, 1941. Rev. ed. Tokyo: Chikuma shob, 1942); Fang Chao-ying, "Fang Kuan-ch'eng," in *Eminent Chinese of the Ch'ing Period (1644-1912)*, edited by Arthur W. Hummel, vol. 1 (Washington, D.C.: The Library of Congress; Washington, D.C.: United States Government Printing Office, 1943), pp. 233-235; Chen Zhengxiang [Cheng-Siang Chen], *Mianhua dili (Geography of Cotton)* [Taibei: Fuming nongye dili yanjiu suo (Institute of Agricultural Geography), 1953], p. 2 and p. 23; Guo Weiqu, *Zhongguo banhua shi lüe* (Beijing: Zhaohua meishu chuban she, 1962), p. 138; Yoshikawa Kôjirô, "Gyodai Menkazu," reprinted in *Yoshikawa Kôjirô zenshû*, vol. 16 (Tokyo: Chikuma shobô, 1970), pp. 206-224, followed by 21 unnumbered pages of plates; Chao Kang, with the assistance of Jessica C.Y. Chao, *The Development of Cotton Textile Production in China* (Cambridge, Mass.: East Asian Research Center, Harvard University, 1977), pp. 1-80, and pp. 317-335 [notes to pp. 1-80]; Zhao Gang and Chen Zhongyi, *Zhongguo mian ye shi* [Taibei: Lianjing chuban shiye gongsi, 1977 (2d printing, 1983)], pp. 1-102; *Catalogue of Chinese Rubbings from Field Museum*, researched by Hoshien Tchen and M. Kenneth Starr, prepared by Alice K. Schneider, photographs by Herta Newton and Field Museum Division of Photography, edited by Hartmut Walravens, Fieldiana: Anthropology, n.s., no. 3, Publication 1327 (Chicago: Field Museum of Natural History, 1981), p. 378, cat. no. 1656; *Zhongguo meishu quanji: Huihua bian*, vol. 19, *Shike xianhua*, compiled by Zhongguo meishu quanji bianji weiyuan hui (Shanghai: Shanghai renmin meishu chuban she, 1988), illustrations section, pp. 118-119, nos. 106-107 [color; 4 selected double-leaves illustrated], text section, pp. 39-40, nos. 106-107 [catalogue entry in Chinese]; Joseph Needham, *Science and Civilisation in China*, vol. 5, *Chemistry and Chemical Technology*, pt. 9, *Textile Technology: Spinning and Reeling*, by Dieter Kuhn (Cambridge and New York: Cambridge University Press, 1988), pp. 57-59, and 187-198; *Shou yi guang xun*, reprinted in *Zhongguo gudai banhua congkan*, compiled and edited by Zheng Zhenduo (Shanghai: Shanghai guji chuban she, 1988), vol. 4, pp. 563-726, with postscript by Shanghai guji chuban she; *Beijing tushu guan cang huaxiang taben huibian*, compiled by Beijing tushu guan shanben bu jinshi zu (Beijing: Shumu wenxian chuban she, 1993), vol. 10, pp. 53-61; *Zhongguo gudai Gengzhi tu (Farming and Weaving Pictures in Ancient China)*, compiled by Zhongguo nongye bowu guan (China Agricultural Museum), edited by Wang Chaosheng [Beijing: Zhongguo nongye chuban she (China Agriculture Press), 1995], pp. 111-125; *Zhongguo shudian 1998 nian qiu ji shukan ziliao paimai hui* (Beijing: Beijing Haiwang cun paimai youxian zeren gongsi, 1998), lot no. 156 [1 selected leaf illustrated; this set of rubbings are mounted in a stitch-bound volume]; *Duoyun xuan '99 qiu ji yishu pin paimai hui: Guji banben zhuanchang (Duo Yun Xuan '99 Autumn Auction of Art Works)* [Shanghai: Shanghai Duoyun xuan yishu pin paimai gongsi (Duo Yun Xuan Art Auctioneer's), 1999], lot no. 644 [2 selected rubbings mounted as facing album leaves illustrated].

45

Illustration of the Clear Jing River and the Muddy Wei River

涇清渭濁圖

Zhongguo gujin diming da cidian, compiled by Zang Lihe et al., edited by Lu Erkui and Fang Yi (Shanghai: Shanghai yinshu guan, 1931), p. 728 and p. 911; Sun Tong, *Guanzhong shuidao ji*, Congshu jicheng chubian ed. (Shanghai: Shangwu yinshu guan, 1936), reprinted as Xibei kaifa shiliao congbian, ser. 1, no. 4 (Tianjin: Tianjin guji chuban she, 1987), pp. 24-26 [in 2 *juan*] and pp. 31-40 [in *juan* 3]; Li Man-kuei, "Tung Kao," in *Eminent Chinese of the Ch'ing Period (1644-1912)*, edited by Arthur W. Hummel, vol. 2 (Washington, D.C.: The Library of Congress; Washington, D.C.: United States Government Printing Office, 1944), pp. 791-792; *Qing shi liezhuan* (80 *juan*), compiled and edited by Taiwan Zhonghua shuju, 2d Taiwan ed. (Taibei: Taiwan Zhonghua shuju, 1983), *juan* 28/1a-3b (in vol. 4); *Qing shi gao liezhuan* (298 *juan*), compiled by Zhao Erxun et al., *juan* 340, Liezhuan, *juan* 127, reprinted in *Qing dai zhuanji congkan*, compiled and edited by Zhou Junfu [Taibei: Mingwen shuju (Ming Wen Book Co., Ltd.), 1985], vol. 92, pp. 7-9; *Qing dai qi bai mingren zhuan* (6 *bian*, *fulu* 5 *zhong*), compiled and edited by Cai Guanluo, *bian* 1, *Zhengzhi, zhengshi*, reprinted in *Qing dai zhuanji congkan*, compiled and edited by Zhou Junfu [Taibei: Mingwen shuju (Ming Wen Book Co., Ltd.), 1985], vol. 194, pp. 224-226; *Beijing tushu guan cang Zhongguo lidai shike taben huibian*, compiled and edited by Beijing tushu guan jinshi zu, vol. 75 (Zhengzhou, Henan: Zhongzhou guji chuban she, 1990), pp. 147-149; *Zhongguo ming shan da chuan cidian*, edited by Shan Shumo et al. (Jinan, Shandong: Shandong jiaoyu chuban she, 1992), pp. 695-696 and p. 729; *Beijing tushu guan cang huaxiang taben huibian*, compiled by Beijing tushu guan shanben bu jinshi zu (Beijing: Shumu wenxian chuban she, 1993), vol. 10, pp. 66-67; Hsieh Chiao-min and Jean Kan Hsieh, *China: A Provincial Atlas* (New York: Macmillan Publishing USA, 1995), pp. 130-132.

46

Illustrations and Records of the Yinxin Stone Dwellings

印心石屋圖説

Zhongguo renming da cidian, compiled and edited by Zang Lihe et al. (Hong Kong: Taixing shuju, 1931), p. 1112; Li Man-kuei, "T'ao Chu," in *Eminent Chinese of the Ch'ing Period (1644-1912)*, edited by Arthur W. Hummel, vol. 2 (Washington, D.C.: The Library of Congress; Washington, D.C.: United States Government Printing Office, 1944), pp. 710-711; R.H. van Gulik, *Chinese Pictorial Art as Viewed by the Connoisseur: Notes on the Means and Methods of Traditional Chinese Connoisseurship of Pictorial Art, Based upon a Study of the Art of Mounting Scrolls in China and Japan* (Rome: Istituto Italiano per il Medio ed Estremo Oriente, 1958), p. 87; *The Cambridge History of China*, edited by Denis Twittchett and John K. Fairbank, vol. 10, *Late Ch'ing, 1800-1911, Part 1*, edited by John K. Fairbank (Cambridge and New York: Cambridge University Press, 1978), pp. 116-162 *passim*; *Zhongguo meishu jia renming cidian*, compiled and edited by Yu Jianhua (Shanghai: Shanghai renmin meishu chuban she, 1981), p. 965; *Qing shi liezhuan* (80 *juan*), compiled and edited by Taiwan Zhonghua shuju, 2d Taiwan ed. (Taibei: Taiwan Zhonghua shuju, 1983), *juan* 37/27b-36b (in vol. 5); *Qing shi gao liezhuan* (298 *juan*), compiled by Zhao Erxun et al., *juan* 379, *Liezhuan, juan* 166, reprinted in *Qing dai zhuanji congkan*, compiled and edited by Zhou Junfu [Taibei: Mingwen shuju (Ming Wen Book Co., Ltd.), 1985], vol. 92, pp. 523-526; *Qing dai qi bai mingren zhuan* (6 *bian, fulu* 5 *zhong*), compiled and edited by Cai Guanluo, *bian* 1, *Zhengzhi, caiwu*, reprinted in *Qing dai zhuanji congkan*, compiled and edited by Zhou Junfu [Taibei: Mingwen shuju (Ming Wen Book Co., Ltd.), 1985], vol. 194, pp. 605-613; *Beijing tushu guan cang huaxiang taben huibian*, compiled by Beijing tushu guan shanben bu jinshi zu (Beijing: Shumu wenxian chuban she, 1993), vol. 10, pp. 74-77.

47

Geographical Map

墜理圖

Édouard Chavannes, "L'instruction d'un futur empereur de Chine en l'an 1193," in *Mémoires concernant l'Asie Orientale, Inde, Asie Centrale, Extrême-Orient, publiés par l'Académie des Inscriptions et Belles-lettres*, tome 1, edited by Émile Senart et al. (Paris: E. Leroux, 1913), pp. 19-64; Joseph Needham, *Science and Civilisation in China*, with the research assistance of Wang Ling [et al.], vol. 3, *Mathematics and the Sciences of the Heavens and the Earth* (Cambridge and New York: Cambridge University Press, 1950), pp. 550-551, and fig. 229 [halftone; entire map illustrated]; Cao Wanru, "Jieshao san fu gu ditu," *Wenwu cankao ziliao*, no. 95 (1958, no. 7) (July 1958), p. 33, continued on p. 30 [see also foldout map between p. 30 and p. 33]; Jin Yingchun and Qiu Fuke, *Zhongguo ditu shihua* (Beijing: Kexue chuban she, 1984), p. 93, and fig. 25; Qian Zheng and Yao Shiying, "Dili tu bei," in *Zhongguo gudai ditu ji: Zhan guo-Yuan [(An Atlas of Ancient Maps in China–From the Warring States to the Yuan Dynasty (476 B.C.-A.D. 1368)]*, edited by Cao Wanru et al. [Beijing: Wenwu chuban she (Cultural Relics Publishing House), 1990], text section, pp. 46-49, with summary in English, "The Tablet of the Geographic Map ('Di li tu bei')," p. 110; *The History of Cartography*, edited by J.B. Harley and David Woodward, vol. 2, bk. 2, *Cartography in the Traditional East and Southeast Asian Societies* (Chicago and London: The University of Chicago Press, 1994), p. 86, fig. 4.11; *Yutu yao lu: Beijing tushu guan cang*

6827 zhong Zhong wai wen gujiu ditu mulu, compiled by Beijing tushu guan shanben tecang bu yutu zu (Beijing: Beijing tushu guan chuban she, 1997), p. 35, no. 0366; *East Asian Books*, Catalogue 19 (London: Sam Fogg Rare Books and Manuscripts, 1998), pp. 72-73, cat. nos. 66; Richard J. Smith, "Mapping China's World: Cultural Cartography in Late Imperial Times," in *Landscape, Culture, and Power in Chinese Society*, edited by Wenhsin Yeh (Berkeley, Calif.: Center for Chinese Studies, Institute of East Asian Studies, University of California, Berkeley, 1998), pp. 60-61; *Zhonghua gu ditu zhenpin xuanji*, compiled and edited by Zhongguo cehui kexue yanjiu yuan (Harbin: Ha'erbin ditu chuban she, 1998), pp. 62-63, no. 48; *China in Ancient and Modern Maps*, compiled by the Ancient Map Research Team of Chinese Academy of Surveying and Mapping (London: Published for Sotheby's Publications by Philip Wilson Publishers Limited, 1998), pp. 74-75, no. 48.

48

Map of the Prefectural City of Pingjiang

平江圖

Qian Yong, "Pingjiang tu bei," *Wenwu*, no. 102 (1959, no. 2) (February 1959), p. 49; Frederick W. Mote, "A Millienium of Chinese Urban History: Form, Time and Space Concept in Soochow," *Rice University Studies* 59, no. 4 (1973), pp. 35-65; *Chinese & Japanese Maps: An Exhibition Organised by the British Library at the British Museum, 1 February-31 December 1974*, catalogue by Yolande Jones, Howard Nelson, [and] Helen Wallis (London: Published for the British Library Board by British Museum Publications Limited, 1974), cat. no. C2; *China cartographica: Chinesische Kartenschätze und europäische Forschungsdokumente: Ausstellung anläßlich des 150. Geburtstages des Chinaforschers Ferdinand von Richthofen*, edited by Lothar Zögner (Berlin: Staatsbibliothek Preußlischer Kulturbesitz; Berlin: Kiepert KG, 1983), p. 61, cat. no. C2; Jin Yingchun and Qiu Fuke, *Zhongguo ditu shihua* (Beijing: Kexue chuban she, 1984), pp. 87-91, 93, and fig. 24; Du Yu, "Cong Song 'Pingjiang tu' kan Pingjiang fu cheng de guimo he buju," *Ziran kexue shi yanjiu (Studies in the History of Natural Sciences)* 8, no. 1 (1989), pp. 90-96; Wang Qianjin, "'Pingjiang tu' de ditu xue yanjiu," *Ziran kexue shi yanjiu (Studies in the History of Natural Sciences)* 8, no. 4 (1989): pp. 378-386 [includes abstract in English, "Cartographical Research on 'Ping Jiang Tu,'" p. 386]; Wang Qianjin, "Nan Song beike Pingjiang tu yanjiu," in *Zhongguo gudai ditu ji: Zhan guo-Yuan [(An Atlas of Ancient Maps in China–From the Warring States to the Yuan Dynasty (476 B.C.-A.D. 1368)]*, edited by Cao Wanru et al. [Beijing: Wenwu chuban she (Cultural Relics Publishing House), 1990], text section, pp. 50-55, with summary in English, "'Ping Jiang Tu,' A Map of Southern Song Dynasty Carved on a Stele," p. 110; Michel Cartier, "Les métamorphoses imaginaires de la Venise chinoise: La ville de Suzhou et ses plans," *Revue de la Bibliothèque nationale*, no. 48 (Summer 1993): pp. 2-9; *The History of Cartography*, edited by J.B. Harley and David Woodward, vol. 2, bk. 2, *Cartography in the Traditional East and Southeast Asian Societies* (Chicago and London: The University of Chicago Press, 1994), p. 141, fig. 6.6; Qian Yucheng, "Song ke 'Pingjiang tu' de bili," *Wenwu*, no. 455 (1994, no. 4) (April 1994), pp. 80-81; *Heyue cang zhen: Zhongguo gu ditu zhan (History through Maps: An Exhibition of Old Maps of China)*, edited by Ding Xinbao (Joseph S.P. Ting) [Hong Kong: Xianggang Linshi shizheng ju (Provisional Urban Council of Hong Kong), 1997], p. 47, cat. no. 3.1 [color illustration], p. 52, cat. no. 3.1 [descriptive text in Chinese], and p. 53, cat. no. 3.1 [descriptive text in English]; *Yutu yao lu: Beijing tushu guan cang 6827 zhong Zhong wai wen gujiu ditu mulu*, compiled by Beijing tushu guan shanben tecang bu yutu zu (Beijing: Beijing tushu guan chuban she, 1997),

p. 320, no. 4004; *Zhonghua gu ditu zhenpin xuanji*, compiled and edited by Zhongguo cehui kexue yanjiu yuan (Harbin: Ha'erbin ditu chuban she, 1998), pp. 58-59, no. 45; *China in Ancient and Modern Maps*, compiled by the Ancient Map Research Team of Chinese Academy of Surveying and Mapping (London: Published for Sotheby's Publications by Philip Wilson Publishers Limited, 1998), pp. 70-71, no. 45; *Zhongguo guojia tushu guan guji zhenpin tulu*, edited by Ren Jiyu (Beijing: Beijing tushu guan chuban she, 1999), p. 275, cat. no. 301 [entire rubbing illustrated].

49

Map of Imperial Territories

輿地圖

Zhongguo lishi ditu ji (The Historical Atlas of China), sponsored by Chinese Academy of Social Sciences, edited by Tan Qixiang, vol. 7, *Yuan, Ming shiqi (The Yuan Dynasty Period, The Ming Dynasty Period)* [N.p. (Beijing): Ditu chuban she (Cartographic Publishing House), 1982], pp. 40-41 [map of 1433], and pp. 42-43 [map of 1582; *Zhongguo gudai ditu ji: Ming dai [(An Atlas of Ancient Maps in China–The Ming Dynasty, 1368-1644)]*, edited by Cao Wanru et al. [Beijing: Wenwu chuban she (Cultural Relics Publishing House), 1995], cat. nos. 12-15, text section, p. 1, nos. 12-15 [catalogue entry by Xu Minggang (in Chinese)], text section, p. 22, nos. 12-15 [catalogue entry by Xu Minggang (in English)]; Zheng Xihuang, "Yang Ziqi ba Yudi tu ji qi tushi fuhao," in *Zhongguo gudai ditu ji: Ming dai [(An Atlas of Ancient Maps in China–The Ming Dynasty, 1368-1644)]*, edited by Cao Wanru et al. [Beijing: Wenwu chuban she (Cultural Relics Publishing House), 1995], text section, pp. 61-64, with summary in English, "'Yu Di Tu' (Terrestrial Map) with a Postscript by Yang Ziqi and Its Legends and Symbols," text section, p. 131; *Yutu yao lu: Beijing tushu guan cang 6827 zhong Zhong wai wen gujiu ditu mulu*, compiled by Beijing tushu guan shanben tecang bu yutu zu (Beijing: Beijing tushu guan chuban she, 1997), p. 36, no. 0368; *Zhonghua gu ditu zhenpin xuanji*, compiled and edited by Zhongguo cehui kexue yanjiu yuan (Harbin: Ha'erbin ditu chuban she, 1998), pp. 84-85, no. 68; *China in Ancient and Modern Maps*, compiled by the Ancient Map Research Team of Chinese Academy of Surveying and Mapping (London: Published for Sotheby's Publications by Philip Wilson Publishers Limited, 1998), pp. 96-97, no. 68.

50

Atlas of Jiangxi Province, with Accompanying Descriptive Notes

江西全省圖説

Zhongguo lishi ditu ji (The Historical Atlas of China), sponsored by Chinese Academy of Social Sciences, edited by Tan Qixiang, vol. 7, *Yuan, Ming shiqi (The Yuan Dynasty Period, The Ming Dynasty Period)* [N.p. (Beijing): Ditu chuban she (Cartographic Publishing House), 1982], pp. 64-65 [map of 1582]; Hsieh Chiao-min and Jean Kan Hsieh, *China: A Provincial Atlas* (New York: Macmillan Publishing USA, 1995), pp. 98-101; *Heyue cang zhen: Zhongguo gu ditu zhan (History through Maps: An Exhibition of Old Maps of China)*, edited by Ding Xinbao (Joseph S.P. Ting) [Hong Kong: Xianggang Linshi shizheng ju

(Provisional Urban Council of Hong Kong), 1997], p. 42, cat. no. 2.1 [descriptive text in Chinese], and p. 43, cat. no. 2.1 [descriptive text in English]; not illustrated; Mei-Ling Hsu, "An Inquiry into Early Chinese Atlases through the Ming Dynasty," in *Images of the World: The Atlas through History*, edited by John A. Wolter and Ronald E. Grim (Washington, D.C.: Library of Congress, 1997), pp. 31-50; *Yutu yao lu: Beijing tushu guan cang 6827 zhong Zhong wai wen gujiu ditu mulu*, compiled by Beijing tushu guan shanben tecang bu yutu zu (Beijing: Beijing tushu guan chuban she, 1997), p. 350, no. 4421; *Zhonghua gu ditu zhenpin xuanji*, compiled and edited by Zhongguo cehui kexue yanjiu yuan (Harbin: Ha'erbin ditu chuban she, 1998), pp. 122-125, nos. 89-91; *China in Ancient and Modern Maps*, compiled by the Ancient Map Research Team of Chinese Academy of Surveying and Mapping (London: Published for Sotheby's Publications by Philip Wilson Publishers Limited, 1998), pp. 134-137, nos. 89-91; *Zhongguo guojia tushu guan (National Library of China)*, edited by Li Zhizhong (Beijing: Zhongguo guojia tushu guan, 1999), p. 14, no. 1 [4 selected leaves illustrated]; *Zhongguo guojia tushu guan guji zhenpin tulu*, edited by Ren Jiyu (Beijing: Beijing tushu guan chuban she, 1999), p. 280, cat. no. 305 [4 selected facing leaves illustrated].

51

Complete Map of Allotted Fields, Human Traces, and Travel Routes Within and Without the Nine Frontiers under Heaven

天下九邊分野人跡路程全圖

Zhongguo gudai ditu ji: Ming dai [(An Atlas of Ancient Maps in China–The Ming Dynasty, 1368-1644)], edited by Cao Wanru et al. [Beijing: Wenwu chuban she (Cultural Relics Publishing House), 1995], cat. no. 146 [halftone], text section, p. 11, no. 146 [catalogue entry by Ren Jincheng (in Chinese)], text section, p. 36, no. 146 [catalogue entry by Ren Jincheng (in English)]; Li Xiaocong, *Ouzhou shoucang bufen Zhongwen gu ditu xulu (A Descriptive Catalogue of Pre-1900 Chinese Maps Seen in Europe)* (Beijing: Guoji wenhua chuban gongsi, 1996), catalogue section, pp. 6-8, cat. no. 00.03, and fig. 2 [halftone illustration]; *Heyue cang zhen: Zhongguo gu ditu zhan (History through Maps: An Exhibition of Old Maps of China)*, edited by Ding Xinbao (Joseph S.P. Ting) [Hong Kong: Xianggang Linshi shizheng ju (Provisional Urban Council of Hong Kong), 1997], p. 24, cat. no. 1.8 [color illustration], p. 32, cat. no. 1.8 [descriptive text in Chinese], and p. 33, cat. no. 1.8 [descriptive text in English]; *Yutu yao lu: Beijing tushu guan cang 6827 zhong Zhong wai wen gujiu ditu mulu*, compiled by Beijing tushu guan shanben tecang bu yutu zu (Beijing: Beijing tushu guan chuban she, 1997), p. 2, no. 0011; Richard J. Smith, "Mapping China's World: Cultural Cartography in Late Imperial Times," in *Landscape, Culture, and Power in Chinese Society*, edited by Wen-hsin Yeh (Berkeley, Calif.: Center for Chinese Studies, Institute of East Asian Studies, University of California, Berkeley, 1998), pp. 75-76; *Zhongguo guojia tushu guan guji zhenpin tulu*, edited by Ren Jiyu (Beijing: Beijing tushu guan chuban she, 1999), p. 282, cat. no. 307 [entire printed map illustrated].

52

Map of the Detached Imperial Residence on the West Lake

西湖行宮圖

Qing neiwu fu zaoban chu yutu fang tumu chubian, compiled by Guoli Beiping gugong bowu yuan wenxian guan (Beiping: Guoli Beiping gugong bowu yuan wenxian guan, 1936), pp. 71-72; *The West Lake Companion* (Beijing: Foreign Languages Press, 1958); Shen Tuqi, *Xi hu gujin tan* (Hangzhou: Zhejiang wenyi chuban she, 1985); *Xi hu (West Lake)*, selected and edited by Chi Changyao (Hangzhou: Zhejiang renmin chuban she, 1990); *Poems of the West Lake: Translations from the Chinese*, translated, with an introduction, by A.C. Graham (London: Wellsweep Press, 1990); *Xi hu zhi*, compiled by Hangzhou shi yuanlin wenwu guanli ju, edited by Shi Diandong (Shanghai: Shanghai guji chuban she, 1995), pp. 605-606; Li Xiaocong, *Ouzhou shoucang bufen Zhongwen gu ditu xulu (A Descriptive Catalogue of Pre-1900 Chinese Maps Seen in Europe)*, Guojia jiaowei quanguo gaoxiao guji zhengli zhongdian xiangmu (Beijing: Guoji wenhua chuban gongsi, 1996), catalogue section, pp. 76-77, cat. no. 05.01.

53

Map of Taiwan

臺灣地圖

Zhongguo lishi ditu ji (The Historical Atlas of China), sponsored by Chinese Academy of Social Sciences, edited by Tan Qixiang, vol. 8, *Qing shiqi (The Qing Dynasty Period)* [N.p. (Beijing): Ditu chuban she (Cartographic Publishing House), 1987], pp. 42-43 [map of 1820]; Hsieh Chiao-min and Jean Kan Hsieh, *China: A Provincial Atlas* (New York: Macmillan Publishing USA, 1995), pp. 105-108; Xia Liming, *Qing dai Taiwan ditu yanbian shi, jian lun yi ge huitu dianfan de zhuanyi licheng*, Mingshan cang, no. 1 (Zhonghe, Taibei county: Zhi shufang chuban she, 1996); Cao Wanru and Jiang Lirong, "Qing Kangxi, Yongzheng he Qianlong shiqi de Taiwan ditu," in *Zhongguo gudai ditu ji: Qing dai [(An Atlas of Ancient Maps in China–The Qing Dynasty (1644-1911)]*, edited by Cao Wanru et al. [Beijing: Wenwu chuban she (Cultural Relics Publishing House), 1997], text section, pp. 79-101, with summary in English, "On the Map of Taiwan During the Reign of Kangxi, Yongzheng and Qianlong of the Qing Dynasty," p. 172; *Heyue cang zhen: Zhongguo gu ditu zhan (History through Maps: An Exhibition of Old Maps of China)*, edited by Ding Xinbao (Joseph S.P. Ting) [Hong Kong: Xianggang Linshi shizheng ju (Provisional Urban Council of Hong Kong), 1997], pp. 40-41, cat. no. 2.4 [color illustration], p. 42, cat. no. 2.4 [descriptive text in Chinese], and p. 44, cat. no. 2.4 [descriptive text in English]; *Yutu yao lu: Beijing tushu guan cang 6827 zhong Zhong wai wen gujiu ditu mulu*, compiled by Beijing tushu guan shanben tecang bu yutu zu (Beijing: Beijing tushu guan chuban she, 1997), p. 371, no. 4712; *Zhonghua gu ditu zhenpin xuanji*, compiled and edited by Zhongguo cehui kexue yanjiu yuan (Harbin: Ha'erbin ditu chuban she, 1998), pp. 194-199, no. 134; *China in Ancient and Modern Maps*, compiled by the Ancient Map Research Team of Chinese Academy of Surveying and Mapping (London: Published for Sotheby's Publications by Philip Wilson Publishers Limited, 1998), pp. 206-211, no. 134; *Zhongguo guojia tushu guan guji zhenpin tulu*, edited by Ren Jiyu (Beijing: Beijing tushu guan chuban she, 1999), pp. 284-285, cat. no. 311 [selected section of handscroll illustrated].

54

Coastal Map of the Seven Maritime Provinces of the Illustrious Dynasty

盛朝七省沿海圖

Names of Places on the China Coast and the Yangtze River, 2d issue [2d ed.], published by order of the Inspector General of Customs (Shanghai: Published at the Statistical Department of the Inspectorate General of Customs, 1904); Ivon A. Donnelly, *The China Coast*, with verse by Joan Power (Tianjin: Tientsin Press, Limited, 1931); *China cartographica: Chinesische Kartenschätze und europäische Forschungsdokumente: Ausstellung anläßlich des 150. Geburtstages des Chinaforschers Ferdinand von Richthofen*, edited by Lothar Zögner (Berlin: Staatsbibliothek Preußischer Kulturbesitz; Berlin: Kiepert KG, 1983), p. 68 and p. 70, cat. no. C14, and color pl. 9; Dian H. Murray, *Pirates of the South China Coast, 1790-1810* (Stanford, Calif.: Stanford University Press, 1987); Cordell D.K. Yee, "A Cartography of Introspection: Chinese Maps as Other Than European," *Asian Art* 5, no. 4 (1992), p. 36, and p. 38, fig. 6; *Yutu yao lu: Beijing tushu guan cang 6827 zhong Zhong wai wen gujiu ditu mulu*, compiled by Beijing tushu guan shanben tecang bu yutu zu (Beijing: Beijing tushu guan chuban she, 1997), p. 84, no. 0896; *Zhongguo guojia tushu guan guji zhenpin tulu*, edited by Ren Jiyu (Beijing: Beijing tushu guan chuban she, 1999), p. 294, cat. no. 322 [selected section of handscroll of a Tongzhi-period (1862-1874) map of the same genre illustrated].

55

Map of Scenic Attractions along the Yangzi River

長江名勝圖

Names of Places on the China Coast and the Yangtze River, 2d issue [2d ed.], published by order of the Inspector General of Customs (Shanghai: Published at the Statistical Department of the Inspectorate General of Customs, 1904); Lyman P. van Slyke, *Yangtze: Nature, History, and the River* (Reading, Mass. and Menlo Park, Calif.: Addison-Wesley Publishing Company, Inc., 1988); *Heyue cang zhen: Zhongguo gu ditu zhan (History through Maps: An Exhibition of Old Maps of China)*, edited by Ding Xinbao (Joseph S.P. Ting) [Hong Kong: Xianggang Linshi shizheng ju (Provisional Urban Council of Hong Kong), 1997], pp. 60-61, cat. no. 4.5 [color illustration], p. 64, cat. no. 4.5 [descriptive text in Chinese], and p. 65, cat. no. 4.5 [descriptive text in English]; *Yutu yao lu: Beijing tushu guan cang 6827 zhong Zhong wai wen gujiu ditu mulu*, compiled by Beijing tushu guan shanben tecang bu yutu zu (Beijing: Beijing tushu guan chuban she, 1997), p. 93, no. 0977; *Zhonghua gu ditu zhenpin xuanji*, compiled and edited by Zhongguo cehui kexue yanjiu yuan (Harbin: Ha'erbin ditu chuban she, 1998), pp. 226-227, no. 149; *China in Ancient and Modern Maps*, compiled by the Ancient Map Research Team of Chinese Academy of Surveying and Mapping (London: Published for Sotheby's Publications by Philip Wilson Publishers Limited, 1998), pp. 238-239, no. 149; *Zhongguo guojia tushu guan guji zhenpin tulu*, edited by Ren Jiyu (Beijing: Beijing tushu guan chuban she, 1999), p. 294, cat. no. 321.

56

Complete Map of the Mountain Retreat for Escaping Summer's Heat

避暑山莊全圖

Lu Sheng, "Chengde Bishu shanzhuang," *Wenwu cankao ziliao*, no. 73 (1956, no. 9) (September 1956), pp. 13-20; *Chengde Bishu shanzhuang*, edited by Chengde shi wenwu ju and Zhongguo renmin daxue Qing shi yanjiu suo (Beijing: Wenwu chuban she, 1980); *Chengde gu jianzhu: Bishu shanzhuang he wai ba miao*, compiled and edited by Tianjin daxue jianzhu xi and Chengde shi wenwu ju [N.p. (Beijing): Zhongguo jianzhu gongye chuban she; Hong Kong: Shenghuo, Dushu, Xinzhi Sanlian shudian Xianggang fendian, 1982]; Fung Ming-chu, "The Establishment of the Outer Eight Temples and the Northwestern Territory Defense of the Early Ch'ing Dynasty," in *Proceedings of the Sixth East Asian Altaistic Conference, December 18-23, 1981, Taipei, China*, edited by Ch'en Chieh-hsien [Taipei: The Taipei City Government (Taibei shi zhengfu), 1983], pp. 115-121; Jin Tao, *Chengde shihua* (Shanghai: Shanghai renmin chuban she, 1983), pp. 35-68; *Bishu shanzhuang sanshi liu jing*, 2d ed. (Beijing: Renmin meishu chuban she, 1984); Anne Chayet, *Les temples de Jehol et leurs modèles tibétains* (Paris: Éditions Recherche sur les Civilisations, 1985); Zhang Yuxin, *Bishu shanzhuang de zaoyuan yishu* (Beijing: Wenwu chuban she, 1991); *Heyue cang zhen: Zhongguo gu ditu zhan (History through Maps: An Exhibition of Old Maps of China)*, edited by Ding Xinbao (Joseph S.P. Ting) [Hong Kong: Xianggang Linshi shizheng ju (Provisional Urban Council of Hong Kong), 1997], p. 64, cat. no. 4.6 [descriptive text in Chinese], and p. 65, cat. no. 4.6 [descriptive text in English]; not illustrated; *Yutu yao lu: Beijing tushu guan cang 6827 zhong Zhong wai wen gujiu ditu mulu*, compiled by Beijing tushu guan shanben tecang bu yutu zu (Beijing: Beijing tushu guan chuban she, 1997), p. 154, no. 1784; *Zhonghua gu ditu zhenpin xuanji*, compiled and edited by Zhongguo cehui kexue yanjiu yuan (Harbin: Ha'erbin ditu chuban she, 1998), pp. 206-207, no. 138; *China in Ancient and Modern Maps*, compiled by the Ancient Map Research Team of Chinese Academy of Surveying and Mapping (London: Published for Sotheby's Publications by Philip Wilson Publishers Limited, 1998), pp. 218-219, no. 138; *Zhongguo guojia tushu guan guji zhenpin tulu*, edited by Ren Jiyu (Beijing: Beijing tushu guan chuban she, 1999), pp. 295-298, cat. no. 323 [entire map and 3 details illustrated]; Philippe Forêt, "The Intended Perception of the Imperial Gardens of Chengde in 1780," *Studies in the History of Gardens & Designed Landscapes* 19, nos. 3-4 (July-December 1999), pp. 343-363.

57

Map of the Routes from Dajianlu to Anterior and Posterior Tsang

自打箭鑪至前後藏途程圖

Arthur de Rosthorn, *On the Tea Cultivation in Western Ssûch'uan and the Tea Trade with Tibet via Tachienlu* (London: Luzac & Co., 1895), pp. 5-40; Claude Madrolle, *Itinéraires dans l'ouest de la Chine, 1895, pour accompagner le journal de l'auteur dans son voyage au Iun-nan, au Tibet chinois et au Se-tch'ouen* (Paris: Augustin Challamel, Éditeur, 1900), map no. 16, unpaginated ["Tà-tsién-loû ting"]; William Carey, *Adventures in Tibet, Including the*

Diary of Miss Annie R. Taylor's Remarkable Journey from Tau-Chau to Ta-Chien-Lu through the Heart of the "Forbidden Land" (New York: The Baker and Taylor Co., 1901); Siegbert Hummel, *Namenkarte von Tibet* [N.p. (Copenhagen): N.p. (E. Munksgaard), n.d. (1950); *Xi zhao tu lüe; Xizang tu kao*, compiled and edited by "Xizang yanjiu" bianji bu (Lhasa, Tibet: Xizang renmin chuban she, 1982), see section entitled *Xizang tu kao*, compiled by Huang Peiqiao (originally published in 1886 and recompiled in 1894), punctuated by Li Peirong, edited by Li Hongnian and Li Wenjiang, pp. 31-268; *Zhongguo lishi ditu ji (The Historical Atlas of China)*, sponsored by Chinese Academy of Social Sciences, edited by Tan Qixiang, vol. 8, *Qing shiqi (The Qing Dynasty Period)* [N.p. (Beijing): Ditu chuban she (Cartographic Publishing House), 1987], pp. 61-62 [map of 1820], and p. 63 [map of 1820]; Keith Dowman, *The Power-Places of Central Tibet: The Pilgrim's Guide* (London and New York: Routledge & Kegan Paul, 1988); Hsieh Chiao-min and Jean Kan Hsieh, *China: A Provincial Atlas* (New York: Macmillan Publishing USA, 1995), pp. 152-154; Li Xiaocong, *Ouzhou shoucang bufen Zhongwen gu ditu xulu (A Descriptive Catalogue of Pre-1900 Chinese Maps Seen in Europe)* (Beijing: Guoji wenhua chuban gongsi, 1996), catalogue section, pp. 88-89, cat. no. 05.11; *Heyue cang zhen: Zhongguo gu ditu zhan (History through Maps: An Exhibition of Old Maps of China)*, edited by Ding Xinbao (Joseph S.P. Ting) [Hong Kong: Xianggang Linshi shizheng ju (Provisional Urban Council of Hong Kong), 1997], p. 43, cat. no. 2.9 [descriptive text in Chinese], and p. 44, cat. no. 2.9 [descriptive text in English]; not illustrated; *Yutu yao lu: Beijing tushu guan cang 6827 zhong Zhong wai wen gujiu ditu mulu*, compiled by Beijing tushu guan shanben tecang bu yutu zu (Beijing: Beijing tushu guan chuban she, 1997), p. 463, no. 5913.

58

Complete Map of the Sacred Peak of the South

南岳全圖

Nan yue zhi (26 *juan*), originally compiled by Li Yuandu, edited by Wang Xiangyu and Ouyang Qian, preface by Guo Songshou dated 1883 [reprint; N.p. (Beijing): Zhongguo shudian, 1990]; *Tianxia Nan yue*, [edited by] Nan yue wenwu guanli suo (Changsha, Hunan: Hunan meishu chuban she, 1984); *Zhongguo ming shan da chuan cidian*, edited by Shan Shumo et al. (Jinan, Shandong: Shandong jiaoyu chuban she, 1992), pp. 945-946; James Robson, "The Southern Marchmount Nanyue Shan: Its Place in Chinese Religious Geography" (Master's thesis, University of California, Santa Barbara, 1993); *Tianxia mingshan cidian (An Encyclopaedia of World-Renowned Peaks and Mounts in China)*, compiled and edited by Wang Shixiong and Li Yuying (Xi'an: Shaanxi renmin jiaoyu chuban she, 1993), pp. 788-792; Frank A. Landt, *Die fünf Heiligen Berge Chinas: Ihre Bedeutung und Bewertung in der Ch'ing-Dynastie* (Berlin: Verlag Dr. Köster, 1994), Abb. 4, pp. 59-77, and pp. 175-184; *Heyue cang zhen: Zhongguo gu ditu zhan (History through Maps: An Exhibition of Old Maps of China)*, edited by Ding Xinbao (Joseph S.P. Ting) [Hong Kong: Xianggang Linshi shizheng ju (Provisional Urban Council of Hong Kong), 1997], pp. 56-57, cat. no. 4.3 [color illustration], p. 64, cat. no. 4.3 [descriptive text in Chinese], and p. 65, cat. no. 4.3 [descriptive text in English]; *Yutu yao lu: Beijing tushu guan cang 6827 zhong Zhong wai wen gujiu ditu mulu*, compiled by Beijing tushu guan shanben tecang bu yutu zu (Beijing: Beijing tushu guan chuban she, 1997), p. 429, no. 5485; *Zhongguo guojia tushu guan guji zhenpin tulu*, edited by Ren Jiyu (Beijing: Beijing tushu guan chuban she, 1999), pp. 302-303, cat. no. 327 [selected section of handscroll illustrated].

59

Rules for Confession in the Place of the Merciful and Compassionate One (Precious Confessional of Emperor Wu of Liang), 10 *juan*, in Tangut Script

西夏文慈悲道場懺法（梁皇寶懺）十卷

Nanjio Bunyiu [Nanjô Bun'yû], *A Catalogue of the Chinese Translation of the Buddhist Tripitaka, the Sacred Canon of the Buddhists in China and Japan, Compiled by Order of the Secretary of State for India* (Oxford: Clarendon Press, 1883. Reprint. Tokyo: Nanjô hakushi kinen kankôkai, 1929), p. 334, no. 1509; *Guoli Beiping tushu guan guan kan (Bulletin of the National Library of Peiping)* 4, no. 3 (May-June 1930) [issued in January 1932], *Xi Xia wen zhuan hao [A Volume on Tangut (Hsi Hsia) Studies]*, 3 unnumbered plates [12 selected leaves, including illustrated frontispiece, from juan 9 illustrated]; Wang Jingru, *Xi Xia yanjiu (Shishiah Studies)*, Guoli zhongyang yanjiu yuan lishi yuyan yanjiu suo dankan (Academia Sinica: The National Research Institute of History and Philology: Monographs), jia zhong (Series A), no. 8 [Beiping: Guoli zhongyang yanjiu yuan lishi yuyan yanjiu suo (The National Research Institute of History and Philology, Academia Sinica), 1932. Reprint. Taibei: Zhongyang yanjiu yuan lishi yuyan yanjiu suo, 1992], vol. 1, pp. 1-14; K.T. Wu, "Chinese Printing under Four Alien Dynasties (916-1368 A.D.)," *Harvard Journal of Asiatic Studies* 13, nos. 3-4 (December 1950): pp. 451-453; *Zhongguo yinben shuji zhanlan mulu*, compiled and edited by Beijing tushu guan (Beijing: Zhongyang renmin zhengfu wenhua bu shehui wenhua shiye guanli ju, 1952), p. 50, no. 269, and p. 51 [halftone; 3 selected leaves illustrated]; *Zhongguo banke tulu*, compiled and edited by Beijing tushu guan, 2d rev. ed. (Beijing: Wenwu chuban she, 1961), vol. 1, p. 53, and vol. 4, pl. 278; Nishida Tatsuo, *Seikago no kenkyû: Seikago no saikôsei to Seika moji no kaidoku (A Study of the Hsi-hsia Language: Reconstruction of the Hsi-hsia Language and Decipherment of the Hsi-hsia Script)*, vol. 2 (Tokyo: Zayû kankôkai, 1966), p. 301, no. 13, and pp. 517-600; Eric D. Grinstead, *Analysis of the Tangut Script* (Lund, Sweden: Studentlitteratur, 1972); Luther Carrington Goodrich, "Tangut Printing," *Gutenberg Jahrbuch* 64 (1976), pp. 64-65; Luc Kwanten, "Tangut Miscellanea, I. On the Inventor of the Tangut Script," *Journal of the American Oriental Society* 97, no. 3 (July-September 1977), pp. 333-335; Luc Kwanten, "The Role of the Tangut in Chinese-Inner Asian Relations," *Acta Orientalia* 39 (1978), pp. 191-198; Zhong Kan, Wu Fengyun, and Li Fanwen, *Xi Xia jian shi* (Yinchuan, Ningxia: Ningxia renmin chuban she, 1979), pp. 141-143; Luc Kwanten and Susan Hesse, *Tangut (Hsi Hsia) Studies: A Bibliography* (Bloomington, Ind.: Research Institute for Inner Asian Studies, Indiana University, 1980); *Xi Xia wenwu*, compiled and edited by Shi Jinbo, Bai Bin, and Wu Fengyun (Beijing: Wenwu chuban she, 1988), pp. 47-48, and figs. 377 and 378 [8 selected leaves illustrated], and pp. 330-331, nos. 377 and 378 [explanatory texts]; Shi Jinbo, *Xi Xia fojiao shi lüe* (Yinzhou, Ningxia: Ningxia renmin chuban she, 1988); Li Wei, *Xi Xia shi yanjiu* (Yinchuan, Ningxia: Ningxia renmin chuban she, 1989); Chen Bingying and Shi Jinbo, "Xi Xia wen," in *Zhongguo minzu gu wenzi tulu*, edited by Zhongguo minzu gu wenzi yanjiu hui (Beijing: Zhongguo shehui kexue chuban she, 1990), pp. 101-136; Evgeny Ivanovich Kychanov, "The State of Great Xia (982-1227 A. D.)," in *Lost Empire of the Silk Road: Buddhist Art from Khara Khoto (X-XIIIth Century)*, edited by Mikhail Piotrovsky [Lugano, Italy: Thyssen-Bornemisza Foundation (Fondazione Thyssen-Bornemisza); Milan: Electa, 1993], pp. 49-58; Kira Fyodorovna Samosyuk, "The Art of the Tangut Empire: A Historical and Stylistic Interpretation," in *Lost Empire of the Silk Road: Buddhist Art from Khara Khoto (X-XIIIth Century)*, edited by Mikhail Piotrovsky [Lugano, Italy: Thyssen-Bornemisza Foundation (Fondazione Thyssen-Bornemisza); Milan: Electa, 1993], pp. 59-88; Nie Hongyin, "Tangutology during

the Past Decades," *Monumenta Serica* 41 (1993), pp. 329-347; Ruth W. Dunnell, "The Hsi Hsia," in *The Cambridge History of China*, vol. 6, *Alien Regimes and Border States, 907-1368*, edited by Herbert Franke and Denis Twitchett (Cambridge and New York: Cambridge University Press, 1994), pp. 154-214; Ruth W. Dunnell, *The Great State of White and High: Buddhism and State Formation in Eleventh-Century Xia* (Honolulu: University of Hawai'i Press, 1996), pp. 63-71; Evgeny Ivanovich Kychanov, "Tangut," in *The World's Writing Systems*, edited by Peter T. Daniels and William Bright (New York and Oxford: Oxford University Press, 1996), pp. 228-230 [bibliography, p. 237]; Ruth W. Dunnell, "The Recovery of Tangut History," *Orientations* 27, no. 4 (April 1996), pp. 28-31; Andrew Dalby, *Dictionary of Languages: The Definitive Reference to More Than 400 Languages* (New York: Columbia University Press, 1998), p. 613.

60

Sutra of the Golden Radiance of the Most Victorious Kings (*Suvarnaprabhasottamaraja-sutra; Qutuγ–tu degedü altan gerel-tü sudur nuγud-un qaγan nere-tü yeke kölgen sudur*), 10 *juan*, in Mongolian Script

蒙文金光明最勝王經十卷

Nanjio Bunyiu [Nanjô Bun'yû], *A Catalogue of the Chinese Translation of the Buddhist Tripitaka, the Sacred Canon of the Buddhists in China and Japan, Compiled by Order of the Secretary of State for India* (Oxford: Clarendon Press, 1883. Reprint. Tokyo: Nanjô hakushi kinen kankôkai, 1929), pp. 41-42, nos. 126-127; *The Suvarnaprabhasa Sutra: A Mahayana Text Called "The Golden Splendour,"* first prepared for publication by the late professor Bunyiu Nanjio [Nanjô Bun'yû], and after his death revised and edited by Hokei Idzumi, under the auspices of The Keimeikwai (Kyoto: The Eastern Buddhist Society, 1931); *Suvarnaprabhasottama-sutra: Das Goldglanz-sutra: Ein Sanskrittext des Mahayana-Buddhismus: Die tibetischen Übersetzungen mit einem Wörterbuch*, herausgegeben von Johannes Nobel, Bd. 1, *Die tibetischen Übersetzungen* [1944], Bd. 2, *Wörterbuch Tibetisch-Deutsch-Sanskrit* [1950] [Leiden: E.J. Brill, 1944-1950 (imprint for Bd. 1: Leiden: E.J. Brill; Stuttgart: W. Kohlhammer, 1944; imprint for Bd. 2: Leiden: E.J. Brill, 1950)]; Pentti Aalto, *Notes on the Altan Gerel (The Mongolian Version of the Suvarnaprabhasa-sutra)*, Studia Orientalia, vol. 14, no. 6 (Helsinki: Societas Orientalis Fennica, 1950); *Zhongguo yinben shuji zhanlan mulu*, compiled and edited by Beijing tushu guan (Beijing: Zhongyang renmin zhengfu wenhua bu shehui wenhua shiye guanli ju, 1952), p. 86, no. 611, and p. 87, no. 623; *Suvarnaprabhasottamasutra: Das Goldglanz-Sutra: Ein Sanskrittext des Mahayana-Buddhismus: I-Tsing's chinesische Version und ihre tibetische Übersetzung*, 2 vols. [Bd. 1, *I-Tsing's chinesische Version, übersetzet, eingeleitet, erläutert und mit einem photomechanischen Nachdruck des chinesischen Textes versehen von J. Nobel; Bd. 2, Die Tibetische übersetzung mit kritischen Ammerkungen herausgegeben.*] (Leiden: E.J. Brill, 1958); *Suvarnaprabhasasutra*, edited by S. [Sitansusekhar] Bagchi, Bauddha-samskrta-granthavali, no. 8 (Darbhanga Mithila Institute of Post-Graduate Studies and Research in Sanskrit Learning, 1967); *The Buddhist Tradition in India, China & Japan*, edited by Wm. Theodore de Bary, with the collaboration of Yoshito Hakeda and Philip Yampolsky (New York: The Modern Library, 1969), pp. 105-108, pp. 266-271, and p. 283; R.E. Emmerick, *The Sutra of Golden Light, Being a Translation of the Suvarnabhasottamasutra* (London: Published for the Pali Text Society by Luzac & Company Ltd., 1970. Reprint. London: The Pali Text Society, 1979);

Walther Heissig, *Catalogue of Mongol Books, Manuscripts and Xylographs*, assisted by Charles Bawden [Copenhagen: The Royal Library, Copenhagen (Det Kongelige Bibliotek, København), 1971], pp. xxv-xxvi, and pp. 204-208, cat. nos. MONG. 395, 479, 440, 556, and 557; Pentti Aalto, "On the Mongol Translations of Buddhist Texts," in *Studies in Indo-Asian Art and Culture*, vol. 1, edited by Perala Ratnam (New Delhi: International Academy of Indian Culture, 1972), pp. 21-26; Claus Oetke, *Die aus dem chinesischen Übersetzten tibetischen Versionen des Suvarnaprabhasasutra: Philologische und linguistische Beiträge zur klassifizierenden Charakterisierunf übersetzter Texte* (Wiesbaden, Germany: Franz Steiner Verlag GmbH, 1977); David Morgan, *The Mongols* (Cambridge, Mass. and Oxford: Blackwell Publishers, Inc., 1986), pp. 123-126; S. Robert Ramsey, *The Languages of China* (Princeton: Princeton University Press, 1987), pp. 194-212; N. Tsultem, *Dekorativno-prikladnoe iskusstvo Mongolii (Mongolian Arts and Crafts) (Arts artisanaux de la Mongolie) (Arte decorativo aplicado de Mongolia)*, edited by D. Bayarsaikhan [Ulan-Bator, Mongolia: Gosizdatel'-stvo (State Publishing House) (Section de la Publication d'État) (Sección de la Publicación del Estado), 1987], unpaginated introductory essays in Russian, English, French, and Spanish, and nos. 54, 55, 56, 57, 58, 59, 116, 117, 118, and 119; Dao Bu, "Huigu shi Menggu wen," in *Zhongguo minzu gu wenzi tulu*, edited by Zhongguo minzu gu wenzi yanjiu hui (Beijing: Zhongguo shehui kexue chuban she, 1990), pp. 295-308; *Qing gong Zang chuan fojiao wenwu (Cultural Relics of Tibetan Buddhism Collected in the Qing Palace)*, edited by Gugong bowu yuan (The Palace Museum) [Beijing: Gugong bowu yuan Zijin cheng chuban she (The Forbidden City Press, The Palace Museum); Hong Kong: Liangmu chuban she (The Woods Publishing Company), 1992], pp. 112-129, cat. nos. 83-95 [introductory text in Chinese and English, and color illustrations with captions in Chinese and English], and pp. 226-230, cat. nos. 83-95 [catalogue entries in Chinese and English]; Alice Sárközi, in collaboration with János Szerb, *A Buddhist Terminological Dictionary: The Mongolian "Mahavyutpatti"* (Budapest: Akadémiai Kiadó, 1995), p. 106, no. 1339, and p. 112, no. 1412, and p. 114, no. 1436, and p. 319, no. 4553; Terese Tse Bartholomew, "Book Covers," in *Mongolia: The Legacy of Chinggis Khan*, by Patricia Berger and Terese Tse Bartholomew (New York: Thames and Hudson Inc., in association with San Francisco: Asian Art Museum of San Francisco, 1995), p. 185, and pp. 188-205, cat. nos. 47-62; Lewis R. Lancaster, "Canonic Texts," in *Mongolia: The Legacy of Chinggis Khan*, by Patricia Berger and Terese Tse Bartholomew (New York: Thames and Hudson Inc., in association with San Francisco: Asian Art Museum of San Francisco, 1995), p. 186-187; Peter Zieme, *Altun yaruq sudur, Vorworte und das erste Buch: Edition und Übersetzung des alttürkischen Version des Goldglanzsutra (Suvarnaprabhasottamasutra)*, Schriften zur Geschichte und Kultur des alten Orients: Berliner Turfantexte, no. 18 (Turnhout, Belgium: Brepols, 1996); William Bright, "The Devanagari Script," in *The World's Writing Systems*, edited by Peter T. Daniels and William Bright (New York and Oxford: Oxford University Press, 1996), pp. 384-390; Mariko Namba Walter, "Kingship and Buddhism in Central Asia" (Ph.D. diss., Harvard University, 1997), pp. 1-358; Andrew Dalby, *Dictionary of Languages: The Definitive Reference to More Than 400 Languages* (New York: Columbia University Press, 1998), pp. 424-426; *Qing gong Zang chuan fojiao wenwu (Cultural Relics of Tibetan Buddhism Collected in the Qing Palace)*, edited by Gugong bowu yuan (The Palace Museum) 2d ed. [Beijing: Zijin cheng chuban she (Forbidden City Publishing House), 1998], pp. 174-195, cat. nos. 83-95 [introductory text in Chinese and English, color illustrations, and catalogue entries in Chinese and English]; *Zhongguo guojia tushu guan (National Library of China)*, edited by Li Zhizhong (Beijing: Zhongguo guojia tushu guan, 1999), p. 15, no. 4 [details of 5 selected folios illustrated]; *Zhongguo guojia tushu guan guji zhenpin tulu*, edited by Ren Jiyu (Beijing: Beijing tushu guan chuban she, 1999), pp. 310-311, cat. no. 336 [illustrated from top to bottom: recessed panel on inner side of bottom sutra cover, recto of first loose folio, and recessed panel on inner side of top sutra cover].

61

Sutra of Reciting the True Names of the Noble Manjusri (*Aryamanjusrinamasangiti*; *'Phags-pa 'Jam-dpal-gyi-mtshan-ya'n-dag-par-brjod-pa*; *Sheng Miaojixiang zhenshi ming jing*) in Sanskrit, Tibetan, and Chinese Scripts
梵、藏、漢三體合璧聖妙吉祥真實名經一卷

Nanjio Bunyiu [Nanjô Bunyû], *A Catalogue of the Chinese Translation of the Buddhist Tripitaka, the Sacred Canon of the Buddhists in China and Japan, Compiled by Order of the Secretary of State for India* (Oxford: Clarendon Press, 1883. Reprint. Tokyo: Nanjô hakushi kinen kankôkai, 1929), p. 227, no. 1032; *Exposition d'ouvrages illustrés de la dynastie Ming (Ming dai banhua shuji zhanlan hui mulu)* [Beijing: Centre franco-chinois d'études sinologiques (Zhong Fa Han xue yanjiu suo), 1944], pp. 99-101, cat. no. 103 [catalogue entries in Chinese and French]; *Zhongguo yinben shuji zhanlan mulu* (Beijing: Zhongyang renmin zhengfu wenhua bu shehui wenhua shiye guanli ju, 1952), p. 59, no. 365, and p. 61 [halftone; 4 selected panels illustrated]; *Manjusri-nama-sangiti in Mongolian, Tibetan, Sanskrit and Chinese, and Sekoddesa in Tibetan and Mongolian*, edited by Raghu Vira [New Delhi: International Academy of Indian Culture, n.d. (1962)]; *Aryamanjusrinamasangiti: Sanskrit & Tibetan Texts*, edited by Durga Das Mukherji (Calcutta: University of Calcutta, 1963); Ronald M. Davidson, "The 'Litany of Names of Manjusri': Text and Translation of the 'Manjusrinamasamgiti,'" in *Tantric and Taoist Studies in Honour of R.A. Stein*, edited by Michel Strickmann (Brussels: Institut Belge des Hautes Études Chinoises, 1981), vol. 1, pp. 1-69; *Chanting the Names of Manjusri: The Manjusri-nama-samgiti, Sanskrit and Tibetan Texts*, translated, with annotation & introduction by Alex Wayman (Boston and London: Shambhala Publications, Inc., 1985); *East Asian Books*, Catalogue 19 (London: Sam Fogg Rare Books and Manuscripts, 1998), p. 84, cat. no. 80; and pp. 90-92, cat. no. 89; and p. 92, cat. no. 92; *Zhongguo guojia tushu guan guji zhenpin tulu*, edited by Ren Jiyu (Beijing: Beijing tushu guan chuban she, 1999), p. 328, cat. no. 354 [illustrated from top to bottom: outer side of top sutra cover, recto of folio 25, and inner side of bottom sutra cover].

62

Three Hundred Icons of Tibetan Buddhism
藏傳佛教三百佛像圖

Sbornik izobrazhenii 300 burkhanov po albomu aziatskago muzeia, edited by Sergei Fedorovich Oldenburg (St. Petersburg: Impr. de l'Académie Impériale des Sciences, 1903. Reprint. Delhi: Motilal Banarsidass Publishers Private Limited, 1992); Lokesh Chandra, *The Three Hundred Gods* [N.p. (New Delhi): N.p. (Lokesh Chandra), n.d. (1965)], unpaginated preface and 2 folded sheets with 150 icons on each sheet; *Ni ma'i 'od zer / Naran-u gerel: Die Biographie des 2. Pekinger lCan skya-Qutuqtu Rol pa'i rdo rje (1717-1786)*, herausgegeben, eingeleitet und zusammengefaßt von Hans-Rainer Kämpfe [Sankt-Augustin, Germany: VGH (Vereinigung für Geschichtswissenschaft Hochasiens) Wissenschaftsverlag GmbH, 1976]; Samuel M. Grupper, "Manchu Patronage and Tibetan Buddhism during the First Half of the Ch'ing Dynasty: A Review Article" [review article of *Ni ma'i 'od zer (Naran-u gerel): Die Biographie des 2. Pekinger LCan skya-Qutuqtu Rol pa'i rdo rje (1717-1786)*, by Hans-Rainer Kämpfe], *The Journal of the Tibet Society* 4 (1984), pp. 47-75; Lokesh Chandra,

Buddhist Iconography of Tibet (Kyoto: Rinsen Book Co., 1986), vol. 1, pp. 58-63, and vol. 2, pp. 683-784; Karl-Heinz Everding, *Die Präexistenzen der lCan skya Qutuqtus: Untersuchungen zur Konstruktion und historischen Entwicklung einer lamaistischen Existenzenlinie* (Wiesbaden, Germany: Otto Harrassowitz, 1988), pp. 15-17, nos. 1.2.2, 1.2.3, 1.2.4, and pp. 28-30, nos. 1.6.1, 1.6.2, and pp. 181-209; Richard P. Palmieri, "Tibetan Xylography and the Question of Movable Type," *Technology and Culture* 32, no. 1 (January 1991), pp. 82-90; *Lalitavajra's Manual of Buddhist Iconography.* [translated by] Sushama Lohia (New Delhi: International Academy of Indian Culture; Delhi: Aditya Prakashan, 1994); Zhangjia Ruobiduoji [Lcan-skya Rol-pa'i-rdo-rje II], *San bai foxiang ji* [text in Tibetan with translation also in Chinese, Latin, and Sanskrit] [N.p. (Beijing): Zhongguo Zang xue chuban she; N.p. (U.S.A.): Meiguo Zhanwang tushu gongsi, 1994]; Andrew Dalby, *Dictionary of Languages: The Definitive Reference to More Than 400 Languages* (New York: Columbia University Press, 1998), pp. 626-628; Evelyn S. Rawski, *The Last Emperors: A Social History of Qing Imperial Institutions* (Berkeley and Los Angeles: University of California Press, 1998), pp. 244-263; *Zhongguo guojia tushu guan guji zhenpin tulu*, edited by Ren Jiyu (Beijing: Beijing tushu guan chuban she, 1999), p. 330, cat. no. 356 [4 selected folios illustrated (2 at top from Tibeto-Mongolian preface; 2 at bottom from iconographic section)].

63

Palace Memorial in Manchu and Chinese Scripts

滿漢合璧奏摺

Zhongguo renming da cidian, compiled and edited by Zang Lihe et al. (Hong Kong: Taixing shuju, 1931), p. 1023; J.K. Fairbank and S.Y. Têng, "On the Types and Uses of Ch'ing Documents," *Harvard Journal of Asiatic Studies* 5, no. 1 (January 1940), pp. 1-37, p. 43, p. 63-65, and pp. 67-68; Silas Hsiu-liang Wu, "The Memorial Systems of the Ch'ing Dynasty (1644-1911)," *Harvard Journal of Asiatic Studies* 27 (1967), pp. 7-75; Silas H.L. Wu, *Communication and Imperial Control in China: Evolution of the Palace Memorial System, 1693-1735* (Cambridge, Mass.: Harvard University Press, 1970), esp. pp. 34-150; Beatrice S. Bartlett, "Imperial Notations on Ch'ing Official Documents in the Ch'ien-lung (1736-1795) and Chia-ch'ing (1796-1820) Reigns [Part One]," *National Palace Museum Bulletin (Gugong Ying wen shuangyue kan)* 7, no. 2 (May-June 1972), pp. 1-13 [see also front cover with color illustration and inside front cover, fig. 1]; Beatrice S. Bartlett, "Imperial Notations on Ch'ing Official Documents in the Ch'ien-lung (1736-1795) and Chia-ch'ing (1796-1820) Reigns, Part Two," *National Palace Museum Bulletin (Gugong Ying wen shuangyue kan)* 7, no. 3 (July-August 1972), pp. 1-13 [see also front and back covers with color illustrations, and inside front cover, fig. 1]; Beatrice S. Bartlett, "Ch'ing Palace Memorials in the Archives of the National Palace Museum," *National Palace Museum Bulletin (Gugong tongxun)* 13, no. 6 (January-February 1979): pp. 1-21 [see also front cover, frontispiece, and back cover]; Zhuang Jifa, *Qing dai zouzhe zhidu* (Taibei: Guoli gugong bowu yuan, 1979), esp. pp. 1-106; *Qing shi liezhuan* (80 *juan*), compiled and edited by Taiwan Zhonghua shuju, 2d Taiwan ed. (Taibei: Taiwan Zhonghua shuju, 1983), *juan* 21/32b-37b (in vol. 3); *Ci lin ji lüe* (11 *juan, fu Ci lin xing shi yun bian*), compiled by Zhu Ruzhen, *juan* 4/7b, reprinted in *Qing dai zhuanji congkan*, compiled and edited by Zhou Junfu [Taibei: Mingwen shuju (Ming Wen Book Co., Ltd.), 1985], vol. 16, p. 156; *Qing shi gao liezhuan* (298 *juan*), compiled by Zhao Erxun et al., *juan* 323, *Liezhuan, juan* 110, reprinted in *Qing dai zhuanji congkan*, compiled and edited by Zhou Junfu [Taibei:

Mingwen shuju (Ming Wen Book Co., Ltd.), 1985], vol. 91, pp. 515-519; *Qing dai qi bai mingren zhuan* (6 *bian, fulu* 5 *zhong*), compiled and edited by Cai Guanluo, bian 1, *Zhengzhi, zhengshi*, reprinted in *Qing dai zhuanji congkan*, compiled and edited by Zhou Junfu [Taibei: Mingwen shuju (Ming Wen Book Co., Ltd.), 1985], vol. 194, pp. 171-174; Ch'en Chieh-hsien, *The Manchu Palace Memorials* (Taibei: Linking Publishing Co. Ltd., 1987), pp. 1-9 and pp. 186-196; S. Robert Ramsey, *The Languages of China* (Princeton: Princeton University Press, 1987), pp. 216-229; Fuli, "Man wen," in *Zhongguo minzu gu wenzi tulu*, edited by Zhongguo minzu gu wenzi yanjiu hui (Beijing: Zhongguo shehui kexue chuban she, 1990), pp. 329-344; Beatrice S. Bartlett, *Monarchs and Ministers: The Grand Council in Mid-Ch'ing China, 1723-1820* (Berkeley and Los Angeles: University of California Press, 1991), esp. pp. 21-22, and pp. 156-158; Endymion Wilkinson, *Chinese History: A Manual* (Cambridge, Mass.: Harvard University Asia Center, 1998), pp. 516-518 and pp. 921-922; *Zhongguo guojia tushu guan guji zhenpin tulu*, edited by Ren Jiyu (Beijing: Beijing tushu guan chuban she, 1999), p. 325, cat. no. 350 [4 selected leaves illustrated].

64

Imperial Patent of Nobility in Manchu and Chinese Scripts

滿漢合璧誥命

Gustav [Gustaaf] Schlegel and Erwin Ritter von Zach, "Zwei Mandschu-Chinesische kaiserliche Diplome," *T'oung Pao*, [ser. 1], vol. 8 (1897), pp. 261-308, accompanied by foldout illustration; *Zhongguo renming da cidian*, compiled and edited by Zang Lihe et al. (Hong Kong: Taixing shuju, 1931), p. 194; Walter Fuchs, "Fan Wen-ch'eng, 1597-1666, und sein Diplom," *Shigaku kenkyû (Sigakukenkyu) (A Review of Historical Studies)* 10, no. 3 (March 1939), pp. 14-36; J.K. Fairbank and S.Y. Têng, "On the Types and Uses of Ch'ing Documents," *Harvard Journal of Asiatic Studies* 5, no. 1 (January 1940), pp. 1-37, and p. 54; Wolfgang Franke, "Patents for Hereditary Ranks and Honorary Titles during the Ch'ing Dynasty," *Monumenta Serica* 7 (1942), pp. 38-67; John L. Mish, "A Manchu-Chinese Scroll, " *Bulletin of The New York Public Library* 52, no. 3 (March 1948), pp. 143-144; John L. Mish, "An Early Manchu-Chinese Patent of Nobility," *Monumenta Nipponica* 10, nos. 1-2 (April 1954), pp. 270-276; *Qing shi liezhuan* (80 *juan*), compiled and edited by Taiwan Zhonghua shuju, 2d Taiwan ed. (Taibei: Taiwan Zhonghua shuju, 1983), *juan* 34/45a-52b (in vol. 5); *Ci lin ji lüe* (11 *juan, fu Ci lin xing shi yun bian*), compiled by Zhu Ruzhen, *juan* 4/48a, reprinted in Qing dai zhuanji congkan, compiled and edited by Zhou Junfu [Taibei: Mingwen shuju (Ming Wen Book Co., Ltd.), 1985], vol. 16, p. 237; *Ba qi wenjing zuozhe kao* (3 *juan*), compiled by Yang Zhongxi, *juan* 59/7a, reprinted in *Qing dai zhuanji congkan*, compiled and edited by Zhou Junfu [Taibei: Mingwen shuju (Ming Wen Book Co., Ltd.), 1985], vol. 17, p. 921; *Qing shi gao liezhuan* (298 *juan*), compiled by Zhao Erxun et al., *juan* 367, *Liezhuan, juan* 154, reprinted in *Qing dai zhuanji congkan*, compiled and edited by Zhou Junfu [Taibei: Mingwen shuju (Ming Wen Book Co., Ltd.), 1985], vol. 92, pp. 380-384; *Qing dai qi bai mingren zhuan* (6 bian, fulu 5 zhong), compiled and edited by Cai Guanluo, bian 2, *Junshi, bianwu*, reprinted in *Qing dai zhuanji congkan*, compiled and edited by Zhou Junfu [Taibei: Mingwen shuju (Ming Wen Book Co., Ltd.), 1985], vol. 195, pp. 641-646; S. Robert Ramsey, *The Languages of China* (Princeton: Princeton University Press, 1987), pp. 216-229; Monique Cohen and Nathalie Monnet, *Impressions de Chine* (Paris: Bibliothèque Nationale, 1992), pp. 118-119, cat. no. 74 [color; selected sections of document illustrated]; *Manmu linlang: Guoli zhongyang tushu guan shanben tecang (A Cornucopia of Rare Editions: The National Central Library's Rare Book Collection)*, compiled by Guoli zhongyang tushu guan (National Central Library) [Taibei: Guoli zhongyang tushu guan (National Central Library), 1993], pp. 128-129 [2 selected sections of handscroll illustrated], p. 152 [catalogue entry in Chinese], and p. 165 [catalogue entry in English]; *East Asian Books*, Catalogue 19 (London: Sam Fogg Rare Books and Manuscripts, 1998), pp. 46-47, cat. nos. 36-37; Andrew Dalby, *Dictionary of Languages: The Definitive Reference to More Than 400 Languages* (New York: Columbia University Press, 1998), pp. 641-643.

65

History of the Six Ancestors in Yi Script

彝文六祖史

Feng Han-yi and John Knight Shryock, ìThe Historical Origins of the Lolo," *Harvard Journal of Asiatic Studies* 3, no. 2 (July 1938), pp. 103-127; *Zhongguo yinben shuji zhanlan mulu*, compiled and edited by Beijing tushu guan (Beijing: Zhongyang renmin zhengfu wenhua bu shehui wenhua shiye guanli ju, 1952), p. 80, nos. 572 and 573, and p. 82 [halftone; 1 selected leaf from no. 572 illustrated]; Wu Zili and Chen Ying, "Yi wen," in *Zhongguo minzu gu wenzi tulu*, edited by Zhongguo minzu gu wenzi yanjiu hui (Beijing: Zhongguo shehui kexue chuban she, 1990), pp. 179-205, esp. p. 181, fig. 159, and p. 377, no. 159; Alain Y. Dessaint, *Minorities of Southwest China: An Introduction to the Yi (Lolo) and Related Peoples and an Annotated Bibliography* [New Haven, Conn.: HRAF (Human Relations Area Files) Press, 1980]; S. Robert Ramsey, *The Languages of China* (Princeton: Princeton University Press, 1987), pp. 250-261; Li Shaoming and and Feng Min, *Yi zu* [N. p. (Beijing): Minzu chuban she, 1993], pp. pp. 7-21; Zhu Chongxian, *Yi zu dianji wenhua* (Beijing: Zhongyang minzu daxue chuban she, 1994), p. 163; Stevan Harrell, "The History of the History of the Yi," in *Cultural Encounters on China's Ethnic Frontiers*, edited by Stevan Harrell (Seattle and London: University of Washington Press, 1995), pp. 63-91; Zhu Chongxian, *Yi zu dianji wenhua yanjiu*, Yi zu dianji wenhua yanjiu congshu (Beijing: Zhongyang minzu daxue chuban she, 1996), p. 68, no. 128, and pp. 266-272; Shi Dingxu, "The Yi Script," in *The World's Writing Systems*, edited by Peter T. Daniels and William Bright (New York and Oxford: Oxford University Press, 1996), pp. 239-243; Andrew Dalby, *Dictionary of Languages: The Definitive Reference to More Than 400 Languages* (New York: Columbia University Press, 1998), pp. 686-687.

66

Palm-Leaf Manuscripts Written in Dai Script with *Narrative Verses of Sariputta* from the *Abhidhamma-pitaka*

傣文刻寫論藏舍利偈頌貝葉經

The Ancient Palm-Leaves Containing the Pragna-paramita-hridaya-sutra and the Ushnisha-vigaya-dharani, edited by F. Max Müller and Bunyiu Nanjio [Nanjô Bunyû], with an appendix by G. Bühler (Oxford: The Clarendon Press, 1884); A.F. Rudolf Hoernle, "An Epigraphical Note on Palm-leaf, Paper and Birch-bark," *Journal of the Asiatic Society of Bengal* 69, pt. 1 (History, Antiquities, &c.), no. 2 (February 29, 1901), pp. 93-134; Mrs. Rhys Davids, *Psalms of the Early Buddhists*, vol. 2, *Psalms of the Brethren* [first published

1913] (Reprint. London: Published for the Pali Text Society by Luzac & Company Ltd., 1964), pp. 340-349; *Zhongguo yinben shuji zhanlan mulu*, compiled and edited by Beijing tushu guan (Beijing: Zhongyang renmin zhengfu wenhua bu shehui wenhua shiye guanli ju, 1952), p. 94, no. 720, and p. 51 [halftone; 3 selected leaves illustrated]; Virendra Kumar, "Preservation of Bark and Palm-leaf Manuscripts," *Herald of Library Science* 2, no. 4 (October 1963), pp. 236-241; Om Prakash Agrawal, "Care and Conservation of Palm-Leaf and Paper Illustrated Manuscripts," in *Palm-leaf and Paper: Illustrated Manuscripts of India and Southeast Asia* by John S. Guy, with an essay by O.P. Agrawal (Melbourne: National Gallery of Victoria, 1982), pp. 84-90; Zhou Yiliang, "Guanyu beiye," *Wenwu*, no. 367 (1986, no. 12) (December 1986), p. 63; S. Robert Ramsey, *The Languages of China* (Princeton: Princeton University Press, 1987), pp. 243-248; Zhang Gongjin, *Dai zu wenhua yanjiu* (Kunming: Yunnan minzu chuban she, 1988), pp. 201-221; Zhang Fusan, "Beiye de wenhua xiangzheng," in *Beiye wenhua lun*, edited by Wang Yizhi and Yang Shiguang (Kunming: Yunnan renmin chuban she, 1990), pp. 1-9; Dao Shixun and Zhang Gongjin, "Lao Dai wen," in *Zhongguo minzu gu wenzi tulu*, edited by Zhongguo minzu gu wenzi yanjiu hui (Beijing: Zhongguo shehui kexue chuban she, 1990), pp. 149-178; Hsieh Shih-chung, "On the Dynamics of Tai/Dai-Lue Ethnicity," in *Cultural Encounters on China's Ethnic Frontiers*, edited by Stevan Harrell (Seattle and London: University of Washington Press, 1995), pp. 301-328; Nyanaponika Thera and Hellmuth Hecker, *Great Disciples of the Buddha: Their Lives, Their Works, Their Legacy*, edited with an introduction by Bhikkhu Bodhi (Boston: Wisdom Publications, in collaboration with Kandy, Sri Lanka: Buddhist Publication Society, 1997), pp. 1-66; *Zhongguo guojia tushu guan guji zhenpin tulu*, edited by Ren Jiyu (Beijing: Beijing tushu guan chuban she, 1999), p. 335, cat. no. 363.

67A-B

Two Dongba Texts of the Naxi People in Geba and Pictographic Scripts

納西族哥巴文、象形文東巴經二種

Joseph F. Rock, *The Ancient Na-khi Kingdom of Southwest China* (Cambridge, Mass.: Harvard University Press, 1947), vols. 1-2; Anthony Jackson, *Na-khi Religion: An Analytical Appraisal of the Na-khi Ritual Texts* (The Hague and Paris: Mouton Publishers, 1979), esp. pp. 59-74; *Dongba wenhua lun ji*, edited by Guo Dalie and Yang Shiguang (Kunming: Yunnan renmin chuban she, 1985); S. Robert Ramsey, *The Languages of China* (Princeton: Princeton University Press, 1987), pp. 264-270; Wang Meitang, "Naxi zu wenxian: Dongba jing," *Wenxian*, no. 32 (1987, no. 2), pp. 230-234; *Ji tian gu ge: Naxi zu Dongba wenxue jicheng*, edited by Yunnan sheng minjian wenxue jicheng bangong shi (Beijing: Zhongguo minjian wenyi chuban she, 1988); Siegbert Hummel, "Die Schrift der Na-Khi," *Zentralasiatische Studien des Seminars für Sprach- und Kulturwissenschaft Zentralasiens der Universität Bonn* 21 (1988), pp. 7-19; He Zhiwu, *Naxi Dongba wenhua* (Changchun, Jilin: Jilin jiaoyu chuban she, 1989), pp. 67-79, and pp. 162-166; He Zhiwu, "Dongba wen he Geba wen," in *Zhongguo minzu gu wenzi tulu*, edited by Zhongguo minzu gu wenzi yanjiu hui (Beijing: Zhongguo shehui kexue chuban she, 1990), pp. 206-224; *Dongba wenhua lun*, compiled and edited by Guo Dalie and Yang Shiguang (Kunming: Yunnan renmin chuban she, 1991); Michael Aris, *Lamas, Princes, and Brigands: Joseph Rock's Photographs of the Tibetan Borderlands of China*, with the assistance of Patrick Booz and contributions by S.B. Sutton and Jeffrey Wagner (New York: China Institute in America, 1992), pp. 25-27, pp. 135-136, and cat. nos. 2.2, 2.3, 2.8, 2.9, 6.4, 6.20, 7.8, 7.9, 7.10, 7.11, 7.12, 7.13; *Naxi zu yanjiu lunwen ji*, edited by Guo Dalie (Beijing: Minzu chuban she, 1992); *Dongba wenhua yishu (The Art of Naxi Dongba Culture)*, compiled by Yunnan sheng shehui kexue yuan Lijiang Dongba wenhua yanjiu suo (Kunming, Yunnan: Yunnan meishu chuban she, 1992); Charles F. McKhann, "Fleshing Out the Bones: Kinship and Cosmology in Naqxi Religion" (Ph.D. diss., The University of Chicago, 1992); *Naxi xiangxing wenzi pu*, compiled by Fang Guoyu, edited by He Zhiwu, 2d ed. (Kunming: Yunnan renmin chuban she, 1995); Charles F. McKhann, "The Naxi and the Nationalities Question," in *Cultural Encounters on China's Ethnic Frontiers*, edited by Stevan Harrell (Seattle and London: University of Washington Press, 1995), pp. 39-62; Emily Chao, "Hegemony, Agency, and Re-presenting the Past: The Invention of Dongba Culture among the Naxi of Southwest China," in *Negotiating Ethnicities in China and Taiwan*, edited by Melissa J. Brown (Berkeley, Calif.: Center for Chinese Studies, Institute of East Asian Studies, University of California, Berkeley, 1996), pp. 208-239; Christine Mathieu, "Lost Kingdoms and Forgotten Tribes: Myths, Mysteries and Mother-right in the History of the Naxi Nationality and the Mosuo People of Southwest China" (Ph.D. thesis, Murdoch University, 1996); *Hafo daxue Hafo-Yanjing tushu guan cang Zhongguo Naxi zu xingxiang wen jingdian fenlei mulu (Annotated Catalog of Naxi Pictographic Manuscripts in the Harvard-Yenching Library, Harvard University)*, compiled by Zhu Baotian (Cambridge, Mass.: Harvard-Yenching Library, Harvard University, 1997), pp. i-xii, and pp. 1-862; Michael Oppitz, *Naxi: Dinge, Mythen, Piktogramme*, mit Zeichen in Bilderschrift von Mu Chen (Zürich: Völkerkundemuseum Zürich, 1997); Andrew Dalby, *Dictionary of Languages: The Definitive Reference to More Than 400 Languages* (New York: Columbia University Press, 1998), pp. 441-442; Mi Chu Wiens, "Sorcerers and Storytellers: Assembling a Modern Rosetta Stone for an Ancient Pictographic Language," *Civilization: The Magazine of the Library of Congress* 6, no. 4 (August-September 1999), p. 95; *Zhongguo guojia tushu guan guji zhenpin tulu*, edited by Ren Jiyu (Beijing: Beijing tushu guan chuban she, 1999), p. 339, cat. no. 365 [illustrated: top cover and 1 selected leaf from another manuscript copy of the *Annals of Creation* in Naxi pictographic script and accompanying Chinese translation].

Yunnan meishu chuban she, 1992); Emily Chao, "Hegemony, Agency, and Re-presenting the Past: The Invention of Dongba Culture among the Naxi of Southwest China," in *Negotiating Ethnicities in China and Taiwan*, edited by Melissa J. Brown (Berkeley, Calif.: Center for Chinese Studies, Institute of East Asian Studies, University of California, Berkeley, 1996), pp. 208-239; Christine Mathieu, "Lost Kingdoms and Forgotten Tribes: Myths, Mysteries and Mother-right in the History of the Naxi Nationality and the Mosuo People of Southwest China" (Ph.D. thesis, Murdoch University, 1996); *Hafo daxue Hafo-Yanjing tushu guan cang Zhongguo Naxi zu xingxiang wen jingdian fenlei mulu (Annotated Catalog of Naxi Pictographic Manuscripts in the Harvard-Yenching Library, Harvard University)*, compiled by Zhu Baotian (Cambridge, Mass.: Harvard-Yenching Library, Harvard University, 1997), pp. i-xii, and pp. 887-890; Michael Oppitz, *Naxi: Dinge, Mythen, Piktogramme*, mit Zeichen in Bilderschrift von Mu Chen (Zürich: Völkerkundemuseum Zürich, 1997).

68A-C

Three Dongba Illustrations from the Naxi People

納西族東巴圖三種

Joseph F. Rock, *The Ancient Na-khi Kingdom of Southwest China* (Cambridge, Mass.: Harvard University Press, 1947), vols. 1-2; Lan Wei, "Dongba hua de zhonglei ji qi tese, " in *Dongba wenhua lun ji*, edited by Guo Dalie and Yang Shiguang (Kunming: Yunnan renmin chuban she, 1985), pp. 412-423; Lan Wei, "Dongba hua yu Dongba wen de guanxi, " in *Dongba wenhua lun ji*, edited by Guo Dalie and Yang Shiguang (Kunming: Yunnan renmin chuban she, 1985), pp. 424-433; He Zhiwu, *Naxi Dongba wenhua* (Changchun, Jilin: Jilin jiaoyu chuban she, 1989), pp. 199-205; *Dongba wenhua lun*, compiled and edited by Guo Dalie and Yang Shiguang (Kunming: Yunnan renmin chuban she, 1991); He Di, "Dongba hua yanjiu," *Duoyun: Zhongguo huihua yanjiu jikan (Art Clouds: Quarterly of Chinese Painting Study)*, no. 29 (1991, no. 2), pp. 51-61; Michael Aris, *Lamas, Princes, and Brigands: Joseph Rock's Photographs of the Tibetan Borderlands of China*, with the assistance of Patrick Booz and contributions by S.B. Sutton and Jeffrey Wagner (New York: China Institute in America, 1992), pp. 25-27, pp. 135-136, and cat. nos. 2.2, 2.3, 2.8, 2.9, 6.4, 6.20, 7.8, 7.9, 7.10, 7.11, 7.12, 7.13; *Naxi zu yanjiu lunwen ji*, edited by Guo Dalie (Beijing: Minzu chuban she, 1992); *Dongba wenhua yishu (The Art of Naxi Dongba Culture)*, compiled by Yunnan sheng shehui kexue yuan Lijiang Dongba wenhua yanjiu suo (Kunming, Yunnan:

Bibliography

主要參考文獻書目

The following bibliography consists of works which were readily available for consultation during the preparation of the catalogue. Given the chronological span and enormous breadth of topics presented in the exhibition, comprehensive bibliographic coverage is not possible. The items listed have been selected from an extensive range of classic texts, facsimile editions, scholarly monographs and articles, exhibition catalogues, standard reference works, and newly published material either for their direct relevance to one or more objects in the exhibition or for their usefulness in providing contextual background.

Pinyin romanization has been utilized throughout, except for the names of authors and titles which originally appeared in print in other forms of romanization. Simplified Chinese characters in Chinese citations have been uniformly converted to their traditional forms, while standard forms used for *kanji* in Japanese citations have been retained as much as possible. Macrons normally used for the transliteration of Japanese names and terms have been substituted with circumflexes.

Compiled by Philip K. Hu

胡廣俊　編

-A-

Aalto, Pentti (1917-). *Notes on the Altan Gerel (The Mongolian Version of the Suvarnaprabhasa-sutra).*Studia Orientalia, edidit Societas Orientalis Fennica, vol. 14, no. 6. Helsinki: Societas Orientalis Fennica [Suomen Itåmainen Seura] [Finnish Oriental Society], 1950.

―――. "On the Mongol Translations of Buddhist Texts." In *Studies in Indo-Asian Art and Culture*, vol. 1, edited by Perala Ratnam, 21-26. Sata-pitaka Series, Indo-Asian Literatures, vol. 95. New Delhi: International Academy of Indian Culture, 1972.

Agrawal, Om Prakash (1931-). "Care and Conservation of Palm-Leaf and Paper Illustrated Manuscripts." In *Palm-leaf and Paper: Illustrated Manuscripts of India and Southeast Asia*, by John S. Guy (1949-), with an essay by O.P. [Om Prakash] Agrawal, 84-90. Exhibition catalogue [National Gallery of Victoria, Melbourne, May 11-July 6, 1982; Art Gallery of Western Australia, Perth, July 23-September 5, 1982; Art Gallery of New South Wales, Sydney, November 5-December 12, 1982]. Melbourne: National Gallery of Victoria, 1982.

Allan, Sarah. *The Shape of the Turtle: Myth, Art, and Cosmos in Early China.* SUNY Series in Chinese Philosophy and Culture, edited by David L. Hall and Roger T. Ames. Albany, N.Y.: State University of New York Press, 1991.

An Siyuan cang shanben beitie xuan (The Chunhuage tie and Rare Rubbings from the Collection of Robert Hatfield Ellsworth). [In Chinese; introductory essay by Qi Gong, 5-8; postscript by An Siyuan (Robert Hatfield Ellsworth), 101.] Exhibition catalogue [Gugong bowu yuan (Palace Museum), Beijing, September 1996]. Beijing: Wenwu chuban she, 1996.
《安思遠藏善本碑帖選》・[收藏者：安思遠]・[啟功・〈真宋本《淳化閣帖》的價值〉・第五頁至第八頁]・[安思遠・〈後記〉・第一百一頁]・[平裝一册]・北京：文物出版社，一九九六年八月第一次印刷・

Ancient China's Technology and Science. Compiled by the Institute of the History of Natural Sciences, Chinese Academy of Sciences. China Knowledge Series. Beijing: Foreign Languages Press, 1983.
《中國古代科技成就》・自然科學史研究所主編・北京：外文出版社，1983年第一版・

Aris, Michael (d. 1999). *Lamas, Princes, and Brigands: Joseph Rock's Photographs of the Tibetan Borderlands of China.* With the assistance of Patrick Booz and contributions by S.B. [Silvia Barry] Sutton and Jeffrey Wagner. Exhibition catalogue [China House Gallery, China Institute in America, New York, April 18-July 31, 1992]. New York: China Institute in America, 1992.

Artefacts of Ancient Chinese Science and Technology. Compiled by the Editorial Board of the Artefacts of Ancient Chinese Science and Technology.[Title on front cover: *Artefacts of Ancient Chinese Science and Technology: National Museum of Chinese History.*] [Translated into English (from the Chinese) by He Fei.] Beijing: Morning Glory Publishers, 1998. [Printer's colophon also in Chinese: *Zhongguo gudai keji wenwu (Yingwen ban).* Edited by "Zhongguo gudai keji wenwu" bianji weiyuan hui. Beijing: Zhaohua chuban she, 1998.]
[《中國古代科技文物》（英文版）・《中國古代科技文物》編輯委員會編・北京：朝華出版社，1998年第一版・]

-B-

Ba qi wenjing zuozhe kao. 3 juan. Compiled by Yang Zhongxi. Reprint [facsimile reproduction]. In *Qing dai zhuanji congkan [Biographical Collections of Ching Dynasty (1644-1912)]*, compiled and edited by Zhou Junfu [Chow Tsin-fu], vol. 17, *Xuelin lei*, no. 19. Taibei: Mingwen shuju (Ming Wen Book Co., Ltd.), 1985.
《八旗文經作者考》・三卷・楊鍾羲撰・[影印本]・《清代傳記叢刊》・第十七冊・〈學林類〉・第十九部（種）・輯者：周駿富・台北：明文書局，民國七十四年五月十日初版・

Baba, Harukichi (1932-). *Kôshi seisekishi.* Tokyo: Daitô bunka kyôkai, 1934.
《孔子聖蹟志》・著者：馬場春吉，大東文化協會，昭和九年八月二十五日發行・

―――. *Kô Mô Seisekizu kan.* [Stitch-bound with colored threads between boards; issued in 1 case.] Tokyo: Santô bunka kenkyûkai, 1940.
《孔孟聖蹟圖鑑》・馬場春吉編著・東京：山東文化研究會，昭和十五年六月壹日發行・

Bagchi, S. [Sitansusekhar], ed. *Suvarnaprabhasasutra.* [Text in Sanskrit; introduction in English, 1-18; and in Hindi, i-xvi.] Bauddha-samskrta-granthavali (Buddhist Sanskrit Texts), no. 8. Darbhanga, Bihar, India: The Mithila Institute of Post-Graduate Studies and Research in Sanskrit Learning, 1967.

Bagley, Robert W. [Robert William]. *Shang Ritual Bronzes in the Arthur M. Sackler Collections.* Ancient Chinese Bronzes in the Arthur M. Sackler Collections, vol. 1. [Issued in slipcase.] Washington, D.C.: The Arthur M. Sackler Foundation; Cambridge, Mass.: Arthur M. Sackler Museum, Harvard University, 1987.

―――. "Shang Archaeology." In *The Cambridge History of Ancient China:*

From the Origins of Civilization to 221 B.C., edited by Michael Loewe and Edward L. Shaughnessy (1952-), 124-231. Cambridge and New York: Cambridge University Press, 1998.

Bai, Bin. *Xi Xia shi lunwen ji.* Yinchuan, Ningxia: Ningxia renmin chuban she, 1984.
《西夏史論文集》‧白濱編‧銀川：寧夏人民出版社，1984 年 7 月第一版‧

Baqiong shi jinshi buzheng. 130 *juan.* Compiled and edited by Lu Zengxiang (1816-1882). [Originally published by Wuxing: Liu shi Xigu lou, 1888.] Edited by Liu Chenggan (1882-1963). 64 vols. [on double-leaves; stitch-bound, Oriental style] in 8 cases. Wuxing: Lu shi Xigu lou, 1925. Reprint [facsimile reproduction of 1925 edition; each page represents 3 leaves of the original; also includes *Baqiong jinshi zhaji* (4 *juan*), compiled by Lu Zengxiang (1816-1882); *Jinshi quwei* (*bufen juan*), compiled by Lu Zengxiang (1816-1882); and *Baqiong shi Yuan jinshi oucun* (*bufen juan*), compiled by Lu Zengxiang (1816-1882)]. Beijing: Wenwu chuban she, 1985.
《八瓊室金石補正》‧[一百三十卷]‧陸增祥撰‧[原版：吳興劉氏希古樓刊]‧[影印版‧據吳興劉氏希古樓一九二五年刊本斷句縮印‧李學勤序‧附陸增祥撰，吳興劉氏希古樓刊《八瓊室金石札記》(四卷)、《金石祛偽》(不分卷)、《八瓊室元金石偶存》(不分卷)]‧北京：文物出版社，1985 年 8 月第一版‧

Barnard, Noel [Ba Na], and Cheung Kwong-yue [Zhang Guangyu]. *Zhong Ri Ou Mei Ao Niu suo jian suo ta suo mo jinwen huibian (Rubbings and Hand Copies of Bronze Inscriptions in Chinese, Japanese, European, American, and Australasian Collections).* [In Chinese and English.] 10 vols. [on double-leaves; stitch-bound, Oriental style] in 2 cases. Taibei: Yee Wen Publishing Coy. Ltd., 1978.
《中日歐美澳組所見所拓所摹金文彙編》‧巴納、張光裕編著‧[綫裝十冊二函]‧台北：藝文印書館，民國六十七年九月‧

Bartholomew, Terese Tse. "Book Covers." In *Mongolia: The Legacy of Chinggis Khan*, by Patricia Berger and Terese Tse Bartholomew, with essays by James Bosson, Lewis R. Lancaster, Morris Rossabi (1941-), [and] Heather Stoddard, 185. New York: Thames and Hudson Inc., in association with San Francisco: Asian Art Museum of San Francisco, 1995.

Bartlett, Beatrice S. [Bai Binju] 白彬菊 . "Imperial Notations on Ch'ing Official Documents in the Ch'ien-lung 乾隆 (1736-1795) and Chia-ch'ing 嘉慶 (1796-1820) Reigns [Part One]." *National Palace Museum Bulletin (Gugong Ying wen shuangyue kan)* 7, no. 2 (May-June 1972): 1-13 [see also front cover with color illustration and inside front cover, fig. 1].

———. "Imperial Notations on Ch'ing Official Documents in the Ch'ien-lung 乾隆 (1736-1795 and Chia-ch'ing 嘉慶 (1796-1820) Reigns, Part Two." *National Palace Museum Bulletin (Gugong Ying wen shuangyue kan)* 7, no. 3 (July-August 1972): 1-13 [see also front and back covers with color illustrations, and inside front cover, fig. 1].

———. "Ch'ing Palace Memorials in the Archives of the National Palace Museum." *National Palace Museum Bulletin (Gugong tongxun)* 13, no. 6 (January-February 1979): 1-21 [see also front cover, frontispiece, and back cover].

———. *Monarchs and Ministers: The Grand Council in Mid-Ch'ing China, 1723-1820.* Berkeley and Los Angeles: University of California Press, 1991.

Beijing daxue tushu guan cang guji shanben shumu. Compiled by Beijing daxue tushu guan. Beijing: Beijing daxue chuban she, 1999.
《北京大學圖書館藏古籍善本書目》‧北京大學圖書館編‧[精裝一冊]‧北京：北京大學出版社，1999 年 6 月第一版‧

Beijing tushu guan cang huaxiang taben huibian. Compiled by Beijing tushu guan shanben bu jinshi zu. [Chief compiler: Ji Yaping.] 10 vols. Beijing: Shumu wenxian chuban she, 1993.
《北京圖書館藏畫像拓本匯編》‧北京圖書館善本部金石組編‧[主編：冀亞平]‧[全十冊]‧北京：書目文獻出版社，1993 年 7 月第一版‧

Beijing tushu guan cang muzhi tapian mulu. Edited by Xu Ziqiang. Compiled by Ji Yaping and Wang Xunwen. Beijing: Zhonghua shuju, 1990.
《北京圖書館藏墓誌拓片目錄》‧徐自強主編‧冀亞平、王巽文編輯‧[精裝一冊]‧北京：中華書局，1991 年 3 月 1 第版‧

Beijing tushu guan cang qingtong qi mingwen taben xuanbian. Compiled and edited by Beijing tushu guan jinshi zu. Beijing: Wenwu chuban she, 1985.
《北京圖書館藏青銅器銘文拓本選編》‧北京圖書館金石組編‧北京：文物出版社，1985 年 10 月第一版‧

Beijing tushu guan cang qingtong qi quanxing tapian ji. Compiled and edited by Beijing tushu guan. 4 vols. Beijing: Beijing tushu guan chuban she, 1997.
《北京圖書館藏青銅器全形拓片集》‧北京圖書館編‧[全四冊‧精裝]‧北京：北京圖書館出版社，1997 年 10 月第 1 版‧

Beijing tushu guan cang Shengping shu xiqu renwu hua ce. [Compiled by Beijing tushu guan; preface by Zhu Jiajin.] Beijing: Beijing tushu guan chuban she, 1997.
《北京圖書館藏昇平署戲曲人物畫冊》‧[著者：北京圖書館‧序：朱家溍]‧北京：北京圖書館出版社，1997 年 10 月第 0 版‧

Beijing tushu guan cang shike xu lu. Edited by Xu Ziqiang. Beijing: Shumu wenxian chuban she,1988.
《北京圖書館藏石刻敘錄》・徐自強主編・北京：書目文獻出版社，一九八八年四月・

Beijing tushu guan cang Zhongguo lidai shike taben huibian. Compiled and edited by Beijing tushu guan jinshi zu. 100 vols. Zhengzhou, Henan: Zhongzhou guji chuban she, 1989-1991.
《北京圖書館藏中國歷代石刻拓本匯編》・北京圖書館金石組編・[全一百冊・精裝]・鄭州：中州古籍出版社，1989 年 5 月第一版至 1991 年第一版・

Beijing tushu guan guan shi ziliao huibian (1909-1949). Compiled and edited by Beijing tushu guan yewu yanjiu weiyuan hui. 2 vols. Beijing: Shumu wenxian chuban she, 1992.
《北京圖書館館史資料匯編（1909-1949）》・北京圖書館業務研究委員會編・[全二冊・精裝]・北京：書目文獻出版社，1992 年 10 月北京第 1 版・

Beijing tushu guan guan shi ziliao huibian (er) (1949-1966). Compiled and edited by Beijing tushu guan guan shi ziliao huibian (er) bianji weiyuan hui. [Chief editor: Zhou Heping; deputy editor: Liu Yiping.] 2 vols. Beijing: Beijing tushu guan chuban she, 1997.
《北京圖書館館史資料匯編（二）（1949-1966）》・北京圖書館館史資料匯編（二）編輯委員會編・[主編：周和平・副主編：劉一平]・[全二冊]・北京：北京圖書館出版社，1997 年 8 月第 1 版・

Beijing tushu guan guji shanben shumu. Compiled by Beijing tushu guan. 5 vols. Beijing: Shumu wenxian chuban she, n.d. [1987].
《北京圖書館古籍善本書目》・北京圖書館編・[全五冊]・北京：書目文獻出版社・[1987 年]・

Beijing tushu guan putong guji zongmu. Compiled and edited by Beijing tushu guan putong guji zu. [Chief editors: Xu Ziqiang and Xue Ying.] [15 vols. projected for complete set.] Beijing: Shumu wenxian chuban she, 1990-[ongoing; most recent volume published 1997].
《北京圖書館普通古籍總目》・北京圖書館普通古籍組編・[主編：徐自強、薛英]・[全套十五卷・精裝]・北京：書目文獻出版社，1990 年 8 月北京第 1 版[第一卷]至[1997 年]・

Beijing tushu guan xin guan jianshe ziliao xuan bian. Compiled by Li Jiarong, Zhu Nan, Li Yidi, and Jin Zhishun. Beijing: Shumu wenxian chuban she, 1992.
《北京圖書館新館建設資料選編》・李家榮、朱南、李以娣、金志舜編・北京：書目文獻出版社，1992 年 9 月北京第 1 版・

Beiye wenhua lun. Edited by Wang Yizhi and Yang Shiguang. Kunming: Yunnan renmin chuban she, 1990.
《貝葉文化論》・王懿之、楊世光編・[精裝一冊]・昆明：雲南人民出版社，1990 年 4 月第 1 版・

Berger, Patricia [Patricia Ann]. "Preserving the Nation: The Political Uses of Tantric Art in China." In *Latter Days of the Law: Images of Chinese Buddhism, 850-1850*, edited by Marsha Weidner, 89-123. Lawrence, Kan.: Spencer Museum of Art, The University of Kansas, in association with Honolulu: University of Hawaii Press, 1994.

———, and Terese Tse Bartholomew. *Mongolia: The Legacy of Chinggis Khan*. With essays by James Bosson, Lewis R. Lancaster, Morris Rossabi (1941-), [and] Heather Stoddard. Catalogue photographs by Kazuhiro Tsuruta. Exhibition catalogue [Asian Art Museum of San Francisco, San Francisco, July 19-October 15, 1995; Denver Art Museum, Denver, November 11, 1995-February 26, 1996; National Geographic Society, Washington, D.C., April 3-July 7, 1996]. New York: Thames and Hudson Inc., in association with San Francisco: Asian Art Museum of San Francisco, 1995.

Berliner, Nancy (1958-). "Wang Tingna and Illustrated Book Publishing in Huizhou." *Orientations* 25, no. 1 (January 1994): 67-75.

———. "The Diverse Roles of Rocks as Revealed in Wood-block Prints." *Orientations* 28, no. 6 (June 1997): 61-68.

Berner, R. Thomas. "The Ancient Chinese Process of Reprography." *Technology and Culture* 38, no. 2 (April 1997): 424-431.

Berry, Margaret (1918-). *The Classic Chinese Novels: An Annotated Bibliography of Chiefly English-language Studies*. Garland Reference Library of the Humanities, vol. 775. New York and London: Garland Publishing, Inc., 1988.

Beyer, Stephan V. (1943-). *The Classical Tibetan Language*. SUNY Series in Buddhist Studies, edited by Matthew Kapstein. Albany, N.Y.: State University of New York Press, 1992.

Bi, Yuan (1730-1797). *Zhongzhou jinshi ji*. 5 *juan*. [With a postscript by Hong Liangji.] Congshu jicheng chu bian, compiled and edited by Wang Yunwu. Shanghai: Shangwu yinshu guan, 1936.
《中州金石記》・五卷・畢沅撰・[洪亮吉後序]・〈叢書集成初編〉・王雲五主編・上海：商務印書館，民國二十五年十二月初版・

Billardon de Sauvigny, Louis Edme (1736-1812). *Histoire naturelle des dorades de la Chine*. Paris: Louis Jorry, 1780 [2 editions, in quarto and in folio].

Birrell, Anne. *Chinese Mythology: An Introduction*. With a foreword by Yuan K'o. Baltimore and London: The Johns Hopkins University Press, 1993.

Bishu shanzhuang sanshi liu jing. [Prefatory text by Li Yimang (1903-1990). Captions on verso of plates.] Zhongguo gudai fengjing banhua congkan. 2d ed. [2d printing]. Beijing: Renmin meishu chuban she, 1984.
《避暑山莊三十六景》·[李一氓供稿]·《中國古代風景版畫叢刊》·北京：人民美術出版社，一九八四年四月第二版第二次印刷·

Bloom, Irene, and Joshua A. Fogel (1950-), eds. *Meeting of Minds: Intellectual and Religious Interaction in East Asian Traditions of Thought: Essays in Honor of Wing-tsit Chan and William Theodore de Bary*. New York: Columbia University Press, 1997.

Blunden, Caroline, and Mark Elvin. *Cultural Atlas of China*. Rev. ed. An Andromeda Book. New York: Checkmark Books, an imprint of Facts on File, Inc., 1998.

Bo, Songnian. "Tan Ming kanben Xixiang ji chatu." *Meishu yanjiu*, no. 8 (1958, no. 4): 45-47 [see also 6 illustrations preceding text].
薄松年·〈談明刊本西廂記插圖〉·《美術研究》·總第八期·一九五八年第四期·第四十五頁至第四十七頁[參見文前圖版六幅]·

Bøckman, Harald. *Naxi Studies in China: A Research Report*. Oslo, Norway: Harald Bøckman, n.d. [1988].

Bodor, John J. *Rubbings and Textures: A Graphic Technique*. An Art Horizons Book. New York and Amsterdam: Reinhold Book Corporation, a subsidiary of Chapman-Reinhold, Inc., 1968.

Bokenkamp, Stephen R. (1949-). *Early Daoist Scriptures*. With a contribution by Peter Nickerson. Taoist Classics, edited by Stephen R. Bokenkamp, no. 1. Berkeley and Los Angeles: University of California Press, 1997.

Boltz, William G. "Early Chinese Writing." *World Archaeology* 17, no. 3 (February 1986): 420-436 [includes abstract, 436].

———. "Lao tzu Tao te ching 老子道德經." In *Early Chinese Texts: A Bibliographical Guide*, edited by Michael Loewe, 269-292. Early China Special Monograph Series, no. 2. N.p.: The Society for the Study of Early China; Berkeley, Calif.: The Institute of East Asian Studies, University of California, Berkeley, 1993.

———. *The Origin and Early Development of the Chinese Writing System*. American Oriental Series, vol. 78. New Haven, Conn.: American Oriental Society, 1994.

———. "Manuscripts with Transmitted Counterparts." In *New Sources of Early Chinese History: An Introduction to the Reading of Inscriptions and Manuscripts*, edited by Edward L. Shaughnessy (1952-), 253-283. Early China Special Monograph Series, no. 3. N.p. [Bethlehem, Pa.]: The Society for the Study of Early China; Berkeley, Calif.: The Institute of East Asian Studies, University of California, Berkeley, 1997.

———. "Language and Writing." In *The Cambridge History of Ancient China: From the Origins of Civilization to 221 B.C.*, edited by Michael Loewe and Edward L. Shaughnessy (1952-), 74-123. Cambridge and New York: Cambridge University Press, 1998.

Bosson, James [James Evert]. "Scripts and Literacy in the Mongol World." In *Mongolia: The Legacy of Chinggis Khan*, by Patricia Berger and Terese Tse Bartholomew, with essays by James Bosson, Lewis R. Lancaster, Morris Rossabi (1941-), [and] Heather Stoddard, 88-95. New York: Thames and Hudson Inc., in association with San Francisco: Asian Art Museum of San Francisco, 1995.

Botanica: The Illustrated A-Z of Over 10,000 Garden Plants and How to Cultivate Them. Consultant: Barbara Segall. Milsons Point, N.S.W., Australia: Mynah, an imprint of Random House Australia Pty Ltd., 1997.

Bright, William (1928-). "The Devanagari Script." In *The World's Writing Systems*, edited by Peter T. Daniels (1951-) and William Bright, 384-390. New York and Oxford: Oxford University Press, 1996.

Bronze Mirrors from Ancient China: Donald H. Graham Jr. Collection. Preface, essay and catalogue by Toru Nakano. Essays by Tseng Yuho Ecke (1924-) and Suzanne Cahill. [Translated (from the Japanese) by Tetsuro Kono and Ace Translation, Honolulu. Edited by Susan Dewar. Glossary and bibliography by Bruce Doar.] N.p. [Honolulu]: N.p. [Donald H. Graham, Jr.], 1994.

Brook, Timothy [Timothy James] (1951-). *Geographical Sources of Ming-Qing History*. Michigan Monographs in Chinese Studies, vol. 58. Ann Arbor, Mich.: Center for Chinese Studies, The University of Michigan, 1988.

Brown, Melissa J., ed. *Negotiating Ethnicities in China and Taiwan*. China Research Monograph, no. 46. Berkeley, Calif.: Center for Chinese Studies, Institute of East Asian Studies, University of California, Berkeley, 1996.

Bryant, Daniel [Daniel Joseph] (1942-). "Wang Shih-chen." In *The Indiana Companion to Traditional Chinese Literature*, edited and compiled by William H. Nienhauser, Jr., vol. 1, 874-876. Bloomington, Ind. and Indianapolis: Indiana University Press, 1986.

Buck, Pearl S. [Pearl Sydenstricker] (1892-1973), trans. *All Men Are Brothers [Shui Hu Chuan]*. Translated from the Chinese by Pearl S. Buck. 2 vols. New York: The John Day Company, 1933.

Buddhist Iconography. Sambhota Series, no. 2. New Delhi: Tibet House, 1989.

Bulling, A. [Anneliese Gutkind] (1900-). *The Decoration of Mirrors of the Han Period: A Chronology*. Artibus Asiae Supplementum, no. 20. Ascona, Switzerland: Artibus Asiae Publishers, 1960.

Bullitt, Judith Ogden. "Princeton's Manuscript Fragments from Tun-huang." *The Gest Library Journal* 3, nos. 1-2 (Spring 1989): 7-29.

Burckhardt, Erwin. *Chinesische Steinabreibungen*. Munich: Hirmer Verlag München, 1961.

Bussotti, Michela. "The 'Gushi huapu 顧氏畫譜,' a Ming Dynasty Wood-Block Printing Masterpiece in the Naples National Library." *Ming Qing yanjiu* 4 (1995): 11-44.

———. "Gravures de l'École de Hui: Étude du livre illustré chinois de la fin du XVIᵉ siècle au milieu du XVIIᵉ siècle." 4 tomes. Thèse de Doctorat (noveau régime), École pratique des hautes études, Section des sciences historiques et philosophiques, 1999.

-C-

Cahill, James F. [James Francis] (1926-), ed. *Shadows of Mt. Huang: Chinese Painting and Printing of the Anhui School*. Exhibition catalogue [University Art Museum, University of California, Berkeley, Berkeley, Calif., January 21-March 22, 1981; The Detroit Institute of Arts, Detroit, July 12-September 13, 1981; Archer M. Huntington Art Gallery, The University of Texas at Austin, Austin, Tex., October 11-November 22, 1981; The Art Museum, Princeton University, Princeton, N.J., December 12, 1981-January 23, 1982]. Berkeley, Calif.: University Art Museum, University of California, Berkeley, 1981.

———. "Chinese Painting: Innovation After 'Progress' Ends." In *China: 5,000 Years: Innovation and Transformation in the Arts*, selected by Sherman Lee, 174-192. New York: Guggenheim Museum Publications, 1998.

Cahill, Suzanne E. [Suzanne Elizabeth]. *Transcendence and Divine Passion: The Queen Mother of the West in Medieval China*. Stanford, Calif.: Stanford University Press, 1993.

Cai, Hongru. "Ming dai zhi mo mingjia Cheng Junfang ji qi 'Mo yuan.'" *Wenwu*, no. 346 (1985, no. 3) (March 1985): 33-35.
蔡鴻茹・〈明代制墨名家程君房及其《墨苑》〉・《文物》・一九八五年第三期・總第三四六號・第三十三頁至第三十五頁・

Cai, Meifen [Tsai Mei-fen]. "Ming dai de mo yu mo shu (Inkcakes and Books on Ink during Ming Dynasty)." In *Zhonghua minguo jianguo bashi nian Zhongguo yishu wenwu taolun hui: Lunwen ji: Qi wu (International Colloquium on Chinese Art History, 1991: Proceedings: Antiquities)*, compiled and edited by Guoli gugong bowu yuan bianji weiyuan hui, pt. 2, 681-725 [in Chinese; includes abstract in English, 683-687; see also 4 unnumbered pages of color plates with 7 illustrations at beginning of volume]. Taibei: Guoli gugong bowu yuan (National Palace Museum), 1992.
蔡玫芬・〈明代的墨與墨書〉・《中華民國建國八十年中國藝術文物討論會：論文集：器物》・國立故宮博物院編輯委員會編輯・台北：國立故宮博物院，民國八十一年六月初版・下册・第六百八十一頁至第七百二十五頁・

The Cambridge Encyclopedia of China. Editor: Brian Hook. Consultant editor: Denis Twitchett. 2d ed. Cambridge and New York: Cambridge University Press, 1991.

The Cambridge History of China. Edited by Denis Twitchett and John K. Fairbank (1907-1991) [and others]. Vol. 1, *The Ch'in and Han Empires, 221 B.C.-A.D. 220*, edited by Denis Twitchett and Michael Loewe [1986]. Vol. 3, *Sui and T'ang China, 589-906, Part 1*, edited by Denis Twitchett [1979]. Vol. 6, *Alien Regimes and Border States, 907-1368*, edited by Herbert Franke and Denis Twitchett [1994]. Vol. 7, *The Ming Dynasty, 1368-1644, Part 1*, edited by Frederick W. Mote and Denis Twitchett [1988]. Vol. 8, *The Ming Dynasty, 1368-1644, Part 2*, edited by Denis Twitchett and Frederick W. Mote [1998]. Vol. 10, *Late Ch'ing, 1800-1911, Part 1*, edited by John K. Fairbank [1978]. Vol. 11, *Late Ch'ing, 1800-1911, Part 2*, edited by John K. Fairbank and Kwang-Ching Liu [1980]. Cambridge and New York: Cambridge University Press, 1979-[continuing].

Cao, Dan. "Lushan xian Han Fan Min que qingli fuyuan." *Wenwu*, no. 157 (1963, no. 11) (November 1963): 65-66 [see also figs. 1-3 following text].
曹丹・〈蘆山縣漢樊敏闕清理復原〉・《文物》・一九六三年第十一期・總第一五七號・第六十五頁至第六十六頁[以及圖版一至三]・

Cao, Wanru. "Jieshao san fu gu ditu." *Wenwu cankao ziliao*, no. 95 (1958, no. 7) (July 1958): 33, continued on 30 [see also foldout map between 30 and 33].
曹婉如・〈介紹三幅古地圖〉・《文物參考資料》・一九五八年第七期・總第九五號・第三十三頁，下接第三十頁[第三十頁與第三十三頁間附圖]・

————. "Maps 2,000 Years Ago and Ancient Cartographical Rules." In *Ancient China's Technology and Science*, compiled by the Institute of the History of Natural Sciences, Chinese Academy of Sciences, 250-257. China Knowledge Series. Beijing: Foreign Languages Press, 1983.

Cao, Zhi. *Zhongguo guji banben xue*. Gaodeng xuexiao wenke jiaocai. Wuchang: Wuhan daxue chuban she, 1992.
《中國古籍版本學》·曹之著·〈高等學校文科教材〉·武昌：武漢大學出版社，1992 年 5 月第 1 版·

Cao Quan bei. [Edited by Feng Tao.] Zhongguo lidai jingdian mingtie jicheng. Beijing: Huaxia chuban she, 1999.
《曹全碑》·[責任編輯：馮濤]·〈中國歷代經典名帖集成〉·[平裝一册]·北京：華夏出版社，一九九九年一月第一版·

Čapek, Abe. *Chinese Stone-Pictures: A Distinctive Form of Chinese Art*. London: Spring Books, 1962.

Carey, William (1861-). *Adventures in Tibet, Including the Diary of Miss Annie R. Taylor's Remarkable Journey from Tau-Chau to Ta-Chien-Lu through the Heart of the "Forbidden Land"*. New York: The Baker and Taylor Co., 1901.

Carlitz, Katherine N. "The Social Uses of Female Virtue in Late Ming Editions of 'Lienü zhuan.'" *Late Imperial China* 12, no. 2 (December 1991): 117-148.

Carter, Thomas Francis (1882-1925). *The Invention of Printing in China and Its Spread Westward*. New York: Columbia University Press, 1925.

————. "The Chinese Background of the European Invention of Printing." *Gutenberg-Jahrbuch* [3. Jahrgang] (1928): 9-14.

————. *The Invention of Printing in China and Its Spread Westward*. Rev. ed. New York: Columbia University Press, 1931.

————. *The Invention of Printing in China and Its Spread Westward*. Revised by L. Carrington [Luther Carrington] Goodrich (1894-1986). 2d ed. New York: The Ronald Press Company, 1955.

Cartier, Michel. "Les métamorphoses imaginaires de la Venise chinoise: La ville de Suzhou et ses plans." *Revue de la Bibliothèque nationale*, no. 48 (Summer 1993): 2-9.

Catalogue of Chinese Rubbings from Field Museum. Researched by Hoshien Tchen [Ch'en Ho-hsien] and M. Kenneth Starr. Prepared by Alice K. Schneider. Photographs by Herta Newton and Field Museum Division of Photography. Edited by Hartmut Walravens (1944-). Fieldiana: Anthropology, n.s., no. 3. Publication 1327. Chicago: Field Museum of Natural History, 1981.

Chang, Kang-i Sun (1944-). "Ming and Qing Anthologies of Women's Poetry and Their Selection Strategies." In *Writing Women in Late Imperial China*, edited by Ellen Widmer and Kang-i Sun Chang, 147-170. Stanford, Calif.: Stanford University Press, 1997.

Chang, K.C. [Kwang-chih Chang] [Zhang Guangzhi] 張光直 (1931-). *Shang Civilization*. New Haven and London: Yale University Press, 1980.

————. *The Archaeology of Ancient China*. 4th ed., rev. and enl. New Haven and London: Yale University Press, 1986.

Chang, Sen-dou (1926-). "Manuscript Maps in Late Imperial China." *The Canadian Geographer* 11, no. 1 (June 1974): 1-14 [includes abstract in English, 1; and abstracts in French, German, and Spanish, 13-14].

Chanting the Names of Manjusri: The Manjusri-nama-samgiti, Sanskrit and Tibetan Texts. Translated, with annotation & introduction by Alex Wayman. Boston and London: Shambhala Publications, Inc., 1985.

Chao, Emily. "Hegemony, Agency, and Re-presenting the Past: The Invention of Dongba Culture among the Naxi of Southwest China." In *Negotiating Ethnicities in China and Taiwan*, edited by Melissa J. Brown, 208-239. China Research Monograph, no. 46. Berkeley, Calif.: Center for Chinese Studies, Institute of East Asian Studies, University of California, Berkeley, 1996.

Chao, Kang [Zhao Gang] 趙岡 (1929-), with the assistance of Jessica C. Y. Chao 陳鍾毅. *The Development of Cotton Textile Production in China*. Harvard East Asian Monographs, no. 74. Cambridge, Mass.: East Asian Research Center, Harvard University, 1977.

Chavannes, Édouard (1865-1918). *Mission archéologique dans la Chine septentrionale: Planches*. 2 pts. [Pt. 1, pl. I-CCLXXXVI; pt. 2, pl. CCLXXXVII-CCCCLXXXVIII; issued in 2 portfolios.] Publication de l'École française d'Extrême-Orient. Paris: Imprimerie nationale; Paris: Ernest Leroux, Éditeur, 1909.

————. "L'instruction d'un futur empereur de Chine en l'an 1193." In *Mémoires concernant l'Asie Orientale, Inde, Asie Centrale, Extrême-Orient*, publiés par l'Académie des Inscriptions et Belles-Lettres, sous la direction de Mm. Senart, Barth, Chavannes, Cordier, membres de l'Institut, tome premier, 19-64, and pls. 5-9. Paris: Ernest Leroux, Éditeur, 1913.

————. Review of *Kêng tschi t'u: Ackerbau und Seidengewinnung in China*:

Ein kaiserliches Lehr- und Mahn-Buch, aus dem Chinesischen übersetzt und mit Erklärungen Versehen von O. [Otto] Franke, mit 102 Tafeln und 57 Illustrationen im Text, by Otto Franke. *T'oung Pao* 14 (1913): 306-309.

———. *Mission archéologique dans la Chine septentrionale*. Tome 1, pt. 1, *La sculpture à l'époque des Han* [1913]. Tome 1, pt. 2, *La sculpture bouddhique* [1915]. Publications de l'École française d'Extrême-Orient, vol. 13, pts. 1-2. Paris: Ernest Leroux, Éditeur, 1913-1915.

Chayet, Anne. *Les temples de Jehol et leurs modèles tibétains*. Synthèse, no. 19. Paris: Éditions Recherche sur les Civilisations, 1985.

Ch'en, Chieh-hsien 陳捷先 . *The Manchu Palace Memorials*. [Title on added title page also in Chinese: *Man wen zouzhe* 滿文奏摺 . Documents in Manchu, romanized Manchu, and English.] Taibei: Linking Publishing Co. Ltd., 1987.

Chen, Jieqi (1813-1884). *Qin qian wenzi zhi yu*. Reorganized by Chen Jikui. Ji'nan, Shandong: Qi Lu shushe, 1991.
《秦前文字之語》・陳介祺著・陳繼揆整理・濟南：齊魯書社，1991 年 4 月第 1 版・

Chen, Warren. "The Emperor Liang Wu-ti and Buddhism." Ph.D. diss., New York University, 1993.

Chen, Zhengxiang [Cheng-Siang Chen]. *Mianhua dili (Geography of Cotton)*. Zuowu dili congkan (Crop Geography Series), no. 2. Taibei: Fuming nongye dili yanjiu suo (Institute of Agricultural Geography), 1953.
《棉花地理》・陳正祥著・〈作物地理叢刊〉・第二號・台北：敷明農業地理研究所，[民國四十二年十月]・

———. *Zhongguo ditu xue shi*. Hong Kong: Shangwu yinshu guan Xianggang fenguan, 1979.
《中國地圖學史》・陳正祥著・香港：商務印書館香港分館，1979 年 3 月初版・

Cheng, Liyao (1932-). *Imperial Gardens*. [Translated (from the Chinese) by Zhang Long.] Ancient Chinese Architecture. Vienna and New York: Springer-Verlag, 1998.

Cheng shi mo yuan. [Compiled by Cheng Dayue (1541-ca. 1616).] Reprint [this edition originally published 1929; preface by Zhou Shaoliang]. 12 vols. [on double-leaves; stitch-bound, Oriental style] in 2 cases. Beijing: Zhongguo shudian, 1990.
《程氏墨苑》・[撰者：程大約]・[影印本・周紹良序]・[綫裝十二册二函]・北京：中國書店，1990 年十月・

Chengde Bishu shanzhuang. Edited by Chengde shi wenwu ju and Zhongguo renmin daxue Qing shi yanjiu suo. Beijing: Wenwu chuban she, 1980.
《承德避暑山莊》・承德市文物局、中國人民大學清史研究所編・北京：文物出版社，1980 年 8 月第一版・

Chengde gu jianzhu: Bishu shanzhuang he wai ba miao. Compiled and edited by Tianjin daxue jianzhu xi (Department of Architecture, Tianjin University) and Chengde shi wenwu ju (Bureau of Relics of Chengde). [Accompanied by a supplement, inserted at the end of the volume, in English, "A Brief Introduction to Ancient Architecture of Chengde (Chengde gu jianzhu, Yingwen fu pian)," unpaginated.] N.p. [Beijing]: Zhongguo jianzhu gongye chuban she (China Building Industry Press); Hong Kong: Shenghuo, Dushu, Xinzhi Sanlian shudian Xianggang fendian [Joint Publishing Co. (Hong Kong)], 1982.
《承德古建築—避暑山莊和外八廟》・天津大學建築系、承德市文物局編著・[北京]：中國建築工業出版社；香港：生活、讀書、新知三聯書店香港分店，一九八二年七月第一版・

Cherniack, Susan. "Book Culture and Textual Transmission in Sung China." *Harvard Journal of Asiatic Studies* 54, no. 1 (June 1994): 5-102.

Cheshire, Horace F. (d. 1921). *Goh, or Wei Chi: A Handbook of the Game and Full Instruction for Play*. Introduction & critical notes by T. Komatsubara. Diagrams and plates (25), illustrative games (12), with notes Japanese and English, many positions and problems discussed. [Title on half-title page: *Handbook of Goh or Wei Chi, The Great Military and Stragetic Game of Eastern Asia, Adapted for European Players: Historical Notes and Appendix*.] Hastings, Eng.: Horace F. Cheshire, 1911.

Cheung, Kwong-yue [Zhang Guangyu] 張光裕 . "Recent Archaeological Evidence Relating to the Origin of Chinese Characters." [Translated (from the Chinese) by Noel Barnard.] In *The Origins of Chinese Civilization*, edited by David N. Keightley (1932-), 323-391. Studies on China, no. 1. Berkeley and Los Angeles: University of California Press, 1983.

Ch'ien, Edward T. [Edward Tzuu]. *Chiao Hung and the Restructuring of Neo-Confucianism in the Late Ming*. Neo-Confucian Studies, sponsored by The Regional Seminar in Neo-Confucian Studies, Columbia University. New York: Columbia University Press, 1986.

Chin shi kyûzô jû shô: Sen'oku seishô besshû (Ten Bronze Bells Formerly in the Collection of Ch'ên Chieh-ch'i, being a Special Volume of the Senoku-seishô, or, The Collection of the Chinese Bronzes of Baron Sumitomo). Explanatory notes by Hamada Kôsaku (1881-1938). 2d ed. (with change in format). [In Japanese and English; on double-leaves; stitch-bound,

Oriental style; in 1 case.] N.p. [Kyoto]: N.p. [Sumitomo Kichizaemon], 1924.
《陳氏舊藏十鐘：泉屋清賞別集》・[解説：濱田青陵]・

China, eine Wiege der Weltkultur: 5000 Jahre Erfindungen und Entdeckungen. [Herausgegber: Arne Eggebrecht. Konzeption: Arne Eggebrecht, Matthias Seidel, Mayke Wagner. Mitarbeit: Monika Geiseler, Matthias Seidel, Mayke Wagner.] Exhibition catalogue [Roemer- und Pelizaeus-Museum, Hildesheim, Germany, July 17-November 27, 1994]. Mainz am Rhein, Germany: Verlag Philipp von Zabern, 1994.

China: 5,000 Years: Innovation and Transformation in the Arts. Selected by Sherman Lee (1918-). [Howard Rogers, general editor; Naomi Richard, consulting editor; Sylvia Moss, editor.] Exhibition catalogue [Solomon R. Guggenheim Museum, New York, February 6-June 3, 1998; Guggenheim Museum Bilbao, Bilbao, Spain, Summer 1998]. New York: Guggenheim Museum Publications, 1998.

China in Ancient and Modern Maps. [Compiled by the Ancient Map Research Team of Chinese Academy of Surveying and Mapping. Translated (from the Chinese) by Chen Gengtao and Wang Pingxiang.] London: Published for Sotheby's Publications by Philip Wilson Publishers Limited, 1998.

Chinese & Japanese Maps: An Exhibition Organised by the British Library at the British Museum, 1 February-31 December 1974. Catalogue by Yolande Jones, Howard Nelson, [and] Helen Wallis. Exhibition catalogue [British Museum, London, February 1-December 31, 1974]. London: Published for the British Library Board by British Museum Publications Limited, 1974.

Chinese Art: Painting, Calligraphy, Stone Rubbing, Wood Engraving. By Werner Speiser, Roger Goepper, and Jean Fribourg. [Translated (from the German) by Diana Imber.] The Universe Library of Antique Art. New York: Universe Books, Inc., 1964.

Chinese Color-Prints from the Painting Manual of the Mustard Seed Garden. With an introduction by Jan Tschichold (1902-1974). Sixteen facsimiles in the size of the originals. [Authorized English translation by Eudo C. Mason; first American ed.] New York: The Beechhurst Press, 1953.

Chinese Goldfish. [By Li Zhen (1954-).] [Colophon page also in Chinese: *Zhongguo jinyu.* Beijing: Waiwen chuban she, 1988.] Beijing: Foreign Languages Press, 1988.
《中國金魚》・北京：外文出版社・1988 年第一版・

Chûgoku kodai hanga ten: Machida shisei 30-shûnen kinen, Nitchû heiwa yûkô jôyaku teiketsu 10-shûnen kinen. Chûgoku hanga 2000-nen ten, dai-

3 bu. Compiled by Machida shiritsu kokusai hanga bijutsukan [and] Takimoto Hiroyuki (1954-). Exhibition catalogue [Machida shiritsu kokusai hanga bijutsukan, Machida, Japan, 1988]. Machida, Japan: Machida shiritsu kokusai hanga bijutsukan, 1988.
《中国古代版画展・町田市制 30 周年記念、日中平和友好条約締結 10 周年記念》・〈中国版画 2000 年展・第 3 部〉・[編集：町田市立国際版画美術館、瀧本弘之]・[主催：町田市立国際版画美術館、中国国家図書館（北京図書館）、中国新疆ウイグル自治区博物館・東京都町田市：町田市立国際版画美術館・1988・

Chûgoku Min Shin no ehon [Chinese illustrated books from the Ming and Ch'ing]. Exhibition catalogue [Ôsaka shiritsu bijutsukan (Osaka Municipal Museum of Fine Arts), Osaka, June 16-July 19, 1987]. Osaka: Ôsaka shiritsu bijutsukan [Osaka Municipal Museum of Fine Arts], 1987.
《中国明清の絵本》・[本図録は、昭和六十二年六月十六日から七月十九日まで、大阪市立美術館にて開催する特別展「中国明清の絵本」展の図録である]・大阪：大阪市立美術館・昭和六十二年六月十六日発行・

Ci lin ji lüe. 11 *juan. Fu Ci lin xing shi yun bian.* Compiled by Zhu Ruzhen (jinshi of 1904). Reprint [facsimile reproduction]. In *Qing dai zhuanji congkan [Biographical Collections of Ching Dynasty (1644-1912)],* compiled and edited by Zhou Junfu [Chow Tsin-fu], vol. 16, Xuelin lei, no. 18. Taibei: Mingwen shuju (Ming Wen Book Co., Ltd.), 1985.
《詞林輯略》・十一卷・附《詞林姓氏輯編》・朱汝珍輯・[影印本]・《清代傳記叢刊》・第十六册・〈學林類〉・第十八部（種）・輯者：周駿富・台北：明文書局・民國七十四年五月十日初版・

Clunas, Craig. "Books and Things: Ming Literary Culture and Material Culture." In *Chinese Studies: Papers Presented at a Colloquium at the School of Oriental and African Studies, University of London, 24-26 August 1987,* edited by Frances Wood (1948-), 136-142. British Library Occasional Papers, no. 10. London: The British Library, 1988.

———. *Superfluous Things: Material Culture and Social Status in Early Modern China.* Urbana and Chicago: University of Illinois Press; Cambridge: Polity Press; Oxford: Basil Blackwell, 1991.

———. *Pictures and Visuality in Early Modern China.* Princeton: Princeton University Press, 1997.

Cohen, Monique. "Le livre illustré en Chine des Ming aux Qing (XVe-XIXe s.)." In *Le livre et l'imprimerie en Extrême-Orient et en Asie du Sud: Actes du Colloque organisé à Paris du 9 au 11 mars 1983,* préparés par Jean-Pierre Drège, Mitchiko Ishigami-Iagolnitzer et Monique Cohen, 57-72. [Revue française d'histoire du livre, nos. 42-43.] Bordeaux: Société des Bibliophiles de Guyenne, 1986.

———, and Nathalie Monnet. *Impressions de Chine.* Exhibition catalogue [Galerie Colbert, Bibliothèque Nationale, Paris, September 8-December

6, 1992]. Paris: Bibliothèque Nationale, 1992.

Cole, Alan [R. Alan]. *Mothers and Sons in Chinese Buddhism*. Stanford, Calif.: Stanford University Press, 1998.

Comentale, Christophe. "Les techniques de l'imprimerie à caractères mobiles (XIᵉ-XVIIIᵉ siècles)." In *Le livre et l'imprimerie en Extrême-Orient et en Asie du Sud: Actes du Colloque organisé à Paris du 9 au 11 mars 1983*, préparés par Jean-Pierre Drège, Mitchiko Ishigami-Iagolnitzer et Monique Cohen, 41-53. [*Revue française d'histoire du livre*, nos. 42-43.] Bordeaux: Société des Bibliophiles de Guyenne, 1986.

Cong Beijing dao Fan'ersai: Zhong Fa meishu jiaoliu (From Beijing to Versailles: Artistic Relations between China and France). [Jointly presented by Xianggang shizheng ju (Urban Council, Hong Kong) and Faguo zhu Xianggang zong lingshi guan (Consulate General of France, Hong Kong). Organized by Xianggang yishu guan (Hong Kong Museum of Art) and Faguo guoli Jimei Yazhou yishu bowu guan (Musée national des arts asiatiques-Guimet). Produced by Xianggang yishu guan (Hong Kong Museum of Art). In Chinese and English.] Exhibition catalogue [Xianggang yishu guan (Hong Kong Museum of Art), Hong Kong, April 29-June 15, 1997]. Hong Kong: Xianggang shizheng ju (Urban Council, Hong Kong), 1997.
《從北京到凡爾賽：中法美術交流》・[香港市政局、法國駐香港總領事館聯合主辦・香港藝術館及法國國立吉美亞洲藝術博物館籌劃・香港藝術館編製]・[特展圖錄・香港藝術館・一九九七年四月二十九日至六月十五日]・香港：香港市政局・一九九七年首次編印・

Conze, Edward (1904-). *Buddhist Scriptures: A Bibliography*. Edited and revised by Lewis Lancaster. Garland Reference Library of the Humanities, vol. 113. New York and London: Garland Publishing, Inc., 1982.

Cotton and Silk Making in Manchu China. Introduction by Mario Bussagli. Excerpts from J.-B. [Jean-Baptiste] Du Halde (1674-1743). [Edited by Laura Casalis and Gianni Guadalupi. Translated from the Italian and the French by Michael Langley. Photographs by Sebastiana Papa.] Iconographia: A Franco Maria Ricci edition. New York: Rizzoli International Publications, Inc., 1980.

Crossley, Pamela Kyle. *The Manchus*. The Peoples of Asia, edited by Morris Rossabi (1941-). Cambridge, Mass. and Oxford: Blackwell Publishers, Inc., 1997.

Crump, J.I. [James Irving] (1921-). *Chinese Theater in the Days of Kublai Khan*. Tucson, Ariz.: The University of Arizona Press, 1980.

Cui, Jian-ying [Cui Jianying]. "The Scope of the Term 'Shan-pen,' the

Identification of Woodblock Editions, and the Organization of Catalogues, in Relation to Traditional Chinese Books." [Translated (from the Chinese) by the *Gest Journal* staff.] The Gest Library Journal 3, no. 3 (Winter 1989-1990): 35-60.

-D-

Dai, Lizhu (1946-). *Zhao Mengfu wenxue yu yishu zhi yanjiu*. Taibei: Xuehai chuban she, 1986.
《趙孟頫文學與藝術之研究》・戴麗珠著・台北：學海出版社・民國七十五年七月初版・

Dalby, Andrew (1947-). *Dictionary of Languages: The Definitive Reference to More Than 400 Languages*. New York: Columbia University Press, 1998.

Daniels, Peter T. (1951-), and William Bright (1928-), eds. *The World's Writing Systems*. New York and Oxford: Oxford University Press, 1996.

David, Percival [Percival Victor], Sir (1892-1964), trans. and ed. *Chinese Connoisseurship: The Ko Ku Yao Lun, The Essential Criteria of Antiquities*. With a facsimile of the Chinese text of 1388. London: Faber and Faber, 1971.

Davids, Rhys, Mrs. [Carolina Augusta Foley Rhys Davids] (1857-1942). *Psalms of the Early Buddhists*. 2 vols. Vol. 1, *Psalms of the Sisters* [first published 1909; reprinted 1932, 1948, and 1964]. Vol. 2, *Psalms of the Brethren* [first published 1913; reprinted 1937, 1951, and 1964.] Reprint. 2 vols. in 1. Unesco Collection of Representative Works. London: Published for the Pali Text Society by Luzac & Company Ltd., 1964.

Davidson, Ronald M. (1950-). "The 'Litany of Names of Manjusri': Text and Translation of the 'Manjusrinamasamgiti.'" In *Tantric and Taoist Studies in Honour of R.A. Stein*, edited by Michel Strickmann (d. 1994), vol. 1, 1-69. Mélanges chinois et bouddhiques, vol. 20. Brussels: Institut Belge des Hautes Études Chinoises, 1981.

de Bary, Wm. Theodore [William Theodore] (1919-), ed. *The Buddhist Tradition in India, China & Japan*. With the collaboration of Yoshito Hakeda and Philip Yampolsky, and with contributions by A.L. Basham, Leon Hurvitz, and Ryusaku Tsunoda. Readings in Oriental Thought. The Modern Library of the World's Best Books, no. 205. New York: The Modern Library, 1969.

———, and Irene Bloom, comps. *Sources of Chinese Tradition*. 2d ed.

Vol. 1. With the collaboration of Wing-tsit Chan (1901-1994) et al., and contributions by Joseph Adler et al. Introduction to Asian Civilizations. New York: Columbia University Press, 1999.

de Rosny, Léon [Léon-Louis-Lucien-Prunol] (1837-1914). *Catalogue de la bibliothèque japonaise de Nordenskiöld, coordonné, revu, annoté et publié par Léon de Rosny et précédé d'une introduction par le marquis d'Hervey de Saint-Denys.* [At head of title: Bibliothèque royale de Stockholm.] Paris: Imprimerie nationale, 1883.

de Rosthorn, A. [Arthur von Rosthorn] (1862-1945). *On the Tea Cultivation in Western Ssûch'uan and the Tea Trade with Tibet viâ Tachienlu.* With sketch map. London: Luzac & Co., 1895.

Delbanco, Dawn Ho. "Nanking and the Mustard Seed Garden Painting Manual." 2 vols. Ph.D. diss., Harvard University, 1981.

———. "Illustrated Books of the Ming Dynasty." *Orientations* 12, no. 11 (November 1981): 23-37.

Denda, Akira (1933-), comp. and ed. *Zôtei Minkan Gen zatsugeki Seishôki mokuroku.* [Tôyôgaku bunken sentâ sôkan, dai-11 shû. Tokyo: Tôkyô daigaku Tôyô bunka kenkyûjo fuzoku Tôyôgaku bunken sentâ kankô iinkai, 1970.] Tôyôgaku bunken sentâ sôkan eiinban, no. 4. Tokyo: Kyôko shoin, 1979.
《增訂明刊元雜劇西廂記目錄》・傳田章編・[〈東洋学文献センター叢刊〉・第11輯・東京：東京大学東洋文化研究所附属東洋学文献センター刊行委員会，昭和45年8月20日発行・〈東洋学文献センター叢刊影印版〉，4・東京：汲古書院・1979年11月30日発行・

Dent-Young, John, and Alex Dent-Young, trans. *The Broken Seals: Part One of "The Marshes of Mount Liang": A New Translation of the "Shuihu Zhuan" or "Water Margin" of Shi Nai'an and Luo Guanzhong.* Hong Kong: The Chinese University Press, 1994.

———, and Alex Dent-Young, trans. *The Tiger Killers: Part Two of "The Marshes of Mount Liang": A New Translation of the "Shuihu Zhuan" or "Water Margin" of Shi Nai'an and Luo Guanzhong.* Hong Kong: The Chinese University Press, 1997.

Dessaint, Alain Y. *Minorities of Southwest China: An Introduction to the Yi (Lolo) and Related Peoples and an Annotated Bibliography.* New Haven, Conn.: HRAF [Human Relations Area Files] Press, 1980.

DeWoskin, Kenneth J. [Kenneth Joel], and J.I. [James Irving] Crump, Jr. (1921-), trans. *In Search of the Supernatural: The Written Record.* Stanford, Calif.: Stanford University Press, 1996.

The Dictionary of Art. Edited by Jane Turner (1956-). 34 vols. New York: Grove's Dictionaries, Inc., 1996.

Dillon, Michael (1949-). *Dictionary of Chinese History.* London: Frank Cass, 1979.

———, ed. *China: A Historical and Cultural Dictionary.* Durham East Asia Series. Richmond, Surrey, Eng.: Curzon Press, 1998.

Ding, Fubao (1874-1952), and Zhou Yunqing, comps. and eds. *Si bu zonglu yiyao bian.* Reprint [originally published by Shangwu yinshu guan, 1955]. 3 vols. [on double-leaves; stitch-bound, Oriental style] in 1 case. Beijing: Wenwu chuban she, 1984.
《四部總錄醫藥編》・丁福保、周雲青編・[重印版・本書系用1955年商務印書館紙型重印]・[綫裝三册一函]・北京：文物出版社，1984年6月第一版・

Doi, Yoshiko (1935-). *Kodai Chûgoku no gazôseki.* Tokyo: Dôhôsha, 1986.
《古代中国の画象石》・土居淑子著・[精装一册]・東京：同朋舎，1986年6月30日発行・

Donnelly, Ivon A. [Ivon Arthur] (1890-). *The China Coast.* With verse by Joan Power. Tianjin: Tientsin Press, Limited, 1931.

Dong, Kaichen. "Horticulture." In *Ancient China's Technology and Science,* compiled by the Institute of the History of Natural Sciences, Chinese Academy of Sciences, 315-328. China Knowledge Series. Beijing: Foreign Languages Press, 1983.

Dong, Zuobin (1895-1963). "Guanyu Dunhuang Tang xieben Miaofa lianhua jing." *Dalu zazhi (The Continent Magazine)* 7, no. 12 (December 31, 1953): 36.
董作賓・〈關於敦煌唐寫本妙法蓮華經〉・《大陸雜誌》・第七卷・第十二期・民國四十二年十二月三十一日・第三十六頁・

Dongba wenhua lun. Compiled and edited by Guo Dalie and Yang Shiguang (1940-). [In Chinese; table of contents also in English.] Kunming: Yunnan renmin chuban she, 1991.
《東巴文化論》・郭大烈、楊世光主編・[精装一册]・昆明：雲南人民出版社，1991年3月第1版・

Dongba wenhua lun ji. Edited by Guo Dalie and Yang Shiguang (1940-). Kunming: Yunnan renmin chuban she, 1985.
《東巴文化論集》・郭大烈、楊世光編・[精装一册]・昆明：雲南人民出版社，1985年6月第一版・

Dongba wenhua yishu (The Art of Naxi Dongba Culture). Compiled by Yunnan sheng shehui kexue yuan Lijiang Dongba wenhua yanjiu suo. [Chief compiler: He Wanbao; deputy compilers: Ma Wen'an, Chen Qi,

and He Zhiwu.] Kunming, Yunnan: Yunnan meishu chuban she, 1992.
《東巴文化藝術》‧雲南省社會科學院麗江東巴文化研究所編‧[主編：和萬寶‧副主編：馬文庵、陳琦、和志武]‧昆明：雲南美術出版社，1992 年 10 月第 1 版‧

Dowman, Keith. *The Power-Places of Central Tibet: The Pilgrim's Guide.* London and New York: Routledge & Kegan Paul, 1988.

Drège, Jean-Pierre. "Le livre manuscrit et les débuts de la xylographie." In *Le livre et l'imprimerie en Extrême-Orient et en Asie du Sud: Actes du Colloque organisé à Paris du 9 au 11 mars 1983*, préparés par Jean-Pierre Drège, Mitchiko Ishigami-Iagolnitzer et Monique Cohen, 19-39. [Revue française d'histoire du livre, nos. 42-43.] Bordeaux: Société des Bibliophiles de Guyenne, 1986.

―――. "Quelques collections 'nouvelles' de manuscrits de Dunhuang." *Cahiers d'Extrême-Asie*, no. 3 (1987): 113-129.

―――. "The Dunhuang and Central Asian Manuscripts and the History of Books." *In Chinese Studies: Papers Presented at a Colloquium at the School of Oriental and African Studies, University of London, 24-26 August 1987*, edited by Frances Wood (1948-), 171-174. British Library Occasional Papers, no. 10. London: The British Library, 1988.

―――. *Les bibliothèques en Chine au temps des manuscrits (jusqu'au Xe siècle).* Publications de l'École française d'Extrême-Orient, vol. 161. Paris: École française d'Extrême-Orient, 1991.

―――. "La lecture et l'écriture en Chine et la xylographie." *Études chinoises: Bulletin de l'Association française d'études chinoises* 10, nos. 1-2 (Spring-Autumn 1991): 77-111.

―――. "Des effets de l'imprimerie en Chine sous la dynastie des Song." *Journal asiatique* 282, no. 2 (1994): 409-442. [Accompanied by summary in English, 442.]

Du, Weisheng. "The Restoration of the Dunhuang Manuscripts in the National Library of China." In *Dunhuang and Turfan: Contents and Conservation of Ancient Documents from Central Asia*, edited by Susan Whitfield and Frances Wood, 29-31. The British Library Studies in Conservation Science, [no. 1], edited by Mirjam M. Foot and Kenneth R. Seddon. [Proceedings of the conference "The Preservation of Material from Cave 17" organized by The British Library, held at the Isle of Thorns Training Centre, University of Sussex, 13-15 October 1993.] London: The British Library, 1996.

Du, Yu. "Cong Song 'Pingjiang tu' kan Pingjiang fu cheng de guimo he buju." *Ziran kexue shi yanjiu (Studies in the History of Natural Sciences)* 8, no. 1 (1989): 90-96.

杜瑜‧〈從宋《平江圖》看平江府城的規模和布局〉‧《自然科學史研究》‧第 卷‧第期‧（年）‧第九十頁至第九十六頁‧

Dunhuang jie yu lu (An Analytical List of the Tun-huang Manuscripts in the National Library of Peiping). [14 zhi.] Compiled and edited by Chen Yuan (1880-1971). Guoli zhongyang yanjiu yuan lishi yuyan yanjiu suo zhuankan, no. 4. 6 vols. [on double-leaves; stitch-bound, Oriental style] in 1 case. Beiping: Guoli zhongyang yanjiu yuan lishi yuyan yanjiu suo (The National Research Institute of History and Philology of Academia Sinica), 1931.
《敦煌劫餘錄》‧[十四帙]‧陳垣編‧[正文卷端題「陳垣校錄」]‧〈國立中央研究院歷史語研究所專刊之四〉‧[裝六冊一函]‧北平：國立中央研究院歷史語研究所，民國二十年三月刊印‧

Dunhuang Tulufan wenwu (Cultural Relics from Dunhuang and Turfan). Jointly presented by Shanghai bowu guan (Shanghai Museum) and Xianggang Zhongwen daxue wenwu guan (Art Gallery, The Chinese University of Hong Kong). [In Chinese and English. Introductory essay by Xie Zhiliu (1910-). Edited by Gao Meiqing (Mayching Kao). Original entries by Zhong Yinlan and Rao Zongyi (Jao Tsung-i). Translated by (from the Chinese) by Gao Meiqing (Mayching Kao).] Exhibition catalogue [Xianggang Zhongwen daxue wenwu guan (Art Gallery, The Chinese University of Hong Kong), Hong Kong, June 24-August 2, 1987]. Shanghai: Shanghai bowu guan (Shanghai Museum); Hong Kong: Xianggang Zhongwen daxue wenwu guan (Art Gallery, The Chinese University of Hong Kong), 1987.
《敦煌吐魯番文物》‧上海博物館、香港中文大學文物館合辦‧[編輯：高美慶‧滬方展品著錄：鍾銀蘭‧港方展品著錄：饒宗頤‧翻譯：高美慶]‧[特展圖錄‧香港中文大學文物館‧一九八七年六月廿四日至八月二日]‧[平裝一冊]‧上海：上海博物館；香港：香港中文大學文物館，一九八七年六月初版‧

Dunhuang xue lunzhu mulu, 1909-1983. Compiled and edited by Xibei shiyuan Dunhuang xue yanjiu suo and Liu Jinbao. Lanzhou, Gansu: Gansu renmin chuban she, 1985.
《敦煌學論著目錄，1909–1983》‧西北師院敦煌學研究所、劉進寶編‧蘭州：甘肅人民出版社，1985 年 5 月第 1 版‧

Dunhuang yishu zongmu suoyin. Compiled and edited by Shangwu yinshu guan. [New ed.] Beijing: Zhonghua shuju, 1983.
《敦煌遺書總目索引》‧商務印書館編‧北京：中華書局，1983 年 6 月新 1 版‧

Dunhuang yishu zuixin mulu. Chief editor: Huang Yongwu. Taibei: Xinwenfeng chuban she, 1986.
《敦煌遺書最新目錄》‧黃永武主編‧[精裝一冊]‧台北：新文豐出版公司，民國七十五年九月台一版‧

Dunnell, Ruth W. (1950-). "The Hsi Hsia." In *The Cambridge History of China*, vol. 6, *Alien Regimes and Border States, 907-1368*, edited by Herbert

Franke and Denis Twitchett, 154-214. Cambridge and New York: Cambridge University Press, 1994.

———. *The Great State of White and High: Buddhism and State Formation in Eleventh-Century Xia.* Honolulu: University of Hawai'i Press, 1996.

———. "The Recovery of Tangut History." *Orientations* 27, no. 4 (April 1996): 28-31.

Duoyun xuan '99 qiu ji yishu pin paimai hui: Guji banben zhuanchang (Duo Yun Xuan '99 Autumn Auction of Art Works). Auction catalogue [Sunday, November 28, 1999 at 4:00 p.m., 2nd Floor Banquet Hall, Shanghai Hilton Hotel]. Shanghai: Shanghai Duoyun xuan yishu pin paimai gongsi (Duo Yun Xuan Art Auctioneer's), 1999.
《朵雲軒' 99秋季藝術品拍賣會：古籍版本專場》 · [1999 年 11 月 28 日（星期日）下午 4：00始 · 上海靜安希爾頓酒店二樓大廳] · [拍賣圖錄 · 平裝一冊] · 上海：上海朵雲軒藝術品拍賣公司，1999 年 ·

Durrant, Stephen W. (1944-). "Lieh-hsien chuan." In *The Indiana Companion to Traditional Chinese Literature*, edited and compiled by William H. Nienhauser, Jr., vol. 1, 566-567 [see also updated bibliography in vol. 2, 365-366]. Bloomington, Ind. and Indianapolis: Indiana University Press, 1986-1998.

-E-

East Asian Books. [Title on front cover: *East Asian Books: China, Japan, Tibet, Nepal, Burma, Thailand, Java*; title on back cover in Chinese: *Dong Ya guji.*] Catalogue 19. [Catalogue by Bob Miller (1954-) et al. (Meher McArthur, Wei Chen-hsuan, and Sam Fogg).] London: Sam Fogg Rare Books and Manuscripts, 1998.

Ebrey, Patricia Buckley (1947-). "Later Han Stone Inscriptions." *Harvard Journal of Asiatic Studies* 40, no. 2 (December 1980): 325-353.

———, ed. *Chinese Civilization: A Sourcebook.* 2d ed., rev. and expanded. New York: The Free Press [a division of Macmillan, Inc.]; Toronto: Maxwell Macmillan Canada; New York and Oxford: Maxwell Macmillan International, 1993.

———. "Some Elements in the Intellectual and Religious Context of Chinese Art." In *China: 5,000 Years: Innovation and Transformation in the Arts*, selected by Sherman Lee, 36-48. New York: Guggenheim Museum Publications, 1998.

Ecke, Tseng Yu-ho [Zeng Youhe] (1923-). *Chinese Calligraphy.* Exhibition

catalogue [Philadelphia Museum of Art, Philadelphia, September 25-November 7, 1971; Nelson Gallery-Atkins Museum, Kansas City, Mo., January 6-February 6, 1972; The Metropolitan Museum of Art, New York, March 14-May 7, 1972]. Philadelphia: Philadelphia Museum of Art; Boston: Boston Book & Art, Publisher, 1971.

———. "The Importance of Ink-Imprints." In *Catalogue of Chinese Rubbings from Field Museum*, researched by Hoshien Tchen [Ch'en Ho-hsien] and M. Kenneth Starr; prepared by Alice K. Schneider; photographs by Herta Newton and Field Museum Division of Photography; edited by Hartmut Walravens (1944-), xxiv-xxvii. Fieldiana: Anthropology, n.s., no. 3. Publication 1327. Chicago: Field Museum of Natural History, 1981.

Edgren, J. Sören [James Sören] (1942-). Catalogue of the Nordenskiöld Collection of Japanese Books in the Royal Library. Acta Bibliothecae Regiae Stockholmiensis, no. 33. Stockholm: N.p. [Kungliga Biblioteket], 1980.

———. *Chinese Rare Books in American Collections.* [With contributions by] Tsuen-hsuin Tsien (1910-), Wang Fang-yu (1913-1997), [and] Wan-go H.C. Weng. Exhibition catalogue [China House Gallery, China Institute in America, New York, October 20, 1984-January 27, 1985]. New York: China Institute in America, 1984.

———. "Southern Song Printing at Hangzhou." *Bulletin of the Museum of Far Eastern Antiquities* 61 (1989): 1-212.

———. "The Traditional Chinese Book: Form & Function." Exhibition pamphlet with a checklist of the exhibition [The Art Museum, Princeton University, Princeton, N.J., April 18-June 4, 1995]. N.p. [Princeton, N. J.]: N.p. [The Art Museum, Princeton University], n.d. [1995].

———. "Books." ["China," §XIII, "Other Arts," 3, (i) "Manuscripts," (ii) "Printed Books."] In *The Dictionary of Art*, edited by Jane Turner (New York: Grove's Dictionaries, Inc., 1996), vol. 7, pp. 62-65.

———. "Prints." ["China," §XIII, "Other Arts," 19, (i) "Tang to Yuan (618-1368)", (ii) "Ming and After (from 1368)."] In *The Dictionary of Art*, edited by Jane Turner (New York: Grove's Dictionaries, Inc., 1996), vol. 7, pp. 117-122.

———. "How to Tell a Book by Its Cover: Interpreting 'Fengmianye' Data in Traditional Chinese Books." Unpublished paper presented at "A Symposium on Visual Dimensions of Chinese Culture," Institute for Advanced Study, Princeton, March 26, 1999.

Egan, Ronald C. (1948-). *The Literary Works of Ou-yang Hsiu (1007-72).*

Cambridge Studies in Chinese History, Literature and Institutions, edited by Patrick Hanan and Denis Twitchett. Cambridge and New York: Cambridge University Press, 1984.

Eitel, Ernest J. [Ernest John] (1838-1908). *Handbook of Chinese Buddhism, Being a Sanskrit-Chinese Dictionary, with Vocabularies of Buddhist Terms in Pali, Singhalese, Siamese, Burmese, Chinese, Tibetan, Mongolian and Japanese.* 2d ed. [First published 1888.] Reprint. New Delhi: Cosmo Publications, 1981.

Elman, Benjamin A. (1946-). "Geographical Research in the Ming-Ch'ing Period." *Monumenta Serica* 35 (1981-1983): 1-18.

Emmerick, R.E. [Ronald E.]. *The Sutra of Golden Light, Being a Translation of the Suvarnabhasottamasutra.* Sacred Books of the Buddhists, vol. 27. London: Published for the Pali Text Society by Luzac & Company Ltd., 1970. Reprint. London: The Pali Text Society, 1979.

Emperor, Scholar, Artisan, Monk: The Creative Personality in Chinese Works of Art. [Catalogue by Paul Moss.] 4 vols. [catalogue volume and 3 separately mounted plates; plate A, *The Seventh Nan-hsün-t'u Handscroll: From Wu-hsi to Suchou (1691-1698)*; plate B, *Prince I's Lan-t'ing Ink Rubbing Compilation (1592)*; plate C, *Beautiful Scenery of Peach Blossom Spring, with Fan Ch'ang-ch'ien's Peach Blossom Spring Poem (1638)*] in 1 slipcase. London: Syndey L. Moss Ltd., 1984.

Emsweller, S.L. [Samuel Leonard] (1898-). "The Chrysanthemum . . . Its Story Through the Ages." *Journal of the New York Botanical Garden* 48, no. 566 (February 1947): 26-29.

Eoyang, Eugene [Eugene Chen] (1939-), trans. "The Great Maudgalyayana Rescues His Mother from Hell." In *Traditional Chinese Stories: Themes and Variations*, edited by Y.W. Ma and Joseph S.M. Lau, 443-455. New York: Columbia University Press, 1978.

Europa und die Kaiser von China, 1240-1816. [Herausgegeber: Berliner Festspiele GmbH. Redaktion: Hendrik Budde, Christoph Müller-Hofstede, Gereon Sievernich. Mitarbeit: Sabine Hollburg, Christoph Schwarz, Gerhard Will.] Exhibition catalogue [Berliner Festspiele, Martin-Gropius-Bau, Berlin, May 12-August 18, 1985]. Frankfurt am Main: Insel Verlag, 1985.

Everding, Karl-Heinz. *Die Präexistenzen der lCan skya Qutuqtus: Untersuchungen zur Konstruktion und historischen Entwicklung einer lamaistischen Existenzenlinie.* Asiatische Forschungen, herausgegeben für das Seminar für Sprach- und Kulturwissenschaft Zentralasiens der Universität Bonn von Walther Heissig, Klaus Sagaster, Veronika Veit und Michael Weiers, unter Mitwirkung von Herbert Franke und

Nikolaus Poppe, Bd. 104. Wiesbaden, Germany: Otto Harrassowitz, 1988.

Exposition d'ouvrages illustrés de la dynastie Ming (Ming dai banhua shuji zhanlan hui mulu). [In Chinese and French. Preface by Du Boqiu (Jean-Pierre Dubosc) (1903-1988); introduction by Fu Xihua (Fou Hsi-houa) (1907-1970).] Exhibition catalogue [Centre franco-chinois d'études sinologiques (Zhong Fa Han xue yanjiu suo), Beijing, July 2-15, 1944]. Beijing: Centre franco-chinois d'études sinologiques (Zhong Fa Han xue yanjiu suo), 1944.
《明代版畫書籍展覽會目錄》· [序：杜柏秋 · 例：傅惜華] · 北京：中法漢學研究所，民國三十三年七月 ·

-F-

Fairbank, J.K. [John King] (1907-1991), and S.Y. [Ssu-yü] Têng (1906-1988). "On the Types and Uses of Ch'ing Documents." *Harvard Journal of Asiatic Studies* 5, no. 1 (January 1940): 1-71.

Farrer, Anne Selina. "The 'Shui-hu chuan': A Study in the Development of Late Ming Woodblock Illustration." 2 vols. Ph.D. thesis, University of London, 1984.

Feng, Han-yi, and J.K. [John Knight] Shryock (1890-). "The Historical Origins of the Lolo." *Harvard Journal of Asiatic Studies* 3, no. 2 (July 1938): 103-127.

Finch, Roger. "The 'Sri-parivarta' (Chapters XVI and XVII) from Sinqu Sali's Uighur Translation of I-tsing's Version of the Suvarnaprabhasottama-sutra." Ph.D. diss., Harvard University, 1976.

Fischer-Schreiber, Ingrid. *The Shambhala Dictionary of Taoism.* Translated [from the German] by Werner Wünsche. Boston: Shambhala Publications, Inc., 1996.

Fong, Wen [Wen C.], ed. *The Great Bronze Age of China: An Exhibition from the People's Republic of China.* Introductory essays by Ma Chengyuan, Wen Fong, Kwang-chih Chang, [and] Robert L. Thorp. Catalogue by Robert W. Bagley, Jenny F. So, [and] Maxwell K. Hearn. Exhibition catalogue [The Metropolitan Museum of Art, New York, April 12-July 9, 1980; Field Museum of Natural History, Chicago, August 20-October 29, 1980; Kimbell Art Museum, Fort Worth, Tex., December 10, 1980-February 18, 1981; Los Angeles County Museum of Art, Los Angeles, April 1-June 10, 1981; Museum of Fine Arts, Boston, July 22-September 30, 1981]. New York: The Metropolitan Museum of Art;

New York: Alfred A. Knopf, Inc., 1980.

———. "Chinese Calligraphy: Theory and History." In *The Embodied Image: Chinese Calligraphy from the John B. Elliott Collection*, by Robert E. Harrist, Jr. and Wen C. Fong, with contributions by Qianshen Bai et al., 28-84. Princeton, N.J.: The Art Museum, Princeton University, 1999.

Forêt, Philippe. "The Intended Perception of the Imperial Gardens of Chengde in 1780." *Studies in the History of Gardens & Designed Landscapes* 19, nos. 3-4 (July-December 1999): 343-363.

Franke, Herbert (1914-). "The Chin Dynasty." In *The Cambridge History of China*, vol. 6, *Alien Regimes and Border States, 907-1368*, edited by Herbert Franke and Denis Twitchett, 215-320. Cambridge and New York: Cambridge University Press, 1994.

Franke, Otto (1863-1946). *Kêng tschi t'u: Ackerbau und Seidengewinnung in China: Ein kaiserliches Lehr- und Mahn-Buch, aus dem Chinesischen übersetzt und mit Erklärungen Versehen von O. [Otto] Franke, mit 102 Tafeln und 57 Illustrationen im Text*. Abhandlungen des Hamburgischen Kolonialinstituts, Bd. 11 (Reihe B, Völkerkunde, Kultuegeschichte und Sprachen, Bd. 8). Hamburg: L. Friederichsen & Co., 1913.

———. "Zur Geschichte des Kêng tschi t'u: Ein Beitrag zue chinesischen Kunstgeschichte und Kunstkritik." *Ostasiatische Zeitschrift* 3 (1914-1915): 169-208.

Franke, Wolfgang (1912-). "Patents for Hereditary Ranks and Honorary Titles during the Ch'ing Dynasty." *Monumenta Serica* 7 (1942): 38-67.

Franklin, Ursula Martius (1921-). "On Bronze and Other Metals in Early China." In *The Origins of Chinese Civilization*, edited by David N. Keightley (1932-), 279-296. Studies on China, no. 1. Berkeley and Los Angeles: University of California Press, 1983.

Fu, Xihua (1907-1970), comp. and ed. *Han dai huaxiang quanji chu bian [Corpus des pierres sculptées Han (estampages), I]*. Bali daxue Beijing Han xue yanjiu suo tu pu congkan (Centre d'études sinologiques, Pékin, Université de Paris), no. 1. [In Chinese and French. Contains 2 lists of plates, one in Chinese and one in French, in folders, and 200 loose leaves of plates. Issued in 1 cloth-covered portfolio.] Beijing: Bali daxue Beijing Han xue yanjiu suo (Centre d'études sinologiques, Pékin, Université de Paris), 1950.
《漢代畫象全集初編》‧傅惜華編‧〈巴黎大學北京漢學研究所圖譜叢刊之一〉‧北京：巴黎大學北京漢學研究所，一九五〇年‧

———, comp. and ed. *Han dai huaxiang quanji er bian [Corpus des pierres sculptées Han (estampages), II]*. Bali daxue Beijing Han xue yanjiu suo tu pu congkan (Centre d'études sinologiques, Pékin, Université de Paris), no. 1. [In Chinese and French. Contains 2 lists of plates, one in Chinese and one in French, in folders, and 200 loose leaves of plates. Issued in 1 cloth-covered portfolio.] Beijing: Bali daxue Beijing Han xue yanjiu suo (Centre d'études sinologiques, Pékin, Université de Paris), 1951.
《漢代畫象全集二編》‧傅惜華編‧〈巴黎大學北京漢學研究所圖譜叢刊之一〉‧北京：巴黎大學北京漢學研究所，一九五一年‧

———. *Qing dai zaju quanmu*. Edited by Zhongguo xiqu yanjiu yuan. Zhongguo xiqu shi ziliao congkan. Zhongguo gudian xiqu zonglu, no. 6. Beijing: Renmin wenxue chuban she, 1981.
《清代雜劇全目》‧傅惜華著‧中國戲曲研究院編‧〈中國戲曲史資料叢刊〉‧〈中國古典戲曲總錄之六〉‧北京：人民文學出版社，1981年2月北京第1版‧

———. *Zhongguo banhua yanjiu zhongyao shumu*. In *Shuhua shulu tieti fukan* [with 3 other titles]. Hong Kong: Xianggang Zhong Mei tushu gongsi, 1969.
《中國版畫研究重要書目》‧錄於《書畫書錄解題附刊》[及其他三種]‧[精裝一册]‧香港：香港中美圖書公司，一九六九年二月出版‧

Fuchs, Walter (1902-1979) "Fan Wen-ch'eng 范文程, 1597-1666, und sein Diplom (誥命)." *Shigaku kenkyû (Sigakukenkyu) (A Review of Historical Studies)* 10, no. 3 (March 1939): 14-36.

———. "Rare Ch'ing Editions of the Keng-chih-t'u." *Huaxi xiehe daxue Zhongguo wenhua yanjiu suo jikan (Studia Serica: Journal of the Chinese Cultural Studies Research Institute, West China Union University)* 6 (1947): 149-157.
[福克司‧〈清代耕織圖珍本考〉‧英文論文]‧《華西協合大學中國文化研究所集刊》‧第六卷‧民國三十六年印行‧第一百四十九頁至第一百五十七頁‧

———. "Der Kupferdruck in China vom 10. bis 19. Jahrhundert." *Gutenberg-Jahrbuch* [25. Jahrgang] (1950): 67-87.

Fung, Ming-chu 馮明珠. "The Establishment of the Outer Eight Temples and the Northwestern Territory Defense of the Early Ch'ing Dynasty." In *Proceedings of the Sixth East Asian Altaistic Conference, December 18-23, 1981, Taipei, China*, edited by Ch'en Chieh-hsien, 115-121. Taipei: The Taipei City Government (Taibei shi zhengfu), 1983.
《第六屆東亞阿爾泰學會會議記錄》‧陳捷先編‧台北：台北市政府，民國七十二年六月印行‧第一百十五頁至第一百二十一頁‧

-G-

Gao, Hanyu, and Shi Bokui. "The Spinning Wheel and the Loom." In

Ancient China's Technology and Science, compiled by the Institute of the History of Natural Sciences, Chinese Academy of Sciences, 504-519. China Knowledge Series. Beijing: Foreign Languages Press, 1983.

Gao, Heng, and Chi Xichao. "Shi tan Mawangdui Han mu zhong de boshu 'Laozi.'" *Wenwu*, no. 222 (1974, no. 11) (November 1974): 1-7.
高亨、池曦朝・〈試談馬王堆漢墓中的帛書《老子》〉・《文物》・一九七四年第十一期・總第二二二號・第一頁至第七頁・

Gao, Wen. *Han bei ji shi*. Kaifeng: Henan daxue chuban she, 1985.
《漢碑集釋》・高文著・開封：河南大學出版社，1985 年 8 月第一版・

Gao Mingben huitu Xin jiaozhu guben Xixiang ji. 6 juan. [By Wang Shifu (fl. 1295-1307); edited and annotated by Wang Jide (ca. 1542-1623); with additional commentaries by Xu Wei (1521-1593).] Reprint [originally published Shanyin: Wang shi Xiangxue ju, 1614]. 6 vols. [on double-leaves; stitch-bound] in 1 case. Beiping: Fujin hushe; Beiping: Donglai shudian, 1929.
《高明本繪圖新校注古本西廂記》・六卷・[民國十八年北平富晉書社、東來閣書店兩家總發行所]・[綫裝六冊一函]・北平：富晉書社；北平：東來閣書店，民國十八年發行・

Giles, Lionel (1875-1958), comp. *An Alphabetical Index to the Chinese Encyclopaedia* 欽定古今圖書集成 *Ch'in Ting Ku Chin T'u Shu Chi Ch'êng*. [In English and Chinese; in double columns.] London: Printed by order of the Trustees of the British Museum, 1911.

————. *Descriptive Catalogue of the Chinese Manuscripts from Tunhuang in the British Museum*. London: Published by the Trustees of the British Museum, 1957.

Goepper, Roger. "Stone Rubbing." In *Chinese Art: Painting, Calligraphy, Stone Rubbing, Wood Engraving*, by Werner Speiser, Roger Goepper, and Jean Fribourg, 245-272. [Translated (from the German) by Diana Imber.] The Universe Library of Antique Art. New York: Universe Books, Inc., 1964.

Goldberg, Stephen J. "Calligraphy." ["China," §IV."] In *The Dictionary of Art*, edited by Jane Turner (New York: Grove's Dictionaries, Inc., 1996), vol. 6, pp. 735-772.

Goodrich, L. Carrington [Luther Carrington] (1894-1986). "Earliest Printed Editions of the Tripitaka." *The Visvabharati Quarterly* 19, no. 3 (Winter 1953-1954): 215-220.

————. "The Origin of Printing." *Journal of the American Oriental Society* 82, no. 4 (October-December 1962): 556-557.

————, and Chaoying Fang (1908-1985), eds. *Dictionary of Ming Biography, 1368-1644*. 2 vols. The Ming Biographical History Project of the Association for Asian Studies. New York and London: Columbia University Press, 1976.

Graham, A.C. [Angus Charles] (1919-1991), trans., with an introd. *Poems of the West Lake: Translations from the Chinese*. [Title on front cover and on title page also in Chinese: *Xi hu shi xuan* 《西湖詩選》. Parallel text in Chinese and English. Calligraphy for the original texts of the poems and that on the title page and front cover by Joseph Lo.] London: Wellsweep Press, 1990.

Grinstead, Eric D. [Eric Douglas] (1921-). *Analysis of the Tangut Script*. Scandinavian Institute of Asian Studies Monograph Series, no. 10. [With summary in Danish, 40-43.] Lund, Sweden: Studentlitteratur, 1972.

Grupper, Samuel M. [Samuel Martin] (1938-). "Manchu Patronage and Tibetan Buddhism during the First Half of the Ch'ing Dynasty: A Review Article." Review article of *Ni ma'i 'od zer (Naran-u gerel): Die Biographie des 2. Pekinger LCan skya-Qutuqtu Rol pa'i rdo rje (1717-1786)*, by Hans-Rainer Kämpfe. *The Journal of the Tibet Society* 4 (1984): 47-75.

Guan cang jing xuan (Shanghai Library Treasures). Compiled and edited by Shanghai tushu guan (Shanghai Library) and Shanghai kexue jishu qingbao yanjiu suo (Institute of Scientific and Technical Information of Shanghai). [In Chinese; some titles of publications also in Latin, French, English, Italian, or Spanish.] Shanghai: Shanghai kexue jishu wenxian chuban she (Shanghai Scientific and Technological Literature Publishing House), 1996.
《館藏精選》・上海圖書館、上海科學技術情報研究所編・[精裝一冊]・上海：上海科學技術文獻出版社，1996 年 11 月第 1 版・

Guben xiaoshuo banhua tulu. Compiled and edited by Shoudu tushu guan. [Chief editor: Jin Peilin. Deputy editor: Zhou Xinhui.] 16 vols. [on double-leaves; stitch-bound, Oriental style] in 2 cases. Beijing: Xianzhuang shuju, 1996.
《古本小說版畫圖錄》・首都圖書館編輯・[主編：金沛霖・副主編：周心慧]・[綫裝十六冊二函]・北京：綫裝書局，一九九六年一月第一版・

Guben xiqu shi da mingzhu banhua quanbian. Compiled and edited by Shoudu tushu guan. [Chief editor: Jin Peilin; deputy editor: Zhou Xinhui.] 2 vols. Beijing: Xianzhuang shuju, 1996.
《古本戲曲十大名著版畫全編》・首都圖書館編輯・[主編：金沛霖・副主編：周心慧]・[精裝二冊]・北京：綫裝書局，一九九六年二月第一版・

Gugong zhencang Kang Yong Qian ciqi tulu (Qing Porcelain of Kangxi, Yongzheng and Qianlong Periods from the Palace Museum Collection). Edited by Li Yihua. Hong Kong: Liangmu chuban she (The Woods Publishing Co.); Beijing: Zijin cheng chuban she (Forbidden City Publishing House), 1989.

《故宮珍藏康雍乾瓷器圖錄》・編輯：李毅華・[精裝一冊]・香港：兩木出版社；北京：紫禁城出版社，一九八九年五月初版・

Guo, Moruo 郭沫若 (1892-1978). *Liang Zhou jinwen ci daxi kaoshi.* [Introduction also in English (translated from the Chinese by John C. Ferguson).] 3 vols. [on double-leaves; stitch-bound, Oriental style] in 1 case. Tokyo: Bunkyûdô shoten, 1935.

《兩周金文辭大系攷釋》・郭沫若譔集・[綫裝三冊一函]・東京：文求堂書店，昭和十年八月二十日發行・

———. "You Wang Xie muzhi de chutu lun dao Lanting xu de zhenwei." [Originally published in *Wenwu* (1965, no. 6)] In *Lanting lun bian.* Compiled by Wenwu chuban she. Beijing: Wenwu chuban she, 1977.

郭沫若・〈由王謝墓志的出土論到蘭亭序的真偽〉・[原載《文物》年第 6 期]・《蘭亭論辨》・文物出版社編輯・北京：文物出版社，1977 年 10 月第一版・第五頁至第三十二頁・

Guo, Weiqu. *Zhongguo banhua shi lüe.* Beijing: Zhaohua meishu chuban she, 1962.

《中國版畫史略》・郭味蕖編著・北京：朝花美術出版社，1962 年 12 月第一版・

Guoli Beiping tushu guan chuban shuji mulu. [Rev. ed.] [Main distributor: Guoli Beiping tushu guan chuban faxing chu. Branch distributor: Guoli Beiping tushu guan Kunming banshi chu.] N.p. [Kunming]: N.p. [Guoli Beiping tushu guan Kunming banshi chu], 1939.

《國立北平圖書館出版書籍目錄》・[重訂本]・[總發行所：國立北平圖書館出版發行處・分發行所：國立北平圖書館昆明辦事處]・[昆明]：[國立北平圖書館昆明辦事處]，民國二十八年十月重訂・

Guoli Beiping tushu guan guan kan (Bulletin of the National Library of Peiping). Vol. 4, no. 3 (May-June 1930) [issued in January 1932], *Xi Xia wen zhuan hao [A Volume on Tangut (Hsi Hsia) Studies].*

《國立北平圖書館館刊》・第四卷・第三號・〈西夏文專號〉・民國十九年五、六月（民國二十一年一月出版）・

Guoli Beiping tushu guan shanben shumu. 4 *juan.* [Compiled and edited by Zhao Wanli (1905-1980). Preface by Fu Zengxiang.] N.p. [Beiping]: N.p. [Guoli Beiping tushu guan], 1933.

《國立北平圖書館善本書目四卷》・[趙萬撰集]・[共和建國二十有二年十二月既望江安傅增湘序]・[北平]：[國立北平圖書館]，民國廿二年十月刊印・

Guoli Beiping tushu guan shanben shumu yi bian xu mu. 4 *juan.* [On double-leaves; stitch-bound, Oriental style.] N.p. [Beiping]: N.p. [Guoli Beiping tushu guan], 1937.

《國立北平圖書館善本書目乙編續目四卷》・[綫裝一冊]・[北平]：[國立北平圖書館]，民國廿六年四月印行・

Guoli zhongyang tushu guan Jin Yuan ben tulu. Compiled and edited by Guoli zhongyang tushu guan. Zhonghua congshu. Taibei: Zhonghua congshu bianshen weiyuan hui, 1961.

《國立中央圖書館金元本圖錄》・編輯者：國立中央圖書館・〈中華叢書〉・台北：中華叢書編審委員會，民國五十年八月印行・

Guoli zhongyang tushu guan Song ben tulu. Compiled and edited by Guoli zhongyang tushu guan. Zhonghua congshu. Taibei: Zhonghua congshu weiyuan hui, 1958.

《國立中央圖書館宋本圖錄》・編輯者：國立中央圖書館・〈中華叢書〉・台北：中華叢書委員會，民國四十七年七月印行・

Guoli zhongyang tushu guan tecang xuan lu. Compiled and edited by Guoli zhongyang tushu guan tecang zu. Rev. ed. Taibei: Guoli zhongyang tushu guan, 1989.

《國立中央圖書館特藏選錄》・編輯者：國立中央圖書館特藏組・[修正版]・台北：國立中央圖書館，民國七十八年八月修正版・

Guy, John S. (1949-). *Palm-leaf and Paper: Illustrated Manuscripts of India and Southeast Asia.* With an essay by O.P. [Om Prakash] Agrawal. Exhibition catalogue [National Gallery of Victoria, Melbourne, May 11-July 6, 1982; Art Gallery of Western Australia, Perth, July 23-September 5, 1982; Art Gallery of New South Wales, Sydney, November 5-December 12, 1982]. Melbourne: National Gallery of Victoria, 1982.

-H-

Han, Sheng. "'Xixiang ji' gujin banben mulu jiyao." In *Xixiang ji xin lun,* compiled and edited by Han Sheng, He Xinhui, and Fan Biao, 161-205. [San Jin wenhua yanjiu congshu bianji weiyuan hui. Chief editor: Zhao Yuting.] Beijing: Zhongguo xiju chuban she, 1992.

寒聲・〈《西廂記》古今版本目錄輯要〉・《西廂記新論》・寒聲、賀新輝、范彪編・第一百六十一頁至第二百零五頁・[三晉文化研究叢書編輯委員會・總編：趙雨亭]・北京：中國戲劇出版社，1992 年 8 月第 1 版・

Hardy, Grant. *Worlds of Bronze and Bamboo: Sima Qian's Conquest of History.* New York: Columbia University Press, 1999.

Hargett, James M. [James Morris] (1948-). "Hsi-hsiang chi." In *The Indiana Companion to Traditional Chinese Literature,* edited and compiled by William H. Nienhauser, Jr., vol. 1, 407-409 [see also updated bibliography in vol. 2, 320-321]. Bloomington, Ind. and Indianapolis:

Indiana University Press, 1986-1998.

Harley, J.B. [John Brian] (1932-1991), and David Woodward (1942-), eds. *The History of Cartography.* Vol. 2, bk. 2, *Cartography in the Traditional East and Southeast Asian Societies.* Associate Editor: Joseph E. Schwartzberg. Assistant Editor: Cordell D.K. Yee (1955-). Chicago and London: The University of Chicago Press, 1994.

Harper, Donald [Donald John]. "Warring States Natural Philosophy and Occult Thought." In *The Cambridge History of Ancient China: From the Origins of Civilization to 221 B.C.,* edited by Michael Loewe and Edward L. Shaughnessy (1952-), 813-884. Cambridge and New York: Cambridge University Press, 1998.

Harrell, Stevan, ed. *Cultural Encounters on China's Ethnic Frontiers.* Studies on Ethnic Groups in China, edited by Steven Harrell. Seattle and London: University of Washington Press, 1995.

————. "The History of the History of the Yi." In *Cultural Encounters on China's Ethnic Frontiers,* edited by Stevan Harrell, 63-91. Studies on Ethnic Groups in China, edited by Steven Harrell. Seattle and London: University of Washington Press, 1995.

Harrist, Robert E., Jr., and Wen C. Fong. *The Embodied Image: Chinese Calligraphy from the John B. Elliott Collection.* With contributions by Qianshen Bai et al. [Dora C.Y. Ching, Chuan-hsing Ho, Cary Y. Liu, Amy McNair, Zhixin Sun, and Jay Xu]. Exhibition catalogue [The Art Museum, Princeton University, Princeton, N.J., March 27-June 27, 1999; Seattle Art Museum, Seattle, February 10-May 7, 2000; The Metropolitan Museum of Art, New York, September 15-January 7, 2001]. Princeton, N.J.: The Art Museum, Princeton University, 1999.

————. "Reading Chinese Calligraphy." In *The Embodied Image: Chinese Calligraphy from the John B. Elliott Collection,* by Robert E. Harrist, Jr. and Wen C. Fong, with contributions by Qianshen Bai et al., 2-27. Princeton, N.J.: The Art Museum, Princeton University, 1999.

He, Di. "Dongba hua yanjiu." *Duoyun: Zhongguo huihua yanjiu jikan (Art Clouds: Quarterly of Chinese Painting Study),* no. 29 (1991, no. 2): 51-61.
易諦·〈東巴畫研究〉·《朵雲：中國繪畫研究季刊》·總第二十九期·一九九一年第二期·第五十一頁至第六十一頁·

He, Zhiwu. *Naxi Dongba wenhua.* Zhongguo shaoshu minzu wenku, edited by Shi Yun. Changchun, Jilin: Jilin jiaoyu chuban she, 1989.
《納西東巴文化》·和志武著·〈中國少數民族文庫〉·史筠主編·[精裝一冊]·長春：吉林教育出版社·1989 年 4 月第 1 版·

Hegel, Robert E. [Robert Earl] (1943-). *Reading Illustrated Fiction in Late Imperial China.* Stanford, Calif.: Stanford University Press, 1998.

————. "The Printing and Circulation of Literary Materials." In *The Indiana Companion to Traditional Chinese Literature,* edited and compiled by William H. Nienhauser, Jr., vol. 2, Charles Hartman, associate editor; Scott W. Galer, assistant editor, 124-132. Bloomington, Ind. and Indianapolis: Indiana University Press, 1998.

Heijdra, Martin [Martin J.] (1956-), and Cao Shuwen. "The World's Earliest Extant Book Printed from Wooden Movable Type? 'Chüan' Seventy-seven of the Tangut Translation of the 'Garland sutra.'" *The Gest Library Journal* 5, no. 1 (Spring 1992): 70-89.

————. "Who Were the Laka? A Survey of Scriptures in the Minority Languages of Southwest China." *The East Asian Library Journal* 8, no. 1 (Spring 1998): [opening illustration on 150] 151-198.

Heissig, Walther. *Catalogue of Mongol Books, Manuscripts and Xylographs.* Assisted by Charles Bawden. Catalogue of Oriental Manuscripts, Xylographs etc. in Danish Collections, founded by Kaare Grønbech, vol. 3. Copenhagen: The Royal Library, Copenhagen [Det Kongelige Bibliotek, København], 1971.

————. *The Religions of Mongolia.* Translated from the German edition by Geoffrey Samuel. Berkeley and Los Angeles: University of California Press, 1980.

Helliwell, David. "Copies et réimpressions sous les dynasties Ming et Qing." In *Le livre et l'imprimerie en Extrême-Orient et en Asie du Sud: Actes du Colloque organisé à Paris du 9 au 11 mars 1983,* préparés par Jean-Pierre Drège, Mitchiko Ishigami-Iagolnitzer et Monique Cohen, 75-86. [Revue française d'histoire du livre, nos. 42-43.] Bordeaux: Société des Bibliophiles de Guyenne, 1986.

————. Review of *Impressions de Chine,* by Monique Cohen and Nathalie Monnet. *The Gest Library Journal* 6, no. 2 (Winter 1993): 93-101.

————. "The Repair and Binding of Old Chinese Books: Translated and Adapted for Western Conservators." [From a manual of traditional restoration techniques by Xiao Zhentang and Ding Yu.] *The East Asian Library Journal* 8, no. 1 (Spring 1998): 27-149.

Henricks, Robert G. (1943-), trans., with an introd. and commentary. *Lao-tzu: Te-tao ching: A New Translation Based on the Recently Discovered Ma-wang-tui Texts.* Classics of Ancient China. New York: Ballantine Books, 1989.

Hervey, George F. [George Frangopulo]. *The Goldfish of China in the XVIII Century*. With a foreword by A.C. Moule (1873-1957). China Society Sinological Series, no. 3. London: The China Society, 1950.

Heyue cang zhen: Zhongguo gu ditu zhan (History through Maps: An Exhibition of Old Maps of China). [Edited by Ding Xinbao (Joseph S.P. Ting).] Exhibition catalogue [Xianggang bowu guan (Hong Kong Museum of History), Hong Kong, 1997]. [In Chinese and English.] Hong Kong: Linshi shizheng ju [Provisional Urban Council], 1997.
《河嶽藏珍：中國古地圖展》・[編輯：丁新豹]・[香港博物館・特展圖錄]・香港：臨時市政局，一九九七年十月首次編印・

Hightower, James R. [James Robert], trans. "The Story of Ying-ying." In *Traditional Chinese Stories: Themes and Variations*, edited by Y.W. Ma and Joseph S.M. Lau, 139-145. New York: Columbia University Press, 1978.

Hirth, Friedrich (1845-1927). *Ueber fremde Einflüsse in der chinesischen Kunst*. Munich and Leipzig: G. Hirth's Verlag, 1896.

Hoernle, A.F. Rudolf [August Friedrich Rudolf] (1841-1918). "An Epigraphical Note on Palm-leaf, Paper and Birch-bark." *Journal of the Asiatic Society of Bengal* 69, pt. 1 (History, Antiquities, &c.), no. 2 (February 29, 1901): 93-134.

Hsieh, Chiao-min (1921-), and Jean Kan Hsieh [Kan Jiaming]. *China: A Provincial Atlas*. [Title and names of authors on title page also in Chinese: *Zhongguo fen sheng ditu ji*; by Xie Juemin and Kan Jiaming. New York: Macmillan Publishing USA, 1995.
《中國分省地圖集》・謝覺民、闞家蘅合著・

Hsieh, Shih-chung. "On the Dynamics of Tai/Dai-Lue Ethnicity." In *Cultural Encounters on China's Ethnic Frontiers*, edited by Stevan Harrell, 301-328. Studies on Ethnic Groups in China, edited by Steven Harrell. Seattle and London: University of Washington Press, 1995.

Hsü, Chin-hsiung [Xu Jinxiong] 許進雄 (1941-). *The Menzies Collection of Shang Dynasty Oracle Bones*. Vol. 1, *A Catalogue*. Toronto: The Royal Ontario Museum, 1972.

———. *The Menzies Collection of Shang Dynasty Oracle Bones*. Vol. 2, *The Text*. [Title and author's name on added title page also in Chinese: *Mingyishi shoucang jiagu shiwen pian* 《明義士收藏甲骨釋文篇》・許進雄著・ Imprint on added title page also in Chinese: Xianggang Zhongwen daxue xiezhu bianjiao; Jianada Huangjia Andalüe bowu guan chuban 香港中文大學協助編校・加拿大皇家安大略博物館出版 .] Toronto: The Royal Ontario Museum, in cooperation with Hong Kong: The Chinese University of Hong Kong, 1977.

———. *Oracle Bones from the White and Other Collections*. [Title and author's name on added title page also in Chinese: *Huaite shi deng shoucang jiagu wenji* 《懷特氏等收藏甲骨文集》・許進雄著・ Imprint on added title page also in Chinese: Huangjia Andalüe bowu guan chuban 加拿大皇家安大略博物館出版 .] [Table of contents, preface, and text of catalogue also in Chinese.] Toronto: The Royal Ontario Museum, 1979.

Hsu, Mei-Ling. "An Inquiry into Early Chinese Atlases through the Ming Dynasty." In *Images of the World: The Atlas through History*, edited by John A. [John Amadeus] (1925-) Wolter and Ronald E. Grim, 31-50. Washington, D.C.: Library of Congress, 1997.

Hsü, Tao-Ching 許道經 . *The Chinese Conception of the Theatre*. Seattle and London: University of Washington Press, 1985.

Hu, Houxuan (1911-1995). "Dalu xian cang zhi jiagu wenzi." *Zhongyang yanjiu yuan Lishi yuyan yanjiu suo jikan (Bulletin of the Institute of History and Philology, Academia Sinica)* 67, pt. 4 (December 1996): 815-876 [includes abstract in English, "The Collection of Oracle Bone Inscriptions on the Chinese Continent," 876].
胡厚宣・〈大陸現藏之甲骨文字〉・《中央研究院歷史語研究所集刊》・第六十七本・第四分・第八百十五頁至第八百七十六頁・友附英文提要・第八百七十六頁犰・

Hu, Yi. "Hu Zhengyan nianpu." In *Shizhu zhai yanjiu wenji: "Shizhu zhai shuhua pu" kanxing sanbai liushi nian jinian*, compiled by Shizhu zhai yishu yanjiu bu, 100-112. Nanjing: Shizhu zhai yishu yanjiu bu, 1987.
胡藝・〈胡正言年譜〉・《十竹齋研究文集：〈十竹齋書畫譜〉刊行三百六十年紀念》・十竹齋藝術研究部編・南京：十竹齋藝術研究部，一九八七年十月・第一百頁至第一百十二頁・

Hu, Zhenqi. "Shanxi sheng bowu guan suo cang Zhaocheng Zang." *Wenwu*, nos. 138-139 (1962, nos. 4-5) (May 1962): 92.
胡振祺・〈山西省博物館所藏趙城藏〉・《文物》・一九六二年第四、五期合刊・總第一三八、一三九號・第九十二頁・

Hua, Rende. "Shitan Shizhu zhai banhua yishu chengjiu de xingcheng yuanyin he gongxian." In *Shizhu zhai yanjiu wenji: "Shizhu zhai shuhua pu" kanxing sanbai liushi nian jinian*, compiled by Shizhu zhai yishu yanjiu bu, 48-52. Nanjing: Shizhu zhai yishu yanjiu bu, 1987.
華仁德・〈試談十竹齋版畫藝術成就的形成原因和貢獻〉・《十竹齋研究文集：〈十竹齋書畫譜〉刊行三百六十年紀念》・十竹齋藝術研究部編・南京：十竹齋藝術研究部，一九八七年十月・第四十八頁至第五十二頁・

———. "The History and Revival of Northern Wei Stele-Style Calligraphy." In *Character & Context in Chinese Calligraphy*, edited by Cary [Cary Yee-Wei] Liu (1955-), Dora C.Y. Ching, and Judith G. Smith

(1941-), 104-131. Princeton, N.J.: The Art Museum, Princeton University, 1999.

Huancui tang yuan jing tu. [Illustrated by Qian Gong. Engraved by Huang Yingzu (1573-1644).] Facsimile reproduction. Beijing: Renmin meishu chuban she, 1981.
《環翠堂園景圖》·[錢貢繪圖·黃應組刻]·[影印本]·北京：人民美術出版社，1981 年·

Huang, Chang. *Qing dai banke yi yu.* N.p. [Ji'nan, Shandong]: Qi Lu shushe, 1992.
《清代版刻一隅》·著者：黃裳·[平裝一冊]·[濟南]：齊魯書社，一九九二年一月第一版·

———. *Huang Chang shuhua.* Edited by Jiang Deming. Selected by Huang Chang. Xiandai shuhua congshu. Beijing: Beijing chuban she, 1996.
《黃裳書話》·作者：黃裳·主編：姜德明·選編：黃裳·〈現代書話叢書〉·[平裝一冊]·北京：北京出版社，1996 年 10 月第 1 版·

Huang, Hongyi. "Shizhu zhai zai Zhongguo wenhua shi shang de diwei." In *Shizhu zhai yanjiu wenji: "Shizhu zhai shuhua pu" kanxing sanbai liushi nian jinian*, compiled by Shizhu zhai yishu yanjiu bu, 41-47. Nanjing: Shizhu zhai yishu yanjiu bu, 1987.
黃鴻儀·〈十竹齋在中國文化上的地位〉·《十竹齋研究文集：〈十竹齋書畫譜〉刊行三百六十年紀念》·十竹齋藝術研究部編·南京：十竹齋藝術研究部，一九八七年十月·第四十一頁至第四十七頁·

Huang, Miaozi (1913-). *Wu Daozi shi ji.* Beijing: Zhonghua shuju, 1991.
《吳道子事輯》·黃苗子編著·北京：中華書局，1991 年 11 月第 1 版·

Hucker, Charles O. (1919-1994). *A Dictionary of Official Titles in Imperial China.* Stanford, Calif.: Stanford University Press, 1985.

Hummel, Arthur W. [Arthur William] (1884-1975). "Accessions to the Division of Chinese Literature." *Report of the Librarian of Congress for the Fiscal Year Ending June 30, 1928* (1928): 272-286 [Part of Appendix 2, "Division of Chinese Literature," 271-316].

———. "Chinese and Other East Asiatic Books Added to the Library of Congress, 1928-1929." *Report of the Librarian of Congress for the Fiscal Year Ending June 30, 1929* (1929): 285-311 [Part of Appendix 2, "Division of Chinese Literature," 285-333].

———. "Division of Orientalia." *Annual Report of the Librarian of Congress for the Fiscal Year Ended June 30, 1938* (1938): 210-248.

———. "Division of Orientalia." *Annual Report of the Librarian of Congress for the Fiscal Year Ended June 30, 1940* (1940): 154-187.

———. "The Development of the Book in China." *Journal of the American Oriental Society* 61, no. 2 (June 1941): 71-76.

———, ed. *Eminent Chinese of the Ch'ing Period (1644-1912).* 2 vols. Washington, D.C.: The Library of Congress; Washington, D.C.: United States Government Printing Office, 1943-1944.

Hummel, Siegbert (1908-). *Namenkarte von Tibet.* [Map has title: *Tibet: Übersicht der Örtlichkeiten in tibetischer Rechtschreibung.*" N.p. [Copenhagen]: N.p. [E. Munksgaard, n.d. [1950].

———. "Die Schrift der Na-Khi." *Zentralasiatische Studien des Seminars für Sprach- und Kulturwissenschaft Zentralasiens der Universität Bonn* 21 (1988): 7-19.

———. "Kailâsa und Mânasarôvar in den Vorstellungen der Na-Khi." *Zentralasiatische Studien des Seminars für Sprach- und Kulturwissenschaft Zentralasiens der Universität Bonn* 22 (1989-1991): 7-19.

Huntington, John C. [John Cooper] (1937-). "A Note on Dunhuang Cave 17, 'The Library,' or Hong Bian's Reliquary Chamber." *Ars Orientalis* 16 (1986): 93-101.

Hurvitz, Leon (1923-), trans. *Scripture of the Lotus Blossom of the Fine Dharma (The Lotus Sutra).* Translated from the Chinese of Kumarajiva by Leon Hurvitz. Prepared for the Columbia College Program of Translations from the Oriental Classics. Buddhist Studies and Translations sponsored by the Columbia University Seminar in Oriental Thought and Religion, with the cooperation of The Institute for Advanced Studies of World Religions. Records of Civilization: Sources and Studies, no. 94. New York: Columbia University Press, 1976. Reprint. New York: Columbia University Press, 1982.

-I-

Irwin, Richard Gregg (1909-). *The Evolution of a Chinese Novel: Shui-hu-chuan.* Harvard-Yenching Institute Studies, no. 10. Cambridge, Mass.: Harvard University Press, 1953.

-J-

Jackson, Anthony. *Na-khi Religion: An Analytical Appraisal of the Na-khi*

Ritual Texts. Religion and Society, edited by Leo Laeyendecker and Jacques Waardenburg, no. 8. The Hague and Paris: Mouton Publishers, 1979.

Jäger, Fritz. "Der angebliche Steindruck des »Kêng-tschi-t'u« vom Jahre 1210." *Ostasiatische Zeitschrift*, n.s. 9 (1933): 1-4.

Ji, Shuying 冀淑英. "The Chinese Union Catalogue of Rare Books and Its Criteria of Inclusion." [Translated from the Chinese by John Cayley.] In *Chinese Studies: Papers Presented at a Colloquium at the School of Oriental and African Studies, University of London, 24-26 August 1987*, edited by Frances Wood (1948-), 161-169. British Library Occasional Papers, no. 10. London: The British Library, 1988.

———. "Guanyu guji shanben de fanwei." *Wenxian*, no. 37 (1988, no. 3): 180-187.
冀淑英・〈關於古籍善本的範圍〉・《文獻》・總第三十七期・一九八八年第三期・第一百八十頁至第一百八十七頁・

Ji tian gu ge: Naxi zu Dongba wenxue jicheng. Edited by Yunnan sheng minjian wenxue jicheng bangong shi. [Consultant: He Wanbao. Chief editor: Ge Agan. Deputy editors: Chen Lie and He Kaixiang.] Beijing: Zhongguo minjian wenyi chuban she, 1988.
《祭天古歌：納西族東巴文學集成》・雲南省民間文學集成辦公室編・[顧問：和萬寶・主編：戈阿干・副主編：陳烈、和開祥]・北京：中國民間文藝出版社，1988年10月第一版・

Jiagu wen he ji. Chief editor: Guo Moruo (1892-1978). Compiled by Zhongguo shehui kexue yuan lishi yanjiu suo. 13 vols. N.p. [Beijing]: Zhonghua shuju, 1978 [vol. 2]-1983 [vol. 12].
《甲骨文合集》・郭沫若主編・中國社會科學院歷史研究所編・[全精裝十三冊]・[北京]：中華書局，1978年10月第一版[第二冊]至1983年6月第一版[第十二冊]・

Jiang, Xingyu (1919-1981). *Ming kan ben Xixiang ji yanjiu*. Beijing: Zhongguo xiju chuban she, 1982.
《明刊本西廂記研究》・蔣星煜著・北京：中國戲劇出版社，1982年8月第1版・

———. *Xixiang ji kaozheng*. Shanghai: Shanghai guji chuban she, 1988.
《西廂記考證》・蔣星煜著・上海：上海古籍出版社，1988年8月第1版・

Jiao, Mingchen. *Dunhuang xie juan shufa yanjiu*. Wen shi zhe xueshu congkan, no. 5. Taibei: Wen shi zhe chuban she, 1997.
《敦煌寫卷書法研究》・焦明晨著・〈文史哲學術叢刊；5〉・台北：文史哲出版社，民國八十六年五月初版・

Jiaye tang cang shu zhi. Compiled by Miao Quansun (1844-1919; *jinshi* of 1876), Wu Changshou (*juren* of 1897), and Dong Kang (1867-). Reorganized and punctuated by Wu Ge. Shanghai: Fudan daxue

chuban she, 1997.
《嘉業堂藏書志》・繆荃孫、吳昌綬、董康撰・吳格整理點校・上海：復旦大學出版社，一九九七年十二月第一版・

Jin, Tao (1940-). *Chengde shihua*. [Illustrations by Dong Yiguo. Photography by Chen Keyin.] Difang shihua. Shanghai: Shanghai renmin chuban she, 1983.
《承德史話》・金濤著・[繪圖：董怡國・攝影：陳克寅]・〈地方史話〉・上海：上海人民出版社，1983年7月第1版・

Jin, Yingchun, and Qiu Fuke. *Zhongguo ditu shihua*. Beijing: Kexue chuban she, 1984.
《中國地圖史話》・金應春、丘富科編著・北京：科學出版社，1984年4月第一版・

Jin, Weinuo (1924-). "'Bunian tu' yu 'Lingyan ge gongchen tu.'" *Wenwu*, no. 144 (1962, no. 10) (October 1962): 13-16.
金維諾・〈"步輦圖"與"凌煙閣功臣圖"〉・《文物》・一九六二年第十期・總第一四四號・第十三頁至第十六頁・

Jin, Yaozhang. "Jing ju jingjiao lian pu de yanbian." In *Zhongguo xiqu lian pu wenji*, compiled and edited by Huang Dianqi, 76-86. Beijing: Zhongguo xiju chuban she, 1994.
金耀章・〈京劇淨臉譜的演變〉・《中國戲曲臉譜文集》・黃殿祺輯・第七十六頁至第八十六頁・北京：中國戲劇出版社，1994年5月第1版・

Jin, Zhang (1884-1939). *Hao liang zhi le ji* [4 juan]. [Prefaces by Jin Cheng (1878-1926) and Jin Zhang. Postcript by Wang Shixiang.] Beijing: Wenwu chuban she, 1985.
《濠梁知樂集》・金章撰輯・[序：金城、金章]・[後記：王世襄]・北京：文物出版社，1985年2月第一版・

Jin, Zhishun. "New Building of National Library of China: A Survey." In *Proceedings of the Fourth International Conference of Directors of National Libraries in Asia and Oceania, December 5-9, 1989*, [compiled by the National Library of China], 22-29. Beijing: National Library of China, 1989.

Jing ju shi yanjiu: Xiqu lunhui (er) zhuanji. Texts supplied by Beijing Jing ju shi yanjiu hui. Edited by Beijing shi xiqu yanjiu suo. Shanghai: Xuelin chuban she, 1985.
《京劇史研究—戲曲論匯（二）專輯》・北京京劇史研究會供稿・北京市戲曲研究所編・上海：學林出版社・1985年12月第1版・

Jingshi tushu guan shanben jianming shumu. [Compiled and edited by Xia Zengyou (1861-1924).] 4 vols. [on double-leaves; stitch-bound, Oriental style] in 1 case. Beijing: Jingshi tushu guan, 1916.
《京師圖書館善本簡明書目》・[夏曾佑編校]・[全四冊・綫裝]・北京：京師圖書

館，民國五年刊印，

Johnson, David, ed. *Ritual Opera, Operatic Ritual: "Mu-lien Rescues His Mother" in Chinese Popular Culture*. Papers from the International Workshop on the Mu-lien Operas, with an additional contribution on the Woman Huang legend by Beata Grant. Publications of the Chinese Popular Culture Project, no. 1. N.p. [Berkeley, Calif.]: N.p. [Chinese Popular Culture Project], 1989.

———. "Actions Speak Louder Than Words: The Cultural Significance of Chinese Ritual Opera." *In Ritual Opera, Operatic Ritual: "Mu-lien Rescues His Mother" in Chinese Popular Culture*, edited by David Johnson, 1-45. Papers from the International Workshop on the Mu-lien Operas, with an additional contribution on the Woman Huang legend by Beata Grant. Publications of the Chinese Popular Culture Project, no. 1. N.p. [Berkeley, Calif.]: N.p. [Chinese Popular Culture Project], 1989.

A Journey into China's Antiquity: National Museum of Chinese History. Compiled by National Museum of Chinese History. 4 vols. Vol. 1, *Palaeolithic Age, Lower Neolithic Age, Upper Neolithic Age, Xia Dynasty, Shang Dynasty, Western Zhou Dynasty, Spring and Autumn Period*. Vol. 2, *Warring States Period, Qin Dynasty, The Western and Eastern Han Dynasties, Three Kingdoms through Western and Eastern Jin to Northern and Southern Dynasties*. Vol. 3, *Sui Dynasty, Tang Dynasty, Five Dynasties and Ten Kingdoms Period, Northern and Southern Song Dynasties*. Vol. 4, *Yuan Dynasty, Ming Dynasty, Qing Dynasty*. [Editor-in-chief: Yu Weichao; editor: Zheng Wenlei.] Beijing: Morning Glory Publishers, 1997.

Ju, Mi [Mi Chu Wiens]. "Ming Qing shiqi Huizhou de ke shu he banhua." In *Nisanjû nendai Chûgoku to tôzai bungei: Ashida Takaaki kyôju kinen ronbunshû*, compiled by Nisanjû nendai Chûgoku to tôzai bungei: Ashida Takaaki kyôju kinen ronbunshû iinkai, reverse pagination, 456-441 [subsidiary pagination in section of articles in Chinese, 3-18]. Tokyo: Tôhô shoten, 1998.
居蜜，〈明清時期徽州的刻書和版画〉，《二三十年代中國と東西文芸：蘆田孝昭教授退休紀念論文集》，編者：蘆田孝昭教授退休紀念論文集編集委員会，東京：東方書店，一九九八年一二月一二日初版第一刷発行，[倒數頁次]，第四百五十六頁至第四百四十一頁，[第三部：中国文学研究（中文），第三頁至第十八頁]，

-K-

Die Kaiserliche Ku-wen-Anthologie von 1685/6 Ku-wen yüan-chien in mandjurische Übersetzung. Herausgegeben von Martin Gimm. Bd. 1,

Kap. 1-24 (Chou- bis Chin-Dynastie). Wiesbaden, Germany: Otto Harrassowitz, 1969.

Kaji, Nobuyuki (1936-). *Kôshi gaden: Seisekizu ni miru Kôshi rur no shôgai to oshie*. Tokyo: Shûeisha, 1991.
《孔子画伝：聖蹟図にみる孔子流浪の生涯の教之》，著者：加地伸行，東京：集英社，一九九一年三月二十五日第一刷発行，

Kan Sô Zen no hi. [Explanatory notes in Japanese by Matsui Joryû (1900-); reproduces the stone rubbings of the Han-dynasty Stele of Cao Quan in a Japanese private collection; original stone in the Shaanxi sheng bowu guan, Xi'an.] Shoseki meihin sôkan, no. 5. Tokyo: Nigensha, 1959 (18th printing, 1973).
《漢曹全碑》，[解説者：松井如流]，[原本：田近憲三藏本]，《書跡名品叢刊》第五回配本，東京：二玄社，一九五九年一月一日初版發行，一九七三年八月三十一日一八刷發行，

Kandai no gazôsen [Exhibition: Figured Bricks in Han Dynasties (202 B.C.-220 A.D.) in the Collection of Tenri Univ. Sankôkan Museum]. Compiled and edited Tenri sankôkan. Tenri gyararî, dai 78-kai ten. Exhibition catalogue [Tenri gyararî (Tenri Gallery), Tenrikyôkan, Tokyo, July 20-October 31,1987]. [In Japanese; title on back cover also in English.] Tokyo: Tenri gyararî (Tenri Gallery), 1987.
《漢代の画像塼》，編集：天理参考館，天理ギャラリー第78回展，[東京天理教館，天理ギャラリー第78回展，漢代画像塼，1987年7月20日―10月31日]，東京：天理ギャラリー，昭和62年7月20日発行，

Kangxi di yu zhi wenji. By the Kangxi emperor (1654-1722; r. 1661-1722). 4 vols. [Vol. 1, *Yu zhi wenji* (40 *juan, zongmu* 4 *juan*). Vol. 2, *Yu zhi wen di er ji* (50 *juan, zongmu* 6 *juan*). Vol. 3, *Yu zhi wen si san ji* (50 *juan, zongmu* 4 *juan*). Vol. 4, *Yu zhi wen di si ji* (36 *juan, zongmu* 4 *juan*).] Zhongguo shi xue congshu, [no. 41], edited by Wu Xiangxiang. [Reprint. Facsimile reproduction of copy in the possession of the National Taiwan University, Taibei; each page represents 4 leaves of the original.] Taibei: Taiwan xuesheng shuju, 1966.
《康熙帝御製文集》，撰者：清玄曄，[《御製文集》，四十卷，總目四卷，校刊者：蔣陳錫、蔣溎謹，編錄者：張玉書等，康熙五十年十一月十四日奉]，[《御製文第二集》，五十卷，總目六卷，校刊者：蔣陳錫、蔣溎謹，編錄者：張玉書等，康熙五十年十一月十四日奉]，[《御製文第三集》，五十卷，總目四卷，校刊者：蔣陳錫、蔣溎謹，編錄者：張玉書等]，[《御製文第四集》，三十六卷，總目四卷，校刊者：蔣陳錫、蔣溎謹，編錄者：允祿等，校對者：方苞，校刊者：朱良裘等，雍正十年十二月初十日奉]，[影印本，據國立臺灣大學藏本影印]，《中國史學叢書》，吳相湘主編，[精裝，全四冊]，台北：台灣學生書局，民國五十五年五月初版，

Karg, Christine U. "Seidespinner und Maulbeerbaum–Die Seidenerzeugung in China." In *China, eine Wiege der Weltkultur: 5000*

Jahre Erfindungen und Entdeckungen, edited by Arne Eggebrecht, 192-199. Mainz am Rhein, Germany: Verlag Philipp von Zabern, 1994.

Karlgren, Bernhard (1889-1978). "The Book of Documents." *Bulletin of the Museum of Far Eastern Antiquities*, no. 22 (1950): 1-81.

Keightley, David N. (1932-). *Sources of Shang History: The Oracle-Bone Inscriptions of Bronze Age China*. Berkeley and Los Angeles: University of California Press, 1978.

————, ed. *The Origins of Chinese Civilization*. With contributions by Noel Barnard et al. Studies on China, no. 1. Berkeley and Los Angeles: University of California Press, 1983.

————. "The Late Shang State: When, Where, and What?" In *The Origins of Chinese Civilization*, edited by David N. Keightley (1932-), 523-564. Studies on China, no. 1. Berkeley and Los Angeles: University of California Press, 1983.

————. "Sacred Characters." In *China: Ancient Culture, Modern Land*, edited by Robert E. Murowchick (1956-), 70-79. Cradles of Civilization. Norman, Okla.: University of Oklahoma Press, 1994.

————. "Shang Oracle-Bone Inscriptions." In *New Sources of Early Chinese History: An Introduction to the Reading of Inscriptions and Manuscripts*, edited by Edward L. Shaughnessy (1952-), 15-55. Early China Special Monograph Series, no. 3. N.p. [Bethlehem, Pa.]: The Society for the Study of Early China; Berkeley, Calif.: The Institute of East Asian Studies, University of California, Berkeley, 1997.

————. "The Shang: China's First Historical Dynasty." In *The Cambridge History of Ancient China: From the Origins of Civilization to 221 B.C.*, edited by Michael Loewe and Edward L. Shaughnessy (1952-), 232-291. Cambridge and New York: Cambridge University Press, 1998.

————. "The Oracle-Bone Inscriptions of the Late Shang Dynasty." In *Sources of Chinese Tradition*, compiled by Wm. Theodore de Bary (1919-) and Irene Bloom, 2d ed., vol. 1, 3-23. New York: Columbia University Press, 1999.

Kinsei Nihon kaiga to gafu, edehon ten: Meiga o unda hanga. [At head of title: *Kaikan 3-shûnen kinen*.] Compiled and edited by Machida shiritsu kokusai hanga bijutsukan. 2 vols. Exhibition catalogue [Machida shiritsu kokusai hanga bijutsukan, Machida, Japan, April 19-June 17, 1990]. Machida, Japan: Machida shiritsu kokusai hanga bijutsukan, 1990.
《近世日本絵画と画譜・絵手本展：名画生んだ版画》・【開館三周年記念】・編集：町田市立国際版画美術館・[平装・全二冊]・[特展圖録・町田市立国際版

画美術館・平成二年四月十九日―六月十七日]・東京都町田市：町田市立国際版画美術館，平成二年（一九九〇年）四月発行・

Der kleine Goldfischteich. Kolorierte Stiche nach chinesischen Aquarellen. [Geleitwort von Franz Kuhn (1884-1961), 25-42.] Insel-Bücherei, no. 255. Leipzig: Insel-Verlag, n.d.

Kobayashi, Hiromitsu, and Samantha J. Sabin. "The Great Age of Anhui Printing." In *Shadows of Mt. Huang: Chinese Painting and Printing of the Anhui School*, edited by James F. Cahill (1926-), 25-33. Berkeley, Calif.: University Art Museum, University of California, Berkeley, 1981.

————. "Figure Compositions in Seventeenth-Century Chinese Prints and Their Influences on Edo-Period Japanese Painting Manuals." Ph.D. diss., University of California, Berkeley, 1987. UMI Order No.: 8726257.

————. "Chûgoku kaigashi ni okeru hanga no igi: Ko shi gafu (1603-nen kan) ni miru rekidai meiga fukusei o megutte." *Bijutsushi*, no. 128 (vol. 39, no. 2) (March 1990): pp. 123-135 [accompanied by résumé in English, "Significances of Pictorial Printing in the History of Chinese Painting–A Study of the 1603 'Gushi huapu' Painting Manual," résumé section, reverse pagination, pp. 1-2].
小林宏光・〈中国絵画史における版画の意義―『顧氏畫譜』（一六〇三年刊）にみる歴代名画複製をめぐって〉・《美術史》・第百二十八册・[第三十九巻・第二期・平成二年三月]・第一百二十三頁至第一百三十五頁・[英文提要・英文提要部分倒数第一頁至第二頁]・

————. "Chûgoku gafu no hakusai, hankoku to wasei gafu no tanjô." In *Kinsei Nihon kaiga to gafu, edehon ten: Meiga o unda hanga*, compiled and edited by Machida shiritsu kokusai hanga bijutsukan, vol. 2, 106-123. Machida, Japan: Machida shiritsu kokusai hanga bijutsukan, 1990.
小林宏光・〈中国画譜の舶載、翻刻と和製画譜の誕生〉・《近世日本絵画と画譜・絵手本展：名画生んだ版画》・編集：町田市立国際版画美術館・東京都町田市：町田市立国際版画美術館，平成二年（一九九〇年）四月発行・第二册・第一百零六頁至第一百二十三頁・

————. *Chûgoku no hanga: Tôdai kara Shindai made (Chinese Woodblock Illustrations from the Tang through the Qing Dynasty)*. Sekai bijutsu sôsho (The Library of World Art History and Artistic Theory), 004. [In Japanese.] Tokyo: Tôshindô, 1995.
《中国の版画：唐代から清代まで》・著者：小林宏光・《世界美術双書》，004・監修：中森義宗、永井信一、小林忠、青柳正規・東京：東信堂，1995年6月10日初版第1刷・

Kohn, Livia (1956-). *Early Chinese Mysticism: Philosophy and Soteriology in the Taoist Tradition*. Princeton: Princeton University Press, 1992.

Kong, Demao (1917-), and Ke Lan. *The House of Confucius*. Translated [from the Chinese] by Rosemary Roberts. Edited and with an introduction by Frances Wood. London and Sydney: Hodder & Stoughton Limited, 1988.

Kong, Xiangxing, and Liu Yiman. *Zhongguo tong jing tudian*. Beijing: Wenwu chuban she, 1992.
《中國銅鏡圖典》・孔祥星、劉一曼・北京：文物出版社，1992 年 1 月第一版・

Koten hyakushu (One Hundred Classics in the Tenri Central Library). Tenri gyararî kaikan jusshûnen kinenten (dai 32-kai ten). Exhibition catalogue [Tenri gyararî (Tenri Gallery), Tenrikyôkan, Tokyo, April 1-June 30, 1972]. [In Japanese; title on back cover also in English.] Tokyo: Tenri gyararî (Tenri Gallery), 1972.
《古典百種》・天理ギャラリー開館十周年記念展（第三十二回）・[東京天理教館・天理ギャラリー・1972 年 4 月 1 日―6 月 30 日]東京：天理ギャラリー，昭和 47 年 3 月 20 日　行・

Kuhn, Dieter (1946-). "Die Darstellungen des 'Keng-chih-t'u' und ihre Wiedergabe in populär-enzyklopädischen Werken der Ming-Zeit." *Zeitschrift der Deutschen Morgenländischen Gesellschaft*, Bd. 126, Heft 2 (1976): 336-367.

Kumar, Virendra. "Preservation of Bark and Palm-leaf Manuscripts." *Herald of Library Science* 2, no. 4 (October 1963): 236-241.

Kwanten, Luc. "Tangut Miscellanea, I. On the Inventor of the Tangut Script." *Journal of the American Oriental Society* 97, no. 3 (July-September 1977): 333-335.

———. "The Role of the Tangut in Chinese-Inner Asian Relations." *Acta Orientalia* 39 (1978): 191-198.

———. *Imperial Nomads: A History of Central Asia, 500-1500*. Philadelphia: University of Pennsylvania Press, 1979.

———, and Susan Hesse. *Tangut (Hsi Hsia) Studies: A Bibliography*. Indiana University Uralic and Altaic Series, edited by Denis Sinor, vol. 137. Bloomington, Ind.: Research Institute for Inner Asian Studies, Indiana University, 1980.

Kychanov, Evgeny Ivanovich. "The State of Great Xia (982-1227 A.D.)." In *Lost Empire of the Silk Road: Buddhist Art from Khara Khoto (X-XIIIth Century)*, edited by Mikhail Piotrovsky, 49-58. Lugano, Italy: Thyssen-Bornemisza Foundation [Fondazione Thyssen-Bornemisza]; Milan: Electa, 1993.

———. "Tangut." In *The World's Writing Systems*, edited by Peter T. Daniels (1951-) and William Bright (1928-), 228-230 [bibliography, 237]. New York and Oxford: Oxford University Press, 1996.

-L-

LaFargue, Michael. *The Tao of the Tao Te Ching: A Translation and Commentary*. SUNY Series in Chinese Philosophy and Culture, edited by David L. Hall and Roger T. Ames. Albany, N.Y.: State University of New York Press, 1992.

Lahiri, Latika. "Kuan-Shih-Yin, Avalokitesvara in Chinese Buddhism." In *Buddhist Iconography*, 142-148. Sambhota Series, no. 2. New Delhi: Tibet House, 1989.

Laing, Ellen Johnston [Ellen Mae Johnston] (1934-). "Ch'ing Dynasty Pictorial Jades and Painting." *Ars Orientalis* 16 (1986): 59-91.

Lan, Wei. "Dongba hua de zhonglei ji qi tese." In *Dongba wenhua lun ji*, edited by Guo Dalie and Yang Shiguang (1940-), 412-423. Kunming: Yunnan renmin chuban she, 1985.
蘭偉・〈東巴畫的種類及其特色〉・《東巴文化論集》・郭大烈、楊世光編・[精裝一冊]・昆明：雲南人民出版社，1985 年 6 月第一版・第四百十二頁至第四百二十三頁・

———. "Dongba hua yu Dongba wen de guanxi." In *Dongba wenhua lun ji*, edited by Guo Dalie and Yang Shiguang (1940-), 424-433. Kunming: Yunnan renmin chuban she, 1985.
蘭偉・〈東巴畫與東巴文的關係〉・《東巴文化論集》・郭大烈、楊世光編・[精裝一冊]・昆明：雲南人民出版社，1985 年 6 月第一版・第四百二十四頁至第四百三十三頁・

Lancaster, Lewis R. "Canonic Texts." In *Mongolia: The Legacy of Chinggis Khan*, by Patricia Berger and Terese Tse Bartholomew, with essays by James Bosson, Lewis R. Lancaster, Morris Rossabi (1941-), [and] Heather Stoddard, 186-187. New York: Thames and Hudson Inc., in association with San Francisco: Asian Art Museum of San Francisco, 1995.

Landt, Frank A. *Die fünf Heiligen Berge Chinas: Ihre Bedeutung und Bewertung in der Ch'ing-Dynastie*. Wissenschaftliche Schriftenreihe Sinologie, Bd. 1. Berlin: Verlag Dr. Köster, 1994.

Lang, Xiuhua. "Qing dai Shengping shu yan'ge." *Gugong bowu yuan yuankan (Palace Museum Journal)*, no. 31 (1986, no. 1): 13-18.
郎秀華・〈清代平署沿革〉・《故宮博物院院刊》・總第三十一期・一九八六年第一期・第十三頁至第十八頁・

Lanting chenlie pin mulu. [Title on front cover: *Lanting daguan.*] [Preface by Li Yan.] Wenwu guan congshu, no. 5. Exhibition catalogue [Xianggang Zhongwen daxue Zhongguo wenhua yanjiu suo wenwu guan (Art Gallery, Institute of Chinese Studies, Chinese University of Hong Kong), Hong Kong, April 10-May 13, 1973]. [Errata slip inserted.] Hong Kong: Xianggang Zhongwen daxue Zhongguo wenhua yanjiu suo wenwu guan [Art Gallery, Institute of Chinese Studies, Chinese University of Hong Kong], n.d. [1973].
《蘭亭陳列品目錄》・[封面標題:《蘭亭大觀》]・[前言:李棪]・文物館叢書之五・[特展圖錄・香港中文大學中國文化研究所文物館・一九七三年四月十日至五月十三日]・香港:香港中文大學中國文化研究所文物館・[一九七三年]・

Lanting lun bian. Compiled by Wenwu chuban she. Beijing: Wenwu chuban she, 1977.
《蘭亭論辨》・文物出版社編輯・北京:文物出版社,1977年10月第一版・

Lasker, Edward. *Modern Chess Strategy, with an Appendix on Go.* Philadelphia: David McKay Company, 1945.

Lau, D.C. [Dim Cheuk] [Liu Dianjue] 劉殿爵, trans. *Confucius: The Analects ("Lun yü").* 2d ed. [Bilingual ed.] Hong Kong: The Chinese University Press, 1992.

Laufer, Berthold (1874-1934). "The Discovery of a Lost Book." *T'oung Pao* 13 (1912): 97-106.

———. *Descriptive Account of the Collection of Chinese, Tibetan, Mongol, and Japanese Books in the Newberry Library.* [Title on front cover: *East Asiatic Collection.*] Publications of the Newberry Library, no. 4. Chicago: The Newberry Library, 1913.

———. *Paper and Printing in Ancient China.* Chicago: Printed for the Caxton Club, 1931.

Lawton, Thomas (1931-). *Chinese Figure Painting.* Freer Gallery of Art, Fiftieth Anniversary Exhibition, vol. 2. Washington, D.C.: Smithsonian Institution, 1973.

———. *A Time of Transition: Two Collectors of Chinese Art.* The Franklin D. Murphy Lectures, no. 12. Lawrence, Kan.: Spencer Museum of Art, The University of Kansas, 1991.

Ledderose, Lothar (1942-). "Rubbings in Art History." In *Catalogue of Chinese Rubbings from Field Museum*, researched by Hoshien Tchen [Ch'en Ho-hsien] and M. Kenneth Starr; prepared by Alice K. Schneider; photographs by Herta Newton and Field Museum Division of Photography; edited by Hartmut Walravens (1944-), xxviii-xxxvi. Fieldiana: Anthropology, n.s., no. 3. Publication 1327. Chicago: Field Museum of Natural History, 1981.

———. "Calligraphy at the Close of the Chinese Empire." In *Art at the Close of China's Empire*, edited by Ju-hsi Chou (1935-), 189-207. *Phœbus: Occasional Papers in Art History*, vol. 8. N.p. [Tempe, Ariz.]: Arizona State University, 1998.

Lee, Thomas H.C. [Li Hongqi] 李弘祺. "Books and Bookworms in Song China: Book Collection and the Appreciation of Books." *Journal of Sung-Yuan Studies*, no. 25 (1995): 193-218.

Li, Chu-tsing (1920-), and James C.Y. Watt, eds. *The Chinese Scholar's Studio: Artistic Life in the Late Ming Period: An Exhibition from the Shanghai Museum.* With contributions by James C.Y. Watt et al. [Chu-tsing Li, Wai-kam Ho, Zhu Xuchu, Wang Qingzheng, and Robert D. Mowry]. Exhibition catalogue [The Asia Society Galleries, The Asia Society, New York, October 15, 1987-January 3, 1988; Seattle Art Museum, Seattle, February 4-March 27, 1988; Arthur M. Sackler Gallery, Smithsonian Institution, Washington, D.C., May 2-June 26, 1988; Nelson-Atkins Museum of Art, Kansas City, Mo., July 30-September 25, 1988]. New York: Thames and Hudson Inc., published in association with New York: The Asia Society Galleries, 1987.

Li, Fuhua (1933-). "'Zhaocheng Jin Zang' yanjiu." *Shijie zongjiao yanjiu (Studies in World Religions)*, no. 46 (1991, no. 4): 1-18.
李富華・〈趙城金藏研究〉・《世界宗教研究》・總第四十六期・一九九一年第四期・第一頁至第十八頁・

Li, Hui-Lin 李惠林 (1911-). *The Garden Flowers of China.* Chronica Botanica, no. 19. New York: The Ronald Press Company, 1959.

Li, Ping. "Jiuhu 'Zhaocheng Jin Zang' de cehua zhe Likong fashi xinglüe–yi 'Huoshan zhi' he Likong fashi zi zhuan de nianpu wei ti." *Wenxian*, no. 64 (1995, no. 2): 109-132.
李憑・〈救護《趙城金藏》的策劃者力空法師行略—以《霍山志》和力空法師自撰的年譜為題〉・《文獻》・總第六十四期・一九九五年第二期・第一百零九頁至第一百三十二頁・

———. "Likong fashi jiuhu 'Zhaocheng Jin Zang' wenti kaoshi." *Wenxian*, no. 65 (1995, no. 3): 94-103.
李憑・〈力空法師救護《趙城金藏》問題考實〉・《文獻》・總第六十五期・一九九五年第三期・第九十四頁至第一百零三頁・

Li, Shaoming, and Feng Min. *Yi zu.* Minzu zhishi congshu. N.p. [Beijing]: Minzu chuban she, 1993.
《彝族》・李紹明、馮敏著・〈民族知識叢書〉・[平裝一冊]・[北京]:民族出版社,1993年11月第1版・

Li, Tiyang. "Qing dai gongting xiju." In *Jing ju shi yanjiu: Xiqu lunhui (er) zhuanji*, texts supplied by Beijing Jing ju shi yanjiu hui, edited by Beijing shi xiqu yanjiu suo, 61-73. Shanghai: Xuelin chuban she, 1985.

《清代宮廷戲劇》・〈京劇史研究─戲曲論匯（二）專輯〉・北京京劇史研究會供稿・北京市戲曲研究所編・上海：學林出版社，1985 年 12 月第 1 版・第六十一頁至第七十三頁・

Li, Wei. *Xi Xia shi yanjiu*. Yinchuan, Ningxia: Ningxia renmin chuban she, 1989.

《西夏史研究》・李蔚[著]・銀川：寧夏人民出版社，1989 年 3 月第 1 版・

Li, Xibi, and Wang Shuwei. *Beijing tushu guan*. Beijing: Beijing chuban she, 1957.

《北京圖書館》・李希泌、王樹偉著・北京：北京出版社，1957 年 12 月第 1 版・

Li, Xiaocong (1947-). *Ouzhou shoucang bufen Zhongwen gu ditu xulu (A Descriptive Catalogue of Pre-1900 Chinese Maps Seen in Europe)*. Guojia jiaowei quanguo gaoxiao guji zhengli zhongdian xiangmu. Beijing: Guoji wenhua chuban gongsi, 1996.

《歐洲收藏部分中文古地圖敘錄》・李孝聰著・〈國家教委全國高校古籍整理重點項目〉・北京：國際文化出版公司，1996 年 8 月第 1 版・

Li, Xueqin (1933-). "Jiagu xue yi bai nian de huigu yu qianzhan." *Wenwu*, no. 500 (1998, no. 1) (January 1998): 33-36 [accompanied by abstract in English, "One Century of Study of Oracle Bone and Shell Inscriptions: Retrospective and Projection," 37].

李學勤・〈甲骨學一百年的回顧與前瞻〉・《文物》・一九九八年第一期・總第五〇〇號・第三十三頁至第三十六頁・英文提要・第三十七頁・

Li, Zhizhong (1927-). "'Shanben' qian lun." *Wenwu*, no. 271 (1978, no. 12) (December 1978): 69-73.

李致忠・〈"善本" 淺論〉・《文物》・一九七八年第十二期・總第二七一號・第六十九頁至第七十三頁・

———. *Gu shu banben xue gailun*. Beijing: Shumu wenxian chuban she, 1990.

《古書版本學概論》・著者：李致忠・北京：書目文獻出版社，1990 年 8 月北京第版・

———. *Song ban shu xu lu*. Beijing: Shumu wenxian chuban she, 1994.

《宋版書敘錄》・李致忠著・北京：書目文獻出版社，1994 年 6 月北京第 1 版・

———. *Gu shu banben jianding*. Beijing: Wenwu chuban she, 1997.

《古書版本鑒定》・李致忠著・[平裝一冊]・北京：文物出版社，1997 年 2 月第一版・

Li shi. 27 *juan*. Compiled by Hong Shi (1117-1184). Preface dated 1167. 8 vols. [on double-leaves; stitch-bound, Oriental style] in 1 case

[facsimile reproduction of the Ming Wanli-period (1573-1619) edition in the possession of the Liu family of Gu'an]. Sibu congkan san bian, vol. 25. Shanghai: Shangwu yinshu guan, 1935. Reprint, with an appendix of errata, *Jiaokan ji*, 1 *juan*. Sibu congkan san bian, vol. 30. Shanghai: Shanghai shudian, 1985.

《隸釋》・二十七卷・宋洪适撰・[南宋乾道三年正月八日洪适自序]・[明萬曆十六年戊子秋八月王雲鷺刻隸識小序]・[上海涵芬樓景印固安劉氏藏明萬曆刊本原書]・〈四部叢刊三編〉・第二十五冊・上海：商務印書館，民國二十四年・[影印本・據商務印書館一九三五年版重印]・〈四部叢刊三編史部〉・第三十冊・[卷一至卷二十七，附校勘記一卷]・上海：上海書店，1985 年 9 月重印・

Li shi, Li xu. [*Li shi*. 27 *juan*; *Li xu*. 21 *juan*.] Compiled by Hong Shi (1117-1184). [Preface to *Li shi* dated 1167. Reprint. Facsmile reproduction of the Hong shi Huimu zhai edition of 1872; most pages represent 2 leaves of the original. Appended with *Wang ben Li shi kan wu* (1 *juan*), compiled by Huang Peilie (1763-1825).] Beijing: Zhonghua shuju, 1985.

《隸釋》、《隸續》・[《隸釋》・二十七卷・《隸續》・二十一卷]・宋洪适撰・[南宋乾道三年正月八日洪适自序《隸釋》]・[影印本・據洪氏晦木齋刻本影印・原刻後附黃丕烈《汪本隸釋刊誤》亦一並付印・北京：中華書局，1985 年 11 月第 1 版・

Liang Qichao tiba moji shufa ji. Compiled and edited by Ji Yaping, Jia Shuangxi, et al. Beijing: Rongbao zhai chuban she, 1995.

《梁啟超題跋墨蹟書法集》・冀亞平、賈雙喜等編・[精裝一冊]・北京：榮寶齋出版社，1995 年 3 月北京第一版・

Liao, Ben (1953-). *Zhongguo xiju tushi*. Zhengzhou, Henan: Henan jiaoyu chuban she, 1996.

《中國戲劇圖史》・廖奔著・[精裝一冊]・鄭州：河南教育出版社，1995 年 8 月第 1 版・

Liao, Xintian [Liao Shin-tyan]. *Qing dai bei xue shufa yanjiu [Research on the Study of Engraving Calligraphy (Pei Hsiue) of Ching Dynasty]*. Meishu luncong, no. 48. [In Chinese; title and chapter headings also in English.] Taibei: Taibei shili meishu guan (Taipei Fine Arts Museum), 1993.

《清代碑學書法研究》・廖新田著・〈美術論叢〉，48・台北：台北市立美術館，民國八十二年六月初版・

Lidai xijian shukan ziliao paimai hui. Auction catalogue [September 14, 1996, Zhongguo shudian, Beijing]. Beijing: Zhongguo shudian, 1996.

《歷代稀見書刊資料拍賣會》・[拍賣品圖錄・中國書店・時間：1996 年 9 月 14 日・星期六下午 1：30・地點：北京琉璃廠西街 57 號，中國書店會議廳]・北京：中國書店，1996 年 9 月 14 日・

Lidai Zhong Kui hua yanjiu. Compiled and edited by Wang Zhende and Li Tianxiu. Tianjin: Tianjin renmin meishu chuban she, 1985.

《歷代鍾馗畫研究》・王振德、李天庥編著・天津：天津人民美術出版社，1985年5月第1版・

Liexian quan zhuan. Zhongguo gudai banhua jingpin xilie congshu. Shijiazhuang, Hebei: Hebei meishu chuban she, 1996.
《列仙全傳》・〈中國古代版畫精品系列叢書〉・[平裝一冊]・石家莊：河北美術出版社，一九九六年八月第一版・

Lin, Li-chiang [Lin Lijiang] (1965-). "The Proliferation of Images: The Ink-Stick Designs and the Printing of the 'Fang-shih mo-p'u' and the 'Ch'eng-shih mo-yüan.'" 2 vols. Ph.D. diss., Princeton University, 1998. UMI Order No.: 9827929.

Lingyan ge gongchen tu. Zhongguo gudai banhua jingpin xilie congshu. Shijiazhuang, Hebei: Hebei meishu chuban she, 1996.
《凌煙閣功臣圖》・〈中國古代版畫精品系列叢書〉・[平裝一冊]・石家莊：河北美術出版社，一九九六年八月第一版・

Linrothe, Rob [Robert N.] (1951-). "New Delhi and New England: Old Collections of Tangut Art." *Orientations* 27, no. 4 (April 1996): 32-41.

Little, Archibald John (1838-1908). *Through the Yang-tse Gorges, or, Trade and Travel in Western China.* 3d and rev. ed., with map and illustrations. London: Sampson Low, Marston & Company Limited, 1898.

Little, Stephen L. (1954-). "The Demon Queller and the Art of Qiu Ying (Ch'iu Ying)." *Artibus Asiae* 46, nos. 1-2 (1985): 5-128.

Liu, Cary [Cary Yee-Wei] (1955-), Dora C.Y. Ching, and Judith G. Smith (1941-), eds. *Character & Context in Chinese Calligraphy.* Princeton, N.J.: The Art Museum, Princeton University, 1999.

Liu, Shaoming [Joseph S.M. Lau] (1934-), Ma Youyuan [Yau-Woon Ma] (1940-), and Hu Wanchuan, eds. *Zhongguo chuantong duanpian xiaoshuo xuanji.* Taibei: Lianjing chuban shiye gongsi, 1979.
《中國傳統短篇小說選集》・編者：劉紹銘、馬幼垣、胡萬川・[精裝、平裝各一冊]・台北：聯經出版事業公司，民國六十八年五月初版・

Liu, Wu-Chi (1907-). *Confucius, His Life and Time.* New York: Philosophical Library, Inc., 1955. Reprint. Westport, Conn.: Greenwood Press, Publishers, 1972.

Le livre et l'imprimerie en Extrême-Orient et en Asie du Sud: Actes du Colloque organisé à Paris du 9 au 11 mars 1983. Préparés par Jean-Pierre Drège, Mitchiko Ishigami-Iagolnitzer et Monique Cohen. [Revue française d'histoire du livre, nos. 42-43.] Bordeaux: Société des Bibliophiles de Guyenne, 1986.

Loewe, Michael. *Ways to Paradise: The Chinese Quest for Immortality.* London and Boston: George Allen & Unwin Ltd., 1979.

———, ed. *Early Chinese Texts: A Bibliographical Guide.* Early China Special Monograph Series, no. 2. N.p.: The Society for the Study of Early China; Berkeley, Calif.: The Institute of East Asian Studies, University of California, Berkeley, 1993.

———, and Edward L. Shaughnessy (1952-), eds. *The Cambridge History of Ancient China: From the Origins of Civilization to 221 B.C.* Cambridge and New York: Cambridge University Press, 1998.

Lohia, Sushama. *Lalitavajra's Manual of Buddhist Iconography.* Satapitaka Series, Indo-Asian Literatures, vol. 379. New Delhi: International Academy of Indian Culture; Delhi: Aditya Prakashan, 1994.

Lokesh Chandra. *The Three Hundred Gods.* [Preface in English; names of gods in Sanskrit and Tibetan; on 2 folded sheets.] N.p. [New Delhi]: N.p. [Lokesh Chandra], n.d. [1965].

———. *Buddhist Iconography of Tibet.* Begun by the late Prof. Raghu Vira (1902-1963). [Thoroughly revised, corrected and re-arranged new edition of The New Tibeto-Mongol Pantheon, Parts 1-20, with detailed index of all the English, Sanskrit, Tibetan and Mongolian names.] [Satapitaka Series, Indo-Asian Languages, vol. 341.] 3 vols. [Explanatory notes in Japanese. Colophon pages of vols. 1 and 2 also in Japanese: ロ—ケーシュ・チャンドラ「チベット佛教　像集成」全3巻・京都：臨川書店，1986年2月25日発行・] 2 vols. Kyoto: Rinsen Book Co., 1986.

Long, Zhuangwei. "'Yuan qu xuan' 'yin shi' tanwei." *Wenxian*, no. 53 (1992, no. 3): 40-49.
龍莊偉・〈《元曲選・音釋》探微〉・《文獻》・總第五十三期・一九九二年第三期・第四十頁至第四十九頁・

Longmen ershi pin. Compiled and edited by Zhongguo shufa bianji zu. Zhongguo shufa. Beijing: Wenwu chuban she, 1980.
《龍門二十品》・編輯者：中國書法編輯組・〈中國書法〉・[布面精裝一冊]・北京：文物出版社，一九八〇年五月一版・

Longmen ershi pin: Beike yu zaoxiang yishu. Edited by Liu Jinglong. [In Chinese and English; translated (from the Chinese) by Liu Zongren and Shao Haiming; photographs by Chen Zhi'an; rubbings by Cao Shesong and Chen Yaoxuan; rubbings photographed by Zheng Hua.] Beijing: Zhongguo shijie yu chuban she (China Esperanto Press), 1995.
《龍門二十品：碑刻與造像藝術》・劉景龍編著・[漢英版・翻譯：劉宗仁、邵海明・攝影：陳志安・拓片印刷：曹社松、陳耀軒・拓片翻拍：鄭華・圖繪製：宋森才]・北京：中國世界語出版社，1995年8月第一版・

Lörincz, László. *Molon Toyin's Journey into the Hell: Altan Gerel's*

Translation. 2 vols. Vol. 1, *Introduction and Transcription*. Vol. 2, *Facsimile*. Monumenta Linguae Mongolicae Collecta, vol. 8, pts. 1-2. Budapest: Akadémiai Kiadó, 1982.

Lu, Huiwen. "Calligraphy of Stone Engravings in Northern Wei Loyang." In *Character & Context in Chinese Calligraphy*, edited by Cary [Cary Yee-Wei] Liu (1955-), Dora C.Y. Ching, and Judith G. Smith (1941-), 78-103. Princeton, N.J.: The Art Museum, Princeton University, 1999.

Lu, Renlong (1963-). "Zhao Mengfu yu daojiao: Jian shu Song mo Yuan chu daojiao fazhan de yixie tezhi." *Shijie zongjiao yanjiu (Studies in World Religions)*, no. 45 (1991, no. 3): 24-34.
盧仁龍・〈趙孟頫與道教—兼述宋末元初道教發展的一些特質〉・《世界宗教研究》・總第四十五期・一九九一年第三期・第二十四頁至第三十四頁・

Lu, Sheng. "Chengde Bishu shanzhuang." *Wenwu cankao ziliao*, no. 73 (1956, no. 9) (September 1956): 13-20.
盧繩・〈承德避暑山莊〉・《文物參考資料》・一九五六年第九期・總第七三號・第十三頁至第二十頁・

Luo, Zhewen. *Ancient Pagodas in China*. Beijing: Foreign Languages Press, 1994.

———. *Zhongguo gu ta*. [Zhongguo chuantong wenhua congshu.] Beijing: Waiwen chuban she, 1994.
《中國古塔》・羅哲文著・〈中國傳統文化叢書〉・北京：外文出版社，1994 年第一版・

Luo, Zhenyu (1866-1940), comp. and ed. *San dai jijin wencun*. Reprint [originally published 1937]. 3 vols. [Includes an explanatory note, vol. 1, 1-4, and an essay by Sun Zhichu, "San dai ji jinwen cun bianzheng," vol. 3, text pages, 1-48.] Beijing: Zhonghua shuju, 1983.
《三代吉金文存》・羅振玉編・[重印版]・[全三冊]・[中華書局編輯部・〈重印說明〉・第一冊・第一頁至第四頁]・[孫稚雛・〈三代吉金文存辨正〉・第三冊・文字部分・第一頁至第四十八頁]・北京：中華書局，1983 年 12 月第 1 版・

Lynn, Richard John. *The Classic of the Way and Virtue: A New Translation of the 'Tao-te ching' of Laozi as Interpreted by Wang Bi*. Translations from the Asian Classics, edited by Wm. Theodore de Bary et al. New York: Columbia University Press, 1999.

-M-

Ma, Chengyuan (1927-). *Ancient Chinese Bronzes*. [Translated from the Chinese by Tang Bowen.] Editor: Hsio-yen Shih. Hong Kong and Oxford: Oxford University Press, 1986.

Ma, Y.W. [Yau-Woon] [Ma Youyuan] 馬幼垣 (1940-), and Joseph S.M. Lau [Liu Shaoming] 劉紹銘 (1934-), eds. *Traditional Chinese Stories: Themes and Variations*. New York: Columbia University Press, 1978.

———, and Tai-loi Ma [Ma Tailai]. "Shui-hu chuan." In *The Indiana Companion to Traditional Chinese Literature*, edited and compiled by William H. Nienhauser, Jr., vol. 1, 712-716 [see also updated bibliography in vol. 2, 416-418]. Bloomington, Ind. and Indianapolis: Indiana University Press, 1986-1998.

Ma, Ziyun (1903-1986). "Chuan ta jifa." *Wenwu*, no. 144 (1962, no. 10) (October 1962): 53-55.
馬子雲・〈傳拓技法〉・《文物》・一九六二年第十期・總第一四四號・第五十三頁至第五十六頁・

———. "Chuan ta jifa (xu)." *Wenwu*, no. 145 (1962, no. 11) (November 1962): 59-62, continued on 52.
馬子雲・〈傳拓技法（續）〉・《文物》・一九六二年第十一期・總第一四五號・第五十九頁至第六十二頁，下接第五十二頁・

———. *Beitie jianding qianshuo*. Beijing: Zijin cheng chuban she, 1986.
《碑帖鑑定淺說》・馬子雲著・北京：紫禁城出版社，1986 年 2 月第 1 版・

———, and Shi Anchang (1945-). *Beitie jianding*. "Zhongguo wenwu jianding" congshu. Guilin, Guangxi: Guangxi shifan daxue chuban she, 1993.
《碑帖鑒定》・馬子雲、施安昌著・《中國文物鑒定》叢書・桂林：廣西師範大學出版社，1993 年 12 月第一版・

Mackerras, Colin P. *The Rise of the Peking Opera, 1770-1870: Social Aspects of the Theatre in Manchu China*. Oxford: Clarendon Press, 1972.

———. *Chinese Drama: A Historical Survey*. Beijing: New World Press, 1990.

Madrolle, Cl. [Claude] (1870-). *Itinéraires dans l'ouest de la Chine, 1895, pour accompagner le journal de l'auteur dans son voyage au Iun-nan, au Tibet chinois et au Se-tch'ouen*. Paris: Augustin Challamel, Éditeur, 1900.

Mair, Victor H. (1943-), ed. *The Columbia Anthology of Traditional Chinese Literature*. Translations from the Asian Classics, [edited by Wm. Theodore de Bary et al.]. New York: Columbia University Press, 1994.

Manjusri-nama-sangiti in Mongolian, Tibetan, Sanskrit and Chinese, and Sekoddesa in Tibetan and Mongolian. [Added titles for the *Manjusri-nama-sangiti* in Sanskrit, Tibetan and Mongolian, and for the *Sekoddesa* in

Tibetan and Mongolian.] Edited by Raghu Vira (1902-1963). Sata-pitaka Series, Indo-Asian Literatures, vol. 18. Mongol-pitaka, being the Mongolian Collectanea in the series of Indo-Asian Literatures forming the Satapitaka, vol. 6. New Delhi: International Academy of Indian Culture, n.d. [1962].

Manmu linlang: Guoli zhongyang tushu guan shanben tecang (A Cornucopia of Rare Editions: The National Central Library's Rare Book Collection). Compiled by Guoli zhongyang tushu guan (National Central Library). Edited by Lu Jintang [Lu Chin-tang] and Song Jiancheng [Soong Chien-cheng]. English translations by Mou Ande [Andrew Morton]. [In Chinese and English; issued in slipcase.] Exhibition catalogue [Guoli zhongyang tushu guan (National Central Library), Taibei, 1993]. Taibei: Guoli zhongyang tushu guan (National Central Library), 1993.
《滿目琳瑯：國立中央圖書館善本特藏》・編著：國立中央圖書館・主編：盧錦堂、宋建成・英譯：牟安德・台北：國立中央圖書館，民國八十二年四月初版・

Mathieu, Christine. "Lost Kingdoms and Forgotten Tribes: Myths, Mysteries and Mother-right in the History of the Naxi Nationality and the Mosuo People of Southwest China." 2 vols. in 3. Ph.D. thesis, Murdoch University, 1996.

Mattos, Gilbert L. [Gilbert Louis] (1939-). "Eastern Zhou Bronze Inscriptions." In *New Sources of Early Chinese History: An Introduction to the Reading of Inscriptions and Manuscripts*, edited by Edward L. Shaughnessy (1952-), 85-123. Early China Special Monograph Series, no. 3. N.p. [Bethlehem, Pa.]: The Society for the Study of Early China; Berkeley, Calif.: The Institute of East Asian Studies, University of California, Berkeley, 1997.

Mawangdui Han mu boshu zhengli xiaozu. "Mawangdui Han mu chutu 'Laozi' shiwen." *Wenwu*, no. 222 (1974, no. 11) (November 1974): 8-20.
馬王堆漢墓帛書整理小組・〈馬王堆漢墓出土《老子》釋文〉・《文物》・一九七四年第十一期・總第二二二號・第八頁至第二十頁・

McKhann, Charles F. [Charles Fremont]. "Fleshing Out the Bones: Kinship and Cosmology in Naqxi Religion." 2 vols. Ph.D. diss., The University of Chicago, 1992.

————. "The Naxi and the Nationalities Question." In *Cultural Encounters on China's Ethnic Frontiers*, edited by Stevan Harrell, 39-62. Studies on Ethnic Groups in China, edited by Steven Harrell. Seattle and London: University of Washington Press, 1995.

McNair, Amy. "Engraved Calligraphy in China: Recension and Reception." *The Art Bulletin* 77, no. 1 (March 1995): 106-114.

————. "So Tan (ca. 250-ca. 325), 'Tao-te ching.'" In *The Embodied Image: Chinese Calligraphy from the John B. Elliott Collection*, by Robert E. Harrist, Jr. and Wen C. Fong, with contributions by Qianshen Bai et al., 90-91, cat. no. 1. Princeton, N.J.: The Art Museum, Princeton University, 1999.

————. "Texts of Taoism and Buddhism and the Power of Calligraphic Style." In *The Embodied Image: Chinese Calligraphy from the John B. Elliott Collection*, by Robert E. Harrist, Jr. and Wen C. Fong, with contributions by Qianshen Bai et al., 224-239. Princeton, N.J.: The Art Museum, Princeton University, 1999.

Mémoires concernant l'Asie Orientale, Inde, Asie Centrale, Extrême-Orient. Publiés par l'Académie des Inscriptions et Belles-Lettres, sous la direction de Mm. [Émile] Senart (1847-1928), [Auguste] Barth (1834-1916), [Édouard] Chavannes (1865-1918), [Henri] Cordier (1849-1925), membres de l'Institut. Tome premier. Paris: Ernest Leroux, Éditeur, 1913.

Mian ye tushuo. 8 juan. 2 vols. [on double-leaves; stitch-bound, Oriental style] in 1 case. Beijing: Nong gongshang bu, 1911.
《棉業圖說》・八卷・[綫裝二冊一函]・北京：農工商部，宣統三年三月印刷科印・

Miaofa lianhua jing tulu (A Special Exhibition of Illustrations of the "Lotus Sutra"). Compiled and edited by Guoli gugong bowu yuan bianji weiyuan hui. [In Chinese; added title page, introductory essay, and list of plates also in English. English translation by Jing Chongyi (Dora C.Y. Ching).] Exhibition catalogue [Guoli gugong bowu yuan (National Palace Museum), Taibei, 1995]. Taibei: Guoli gugong bowu yuan, 1995.
《妙法蓮花經圖錄》・編輯部：國立故宮博物院編輯委員會・[英文翻譯：經崇儀]・[特展圖錄・國立故宮博物院・台北・民國八十四年]・台北：國立故宮博物院，民國八十四年元月初版・

Ming dai banben tulu chu bian. [12 juan.] Compiled by Pan Chengbi and Gu Tinglong. 4 vols. [on double-leaves; stitch-bound, Oriental style] in 1 case. Qi Lu daxue guoxue yanjiu suo zhuanzhu huibian, no. 4. N.p. [Shanghai]: Kaiming shudian, n.d. [1941].
《明代版本圖錄初編》・[十二卷]・編著者：潘承弼、顧廷龍・《齊魯大學國學研究所專著彙編之四》・[綫裝四冊一函]・[上海]・開明書店，[民國三十年]・

Ming dai banhua xuan: Chu ji. Compiled and edited by Chang Bide. 2 vols. [on double-leaves; stitch-bound, Oriental style] in 1 case. Taibei: Guoli zhongyang tushu guan, 1969.
《明代版畫選：初輯》・編纂者：昌彼得・[綫裝二冊一函]・台北：國立中央圖書館，民國五十八年三月初版・

Ming dai banhua yishu tushu tezhan zhuanji (Exhibition of Graphic Art in Printed Books of the Ming Dynasty). Edited by Guoli zhongyang tushu guan (National Central Library). Sponsored by Xingzheng yuan

wenhua jianshe weiyuan hui (Council for Cultural Planning and Development, Executive Yuan). Organized by Guoli zhongyang tushu guan (National Central Library). [Chief editor: Pan Yuanshi (P'an Yuan-shih). English translator: Andrew Morton (Mou Ande).] Exhibition catalogue [Guoli zhongyang tushu guan (National Central Library), Taibei, December 23, 1989-January 8, 1990]. Taibei: Guoli zhongyang tushu guan (National Central Library), 1989.
《明代版畫藝術圖書特展專輯》‧國立中央圖書館編‧[策劃主辦單位：行政院文化建設委員會‧承辦單位：國立中央圖書館‧執行主編：潘元石‧英譯：牟安德‧特展圖錄‧國立中央圖書館‧台北‧民國78年12月23日—79年1月8日]‧台北：國立中央圖書館，民國七十八年十二月‧

Ming dai banke zonglu. 8 juan. [Appended by *Ming dai banke zonglu shuming suoyin.*] Compiled and edited by Du Xinfu. Reviewed and corrected by Zhou Guangpei and Jiang Xiaoda. 8 vols. [on double-leaves; stitch-bound, Oriental style] in 1 case. Yangzhou: Jiangsu Guangling guji keyin she, 1983.
《明代版刻綜錄》‧八卷‧[附《明代版刻綜錄書名索引》]‧杜信孚纂輯‧周光培、蔣孝達參校‧[線裝八册一函]‧揚州：江蘇廣陵古籍刻印社，一九八三年五月第一版‧

Ming Rongyu tang ke Shuihu zhuan tu. Compiled and edited by Zhonghua shuju Shanghai bianji suo. [Introductory remarks by Zhonghua shuju Shanghai bianji suo.] [Facsimile reproduction of illustrations from the copy in the possession of the Beijing tushu guan.] [On double-leaves; stitch-bound, Oriental style.] Beijing: Zhonghua shuju, 1965.
《明容與堂刻水滸傳圖》‧中華書局上海編輯所編輯‧[公元一九六五年十月中華書局上海編輯所據北京圖書館藏本影印版匡尺寸悉準原書]‧[出版說明：中華書局上海編輯所，一九六五年八月]‧[線裝一册]‧北京：中華書局，一九六五年十二月第一版‧

Mish, John L. (1909-1983). "A Manchu-Chinese Scroll." *Bulletin of The New York Public Library* 52, no. 3 (March 1948): 143-144.

————. "An Early Manchu-Chinese Patent of Nobility." *Monumenta Nipponica* 10, nos. 1-2 (April 1954): 270-276.

Mizuho no kuni Nihon: Shiki kôsakuzu no sekai. By Reizei Tamehito (1944-), Kôno Michiaki (1938-), Iwasaki Takehito (1958-), [Namiki Seishi (1955-)]. Kyoto: Tankôsha, 1996.
《瑞穂の国‧日本—四季耕作図の世界》‧著者：冷泉為人、河野通明、岩崎竹彦、並木誠士‧京都：淡交社，1996年12月23日初版発行‧

Mizuno, Kôgen (1901-). *Buddhist Sutras: Origin, Development, Transmission.* Tokyo: Kôsei Publishing Co., 1982.

Montell, Gösta (1899-). "Kêng chih t'u: 'Illustrations of Husbandry

and Weaving.'" *Ethnos* 5, nos. 3-4 (1940): 165-183.

Morgan, David. *The Mongols.* The Peoples of Europe, edited by James Campbell and Barry Cunliffe. Cambridge, Mass. and Oxford: Blackwell Publishers, Inc., 1986 [1998 printing].

Mote, Frederick W. (1922-). "A Millienium of Chinese Urban History: Form, Time and Space Concept in Soochow." *Rice University Studies* 59, no. 4 (1973): 35-65.

————, and Hung-lam Chu. *Calligraphy and the East Asian Book.* With the collaboration of Ch'en Pao-chen, W.F. Anita Siu, and Richard Kent. Edited by Howard L. Goodman. Exhibition catalogue [The Art Museum, Princeton University, Princeton, N.J., 1988]. Boston and Shaftesbury, Dorset, Eng.: Shambhala Publications, Inc., 1988.

Moule, A.C. [Arthur Christopher] (1873-1957). "A Version of the Book of Vermilion Fish." *T'oung Pao* 39, livr. 1-3 (1949): 1-82.

Mu, Xiaotian. "Shizhu zhai de banhua yishu." In *Shizhu zhai yanjiu wenji: "Shizhu zhai shuhua pu" kanxing sanbai liushi nian jinian,* compiled by Shizhu zhai yishu yanjiu bu, 63-65. Nanjing: Shizhu zhai yishu yanjiu bu, 1987.
穆孝天‧〈十竹齋的版畫藝術〉‧《十竹齋研究文集：〈十竹齋書畫譜〉刊行三百六十年紀念》‧十竹齋藝術研究部編‧南京：十竹齋藝術研究部，一九八七年十月‧第六十三頁至第六十五頁‧

Mukherji, Durga Das, ed. *Aryamanjusrinamasangiti: Sanskrit & Tibetan Texts.* [In Sanskrit and Tibetan; introductory matter and some notes in English.] Calcutta: University of Calcutta, 1963.

Mulian jiu mu quan shan xiwen. [Compiled by Zheng Zhizhen (fl. 1582).] 3 vols. Quan Ming chuanqi, [no. 68]. Zhongguo xiju yanjiu ziliao, ser. 1. Editor-in-chief: Lin Youshi. Taibei: Tianyi chuban she, n.d. [1983].
《目連救母勸善戲文》‧[鄭之珍撰]‧[全三册]‧〈全明傳奇〉‧[第六十八部]‧〈中國戲劇研究資料第一輯〉‧主編：林侑蒔‧台北：天一出版社，[民國七十二年]‧

Müller, F. Max [Friedrich Max] (1823-1900), and Bunyiu Nanjio [Nanjô Bunyû] (1849-1927), eds. *The Ancient Palm-Leaves Containing the Pragna-paramita-hridaya-sutra and the Ushnisha-vigaya-dharani.* With an appendix by G. [Georg] Bühler (1837-1898). Anecdota Oxoniensia: Texts, Documents, and Extracts Chiefly from Manuscripts in the Bodleian and Other Oxford Libraries, Aryan Series, vol. 1, pt. 3. Oxford: The Clarendon Press, 1884.

Müller, Marie-Pierre. ""Problèmes de l'étude du commerce du livre." In *Le livre et l'imprimerie en Extrême-Orient et en Asie du Sud: Actes du Colloque organisé à Paris du 9 au 11 mars 1983,* préparés par Jean-Pierre

Drège, Mitchiko Ishigami-Iagolnitzer et Monique Cohen, 87-92. [Revue française d'histoire du livre, nos. 42-43.] Bordeaux: Société des Bibliophiles de Guyenne, 1986.

Murano, Senchu, trans. *The Sutra of the Lotus Flower of the Wonderful Law.* Translated from Kumarajiva's version of the *Saddharmapundarika-sutra* by Senchu Murano. [Title on title page also in Chinese characters: *Miaofa lianhua jing* 妙法蓮華經 .] Tokyo: Nichiren Shu Headquarters, 1974.

Murowchick, Robert E. (1956-), ed. *China: Ancient Culture, Modern Land.* Cradles of Civilization. Norman, Okla.: University of Oklahoma Press, 1994.

Murray, Dian H. (1949-). *Pirates of the South China Coast, 1790-1810.* Stanford, Calif.: Stanford University Press, 1987.

Murray, Julia K. "Gaozong." In *The Dictionary of Art*, edited by Jane Turner, vol. 12, 52. New York: Grove's Dictionaries, Inc., 1996.

—————. "Illustrations of the Life of Confucius: Their Evolution, Functions, and Significance in Late Ming China." *Artibus Asiae* 62, nos. 1-2 (1997): 73-134.

-N-

Nakamura, Kyûshirô. "Gengzhi tu zhong suo jian Song dai zhi fengsu yu Xiyang hua zhi yingxiang." Translated from the Japanese by Zhao Yashu. *Shihuo yuekan (Shih-huo Monthly)* 3, no. 4 (July 1973): 187-194.
中村久四郎・〈耕織圖中所見宋代之風俗與西洋畫之影響〉・趙雅書譯・《食貨月刊》・復刊第三卷・第四期・民國六十二年六月十五日出版・第一百八十七頁至第一百九十四頁・

Nakanishi, Akira. *Writing Systems of the World: Alphabets, Syllabaries, Pictograms.* Rutland, Vt. and Tokyo: Charles E. Tuttle Company, Inc., 1980.

Names of Places on the China Coast and the Yangtze River. 2d issue [2d ed.]. Published by order of the Inspector General of Customs. [At head of title: China. Imperial Maritime Customs. III.–Miscellaneous Series, no. 10.] Shanghai: Published at the Statistical Department of the Inspectorate General of Customs, 1904.

Nanjio, Bunyiu [Nanjô Bunyû] 南條文雄 (1849-1927). *A Catalogue of the Chinese Translation of the Buddhist Tripitaka, the Sacred Canon of the Buddhists in China and Japan, Compiled by Order of the Secretary of State for India.* [Added title page in Japanese: *Dai Min sanzô shôgyô mokuroku* 大明三藏聖教目錄 .] [With double-columned pages, each column being paginated.] Oxford: Clarendon Press, 1883.
《大明三藏聖教目錄》・日本真宗南條文雄譯補・明治十六年癸未鐫・英國牛津大學校印書局刊行・[原著者：南條文雄・著作權相續者：南條文英・訂補者代表：常盤大定・東京：南條博士記念刊行會，昭和四年五月拾日發行]・

Nan yue zhi. 26 *juan.* Originally compiled by Li Yuandu (1821-1887). Edited by Wang Xiangyu and Ouyang Qian. Preface by Guo Songshou dated 1883. [Appended by: *Zengbu Nan yue zhi.* 2 *juan.* Compiled by Li Zirong. Edited by Zheng Fukang. Recompiled by Wang Xiangyu and Ouyang Qian. Preface by Chen Jiayan dated 1923.] [Appended by: *Xu zeng Nan yue zhi wenji.* 2 *juan.* Compiled by Wang Xiangyu. Edited by Li Zirong and Zheng Fukang. Supplement by Wang Xiangyu. Postscript by Tan Dejun dated 1924.] Reprint. Haiwang cun guji congkan. N.p. [Beijing]: Zhongguo shudian, 1990.
《南嶽誌》[《南嶽志》]・二十六卷・李元度原輯・王香余、歐陽謙校刊・清光緒九年郭嵩燾序・[附《增補南嶽志》]・二卷・李子榮編次・鄭阜康參閱・王香余、歐陽謙全輯・民國十二年陳嘉序]・[附《續增南嶽志文集》・二卷・王香余撰・李子榮、鄭阜康鑒定・王香余補輯・書後民國十三年譚德峻撰]・[影印版]・〈海王古籍叢刊〉・[北京]：中國書店，1990年12月第1版・

Naquin, Susan, and Evelyn S. [Evelyn Sakakida] Rawski. *Chinese Society in the Eighteenth Century.* New Haven and London: Yale University Press, 1987.

The National Library of Peiping and Its Activities. Beiping: National Library of Peiping, 1931.

Naxi xiangxing wenzi pu. Compiled by Fang Guoyu. Edited by He Zhiwu. 2d ed. Kunming: Yunnan renmin chuban she, 1995.
《納西象形文字譜》・方國瑜編撰・和志武參訂・[精裝一册]・昆明：雲南人民出版社，1995年10月第2版第3次印刷・

Naxi zu yanjiu lunwen ji. Edited by Guo Dalie. Beijing: Minzu chuban she, 1992.
《納西族研究論文集》・郭大烈編・北京：民族出版社，1992年10月第1版・

Needham, Joseph (1900-1994). *Science and Civilisation in China.* With the research assistance of Wang Ling [et al.]. Vol. 1, *Introductory Orientations* [1954 (reprinted 1961). Vol. 3, *Mathematics and the Sciences of the Heavens and the Earth* [1959]. Vol. 5, *Chemistry and Chemical Technology*, pt. 1, *Paper and Printing*, by Tsien Tsuen-hsuin [Qian Cunxun] [1985], pt. 2, *Spagyrical Discovery and Invention: Magisteries of Gold and Immortality* [1974], pt. 3, *Spagyrical Discovery and Invention: Historical Survey, from Cinnabar Elixirs to Synthetic Insulin* [1976], pt. 4, *Spagyrical*

Discovery and Invention: Apparatus, Theories and Gifts [1980], pt. 9, *Textile Technology: Spinning and Reeling*, by Dieter Kuhn [1988]. Vol. 6, *Biology and Biological Technology*, pt. 1, *Botany*, with the collaboration of Lu Gwei-djen and a special contribution by Huang Hsing-tsung [1986], pt. 2, *Agriculture*, by Francesca Bray [1984]. Cambridge and New York: Cambridge University Press, 1954-[continuing].

Nelson, Howard G.H. "Maps from Old Cathay." *The Geographical Magazine* 47, no. 11 (August 1975): 702-711.

———. "Manchu Books: An Exhibition at the British Library From 1 March to 30 June 1977." *Manchu Studies Newsletter*, nos. 1-2 (1977-1978): 43-54.

Ni ma'i 'od zer / Naran-u gerel: Die Biographie des 2. Pekinger lCan skya-Qutuqtu Rol pa'i rdo rje (1717-1786). Herausgegeben, eingeleitet und zusammengefaßt von Hans-Rainer Kämpfe. Monumenta Tibetica Historica, herausgegeben von D. Schuh et al. [L. Petech, R.A. Stein, G. Uray, R.O. Meisezahl, H.R. Kämpfe], Abteilung 2: Vitae, herausgegeben von L. Petech, Bd. 1. Sankt-Augustin, Germany: VGH [Vereinigung für Geschichtswissenschaft Hochasiens] Wissenschaftsverlag GmbH, 1976.

Nie, Hongyin 聶鴻音. "Tangutology during the Past Decades." *Monumenta Serica* 41 (1993): 329-347.

Nienhauser, William H., ed. and comp. *The Indiana Companion to Traditional Chinese Literature*. 2 vols. [Vol. 1, Charles Hartman, associate editor for poetry; Y.W. Ma, associate editor for fiction; Stephen H. West (1944-), associate editor for drama (1986; reissued 1998); vol. 2, Charles Hartman, associate editor; Scott W. Galer, assistant editor (1998).] Bloomington, Ind. and Indianapolis: Indiana University Press, 1986-1998.

Nisanjû nendai Chûgoku to tôzai bungei: Ashida Takaaki kyôju kinen ronbunshû. Compiled by Nisanjû nendai Chûgoku to tôzai bungei: Ashida Takaaki kyôju kinen ronbunshû iinkai. Tokyo: Tôhô shoten, 1998.
《二三十年代中国と東西文芸：蘆田孝昭教授退休紀念論文集》・編者：蘆田孝昭教授退休紀念論文集編集委員会・東京：東方書店，一九九八年一二月一二日初版第一刷発行・

Nishida, Tatsuo (1928-). *Seikago no kenkyû: Seikago no saikôsei to Seika moji no kaidoku (A Study of the Hsi-hsia Language: Reconstruction of the Hsi-hsia Language and Decipherment of the Hsi-hsia Script)*. 2 vols. [Vol. 1 (1964); vol. 2 (1966)]. [In Japanese; summary and decipherment of the Hsi-hsia script also in English: vol. 2, 509-600, "A Study of Hsi-hsia Language: Reconstruction of the Hsi-hsia Language and Decipherment

of the Hsi-hsia Script"; English summary and English translations of the Hsi-hsia works undertaken by Philip Yampolsky and Burton Watson.] Tokyo: Zayûhô kankôkai (The Zauho Press), 1964-1966.
《西夏語の研究：西夏語の再構成と西夏文字の解読》・西田龍雄著・[上、下巻]・東京：座右宝刊行会，昭和39年6月30日発行[上巻]，昭和41年4月10日発行[下巻]・

———. *Seika moji no hanashi: Shiruku rôdo no nazo*. Tokyo: Taishûkan shoten, 1989.
《西夏文字話》・西田龍雄著・東京：大修館書店，1989年2月15日初版　行・

Nivison, David Shepherd. "The Classical Philosophical Writings." In *The Cambridge History of Ancient China: From the Origins of Civilization to 221 B.C.*, edited by Michael Loewe and Edward L. Shaughnessy (1952-), 745-812. Cambridge and New York: Cambridge University Press, 1998.

Norman, Jerry (1936-). *A Concise Manchu-English Lexicon*. Publications on Asia of the School of International Studies, no. 32. Seattle and London: University of Washington Press, 1978.

Nouvelles contributions aux études de Touen-houang. Sous la direction de Michel Soymié. Ouvrage publié avec le concours du Centre National de la Recherche Scientifique. Centre de Recherches d'Histoire et de Philologie de la IVe Section de l'École pratique des Hautes Études, no. 2. Hautes Études Orientales, no. 17. [Publication de l'Équipe de Recherche associée au Centre National de la Recherche Scientifique, E.R.A. 438, Documents de Touen-houang.] Geneva: Librairie Droz S.A., 1981.

Nyanaponika, Thera, and Hellmuth Hecker. *Great Disciples of the Buddha: Their Lives, Their Works, Their Legacy*. Edited with an introduction by Bhikkhu Bodhi. Boston: Wisdom Publications, in collaboration with Kandy, Sri Lanka: Buddhist Publication Society, 1997.

Nylan, Michael. "Calligraphy, the Sacred Text and Test of Culture." In *Character & Context in Chinese Calligraphy*, edited by Cary [Cary Yee-Wei] Liu (1955-), Dora C.Y. Ching, and Judith G. Smith (1941-), 16-77. Princeton, N.J.: The Art Museum, Princeton University, 1999.

-O-

Oertling, Sewall Jerome, II. "Ting Yün-p'eng: A Chinese Artist of the Late Ming Dynasty." Ph.D. diss., The University of Michigan, 1980. UMI Order No.: 8025740.

Oetke, Claus. *Die aus dem chinesischen Übersetzten tibetischen Versionen des Suvarnaprabhasasutra: Philologische und linguistische Beiträge zur klassifizierenden Charakterisierunf übersetzter Texte*. Alt- und Neu-Indische Studien, herausgegeben vom Seminar für Kultur und Geschichte Indiens an der Universität Hamburg, no. 18. Wiesbaden, Germany: Franz Steiner Verlag GmbH, 1977.

Oldenburg, Sergei Fedorovich (1863-1934), ed. *Sbornik izobrazhenii 300 burkhanov po albomu aziatskago muzeia*. Bibliotheca Buddhica, no. 5. [Introduction in Russian.] St. Petersburg: Impr. de l'Académie Impériale des Sciences, 1903. Reprint. Delhi: Motilal Banarsidass Publishers Private Limited, 1992.

Oppitz, Michael. *Naxi: Dinge, Mythen, Piktogramme*. Mit Zeichen in Bilderschrift von Mu Chen. Zürich: Völkerkundemuseum Zürich, 1997.

Otani, Takeo. "Gengzhi tu zhi yanjiu." Translated from the Japanese by Zhao Yashu. *Shihuo yuekan (Shih-huo Monthly)* 3, no. 5 (August 1973): 220-227.
大健夫・〈耕織圖之研究〉・趙雅書譯・《食貨月刊》・復刊第三卷・第五期・民國六十二年八月十五日出版・第二百二十頁至第二百二十七頁・

-P-

Paine, Robert, Jr. "The Ten Bamboo Studio: Its Early Editions, Pictures, and Artists." *Archives of the Chinese Art Society of America* 5 (1951): 39-54.

Pal, Pratapaditya (1935-), and Julia Meech-Pekarik. *Buddhist Book Illuminations*. [Issued in slipcase.] New York: Ravi Kumar Publishers; New York: Hacker Art Books, Inc., 1988.

Palm-leaf and Other Manuscripts in Indian Languages (Proceedings of the National Seminar). General editors: Shu Hikosaka, G. John Samuel. Editors: A. Pandurangam, P. Maruthanayagam. 11th, 12th and 13th January 1995 at Pondicherry University. Organised jointly by Institute of Asian Studies and Pondicherry University. [Editorial assistance: V. Ganesan, J. Kalpana.] [Institute of Asian Studies, Publication no. 42.] Madras: Institute of Asian Studies, 1996.

Palmieri, Richard P. "Tibetan Xylography and the Question of Movable Type." *Technology and Culture* 32, no. 1 (January 1991): 82-90.

Pan, Jixing. *Zhongguo zao zhi jishu shi gao*. Beijing: Wenwu chuban she, 1979.

《中國造紙技術史稿》・潘吉星著・北京：文物出版社，1979 年 3 月第一版・

————. "The Invention and Development of Papermaking." In *Ancient China's Technology and Science*, compiled by the Institute of the History of Natural Sciences, Chinese Academy of Sciences, 176-183. China Knowledge Series. Beijing: Foreign Languages Press, 1983.

————. "The Origin of Papermaking in the Light of Scientific Research on Recent Archaeological Discoveries." In *Chinese Studies: Papers Presented at a Colloquium at the School of Oriental and African Studies, University of London, 24-26 August 1987*, edited by Frances Wood (1948-), 176-180. British Library Occasional Papers, no. 10. London: The British Library, 1988.

————. "Yinshua shu de qiyuan di: Hanguo haishi Zhongguo" *Ziran kexue shi yanjiu (Studies in the History of Natural Sciences)* 16, no. 1 (1997): 50-68 [includes abstract in English, "The Birthplace of Printing: Korea or China", 66-68].
潘吉星・〈印刷術的起源地：韓國還是中國？〉・《自然科學史研究》・第 16 卷・第 1 期・（1997 年）・第五十頁至第六十八頁・

Pan, Yuanshi. "Shizhu zhai shuhua pu." In *Ming dai banhua yishu tushu tezhan zhuanji (Exhibition of Graphic Art in Printed Books of the Ming Dynasty)*, edited by Guoli zhongyang tushu guan (National Central Library), 230-247, accompanied by abstract in English, "The Graphic Art Album Shih Chu Chai Shu-hua P'u" [translated from the Chinese by Andrew Morton], 340-341. Exhibition catalogue [Guoli zhongyang tushu guan (National Central Library), Taibei, December 23, 1989-January 8, 1990]. Taibei: Guoli zhongyang tushu guan (National Central Library), 1989.
潘元石・〈十竹齋書畫譜〉・《明代版畫藝術圖書特展專輯》・國立中央圖書館編・[策劃主辦單位：行政院文化建設委員會・承辦單位：國立中央圖書館・執行主編：潘元石・英譯：牟安德・特展圖錄・國立中央圖書館・台北・民國年月日一年月日]・台北：國立中央圖書館，民國七十八年十二月・第二百三十頁至第二百四十七頁・英文提要・第三百四十頁至第三百四十一頁・

Pang, Tatiana A. *A Catalogue of Manchu Materials in Paris: Manuscripts, Blockprints, Scrolls, Rubbings, Weapons*. Wiesbaden, Germany: Harrassowitz Verlag in Kommission, 1998.

Peake, Cyrus H. "The Origin and Development of Printing in China in the Light of Recent Research." *Gutenberg-Jahrbuch* [10. Jahrgang] (1935): 9-17.

————. "Additional Notes and Bibliography on the History of Printing in the Far East." *Gutenberg-Jahrbuch* [14. Jahrgang] (1939): 57-61.

Pekin toshokan zô Tonkô isho sômokuroku. Compiled and edited by Nakata

Tokurô. Revised by Inokuchi Taijun. Kyoto: Hôyû shoten, 1989. 《北京圖書館藏敦煌遺書目錄》・中田篤郎編・井口泰淳監修・京都：朋友書店，一九八九年十二月十日發行・

Pelliot, Paul (1878-1945). "À propos du 'Keng tche t'ou.'" In *Mémoires concernant l'Asie Orientale, Inde, Asie Centrale, Extrême-Orient,* publiés par l'Académie des Inscriptions et Belles-Lettres, sous la direction de Mm. Senart, Barth, Chavannes, Cordier, membres de l'Institut, tome premier, 65-122, and pls. 10-61. Paris: Ernest Leroux, Éditeur, 1913.

———. *Les débuts de l'imprimerie en Chine.* Œuvres posthumes de Paul Pelliot, no. 4, publiées sous les auspices de l'Académie des Inscriptions et Belles-Lettres et avec le concours du Centre National de la Recherche Scientifique. [Avertissement par Robert des Rotours.] Paris: Imprimerie Nationale; Paris: Librairie d'Amérique et d'Orient Adrien-Maisonneuve, 1953.

Perkins, Dorothy. *Encyclopedia of China: The Essential Reference to China, Its History and Culture.* A Roundtable Press Book. New York: Facts On File, Inc., 1999.

Petech, Luciano. *China and Tibet in the Early XVIIIth Century: History of the Establishment of Chinese Protectorate in Tibet.* 2d rev. ed., with 2 folding maps. T'oung Pao Monographies, no. 1. Leiden: E.J. Brill, 1972.

Petrucci, Raphael (1872-1917), trans. and comm. *Le Kie tseu yuan houa tchouan: Traduit et commenté par R. Petrucci: Introduction générale.* Leiden: E.J. Brill, 1912.

Pfandt, Peter, comp. *Mahayana Texts Translated into Western Languages: A Bibliographical Guide.* Compiled by Peter Pfandt on behalf of the Religionswissenschaftliches Seminar der Universität Bonn. Bonn, Germany: The Director, Religionswissenschaftliches Seminar der Universität Bonn, in Kommission bei Cologne: E.J. Brill, 1983.

Pimpaneau, Jacques. *Promenade au Jardin des Poiriers: L'opéra chinois classique.* Ouvrage publié avec le concours de la Caisse Nationale des Lettres. Paris: Musée Kwok On, 1983.

Piotrovsky, Mikhail, ed. *Lost Empire of the Silk Road: Buddhist Art from Khara Khoto (X-XIIIth Century).* Exhibition catalogue [Fondazione Thyssen-Bornemisza, Villa Favorita, Lugano, Italy, June 25-October 31, 1993]. Lugano, Italy: Thyssen-Bornemisza Foundation [Fondazione Thyssen-Bornemisza]; Milan: Electa, 1993.

Plaks, Andrew H. (1945-). *The Four Masterworks of the Ming Novel.* [Title on title page also in Wade-Giles romanization and in Chinese characters:

Ssu ta ch'i-shu 四大奇書.] Princeton: Princeton University Press, 1987.

Po, Sung-nien, and David [David George] Johnson (1938-). *Domesticated Deities and Auspicious Emblems: The Iconography of Everyday Life in Village China: Popular Prints and Papercuts from the Collection of Po Sung-nien.* Publications of the Chinese Popular Culture Project, no. 2. Exhibition catalogue [Library, Graduate Theological Union, Berkeley, Calif., 1991]. N.p. [Berkeley, Calif.]: N.p. [Chinese Popular Culture Project], 1992.

Pommeranz-Liedtke, Gerhard. *Die Weisheit der Kunst: Chinesische steinabreibungen.* [On double-leaves; bound between cloth-covered boards.] N.p. [Leipzig, Germany]: Erschienen im Insel-Verlag, 1963.

Powers, Martin J. [Martin Joseph] (1949-). "Pictorial Art and Its Public in Early Imperial China." *Art History* 7, no. 2 (June 1984): 135-163.

———. *Art and Political Expression in Early China.* New Haven and London: Yale University Press, 1991.

Prebish, Charles S. *Historical Dictionary of Buddhism.* Historical Dictionaries of Religions, Philosophies, and Movements, edited by Jon Woronoff, no. 1. Metuchen, N.J. and London: The Scarecrow Press, Inc., 1993.

The Prints of the Ten Bamboo Studio, Followed by Plates from the Kaempfer Series and Perfect Harmony. Presentation and Commentary by Joseph Vedlich. [Title on half-title-page: *The Ten Bamboo Studio: A Chinese Masterpiece.*] [Translated (from the French) by Peter J. Tallon.] N.p.: Crescent Books, a division of Crown Publishers, Inc., 1979.

Proceedings of the Fourth International Conference of Directors of National Libraries in Asia and Oceania, December 5-9, 1989. [Added title page also in Chinese: *Di si jie Yazhou he Dayangzhou guojia tushu guan guanzhang guoji huiyi huiyi lu, 1989 nian 12 yue 5 ri-9 ri, Beijing.*] [Compiled by the National Library of China.] Beijing: National Library of China, 1989. 《第四屆亞洲和大洋洲國家圖書館館長國際會議會議錄・1989年12月5日—9日・北京》・北京：中國國家圖書館，1989年・

Proceedings of the Sixth East Asian Altaistic Conference, December 18-23, 1981, Taipei, China. [Added title page in Chinese: *Di liu jie Dong Ya A'ertai xuehui huiyi jilu.*] Edited by Ch'en Chieh-hsien. Taipei: The Taipei City Government (Taibei shi zhengfu), 1983. 《第六屆東亞阿爾泰學會會議記錄》・陳捷先編・台北：台北市政府，民國七十二年六月印行・

Pulleyblank, Edwin G. [Edwin George] (1922-). *Outline of Classical Chinese Grammar.* Vancouver: UBC Press, 1995.

-Q-

Qian, Cunxun [Tsien Tsuien-hsuin]　錢存訓 (1910-). *Yinshua faming qian de Zhongguo shu he wenzi jilu*. Beijing: Yinshua gongye chuban she, 1988.
《印刷發明前的中國書和文字記錄》・錢存訓著・鄭如斯增訂・[本書系根據周寧森博士之中文譯稿《書與竹帛》增訂而成]・北京：印刷工業出版社，1988年1月第一版・

———. *Zhong Mei shu yuan*. Taibei: Wenhua tushu guan guanli zixun youxian gongsi, 1998.
《中美書緣》・錢存訓著・[精裝、平裝各一冊]・台北：文華圖書館管理資訊有限公司，民國八十七年八月初版・

Qian, Yong. "Pingjiang tu bei." *Wenwu*, no. 102 (1959, no. 2) (February 1959): 49.
錢鏞・〈平江圖碑〉・《文物》・一九五九年第二期・總第一〇二號・第四十九頁・

Qian, Yucheng. "Song ke 'Pingjiang tu' de bili." *Wenwu*, no. 455 (1994, no. 4) (April 1994): 80-81.
錢玉成・〈宋刻《平江圖》的比例〉・《文物》・一九九四年第四期・總第四五五號・第八十頁至第八十一頁・

Qian, Zheng, and Yao Shiying. "Dili tu bei." In *Zhongguo gudai ditu ji: Zhan guo-Yuan [(An Atlas of Ancient Maps in China–From the Warring States to the Yuan Dynasty (476 B.C.-A.D. 1368)]*, edited by Cao Wanru, Zheng Xihuang, Huang Shengzhang, Niu Zhongxun, Ren Jincheng, and Ju Deyuan, text section, 46-49, with summary in English, "The Tablet of the Geographic Map ('Di li tu bei')," 110. Beijing: Wenwu chuban she (Cultural Relics Publishing House), 1990.
錢正、姚世英・〈墬理圖碑〉・《中國古代地圖集：戰國—元》・曹婉如、鄭錫煌、黃盛璋、鈕仲勛、任金城、鞠德源編・北京：文物出版社，1990年7月第1版・第四十六頁至第四十九頁・英文提要・第一百十頁・

Qin Han wadang (Eave Tiles of the Qin and Han Dynasties). Compiled and edited by Xi'an shi wenwu guanli weiyuan hui (Xian Municipal Administrative Commission for Cultural Relics). [Preface by Fu Jiayi; explanatory notes by Wang Hanzhen; photography by Zheng Yianyu; translations by Mu Shanpei and Zhou Shizhong.] Shaanxi gudai meishu xunli (Shaanxi Ancient Fine Arts Series), no. 5. [In Chinese and English.] N.p. [Xi'an]: Shaanxi renmin meishu chuban she, [title page dated 1984] 1985.
《秦漢瓦當》・西安市文物管理委員會編・傅嘉儀撰序・王漢珍圖版解說・鄭天禹攝影・穆善培、周式中翻譯・〈陝西古代美術巡禮〉，5・[漢英版]・[西安]：陝西人民美術出版社，1985年7月第1版・

Qinding Gujin tushu jicheng. 10,000 *juan*; *mulu* 40 *juan*. Compiled and edited by Jiang Tingxi (1669-1732) et al. [Originally published in Beijing: Wuying dian, 1726.] Reprint [facsimile reproduction; each page represents 9 leaves of the original; with a supplement, *Gujin tushu jicheng kaozheng*, 8 vols.]. 808 vols. [on double-leaves; stitch-bound, Oriental style] in 102 cases. Shanghai: Zhonghua shuju, 1934.
《欽定古今圖書集成》・一萬卷・目錄四十卷・蔣廷錫等奉・[六彙編・三十二典・六千一百九部・共一萬卷・附《古今圖書集成考證》八冊]・[影印本]・以原書九葉合一葉・全線裝八百零八冊一百零二函・上海：中華書局，民國二十三年十月影印・

Qing dai banben tulu. Compiled and edited by Huang Yongnian and Jia Erqiang. Guojia jiaoyu weiyuan hui quanguo gaodeng yuanxiao guji zhengli yanjiu gongzuo weiyuan hui zizhu xiangmu. 5 vols. [on double-leaves; stitch-bound, Oriental style] in 1 case. Hangzhou: Zhejiang renmin chuban she, 1997.
《清代版本圖錄》・黃永年、賈二強撰集・〈國家教育委員會全國高等院校古籍整理研究工作委員會資助項目〉・[線裝五冊一函]・杭州：浙江人民出版社，一九九七年五月第一版・

Qing dai gongting huihua. Chief editor: Nie Chongzheng. Gugong bowu yuan cang wenwu zhenpin quanji, vol. 14. [In Chinese; captions also in English.] Hong Kong: Shangwu yinshu guan [The Commercial Press (Hong Kong) Ltd.], 1996.
《清代宮廷繪畫》・主編：聶崇正・〈故宮博物院藏文物珍品全集〉，14・[精裝一冊]・香港：商務印書館（香港）有限公司，1996年12月第1版・

Qing dai neifu ke shu mulu jieti. Compiled and edited by Gugong bowu yuan tushu guan and Liaoning sheng tushu guan. Beijing: Zijin cheng chuban she, 1995.
《清代內府刻書目錄解題》・故宮博物院圖書館、遼寧省圖書館編著・北京：紫禁城出版社，1995年9月第一版・

Qing dai qi bai mingren zhuan. 6 *bian, fulu* 5 *zhong*. Compiled and edited by Cai Guanluo. Reprint [facsimile reproduction]. In *Qing dai zhuanji congkan [Biographical Collections of Ching Dynasty (1644-1912)]*, compiled and edited by Zhou Junfu [Chow Tsin-fu], vols. 194-196, *Zonglu lei*, no. 9. Taibei: Mingwen shuju (Ming Wen Book Co., Ltd.), 1985.
《清代七百名人傳》・六編附錄五種・蔡冠洛編纂・[影印本]・《清代傳記叢刊》・第一百九十四至第一百九十六冊・〈綜錄類〉・第九部（種）・輯者：周駿富・台北：明文書局，民國七十四年五月十日初版・

Qing dai zhuanji congkan [Biographical Collections of Ching Dynasty (1644-1912)]. [150 *bu* (*zhong*), *fulu* 17 *zhong*.] Compiled and edited by Zhou Junfu [Chow Tsin-fu]. 202 vols. Taibei: Mingwen shuju (Ming Wen Book Co., Ltd.), 1985.
《清代傳記叢刊》・[一百五十部（種）・附錄十七種・輯者：周駿富・[精裝二〇

二冊]・台北：明文書局，民國七十四年五月十日初版・

Qing gong Zang chuan fojiao wenwu (Cultural Relics of Tibetan Buddhism Collected in the Qing Palace). Edited by Gugong bowu yuan (The Palace Museum). [Editorial board: Yang Xin, Wang Jiapeng, Liu Lu, and Hu Jianzhong.] [English translation: Chen Guansheng and Li Peizhu.] Exhibition catalogue [Palace Museum, Beijing, August 1992]. [In Chinese and English.] Beijing: Gugong bowu yuan Zijin cheng chuban she (The Forbidden City Press, The Palace Museum); Hong Kong: Liangmu chuban she (The Woods Publishing Company), 1992.
《清宮藏傳佛教文物》・故宮博物院主編・[編委會：楊新、王家鵬、劉璐、胡建中]・[翻譯：陳觀勝、李培茱]・特展圖錄・〈清宮藏傳佛教藝術展覽〉・故宮博物院・一九九二年八月・北京：故宮博物院紫禁城出版社；香港：兩木出版社，一九九二年八月初版・

Qing gong Zang chuan fojiao wenwu (Cultural Relics of Tibetan Buddhism Collected in the Qing Palace). Edited by Gugong bowu yuan (The Palace Museum). [Editorial board: Yang Xin, Wang Jiapeng, Liu Lu, and Hu Jianzhong.] [English translation: Chen Guansheng and Li Peizhu.] Exhibition catalogue [Palace Museum, Beijing, August 1992]. [In Chinese and English.] 2d ed. Beijing: Zijin cheng chuban she (Forbidden City Publishing House), 1998.
《清宮藏傳佛教文物》・故宮博物院主編・[編委會：楊新、王家鵬、劉璐、胡建中]・[翻譯：陳觀勝、李培茱]・[修訂版]・北京：紫禁城出版社，1998 年 7 月第二版第一次印刷・

Qing neiwu fu zaoban chu yutu fang tumu chubian. Compiled by Guoli Beiping gugong bowu yuan wenxian guan. Beiping: Guoli Beiping gugong bowu yuan wenxian guan, 1936.
《清內務府造辦處輿圖房圖目初編》・編輯者：國立北平故宮博物院文獻館・[平裝一冊]・北平：國立北平故宮博物院文獻館，民國二十五年五月出版・

Qing shi gao liezhuan. 298 *juan*. Compiled by Zhao Erxun (1844-1927) et al. Reprint [facsimile reproduction]. In *Qing dai zhuanji congkan [Biographical Collections of Ching Dynasty (1644-1912)]*, compiled and edited by Zhou Junfu [Chow Tsin-fu], vols. 89-95, *Zonglu lei*, no. 1. Taibei: Mingwen shuju (Ming Wen Book Co., Ltd.), 1985.
《清史稿列傳》・二百九十八卷・趙爾巽等撰・[影印本]・《清代傳記叢刊》・第八十九至第九十五冊・〈綜錄類〉・第一部（種）・輯者：周駿富・台北：明文書局，民國七十四年五月十日初版・

Qing shi liezhuan. 80 *juan*. [Originally compiled by Qing guoshi guan. First published 1928. Reprint (facsimile reproduction) of copy in the possession of the National Palace Museum, Taibei.] Compiled and edited by Taiwan Zhonghua shuju. 2d Taiwan ed. 10 vols. Taibei: Taiwan Zhonghua shuju, 1983.
《清史列傳》・八十卷・[清國史館原編・原出現於民國十七年・據台北國立故宮

博物院影印本]・臺灣中華書局編輯部編・[臺二版]・[全十冊・精裝]・台北：臺灣中華書局，民國七十二年二月臺二版・

Qu, Tunjian. "Ming Qing shiqi Huizhou ke shu jianshu." *Wenxian*, no. 38 (1988, no. 4): 242-251.
瞿屯建・〈明清時期徽州刻書簡述〉・《文獻》・總第三十八期・一九八八年第四期・第二百四十二頁至第二百五十一頁・

-R-

Ramsey, S. Robert (1941-). *The Languages of China*. Princeton: Princeton University Press, 1987.

Rawski, Evelyn S. [Evelyn Sakakida]. *The Last Emperors: A Social History of Qing Imperial Institutions*. A Philip E. Lilienthal Book. Berkeley and Los Angeles: University of California Press, 1998.

Rawson, Jessica. *Chinese Bronzes: Art and Ritual*. Exhibition catalogue [Burrell Collection, Glasgow; Sainsbury Centre for Visual Arts, University of East Anglia]. London: Published for the Trustees of the British Museum in association with the Sainsbury Centre for Visual Arts, University of East Anglia, by British Museum Publications Ltd., 1987.

————. *Western Zhou Ritual Bronzes from the Arthur M. Sackler Collections*. 2 vols. Ancient Chinese Bronzes from the Arthur M. Sackler Collections, vol. 2. [Issued in slipcase.] Washington, D.C.: The Arthur M. Sackler Foundation; Cambridge, Mass.: Arthur M. Sackler Museum, Harvard University, 1990.

————. "Western Zhou Archaeology." In *The Cambridge History of Ancient China: From the Origins of Civilization to 221 B.C.*, edited by Michael Loewe and Edward L. Shaughnessy (1952-), 352-449. Cambridge and New York: Cambridge University Press, 1998.

Ren, Daobin. *Zhao Mengfu xinian*. N.p. [Zhengzhou, Henan]: Henan renmin chuban she, 1984.
《趙孟頫系年》・任道斌著・[鄭州]：河南人民出版社，1984 年 7 月第 1 版・

Rhie, Marylin M., and Robert A.F. Thurman. *Worlds of Transformation: Tibetan Art of Wisdom and Compassion*. Foreword by His Holiness the Dalai Lama. With an essay by David P. Jackson. Senior editor: Robert A.F. Thurman. Editor, art director: Thomas F. Yarnall. Associate Editor: Barbara K. Rona. Rubin Collections Administrator: Moke Mokotoff. New York: Tibet House, in association with The Shelley and Donald

Rubin Foundation, 1999.

Robson, James. "The Southern Marchmount Nanyue Shan: Its Place in Chinese Religious Geography." Master's thesis, University of California, Santa Barbara, 1993.

Rock, Joseph F. [Joseph Francis Charles] (1884-1962). *The Ancient Na-khi Kingdom of Southwest China*. 2 vols. Harvard-Yenching Institute Monograph Series, vols. 8-9. Cambridge, Mass.: Harvard University Press, 1947.

———. *A Na-khi–English Encyclopedic Dictionary*. 2 pts. in 2 vols. Pt. 1 [1963]. Pt. 2, *Gods, Priests, Ceremonies, Stars, Geographical Names* [1972]. Serie Orientale Roma, no. 28, pts. 1-2. Rome: Istituto Italiano per il Medio ed Estremo Oriente, 1963-1972.

Rong, Geng (1894-1983), comp. *Jinwen bian*. [Originally published in 1925. First revised in 1939, then revised again and edited by Zhongguo kexue yuan kaogu yanjiu suo.] Edited by Zhongguo kexue yuan kaogu yanjiu suo. Kaogu xue zhuankan yi zhong, no. 9. Beijing: Kexue chuban she, 1959.
《金文編》・編著者：容庚・[初版本在一九二五年印行・一九三九年再版有所增修，此重印版誤者增訂，中國科學院考古研究所校訂]・編輯者：中國科學院考古研究所・〈考古學專刊乙種第九號〉・北京：科學出版社，1995年5月第一版・

Roosa, Mark. "Naxi Manuscripts Pose Preservation Challenges." *The Library of Congress Information Bulletin* 58, no. 6 (June 1999): 141.

-S-

Samosyuk, Kira Fyodorovna. "The Art of the Tangut Empire: A Historical and Stylistic Interpretation." In *Lost Empire of the Silk Road: Buddhist Art from Khara Khoto (X-XIIIth Century)*, edited by Mikhail Piotrovsky, 59-88. Lugano, Italy: Thyssen-Bornemisza Foundation [Fondazione Thyssen-Bornemisza]; Milan: Electa, 1993.

San bai fo xiang ji. Compiled by Zhangjia Ruobi Duoji [Lcan-skya Rol pa'i rdo rje] (1717-1786). [Reorganized by Lü Tiegang; edited and revised by Chen Qingying.] N.p. [Beijing]: Zhongguo Zang xue chuban she; N.p. [U.S.A.]: Meiguo Zhanwang tushu gongsi, 1994.
《三百佛像集》・章嘉・若必多吉編・[呂鐵鋼整理・陳慶英校訂]・[北京]：中國藏學出版社；[美國]：美國展望圖書公司，1994年3月第1版・

Sanskrit Texts from the Imperial Palace at Peking in the Manchurian, Chinese, Mongolian and Tibetan Scripts. Edited by Lokesh Chandra from the collection of Raghu Vira (1902-1963). 22 pts. Sata-pitaka Series, Indo-Asian Literatures, vol. 71 (pts. 1-22). New Delhi: Institute for the Advancement of Science and Culture, 1966-1976.

Sárközi, Alice, in collaboration with János Szerb. *A Buddhist Terminological Dictionary: The Mongolian "Mahavyutpatti"*. Bibliotheca Orientalis Hungarica, edited by György Hazai, vol. 42. [Also published as vol. 130 of the series *Asiatische Forrschungen* by Harrassowitz Verlag, Wiesbaden, Germany, as a joint edition with Akadémiai Kiadó, Budapest.] Budapest: Akadémiai Kiadó, 1995.

Satô, Kazuyoshi. "'Seisekizu' no rekishi." In *Kôshi gaden: Seisekizu ni miru Kôshi rurô no shôgai to oshie*, by Kaji Nobuyuki (1936-), 160-165. Tokyo: Shûeisha, 1991.
佐藤一好・〈『聖蹟図』の歴史〉・《孔子画伝：聖蹟図にみる孔子流浪の生涯と教之》・著者：加地伸行・東京：集英社，一九九一年三月二十五日第一刷発行・第160頁至第165頁・

Schierlitz, Ernst (1902-). "Zur Technik der Holztypendrucke aus dem Wu-ying-tien in Peking." *Monumenta Serica* 1, fasc. 1 (1935): 17-38.

Schlegel, Gustav [Gustaaf] (1840-1903), and Erwin Ritter von Zach (1872-1942). "Zwei Mandschu-Chinesische kaiserliche Diplome." *T'oung Pao*, [ser. 1], vol. 8 (1897): 261-308, accompanied by foldout illustration.

Schmidt, J.D. [Jerry Dean] (1946-). "Ching chü." In *The Indiana Companion to Traditional Chinese Literature*, edited and compiled by William H. Nienhauser, Jr., vol. 1, 316-318 [see also updated bibliography in vol. 2, 292]. Bloomington, Ind. and Indianapolis: Indiana University Press, 1986-1998.

Schubert, Johannes. "Typographia Tibetana." *Gutenberg-Jahrbuch* [25. Jahrgang] (1950): 280-298.

"Seishôki to Mindai no sashiebon" ten [Exhibition of the "Hsi-hsiang chi" ("Seishôki") and illustrated books of the Ming period]. Compiled and edited by Machida shiritsu kokusai hanga bijutsukan [Machida City Museum of Graphic Arts]. [With an essay by Chang Kuo-feng, "'Seishôki' no rekishi" (translated from the Chinese), unpaginated, preceding section with color plates.] Exhibition catalogue [Machida shiritsu kokusai hanga bijutsukan (Machida City Museum of Graphic Arts), Machida, Japan, 1993]. Machida, Japan: Machida shiritsu kokusai hanga bijutsukan [Machida City Museum of Graphic Arts], 1993.
《「西廂記と明代の挿絵本」展》・編集：町田市立国際版画美術館・[張国風・〈『西廂記』の歴史〉・訳：仲祐理子]・東京都町田市：町田市立国際版画美術館，1993年発行・

Shanben cangshu yinzhang xuancui. Compiled by Guoli zhongyang tushu

guan tecang zu. Taibei: Guoli zhongyang tushu guan, 1988.
《善本藏書印章選粹》‧編輯者：國立中央圖書館特藏組‧台北：國立中央圖書館，民國七十七年六月初版‧

Shang Zhou gu wenzi duben. Compiled and edited by Liu Hsiang et al. [Chen Kang, Chen Chusheng, and Dong Kun]. Checked by Li Xueqin. Beijing: Yuwen chuban she, 1989.
《商周古文字讀本》‧劉翔、陳抗、陳初生、董琨編著‧李學勤審訂‧北京：語文出版社，1989 年 9 月第 1 版‧

Shang Zhou qingtong qi mingwen xuan. Compiled by Shanghai bowu guan Shang Zhou qingtong qi mingwen xuan bianxie zu. 4 vols. Vol. 1, *Shang, Xi Zhou qingtong qi mingwen* [1986]. Vol. 2, *Dong Zhou qingtong qi mingwen* [1987]. Vol. 3, *Shang, Xi Zhou qingtong qi mingwen shiwen ji zhushi,* edited by Ma Chengyuan; compiled by Chen Peifen, Pan Jianming, Chen Jianmin, and Pu Maozuo [1988]. Vol. 4, *Dong Zhou qingtong qi mingwen shiwen ji zhushi,* edited by Ma Chengyuan; compiled by Chen Peifen, Pan Jianming, Chen Jianmin, and Pu Maozuo [1990]. Beijing: Wenwu chuban she, 1986-1990.
《商周青銅器銘文選》‧上海博物館商周青銅器銘文選編寫組‧[全四冊]‧[第一卷‧〈商、西周青銅器銘文〉]‧[第二卷‧〈東周青銅器銘文〉]‧[第三卷‧〈商、西周青銅器銘文釋文及注釋〉‧主編：馬承源‧編撰：陳佩芬、潘建明、陳建敏、濮茅左]‧[第四卷‧〈東周青銅器銘文釋文及注釋〉‧主編：馬承源‧編撰：陳佩芬、潘建明、陳建敏、濮茅左]‧北京：文物出版社，1986 年 8 月第一版[第一冊]，1987 年 9 月第一版[第二冊]，1988 年 4 月第一版[第三冊]，1990 年 4 月第一版[第四冊]‧

Shanghai bowu guan cang qingtong qi. Compiled and edited by Shanghai bowu guan. 2 vols. Shanghai: Shanghai renmin meishu chuban she, 1964.
《上海博物館藏青銅器》‧上海博物館編‧[精裝全二冊]‧上海：上海人民美術出版社，一九六四年一月第一版‧

Shaughnessy, Edward L. (1952-). *Sources of Western Zhou History: Inscribed Bronze Vessels.* Berkeley and Los Angeles: University of California Press, 1991.

———, ed. *New Sources of Early Chinese History: An Introduction to the Reading of Inscriptions and Manuscripts.* Early China Special Monograph Series, no. 3. N.p. [Bethlehem, Pa.]: The Society for the Study of Early China; Berkeley, Calif.: The Institute of East Asian Studies, University of California, Berkeley, 1997.

———. "Introduction." In *New Sources of Early Chinese History: An Introduction to the Reading of Inscriptions and Manuscripts,* edited by Edward L. Shaughnessy (1952-), 1-14. Early China Special Monograph Series, no. 3. N.p. [Bethlehem, Pa.]: The Society for the Study of Early China; Berkeley, Calif.: The Institute of East Asian Studies, University of California, Berkeley, 1997.

———. "Western Zhou Bronze Inscriptions." In *New Sources of Early Chinese History: An Introduction to the Reading of Inscriptions and Manuscripts,* edited by Edward L. Shaughnessy (1952-), 57-84. Early China Special Monograph Series, no. 3. N.p. [Bethlehem, Pa.]: The Society for the Study of Early China; Berkeley, Calif.: The Institute of East Asian Studies, University of California, Berkeley, 1997.

———. "Calendar and Chronology." In *The Cambridge History of Ancient China: From the Origins of Civilization to 221 B.C.,* edited by Michael Loewe and Edward L. Shaughnessy (1952-), 19-29. Cambridge and New York: Cambridge University Press, 1998.

———. "Western Zhou History." In *The Cambridge History of Ancient China: From the Origins of Civilization to 221 B.C.,* edited by Michael Loewe and Edward L. Shaughnessy (1952-), 292-351. Cambridge and New York: Cambridge University Press, 1998.

Shaw, Shiow-jyu Lu (1944-). *The Imperial Printing of Early Ch'ing China, 1644-1805.* Studies in East Asian Librarianship. Asian Library Series, no. 20. N.p. [San Francisco]: Chinese Materials Center, 1983.

Shen, Jin [Chun Shum] (1945-). *Meiguo Hafo daxue Hafo Yanjing tushu guan Zhongwen shanben shu zhi.* Hafo Yanjing tushu guan shumu congkan [Harvard-Yenching Library Bibliographical Series], no. 7. Shanghai: Shanghai cishu chuban she, 1999.
《美國哈佛大學哈佛燕京圖書館中文善本書志》‧沈津著‧〈哈佛燕京圖書館書目叢刊第七種〉‧上海：上海辭書出版社，1999 年 2 月第 1 版‧

Shen, Tuqi. *Xi hu gujin tan.* Xi hu wenyi congshu. Hangzhou: Zhejiang wenyi chuban she, 1985.
《西湖古今談》‧申屠奇編著‧〈西湖文藝叢書〉‧杭州：浙江文藝出版社，1985 年 5 月第 1 版‧

Shen, Zhiyu. "Ba 'Luoxuan biangu jian pu.'" *Wenwu,* no. 165 (1964, no. 7) (July 1964): 7-9, and pl. 1.
沈之瑜‧〈跋《蘿軒變古箋譜》〉‧《文物》‧一九六四年第七期‧總第一六五號‧第七頁至第九頁，以及圖版壹‧

Sheng ji tu. Compiled and edited by Gong Fada and Xiao Yu. Wuhan: Hubei jiaoyu chuban she, 1994.
《聖蹟圖》‧龔發達、肖玉編‧[平裝一冊]‧武漢：湖北教育出版社，1994 年 9 月第 1 版‧

Sheng ji zonglu. Compiled by Zhao Ji [Emperor Huizong (1082-1135; r. 1101-1125) and eleven members of the Imperial College of Physicians between 1111 and 1118]. 2 vols. Beijing: Renmin weisheng chuban she, 1962 [2d printing, 1982].

《聖濟總錄》・趙佶[宋徽宗]編・[精裝上、下二冊]・北京：人民衛生出版社，1962 年 10 月第 1 版，1982 年 3 月第 1 版第 2 次印刷・

Shi, Anchang. "Guanyu Wu Zetian zao zi de wushi yu jiegou." *Gugong bowu yuan yuankan (Palace Museum Journal)*, no. 26 (1984, no. 4): 84-90.
施安昌・〈關於武則天造字的誤識與結構〉・《故宮博物院院刊》・總第二十六期・一九八四年第四期・第八十四頁至第九十頁・

———. "Dunhuang xie jing duandai fafan, jian lundi bian zi qun de guilü." *Gugong bowu yuan yuankan (Palace Museum Journal)*, no. 30 (1985, no. 4): 58-66.
施安昌・〈敦煌寫經斷代發凡—兼論敵變字群的規律〉・《故宮博物院院刊》・總第二十六期・一九八四年第四期・第八十四頁至第九十頁・

Shi, Dingxu. "The Yi Script." In *The World's Writing Systems*, edited by Peter T. Daniels (1951-) and William Bright (1928-), 239-243. New York and Oxford: Oxford University Press, 1996.

Shi Nai'an (ca. 1290-ca. 1365), and Luo Guanzhong (ca. 1330-ca. 1400). *Outlaws of the Marsh: An Abridged Version*. Translated [from the Chinese] by Sidney Shapiro. [Based on the unabridged version of *Outlaws of the Marsh* published by the Foreign Languages Press, Beijing, 1980.] Hong Kong: The Commercial Press (Hong Kong) Ltd., 1986 [4th impression, 1996].

———, and Luo Guanzhong (ca. 1330-ca. 1400). *Rongyu tang ben Shuihu zhuan*. Edited and punctuated by Ling Geng, Heng He, and Diao Ning. 2 vols. Shanghai: Shanghai guji chuban she, 1988.
《容與堂本水滸傳》・施耐庵、羅貫中著・凌賡、恆鶴、刁寧校點・[全二冊・精裝]・上海：上海古籍出版社，1988 年 11 月第 1 版・

Shi, Jinbo. *Xi Xia fojiao shi lüe*. Yinzhou, Ningxia: Ningxia renmin chuban she, 1988.
《西夏佛教史略》・史金波著・銀州：寧夏人民出版社，1988 年 8 月第 1 版・

Shi, Tingyong. *Zhongguo guji banben gaiyao*. Edited by Zhang Xiumin. Tianjin: Tianjin guji chuban she,1987.
《中國古籍版本概要》・施廷鏞著・張秀民校・天津：天津古籍出版社，1987 年 8 月第 1 版・

Shi'er yan zhai jinshi guoyan lu. 18 *juan*. With supplement, *Shi'er yan zhai jinshi guoyan xu lu*, 6 *juan*. Compiled and edited by Wang Yun (1816-). [Preface by Wang Yun dated 1886.] Reprint. 8 vols. [on doubleleaves; stitch-bound, Oriental style] in 1 case. Yangzhou: Chen Henghe shulin, 1931.
《十二硯齋金石過眼錄》・十八卷・附《十二硯齋金石過眼續錄》・六卷・汪鋆編輯・[綫裝八冊一函]・揚州：陳恒和書林，民國二十年藏板・

Shih, Chung-wen. *The Golden Age of Chinese Drama: Yüan "Tsa-chü"*. Princeton University Press, 1976.

Shike shiliao xin bian. Compiled by Xinwenfeng chuban gongsi bianji bu. 30 vols. Taibei: Xinwenfeng chuban gongsi, 1977.
《石刻史料新編》・編輯者：新文豐出版公司編輯部・[精裝全三十冊]・台北：新文豐出版公司，民國六十六年十二月初版・

Shike shiliao xin bian: Di er ji. Compiled by Xinwenfeng chuban gongsi bianji bu. 20 vols. Taibei: Xinwenfeng chuban gongsi, 1979.
《石刻史料新編：第二輯》・編輯者：新文豐出版公司編輯部・[精裝全二十冊]・台北：新文豐出版公司，民國六十八年六月初版・

Shike shiliao xin bian: Di san ji. Compiled by Xinwenfeng chuban gongsi bianji bu. 40 vols. Taibei: Xinwenfeng chuban gongsi, 1986.
《石刻史料新編：第三輯》・編輯者：新文豐出版公司編輯部・[精裝全四十冊]・台北：新文豐出版公司，民國七十五年七月台一版・

Shike tiba suoyin. Edited by Yang Dianxun. Rev. ed. [originally published 1941]. Shanghai: Shangwu yinshu guan, 1957.
《石刻題跋索引》・楊殿珣編・[增訂本]・上海：商務印書館，1941 年 9 月初版，1957 年 11 月重印第 1 版・

Shizhu zhai yanjiu wenji: "Shizhu zhai shuhua pu" kanxing sanbai liushi nian jinian. Compiled by Shizhu zhai yishu yanjiu bu. Nanjing: Shizhu zhai yishu yanjiu bu, 1987.
《十竹齋研究文集：〈十竹齋書畫譜〉刊行三百六十年紀念》・十竹齋藝術研究部編・南京：十竹齋藝術研究部，一九八七年十月・

A Short Sketch of the National Library of Peiping. Beiping: National Library of Peiping, 1931.

Shuihu yanjiu lunwen ji. Edited by Zuojia chuban she bianji bu. Beijing: Zuojia chuban she, 1957.
《水滸研究論文集》・作家出版社編輯部編・北京：作家出版社，一九五七年・

Si, Xi. "Xiuzhen xing de Gengzhi tu: Jian tan woguo xiri nonggeng fangshi." *Gugong wenwu yuekan (The National Palace Museum Monthly of Chinese Art)*, no. 13 (vol. 2, no. 1) (April 1984): 11-17.
似熹・〈袖珍型的耕織圖—兼談我國昔日農耕方式〉・《故宮文物月刊》・第十三號・第二卷第一期・民國七十三年四月・第十一頁至第十七頁・

Sickman, Laurence [Laurence Chalfant Stevens] (1906-1988). "Notes on Chinese Rubbings." *Parnassus* 9, no. 1 (January 1937): [opening illustration on 8] 9-12.

Simon, Walter, and Howard G.H. Nelson. *Manchu Books in London: A Union Catalogue*. London: Published for the British Library by British Museum Publications Limited, 1977.

Siu, Wai-fong Anita. "Ink-making in China." *Orientations* 28, no. 6 (June 1997): 54-60.

Smith, Richard J. [Richard Joseph] (1944-). *Chinese Maps: Images of 'All under Heaven.'* Images of Asia [China titles], edited by Nigel Cameron and Sylvia Fraser-Lu. Hong Kong and Oxford: Oxford University Press, 1996.

————. "Mapping China's World: Cultural Cartography in Late Imperial Times." In *Landscape, Culture, and Power in Chinese Society*, edited by Wen-hsin Yeh, 52-109. China Research Monograph, no. 49. Berkeley, Calif.: Center for Chinese Studies, Institute of East Asian Studies, University of California, Berkeley, 1998.

Snellgrove, David L. *Indo-Tibetan Buddhism: Indian Buddhists and Their Tibetan Successors.* London: Serindia Publications [published in association with Shambhala Publications Inc.], 1987.

Sô Zen no hi: Gokan. [Explanatory notes in Japanese by Nishibayashi Shôichi (1932-); reproduces the stone rubbings of the Han-dynasty Stele of Cao Quan in the Mitsui bunko, Tokyo; original stone in the Shaanxi sheng bowu guan, Xi'an.] Chûgoku hôsho sen, no. 8. Tokyo: Nigensha, 1988.
《曹全碑：後漢》•［原本：三井文庫藏•解說：西林昭一]•〈中國法書選〉，8•東京：二玄社•1988年3月10日初版第1刷發行•

Song Zang yizhen xu mu. [Preface by Ye Gongchuo (1880-1968). Caption title: *Yingyin Song Zang yizhen mulu.* Essay by Jiang Weixin, "Jin Zang diaoyin shimo kao," *fulu 1a-21b; Fu* "Guangsheng si Da Zang jing jianmu," *fulu* 21b-42b; Postface by Ouyang Jian, *fulu* 42b-43a, dated 1936.] [Text on double-leaves; stitch-bound, Oriental style, with 7 leaves of plates.] N.p. [Shanghai]: N.p. [Yingyin Song ban Zang jing hui]], n.d. [1936].
《宋藏遺珍敘目》•［序：葉恭綽]•［〈影印宋藏遺珍目錄〉]•蔣唯心•〈金藏雕印始末考〉]•［〈附廣勝寺大藏經簡目〉]•［跋：歐陽漸•民國二十五年五月朔]•［裝一冊]•［上海]：［影印宋版藏經會]，［民國二十五年]•

Soothill, William Edward (1861-1935), and Lewis Hodous (1872-1949), comps. *A Dictionary of Chinese Buddhist Terms, with Sanskrit and English Equivalents and a Sanskrit-Pali Index.* [First published 1937.] Reprint. Richmond, Surrey, Eng.: Curzon Press, 1995.

Space & Place: Mapmaking East and West: Four Hundred Years of Western and Chinese Cartography from the Library of Congress, Geography and Map Division, and the Collection of Leonard & Juliet Rothman. Exhibition catalogue by Cordell D.K. Yee (1955-), with Alexander Bowles, Heather Deutsch, and Sarah Jane Fremont. Exhibition catalogue [The Elizabeth Myers Mitchell Art Gallery, St. John's College, Annapolis, Md., April 12-June 16, 1996]. Annapolis, Md.: St. John's College Press, 1996.

Stary, Giovanni. *Manchu Studies: An International Bibliography.* 3 vols. Vol. 1, *Catalogues, Bibliographies, Geography, Ethnography, Religion, History.* Vol. 2, *Language, Literature, Sibe-Manchu.* Vol. 3, *Indices.* Wiesbaden, Germany: Kommissionsverlag Otto Harrassowitz, 1990.

Strassberg, Richard E. (1948-), trans. with annotations and an introduction. *Inscribed Landscapes: Travel Writing from Imperial China.* Berkeley and Los Angeles: University of California Press, 1994.

Steinhardt, Nancy Shatzman. "Chinese Cartography and Calligraphy." *Oriental Art* 43, no. 1 (Spring 1997): 10-20.

Strickmann, Michel (d. 1994), ed. *Tantric and Taoist Studies in Honour of R.A. Stein.* Vol. 1. Mélanges chinois et bouddhiques, vol. 20. Brussels: Institut Belge des Hautes Études Chinoises, 1981.

Su, Bai. "Nan Song de diaoban yinshua." *Wenwu*, no. 135 (1962, no. 1) (January 1962): 15-28.
宿白•〈南宋的雕版印刷〉•《文物》•一九六二年第一期•總第一三五號•第十五頁至第二十八頁•

Sueki, Yasuhiro. *Bibliographical Sources for Buddhist Studies from the Viewpoint of Buddhist Philology.* Bibliographia Indica et Buddhica, no. 3. Tokyo: The International Institute for Buddhist Studies of The International College for Advanced Buddhist Studies, 1998.

Sui Tang huajia shiliao. Compiled and edited by Chen Gaohua (1938-). Beijing: Wenwu chuban she, 1987.
《隋唐畫家史料》•陳高華編•北京：文物出版社•1987年10月第一版•

Sun, Tong (fl. 1808). *Guanzhong shuidao ji.* [4 *juan.*] Congshu jicheng chubian, edited by Wang Yunwu (1888-). Shanghai: Shangwu yinshu guan, 1936. Reprint [facsimile reproduction; on double-leaves; stitch-bound, Oriental style]. Xibei kaifa shiliao congbian, ser. 1, no. 4. Tianjin: Tianjin guji chuban she, 1987.
《關中水道記》•四卷•孫彤撰•〈叢書集成初編〉•王雲五主編•上海：商務印書館•民國二十五年十二月初版•［影印版•本館據問影樓輿地叢書本排印•初編各叢書僅有此本]•〈西北開發史料叢編第一輯〉，4•［綫裝一冊]•天津：天津古籍出版社•一九八七年十月•

Sun, Zhixin. "A Quest for the Imperishable: Chao Meng-fu's Calligraphy for Stele Inscriptions." In *The Embodied Image: Chinese Calligraphy from the John B. Elliott Collection*, by Robert E. Harrist, Jr. and Wen C. Fong, with contributions by Qianshen Bai et al., 302-319. Princeton, N.J.: The Art Museum, Princeton University, 1999.

A Sung Bibliography (Bibliographie des Sung). Initiated by Étienne Balazs (1905-1963). Edited by Yves Hervouet. [Title on added half-title page also in Chinese: *Song dai shu lu* 宋代書錄 ; introduction and instructions to the reader in English and French; bibliographic entries in English or French; errata slip inserted.] Hong Kong: The Chinese University Press, 1978.

The Suvarnaprabhasa Sutra: A Mahayana Text Called "The Golden Splendour." First prepared for publication by the late professor Bunyiu Nanjio, and after his death revised and edited by Hokei Idzumi, under the auspices of The Keimeikwai. [Added title page in Japanese: 梵文金光明最勝王經・南條文雄、泉芳璟校訂・財團法人啟明會補助出版・東方佛教協會發行 .] [Foreword by Hokei Idzumi in English and Japanese; introduction in English; table of contents partially in English and partially in Sanskrit; text in Sanskrit, with some notes in English.] Kyoto: The Eastern Buddhist Society, 1931.

Suvarnaprabhasottama-sutra: Das Goldglanz-sutra: Ein Sanskrittext des Mahayana-Buddhismus: Die tibetischen Übersetzungen mit einem Wörterbuch. Herausgegeben von Johannes Nobel (1887-1960). 2 vols. Bd. 1, *Die tibetischen Übersetzungen* [1944]. Bd. 2, *Wörterbuch Tibetisch-Deutsch-Sanskrit* [1950]. [Introductory matter in German.] Leiden: E.J. Brill, 1944-1950 [Imprint for Bd. 1: Leiden: E.J. Brill; Stuttgart: W. Kohlhammer, 1944; imprint for Bd. 2: Leiden: E.J. Brill, 1950].

Sze, Mai-mai. *The Tao of Painting: A Study of the Ritual Disposition of Chinese Painting; with a Translation of the "Chieh Tzu Yüan Hua Chuan" or "Mustard Seed Garden Manual of Painting," 1679-1701.* 2 vols. Vol. 1, *The Tao of Painting.* Vol. 2, *The Chieh Tzu Yüan Hua Chuan.* Bollingen Series, no. 49. New York: Pantheon Books Inc., 1956.

———. *The Tao of Painting: A Study of the Ritual Disposition of Chinese Painting; with a Translation of the "Chieh Tzu Yüan Hua Chuan" or "Mustard Seed Garden Manual of Painting," 1679-1701.* 2d ed. (with corrections). 2 vols. in 1. Bollingen Series, no. 49. New York: Pantheon Books Inc., 1963.

-T-

Tang shi da cidian. Edited by Zhou Xunchu. [Co-edited by Mo Lifeng and Yan Jie.] N.p. [Nanjing]: Jiangsu guji chuban she, 1990.
《唐詩大辭典》・周勛初主編・[副主編：莫礪鋒、嚴杰]・[南京]：江蘇古籍出版社，1990 年 11 月第 1 版・

Tang shi shu lu. Compiled and edited by Chen Bohai and Zhu Yi'an. Tang shi xue yanjiu congshu. Ji'nan, Shandong: Qi Lu shu she, 1988.
《唐詩書錄》・陳伯海、朱易安編撰・《唐詩學研究叢書》・濟南：齊魯書社，

1988 年 12 月第 1 版・

Tao, Xiang (1871-1940). "Ming Wuxing Min ban shumu." *Qinghe* 5, no. 13 (cumulative no. 109) (1937): 1-10.
陶湘・〈明吳興閔板書目〉・《青鶴》・第五卷・第十三期・即一百〇九期・民國二十六年・第一頁至第十頁・

Tay, C.N. "Kuan-Yin: The Cult of Half Asia." *History of Religions* 16, no. 2 (November 1976): 147-177.

Teiser, Stephen F. "The Ritual Behind the Opera: A Fragmentary Ethnography of the Ghost Festival, A.D. 400-1900." In *Ritual Opera, Operatic Ritual: "Mu-lien Rescues His Mother" in Chinese Popular Culture,* edited by David Johnson, 191-223. Papers from the International Workshop on the Mu-lien Operas, with an additional contribution on the Woman Huang legend by Beata Grant. Publications of the Chinese Popular Culture Project, no. 1. N.p. [Berkeley, Calif.]: N.p. [Chinese Popular Culture Project], 1989.

———. "Hymns for the Dead in the Age of the Manuscript." *The Gest Library Journal* 5, no. 1 (Spring 1992): 26-56.

Tiangong kaiwu: Zhongguo gudai keji wenwu zhan (Heavenly Creations: Gems of Ancient Chinese Inventions). Jointly presented by Xianggang linshi shizheng ju (Provisional Urban Council, Hong Kong) and Zhongguo lishi bowu guan (National Museum of Chinese History). Organized by Xianggang lishi bowu guan (Hong Kong Museum of History). Produced by Xianggang lishi bowu guan (Hong Kong Museum of History). [Chief editor: Kong Xiangxing. Chief curator: Ding Xinyue (Joseph S.P. Ting).] [In Chinese and English.] Exhibition catalogue [Xianggang lishi bowu guan (Hong Kong Museum of History), September 29, 1998-January 3, 1999]. Hong Kong: Xianggang linshi shizheng ju (Provisional Urban Council, Hong Kong), 1998.
《天工開物─中國古代科技文物展》・香港臨時市政局、中國歷史博物館聯合主辦・香港歷史博物館籌劃・[香港歷史博物館編製]・[主編：孔祥星]・[總館長：丁新豹]・香港：香港臨時市政局，一九九八年九月首次編印・

Tianxia mingshan cidian (An Encyclopaedia of World-Renowned Peaks and Mounts in China). [In Chinese.] Compiled and edited by Wang Shixiong and Li Yuying. Xi'an: Shaanxi renmin jiaoyu chuban she, 1993.
《天下名山詞典》・王世雄、李玉英主編・西安：陝西人民教育出版社，1993 年 7 月第 1 版・

Tianxia Nan yue. [Edited by] Nan yue wenwu guanli suo. San Xiang lansheng lüyou congshu. Changsha, Hunan: Hunan meishu chuban she, 1984.
《天下南岳》・友編者仈：南岳文物管理所・《三湘攬勝旅游叢書》・長沙：湖南美術出版社，1984 年 4 月第 1 版・

Tillman, Hoyt Cleveland, and Stephen H. West (1944-), eds. *China under Jurchen Rule: Essays on Chin Intellectual and Cultural History*. SUNY Series in Chinese Philosophy and Culture, edited by David L. Hall and Roger T. Ames. Albany, N.Y.: State University of New York Press, 1995.

Ting, Wen-Yuan. "Von der alten chinesischen Buchdruckerkunst." *Gutenberg-Jahrbuch* [4. Jahrgang] (1929): 9-17.

Trésors de Chine et de Haute Asie: Centième anniversaire de Paul Pelliot. [Preface by Georges Le Rider. Introduction and catalogue entries by Marie-Rose Séguy.] Exhibition catalogue [Bibliothèque nationale, Paris, September 20-December 28, 1979]. Paris: Bibliothèque nationale, 1979.

Tschichold, Jan. *Chinese Color Prints from the Ten Bamboo Studio*. Translated by Katherine Watson. London: Lund Humphries, 1972.

Tseng, Yuho [Zeng Youhe] [Tseng Yu-ho Ecke] (1923-). *A History of Chinese Calligraphy*. Hong Kong: The Chinese University Press, 1993.

Tsien, Tsuen-hsuin [Qian Cunxun] 錢存訓 (1910-). "A History of Bibliographic Classification in China." *The Library Quarterly* 22, no. 4 (October 1952): 307-324.

————. *Written on Bamboo and Silk: The Beginnings of Chinese Books and Inscriptions*. The University of Chicago Studies in Library Science. Chicago: The University of Chicago Press, 1962.

————. "Technical Aspects of Chinese Printing." In Sören Edgren, *Chinese Rare Books in American Collections*, 16-25. New York: China Institute in America, 1984.

Tsultem, N. [Niamosoryn] (1924-). *Dekorativno-prikladnoe iskusstvo Mongolii (Mongolian Arts and Crafts) (Arts artisanaux de la Mongolie) (Arte decorativo aplicado de Mongolia)*. Edited by D. Bayarsaikhan. [Prefatory matter and legends in Russian, English, French, and Spanish. Title also in Mongolian on cover and spine: Monggol-un goyul cimeglel-un uralig.] Ulan-Bator, Mongolia: Gosizdatel'-stvo (State Publishing House) (Section de la Publication d'État) (Sección de la Publicación del Estado), 1987.

Tu, Long (1542-1605). *Kaopan yu shi*. 4 *juan*. [First published in 1592; reprint of typeset and punctuated edition]. Congshu jicheng chubian, vol. 1559 [with 3 other titles]. Beijing: Zhonghua shuju, 1985. 《考槃餘事》・屠隆著・〈叢書集成初編〉・第一五五九冊（及其他三種）・北京：中華書局，一九八五年北京新一版・

Tung, Tso-pin [Dong Zuobin] (1895-1963). *Fifty Years of Studies in Oracle Inscriptions*. [Translated from the Chinese by Paul Yang (chapters 1, 2, and 5) and the Centre for East Asian Cultural Studies (chapters 3 and 4).] Tokyo: Centre for East Asian Cultural Studies, 1964.

Twitchett, Denis C. [Denis Crispin]. *Printing and Publishing in Medieval China*. [Based on a talk given to The Wynkyn de Worde Society at Stationers' Hall London on 28 September 1977.] New York: Frederic C. Beil, Publisher, 1983.

-U-

Unschuld, Paul U. [Paul Ulrich] (1943-). *Medicine in China: A History of Ideas*. Comparative Studies of Health Systems and Medical Care. Berkeley and Los Angeles: University of California Press, 1985.

————, comp. and trans. *Introductory Readings in Classical Chinese Medicine: Sixty Texts with Vocabulary and Translation, a Guide to Research Aids and a General Glossary*. Dordrecht, the Netherlands, and Boston: Kluwer Academic Publishers, 1988.

————, ed. *Approaches to Traditional Chinese Medical Literature: Proceedings of an International Symposium on Translation Methodologies and Terminologies*. Dordrecht, the Netherlands, and Boston: Kluwer Academic Publishers, 1989.

-V-

Valder, Peter. *The Garden Plants of China*. Balmain, N.S.W., Australia: Florilegium, 1999.

van der Kuijp, Leonard W.J. "The Tibetan Script and Derivatives." In *The World's Writing Systems*, edited by Peter T. Daniels (1951-) and William Bright (1928-), 431-441. New York and Oxford: Oxford University Press, 1996.

van Gulik, R.H. [Robert Hans] (1910-1967). *Chinese Pictorial Art as Viewed by the Connoisseur: Notes on the Means and Methods of Traditional Chinese Connoisseurship of Pictorial Art, Based upon a Study of the Art of Mounting Scrolls in China and Japan*. With 160 plates, and 42 actual samples of Chinese and Japanese paper, in pocket. [Title on title page also in Chinese: *Shuhua jianshang huibian* 《書畫鑑賞彙編》.] Serie Orientale Roma, vol. 19. Rome: Istituto Italiano per il Medio ed Estremo Oriente, 1958.

van Slyke, Lyman P. *Yangtze: Nature, History, and the River*. A Portable Stanford Book. Reading, Mass. and Menlo Park, Calif.: Addison-Wesley Publishing Company, Inc., 1988.

von Falkenhausen, Lothar [Lothar Alexander] (1959-). *Suspended Music: Chime-Bells in the Culture of Bronze Age China*. Berkeley and Los Angeles: University of California Press, 1993.

von Franz, Rainer. "Ou-yang Hsiu." In *The Indiana Companion to Traditional Chinese Literature*, edited and compiled by William H. Nienhauser, Jr., vol. 1, 639-641 [see also updated bibliography in vol. 2, 386-387]. Bloomington, Ind. and Indianapolis: Indiana University Press, 1986-1998.

-W-

Wadang huibian. Compiled and edited by Qian Juntao, Zhang Xingyi, and Xu Mingnong. Shanghai: Shanghai renmin meishu chuban she, 1988.
《瓦當匯編》・編者：錢君匋、張星逸、許明農・上海：上海人民美術出版社，一九八八年六月第一版・

Wallis, Helen (1924-1995). "Missionary Cartographers to China." *The Geographical Magazine* 47, no. 12 (September 1975): 751-759.

―――. "Chinese Maps and Globes in the British Library and the Phillips Collection." In *Chinese Studies: Papers Presented at a Colloquium at the School of Oriental and African Studies, University of London, 24-26 August 1987*, edited by Frances Wood, 88-95. British Library Occasional Papers, no. 10. London: The British Library, 1988.

Walter, Mariko Namba. "Kingship and Buddhism in Central Asia." Ph.D. diss., Harvard University, 1997. UMI Order No.: 9733435.

Wang, Bomin. *Wu Daozi*. Zhongguo huajia congshu. Shanghai: Shanghai renmin meishu chuban she, 1958.
《吳道子》・王伯敏著・〈中國畫家叢書〉・上海：上海人民美術出版社，一九五八年一月第一版・

―――. "Hu Zhengyan ji qi Shizhu zhai de shuiyin muke." In *Shizhu zhai yanjiu wenji: "Shizhu zhai shuhua pu" kanxing sanbai liushi nian jinian*, compiled by Shizhu zhai yishu yanjiu bu, 2-9. Nanjing: Shizhu zhai yishu yanjiu bu, 1987.
王伯敏・〈胡正言及其十竹齋的水印木刻〉・《十竹齋研究文集：〈十竹齋書畫譜〉刊行三百六十年紀念》・十竹齋藝術研究部編・南京：十竹齋藝術研究部，

一九八七年十月・第二頁至第九頁・

Wang, Chia Chi Jason. "The Iconography of Zhong Kui in Chinese Painting." Masterís thesis, University of California, Berkeley, 1991.

Wang, Chunyuan. *Zhongguo jinyu (Chinese Goldfish)*. [In Chinese; title on front cover also in English.] Beijing: Jindun chuban she, 1994.
《中國金魚》・王春元著・北京：金盾出版社，1994 年 3 月第 1 版・

Wang, Fang-yu [Wang Fangyu] (1913-1997). "Book Illustration in Late Ming and Early Qing China." In Sören Edgren, *Chinese Rare Books in American Collections*, 31-43. New York: China Institute in America, 1984.

Wang, Françoise. "Contribution des bibliophiles éditeurs au monde chinois intellectuel pré-moderne." In *Le livre et l'imprimerie en Extrême-Orient et en Asie du Sud: Actes du Colloque organisé à Paris du 9 au 11 mars 1983*, préparés par Jean-Pierre Drège, Mitchiko Ishigami-Iagolnitzer et Monique Cohen, 95-108. [Revue française d'histoire du livre, nos. 42-43.] Bordeaux: Société des Bibliophiles de Guyenne, 1986.

Wang, Jing (1950-). *The Story of Stone: Intertextuality, Ancient Chinese Stone Lore, and the Stone Symbolism of "Dream of the Red Chamber," "Water Margin," and "The Journey to the West."* Post-Contemporary Interventions, edited by Stanley Fish and Fredric Jameson. Durham, N.C. and London: Duke University Press, 1992.

Wang, Jingru. *Xi Xia yanjiu (Shishiah Studies)*. 3 vols. Vol. 1 [1932]; vol. 2 [1933]; vol. 3 [1933]. Guoli zhongyang yanjiu yuan lishi yuyan yanjiu suo dankan (Academia Sinica: The National Research Institute of History and Philology: Monographs), jia zhong (Series A), nos. 8, 11, and 13. Beiping: Guoli zhongyang yanjiu yuan lishi yuyan yanjiu suo (The National Research Institute of History and Philology, Academia Sinica), 1932-1933. Reprint. 3 vols. Taibei: Zhongyang yanjiu yuan lishi yuyan yanjiu suo, 1992.
《西夏研究》・王靜如著・[全三輯・第一輯（民國二十一年）・第二輯（民國二十二年）・第三輯（民國二十二年）]・〈國立中央研究院歷史語研究所單刊甲種〉之八、十一、十三・北平：國立中央研究院歷史語研究所，民國二十一年至二十二年初版・[影印版・全三冊]・台北：中央研究院歷史語研究所，民國八十一年十月景印一版・

Wang, Lianqi. "Zhao Mengfu shufa yishu jian lun." In *Zhao Mengfu yanjiu lunwen ji*, edited by Shanghai shuhua chuban she, 777-806. Shanghai: Shanghai shuhua chuban she, 1995.
王連起・〈趙孟頫書法藝術簡論〉・《趙孟頫研究論文集》・編者：本社[上海書畫出版社]・上海：上海書畫出版社，1995 年 3 月第一版・第七百七十七頁至第八百零六頁・

Wang, Meitang. "Naxi zu wenxian: Dongba jing." *Wenxian*, no. 32 (1987, no. 2): 230-234.

王梅堂・〈納西族文獻—東巴經〉・《文獻》・總第三十二期・一九八七年第二期・第二百三十頁至第二百三十四頁・

Wang, Nancy. "Research Materials in the National Palace Museum." In *Chinese Studies: Papers Presented at a Colloquium at the School of Oriental and African Studies, University of London, 24-26 August 1987*, edited by Frances Wood (1948-), 152-159. British Library Occasional Papers, no. 10. London: The British Library, 1988.

Wang, Qi. "Zhongguo gudai banhua zhong de renwu xingxiang." *Meishu yanjiu*, no. 6 (1958, no. 2): 39-48.

王琦・〈中國古代版畫中的人物形象〉・《美術研究》・總第六期・一九五八年第二期・第三十九頁至第四十八頁・

Wang, Qianjin. "'Pingjiang tu' de ditu xue yanjiu." *Ziran kexue shi yanjiu (Studies in the History of Natural Sciences)* 8, no. 4 (1989): 378-386 [includes abstract in English, "Cartographical Research on 'Ping Jiang Tu,'" 386].

汪前進・《《平江圖》的地圖學研究〉・《自然科學史研究》・第8卷・第4期・（1989年）・第三百七十八頁至第三百八十六頁・

———. "Nan Song beike Pingjiang tu yanjiu." In *Zhongguo gudai ditu ji: Zhan guo-Yuan [(An Atlas of Ancient Maps in China–From the Warring States to the Yuan Dynasty (476 B.C.-A.D. 1368)]*, edited by Cao Wanru, Zheng Xihuang, Huang Shengzhang, Niu Zhongxun, Ren Jincheng, and Ju Deyuan, text section, 50-55, with summary in English, "'Ping Jiang Tu,' A Map of Southern Song Dynasty Carved on a Stele," 110. Beijing: Wenwu chuban she (Cultural Relics Publishing House), 1990.

汪前進・〈南宋碑刻平江圖研究〉・《中國古代地圖集：戰國—元》・曹婉如、鄭錫煌、黃盛璋、鈕仲勛、任金城、鞠德源編・北京：文物出版社，1990年7月第1版・第五十頁至第五十五頁・英文提要・第一百十頁・

Wang, Qingzheng. "The Arts of Ming Woodblock-printed Images and Decorated Paper Albums." In *The Chinese Scholar's Studio: Artistic Life in the Late Ming Period: An Exhibition from the Shanghai Museum*, edited by Chu-tsing Li (1920-) and James C.Y. Watt, 56-61. New York: Thames and Hudson Inc., published in association with New York: The Asia Society Galleries, 1987.

Wang, Renbo. "Shi lun Yungang, Longmen shiku Bei Wei zhuyao zaoxiang ticai yu fojiao shi zhu wenti." In *Shanghai bowu guan jikan*, no. 7, 272-288. Shanghai: Shanghai shuhua chuban she, 1996.

王仁波・〈試論雲岡、龍門石窟北魏主要造像題材與佛教史諸問題〉・《上海博物館集刊》・第七期・上海：上海書畫出版社，1996年9月第1版・第二百七十二頁至第二百八十八頁・

Wang, Ruo. "Shi tan 'paiji' chansheng de niandai." *Wenxian*, no. 67 (1996, no. 1): 192-195.

王若・〈試談"牌記"產生的年代〉・《文獻》・總第六十七期・一九九六年第一期・第一百九十二頁至第一百九十五頁・

Wang, Shifu (fl. 1295-1307). *Xixiang ji.* [6 *juan*; caption title: *Xin jiaozhu guben Xixiang ji*; running title: *Jiaozhu guben Xixiang ji.* Edited and annotated by Wang Jide (d. 1623); with additional commentaries by Xu Wei (1521-1593); illustrations by Qian Gu (1508-ca. 1578) and copied by Ru Wenshu (fl. early 17th century); woodblocks engraved by Huang Yingzu (1563 or 1573-1644).] Compiled and edited by Guoli gugong bowu yuan bianji weiyuan hui. Ming dai banhua congkan, no. 4. [Facsimile reproduction of the copy of the 1614 edition of the *Xin jiaozhu guben Xixiang ji* published by Xiangxue ju in the possession of Guoli gugong bowu yuan (National Palace Museum).] Taibei: Guoli gugong bowu yuan, 1988.

《西廂記》・〈明代版畫叢刊，四〉・[影印本・影印明萬曆四十二年（1614年）王氏香雪居刻本《新校注古本西廂記六卷》・元王實甫撰・明王驥德校注・明徐渭附解・明錢穀畫・明汝文淑摹圖・明黃應光刻・明王伯良序]・台北：國立故宮博物院，民國七十七年六月初版・

———. *The Moon and the Zither: "The Story of the Western Wing."* Edited and translated with an introduction by Stephen H. West (1944-) and Wilt L. Idema. With a study of its woodblock illustrations by Yao Dajuin. Berkeley and Los Angeles: University of California Press, 1991.

Wang, Yong (1899-1956). "Guoli Beiping tushu guan cang Qing neige daku yutu mulu." *Guoli Beiping tushu guan guankan (Bulletin of the National Library of Peiping)* 6, no. 4 (July-August 1932): 45-72.

王庸・〈國立北平圖書館藏清內閣大庫輿圖目錄〉・《國立北平圖書館館刊》・第六卷・第四號・民國二十一年七、八月・第四十五頁至第七十二頁・

———, comp. and ed. *Zhongguo dili tuji congkao.* [Originally published in 1947. Reprint, with corrections.] Shanghai: Shangwu yinshu guan, 1956 [2d printing, 1957].

《中國地理圖籍叢考》・王庸編・[1947年6月初版]・[修訂本]・上海：1956年4月重印第1版，1957年10月上海第2次印刷・

Wang, Zhizhang (1903-), comp. and ed. *Qing Shengping shu zhi lüe.* 2 vols. in 1. N.p. [Beiping]: Guoli Beiping yanjiu yuan shi xue tanjiu hui, 1937.

《清昇平署志略》・王芷章編纂・[上、下二冊]・[北平]：國立北平研究院史學研究會，民國二十六年四月初版・

Wang, Zichun. "Sericulture." In *Ancient China's Technology and Science*, compiled by the Institute of the History of Natural Sciences, Chinese Academy of Sciences, 305-314. China Knowledge Series. Beijing: Foreign Languages Press, 1983.

Wang, Zhongmin 王重民 (1903-1975). *A Descriptive Catalog of Rare*

Chinese Books in the Library of Congress. [Title on front covers, spines, and title pages of each volume also in Chinese: *Guohui tushu guan cang Zhongguo shanben shulu* 《國會圖書館藏中國善本書錄》] Edited by T.L. Yuan. 2 vols. Washington, D.C.: Library of Congress, 1957.

———. *Zhongguo shanben shu tiyao.* Shanghai: Shanghai guji chuban she, 1983.
《中國善本書提要》・王重民撰・[精裝一冊]・上海：上海古籍出版社，1983 年 8 月第 1 版・

———. *Zhongguo shanben shu tiyao bubian.* Beijing: Beijing tushu guan chuban she, 1991 [2d printing, 1997].
《中國善本書提要補編》・王重民撰・[精裝一冊]・北京：北京圖書館出版社，1991 年 12 月第 1 版，1977 年 12 月第 2 次印刷・

Wang, Ziyun. "Tang dai de shike xianhua." *Wenwu cankao ziliao*, no. 68 (1956, no. 4) (April 1956): 29-33 [see also illustration on 28].
王子雲・〈唐代的石刻線畫〉・《文物參考資料》・一九五六年第四期・總第六八號・第二十九頁至第三十三頁[第二十八頁附圖]・

Watson, Burton (1925-), trans. *The Lotus Sutra.* Translations from the Asian Classics, edited by Wm. Theodore de Bary et al. New York: Columbia University Press, 1993.

Watson, William (1917-). *The Arts of China to AD 900.* Yale University Press Pelican History of Art. New Haven and London: Yale University Press, 1995.

Wei, Yinru. "Manhua Shizhu zhai yishu." In *Shizhu zhai yanjiu wenji: "Shizhu zhai shuhua pu" kanxing sanbai liushi nian jinian*, compiled by Shizhu zhai yishu yanjiu bu, 10-13. Nanjing: Shizhu zhai yishu yanjiu bu, 1987.
曾景初・〈漫話十竹齋藝術〉・《十竹齋研究文集：〈十竹齋書畫譜〉刊行三百六十年紀念》・十竹齋藝術研究部編・南京：十竹齋藝術研究部・一九八七年十月・第十頁至第十三頁・

Weidner, Marsha [Marsha Smith], ed. *Latter Days of the Law: Images of Chinese Buddhism, 850-1850.* Preface by Sherman E. Lee. Essays by Patricia Berger, Richard K. Kent, Julia K. Murray, Marsha Weidner, [and] Chün-fang Yü. Exhibition catalogue [Helen Foresman Spencer Museum of Art, University of Kansas, Lawrence, Kan., August 27-October 9, 1994; Asian Art Museum of San Francisco, San Francisco, November 30, 1994-January 29, 1995]. Lawrence, Kan.: Spencer Museum of Art, The University of Kansas, in association with Honolulu: University of Hawaii Press, 1994.

Wen, Xingzhen. "Kangxi yu nongye." *Gugong bowu yuan yuankan (Palace Museum Journal)*, no. 19 (1983, no. 1): 20-30.
聞性真・〈康熙與農業〉・《故宮博物院院刊》・總第十九期・一九八三年第一期・第二十頁至第三十頁・

Weng, Wan-go H.C. 翁萬戈. "Chinese Type Design and Calligraphy." In Sören Edgren, *Chinese Rare Books in American Collections*, 26-30. New York: China Institute in America, 1984.

Wenmei zhai shi jian pu. [Title on cover of case and on title slips: *Bai hua shi jian pu.*] [With illustrations by Zhang Zhaoxiang.] Reprint [facsimile reproduction of original published by Tianjian: Wenmei zhai, 1911]. 2 vols. [on double-leaves; stitch-bound, Oriental style] in 1 case. Beijing: Zhongguo shudian, 1992.
《文美齋詩箋譜》・[又稱《百花詩箋譜》]・[繪畫：張兆祥]・[原版清宣統三年歲次辛亥五月天津文美齋刊成]・[影印版]・北京：中國書店，一九九二年七月・

West, Andrew C. [Andrew Christopher] (1960-). *Catalogue of the Morrison Collection of Chinese Books.* [Added title page also in Chinese: *Malixun cang shu shumu; Wei An bian; Lundun daxue Ya Fei xueyuan*, 1998.] London: School of Oriental and African Studies, University of London, 1998.
《馬禮遜藏書書目》・魏安編・倫敦大學亞非學院，1998 年・

West, Stephen H. [Stephen Harry] (1944-). "Tsa-chü." In *The Indiana Companion to Traditional Chinese Literature*, edited and compiled by William H. Nienhauser, Jr., vol. 1, 774-783 [see also updated bibliography in vol. 2, 436-439]. Bloomington, Ind. and Indianapolis: Indiana University Press, 1986-1998.

The West Lake Companion. [In English; colophon page also in Chinese.] Beijing: Foreign Languages Press, 1958.
《西湖勝蹟》・北京：外文出版社，1958 年 4 月第一版・

Whitfield, Roderick (1937-), and Anne Farrer. *Caves of the Thousand Buddhas: Chinese Art from the Silk Route.* Edited by Anne Farrer. With contributions by S.J. Vainker and Jessica Rawson. Exhibition catalogue [The British Museum, London, 1990]. New York: George Braziller, Inc., 1990.

———, ed. *The Problem of Meaning in Early Chinese Ritual Bronzes.* Colloquies on Art & Archaeology in Asia, no. 15. London: Percival David Foundation of Chinese Art, School of Oriental and African Studies, University of London, 1993.

Whitfield, Susan, and Frances Wood, eds. *Dunhuang and Turfan: Contents and Conservation of Ancient Documents from Central Asia.* The British Library Studies in Conservation Science, [no. 1], edited by Mirjam M. Foot and Kenneth R. Seddon. [Proceedings of the conference "The Preservation of Material from Cave 17" organized by The British Library, held at the Isle of Thorns Training Centre, University of Sussex, 13-15 October 1993.] London: The British Library, 1996.

Widmer, Ellen, and Kang-i Sun Chang (1944-), eds. *Writing Women in Late Imperial China*. Stanford, Calif.: Stanford University Press, 1997.

Wiens, Mi Chu [Ju Mi]. "Living Pictographs: Asian Scholar Unlocks Secrets of the Naxi Manuscripts." *The Library of Congress Information Bulletin* 58, no. 6 (June 1999): 140-142.

———. "Sorcerers and Storytellers: Assembling a Modern Rosetta Stone for an Ancient Pictographic Language." *Civilization: The Magazine of the Library of Congress* 6, no. 4 (August-September 1999): 95.

Wilkinson, Endymion [Endymion Porter]. *Chinese History: A Manual*. Harvard-Yenching Institute Monograph Series, no. 46. Cambridge, Mass.: Harvard University Asia Center, 1998.

Wills, John E. [John Elliot], Jr. (1936-). *Mountain of Fame: Portraits in Chinese History*. Princeton: Princeton University Press, 1994.

Wilson, Thomas A. (1954-). *Genealogy of the Way: The Construction and Uses of the Confucian Tradition in Late Imperial China*. Stanford, Calif.: Stanford University Press, 1995.

With, Karl (1891-1980). *Chinesische Steinschnitte*. Leipzig: Verlag von E. A. Seemann, 1922.

Wolter, John A. [John Amadeus] (1925-), and Ronald E. Grim, eds. *Images of the World: The Atlas through History*. Washington, D.C.: Library of Congress, 1997.

Wong, Dorothy C. "The Beginnings of the Buddhist Stele Tradition in China." Ph.D. diss., Harvard University, 1995. UMI Order No.: 9609180.

Wong, Yanchung. "Bronze Mirror Art of the Han Dynasty." [Translated from the Chinese by Christopher Homfray.] *Orientations* 19, no. 12 (December 1988): 42-53.

Wood, Frances (1948-). *Chinese Illustration*. London: The British Library, 1985.

———, ed. *Chinese Studies: Papers Presented at a Colloquium at the School of Oriental and African Studies, University of London, 24-26 August 1987.* Sponsored jointly by the British Library, the School of Oriental and African Studies, University of London and the China Library Group. British Library Occasional Papers, no. 10. London: The British Library, 1988.

———. "Two Thousand Years at Dunhuang." In *Dunhuang and Turfan: Contents and Conservation of Ancient Documents from Central Asia*, edited by Susan Whitfield and Frances Wood (1948-), 1-6. The British Library Studies in Conservation Science, [no. 1], edited by Mirjam M. Foot and Kenneth R. Seddon. [Proceedings of the conference "The Preservation of Material from Cave 17" organized by The British Library, held at the Isle of Thorns Training Centre, University of Sussex, 13-15 October 1993.] London: The British Library, 1996.

Wu, Haokun, and Pan You. *Zhongguo jiagu xue shi*. Zhongguo wenhua shi congshu, edited by Zhou Gucheng. Shanghai: Shanghai renmin chuban she, 1985.
《中國甲骨學史》・吳浩坤、潘悠著・〈中國文化史叢書〉・周城主編・上海：上海人民出版社，1985 年 12 月第 1 版・

Wu, Hung [Wu Hong] 巫鴻 (1945-). *The Wu Liang Shrine: The Ideology of Early Chinese Pictorial Art*. Stanford, Calif.: Stanford University Press, 1989.

———. *Monumentality in Early Chinese Art and Architecture*. Stanford, Calif.: Stanford University Press, 1995.

Wu, Junfa. "Qiao duo tiangong de Shizhu zhai shuiyin muke." In *Shizhu zhai yanjiu wenji: "Shizhu zhai shuhua pu" kanxing sanbai liushi nian jinian*, compiled by Shizhu zhai yishu yanjiu bu, 57-59. Nanjing: Shizhu zhai yishu yanjiu bu, 1987.
吳俊發・〈巧奪天工的十竹齋水印木刻〉・《十竹齋研究文集：〈十竹齋書畫譜〉刊行三百六十年紀念》・十竹齋藝術研究部編・南京：十竹齋藝術研究部，一九八七年十月・第五十七頁至第五十九頁・

Wu, Kwang Tsing [K.T. Wu] [Wu Kuang-ch'ing] 吳光清 (1905-). "Ming Printing and Printers." *Harvard Journal of Asiatic Studies* 7 (1942-1943): 203-260.

———. "Chinese Printing under Four Alien Dynasties (916-1368 A.D.)." *Harvard Journal of Asiatic Studies* 13, nos. 3-4 (December 1950): 447-523.

———. "The Development of Typography in China during the Nineteenth Century." *The Library Quarterly* 22, no. 3 (July 1952): 288-301.

———. "Illustrations in Sung Printing." *The Quarterly Journal of the Library of Congress* 28, no. 3 (July 1971): 173-195.

———. "Ch'eng Ta-yüeh." In *Dictionary of Ming Biography, 1368-1644*, edited by L. Carrington Goodrich (1894-1986) and Chaoying Fang (1908-1985), vol. 1, 212-215. New York and London: Columbia University

Press, 1976.

Wu, Shuping, comp. and ed. *Zhongguo lidai huapu huibian*. 16 vols. Tianjin: Tianjin guji chuban she, 1997.
《中國歷代畫譜匯編》・吳樹平編・[全十六冊]・天津：天津古籍出版社，1997年2月第1版・

Wu, Silas Hsiu-liang 吳秀良 (1929-). "The Memorial Systems of the Ch'ing Dynasty (1644-1911)." *Harvard Journal of Asiatic Studies* 27 (1967): 7-75.

————. *Communication and Imperial Control in China: Evolution of the Palace Memorial System, 1693-1735*. Harvard East Asian Series, no. 51. Cambridge, Mass.: Harvard University Press, 1970.

-X-

Xi hu (West Lake). Selected and edited by Chi Changyao. [In Chinese and English. Chinese text by Shen Tuqi. English text by Xu Qiping, Xue Chen, and Wen Ying.] Hangzhou: Zhejiang renmin chuban she, 1990.
《西湖》・池長堯選編・[中文：申屠奇・英文：徐齊平、薛琛、聞鶯]・杭州：浙江人民出版社，1990年8月第一版・

Xi hu zhi. Compiled by Hangzhou shi yuanlin wenwu guanli ju. Edited by Shi Diandong. Shanghai: Shanghai guji chuban she, 1995.
《西湖志》・杭州市園林文物管理局編・施奠東主編・上海：上海古籍出版社，1995年12月第1版・

Xi Xia wenwu. Compiled and edited by Shi Jinbo, Bai Bin, and Wu Fengyun. Beijing: Wenwu chuban she, 1988.
《西夏文物》・史金波、白濱、吳峰雲編著・北京：文物出版社，1988年3月第1版・

Xi zhao tu lüe; Xizang tu kao. Compiled and edited by "Xizang yanjiu" bianji bu. Xizang yanjiu congkan. [Incorporates *Xi zhao tu lüe*, compiled by Songyun (1752-1835) (originally published in 1798 and recompiled in 1847), edited by Wu Fengpei, 1-29; *Xizang tu kao*, compiled by Huang Peiqiao (fl. 1886) (originally published in 1886 and recompiled in 1894), punctuated by Li Peirong, edited by Li Hongnian and Li Wenjiang, 31-268; appended by Cheng Fengxiang, "Kemu xi'nan qun shuo bian yi," 269-281 (extracted from *Chuan Zang you zong huibian* 7).] Lhasa, Tibet: Xizang renmin chuban she, 1982.
《〈西招圖略〉；〈西藏圖考〉》・《西藏研究》編輯部編輯・《西藏研究叢刊》・[《西招圖略》・松筠撰・吳豐培校訂・正文第一頁至第二十九頁]・[《西藏圖考》

・黃沛翹撰・李培榮付梓・李宏年、李文江同校・第三十一頁至第二百六十八頁]・[附：程鳳翔・〈喀木西南群說辨異〉・第二百六十九頁至第二百八十一頁・選自中央民族學院圖書館編《川藏游踪匯編》七]・拉薩：西藏人民出版社，一九八二年・

Xia, Liming. *Qing dai Taiwan ditu yanbian shi, jian lun yi ge huitu dianfan de zhuanyi licheng*. Mingshan cang, no. 1. Zhonghe, Taibei county: Zhi shufang chuban she, 1996.
《清代臺灣地圖演變史，兼論一個繪圖典範的轉移歷程》・夏黎明著・〈名山藏〉，・台北縣中和市：知書房出版社，1996年6月初版・

Xia, Wei. "The Huizhou Style of Woodcut Illustration." *Orientations* 25, no. 1 (January 1994): 61-66.

Xia, Zhifeng, and Zhang Binyuan. *Zhongguo gu ta*. Zaoxing wenhua congshu, edited by Luo Qi and Xu Encun. Hangzhou: Zhejiang renmin chuban she, 1996.
《中國古塔》・夏志峰、張斌遠著・〈造型文化叢書〉・主編：洛齊、徐恩存・杭州：浙江人民出版社，1996年10月第1版・

Xiao, Ping. "Shizhu zhai de huajia shijie: 'Shizhu zhai shuhua pu' huajia zhi yanjiu." In *Shizhu zhai yanjiu wenji: "Shizhu zhai shuhua pu" kanxing sanbai liushi nian jinian*, compiled by Shizhu zhai yishu yanjiu bu, 75-78. Nanjing: Shizhu zhai yishu yanjiu bu, 1987.
蕭平・〈十竹齋的畫家世界—《十竹齋書畫譜》畫家之研究〉・《十竹齋研究文集：〈十竹齋書畫譜〉刊行三百六十年紀念》・十竹齋藝術研究部編・南京：十竹齋藝術研究部，一九八七年十月・第七十五頁至第七十八頁・

Xidi shumu. 6 juan [5 juan, tiba 1 juan]. Compiled and edited by Beijing tushu guan. [Preface by Zhao Wanli (1905-1980). Colophons to collected editions by Zheng Zhenduo (1898-1958).] 6 vols. [on double-leaves; stitch-bound, Oriental style] in 1 case]. N.p. [Beijing]: Wenwu chuban she, 1963.
《西諦書目》・[五卷・題跋一卷]・編著者：北京圖書館・[《西諦書目序》：趙萬・〈西諦題跋〉：鄭振鐸]・[綫裝六冊一函]・[北京]：文物出版社，一九六三年十月第一版・

Xin bian Qin Han wadang tulu. Compiled and edited by Shaanxi sheng kaogu yanjiu suo Qin Han yanjiu shi. Xi'an: San Qin chuban she, 1986.
《新編秦漢瓦當圖錄》・陝西省考古研究所秦漢研究室編・西安：三秦出版社，1986年12月第1版・

Xing, Runchuan. "The Invention and Development of Printing and Its Dissemination Abroad." In *Ancient China's Technology and Science*, compiled by the Institute of the History of Natural Sciences, Chinese Academy of Sciences, 383-391. China Knowledge Series. Beijing: Foreign Languages Press, 1983.

Xixiang ji jianshang cidian. Compiled and edited by He Xinhui and Zhu Jie. San Jin wenhua yanjiu congkan. N.p. [Beijing]: Zhongguo funü chuban she, 1990.

《西廂記鑒賞辭典》・賀新輝、朱捷編著・〈三晉文化研究叢刊〉・[北京]：中國婦女出版社，1990 年 5 月北京第一版・

Xixiang ji xin lun. Compiled and edited by Han Sheng, He Xinhui, and Fan Biao. Xixiang ji yanjiu wenji. San Jin wenhua yanjiu congshu. [San Jin wenhua yanjiu congshu bianji weiyuan hui. Chief editor: Zhao Yuting.] Beijing: Zhongguo xiju chuban she, 1992.

《西廂記新論》・寒聲、賀新輝、范彪編・〈西廂記研究文集〉・〈三晉文化研究叢書〉・[三晉文化研究叢書編輯委員會・總編：趙雨亭]・北京：中國戲劇出版社，1992 年 8 月第 1 版・

Xu, Shuofang. *Wan Ming qujia nianpu*. 3 vols. Vol. 1, *Suzhou juan*. Vol. 2, *Zhejiang juan*. Vol. 3, *Gan Wan juan*. Hangzhou: Zhejiang guji chuban she, 1993.

《晚明曲家年譜》・徐朔方著・[全三卷・第一卷：〈蘇州卷〉・第二卷：〈浙江卷〉・第三卷：〈贛皖卷〉]・[精裝三冊]・杭州：浙江古籍出版社，1993 年 12 月第 1 版・

Xu, Xitai, Lou Yudong, and Wei Jiaozu. *Zhou Qin Han wadang*. Beijing: Wenwu chuban she, 1988.

《周秦漢瓦當》・[著者]：徐錫台、樓宇棟、魏效祖・北京：文物出版社，1998年10 月第一版・

-Y-

Yan, Wenbian, and Zheng Peng. "Beiye jing: Dai zu wenhua de baocang." In *Beiye wenhua lun*, edited by Wang Yizhi and Yang Shiguang, 10-18. Kunming: Yunnan renmin chuban she, 1990.

岩温扁、征鵬・〈貝葉經—傣族文化的寶藏〉・《貝葉文化論》・王懿之、楊世光編・[精裝一冊]・昆明：雲南人民出版社，1990年4月第1版・第十頁至第十八頁・

Yang, Boda (1927-). "Shi lun Shandong huaxiang shi de kefa." *Gugong bowu yuan yuankan (Palace Museum Journal)*, no. 38 (1987, no. 4): 3-24 [see also 2 illustrations on inside front cover].

楊伯達・〈試論山東畫像石的刻法〉・《故宮博物院院刊》・總第三十八期・一九八七年第四期・第三頁至第二十四頁[附封面內圖版一、二]・

Yang, Yanping. "Song dai de Jiangxi ke shu." *Wenxian*, no. 69 (1996, no. 3): 174-188.

楊晏平・〈宋代的江西刻書〉・《文獻》・總六十九第期・一九九六年第三期・第一百七十四頁至第一百八十八頁・

Yangzheng tujie. 2 *juan*. Compiled by Jiao Hong (1541-1620; *jinshi* of 1589). Explanatory text by Wu Jixu. [First published 1593; facsimile reprint of Qing manuscript copy; issued with 2 other titles.] Wanwei biecang, vol. 62. N.p. [Nanjing]: Jiangsu guji chuban she, 1988.

《養正圖解》・上、下二卷・焦竑撰・吳繼序解說・[原刊於明萬曆二十一年（年）・據清抄本影印版，及其他二種]・〈宛委別藏〉・阮元輯・[全一百二十冊]・第六十二冊・[南京]：江蘇古籍出版社，一九八八年二月第一版・

Yao, Dajuin. "The Mu-lien Operas: A Selective Bibliography." In *Ritual Opera, Operatic Ritual: "Mu-lien Rescues His Mother" in Chinese Popular Culture*, edited by David Johnson, 312-324. Papers from the International Workshop on the Mu-lien Operas, with an additional contribution on the Woman Huang legend by Beata Grant. Publications of the Chinese Popular Culture Project, no. 1. N.p. [Berkeley, Calif.]: N.p. [Chinese Popular Culture Project], 1989.

Yao, Tao-chung. "Buddhism and Taoism under the Chin." In *China under Jurchen Rule: Essays on Chin Intellectual and Cultural History*, edited by Hoyt Cleveland Tillman and Stephen H. West (1944-), 145-180. SUNY Series in Chinese Philosophy and Culture, edited by David L. Hall and Roger T. Ames. Albany, N.Y.: State University of New York Press, 1995.

Ye, Gongchuo (1880-1968). "Lidai Zang jing kao lüe." In *Zhang Jusheng xiansheng qishi shengri jinian lunwen ji*, compiled and edited by Cai Yuanpei (1868-1940), Hu Shi (1891-1962), and Wang Yunwu (1888-), 25-42, and 20 unnumbered pages of illustrations. Shanghai: Shangwu yinshu guan, 1937.

葉恭綽・〈歷代藏經考略〉・《張菊生先生七十生日紀念論文集》・蔡元培、胡適、王雲五編輯・上海：商務印書館，民國二十六年一月初版・第二十五頁至第四十二頁・附圖版二十頁・

Yee, Cordell D.K. (1955-). "A Cartography of Introspection: Chinese Maps as Other Than European," *Asian Art* 5, no. 4 (1992): 29-47.

———. "Reinterpreting Traditional Chinese Geographical Maps." In *The History of Cartography*, vol. 2, bk. 2, *Cartography in the Traditional East and Southeast Asian Societies*, edited by J.B. Harley (1932-1991) and David Woodward (1942-) [with Joseph E. Schwartzberg, associate editor; and Cordell D.K. Yee, assistant editor], 35-70. Chicago and London: The University of Chicago Press, 1994.

———. "Chinese Maps in Political Culture." In *The History of Cartography*, vol. 2, bk. 2, *Cartography in the Traditional East and Southeast Asian Societies*, edited by J.B. Harley (1932-1991) and David Woodward (1942-) [with Joseph E. Schwartzberg, associate editor; and Cordell D. K. Yee, assistant editor], 71-95. Chicago and London: The University of Chicago Press, 1994.

——. "Taking the World's Measure: Chinese Maps between Observation and Text." In *The History of Cartography*, vol. 2, bk. 2, *Cartography in the Traditional East and Southeast Asian Societies*, edited by J.B. Harley (1932-1991) and David Woodward (1942-) [with Joseph E. Schwartzberg, associate editor; and Cordell D.K. Yee, assistant editor], 96-127. Chicago and London: The University of Chicago Press, 1994.

——. "Chinese Cartography among the Arts: Objectivity, Subjectivity, Representation." In *The History of Cartography*, vol. 2, bk. 2, *Cartography in the Traditional East and Southeast Asian Societies*, edited by J.B. Harley (1932-1991) and David Woodward (1942-) [with Joseph E. Schwartzberg, associate editor; and Cordell D.K. Yee, assistant editor], 128-169. Chicago and London: The University of Chicago Press, 1994.

——. "Traditional Chinese Cartography and the Myth of Westernization." In *The History of Cartography*, vol. 2, bk. 2, *Cartography in the Traditional East and Southeast Asian Societies*, edited by J.B. Harley (1932-1991) and David Woodward (1942-) [with Joseph E. Schwartzberg, associate editor; and Cordell D.K. Yee, assistant editor], 170-202. Chicago and London: The University of Chicago Press, 1994.

——. "Concluding Remarks: Foundations for a Future History of Chinese Mapping." In *The History of Cartography*, vol. 2, bk. 2, *Cartography in the Traditional East and Southeast Asian Societies*, edited by J.B. Harley (1932-1991) and David Woodward (1942-) [with Joseph E. Schwartzberg, associate editor; and Cordell D.K. Yee, assistant editor], 228-231. Chicago and London: The University of Chicago Press, 1994.

——. "Space and Place: Ways of World-making." In *Space & Place: Mapmaking East and West: Four Hundred Years of Western and Chinese Cartography from the Library of Congress, Geography and Map Division, and the Collection of Leonard & Juliet Rothman*, exhibition catalogue by Cordell D.K. Yee, with Alexander Bowles, Heather Deutsch, and Sarah Jane Fremont, 7-16. Annapolis, Md.: St. John's College Press, 1996.

Yeh, Wen-hsin, ed. *Landscape, Culture, and Power in Chinese Society*. China Research Monograph, no. 49. Berkeley, Calif.: Center for Chinese Studies, Institute of East Asian Studies, University of California, Berkeley, 1998.

Yin, Runsheng. "Pinglun Fang Yulu yu Cheng Junfang liang jia mo dian." *Gugong bowu yuan yuankan (Palace Museum Journal)*, no. 14 (1981, no. 4): 44-48.
尹潤生・〈評論方于魯與程君房兩家墨店〉・《故宮博物院院刊》・總第十四期・一九八一年第四期・第四十頁至第四十八頁・

Yin Zhou jinwen jicheng. Compiled and edited by Zhongguo shehui kexue yuan kaogu yanjiu suo. Kaogu xue tekan. 18 vols. N.p. [Beijing]: Zhonghua shuju, 1984-1994.
《殷周金文集成》・中國社會科學院考古研究所編・《考古學特刊》・[全十八册・精裝]・[北京]：中華書局，1984年8月第1版至1994年12月第1版・

Ying sui ji fu: Yuan cang Zhong Kui ming hua tezhan (Blessings for the New Year: Catalogue to the Special Exhibition of Paintings of Chung K'uei). Compiled and edited by Guoli gugong bowu yuan bianji weiyuan hui. [Organized by Liu Fangru. In Chinese; title page, table of contents, and introduction also in English. Text by Liu Fangru. English translation by Donald E. Brix.] Taibei: Guoli gugong bowu yuan (National Palace Museum), 1997.
《迎歲集福：院藏鍾馗名畫特展》・編輯者：國立故宮博物院編輯委員會・[文字撰述：劉芳如・[英文翻譯：蒲思棠]・台北：國立故宮博物院，民國八十六年二月初版・

Yoshikawa, Kôjirô (1904-1980). *Yoshikawa Kôjirô zenshü.* 24 vols. [Chiefly in Japanese; some articles in English and German.] Tokyo: Chikuma shob, 1968-1976.
《吉川幸次郎全集》・著者：吉川幸次郎・[全精裝二十四卷]・東京：筑摩書房・昭和四十三年十一月十五日発行[第一卷]至昭和五十一年十二月十五日一刷発行[第二十四卷]・

You xiang Liexian quan zhuan. [Compiled and edited by Wang Yunpeng (fl. 1600).] Zhongguo minjian xinyang ziliao huibian, edited by Wang Qiugui and Li Fengmao, ser. 1, vol. 6. Zheng bian, no. 5. [Facsimile reproduction of 1600 edition compiled and edited by Wang Yunpeng.] Taibei: Taiwan Xuesheng shuju, 1989.
《有象列仙全傳》・編輯者：汪雲鵬・《中國民間信仰資料彙編》・王秋桂、李豐楙主編・第一輯第册・正編第種・[影印本・據明萬曆二十八年（1600年）汪雲鵬刊本影印]・台北：台灣學生書局，民國七十八年十一月景印初版・

Yü, Chün-fang. "Feminine Images of Kuan-yin in Post-Tang China." *Journal of Chinese Religions*, no. 18 (Fall 1990): 61-89.

——. "Guanyin: The Chinese Transformation of Avalokiteshvara." In *Latter Days of the Law: Images of Chinese Buddhism, 850-1850*, edited by Marsha Weidner, 151-181. Lawrence, Kan.: Spencer Museum of Art, The University of Kansas, in association with Honolulu: University of Hawaii Press, 1994.

——. "The Cult of Kuan-yin in Ming-Ch'ing China: A Case of Confucianization of Buddhism" In *Meeting of Minds: Intellectual and Religious Interaction in East Asian Traditions of Thought: Essays in Honor of Wing-tsit Chan and William Theodore de Bary*, edited by Irene Bloom and Joshua A. Fogel (1950-), 144-174. New York: Columbia University Press, 1997.

Yu, Hailan. "Qing dai hua jian yishu." *Duoyun (Flowery Cloud)*, no. 7

(November 1984): 158-159.

俞海藍・〈清代畫箋藝術〉・《朵雲》・第七集・一九八四年十一月・第一百五十八頁至第一百五十九頁・

Yu, Shenchu. *Zhongguo yi xue jianshi*. Fuzhou: Fujian kexue jishu chuban she, 1983.

《中國醫學簡史》・俞慎初著・福州：福建科學技術出版社，1983 年 12 月第 1 版・

Yutu yao lu: Beijing tushu guan cang 6827 zhong Zhong wai wen gujiu ditu mulu. Compiled by Beijing tushu guan shanben tecang bu yutu zu. Beijing: Beijing tushu guan chuban she, 1997.

《輿圖要錄：北京圖書館藏種中外文古舊地圖目錄》・北京圖書館善本特藏部輿圖組編・[精裝一冊]・北京：北京圖書館出版社，1997 年 12 月第 1 版・

Yu zhi Gengzhi tu. [Illustrated by Jiao Bingzhen (act. 1680-1720), with preface and poetic inscriptions by the Kangxi emperor (1654-1722; r. 1661-1722).] 2 vols. [on double-leaves; stitch-bound, Oriental style] in 1 case. [2d lithographic edition.] Shanghai: Dianshi zhai, 1886.

《御製耕織圖》・[焦秉貞繪・清聖祖序、題詩]・[石印本・裝二冊一函]・上海：點石齋，光緒十二年正月第二次石印・

Yu zhi Gengzhi tu. Illustrated by Jiao Bingzhen (act. 1680-1720). [Facsimile reproduction; album mounted in accordion style; issued in slipcase.] Beijing: Zhongguo shudian, 1998.

《御製耕織圖》・焦秉貞繪・[影印本・一函一冊]・北京：中國書店出版社，一九九八年六月・

Yuan, Weichun. *Qin Han bei shu*. Beijing: Beijing gongyi meishu chuban she, 1990.

《秦漢碑述》・袁維春撰・北京：北京工藝美術出版社，一九九〇年十二月第一版・

Yuan dai huajia shiliao. Compiled and edited by Chen Gaohua (1938-). Shanghai: Shanghai renmin meishu chuban she, 1980.

《元代畫家史料》・陳高華編著・上海：上海人民美術出版社，1980 年 5 月第 1 版・

Yuan qu xuan jiaozhu. Edited by Wang Xueqi. 4 vols. in 8. Shijiazhuang, Hebei: Hebei jiaoyu chuban she, 1994.

《元曲選校注》・王學奇主編・[全四冊，每冊分上、下部，共八部]・[精裝]・石家莊：河北教育出版社，1994 年 6 月第 1 次印刷・

-Z-

Zeitlin, Judith T. "The Secret Life of Rocks: Objects and Collectors in the Ming and Qing Imagination." *Orientations* 30, no. 5 (May

1999): 40-47.

Zeng, Jingchu. "Qiantan Shizhu zhai yishu." In *Shizhu zhai yanjiu wenji: "Shizhu zhai shuhua pu" kanxing sanbai liushi nian jinian*, compiled by Shizhu zhai yishu yanjiu bu, 14-17. Nanjing: Shizhu zhai yishu yanjiu bu, 1987.

曾景初・〈淺談十竹齋藝術〉・《十竹齋研究文集：〈十竹齋書畫譜〉刊行三百六十年紀念》・十竹齋藝術研究部編・南京：十竹齋藝術研究部，一九八七年十月・第十四頁至第十七頁・

Zhang, Binglun. "Researches in Heredity and Breeding." In *Ancient China's Technology and Science*, compiled by the Institute of the History of Natural Sciences, Chinese Academy of Sciences, 281-291. China Knowledge Series. Beijing: Foreign Languages Press, 1983.

Zhang, Bojin. *Guo ju yu lian pu*. [On double-leaves; stitch-bound, Oriental style, in 1 case.] Taibei: Mei Ya shuban gufen youxian gongsi, 1969.

《國劇與臉譜》・編著者：張伯謹・[綫裝全一冊]・台北：美亞書版股份有限公司，民國五十八年十一月初版・

Zhang, Erbin. "'Shizhu zhai shuhua pu' dui Zhongguo huapu xue de yanjiu jiazhi." In *Shizhu zhai yanjiu wenji: "Shizhu zhai shuhua pu" kanxing sanbai liushi nian jinian*, compiled by Shizhu zhai yishu yanjiu bu, 70-74. Nanjing: Shizhu zhai yishu yanjiu bu, 1987.

張爾賓・〈《十竹齋書畫譜》對中國畫譜學的研究價值〉・《十竹齋研究文集：〈十竹齋書畫譜〉刊行三百六十年紀念》・十竹齋藝術研究部編・南京：十竹齋藝術研究部，一九八七年十月・第七十頁至第七十四頁・

Zhang, Fusan. "Beiye de wenhua xiangzheng." In *Beiye wenhua lun*, edited by Wang Yizhi and Yang Shiguang, 1-9. Kunming: Yunnan renmin chuban she, 1990.

張福三・〈貝葉的文化象征〉・《貝葉文化論》・王懿之、楊世光編・[精裝一冊]・昆明：雲南人民出版社，1990 年 4 月 1 第版・第一頁至第九頁・

Zhang, Gongjin (1933-). *Dai zu wenhua yanjiu*. Kunming: Yunnan minzu chuban she, 1988.

《傣族文化研究》・張公瑾著・昆明：雲南民族出版社，1988 年 2 月第 1 版・

Zhang, Guobiao. "Hu Zhengyan de yishu zhi lu." In *Shizhu zhai yanjiu wenji: "Shizhu zhai shuhua pu" kanxing sanbai liushi nian jinian*, compiled by Shizhu zhai yishu yanjiu bu, 90-93. Nanjing: Shizhu zhai yishu yanjiu bu, 1987.

張國標・〈胡正言的藝術之路〉・《十竹齋研究文集：〈十竹齋書畫譜〉刊行三百六十年紀念》・十竹齋藝術研究部編・南京：十竹齋藝術研究部，一九八七年十月・第九十頁至第九十三頁・

Zhang, Renhe. *"Xixiang ji" lunzheng*. Dongbei shifan daxue wenku.

Changchun, Jilin: Dongbei shifan daxue chuban she, 1995.

《〈西廂記〉論證》・張人和著・〈東北師範大學文庫〉・長春：東北師範大學出版社，1995 年 8 月第 1 版・

Zhang, Shaohua. *Beijing jinyu.* 2d rev. ed. Beijing: Beijing chuban she, 1987.

《北京金魚》・張紹華著・[增訂本]・北京：北京出版社，1987 年 4 月第 2 版・

Zhang, Tiexian. "Dunhuang gu xieben congtan." *Wenwu,* no. 149 (1963, no. 3) (March 1963): 7-11.

張鐵弦・〈敦煌古寫本叢談〉・《文物》・一九六三年第三期・總第一四九號・第七頁至第十一頁・

Zhang, Xiulan. "Ji Zhaocheng Zang lingben." *Wenwu,* no. 331 (1983, no. 12) (December 1983): 88-89.

張秀蘭・〈記趙城藏零本〉・《文物》・一九八三年第十二期・總第三三一號・第八十八頁至第八十九頁・

Zhang, Xiumin. "Liao, Jin, Xi Xia ke shu jianshi." *Wenwu,* no. 103 (1959, no. 3) (March 1959): 11-18.

張秀民・〈遼、金、西夏刻書簡史〉・《文物》・一九五九年第三期・總第一〇三號・第十一頁至第十八頁・

———. "Ming dai Nanjing de yinshu." *Wenwu,* no. 294 (1980, no. 11) (November 1980): 78-83.

張秀民・〈明代南京的印書〉・《文物》・一九八〇年第十一期・總第二九四號・第七十八頁至第八十三頁・

Zhang, Yuxin. *Bishu shanzhuang de zaoyuan yishu.* Beijing: Wenwu chuban she, 1991.

《避暑山莊的造園藝術》・張羽新著・北京：文物出版社，1991 年 1 月第一版・

Zhang, Zhongjiang. *Lidai jinü yu shige.* Huadeng congshu. Taoyuan, Taiwan: Zhiquan chuban she, n.d. [1966].

《歷代妓女與詩歌》・張忠江編著・〈華燈叢書〉・[台灣]桃園・志全出版社，[民國五十五年]・

Zhang Jusheng xiansheng qishi shengri jinian lunwen ji. Compiled and edited by Cai Yuanpei (1868-1940), Hu Shi (1891-1962), and Wang Yunwu (1888-). Shanghai: Shangwu yinshu guan, 1937.

《張菊生先生七十生日紀念論文集》・蔡元培、胡適、王雲五編輯・上海：商務印書館，民國二十六年一月初版・

Zhao, Chengze. "Silk and Silk Textile Technology." In *Ancient China's Technology and Science,* compiled by the Institute of the History of Natural Sciences, Chinese Academy of Sciences, 520-533. China Knowledge Series. Beijing: Foreign Languages Press, 1983.

Zhao, Gang (1929-), and Chen Zhongyi. *Zhongguo mian ye shi.* Taibei:

Lianjing chuban shiye gongsi, 1977 [2d printing, 1983].

《中國棉業史》・趙岡、陳鍾毅著・[平裝一冊]・台北：聯經出版事業公司，民國六十六年七月初版・[民國七十二年九月第二次印行]・

Zhao, Yashu. "Gengzhi tu yu Gengzhi tu shi (yi)." *Shihuo yuekan (Shih-huo Monthly)* 3, no. 7 (October 1973): 331-335.

趙雅書・〈耕織圖與耕織圖詩（一）〉・《食貨月刊》・復刊第三卷・第七期・民國六十二年十月十五日出版・第三百三十一頁至第三百三十五頁・

———. "Gengzhi tu yu Gengzhi tu shi (er)." *Shihuo yuekan (Shih-huo Monthly)* 3, no. 9 (November 1973): 409-426.

趙雅書・〈耕織圖與耕織圖詩（二）〉・《食貨月刊》・復刊第三卷・第九期・民國六十二年十二月十五日出版・第四百零九頁至第四百二十六頁・

———. "Gengzhi tu yu Gengzhi tu shi (san)." *Shihuo yuekan (Shih-huo Monthly)* 3, no. 11 (February 1974): 526-531.

趙雅書・〈耕織圖與耕織圖詩（三）〉・《食貨月刊》・復刊第三卷・第十一期・民國六十三年二月十五日出版・第五百二十六頁至第五百三十一頁・

———. "Gengzhi tu yu Gengzhi tu shi (si)." *Shihuo yuekan (Shih-huo Monthly)* 4, no. 5 (August 1974): 192-201.

趙雅書・〈耕織圖與耕織圖詩（四）〉・《食貨月刊》・復刊第四卷・第五期・民國六十三年八月一日出版・第三百三十一頁至第三百三十五頁・

Zhao Mengfu xiaokai Daode jing zhenji. [Compiled and edited by Shanghai shuhua chuban she.] Lidai fashu cuiying. Shanghai: Shanghai shuhua chuban she, 1986 [6th printing, 1999].

《趙孟頫小楷道德經真蹟》・[上海書畫出版社編]・〈歷代法書萃英〉・[平裝一冊]・上海：上海書畫出版社，1986 年 3 月第 1 版，1999 年 3 月第 6 次印刷・

Zhao Mengfu yanjiu lunwen ji. Edited by Shanghai shuhua chuban she. Shanghai: Shanghai shuhua chuban she, 1995.

《趙孟頫研究論文集》・編者：本社[上海書畫出版社]・上海：上海書畫出版社，1995 年 3 月第一版・

Zheng, Shangxian. "Zang Jinshu gaiding 'Yuan qu xuan' kao." *Wenxian,* no. 40 (1989, no. 2): 50-56.

鄭尚憲・〈臧晉叔改訂《元曲選》考〉・《文獻》・總第四十期・一九八九年第二期・第五十頁至第五十六頁・

Zheng, Xihuang. "Yang Ziqi ba Yudi tu ji qi tushi fuhao." In *Zhongguo gudai ditu ji: Ming dai [(An Atlas of Ancient Maps in China–The Ming Dynasty, 1368-1644)],* edited by Cao Wanru et al., text section, 61-64, with summary in English, ""Yu Di Tu' (Terrestrial Map) with a Postscript by Yang Ziqi and Its Legends and Symbols," text section, 131. Beijing: Wenwu chuban she (Cultural Relics Publishing House), 1995.

鄭錫煌・〈楊子器跋輿地圖及其圖式符號〉・《中國古代地圖集：明代》・曹婉如、鄭錫煌、黃盛璋、鈕仲勛、任金城、秦國經、胡波編・北京：文物出版社，

1995 年 10 月第一版・第六十一頁至第六十四頁・英文提要・第一百三十一頁・

Zheng, Zhenduo (1898-1958), comp. and ed. *Zhongguo gudai muke hua xuan ji*. [With an explanatory text by Li Pingfan and Liu Yushan; preface by Zheng Zhenduo.] 10 vols. [on double-leaves; stitch-bound, Oriental style] in 1 case within another case. Beijing: Renmin meishu chuban she, 1985.
《中國古代木刻畫選集》・鄭振鐸編著・[出版説明：李平凡、劉玉山・鄭振鐸序]・[線裝十冊一函]・北京：人民美術出版社，一九八五年二月出版・

―――. *Zheng Zhenduo shuhua*. Edited by Jiang Deming. Selected by Zheng Erkang. Xiandai shuhua congshu. Beijing: Beijing chuban she, 1996.
《鄭振鐸書話》・作者：鄭振鐸・主編：姜德明・選編：鄭爾康・〈現代書話叢書〉・[平裝一冊]・北京：北京出版社，1996 年 10 月第 1 版・

Zhiwu mingshi tukao. 38 juan. *Fu Zhiwu mingshi tukao changbian*. 22 juan. By Wu Qijun (1789-1847). Edited by Lu Yinggu. [Preface by Lu Yinggu dated 1848. Rev. ed. Shanghai: Shangwu yinshu guan, 1919. 2d revised ed. (reduced format). 2 vols. Shanghai: Shangwu yinshu guan, 1933.] Reprint. 18 vols. Wanyou wenku huiyao, edited by Wang Yunwu, vols. 536-553. Taibei: Taiwan Shangwu yinshu guan, 1965.
《植物名實圖考》・三十八卷・附《植物名實圖考長編》・二十二卷・吳其濬著・陸應穀校刊・[道光二十八年陸應穀序]・[上海商務印書館民國八年十二月重校付印本初版]・上海商務印書館民國二十二年十一月縮本初版・二冊・[影印本]・〈萬有文庫薈要〉・王雲五主編・第五百三十六冊至第五百五十三冊・[平裝十八冊]・台北：臺灣商務印書館，民國五十四年十一月臺一版・

Zhong, Kan, Wu Fengyun, and Li Fanwen. *Xi Xia jian shi*. Yinchuan, Ningxia: Ningxia renmin chuban she, 1979.
《西夏簡史》・鍾侃、吳峰雲、李范文著・銀川：寧夏人民出版社，1979 年 11 月第 1 版・

Zhong Kui bai tu. Chief editor: Wang Lanxi. Deputy editor: Wang Shucun. [Table of contents in Chinese and English. Spine title also in English: *A Hundred Paintings Concerning Zhong Kui*.] Guangzhou: Lingnan meishu chuban she, 1990.
《鍾馗百圖》・主編：王蘭西・副主編：王樹村・廣州：嶺南美術出版社，1990 年 10 月第一版・

Zhongguo banhua shi tulu. Compiled by Zheng Zhenduo (1898-1958). 20 vols. [on double-leaves; stitch-bound, Oriental style] in 5 cases. [Facsimile reproductions. Originally projected as a set of 24 vols. Vols. 14, 19, 22, and 24 were never published.] Shanghai: Zhongguo banhua shi she, 1940-1942.
《中國版畫史圖錄》・鄭振鐸編著・[二十冊五函・原計劃一套二十四冊・第十四、十九、二十二、二十四冊未刊]・上海：中國版畫史社，民國二十九年至三十一年・

Zhongguo banke tulu. Compiled and edited by Beijing tushu guan. 2d rev. ed. 8 vols. [on double-leaves; stitch-bound, Oriental style] in 1 case. Beijing: Wenwu chuban she, 1961.
《中國版刻圖錄》・北京圖書館編・[增訂本]・[裝八冊一函]・北京：文物出版社，一九六一年三月再版・

Zhongguo banke zonglu. Compiled and edited by Yang Shengxin. N.p. [Xi'an]: Shaanxi renmin chuban she, 1987.
《中國版刻綜錄》・楊繩信編著・[西安]：陝西人民出版社，一九八七年六月第一版・

Zhongguo gu ditu jingxuan (A Selection of China's Ancient Maps). Editor-in-chief: Liu Zhenwei. Deputy editors-in-chief: Wang Ruo, Jiang Tonghua. [Text by Wang Qianjin. Translation by Feng Qionghuan.] [In Chinese; title on title-page, foreword by Liu Zhenwei, general information, table of contents, and captions to illustrations also in English.] Beijing: Zhongguo shijie yu chuban she (China Esperanto Press), 1995.
《中國古地圖精選》・主編：劉鎮偉・副主編：王若、姜桐華・[撰文：汪前進・翻譯：馮瓊歡]・北京：中國世界語出版社，1995 年 3 月第一版・

Zhongguo gudai banhua congkan. Compiled and edited by Zheng Zhenduo (1898-1958). 4 vols. [Vol. 1, *Xin ding San li tu, Tianzhu ling qian, Taiyin da quan ji, Sheng ji tu, Lidai guren xiangzan, Wu jing zongyao qian ji*; vol. 2, *Jiu huang bencao, Riji gushi, Zhongyi Shuihu zhuan chatu, Bianmin tu zuan*; vol. 3, *Liexian quan zhuan, Gu shi hua pu, Hanhan zhai jiu pai, Tiangong kaiwu*; vol. 4, *Yuan Ming xiqu yezi, Lisao tu, Lingyan ge gongchen tu, Wushuang pu, Baiyue ningyan, Shouyi guangxun*]. Shanghai: Shanghai guji chuban she, 1988.
《中國古代版畫叢刊》・鄭振鐸編・[全四冊]・[第一冊・《新定三禮圖、天竺靈籤、太音大全集、聖跡圖、歷代古人像贊、武經總要前集》・第二冊・《救荒本草、日記故事、忠義水滸傳插圖、便民圖纂》・第三冊・《列仙全傳、顧氏畫譜、醉醉齋酒牌、天工開物》・第四冊・《元明戲曲葉子、離騷圖、凌煙閣功臣圖、無雙譜、白嶽凝煙、授衣廣訓》]・上海：上海古籍出版社，1988 年 8 月第 1 版・

Zhongguo gudai banhua congkan er bian. Compiled and edited by Shanghai guji chuban she. 9 vols. in 10 [Vol. 1, *Meihua xishen pu, Yinshan zhengyao (fu Yuan ke Yinshan zhengyao can juan), Shanhai jing tu*; vol. 2, *Shi shi yuanliu, Shuilu daochang shengui tuxiang, Muniu tu*; vol. 3, *Kong sheng jiayu tu, Kong men rujiao liezhuan*; vol. 4, *Gujin lienü zhuan pinglin, Qinglou yunyu*; vol. 5, *Gui fan*; vol. 6, pts. 1-2, *Cheng shi mo yuan*; vol. 7, *Tang shi hua pu, Shi yu hua pu, Yuan qu xuan tu*; vol. 8, *Hainei qi guan, Ming shan tu, Taiping shanshui tuhua, Gu She shanchuan tu*; vol. 9, *Ruishi liangying*]. Shanghai: Shanghai guji chuban she, 1994.
《中國古代版畫叢刊二編》・上海古籍出版社編・[全九輯十冊]・[第一輯・《梅花喜神譜、飲膳正要（附元刻飲膳正要殘卷）、山海經圖》・第二輯・《釋氏源流、

水陸道場神鬼圖像、牧牛圖〉‧第三輯‧《孔聖家語圖、孔門儒教列傳》‧第四輯‧《古今列女傳評林》‧第五輯‧《閨範》‧第六輯，分上、下冊‧《程氏墨苑》‧第七輯‧《唐詩畫譜、詩餘畫譜、元曲選圖》‧第八輯‧《海內奇觀、名山圖、太平山水圖畫、古歙山川圖》‧第九輯‧《瑞世良英》]‧上海：上海古籍出版社，1994 年 10 月第 1 版‧

Zhongguo gudai cang shu yu jindai tushu guan shiliao (Chunqiu zhi Wusi qianhou). Compiled and edited by Li Xibi and Zhang Shuhua. Beijing: Zhonghua shuju, 1982.
《中國古代藏書與近代圖書館史料（春秋至五四前後）》‧李希泌、張椒華編‧北京：中華書局，1982 年 2 月第 1 版‧

Zhongguo gudai ditu ji: Ming dai [(An Atlas of Ancient Maps in China–The Ming Dynasty (1368-1644)]. Edited by Cao Wanru, Zheng Xihuang, Huang Shengzhang, Niu Zhongxun, Ren Jincheng, Qin Guojing, and Hu Bangbo. Beijing: Wenwu chuban she (Cultural Relics Publishing House), 1995.
《中國古代地圖集：明代》‧曹婉如、鄭錫煌、黃盛璋、鈕仲勛、任金城、秦國經、胡波編‧北京：文物出版社，1995 年 10 月第一版‧

Zhongguo gudai ditu ji: Qing dai [(An Atlas of Ancient Maps in China–The Qing Dynasty (1644-1911)]. Edited by Cao Wanru, Zheng Xihuang, Huang Shengzhang, Niu Zhongxun, Ren Jincheng, Qin Guojing, and Wang Qianjin. Beijing: Wenwu chuban she (Cultural Relics Publishing House), 1997.
《中國古代地圖集：清代》‧曹婉如、鄭錫煌、黃盛璋、鈕仲勛、任金城、秦國經、汪前進編‧北京：文物出版社，1997 年 12 月 1 第版‧

Zhongguo gudai ditu ji: Zhan guo-Yuan [(An Atlas of Ancient Maps in China–From the Warring States to the Yuan Dynasty (476 B.C.-A.D. 1368)]. Edited by Cao Wanru, Zheng Xihuang, Huang Shengzhang, Niu Zhongxun, Ren Jincheng, and Ju Deyuan. Beijing: Wenwu chuban she (Cultural Relics Publishing House), 1990.
《中國古代地圖集：戰國—元》‧曹婉如、鄭錫煌、黃盛璋、鈕仲勛、任金城、鞠德源編‧北京：文物出版社，1990 年 7 月第 1 版‧

Zhongguo gudai fojiao banhua ji. Chief editor: Zhou Xinhui. Co-editors: Chen Jian and Ma Wenda. 3 vols. [Vol. 1, *Tang zhi Yuan fojiao banhua*. Vol. 2, *Ming dai fojiao banhua*. Vol. 3, *Qing ji Min chu fojiao banhua*.] Beijing: Xueyuan chuban she, 1998.
《中國古代佛教版畫集》‧主編：周心慧‧副主編：陳堅、馬文大‧[精裝全三冊‧第一冊：〈唐至元佛教版畫〉‧第二冊：〈明代佛教版畫〉‧第三冊：〈清及民初佛教版畫〉]‧北京：學苑出版社，一九九八年五月北京第一版‧

Zhongguo gudai Gengzhi tu (Farming and Weaving Pictures in Ancient China). Compiled by Zhongguo nongye bowu guan (China Agricultural Museum). Edited by Wang Chaosheng. Zhongguo nongye bowu guan congshu, edited by Zhongguo nongye bowu guan. [In Chinese and English.] Beijing: Zhongguo nongye chuban she (China Agriculture Press), 1995.
《中國古代耕織圖》‧中國農業博物館編‧主編：王潮生‧〈中國農業博物館叢書〉‧[精裝一冊]‧北京：中國農業出版社，1995 年 12 月第 1 版‧

Zhongguo gudai yinshua shi tuce (An Illustrated History of Printing in Ancient China). Compiled by Zhongguo yinshua bowu guan (The Printing Museum of China). Edited by Luo Shubao. Translated by Chen Shanwei (Chan Sin-wai). Hong Kong: Xianggang chengshi daxue chuban she (City University of Hong Kong Press); Beijing: Wenwu chuban she (Cultural Relics Publishing House), 1998.
《中國古代印刷史圖冊》‧中國印刷博物館編‧羅樹寶主編‧陳善偉譯‧[漢英版]‧香港：香港城市大學出版社；北京：文物出版社，1998 年‧

Zhongguo gudai zhuan wen. Compiled and edited by Wang Yong and Li Miao. Beijing: Zhishi chuban she, 1990.
《中國古代磚文》‧王鏞、李淼編撰‧北京：知識出版社，一九九○年十二月第一版‧

Zhongguo gudian wenxue banhua xuanji. Edited by Fu Xihua (1907-1970). 2 vols. Shanghai: Shanghai renmin meishu chuban she, 1981.
《中國古典文學版畫選集》‧傅惜華編‧[上下兩冊]‧上海：上海人民美術出版社，一九八一年十二月第一版‧

Zhongguo guji shanben shumu: Zi bu. Compiled and edited by Zhongguo guji shanben shumu bianji weiyuan hui. 8 vols. [on double-leaves; stitch-bound, Oriental style] in 1 case. Shanghai: Shanghai guji chuban she, 1994.
《中國古籍善本書目：子部》‧中國古籍善本書目編輯委員會編‧[線裝八冊一函]‧上海：上海古籍出版社，1994 年 12 月第 1 版‧

Zhongguo gujin diming da cidian. Compiled by Zang Lihe et al. Edited by Lu Erkui and Fang Yi. Shanghai: Shanghai yinshu guan, 1931.
《中國古今地名大辭典》‧臧勵龢等編輯‧陸爾奎、方毅校訂‧上海：商務印書館，民國二十年五月初版‧

Zhongguo guojia tushu guan (National Library of China). [Adviser: Ren Jiyu. Editor-in-Chief: Li Zhizhong. Supervisors: Liu Huiping and Suo Kuihuan. Text writers: Tang Gengsheng and Zhang Yan. Translator: Gu Ben.] [In Chinese and English.] Beijing: Zhongguo guojia tushu guan, 1999.
《中國國家圖書館》‧[顧問：任繼愈‧主編：李志忠‧監制：劉惠平、索奎桓‧撰文：湯更生、張彥‧譯文：顧　]‧[平裝一冊]‧北京：中國國家圖書館，1999 年編輯‧

Zhongguo guojia tushu guan guji zhenpin tulu. Chief editor: Ren Jiyu. [Planning: Ren Jiyu, Zhou Heping, Sun Beixin, and Li Zhizhong. Co-editors: Huang Runhua, Chen Hanyu, Chen Xingzhen, Zhang Zhiqing,

Guo Youling.] Beijing: Beijing tushu guan chuban she, 1999.

《中國國家圖書館古籍珍品圖錄》・主編：任繼愈・[策劃：任繼愈、周和平、孫蓓欣、李志忠・副主編：黃潤華、陳漢玉、陳杏珍、張志清、郭又陵]・[精裝、平裝各一冊]・北京：北京圖書館出版社，1999 年 9 月第 1 版・

Zhongguo Han dai huaxiang shi huaxiang zhuan wenxian mulu. Compiled and edited by Shenzhen bowu guan. Beijing: Wenwu chuban she, 1995.

《中國漢代畫像石畫像磚文獻目錄》・深圳博物館編・北京：文物出版社，1995 年 5 月第一版・

Zhongguo hua jing (China Floral Encyclopaedia). Edited by Chen Junyu and Cheng Xuke. [In Chinese; title also in English; scientific names also in Latin.] Shanghai: Shanghai wenhua chuban she, 1990.

《中國花經》・陳俊愉、程緒珂主編・[精裝一冊]・上海：上海文化出版社，1990 年 8 月第 1 版・

Zhongguo Jiade '95 chun ji paimai hui: Guji shanben (China Guardian '95 Spring Auctions: Rare Books). Auction catalogue [Wednesday, May 10, 1995 at 10:00 a.m. (Lots 391 to 494) at Ballroom, The Great Wall Sheraton Hotel, Beijing)]. Beijing: Zhongguo Jiade guoji paimai youxian gongsi (China Guardian Auctions Co., Ltd.), 1995.

《中國嘉德' 95 春季拍賣會：古籍善本》・[一九九五年五月十日星期三上午十點・北京・長城飯店・大宴會廳・拍賣品號]・[拍賣圖錄・平裝一冊]・北京：中國嘉德國際拍賣有限公司，1995 年・

Zhongguo jing ju shi. Compiled and edited by Beijing shi yishu yanjiu suo and Shanghai yishu yanjiu suo. Zhongguo xiqu juzhong shi congshu. Vols. 1-2. Beijing: Zhongguo xiju chuban she, 1990.

《中國京劇史》・北京市藝術研究所、上海藝術研究所編著・〈中國戲曲劇種史叢書〉・[上、中冊]・北京：中國戲劇出版社，1990 年 1 月北京第 1 版（上卷），1990 年 11 月第 1 版（中卷）・

Zhongguo jing ju shi tulu. Chief editor: Jin Yaozhang. Deputy editors: Zhang Jie and Liu Dongfeng. Shijiazhuang, Hebei: Hebei jiaoyu chuban she, 1994.

《中國京劇史圖錄》・主編：金耀章・副主編：張杰、劉東風・石家莊：河北教育出版社，1994 年 11 月第 1 版・

Zhongguo kaishu ming tie jinghua. Chief editor: Ouyang Zhongshi. 3 vols. Zhongguo shufa ming tie jinghua. Beijing: Beijing chuban she, 1994.

《中國楷書名帖精華》・主編：歐陽中石・[全三冊]・〈中國書法名帖精華叢書〉・北京：北京出版社，一九九四年六月第一版・

Zhongguo lishi dili xue lunzhu suoyin (1900-1980). Compiled and edited by Du Yu and Zhu Lingling. Beijing: Shumu wenxian chuban she, 1986.

《中國歷史地理學論著索引（1900–1980）》・杜瑜、朱玲玲編・北京：書目文獻
出版社，1986 年 4 月北京第 1 版・

Zhongguo lishi ditu ji (The Historical Atlas of China). Sponsor: Chinese Academy of Social Sciences. Chief editor: Tan Qixiang. 8 vols. Vol. 6, Song, Liao, Jin shiqi (The Liao Dynasty and Northern Song Dynasty Period, The Jin Dynasty and Southern Song Dynasty Period) [1982]. Vol. 7, Yuan, Ming shiqi (The Yuan Dynasty Period, The Ming Dynasty Period) [1982]. Vol. 8, Qing shiqi (The Qing Dynasty Period) [1987]. N.p. [Beijing]: Ditu chuban she (Cartographic Publishing House), 1982-1987.

《中國歷史地圖集》・主辦單位：中國社會科學院・主編：譚其驤・[精裝本・全八冊]・[第六冊：〈宋、遼、金時期〉・第七冊：〈元、明時期〉・第八冊：〈清時期〉]・[北京]：地圖出版社，1982 年 10 月第 1 版[第一冊]至 1987 年 10 月第 1 版[第八冊]・

Zhongguo meishu quanji: Diaosu bian. Vol. 11, Longmen shiku diaoke. Compiled by Zhongguo meishu quanji bianji weiyuan hui. [Editor-in-chief: Wen Yucheng. Deputy editor: Li Wensheng.] Shanghai: Shanghai renmin meishu chuban she, 1988.

《中國美術全集・雕塑編》・第十一冊・《龍門石窟雕刻》・中國美術全集編輯委員會編・[本卷主編：溫玉成・本卷副主編：李文生]・上海：上海人民美術出版社，一九八八年六月第一版・

Zhongguo meishu quanji: Huihua bian. Vol. 18, Huaxiang shi huaxiang zhuan. Compiled by Zhongguo meishu quanji bianji weiyuan hui. [Editor-in-chief: Chang Renxia.] Shanghai: Shanghai renmin meishu chuban she, 1988.

《中國美術全集・繪畫編》・第十八冊・《畫像石畫像磚》・中國美術全集編輯委員會編・友本卷主編：常任俠狁・上海：上海人民美術出版社，一九八八年四月第一版・

Zhongguo meishu quanji: Huihua bian. Vol. 19, Shike xianhua. Compiled by Zhongguo meishu quanji bianji weiyuan hui. [Consultant: Wang Ziyun; editor-in-chief: Wang Shucun.] Shanghai: Shanghai renmin meishu chuban she, 1988.

《中國美術全集・繪畫編》・第十九冊・《石刻畫》・中國美術全集編輯委員會編・[本卷顧問：王子雲・本卷主編：王樹村]・上海：上海人民美術出版社，一九八八年十月第一版・

Zhongguo meishu quanji: Huihua bian. Vol. 20, Banhua. Compiled by Zhongguo meishu quanji bianji weiyuan hui. [Editor-in-chief: Wang Bomin.] Shanghai: Shanghai renmin meishu chuban she, 1988.

《中國美術全集・繪畫編》・第二十冊・《版畫》・中國美術全集編輯委員會編・[本卷主編：王伯敏]・上海：上海人民美術出版社，一九八八年第一版・

Zhongguo meishu quanji: Shufa zhuanke bian. Vol. 1, Shang Zhou zhi Qin Han shufa. Compiled by Zhongguo meishu quanji bianji weiyuan hui. [Editor-in-chief: Qi Gong.] Beijing: Renmin meishu chuban she, 1987.

《中國美術全集・書法篆刻編》・第一冊・《商周至秦漢書法》・中國美術全集編

輯委員會編・[本卷主編：啟功]・北京：人民美術出版社，一九八七年十二月第
一版・

Zhongguo meishu quanji: Shufa zhuanke bian. Vol. 2, *Wei Jin Nanbei chao shufa.* Compiled by Zhongguo meishu quanji bianji weiyuan hui. [Editor-in-chief: Qi Gong.] Beijing: Renmin meishu chuban she, 1986.
《中國美術全集・書法篆刻編》・第二冊・《魏晉南北朝書法》・中國美術全集編輯委員會編・[本卷主編：啟功]・北京：人民美術出版社，一九八六年七月第一版・

Zhongguo meishu quanji: Shufa zhuanke bian. Vol. 4, *Song Jin Yuan shufa.* Compiled by Zhongguo meishu quanji bianji weiyuan hui. [Editor-in-chief: Shen Peng.] Beijing: Renmin meishu chuban she, 1986.
《中國美術全集・書法篆刻編》・第四冊・《宋金元書法》・中國美術全集編輯委員會編・[本卷主編：沈鵬]・北京：人民美術出版社，一九八六年七月第一版・

Zhongguo meishu jia renming cidian. Compiled and edited by Yu Jianhua (1895-1979). Shanghai: Shanghai renmin meishu chuban she, 1981.
《中國美術家人名辭典》・俞劍華編・上海：上海人民美術出版社，一九八一年十二月第一版・

Zhongguo ming shan da chuan cidian. Chief editor: Shan Shumo. Deputy editors: Ge Minqing and Sun Wenchang. Jinan, Shandong: Shandong jiaoyu chuban she, 1992.
《中國名山大川辭典》・主編：單樹模・副主編：葛敏卿、孫文昌・濟南：山東教育出版社，1992年12月第1版・

Zhongguo minjian xinyang ziliao huibian. Ser. 1. Edited by Wang Qiugui and Li Fengmao. 31 vols. Taibei: Taiwan Xuesheng shuju, 1989.
《中國民間信仰資料彙編》・第一輯・王秋桂、李豐楙主編・[全精裝三十一冊]・台北：台灣學生書局，民國七十八年十一月景印初版・

Zhongguo minzu gu wenzi tulu. Edited by Zhongguo minzu gu wenzi yanjiu hui. Beijing: Zhongguo shehui kexue chuban she, 1990.
《中國民族古文字圖錄》・中國民族古文字研究會編・北京：中國社會科學出版社，1990年12月第1版・

Zhongguo renming da cidian. Compiled and edited by Zang Lihe et al. Hong Kong: Taixing shuju, 1931.
《中國人名大辭典》・臧勵龢等編輯・香港：泰興書局，一九三一年四月版・

Zhongguo shenhua chuanshuo cidian. Compiled and edited by Yuan Ke. Shanghai: Shanghai cishu chuban she, 1985.
《中國神話傳說詞典》・袁珂編著・上海：上海辭書出版社，1985年6月第1版・

Zhongguo shenxian huaxiang ji. Compiled and edited by Cheng Yin. Shanghai: Shanghai guji chuban she, 1996.
《中國神仙畫像集》・成寅編・上海：上海古籍出版社，1996年4月第1版・

Zhongguo shu shi. Compiled and edited by Zheng Rusi and Xiao Dongfa. Zhongyang guangbo dianshi daxue tushu guan xue zhuanye yongshu. Beijing: Shumu wenxian chuban she, 1987. Reprint (6th printing). Beijing: Beijing tushu guan chuban she, 1998.
《中國書史》・鄭如斯、肖東發編著・〈中央廣播電視大學圖書館學專業用書〉・北京：書目文獻出版社，1987年6月第1版・[重印本]・[平裝 一冊]・北京：北京圖書館出版社，1998年4月第6次印刷・

Zhongguo shudian 1998 nian chun ji shukan ziliao paimai hui. Auction catalogue [May 8, 1998 at 1:30 p.m., Zhongguo shudian (Cathay Bookshop), Beijing]. Beijing: Beijing Haiwang cun paimai youxian zeren gongsi, 1998.
《中國書店年春季書刊資料拍賣會》・[1998年5月8日（星期五）下午1：30分始]・[拍賣圖錄・平裝 一冊]・北京：北京海王村拍賣責任公司，1998年・

Zhongguo shudian 1998 nian qiu ji shukan ziliao paimai hui. Auction catalogue [October 29, 1998 at 1:30 p.m., Zhongguo shudian (Cathay Bookshop), Beijing]. Beijing: Beijing Haiwang cun paimai youxian zeren gongsi, 1998.
《中國書店年秋季書刊資料拍賣會》・[1998年10月29日（星期四）下午1：30分始]・[拍賣圖錄・平裝 一冊]・北京：北京海王村拍賣責任公司，1998年・

Zhongguo shufa wenhua daguan. Edited by Jin Kaicheng and Wang Yuechuan. [In Chinese; preface also in English.] Zhongguo wenhua daguan xilie (Grand Exposition of Chinese Culture Series). Beijing: Beijing daxue chuban she, 1995.
《中國書法文化大觀》・金開誠、王岳川主編・〈中國文化大觀系列〉・[精裝一冊]・北京：北京大學出版社，1995年1月第一版・

Zhongguo xiqu lian pu wenji. Compiled and edited by Huang Dianqi. [Preface by Weng Ouhong.] Beijing: Zhongguo xiju chuban she, 1994.
《中國戲曲臉譜文集》・黃殿祺輯・[翁耦虹序]・北京：中國戲劇出版社，1994年5月1第版・

Zhongguo weiqi (Chûgoku no igo) (China Weiqi). Edited by Liu Shancheng. Proofread by Shurong qi yuan. Chengdu: Sichuan kexue jishu chuban she; Chengdu: Shurong qi yi chuban she, 1985.
《中國圍棋》（《中国の囲碁》）・主編：劉善承・校審：蜀蓉棋院・[精裝一冊]・成都：四川科學技術出版社；成都：蜀蓉棋藝出版社，1985年7月第一版・

Zhongguo yinben shuji zhanlan mulu. Compiled and edited by Beijing tushu guan. [Introduction by Zheng Zhenduo (1898-1958), 1-4.] [Stitch-bound, with paper covers.] Beijing: Zhongyang renmin zhengfu wenhua bu shehui wenhua shiye guanli ju, 1952.
《中國印本書籍展覽目錄》・北京圖書館編・[引言：鄭振鐸，第一頁至第四頁]・[紙面裝一冊]・北京：中央人民政府文化部社會文化事業管理局，一九五二年十月・

Zhongguo yinshua shi lun cong: Shi pian (The Encyclopedia of Chinese Printing History). Chief editor: Xu Yingjian (Jerry Y.C. {Jerry Ying-Chien} Sheu). Compiled and edited by Guoli Taiwan Shifan daxue tuwen chuanbo jishu xue xi (Department of Graphic Communication & Printing Technology, National Taiwan Normal University). [English translations revised by Gu Boyan (Poyen Koo) and Cai Xitao (Shir-Tau Tsai).] 2 vols. [Vol. 1, Shi bu; vol. 2, Shi bu fu lu]. [Issued in slipcase.] Taibei: Zhongguo yinshua xuehui (China Graphic Arts Association), 1997.

《中國印刷史論叢：史篇》·主編：許瀛鑑·編輯者：國立台灣師範大學圖文傳播技術學系·[翻譯訂正：顧柏岩、蔡錫濤]·[上、下冊·精裝]·[上冊：〈史部〉·下冊：〈史部附錄〉]·台北：中國印刷學會，一九九七年九月二十八日初版·

Zhongguo yi xue da cidian. Compiled and edited by Xie Guan (1880-1950) et al. Reprint [originally published Shanghai: Shangwu yinshu guan, 1921]. 4 vols. N.p. [Beijing]: Zhongguo shudian, 1988.

《中國醫學大辭典》·謝觀等編纂·[影印本·據一九二一年商務印書館版影印·全四冊·精裝]·[北京]：中國書店，1998年2月第1版·

Zhonghua Da zang jing (Han wen bufen). Compiled and edited by Zhonghua Da zang jing bianji ju. 106 vols. Beijing: Zhonghua shuju, 1984-1996.

《中華大藏經（漢文部分）》·中華大藏經編輯局編·[全一〇六冊]·北京：中華書局，1984年4月第1版[第一冊]至1996年6月第1版[第一〇六冊]·

Zhonghua gu ditu zhenpin xuanji. Compiled and edited by Zhongguo cehui kexue yanjiu yuan. Harbin: Ha'erbin ditu chuban she, 1998.

《中國古地圖珍品選集》·中國測繪科學研究院編纂·[精裝一冊]·哈爾濱：哈爾濱地圖出版社，1998年1月第1版·

Zhonghua minguo chuantong banhua yishu (The Traditional Art of Chinese Woodblock Prints). Organized by Xingzheng yuan wenhua jianshe weiyuan hui (Council for Cultural Planning and Development, Executive Yuan). [Special writer: Pan Yuanshi (Pan Yuan-shih). Chief editor: Huang Cailang (Huang Tsai-lang). Translators: Shi Dawei (David Kamen) and Mou Ande (Andrew Morton).] [In Chinese and English.] Taibei: Xingzheng yuan wenhua jianshe weiyuan hui (Council for Cultural Planning and Development, Executive Yuan), 1986.

《中華民國傳統版畫藝術》·行政院文化建設委員會策劃·[特約撰述：潘元石·執行主編：黃才郎·翻譯：石大為、牟安德]·台北：行政院文化建設委員會，民國七十五年七月一日發行·

Zhonghua minguo jianguo bashi nian Zhongguo yishu wenwu taolun hui: Lunwen ji: Qi wu (International Colloquium on Chinese Art History, 1991: Proceedings: Antiquities). Compiled and edited by Guoli gugong bowu yuan bianji weiyuan hui. 2 pts. [issued in 1 slipcase]. [In Chinese and English.] Taibei: Guoli gugong bowu yuan (National Palace Museum),

1992.

《中華民國建國八十年中國藝術文物討論會：論文集：器物》·國立故宮博物院編輯委員會編輯·[上、下冊]·[精裝二冊一套]·台北：國立故宮博物院，民國八十一年六月初版·

Zhonghua shenmi wenhua cidian. Editor-in-chief: Wu Kang. Deputy editors-in-chief: Su Jianke, Zhang Yaxun, Zhang Keming, and Li Changgeng. Haikou, Hainan: Hainan chuban she, 1993.

《中國神秘文化辭典》·主編：吳康·副主編：蘇建科、張亞勛、張克明、李長庚·[精裝一冊]·海口：海南出版社，1993年4月第1版·

Zhou, Xinhui. "Zhongguo fojiao banhua shi zonglun." In *Zhongguo gudai fojiao banhua ji*, chief editor: Zhou Xinhui, co-editors: Chen Jian and Ma Wenda, vol. 1, introductory text section, 1-67. Beijing: Xueyuan chuban she, 1998.

周心慧·〈中國佛教版畫史綜論〉·《中國古代佛教版畫集》·主編：周心慧·副主編：陳堅、馬文大·北京：學苑出版社，一九九八年五月北京第一版·第一冊·論文部分·第一頁至第六十七頁·

———. *Zhongguo gudai banke banhua shi lun ji*. Beijing: Xueyuan chuban she, 1998.

《中國古代版刻版畫史論集》·周心慧著·[平裝一冊]·北京：學苑出版社，1998年10月北京第1版·

Zhou, Yiliang. "Guanyu beiye." *Wenwu*, no. 367 (1986, no. 12) (December 1986): 63.

周一良·〈關於葉〉·《文物》·一九八六年第十二期·總第三六七號·第六十三頁·

Zhou, Wu (1921-1990). "Wang Tingna yu Hu Zhengyan: Ji Ming dai liang wei chuban jia." *Duoyun*, no. 2 (November 1981): 154-156.

周蕪·〈汪廷訥與胡正言—記明代兩位出版家〉·《朵雲》·第二集·一九八一年十一月·第一百五十四頁至第一百五十六頁·

———. "Hui pai banhua." *Duoyun*, no. 4 (November 1982): 140-145, continued on 147.

周蕪·〈徽派版畫〉·《朵雲》·第四集·一九八二年十一月·第一百四十頁至第一百四十五頁，下轉第一百四十七頁·

———, comp. and ed. *Hui pai banhua shi lun ji*. Hefei, Anhui: Anhui renmin chuban she, 1984.

《徽派版畫史論集》·周蕪編著·合肥：安徽人民出版社，1984年1月第1版·

———, comp. and ed. *Zhongguo gudai banhua bai tu*. Beijing: Renmin meishu chuban she, 1984.

《中國古代版畫百圖》·周蕪編著·北京：人民美術出版社，一九八四年五月第一版·

———, comp. and ed. *Zhongguo guben xiqu chatu xuan*. Tianjin: Tianjin renmin meishu chuban she, 1985.

《中國古本戲曲插圖選》·周蕪編著·天津：天津人民美術出版社，一九八五年四月第一版·

———. "Guanyu 'Shizhu zhai shuhua pu' yuan kanben wenti." In *Shizhu zhai yanjiu wenji: "Shizhu zhai shuhua pu" kanxing sanbai liushi nian jinian*, compiled by Shizhu zhai yishu yanjiu bu, 28-29. Nanjing: Shizhu zhai yishu yanjiu bu, 1987.

周蕪·〈關於《十竹齋書畫譜》原刊本問題〉·《十竹齋研究文集：〈十竹齋書畫譜〉刊行三百六十年紀念》·十竹齋藝術研究部編·南京：十竹齋藝術研究部，一九八七年十月·第二十八頁至第二十九頁·

———, comp. and ed. *Zhongguo banhua shi tulu*. 2 vols. Zhongguo meishu shi tulu congshu. Shanghai: Shanghai renmin meishu chuban she, 1988.

《中國版畫史圖錄》·周蕪編·[上、下冊]·《中國美術史圖錄叢書》·上海：上海人民美術出版社，1988年10月第1版·

———, comp. and ed. *Jinling gu banhua (Ancient Woodblock Prints in Jinling)*. [In Chinese; title on added title page also in English.] Nanjing: Jiangsu meishu chuban she, 1993.

《金陵古版畫》·周蕪編著·[精裝一冊]·南京：江蘇美術出版社，1993年6月第1版·

Zhu, Baotian (1931-), comp. *Hafo daxue Hafo-Yanjing tushu guan cang Zhongguo Naxi zu xingxiang wen jingdian fenlei mulu (Annotated Catalog of Naxi Pictographic Manuscripts in the Harvard-Yenching Library, Harvard University)*. Hafo-Yanjing tushu guan shumu congkan (Harvard-Yenching Library Bibliographical Series), no. 5. Cambridge, Mass.: Harvard-Yenching Library, Harvard University, 1997.

《哈佛大學哈佛燕京圖書館藏中國納西族形象文經典分類目錄》·朱寶田編·〈哈佛燕京圖書館書目叢刊第五種〉·哈佛大學哈佛燕京圖書館出版·

Zhu, Chongxian. *Yi zu dianji wenhua*. Beijing: Zhongyang minzu daxue chuban she, 1994.

《彝族典籍文化》·朱崇先著·北京：中央民族大學出版社，1994年8月第1版·

———. *Yi zu dianji wenhua yanjiu*. Yi zu dianji wenhua yanjiu congshu. Beijing: Zhongyang minzu daxue chuban she, 1996.

《彝族典籍文化研究》·朱崇先著·〈彝族典籍文化研究叢書〉·北京：中央民族大學出版社，1996年6月第1版·

Zhu, Hengfu. "Ming Qing Mulian xi taiben liubian kao." *Wenxian*, no. 52 (1992, no. 2): 42-58.

朱恒夫·〈明清目連戲台本流編考〉·《文獻》·總第五十二期·一九九二年第二期·第四十二頁至第五十八頁·

———. "Mulian gushi zai shuochang wenxue zhong zhi liubian kao." *Wenxian*, no. 56 (1993, no. 2): 27-47.

朱恒夫·〈目連故事在說唱文學中之流編考〉·《文獻》·總第五十六期·一九九三年第二期·第二十七頁至第四十七頁·

Zhu sha yu pu. Compiled by Zhang Qiande [Zhang Zhao] (1577-1643). Manuscript dated 1596. [Typeset ed.] In *Meishu congshu*, ser. 2, no. 10 [vol. 20]: 125-134. Taibei: Guangwen shuju, 1963.

《硃砂魚譜》·張丑[原名：張謙德]撰·[丙申夏仲六日序]·[依寫本刊]·錄於《美術叢書》·黃賓虹、鄧實編·二集·第十輯·第一百二十五頁至第一百三十四頁·台北：廣文書局，民國五十二年元月初版·

Zhuang, Jifa. *Qing dai zouzhe zhidu*. Gugong congkan jia zhong, no. 15. Taibei: Guoli gugong bowu yuan, 1979.

《清代奏摺制度》·莊吉發著·〈故宮叢刊甲種之十五〉·台北：國立故宮博物院，民國六十八年九月初版·

Zieme, Peter. *Altun yaruq sudur, Vorworte und das erste Buch: Edition und Übersetzung des alttürkischen Version des Goldglanzsutra (Suvarnaprabhasottamasutra)*. Schriften zur Geschichte und Kultur des alten Orients: Berliner Turfantexte, no. 18. Turnhout, Belgium: Brepols, 1996.

Zögner, Lothar, ed. *China cartographica: Chinesische Kartenschätze und europäische Forschungsdokumente: Ausstellung anläßlich des 150. Geburtstages des Chinaforschers Ferdinand von Richthofen*. [Ausstellung und Katalog: Lothar Zögner, unter Mitarbeit von G.K. Zögner und Wen-tien Wang. Mit Beiträgen von Ulrich Freitag et al. (Eduard Imhof, Albert Kolb, Peter Thiele. Dia-Schau: Zusammenstellung und Texte Peter Thiele.] Ausstellungskataloge, no. 19. Exhibition catalogue [Staatsbibliothek Preußischer Kulturbesitz, Berlin, October 7-November 26, 1983; Wissenschaftszentrum, Bonn, April 5-May 6, 1984]. [Errata slip inserted.] Berlin: Staatsbibliothek Preußischer Kulturbesitz; Berlin: Kiepert KG, 1983.

Zurndorfer, Harriet T. [Harriet Thelma]. *China Bibliography: A Research Guide to Reference Works about China Past and Present*. Leiden and New York: E.J. Brill, 1995. Paperback ed. Honolulu: University of Hawaii Press, 1999.

Zwalf, W. [Wladimir], ed. *Buddhism: Art and Faith*. Exhibition catalogue [The British Museum, London, 1985]. London: Published by British Museum Publications Limited for the Trustees of the British Museum and the British Library Board, 1985.

書　　　名：中國國家圖書館善本特藏珍品蒞美展覽圖錄

編　　　著：胡廣俊

中方編委會名單：

黃潤華、張志清、陳漢玉、陳紅彥、趙前

冀亞平、蘇品紅、鄭賢蘭、程有慶

致　　　辭：周和平

策　　　劃：孫利平

責任編輯：姜成安

執行編輯：鄭文蕾

裝幀設計：王晨、徐竣

攝　　　影：馮金川、趙純厚（北京佳貝圖片交流中心）

出　　　版：皇后區公共圖書館（紐約）、中國國家圖書館（北京）、朝華出版社（北京）聯合出版

發　　　行：美國藝術資源有限公司（Art Media Resources, Ltd.）

制　　　版：北京利豐雅高長城電分制版中心

印　　　刷：北京嘉彩印刷有限公司

開　　　本：899 x 1194 mm、　12 開

印　　　張：30

封　　　面：300 克玻璃卡

正　　　文：128 克亞粉紙

版　　　次：2000 年 2 月第 1 版，2000 年 2 月第 1 次印刷

I S B N：　0-964-53371-5